COMPREHENSIVE, AUTHORITATIVE, easy to consult—and the only work of its kind on American writing: this invaluable survey of criticism centering on 174 American authors who wrote or came to prominence after 1900 fills a long empty gap in the reference bookshelf.

Any reader who has ever wondered what the critics wrote of Faulkner, Hemingway, or Robert Frost when they were "new writers" now has a unique opportunity to find out quickly and easily. Ezra Pound on Frost; Carl Van Doren and Sherwood Anderson on Sinclair Lewis; Paul Rosenfeld on Fitzgerald and Sandburg; Walter Lippman on Upton Sinclair—critical comments on writers or on an individual play or novel are now immediately available without the need for checking through literary histories or back issues of magazines or newspapers. The added Supplement to this edition contains up-to-date critical comments on these writers, some of whom are now deceased.

The critical excerpts have been culled systematically from the writings of outstanding critics in periodicals, both general and scholarly, and in books. These excerpts reflect the sweep and variety of the literary taste and critical standards of our century.

Here in this one well-planned volume are evaluations in chronological sequence of every major literary performance of the past sixty years. Full bibliographic information allows the reader to go to the source for more detailed criticism if he wishes. The Index to Critics permits the reader to find quickly all the authors on which each critic has written.

Besides authors of our own time and the early century, *A Library of Literary Criticism* gives full coverage to writers like Henry James, Mark Twain, and Emily

continued on back flap

A LIBRARY OF LITERARY CRITICISM

A LIBRAR

Third Edition

WITH INDEX TO CRITICS
AND SUPPLEMENT

Frederick Ungar Publishing Co., New York

F LITERARY CRITICISM

Modern American Literature

Compiled and edited by
DOROTHY NYREN

Publishing Department
American Library Association

FOREWORD

When Charles Wells Moulton completed in 1905 the last of the eight volumes of his *Library of Literary Criticism of English and American Authors,* English literature was undeniably more important than its American counterpart. Quite sensibly he decided to devote most of his useful compendium to commentaries on English authors.

America had already had some important writers: Cooper, Whitman, Poe, Melville, Hawthorne, Emerson and Thoreau, but our great stylists were few in comparison with those of England and even the names of those few were not widely known. It has happened, fortunately, that this is no longer the case. During the past half century American literature has grown greatly in quantity and in importance. Henry James and Mark Twain have become major figures since Moulton edited his serviceable volumes. We have had generations of writers from "Bitter Bierce" and Jack London to the Beatniks on the West Coast, from Dreiser to James Jones and Saul Bellow in the Middle West, from Cabell to Faulkner and Penn Warren in the South, and from the comfortable gentility of Edith Wharton to the uncomfortable acerbity of James Gould Cozzens in the East. It is time indeed that "American Authors" be brought up to date.

Following Moulton's idea (but not in all details his method), the editor has systematically reviewed the critical accompaniment to the major literary preformances of the past half century and more, going through the literature of criticism as it appeared in the popular and scholarly journals and in books, and choosing excerpts which reflected the sweep and variety of the literary taste, critical standards, and attitudes of the period. The over-all result is, it is hoped, a fairly definitive critical key to twentieth-century American writing through the 1950's.

One hundred and seventy American authors who wrote or became prominent after 1904 are included in this survey of significant criticism. Most of the authors in this volume may be found in Stanley Kunitz's *Twentieth-Century Authors* and its *First Supplement,* which should be consulted for biographical information.

A Library of Literary Criticism: Modern American Literature is intended primarily as a reference tool for school, library, or home, for the use of scholars and students as well as browsers. Each citation is accompanied by full bibliographical information indicating its source. A highly selective list of books by the author being considered is also appended to each group of citations as suggestions for first readings in the author himself. It must be remembered, above all, that a guide of this sort becomes valuable only when used in connection with a careful reading of the books under discussion.

The editor expresses her gratitude to the numerous publishers who made this book possible by granting permission to use quotations from their publications. While it has not always been possible to obtain permission to use desired quotations, cooperation from those owning copyrighted material has been, with few exceptions, generous and helpful.

D. N.

NOTE ON THIRD EDITION

The Supplement added in this third edition is intended to bring to the reader's attention additional materials that have become important in the three years following the previous edition. There are complete sections on Joseph Heller, J. F. Powers, Philip Roth, and John Updike. Material has been added for sixteen other writers. Attention has been focused on the reputation of writers, such as Robert Frost and Ernest Hemingway, whose total work is now being reassessed; writers, such as Henry Miller and James Baldwin, whose books are of major current interest; and writers, such as Herbert Gold and Bernard Malamud, the growth of whose talents must be watched with continuing interest.

D. N.

PERIODICALS REPRESENTED

See supplementary listings at end.

Where no abbreviation is indicated, the magazine references are listed in full.

	Accent
AHR	American Historical Review
AL	American Literature
Am	America
AM	American Mercury
AnR	Antioch Review
AQ	Arizona Quarterly
AR	American Review
AS	American Scholar
At	Atlantic Monthly
Bkm	Bookman
BkmL	Bookman (London)
	Century
	Chimera
CC	Christian Century
CE	College English
CF	Canadian Forum
Cmty	Commentary
Com	Commonweal
Crit	Criterion
	Critic
CS	Chicago Sun Book Week
CSM	Christian Science Monitor
CW	Catholic World
	Dial
DR	Dublin Review
EJ	English Journal
ER	Evergreen Review
	Forum
Fm	Freeman
Harper	Harper's Magazine
	Holiday
HdR	Hudson Review
HR	Hopkins Review
	Horizon
IW	Independent Woman
JELH	Journal of English Literary History
JHI	Journal of the History of Ideas
JSS	Jewish Social Studies
KR	Kenyon Review
LJ	Library Journal

LM	London Mercury
LR	Literary Review
LtR	Little Review
MP	Modern Philology
NAR	North American Review
	Nation
NC	Nineteenth Century
NEQ	New England Quarterly
NMQ	New Mexico Quarterly
NR	New Republic
NSN	New Statesman and Nation; later Statesman and Nation
Nwk	Newsweek
NWW	New World Writing
NYEP	New York Evening Post Book Section
NYHT	New York Herald Tribune Book Section
NYHT ts	New York Herald Tribune Theater Section
NYT	New York Times Book Section
NYT mag	New York Times Magazine Section
NYT ts	New York Times Theater Section
OM	Overland Monthly
	Outlook
Per	Perspectives U.S.A.
	Phylon
PMLA	Publications of the Modern Language Association
	Poetry
PR	Partisan Review
PS	Pacific Spectator
Ren	Renascence
	Reporter
SAQ	South Atlantic Quarterly
Scy	Scrutiny
SLM	Southern Literary Messénger
SoR	Southern Review
Spec	Spectator

SR	Saturday Review of Litera-ture, later Saturday Review	*UTQ*	University of Toronto Quarterly
SwR	Sewanee Review	*VQR*	Virginia Quarterly Review
SWR	Southwest Review	*YR*	Yale Review (copyright Yale University Press)
TA	Theatre Arts Time		

ADDITIONAL PERIODICALS

	Critique	*NYR*	New York Review of Books
MR	Massachusetts Review		
NY	New Yorker	*WLB*	Wilson Library Bulletin

AUTHORS ADDED IN SUPPLEMENT

Heller, Joseph
Powers, J. F.
Roth, Philip
Updike, John

AUTHORS COVERED

Adams. Henry
Agee, James
Aiken, Conrad
Algren, Nelson
Anderson, Maxwell
Anderson, Sherwood
Auchincloss, Louis
Auden, W. H.
Babbitt, Irving
Baldwin, James
Barnes, Djuna
Barry, Philip
Behrman, S. N.
Bellow, Saul
Benét, Stephen Vincent
Bierce, Ambrose
Bishop, Elizabeth
Bishop, John Peale
Blackmur, Richard
Bodenheim, Maxwell
Bogan, Louise
Bowles, Paul
Boyle, Kay
Brooks, Cleanth
Brooks, Van Wyck
Buck, Pearl
Burke, Kenneth
Burns, John Horne
Cabell, James Branch
Caldwell, Erskine
Capote, Truman
Cather, Willa
Ciardi, John
Clark, Walter Van Tilburg
Cowley, Malcolm
Cozzens, James Gould
Crane, Hart
Crane, Stephen
Cullen, Countee
Cummings, E. E.
Dickinson, Emily
Doolittle, Hilda

Dos Passos, John
Dreiser, Theodore
Eberhart, Richard
Edmonds, Walter
Eliot, T. S.
Ellison, Ralph
Farrell, James T.
Fast, Howard
Faulkner, William
Fearing, Kenneth
Fisher, Dorothy Canfield
Fisher, Vardis
Fitzgerald, F. Scott
Fitzgerald, Robert
Fletcher, John Gould
Fowlie, Wallace
Frost, Robert
Garland, Hamlin
Garrigue, Jean
Ginsberg, Allen
Glasgow, Ellen
Gold, Herbert
Goyen, William
Gregory, Horace
Guthrie, A. B., Jr.
Hayes, Alfred
Hearn, Lafcadio
Hellman, Lillian
Hemingway, Ernest
Hersey, John
Howard, Sidney
Howells, William Dean
Hughes, Langston
Inge, William
Jackson, Shirley
James, Henry
Jarrell, Randall
Jeffers, Robinson
Jones, James
Kantor, MacKinlay
Kerouac, Jack
Kingsley, Sidney

Kreymborg, Alfred
Kunitz, Stanley
Lardner, Ring
Levin, Meyer
Lewis, Sinclair
Lewisohn, Ludwig
Lindsay, Vachel
London, Jack
Lowell, Amy
Lowell, Robert
McCarthy, Mary
McCullers, Carson
MacLeish, Archibald
Mailer, Norman
Malamud, Bernard
March, William
Markham, Edwin
Marquand, John P.
Masters, Edgar Lee
Mencken, H. L.
Millay, Edna St. Vincent
Miller, Arthur
Miller, Henry
Moody, William Vaughan
Moore, Marianne
Moore, Merrill
Morris, Wright
Nin, Anais
Norris, Frank
O'Connor, Flannery
Odets, Clifford
O'Neill, Eugene
Parker, Dorothy
Patchen, Kenneth
Porter, Katherine Anne
Pound, Ezra
Ransom, John Crowe
Rexroth, Kenneth
Rice, Elmer
Richter, Conrad
Roberts, Elizabeth Madox
Roberts, Kenneth
Robinson, Edwin Arlington

Roethke, Theodore
Rukeyser, Muriel
Salinger, J. D.
Sandburg, Carl
Santayana, George
Saroyan, William
Sarton, May
Schulberg, Budd
Schwartz, Delmore
Scott, Winfield Townley
Shapiro, Karl
Shaw, Irwin
Sherwood, Robert
Sinclair, Upton
Stafford, Jean
Stegner, Wallace
Stein, Gertrude
Steinbeck, John
Stevens, Wallace
Styron, Wallace
Tate, Allen
Taylor, Peter
Thurber, James
Trilling, Lionel
Twain, Mark
Van Doren, Mark
Van Druten, John
Viereck, Peter
Warren, Robert Penn
Welty, Eudora
Wescott, Glenway
West, Nathanael
Wharton, Edith
Wheelock, John Hall
Wheelwright, John Brooks
Wilbur, Richard
Wilder, Thornton
Williams, Tennessee
Williams, William Carlos
Wilson, Edmund
Winters, Yvor
Wolfe, Thomas
Wright, Richard

ADAMS, HENRY (1838–1918)

The value of the work of Henry Adams is that he was a scholar who saw the difference between knowledge and ignorance, an historian who studied the sequence of cause and effect, and a mystic who entered at times into the world of the "other reality," where there is neither cause and effect, nor object and subject.

Like all mystics it was the "other" reality which he prized most, although—like all intelligent mystics—he also valued highly the world in which we live.

Kirsopp Lake. At. April, 1924. p. 529

This gentleman from the House of Adams is preeminently a modern American scholar. He had a singular capacity for original research and polished presentation. He was both a student of history and a literary artist and in all his work he combined his abilities in the one with his powers in the other. To match his breadth and depth of knowledge he had a keen critical sense and a clear judicial mind. He had creative imagination, a sensitive appreciation of significant form, and a remarkable skill in removing the clutter of details and depicting essentials. He was a master of facts, pursuing his ideas with minute research and solid reasoning. He was a superb maker of phrases, but he sketched with accuracy and precision, coloring his narrative with his own personality and toning his portraits with insight and understanding.

Marian D. Irish. AS. March, 1932. pp. 223–4

Henry Adams recapitulated on American soil the romantic tradition of Europe. This tradition included aesthetic pessimism, in which framework he built up a personality-image which he came to enjoy artistically. The image was that of the failure, the heroic failure. He came to enjoy the spectacle doubly: on the stage as an actor, from the wings as an onlooker who revels in the gaping audiences. . . . Adams's failure was only a pen and paper failure. He wrote "a terribly ironic estimate of himself" because it pleased his artistic fancy to do so.

Max I. Baym. AS. Winter, 1945. pp. 87–8

Pessimism was both a pose and a habit of mind with Henry Adams. Only fools and great statesmen were paid to be optimists. Furthermore, as Adams remarked, "no one can afford to pose as an optimist, short of an income of a hundred thousand a year." Adams had about twenty-five thousand and considered himself to be neither a great statesman nor a fool; thus, pessimism was for him the only dignified pose. And dignity was important, as well as required. However, something of his pessimism was genuine because his scientific and metaphysical speculations had convinced him that the cherished assumptions of his culture and tradition were totally wrong, and worse than useless; because by stubbornly defending the old notions of order, unity, the unique value of the individual, freedom of the will, one would only hasten the acceleration towards the inevitable catastrophe of all civilization.

Gerrit H. Roelofs. *JELH*. Sept., 1950. p. 231

It is dangerously easy to overstress the near-tragic quality of the aging scholar, caught as never before in the impingement of beauty but knowing, too, the final ineffectuality of its comfort for one whose mind insisted on discovering monstrosity and chaos on every side. He still was one to relish good food and drink, to enjoy the company of handsome women and vigorous men and stimulate them by questions and banter. He was by no means the bitter, broken prophet that many critics, gullibly misreading his own account, have pronounced him to be. . . . One comprehends Adams most clearly as a man who to the last felt and not quite successfully defied the personal and universal disorder encroaching upon a sensitive dweller in the nineteenth and twentieth centuries. His dilemma was at once individual and typical.

Robert A. Hume. *Runaway Star* (Cornell). 1951.

pp. 35–6

He was very shy of self-revelation. Some of it came out, disguised, in the novels, biographies, and *History*. He could be more naked, for instance in *Esther* than in the first-person books, *Mont-St.-Michel* and *The Education. Democracy* is his political ordeal; *Esther,* his own, as well as his wife's religious plight. And where one might least expect to find it, in the heavily documented, nine-volume *History of the United States,* there are passages of lyrical intensity which tell us as much about the subjective Henry Adams as any of (his) letters.

Elizabeth Stevenson. *Nation.* Jan. 26, 1952. p. 87

Adams was not a likeable man; he was an important man. Like the intellectuals who would model themselves on his legend, he cultivated his snobbism too lovingly; he was something of what the Germans call *ein Besserwisser;* and his attitudes always seem a bit disassociated from his individual experience. In his own life he suffered the destructive split between literary and political vocations which has since become so prevalent. . . . But it was greatly to his credit that even as he submitted to this split, he did not approve of it; he knew that for the intellectual, health is possible only through a unity of the two parts, even if a unity in tension.

Irving Howe. NR. Sept. 22, 1952. p. 26

The greatness of the mind of Adams himself is in the imaginative reach of the effort to solve the problem of the meaning, the use, or the value of its own energy. The greatness is in the effort itself, in variety of response deliberately made to every possible level of experience. It is in the acceptance, with all piety, of ignorance as the humbled form of knowledge; in the pursuit of divers shapes of knowledge—the scientific, the religious, the political, the social and trivial—to the point where they add to ignorance, when the best response is silence itself. That is the greatness of Adams as a type of mind. As it is a condition of life to die, it is a condition of thought, in the end, to fail. Death is the expense of life and failure is the expense of greatness.

R. P. Blackmur. The Lion and the Honeycomb
(Harcourt). 1955. p. 95

To agree that after his wife's death Adams devoted his talent to indicting the universe that had produced her and destroyed her is, of course, to over-simplify. Yet, once the History is finished, everything else of import seems to turn upon the theme of conflict between tranquillity and force. . . . This gifted man was in some sense the child of Byron and Voltaire. There was something in him elementary as well as ironical. A hostile critic might plausibly demonstrate that, because it was outrageous of the universe to·deal with Mr. and Mrs. Henry Adams as the universe had done, the scholar would condemn the universe. The rebelliousness, the self-incrimination, the irony of the mature Byron are paralleled by Adams, the principal difference being that in the American these qualities were held in restraint as judgments, not hurled at the target as weapons.

Howard Mumford Jones. Nation. Dec. 24, 1955.
pp. 558–9

Henry Adams had a rich and sensitive mind and was, behind his misanthropic exterior, a deeply humane individual. He had been formed rather rigidly in the heavy heritage of his Presidential ancestry and of New England dogma; and by the most subtle and delicate process he achieved, within his sensibility, a system of feathery balances, so that the discharge of his emotions might be propped by flying buttresses and filtered through his stained-glass windows. His mind was like the cathedrals he came to study; it was no accident that he turned to them.

Leon Edel. SR. Dec. 10, 1955. p. 15

Mont-Saint-Michel and Chartres

Scenery, psychology, history, literature, poetry, art—all these are materials for the story he relates. But the controlling purpose of the narrative is to show, in its own form as in its subject, how vast a world can
be found by the senses and how great a work the intellect may do
when it serves the highest vision of the imagination and defies, knowingly, the terrors of fact which always beset that vision. Because the
pilgrim-artist has discovered the realm of tragedy, the tourist-historian
of *Mont-Saint-Michel and Chartres* works in a realm beyond that
which can be marked out by any particular theory of history. The
naïvete of the Romanesque, the refinement of the Transition, the scientific modernity of the Gothic all had their appeal to him because
he saw them as phases of life which he had experienced in his role of
human being as well as in his capacity as scholar. His aspiration expressed itself in the very shape of his composition, but the anguish of
his doubt was also there, almost buried out of sight, in the continual
presence of time that foreshadowed the end of love.

J. C. Levenson. *The Mind and Art of Henry Adams*
(Houghton). 1957. p. 288

The Education of Henry Adams

The Education of Henry Adams, conceived as a study of the philosophy of history, turns out in fact to be an *apologia pro vita sua,* one of
the most self-centered and self-revealing books in the language.

The revelation is not indeed of the direct sort that springs from frank
and insouciant spontaneity. Since the revelation was not intended, the
process is tortuous in the extreme. It is a revelation that comes by the
way, made manifest in the effort to conceal it, overlaid by all sorts of
cryptic sentences and self-deprecatory phrases, half hidden by the protective coloring taken on by a sensitive mind commonly employing
paradox and delighting in perverse and teasing mystification. . . . The
Education is in fact the record, tragic and pathetic underneath its genial irony, of the defeat of fine aspirations and laudable ambitions. It is
the story of a life which the man himself, in his old age, looked back
upon as a broken arch.

Carl Becker. *AHR.* April, 1919. pp. 4245–6

In a manner he was a microcosm of American history, for what of
history his family had not actually made, he had written or had watched.
America knew him not, but he had known America; and his autobiography stands in a class with that of Benjamin Franklin. He described it
as "the education of Henry Adams," a process he seems to have aban-

doned in despair; but the reading of the book will give an American a European education, and a European an American one.

Shane Leslie. DR. June, 1919. p. 218

Henry Adams, very early, became too pessimistic and cynical to go on being a participant. He chose, instead, a place on the sidelines, and from there set about recording the minutes of all the unsavory transactions of America's public life. The picture of such proceedings which Adams drew, or at least suggested, in the *Education* is a final one. For not only were its revelations damning, but its sources were unimpeachable. It was the indictment of a supremely placed worldling who had listened at the most private keyholes, who had been told—or allowed to guess—the secrets of those who worked behind the scenes. Scarcely anyone else who did so little knew so much. Adams's indictment stands: the great documentary merit of the *Education* is its demonstration of what nineteenth-century America had become, and by what process, and on what terms.

Louis Kronenberger. NR. March 15, 1939. p. 156

See *The Henry Adams Reader;* also *The Education of Henry Adams* (autobiography) and *Mont-Saint-Michel and Chartres* (long essay).

AGEE, JAMES (1909–1955)

Mr. Agee's delight has been in literature. He has no simple and direct view of a real scene, no sensuous world of experience save books. . . . Mr. Agee is, I take it, Anglo-Catholic, scholarly, classical in his desire to be in the stream of literary tradition. . . . There is little perception in his work except for words and their values. Nevertheless his music, his exquisite choice of phrase and word, will gain him recognition.

Eda Lou Walton. NYHT. Dec. 9, 1934. p. 19

Fortunately for the general reader, Mr. Agee is not only a poet but a corking good journalist when he needs to be. . . . With the combined sensitive perception of a poet, the exact, almost microscopic recording of a scientist, and the generic sharpness of observation making a good reporter, Agee shows us places and things, camera-eye plain. . . . Mr. Agee's main literary weaknesses (as well as his virtues) stem mostly from his influence by and allegiance to such writers as Joyce, Kafka and Céline.

Ruth Lechlitner. NYHT. Aug. 24, 1941. p. 10

Mr. Agee does a good deal to antagonize the reader. There are too many tongues, too many attitudes, too many awarenesses on the subjective side (perhaps defenses would be more precise); even the sincerity is too much, is too prostrate. And yet, visible through all this, are some unmistakable virtues: Mr. Agee, at times, writes brilliantly . . . ; he is extraordinarily sensitive and aware and, above all, concerned with that deeper honesty that assembles before itself all those minute rationalizations and nuances of feeling that are always a kind of havoc inside ourselves.

Harvey Breit. *NR*. Sept. 15, 1941. p. 348

James Agee was born in the South and retains the pride and piety and love of language of the Southern writer. . . . Genius he surely had; the trouble perhaps lay in his trying to read that genius into things not of his own making. In a vague way his instinct resembled that of Proust, whose genius was of a kind that could only portray genius, nothing but genius, whether in painters, duchesses, or elevator boys. Yet where Proust actually recreated his powers, Agee was content to delegate his.

F. W. Dupee. *Nation*. April 28, 1951. p. 400

James Agee . . . was a writer who gave all of himself . . . to every medium that he worked in—poetry, fiction, reportage, criticism, movies, television. He was not only one of the most gifted writers in the United States, but such a natural as a writer that he found a creative opportunity in every place where drearier people pitied themselves for potboiling. . . . Agee was a writer who actually did better in popular and journalistic media—where certain objective technical requirements gave him a chance to create something out of his immense tenderness and his high sense of comedy than when he let himself go in purely speculative lyricism. He was a natural literary craftsman, not a literary intellectual, and it was only *avant-garde* associations that ever misled him. His most beautiful poems—like the title poem of his first book, *Permit Me Voyage*—are those which are most traditional in form.

Alfred Kazin. *NYT*. Nov. 17, 1957. p. 5

Agee was a very gifted and versatile writer; his best-known work is *Let Us Now Praise Famous Men,* an account of sharecroppers in the depression, with photographs by Walker Evans. He wrote for motion pictures and was the finest critic of films this country has produced. . . . The most remarkable thing about Agee's new book—*A Death in the Family*—is that it is exactly the kind of novel that a great many people have tried to write and have not been able to bring off, at least not the way Agee does. The subject is extremely simple: a man dies. There is no plot or story, just an account of the reactions of his relatives and one friend. But the writing is brilliant, because it manages to be so sensitive to every nuance of emotion without ever going soft.

Paul Pickrel. *Harper*. Dec., 1957. p. 88

The posthumously published *A Death in the Family* is Agee's final item of his career in letters, a novel on which he had been at work for eight years. It does not give him any new importance as an American writer, but it does bring to a delicate and satisfactory flowering his very great ability to create the qualities and nuances of private feeling. . . . There are moments of grief and loss in everyone's life which one cannot live with, but can only recover from. And they are, oddly, the moments when one recognizes one's feelings to have been most alive. The success of *A Death in the Family* is that it brings to the surface of the reader's consciousness these forgotten, rejected moments—his own tender, unusable anguish.

David L. Stevenson. *Nation*. Dec. 14, 1957.
pp. 460–1

The late James Agee was a writer at the opposite end of the literary spectrum to James Jones. He had a poet's sensitivity to and mastery of language; a depth of awareness which rescued ordinary happenings from banality and drew out of them their universal significance; the capacity to be tender without being mawkish, to celebrate life without sententiousness.

Charles Rolo. *At*. Jan., 1958. p. 79

See *Permit Me Voyage* (poetry), *Let Us Now Praise Famous Men* (documentary), and *The Morning Watch* and *A Death in the Family* (novels).

AIKEN, CONRAD (1889–   )

He was master of a smooth limpid flow of verse narrative from the beginning. He did not have to learn and unlearn his technique. It was an authentic gift. Such a poet is rare enough even in England, still rarer in America. . . . Now it seems to me that, apart from his incontestable gifts as a prosodist and word-controller, Conrad Aiken's mind has up to the present worked on somewhat too narrow a basis. His poems, in short, are variations of but one idea—the idea of sexual disillusionment.

John Gould Fletcher. *Dial*. March 28, 1918.

pp. 291–2

Apparently he believes in poetry as a craft, a sport, a profession—like boxing or magic—which must be thoroughly studied before it can be improved. He examines other poets accordingly, not to imitate them, but to learn their tricks. He never echoes. Sometimes he uses the devices of other poets as a vehicle for his own expression, but in any case he mingles them with devices of his own discovery so that he does not merely live in a tradition; he aids with his proper hands in building it.

Malcom Cowley. *Dial*. Nov., 1922. p. 564

He has gone as far as possible in the direction of spiritual disorder, without plunging into madness. He has made the case for sensitive living today as bad as possible. His disillusion is fearful and complete, his melancholy incurable. He always manages to disclose the worst side of things, to use his knowledge to increase confusion. And yet this later poetry of Aiken's is so honest, extravagant and inspired, that it is actually invigorating. It is so much richer than pale moderation. It carries us triumphantly to the metaphysical bottom. Now we can say that the bitterest songs have been sung.

Houston Peterson. *The Melody of Chaos*
(Longmans). 1931. p. 280

His has been a stubborn and, in many ways, heroic journey inward, following the Freudian stream. The political and social forces of our time have failed to touch him at his creative centers, though I do not doubt his intellectual awareness of them. What needs to be kept in mind is that the seemingly inexhaustible fertility of his imagination would seem to indicate that the course he has chosen may be, for him, the proper course. . . . His vision is of the shadows in the cave, and the cave itself impalpable as fog, of the swirling of phantoms, the dance of atoms, the blind gusts of desire. . . . What holds the dissolving cloud-rack together is memory, the persistence of mind.

Stanley J. Kunitz. *Poetry*. May, 1937. pp. 103–4

Conrad Aiken's early association with the Imagists obscures rather than clarifies the basic movement of his spirit. He was never in any real sense an Imagist, although certain early poems have a harsh reality that made them seem fresh and novel. But he turned quickly away from such external realism to a solitary devotion to the creation of poetry that should come as close as possible to the art of music. To this end, he cultivated the flowing repetitious movement of symphonic music, the emphases on emotion and feeling at the expense of thought, and the substitution of emotional coherence for the logical coherence conventional in poetry.

Fred B. Millett. *Contemporary American Authors* (Harcourt). 1940. p. 144

Probably no poet has been more concerned with music than Conrad Aiken, or has used it more fruitfully. The interest is visible even in the titles of his poems, where we find nocturnes, tone-poems, variations, dissonants, and symphonies. . . . The formal arrangement of a good deal of his poetry is based on musical principles rather than on the more widely accepted poetic ones. His symbols are developed and combined in ways analogous to the composer's handling of themes. He has given us, here and there, enough information about the theoretical basis of his work to make it clear that the musical analogues are deliberately and skilfully cultivated. And, finally, this poetry based on music is alive with musical references which reinforce both the implications of its structure and a philosophy in which music is that epitome of the individual and the universe which it was to Schopenhauer.

Calvin S. Brown. *Music and Literature* (Georgia). 1948. p. 195

The voice of Mr. Aiken—in his prose as in his poetry—has never been a loud one. His work is melodically beguiling rather than demandingly active. Quietly it reveals to us hidden facets of our behavior, recalls old and lost desires. The range is perhaps too narrow, the characters have too cultivated a sensibility, the disillusionment is too complete, the defeat is too Calvinistically inevitable. Gehenna is the recurrent symbol, *Feldeinsamkeit* the persistent mood. But within his range Mr. Aiken works with precision and persuasiveness.

E. J. Fitzgerald. *SR.* Sept. 16, 1950. p. 16

As long ago as the First World War, Conrad Aiken was writing of the poet as being "a curious blending of the psychoanalyst and patient." In novels, short stories, and a prolific poetry, all Aiken's work has exemplified the doctrine. He very early grafted upon traditional romanticism the golden bough of Freud. And somehow the undeviating process has made him one of the most distinguished unassessed writers of our era—perhaps the most distinguished.

Winfield Townley Scott. *SR.* Oct. 11, 1952. p. 26

Where other modern poets take the modern image of the cosmos as, at most, a point of departure, or a background irrelevant to human concerns and values, in Aiken's work it is always present as an inevitable awareness, as a kind of cold night which surrounds all things, like the sky itself. . . . But no matter how great the darkness, one cannot live by darkness. One must confront the darkness of existence—the silence of the stars, the depths of the atom, the gulf between each conscious being with all the attitudes which the imagination makes possible. This is the essential center of Aiken's poetry.

Delmore Schwartz. *NR*. Nov. 2, 1953. pp. 24–5

Aiken has sought his style in many directions, his experiments ranging from the diffuse allusiveness of Senlin to the archaic slam-bang theatrics of John Deth. Through every change, however, his devotion has been to the idea of the symphonic tone-poem, to a dissolving watery music, to a rain-swept and fog-abstracted landscape of the psyche. He has sought, in his own phrase, an "absolute poetry."

The weakness of that poetry seems to have centered from the beginning in its excess of melody and in the indefinitiveness of tone. . . . There is not much of the "real world"—whatever that is—in Aiken, but certainly one is persuaded that he has found music for everything that dreams.

John Ciardi. *Nation*. Nov. 14, 1953. p. 410

He is in the tradition of Romantic poets from Shelley to Swinburne but with the manners and sensibility of one who knows London's twentieth-century Bloomsbury as well as Boston Common. If one thinks or speaks of such a thing as "poetic talent," there is more of that almost indefinable quality in a half dozen pages of Mr. Aiken's book (*Collected Poems*) than can be unearthed in whole volumes written by hundreds of his younger contemporaries. . . . As poet Mr. Aiken's gifts are rich and obvious, but the flaw among his gifts is not a superficial one. His deep lapses into flabby diction indicate that somewhere below the surface of his poems a flabby moral attitude exists.

Horace Gregory. *NYT*. Dec. 20, 1953. p. 5

How does the bard sing? In the easiest external forms of any modern poet of stature. He sings by nature and training out of the general body of poetry in English. He writes from the cumulus of cliché in the language, always, for him, freshly felt, as if the existing language were the only reality outside himself there were. There is hardly ever in his work the stinging twist of new idiom, and the sometimes high polish of his phrasing comes only from the pressure and friction of his mind upon his metres. . . . Aiken depends on the force of his own mind and the force of metrical form to refresh his language.

The cumulus upon which he really works is the cumulus of repetition, modulation by arrangement, pattern, and overtone. He writes as if the words were spoken to let the mind under the words sing. He writes as if it were the song of the mind that puts meaning in the words.

R. P. Blackmur. *At.* Dec., 1953. p. 82

Whatever stature the work of Conrad Aiken may ultimately assume in the long run of criticism, we can affirm now, that he is one of the supreme technicians of modern English poetry. There are few writers, either in prose or in verse, who can challenge his mastery of language, who give us anything comparable to his assurance in controlling the most powerful and varied and nervous resources of expression. His writing has the inevitability of the highest art; it is, rhetorically, definitive.

Dudley Fitts. *NR.* Dec. 26, 1955. p. 19

Aiken is a kind of Midas: everything he touches turns to verse. Reading his poems is like listening to Delius—one is experiencing an unending undifferentiating wash of fairly beautiful sounds—or like watching a fairly boring, because almost entirely predictable kaleidoscope; a kaleidoscope all of whose transmutations are veiled, misty, watered-down. These are the metamorphoses of a world where everything *blurs* into everything else, where the easy, automatic, lyric, elegiac, nostalgic tone of the verse turns everything into itself, as the diffused, Salon photography of the first part of this century turned everything into Salon photographs.

Randall Jarrell. *YR.* Spring, 1956. pp. 479–80

Fiction

A neurologist tells us that, given the present rate of increase in nervous diseases, the civilized world will be insane in a couple of centuries. Mr. Aiken's work is a prophecy of that grim failure. His detachment, his underemphasis, his humor are in a way deceptive, and conceal from us the fact that many of his characters, even those who are so like ourselves that we exclaim, "There but for the grace of God go I," are on, or beyond, the verge. There is no heaviness or melodrama in their tragedy; they may even amuse us. But they are lost people in a sense more real than figurative, lost to the world, sometimes even lost to themselves.

R. M. Lovett. *NR.* May 30, 1934. p. 80

In contrast to most of his contemporaries in fiction, he peoples his books with civilized, educated, extraordinarily alert and sensitive human beings. They live in the modern world. When they are abnormal it is not the abnormality of degeneracy, but of the hypersensitive personality. Though in general they are characters untouched by the social, political and economic conflicts of contemporary life, they are vitally alive, and are depicted with a realism that is rendered palatable by the author's flawless prose.

Clayton Hoagland. *SLM*. April, 1940. p. 260

A story by Conrad Aiken is a horror wrapped in actuality, a fantasy all rooted and real, all rooted in a real detail. . . . Just as the structure of these stories characteristically develops in the effort of the material to assert a reality beyond or below its mundane shape, so their drama struggles to break over the edge of its own limitations. . . . We have, I think, no other body of contemporary fiction like this—so centrally coherent, its very coherence derived from a contemplation of the intransigence of that incoherence that lies scattered on all sides of us, and above and below.

Mark Schorer. *NR*. March 31, 1952. pp. 19–20

See *Collected Poems* and *A Letter from Li Po* (poetry); *Short Stories; Ushant* (autobiography); and *Blue Voyage* (novel).

ALGREN, NELSON (1909–   )

Nelson Algren is one of God's angry and gifted men, a Chicagoman— and maybe a Chicago-firster—to the bitter end. As his admirers know, his fiction is a heady, curious blend of skidrow Chicago talk and poetic insight. He writes like no one else in America today.

Budd Schulberg. *NYT*. Oct. 21, 1951. p. 3

The point is that Algren's typical figures are failures even at vice. They are the underdogs of sin, the small souls of corruption, the fools of poverty, not of wealth and power. Even the murders they commit, out of blind rage or through sheer accident—or through another ironic twist of their impoverished destiny—are not important. . . . Thus Algren's work represents an extreme phase of the native American realism which opened in the 1900's. . . . And there are obvious limitations and aesthetic dangers in the social area and the kind of human material that Algren has made his own.

Maxwell Geismar. *EJ*. March, 1953. pp. 124–5

It might be said that Algren's novels are weak in structure, and that they evince a lack of good constructive sense and an inability to maintain a narrative pace. Algren writes all around a character and gradually you realize that his character is real. He is atmospheric and impressionistic.

James Farrell. *NR*. May 21, 1956. p. 19

Algren's is a world of exotics—the last jungle inhabited by the last of the Noble Savages, the final goal of literary tourism.

It is, then, as an exotic, a romantic purveyor of escape literature that Algren must be read—this apparent "realist" whose fictional world is at the ultimate remove from any reality his readers know. Beyond Tahiti and Samoa, there exists the last unexplored island: Ultima Skid Row, on which nothing is merely dull, grimy, and without savor, but all grotesque and titillating in the lurid light of Algren's "poetic" prose.

Leslie A. Fiedler. *Reporter*. July 12, 1956. p. 44

Never Come Morning

It is a novel about depressed people by a depressed man, and it is most convincing in its complete unity of action, mood, and form. . . . The whole narrative is pervaded by a feeling of loss rather than of bitterness or horror. And Algren's realism is so paced as to avoid the tedium of the naturalistic stereotype, of the literal copying of surfaces. He knows how to select, how to employ factual details without letting himself be swamped by them, and finally, how to put the slang his characters speak to creative uses so that it ceases to be an element of mere documentation and turns into an element of style.

Philip Rahv. *Nation*. April 18, 1942. pp. 466–7

The scene in *Never Come Morning* that most people will remember is the rape of Bruno's girl in the cellar. . . . There are other scenes as brutal. . . . But the really good scenes are quieter; they are still lifes and genre pictures instead of being sensational films—the girls sitting around the juke box in Mama Topak's flat, the boys playing under the El, the look of Chicago streets in the rain, the tall corn growing between the slag heaps down by the river. It is this poetry of familiar things that is missing in the other Chicago novels and that shows the direction of Algren's talent. In spite of the violent story he tells—and tells convincingly—he is not by instinct a novelist. He is a poet of the Chicago slums, and he might well be Sandburg's successor.

Malcolm Cowley. *NR*. May 4, 1942. pp. 613–4

The Man with the Golden Arm

The Man with the Golden Arm . . . seems to declare that admirable human qualities have little—or perhaps a negative bearing on social status and that the poetry of human relationships appears most richly where people are stripped down to the core of survival and have not strength or use for complicated emotions. Living on the barest edge of physical survival, his people simply have no use for vanity, sanctimoniousness, or prestige; being free and pure, their loves and affections are beautiful. . . . Society has become a jungle of viciousness and injustice beyond reclamation; only the waifs and strays merit attention because only they are capable of tender and beautiful feelings. One may be deeply moved by *The Man with the Golden Arm* but must, I believe, finally regard it as irresponsible and inaccurate—a sentimental contrivance that has little to do with reality but rather explores a cul-de-sac in the author's imagination.

Charles Child Walcutt. *American Literary Naturalism*
(Minnesota). 1956. pp. 298–9

A Walk on the Wild Side

Algren's narrative . . . flickers to life only intermittently among the lay sermons and the miscellaneous information about jails and whorehouses. *A Walk on the Wild Side* is . . . documented, out of the same sense, I suppose, which compels popular magazine fiction, the notion that "truth" resides in avoiding inaccuracies; in knowing, for instance, exactly what equipment a New Orleans prostitute of the '30's would have had on her table. It is all part of the long retreat of the imagination before science, or our surrender to information.

Leslie A. Fiedler. *PR*. June, 1956. p. 361

A Walk on the Wild Side is in an American tradition of emotional giantism: its comedy is farce, its joys are orgies, the feats of its characters Bunyanesque, the sexuality is prodigious, their sorrow a wild keening almost too high for ordinary ears. Dove Linkhorn is pioneer stock gone bad, grown up and gone to seed, caught in a neon-lit jungle in a time of break-down. The picture of Dove burning out his dammed up, useless energies in a bonfire of lust and violence is one of the most extraordinary in contemporary fiction.

Milton Rugoff. *NYHT*. May 20, 1956. p. 4

The Chicago School of Realism has a new headmaster who frames his materials in back-country balladry and earthy lyricism. Enveloping pornography, as bluntly couched as ever, has now become incidental to the journalist's desire to get the facts and the historian's need to relate them to human affairs. To complete the effect, one could only ask for Toulouse-Lautrec illustrations and Louis Armstrong music. . . . *A Walk on the Wild Side* will be too rough for frail sightseers, but a participant's backward look at a wild 1931 landscape with figures seems worth the effort.

James Kelly. *SR*. May 26, 1956. p. 16

See *Somebody in Boots, Never Come Morning, The Man with the Golden Arm,* and *A Walk on the Wild Side* (novels); also *The Neon Wilderness* (short stories).

ANDERSON, MAXWELL (1888–1959)

Mr. Anderson's uncommon virtues and regrettable shortcomings are once more visible (in *The Wingless Victory* and *High Tor*). Both contain much lovely song. Both . . . disclose a mind and a point of view infinitely superior to the playwrighting general. And the second combines with its other qualities a sound originality and a small measure of that precious after-image, a small measure of the day-after recollective warmth, which in its full is the stamp and mark of important drama. But both the superior second as well as the inferior first, lack the strong, taut, purple cords to tie up and bind closely into a whole their isolatedly commendable elements and their periodic stirring notes of dramatic music.

George Jean Nathan. *SR*. Jan. 30, 1937. p. 19

Mr. Anderson, it seems to me, in his own plays has given the most striking confirmation of the obsolescence of verse technique. He is capable of writing well—in prose, and when he is close to real American speech. But in these recent plays he writes badly. I do not mean that he is technically incompetent; but he writes badly because English blank verse no longer has any relation whatsoever to the language or tempo of our lives, and because, as soon as he tries to use it, he has no resources but a flavorless imagery which was growing trite in our grandfathers' time.

Edmund Wilson. *NR*. June 23, 1937. p. 194

Maxwell Anderson has been at his best, in recent years, when he was angry. But because his language lacks any basis for hope, for a constructive point of view towards what disgusts him, it must in the end turn back upon itself, and render him peevish and despairing. Fine words and despair are not enough on which to nurture a dramatic talent; Anderson's latest plays show a marked decline. Yet his great gift is apparent whenever he permits himself to write immediately and simply about human beings.

Eleanor Flexner. American Playwrights (Simon).
1938. pp. 128–9

In eleven plays "poetic" from beginning to end, Maxwell Anderson, America's chief verse writer for the theatre, has produced very little poetry. . . . Consciously or otherwise, Mr. Anderson seems more interested in arguing for his philosophy of life than in any particular happening, past or present. Each of the full-length plays turns upon a love story, essentially the same in all. A potentially perfect romance is frustrated by another need, political (the crown in *Elizabeth, Mary,* etc.), social (*Wingless Victory, Winterset*), or private (*High Tor, Key Largo*). While an assortment of contemporary topics are touched upon—the decay of aristocracy, race prejudice, class injustice, revolution, and absolution—the mechanism of the play is always the love affair, and the issue always a certain omnipresent danger of "dying within."

Harold Rosenberg. Poetry. Jan., 1941. pp. 258–60

Maxwell Anderson's independence set him apart from his time. Not only as a literary craftsman—since he alone was writing poetic and romantic tragedies—but in other respects, he was an alien voice. In an age of increasing collectivism this voice could be heard praising individualism, independence, and the frontier spirit. In an age of increasing governmentalism he could still maintain that the best government was that which governed least. As the last champion of what almost amounts to a laissez-faire and rugged individualism, he is an isolated figure, almost an anachronism.

Vincent Wall. SwR. July, 1941. p. 339

I am sure of this: the Anderson plays are declining in theatrical effectiveness but rising steadily in intellectual significance. If he is not an original thinker, Mr. Anderson has at least dug his teeth into a great subject; he has gradually moved beyond the crudely American conception of freedom as license to buy and sell anything at a profit to an Emersonian vision of the "infinitude of the private man." And always one feels—here is the peculiar appeal of the dramas—that he has achieved insight by staring hard at facts. Only Sean O'Casey among his contemporaries can hammer as much of the crude stuff of living into poetry for the stage.

Edward Foster. SwR. Jan., 1942. p. 100

As Mr. Anderson's art matured . . . he evolved at the end of the first decade a working group of principles which were later stated as explicit theory. . . . This theory conceives of drama as having a high destiny, not only in its obligation to reflect a moral universe, but also in its function as inspirer of man's faith and as prophet of his future. The dramas Mr. Anderson wrote during his first decade did not fulfill these high purposes; nor did some of those he wrote during the second decade. But there are half a dozen plays from the later period which come close to his ideal and three or four which realize it fully; among the latter are *Mary of Scotland, Winterset,* and *Key Largo.*

Allan H. Halline. *AL.* May, 1944. p. 81

Mr. Anderson really discovered himself, I think, in the historical plays. Here he developed his characteristic verse-form—a rather rough blank verse with a sort of tumbling, hurrying rhythm, like that of a tossing sea —a verse that can be used in colloquial realistic scenes, but that is capable of rising to high levels of imaginative beauty. Here also, through the study of historical figures and the attempt to recreate and interpret them, he gained a firmer grasp on character than he had shown in his earlier plays—a more penetrating insight, and greater skill in revealing character through speech. And here, too, I think he learned to simplify and clarify his story, just because the material with which he was dealing was so complex that severe simplification was necessary.

Homer E. Woodbridge. *SAQ.* Jan., 1945. p. 60

Many persons who do not count themselves among his most enthusiastic admirers would probably be willing to admit that he has succeeded more fully than any of our other dramatists in persuading a large popular audience to follow him gladly beyond the rather narrow circle of subjects, attitudes, and methods within which it has grown accustomed to remain confined. . . . Something of the same sort may be said of his verse which found ready comprehension in part because it did not, like so much modern poetry, require for its comprehension a familiarity with a modern tradition of which four-fifths of the theater-going public is completely ignorant. It has at least the primary virtue of dramatic verse inasmuch as it is easily speakable and easily understood when spoken.

Joseph Wood Krutch. *American Drama since 1918* (Braziller). 1957. p. 305

See *What Price Glory?, Winterset, Mary of Scotland, Elizabeth the Queen, High Tor,* and *Key Largo* (plays).

ANDERSON, SHERWOOD (1876–1941)

He sits across the table from you as you read. You can almost hear him breathe. It is all so real. This is the way people feel and the way they think, the way a story of this kind must be told. And though this may not be all the world, the world of flowers and ships at sea, it is the frustrated world of the artist, driven back upon himself, and the repressed world of youth. And between the lines there is something—call it symbolism, atmosphere, the mystery of being, what you will—that is in all of Anderson's stories. . . . To him the world is—close-knit, throbbing, pulsating with one life, men and animals, trees, clouds, earth, the whole of nature. And it is this throb, the pulse of creation, that makes the rhythm of his prose.

> Charles C. Baldwin. *The Men Who Make Our Novels*
> (Dodd). 1919. p. 27

Out of . . . fallen creatures, Sherwood Anderson has made the pure poetry of his tales. He has taken the words surely, has set them fiercely end to end, and underneath his hand there has come to be a surface as clean and fragrant as that of joyously made things in a fresh young country. The vocabulary of the simplest folk; words of a primer, a copy-book quotidianness, form a surface as hard as that of pungent fresh-placed boards of pine and oak. Into the ordered prose of Anderson the delicacy and sweetness of growing corn, the grittiness and firmness of black earth sifted by the fingers, the broad-breasted power of great laboring horses, has wavered again. The writing pleases the eye. It pleases the nostrils. It is moist and adhesive to the touch, like milk.

> Paul Rosenfeld. *Port of New York* (Harcourt). 1924.
> p. 176

The thing which captures me and will not let me go is the profound sincerity, the note of serious, baffled, tragic questioning which I hear above its laughter and tears. It is, all through, an asking of the question which American literature has hardly as yet begun to ask. "What for?" . . . It is that spirit of profound and unresisting questioning which has made Russian literature what it is. "Why? why? why?" echoes insistently through all their pages. . . . It echoes, too, in this book, like a great bell pealing its tremendous question to an unanswering sky, and awakening dangerously within one's self something that one has carefully laid to sleep—perhaps one's soul, who knows?

> Floyd Dell. *Looking at Life* (Knopf). 1924. pp. 83–4

Sherwood Anderson is something of an anomaly. He has been more daring than any of his contemporaries in his attempts to get to the basic facts about people. He has tried to explore deeper into human emotions and reactions than they. He has tried to seize on the important, significant moments in the dull and drab lives that go on about him. In his search for the until recently disguised facts about modern life, and in his statement of human problems he stands shoulder to shoulder with the best of his contemporaries the world over. But if he has attempted much, he has often failed. In his disposal of these facts and in his interpretation of these problems he often goes as far off the track as did the writers of the Pollyanna school. His work contains more sentimental alloy than that of any other "serious" modern writer.

Cleveland B. Chase. *Sherwood Anderson* (McBride).
1927. pp. 4–5

To the student of human nature under the conditions of provincial neo-Puritanism there must always belong a high interest to these documents with their toneless murmur as of one who has exhausted eloquence and passion and found them of no avail, with their tortured sense of life as a thing immitigably ugly and mean, with their delineation of dull misery so ground into the bone that it no longer knows itself for what it is. Nowhere in all these pages of Anderson will this student find a breath of freedom or of joy—never the record of an hour of either passion or serenity. Life is walled in; it is imprisoned from itself, from the sources without which it withers and dies. Who will knock down the walls? There is no one, least of all the author himself.

Ludwig Lewisohn. *Expression in America* (Harper).
1932. p. 484

(Hemingway and Gertrude Stein) disagreed about Sherwood Anderson. Gertrude Stein contended that Sherwood Anderson had a genius for using the sentence to convey a direct emotion, this was in the great American tradition, and that really except Sherwood there was no one in America who could write a clear and passionate sentence. Hemingway did not believe this, he did not like Sherwood's taste. Taste has nothing to do with sentences, contended Gertrude Stein.

Gertrude Stein. *The Autobiography of Alice B. Toklas*
(Harcourt). 1933. p. 268

Anderson turned fiction into a substitute for poetry and religion, and never ceased to wonder at what he had wrought. He had more intensity than a revival meeting and more tenderness than God; he wept, he chanted, he loved indescribably. There was freedom in the air, and he would summon all Americans to share it; there was confusion and mystery on the earth, and he would summon all Americans to wonder at it. He was clumsy and sentimental; he could even write at times as if he were finger-painting; but at the moment it seemed as if he had sounded the depths of common American experience as no one else could.

There was always an image in Anderson's books—an image of life as a house of doors, of human beings knocking at them and stealing through one door only to be stopped short before another as if in a dream. Life was a dream to him, and he and his characters seemed always to be walking along its corridors. Who owned the house of life? How did one escape after all? No one in his books ever knew, Anderson least of all. Yet slowly and fumblingly he tried to make others believe, as he thought he had learned for himself, that it was possible to escape if only one laughed at necessity.

> Alfred Kazin. *On Native Grounds* (Reynal). 1942.
> pp. 210-1

Read for moral explication as a guide to life, his work must seem unsatisfactory; it simply does not tell us enough. But there is another, more fruitful way of reading his work: as an expression of a sensitive witness to the national experience and as the achievement of a story teller who created a small body of fiction unique in American writing for the lyrical purity of its feeling. So regarded his best work becomes a durable part of the American literary structure. . . . While Steinbeck and Saroyan could enlarge on his occasional sentimentalism and Hemingway could tighten and rigidify his style, no American writer has yet been able to realize that strain of lyrical and nostalgic feeling which in Anderson's best work reminds one of another and greater poet of tenderness, Turgeniev. At his best Anderson creates a world of authentic sentiment, and while part of the meaning of his career is that sentiment is not enough for a writer, the careers of those that follow him—those who swerve to Steinbeck's sentimentalism or Hemingway's toughness—illustrate how rare a genius sentiment still is in our literature.

> Irving Howe. *Sherwood Anderson* (Sloane). 1951.
> pp. 249, 255

Winesburg, Ohio

Winesburg, Ohio is a primer of the heart and mind, the emotions and the method of Sherwood Anderson. It is the most compact, the most unified, the most revealing of all his books. It is his most successful effort technically, for in it he has told the story of one community in terms of isolated short stories. . . . The author presents the impression that he is discovering for the first time the situations that he reveals to the reader, consequently he leads up to them as haltingly, as slowly as a child opening a door and entering an old, unused room. In the end the effect is cumulative and powerful.

Harry Hansen. *Midwest Portraits* (Harcourt). 1923.
pp. 147–8

Winesburg, Ohio is a psychological document of the first importance; no matter that it is an incomplete picture of modern American life, it is an honest and penetrating one done with bold and simple strokes. These pictures represent the finest combination Anderson has yet achieved of imagination, intuition and observation welded into a dramatic unity by painstaking craftsmanship. They are one of the important products of the American literary renascence and have probably influenced writing in America more than any other book published within the last decade. They made and they sustain Anderson's reputation as an author worthy of comparison with the great short story writers.

Cleveland B. Chase. *Sherwood Anderson* (McBride).
1927. pp. 51–2

We must enter the realm of myth if we are to penetrate deeply into the form of *Winesburg*. . . . The myth of *Winesburg* concerns the legendary American small town, the town represented in the popular tradition as the lazy, gentle village of the Christian virtues. . . . The author's intention is to replace the myth of the small town Christian virtues with the myth of the "grotesques." It is important to remember that the "grotesques" are not merely small town characters. They are universal people, defeated by their false ideas and dreams. . . . The "grotesque" is neither misshapen nor abnormal. He is an unintegrated personality, cut off from society and adrift in his own mind.

James Schevill. *Sherwood Anderson* (Denver). 1951.
pp. 100–103

Poor White

Poor White belongs among the few books that have restored with memorable vitality the life of an era, its hopes and desires, its conflicts between material prosperity and ethics, and its disillusionments, in a manner that stimulates the historical imagination. . . . No novel of the American small town in the Middle West evokes in the minds of its readers so much of the cultural heritage of its milieu as does *Poor White;* nor does Anderson in his later novels ever recapture the same richness of association, the ability to make memorable each scene in the transition from an agrarian way of living to a twentieth-century spectacle of industrial conflict with its outward display of physical comfort and wealth.

> Horace Gregory. Introduction to *The Portable*
> *Sherwood Anderson* (Viking). 1949. pp. 16, 22

In *Poor White* Anderson has given untainted expression to the persistent American myth of isolation: the society that has made money its dominant objective indicates its self-doubt and guilt by stubbornly insisting that the wealthy are unhappy; the society that believes, as no other, in success yet feels a need to brand it with disapproval. Hugh McVey, combining two main constituents of American character, Ford's mindless inventiveness and Lincoln's lonely brooding, has been driven to his work largely by the barrenness of his life; which is to say that the rise of American industrial society is the culmination of previous failure in sociality and that in such a society work is intimately related to the absence of creative activity. The central symbol of the book, through which it gains a quality of muted pathos, is the basket woven in desperation: the basket that is neither produce nor commodity but token of despair.

> Irving Howe. *Sherwood Anderson* (Sloane). 1951.
> p. 129

See *Winesburg, Ohio* and *The Triumph of the Egg* (short stories); also *Poor White, Many Marriages,* and *Dark Laughter* (novels).

AUCHINCLOSS, LOUIS (1917–   )

He is wonderfully adept at showing the conflicts between personalities; at exposing the tyrannies, the dominations, the iron fingers in the velvet gloves of courtesy and social convention and family relationships. . . . His style is fluent, cultivated, urbane. . . . He has wit and irony; he has also a real understanding of and pity for the seekers of their own hurt.

> Sara Henderson Hay. *SR*. Oct. 14, 1950. pp. 37–8

In this novel (*Sybil*), his first, Mr. Auchincloss shows many faults. His style is rather flat, and at times even clumsy; he has a sharp eye, but seldom describes what he observes with quite enough flair or wit. His heroine, furthermore, is a little too sensitive to ring true, a little too much the faithful recorder of her creator's feelings and ideas.

In spite of its limitations, however, *Sybil* is one of the most promising

American novels in a long time. This is because Mr. Auchincloss succeeds in giving us vivid portraits of nearly every one of the people in
his story. . . . Mr. Auchincloss shows them no mercy, spares them
none of their faults, and yet manages to give a little twist of tenderness,
an unexpectedly sympathetic turn, to each of them.

James Yaffe. *YR*. Spring, 1952. p. vi

With his four previous books, Louis Auchincloss has won a solid reputation as a polished and eminently civilized writer with a cool, discerning eye and a quietly satiric sense of humor. *The Romantic Egoists,* in
addition to these qualities, has a somewhat higher voltage than Mr.
Auchincloss has hitherto succeeded in generating. The writing is more
pointed; some of the characterizations are stronger; the storytelling
has more pull and it achieves a sharper impact.

Charles J. Rolo. *At*. July, 1954. p. 83

The Romantic Egoists is a book of quite remarkable distinction and
solidity. The method is rather like Anthony Powell's—there is a similar
dry reticence, a similar quiet building up of surprises from everyday
incidents. But where Mr. Powell sticks out his legs and beams at you,
Mr. Auchincloss, being a *New Yorker* writer, screws the pressure up till
something explodes—and in his case that something is not just another taut nerve, it is a new idea. Not all the sketches are equally
thought-provoking; one or two are a trifle self-satisfied. But most of
them are brilliant essays in that most difficult theme, change of character. Butterflies turn into caterpillars, stones into bread, faces into stone.
Hardly anyone has the nerve to contemplate these things. Mr. Auchincloss, cucumber-cool, can watch them happening to himself.

Mary Scutton. *NSN*. Oct. 9, 1954. p. 449

Apart from his knowledge of the law, Mr. Auchincloss probably knows
more about traditional New York City society than any other good
novelist now working. Furthermore, he seems to believe in the continuing importance of what is left of such society, and the values it
attempts to preserve and hand down. It is precisely the background of
such belief that makes his satirical jibes so entertaining, and makes
the rather neat, foursquare world of his books so comfortable to read
about. *The Great World and Timothy Colt* appeals in part, perhaps un-
intentionally, to the escapist impulse; but it also shows how traditional
writing methods and social attitudes can throw a refreshing light on
parts of the contemporary scene.

John Brooks. *NYT*. Oct. 21, 1956. p. 50

Louis Auchincloss . . . has a direct acquaintance with investment banking and . . . has made himself a skilful craftsman. In several novels and a couple of collections of short stories he has written authoritatively and persuasively about a small but important segment of American business. . . . Auchincloss is a deft prober, and he shows us how a sense of inadequacy and guilt can be created and how it can shape a life. To me the psychological problem to which he addresses himself in *Venus in Sparta* is less interesting than the ethical problem with which he was concerned in his preceding novel, *The Great World and Timothy Colt*. In its portrayal of a particular milieu, however, of a world in which there not only is money but has been money for several generations, the novel demonstrates that Auchincloss knows his stuff and knows how to use it to literary advantage.

Granville Hicks. SR. Sept. 20, 1958. p. 18

It is obviously high time someone pointed out that he is one of our very best young novelists. This is far more than a matter of his knowledge of "the highest stratum of American society" or his alleged resemblance to Edith Wharton. It is true that Mr. Auchincloss knows a good deal about the successful and indifferent children of the earth . . . these people he represents with such complete and quiet understanding that it is easy to overlook their horror and their ultimate pathos.

What moves Mr. Auchincloss is the miracle of the developing heart flourishing incongruously in the great world. . . . Their honesty is his comedy.

Arthur Mizener. NYT. Sept. 21, 1958. p. 4

See *The Romantic Egoists* (short stories); also *The Great World and Timothy Colt* and *Venus in Sparta* (novels).

AUDEN, W. H. (1907–)

Mr. W. H. Auden is a courageous poet. He is trying to find some way of living and expressing himself that is not cluttered with stale conventions and that is at once intellectually valid and emotionally satisfying. In order to do so he is obliged to hack his way in zigzag fashion through a stifling jungle of outworn notions which obstruct progress. . . . The only difficulty in following him is that he seems to be perpetually mixing up two levels of experience, private and public. Publicly he tries to persuade us that the world is a farce, privately we feel that he regards it largely as a tragedy.

John Gould Fletcher. Poetry. May, 1933. pp. 110–1

Auden is a stylist of great resourcefulness. He has undoubtedly drawn heavily on the experimenters of the past decade, Eliot, Pound, Graves, and Riding in verse, and Joyce and Woolf (especially *The Waves*) in prose. But he is not an imitator, for very rarely has he failed to assimilate completely what the model had to give. He is not a writer of one style. The lyrics written in short lines display an aptitude for economy of statement that is almost ultimate; he has sometimes paid for this by an insoluble crabbedness or a grammatical perversity in the unsuccessful pieces, but a few of this type are among his best poems. On the whole, he is most effective in the poems using a long line, poems where the difficulty his verse offers is more often legitimate, that is, derives from an actual subtlety of thought and effect rather than from a failure in technical mastery.

Robert Penn Warren. *AR*. May, 1934. p. 226

Mr. Auden's ideas are not so important as the way in which he expresses them. In his early work he is frequently obscure, not only because of the presence of private jokes which only a few intimates may understand, but because he oversimplifies the communication of complex experiences. He has used the imagery of psychoanalysis for the illumination of the subconscious mind and has left the uninitiated bewildered. . . . It is, of course, still too early to prophesy Mr. Auden's ultimate position. . . . But there can be no doubt that the corpus of his good work, already large enough to merit serious attention, communicates the truth as he has seen it.

James G. Southworth. *SwR*. April, 1938. p. 205

As a technical virtuoso, W. H. Auden has no equal in contemporary English or American poetry; and no equal in French, if we except Louis Aragon. There has been no one since Swinburne or Hugo who rhymed and chanted with the same workmanlike delight in his own skill. . . . He combines a maximum of virtuosity with . . . you could hardly say a maximum, but still a considerable density of meaning. . . . Whether you approach his work through his theology or his virtuosity, he is one of the most important living poets.

Malcolm Cowley. *Poetry*. Jan., 1945. pp. 202–9

In the poems written since Auden came to America the effects are clarified, the ambiguities have all but disappeared. The music hall improvisations which he favors—the purposeful blend of casual horror and baleful doggerel—sometimes make him seem the Freudian's Noel Coward; but the combination of acridity and banality is unsurpassably his own. No living poet has succeeded so notably in the fashioning of metropolitan eclogues. . . . The virtuoso has extended his range, and cleverness is no longer the dominant note. Versatile but no longer special, elaborate without being finicky, Auden has become not only the most eloquent and influential but the most impressive poet of his generation.

Louis Untermeyer. *SR*. Apr. 28, 1945. p. 10

When we compare the Auden of the *Collected Poetry* with the Eliot of *The Waste Land,* we find in Auden more vigor, more scope, greater tension, but less fulfillment. This is natural enough, for Auden is in the middle of the arena riding a wildly bucking horse, whereas Eliot, on the sidelines, has just completed the examination of his horse's broken leg and has shot the horse neatly through the head.

Dan S. Norton. *VQR*. Summer, 1945. pp. 435–6

The best poet of the Auden generation is Auden. His *Poems* (1930) reveal a new social consciousness in original rhymes, conversational or jazz techniques, and unlimited sensitivity. By these rhymes, and by suitable images of deserted factories, frontiers, invalid chairs, glaciers, and schoolboy games, Auden suggests the death of his class. Ideas for improvement, resembling those of D. H. Lawrence, stop short of Marx, who had little use for the individual change of heart that Auden prescribes.

William York Tindall. *Forces in Modern British Literature* (Knopf). 1947. pp. 56–7

He has a brain nimble, alert, never-resting; perception, alive and darting; an imagination which sweeps over his world of perceived things with bewildering brilliance; he has humour which turns to satire; passion, which often consumes itself in scorn. In poetry he may be intensely serious or he may be playing a game in the use of words. His play is grim and and his seriousness playful, and you can never be sure where the fireworks will lead you. In much of his work scorn is the predominant note—scorn of shallow emotion, philanthropic pretension, plutocratic display, slickness, trite phrases, borrowed metaphors, sentimentality, secret vice—and these are things which distract his attention when pure beauty is ready to move him.

R. A. Scott-James. *Fifty Years of English Literature* (Longmans). 1951. p. 216

We may sometimes feel that his view is distorted, that, for example, he thinks more are frustrated today than are in fact frustrated, or that he does not give sufficient weight, especially at present, to the surrounding

evidence of human goodness as against the evidence of human sin.
. . . Nevertheless, he is a significant figure, and in nothing more than
in his sensitivity to the tensions of the age. . . . Auden is at one of
the frontiers of this anxiety-torn world; he is one of those who play out
in themselves, with unusual and revealing clarity, struggles to which,
whether we recognize it or not, we are all committed.

Richard Hoggart. *Auden* (Chatto and Windus).
1951. pp. 218–9

Auden's ideas have changed as strikingly as his way of life has remained the same. There is a dualistic idea running through all his work
which encloses it like the sides of a box. This idea is Symptom and
Cure. . . . The symptoms have to be diagnosed, brought into the
open, made to weep and confess. . . . They may be related to the
central need of love. . . . It is his conception of the Cure which has
changed. At one time Love, in the sense of Freudian release from inhibition; at another time a vaguer and more exalted idea of loving; at
still another the Social Revolution; and at yet a later stage, Christianity. Essentially the direction of Auden's poetry has been towards the
defining of the concept of Love.

Stephen Spender. *At.* July, 1953. p. 75

Perhaps Auden has always made such impossibly exacting moral demands on himself and everybody else partly because it kept him from
having to worry about more ordinary, moderate demands; perhaps he
had preached so loudly, made such extraordinary sweeping gestures, in
order to hide himself from himself in the commotion. But he seems,
finally, to have got tired of the whole affair, to have become willing to
look at himself *without doing anything about it,* not even shutting his
eyes or turning his head away. In some of the best of his later poems
he accepts himself for whatever he is, the world for whatever it is,
with experienced calm; much in these poems is accurate just as observed, relevant, inescapable fact, not as the journalistic, local-color, in-
the-know substitute that used to tempt Auden almost as it did Kipling.
The poet is a man of the world, and his religion is of so high an order,
his morality so decidedly a meta-morality, that they are more a way of
understanding everybody than of making specific demands on anybody.

Randall Jarrell. *YR.* Summer, 1955. p. 607

Mr. Auden . . . identifies himself with the humanity of suffering,
neurosis, and fear. He is a tragic poet who does not particularly care
about the dignity of tragedy. His poetry, by turns rhetorical and colloquial, is always about to slip into bathos. Like its creator it is not

concerned with correct attitudes. I hope I shall not be misunderstood if I say that it is Mr. Auden's readiness to risk a thoroughly bad poem that makes him a far greater poet than Mr. Empson, the most original English poet, in fact, to appear during the last thirty years.

Anthony Hartley. *Spec.* Dec. 9, 1955. p. 816

As our undoubted master of poetic resources, Auden has experimented with every device that would flat the poem into a true statement of the human position as he sees it. Meter, diction, imagery—every device of Auden's great skill (even his flippancy) is a speaking way of refusing to belie the truth with false compare. . . . In the native motion of his genius . . . Auden implicitly warns us away from the stereotyped affirmation of the good, the true, and the beautiful. He is not against the good, the true, and the beautiful, as some foolish critics have argued. Rather, he asks us to weigh these values in mortal fear of smudging them with prettiness, and with an instinctive recognition of the fact that, being human, our feelings are subtle, various, and often conflicting.

John Ciardi. *SR*. Feb. 18, 1956. p. 48

See *The Collected Poetry, The Age of Anxiety, Nones,* and *The Shield of Achilles* (poetry).

BABBITT, IRVING   (1865–1933)

The distinction of Professor Irving Babbitt is that he endeavours to acquire the now unfashionable but not outworn Socratic virtues: he works for an attitude toward letters and the life of which letters are symptomatic that shall be comprehensive, cohesive and based upon perceptions of wholes.

This direction and this effort enables him to outrank almost all his colleagues in American literary criticism. . . . It is Professor Babbitt's Socratic merit that he has succeeded in charting the contemporary chaos and in constructing for himself a unifying attitude.

Gorham B. Munson. *Crit.* June, 1926. pp. 494-6

It is an unpleasant task to profess skepticism about the value of a group of writers who are aiming at the betterment of conduct. The philosophical difficulties that may inhere in Mr. Babbitt's particular defense of sane conduct, I do not feel myself competent to discuss. . . . The ethical code of the Humanists is probably sound enough, but, however sound these abstractions may be, they are of no use to the Humanists or to us so long as they retain the status of pure abstractions; the abstractions remain what Mr. Tate has called wisdom in a vacuum. The arbitrary and mechanical application of these principles to organic experience, whether the experience be literary or non-literary, does not constitute a discipline but rather a pedantic habit.

Yvor Winters. The Critique of Humanism, edited by
C. Hartley Grattan (Brewer). 1930. pp. 329–32

Professor Babbitt's doctrine is a compound of snobbery of the kind I find most irritating. Yet it has some elements in it of sense, even if these elements happen to be platitudes which my iceman, cigar dealer, grocer, butcher, bootlegger, garbage man and dentist already know; i.e., that it is best to keep temperate and thrifty, not to let your temper run away with you, not to make a nuisance of yourself, not to get up in the air over trifles, to see that your family gets properly fed and clothed, to pay your bills and not violate the laws. But what is new or Humanistic about that? Not a single person among my personal acquaintance has ever abandoned a child, although quite a few of them have read Rousseau.

Burton Rascoe. The Critique of Humanism, edited by
C. Hartley Grattan (Brewer). 1930. p. 123

There is no doubt that his aim is the same as that of Brunetière. He attacks the same multiform manifestations of naturalistic relativity. He agrees with him that "there is needed a principle of restraint in human nature (<i>un principe refrénant</i>)," that something must be opposed to "the mobility of our impressions, the unruliness of our individual sense, and the vagrancy of our thought." Brunetière, however, finally came to seek this principle of restraint in revealed religion. Babbitt does not deny that it may be found there, but the conversion of Brunetière is for him an occasion for insisting that the immediate data of consciousness reveal such a principle of restraint at work within the individual, whether or not he believes in revealed religion. Thus Babbitt finds a way to ground his humanism purely on individualism.

Louis J. A. Mercier. The Challenge of Humanism
(Oxford). 1933. pp. 60–1

How perfectly he knew each of those great, queer but powerful beasts, the modernist ideas, how convincingly he set forth the origin, growth, and present shape of each. How admirably he described their skill in concealing themselves, or in appearing innocent while stalking their prey. And how he dissected them all, showing their powerful muscles, their great fangs, and their sacks of poison. . . . To hear him was to understand the modern world.

In his astonishing power of understanding and analysing his enemy, his skill in diagnosing the modernist disease, lies his unique importance.

Hoffman Nickerson. *Crit.* Jan., 1934. p. 194

The astonishing fact, as I look back over the years, is that he seems to have sprung up, like Minerva, fully grown and armed. No doubt he made vast additions to his knowledge and acquired by practice a deadly dexterity in wielding it, but there is something almost inhuman in the immobility of his central ideas. He has been criticized for this and ridiculed for harping everlastingly on the same thoughts, as if he lacked the faculty of assimilation and growth. On the contrary, I am inclined to believe that the weight of his influence can be attributed in large measure to just this tenacity of mind. In a world visibly shifting from opinion to opinion and, as it were, rocking on its foundation, here was one who never changed or faltered in his grasp of principles, whose latest words can be set beside his earliest with no apology for inconsistency, who could always be depended on.

Paul Elmer More. *UTQ*. Jan., 1934. pp. 132–3

His own manner of speech was of the substantial order, straight forward, unadorned, unimaged, owing its flashes of color either to quotations artfully interwoven or to the antics of a playful humor, which in lighter vein regaled itself by caricaturing and distorting any illogical statement or any lapse from good sense in one's hurried interjections. He had, in dialoguing, a mischievous fondness for playing out the game of argument to a finish and inflicting a sudden and disastrous checkmate on any unwary advances of his opponent—a process not always relished by those whose sense of humor was less active than his own.

William F. Giese. *AR*. Nov., 1935. p. 78

Though Babbitt became identified in the public mind with one cause, that which bore the never fully elucidated name humanism, it was recognized in the academic world that he was also the proponent of a cause in one sense larger and more catholic—the cause of the humane study and teaching of literature. At Harvard he fought, in behalf of every American professor who believes that his function comprehends interpretation and criticism, against all who would restrict the academic office to fact-finding, fact-compilation, fact-reporting. Frequently viewed as a reactionary, he defended an academic freedom precious and perishable—the freedom to judge.

Austin Warren. *Com.* June 26, 1936. p. 236

In exposing an idea he would often use a peculiar and significant gesture. His right hand, rising beside its shoulder with spread fingers and outward palm, would make short lateral pushes in the air. There was not the slightest volitant or undulatory motion of the arm—no concession to flying, no fluent gracefulness. Those shoves of the open hand into space—into the spaces of thought—were rigid and impersonal. They insisted that the principle on which he talked was patently universal, belonging to everyone and no one. As for wrong opposing notions, his fingers would sweep them down and away, one after another, while his tongue attacked them.

G. R. Elliott. *AR*. Nov., 1936. p. 41

His opinions were hard-set, his statements clean-cut and definitive. There was no budging him from his positions. This is what made him a precious friend for me, though I did not share in all his principles or judgements. He was the touchstone on which to assay your own thoughts, when you wanted the stimulus of contradiction—always based on deep reflection, fortified by vast learning, ordered by nimble didacticism. His militant spirit (equal to his athletic strength), and his dogmatic peremptoriness (marked on his deep-set features), displeased some. I felt always attracted to his decided personality. . . . The geniality of his smile and wink took away the sharp edge of his obstinacy.

C. Cestre. *Irving Babbitt,* edited by Frederick
Manchester (Putnam). 1941. p. 55

The humanistic point of view is auxiliary to and dependent upon the religious point of view. For us, religion is Christianity; and Christianity implies, I think, the conception of the Church. It would be not only interesting but invaluable if Professor Babbitt, with his learning, his great ability, his influence, and his interest in the most important questions of the time, could reach this point. . . . Such a consummation is impossible. Professor Babbitt knows too much; and by that I do not mean erudition or information or scholarship. I mean that he knows too many religions and philosophies, has assimilated their spirit too thoroughly (there is probably no one in England or America who understands early Buddhism better than he) to be able to give himself to any.

T. S. Eliot. *Selected Essays* (Harcourt). 1950.
pp. 427–8

See *The New Laocoon, Rousseau and Romanticism,* and *On Being Creative* (criticism).

BALDWIN, JAMES (1924–   )

Go Tell It on the Mountain's beauty is the beauty of sincerity and of the courageous facing of hard, subjective truth. This is not to say that there is nothing derivative—of what first novel can this be said?—but James Baldwin's critical judgments are perspicacious and his esthetic instincts sound, and he has read Faulkner and Richard Wright and, very possibly, Dostoevski to advantage. A little of each is here—Faulkner in the style, Wright in the narrative, and the Russian in the theme. And yet style, story, and theme are Baldwin's own, made so by the operation of the strange chemistry of talent which no one fully understands.

                                                    J. Saunders Redding. *NYHT*. May 17, 1953. p. 5

There are many strong and powerful scenes in this work (*Go Tell It on the Mountain*). Mr. Baldwin has his eye clearly on the full values that his sincere characters possess, though these values often are tossed aside and trampled. His people have an enormous capacity for sin, but their capacity for suffering and repentance is even greater. I think that is the outstanding quality of this work, a sometimes majestic sense of the failings of men and their ability to work through their misery to some kind of peaceful salvation. Certainly the spark of the holy fire flashes even through their numerous external misfortunes.

                                                    T. E. Cassidy. *Com*. May 22, 1953. p. 186

Go Tell It on the Mountain is an attempt by a Negro to write a novel about Negroes which is yet not a Negro novel. "I wanted," he says, "my people to be people first, Negroes almost incidentally." In this he is eminently successful, yet, paradoxically, he at the same time manages to convey more of the essential story of the American Negro than do most avowedly historical or avowedly hortatory books on the subject. . . . *Go Tell It on the Mountain* is impressive not only for its psychology or saga, but for its construction, which employs a skillful time-shift, and for a style rich in metaphor and in a sad eloquence.

                                                    John Henry Raleigh. *NR*. June 22, 1953. p. 21

Go Tell It on the Mountain may be the most important novel written about the American Negro. . . . Although *Go Tell It on the Mountain* is meticulously planned, and every episode is organic to the governing conception, it is not primarily a novel of delicate relations, subtle qualifications, and minutely discriminated personalities. There is instead a force above the characters and their relations—adequately realized though they are—which creates an impression of terrible uniformity and strangeness. One of the best things this novel does is capture all the uniqueness, foreignness, and exoticism of Negro life. Like an anthropologist, Mr. Baldwin shows us these people under the aspect of homogeneity; their individual lives represent their collective fate. . . . Mr. Baldwin shows the basic separateness of his people without making them depersonalized savages.

Steven Marcus. *Cmty.* Nov., 1953. pp. 459–61

Mr. Baldwin has been enraged into a style; the harshness of his lot, his racial sensitivity, and the sense of alienation and displacement that is frequently the fate of intellectuals in this country has moved him to portray in lyrical, passionate, sometimes violent prose the complex, oblique, endless outrages by which a man, particularly a black man, can be made to feel outside the established social order.

Dachine Rainer. *Com.* Jan. 13, 1956. p. 385

Few American writers handle words more effectively in the essay form than James Baldwin. To my way of thinking, he is much better at provoking thought in an essay than he is at arousing emotion in fiction. I much prefer *Notes of a Native Son* to his novel *Go Tell It on the Mountain,* where the surface excellence and poetry of his writing did not seem to me to suit the earthiness of his subject matter. In his essays, words and material suit each other. The thought becomes poetry, and the poetry illuminates the thought.

Langston Hughes. *NYT.* Feb. 26, 1956. p. 26

His most conspicuous gift is his ability to find words that astonish the reader with their boldness even as they overwhelm him with their rightness.

The theme of *Giovanni's Room* is delicate enough to make strong demands on all of Mr. Baldwin's resourcefulness and subtlety. . . . Much of the novel is laid in scenes of squalor, with a background of characters as grotesque and repulsive as any that can be found in Proust's *Cities of the Plain,* but even as one is dismayed by Mr. Baldwin's materials, one rejoices in the skill with which he renders them. . . . Mr. Baldwin's subject (is) the rareness and difficulty of love, and, in his rather startling way, he does a great deal with it.

Granville Hicks. *NYT.* Oct. 14, 1956. p. 5

James Baldwin, the young American writer whose first novel *Go Tell It on the Mountain* received wide critical praise, has chosen the special, tortured world of the homosexual as the subject of his second (*Giovanni's Room*). . . . Mr. Baldwin has taken a very special theme and treated it with great artistry and restraint. While he is franker about the physical aspects of male love than other writers who have written on the subject, he manages to retain a very delicate sense of good taste so that his characters never really offend us even when they appear most loathesome, most detestable. This truly remarkable achievement is possible because of Mr. Baldwin's intense sincerity and genuine ability to understand and to pity the wretches involved.

David Karp. *SR*. Dec. 1, 1956. p. 34

Giovanni's Room is the best American novel dealing with homosexuality I have read. . . . James Baldwin successfully avoids the cliché literary attitudes: over-emphasis on the grotesque and the use of homosexuality as a facile symbol for the estrangement which makes possible otherwise unavailable insights into the workings of "normal" society. . . . Baldwin insists on the painful, baffling complexity of things. . . . The complexities are of course most numerous in the treatment of the relationship between David and Giovanni. The void of mutual lovelessness . . . is the central pain of homosexual relationships.

William Esty. *NR*. Dec. 17, 1956. p. 26

Though Baldwin has abandoned the primitive Calvinism on which he was reared, its dogma still has him in thrall. Everything he has written is filled with a sense of human depravity, a deterministic view of the universe, a hopeless search for salvation, and a conviction that unregenerate, alienated modern man is doomed. . . . Baldwin's style is, perhaps, his greatest strength; he is never obvious, banal, or trite. And the determinism and outraged horror with which he views life crops up in a hundred images and ironies. . . . In Baldwin the culminating effect is one of damnation; wretched man is dragged before the bar and condemned to endless fires of guilt and fear. It is the New Calvinism dramatized.

Charles H. Nichols. *Cmty*. Jan., 1957. pp. 94–5

See *Go Tell It on the Mountain* and *Giovanni's Room* (novels); also *Notes of a Native Son* (essays).

See Supplement at end of text for additional material.

BARNES, DJUNA (1900–   )

A facetious commentator has said of Miss Barnes that she has a white pine mind with a mahogany finish, which for all its disrespect, is a fairly accurate description of the surface brilliance which glosses the simple, soft, and human intimations of beauty, truth, and pathos in Miss Barnes's work. Her prose is firm, vibrant, and rhythmical and her poetry ambiguous but melodious. Her stories, playlets, and dialogues are for the most part no more than a succession of brilliant, unrelated, ironic comments in an unintegrated design. . . . In escaping the commonplace, the platitude, the cliché and the formula she has retreated so far into ironic and disillusioned disdain that she has seemingly nothing left but a will for acrid observation and grim absurdities.

Burton Rascoe. *NYHT*. Oct. 14, 1923. p. 25

In the details of Djuna Barnes's stories there is a great deal of fine observation, clearly as well as beautifully phrased. It is the larger outlines of her stories that are obscure. This is perhaps because she sees in detail what the rest of us see, but feels about life as a whole differently from the rest of us. . . . The whole book (*A Book*), when one has ceased to ponder its unintelligibilities, leaves a sense of the writer's deep temperamental sympathy with the simple and mindless lives of the beasts: it is in dealing with their lives, and with the lives of men and women in moods which approach such simplicity and mindlessness, that she attains a momentary but genuine power.

Floyd Dell. *Nation*. Jan. 2, 1924. pp. 14–15

No one need be entirely unhappy this fall with such a book as *Ryder* newly come into the world—no one, at least, with a clear head and a stout stomach. Here are nimble wit, gay humor, trenchant satire, and, above all, a grandiose imagination creating a robustious world of loose-tongued, free-living characters such as have hardly ventured on paper for a century. . . . *Ryder* is certainly the most amazing book ever written by a woman. That much abused word "Rabelaisian" . . . is here perfectly in place. In fact, *Ryder* is more "Rabelaisian" than Rabelais himself.

Ernest Sutherland Bates. *SR*. Nov. 17, 1928. p. 376

(In *Nightwood*) the web of entanglement is naturally and inevitably woven, and the action progresses powerfully to its horrible conclusion. Though the characters are plainly and obtrusively psychopaths, the quality of the book does not derive from that particular, which is simply the mechanism of the tragedy, but from the force and distinction of Miss Barnes's writing. Her style is richly poetic; sometimes it becomes oppressive from a too conscious refinement of perception and language, but for the most part her wit and passion rescue it from its faults. In some passages the intensity of pity and terror effects something akin to genuine catharsis; in others, where the scope of implication contracts to the particular dilemma of the characters, a kind of hysteria results that leaves the reader merely horrified.

Philip Horton. *NR*. March 31, 1937. p. 247

If genius is perfection wrought out of anguish and pain and intellectual flagellation, then Djuna Barnes's novel *Nightwood* is a book of genius. In language, in philosophy, in the story it unfolds, she has woven a dark tapestry of spiritual and emotional disintegration whose threads never outrage each other in clashing disharmony. No gayety and no light falls upon her pattern, which is not to say that her pages are devoid of laughter or humor. For humor she has in abundance but it runs deep in hidden places and the laughter it evokes is tragic. If she has been ruthless and cruel to herself in writing this book out of the rich essence of her knowledge and her thinking and her experience, she has the compensating reward of compelling the thoughtful reader into attention to what she has to say and her manner of saying it. Her prose is lyrical to a degree where it seems of another age and another world but at the same time it does not lose kinship with the earthiness of humans.

Rose C. Feld. *NYHT*. March 7, 1937. p. 4

In her novel (*Nightwood*) poetry is the bloodstream of the universal organism, a poetry. that derives its coherence from the meeting of kindred spirits. The "alien and external" are, more than ever, props; they form the hard rock on which Miss Barnes's metaphysically minded characters stand and let their words soar. The story of the novel is like the biological routine of the body; it is the pattern of life, something that cannot be avoided, but it has the function of a spring, and nothing more. It is in their release from mere sensation, or rather the expression of such an attempted release, that Miss Barnes's characters have their being.

Alfred Kazin. *NYT*. March 7, 1937. p. 6

This (writer) stares away from her in a rigor of horror, probing distance with fixed eyes in the hope that it will yield a niche where the contemporary mind, trained on distrust and disgust, can lose itself in stretches of time beyond our time. . . . For brilliance and formal beauty few novels of any age can compare with it (*Nightwood*). But one must also say how desperate it is.

Mark Van Doren. *Nation*. April 3, 1937. pp. 382–3

In *Nightwood,* as in the work of Braque and the later abstract painters, the naturalistic principle is totally abandoned: no attempt is made to

convince us that the characters are actual flesh-and-blood human beings. We are asked only to accept their world as we accept an abstract
painting . . . as an autonomous pattern giving us an individual vision
of reality, rather than what we might consider its exact reflection. . . .
The eight chapters of *Nightwood* are like searchlights, probing the
darkness each from a different direction, yet ultimately focusing on
and illuminating the same entanglement of the human spirit. . . .
(*Nightwood*) combines the simple majesty of a medieval morality play
with the verbal subtlety and refinement of a symbolist poem.

> Joseph Frank. *SwR*. Summer, 1945. pp. 435, 438,
> 455–6

The Antiphon is unmistakably the work of a mind of distinction and
stature. I was not so much moved as shaken by the spectres it raises.
But is it, as a work of art, successful? Is it really comparable with Webster, or is the style a sham Jacobean, or a sham Eliot-Jacobean make.
. . . The speeches of the characters are never, in the true sense,
dramatic, shaped by a living emotion. For all the sombre violence of
imagery, they are aggregates of fancy, not imaginative expression
proceeding from an inner unity of condition and thought.

> Kathleen Raine. *NSN*. Feb. 8, 1958. p. 174

In *Nightwood,* published in 1936, Djuna Barnes gave us a novel of extraordinary and appalling force, a study of moral degeneration recited
in a rhetoric so intensely wrought, so violent and so artificial, that it dis-
couraged all but the hardiest readers and became a kind of symbol of
sinister magnificence. *The Antiphon*, a verse play in three acts, repeats
the oratorical modes of the novel, though with less obscurity and with
some reduction of queerness. It is still difficult, perversely wayward;
but it does make concessions to ordinary humanity, and there are in it
moments of poetry and true excitement. It is scarcely a play: one cannot imagine it on any stage this side of Chaos and Old Night; but it is
dramatic poetry of a curious and sometimes high order.

> Dudley Fitts. *NYT*. April 20, 1958. p. 22

See *A Book* (miscellany), *Ryder* and *Nightwood* (novels), and *The Antiphon* (play).

BARRY, PHILIP   (1896–1949)

Mr. Barry has had the best preparation that America can give. He
has been educated by our professors and theorists and has built upon

the foundation thus attained with experience in the hard school of Broadway. If he allows nothing to turn him aside from it, he may yet write a great play. . . . His knowledge of the technique, his ability to write sincere and moving dialogue, his poetic sensitivity, the acting quality of his work, his varied experience, all forecast an achievement of which America may be proud.

Carl Carmer. TA. Nov., 1929. p. 826

The characteristic cleverness and brightness of Philip Barry's dialogue have tended to obscure the similarity of pattern of his plays. He deals for the most part with the individual's revolt against conventional pressure for social conformity and attempts to force him into a pattern of behavior to which he is inimical. Most frequently his antagonist is "business" and everything it stands for: its goal, way of life, its hostility to originality and individuality. To Barry "big business" represents everything he abhors in modern life.

Eleanor Flexner. American Playwrights (Simon).
1938. p. 249

Before the emergence of S. N. Behrman, Mr. Barry was our best writer of polite comedy. The true gift was his, but he valued it so little that he was said to have only contempt for Paris Bound, one of the earliest as well as one of the best of his pieces, and he gradually sacrificed success to two tendencies incompatible not only with the spirit of comedy but also, it would seem, with each other. Increasingly Mr. Barry became a snob and a mystic. His later plays were full of yearning elegants who seemed equally concerned with the meaning of the universe and with what the well-dressed man will wear—in his head as well as on it.

Joseph Wood Krutch. Nation. Dec. 24, 1938. p. 700

I carefully reread what Mr. John Anderson, Mr. John Mason Brown, and Mr. Brooks Atkinson had in their various columns seen fit to record (about Here Come the Clowns). . . . I was compelled to admire the diffused and sociable precision with which they expressed their respect for the playwright's intentions, past achievements, forward-looking subject matter and approach, and the equally exact conveyance of the tedium they felt at his present effort. Each of these reviews of theirs conveyed also the sense we get of fine intervals as such, of genuine and thrilling inventions now and then. . . . That the critics wished the author well was clear, and wished his play well, and clearly too they could not find their way in it. Which . . . is pretty much the way I feel about it.

Stark Young. NR. Dec. 28, 1938. p. 230

On the whole Mr. Barry has written an interesting play (*The Philadelphia Story*), with shrewd touches of character, and much humour. Moreover, Mr. Barry's heart and brain are both on the side of the angels, which is something in this day of inverted values in the theatre. . . . Also Mr. Barry can write admirable dialogue, though at times his tendency to preciosity is evident. In fact this latter tendency is his greatest artistic sin. But despite this fault Mr. Barry has written his best comedy since *Holiday,* though not his finest play—that is *Here Comes the Clowns.*

Glenville Vernon. *Com.* April 14, 1939. p. 692

Phil was as serious at heart as he was gay on the surface. He was at once a conformist and a non-conformist, a sophisticate and a romantic. He was a good American from Rochester who never ceased to be Irish. The accent of his spirit, regardless of the accent of his speech, remained Gaelic. The fey quality was there, the ability to see the moon at midday. He had the Irish gift for both anger and sweetness, and the Irish ferment in his soul. He was a Catholic whose thinking was unorthodox and restless. Even in his comedies, when apparently he was being audacious, he employed the means of Congreve to preach sermons against divorce which would have won a Cardinal's approval.

John Mason Brown. *SR*. Dec. 24, 1949. p. 26

Barry was essentially a writer of comedy, and repartee was his stock in trade. He did however aspire to a greater seriousness, and there are passages in *Hotel Universe* and *Here Come the Clowns* which indicate ability in that direction. The difficulty, whenever he attempted heavier fare, was that he seemed to walk on tiptoe, perhaps in fear that he would be laughed at, and his work always seems to be trying to anticipate that possibility by getting in the first laugh. It moves gingerly among the more disturbing moral problems, darting and feinting, always ready to withdraw into the security of a smart remark, as though to indicate that the author has not lost his sense of humor or got himself out of his depth.

Walter Kerr. *Com.* Jan. 26, 1951. p. 398

Barry's was a healing art at a time when dramatic art was mostly dissonance. Perhaps Barry felt the need for healing too greatly himself to add to the dissonance and to widen the rifts in the topography of the modern, specifically contemporary American, scene. Whatever the reason, and regardless of the risk of indecisiveness, Barry sought balm in Gilead, found it somehow, and dispensed it liberally—and with gentlemanly tact. . . . It was not the least of Barry's merits, a mark of both his breeding and manliness, that his manner was generally bright and brisk and that the hand he stretched out to others, as if to himself, was as firm as it was open.

John Gassner. TA. Dec., 1951. p. 89

Certainly it falls far short to dismiss Barry as a witty writer of high comedy of manners, bantering, facile, and superficial. He was that and more. Beneath his flippancy and "chit-chat" was a sensitive and deeply spiritual writer coming to grips with the psychology of his times and expressing a yearning for maturity and emotional wholeness. No other American playwright was able to transmute the raw elements of unconscious life into a work of art so delicate, so subtly ingratiating, and so fresh in form, as did Philip Barry. If these are the criteria of greatness, *Hotel Universe* belongs among the great plays.

W. David Sievers. Freud on Broadway (Heritage).
1955. p. 211

See *Holiday, The Philadelphia Story, Here Come the Clowns,* and *Hotel Universe* (plays).

BEHRMAN, S. N. (1893–   )

In this American play (*The Second Man*) the talk is fresh, the epigrams are not machine made but seem spontaneous and in keeping with the character, and there is a merry note of satirical burlesque in the melodramatic episodes introduced into the story. . . . This play may owe much to *The Importance of Being Earnest* (as it owes something, also, to *Man and Superman*), but it is no mere rehash of ancient styles. It is much more the ironic Yankee burlesque-comedy of Hoyt and Cohan touched with literary distinction and a hint—just a pleasant hint—of thoughtfulness.

Walter Prichard Eaton. NYHT. June 26, 1927. p. 12

Mr. Behrman . . . remains one of the few playwrights that we have ever had in America who does not cause embarrassment to dramatist, actors, and audience when he indulges in brains or sophisticated statement. . . . He is one of those rare authors in the theatre who do not mistrust civilized society and do not think that Times Square must understand or no tickets will be sold. He has sensed the fact that in our theatre there is a genuine opening for such dramatists as might leave the mass of theatre-goers confounded or displeased; for him the French proverb, "Pour les sots acteurs Dieu créa les sots spectateurs," extends to audiences and plays, and he has taken the bold risk of failing in his own way instead of failing in somebody else's.

Stark Young. *NR*. Dec. 28, 1932. p. 188

The remarkable thing about Mr. Behrman is . . . the clarity with which he realizes that we must ultimately make our choice between judging men by their heroism or judging them by their intelligence, and the unfailing articulateness with which he defends his determination to choose the second alternative. . . . Mr. Behrman's plays are obviously "artificial"—both in the sense that they deal with an artificial and privileged section of society and in the sense that the characters themselves are less real persons than idealized embodiments of intelligence and wit. . . . No drawing room ever existed in which people talked so well or acted so sensibly at last, but this idealization is the final business of comedy.

Joseph Wood Krutch. *Nation*. July 19, 1933.
pp. 74–6

You must grant S. N. Behrman the privilege of writing plays on his own terms, if you want to enjoy them in the theatre. His dramas have little plot and less action. People come and go as often as they do in other men's plays; they meet and part and meet again, but they do so because the conversation—which is the alpha and omega of Behrman's playwriting—needs a shift in emphasis or in attack, rather than because of any change in the aspect of the situation. You cannot fairly say that his plays are "not about anything," for they fairly bristle with the contemporary, social, economic, controversial things they are about. But his drama is in his talk, and it would be well for people who think they do not like "talky" plays to consider carefully what Behrman can do with talk, before they decide too definitely that many words never made a play.

Edith J. R. Isaacs. *TA*. April, 1936. p. 258

Behrman is a man of rather emotional, almost lyrical and, if you will, sentimental nature, embarrassed by a sense that this nature is not quite smart enough for the society in which he finds himself and in which he would like to occupy a favored place. Thinking of himself—and he is preoccupied with the subject—he is ready to weep, but society, he believes, would consider such behavior unseemly. Looking at the world, he is almost ready to cry out or at least to heave so profound a sigh that the sound might be construed as a protest, so he suppresses his impulse and flicks our consciousness with a soft wit that contains as much self-depreciation as mockery. He tries to chide his world with a voice that might be thought to belong to someone else—a person far more brittle, debonair, urbane than he knows himself to be.

Harold Clurman. NR. Feb. 18, 1952. pp. 22–3

Something deeper than style alone distinguishes him from our many purveyors of light entertainment, including those who have at one time or another made a speciality of skepticism and debunking. That something is his habit of balancing the score. It makes him not merely a judicious but an acute playwright rather than a merely congenial one. He always remains *two* men; one man makes the positive observations, the second proposes the negative ones. . . . Behrman's art of comedy, including his so-called comic detachment, consists of an ambivalence of attitudes that has its sources in the simultaneous possession of a nimble mind and a mellow temperament.

John Gassner. TA. May, 1952. pp. 96–7

Providence Street, the background for most of (*The Worcester Account*), is the scene of Mr. Behrman's early life. . . . To one who comes, as I do, from a similar place, the half-ghetto of an American city, these people are immediately familiar. I recognize them in Mr. Behrman's skillful reproduction and wonder why they often appear shortened, flattened, and lacking in vigor and primitive idiosyncrasy. They have been written of with charm and in the process have emerged somewhat tamed and weakened. Somehow the charm does not seem to belong to them; it is not their native charm but one which the author has lent them, returning to them after long separation. The air of nostalgia which pervades the book is often appealing but many times emphasizes the quaintness of Providence Street rather than its difficulty and poverty.

Saul Bellow. SR. Nov. 20, 1954. p. 41

See *Four Plays*.

BELLOW, SAUL (1915–   )

It was of Dostoevsky that André Gide once said all factions could find something in him to support their claims but no one faction could claim him exclusively. Some of this holds true for Saul Bellow. He came up as a writer out of the tough, tight literary magazines, established his beachhead, as it were, and is now successfully fanning out into the broader and brighter domains; his talents, valued from the start by the severer literary critics, have gradually begun to be noticed by greater numbers of the ordinary, intelligent vintage. Mr. Bellow's work contains innumerable diverse elements, it has variousness and is against the grain. His readers, therefore, are to be found anywhere and everywhere and they can be anyone at all.

Harvey Breit. *The Writer Observed* (World). 1956.
p. 271

Saul Bellow views the past in an almost anthropological way. He finds no moral in it, but rather senses the shaping force of heredity and social circumstances upon man, the isolation and burden of human life, the natural ruins of time, and the continuity of human history. Like James Joyce, a chronicler of the city, Bellow attempts to discover pattern and meaning in the hidden fantasies of man living in a mechanized urban world where the daily routine obscures private realities and where normal human reactions are expected to be proper, abstractions systematized by a code of social behavior, not deeply felt, emotional or genuine. . . . Altogether Bellow seems more suited by temperament and ability than any writer of his generation to create for America "the uncreated conscience" of modern man.

Edward Schwartz. *NR*. Dec. 3, 1956. pp. 20–1

The suffering, the humility, the moral goodness in his books, the honest and ironic realization of human weakness: these are the traits that appeal to us. But this note of resignation, of acceptance does not appear in Bellow's work after the violence and passions of life, as it commonly does in the work of major artists. It appears in Bellow's fiction *instead* of the emotional storm and stress it should transcend. The central image of the hero in his novels and stories is not indeed that of the rebellious son, but of the suffering, the tormented, and the conforming son.

To use the phraseology of Salinger, this hero is the good boy, the sad sack; or to use the terms of depth psychology, he is the castrated son. . . . There is something in Bellow's accent that may remind us of the innocent and childlike spirit of a Stephen Crane, consumed as the earlier writer was also by the flames of his oedipal and religious conflict.

Maxwell Geismar. *American Moderns* (Hill and
Wang). 1958. pp. 221–4

In all his work thus far Bellow has been moving toward a hedged affirmation: an insistence upon the importance and possibility of such fulfillment with a recognition always of its cost. In qualified terms he has revived the cult of personality and, paradoxically, given us the clue to the social history of the post-war years. Preoccupied with what it feels like, what it takes, what it means to be a human being, Bellow has made the man the vital center of his work. No guiding philosophical conception shapes his image of man; he is concerned with man alive. . . . Bellow wants no confining philosophy or myth . . . has no patience with passing social phenomena . . . finds the essentials of human experience in human beings seeking themselves and seeking love. And fleeing annihilation. That fate awaits the corporate, tabulated man whose identity has been surrendered. Bellow's fiction is surely a response to his need and ours to push back the many-faced Leviathan. It is a reaction against the loss of community in modern America. In its ultimate atomization it is social history.

Chester E. Eisenger. *Accent.* Summer, 1958.
pp. 202–3

The Victim

What Mr. Bellow attempts is to compress into an arena the size of two human souls the agony of mind which has ravaged millions of Jews in our century. *The Victim* rates as a subtle and thoughtful contribution to the literature of 20th century anti-Semitism.

Richard Match. *NYHT.* Nov. 23, 1947. p. 10

The Victim . . . is hard to match in recent fiction, for brilliance, skill, and originality. . . . *The Victim* is solidly built of fine, important ideas; it also generates fine and important, if uncomfortable, emotions.

Diana Trilling. *Nation.* Jan. 3, 1948. pp. 24–5

The Victim depended much on intensification of effect, by limitations on time, by rigid economy in structure of scene, by placement and juxtaposition of scenes, by the unsaid and the withheld, by a muting of action, by a scrupulously reserved style. The novel proved that the author had a masterful control of the method, not merely fictional good manners, the meticulous good breeding which we ordinarily damn by the praise "intelligent."

Robert Penn Warren. *NR.* Nov. 2, 1953. p. 22

The Adventures of Augie March

Reading *The Adventures of Augie March* in 1953 must be a good deal like reading *Ulysses* in 1920. . . . Tentatively: Saul Bellow is perhaps a great novelist, *The Adventures of Augie March* perhaps a great novel. If *The Adventures of Augie March* is great, it is great because of its comprehensive, not-naturalistic survey of the modern world, its wisely inconclusive presentation of its problems; because its author dares to let go (as so many very good and very neat modern writers do not); because the style of its telling makes the sequence of events seem real even when one knows they couldn't be; because the novel is intelligently and ambitiously conceived as a whole that esthetically comprehends its parts; because it is an achievement in and a promise of the development of a novelist who deserves comparison only with the best, even at this early stage of his development.

Harvey Curtis Webster. *SR*. Sept. 19, 1953. pp. 13–4

Augie introduces the most startling extremes of realism with cheerful casualness. He does not hold them against life itself. There is a great deal of vigorous love-making, explicitly described, but with a joy and attractiveness very rare in recent fiction. . . . Not since Dos Passos's *U.S.A.* has there been in a novel such an enormous range of discriminating reporting as in this one. . . . The crowding of descriptive epithets and hyphenizations recalls Hopkins.

Robert Gorham Davis. *NYT*. Sept. 20, 1953.
pp. 1, 36

If such a novel is to be fully effective the sense of dramatic improvisation must be a dramatic illusion, the last sophistication of the writer, and . . . the improvisation is really a pseudo-improvisation, and . . . the random scene or casual character that imitates the accidental quality of life must really have a relevance, and . . . the discovery, usually belated, of this relevance, is the characteristic excitement of the genre. That is, in this genre the relevance is deeper and more obscure and there is, in the finest examples of the genre, a greater tension between the random life force of the materials and the shaping intuition of the writer.

It is the final distinction, I think, of *The Adventures of Augie March* that we do feel this tension, and that it is a meaningful fact.

Robert Penn Warren. *NR*. Nov. 2, 1953. p. 22

Saul Bellow's new novel is a new kind of book. The only other American novels to which it can be compared with any profit are *Huckleberry Finn* and *U.S.A.*, and it is superior to the first by virtue of the complexity of its subject matter and to the second by virtue of a realized unity of composition. In all three books, the real theme is America, a fact which is not as clear in this new book as it is in its predecessors, perhaps because of its very newness. . . . *The Adventures of Augie March* is a new kind of book first of all because Augie March possesses a new attitude toward experience in America: instead of the blindness of affirmation and the poverty of rejection, Augie March rises from the streets of the modern city to encounter the reality of experience with an attitude of satirical acceptance, ironic affirmation, and comic transcendence of affirmation and rejection.

Delmore Schwartz. PR. Jan., 1954. pp. 112–3

Mr. Saul Bellow's *The Adventures of Augie March* is (a) study in the spiritual picaresque, a later form of the traditional *bildungsroman* in which the *picaro* or hero is consciousness rather than swashbuckling rogue, and so is required, as the rogue is not, to develop, deepen, strike through its first illusion to the truth which, at the end of the road, it discovers to be its fate. But *Augie March* begins with the aphorism, "Man's character is his fate," and ends with the aphorism, 'Man's fate is his character." The learning is in the transposition. Man's fate is that he shall inherit, be stuck with, his character. The movement which the transposition represents is the movement from the naturalist to the existentialist, from what is determined to what is accepted or chosen.

John W. Aldridge. In Search of Heresy (McGraw).
1956. pp. 131–2

Henderson the Rain King

Henderson the Rain King differs from *Augie March* in many interesting ways. In the earlier novel Bellow uses a loose structure to illustrate, through a long series of essentially realistic episodes, the vast possibilities of contemporary life. Beginning in poverty and illegitimacy, Augie ranges far, horizontally and vertically, to end in uncertainty. Henderson, on the other hand, born to every advantage, has lived fifty-five years of unquiet desperation. Of Augie's kind of patient pilgrimage he has never been capable. He is driven by the voice that cries, "I want, I want," and the story of his search is both romantic and dramatic. I cannot say that *Henderson the Rain King* is a better book than *Augie March:* the denseness of the experience in the earlier novel is something almost unparalleled in contemporary literature. But it is a wonderful book for Bellow to have written after writing *Augie March*. It is a book that should be read again and again, and each reading, I believe, will yield further evidence of Bellow's wisdom and power.

Granville Hicks. SR. Feb. 21, 1959. p. 20

Anyone unfamiliar with Mr. Bellow's earlier work would, I think, immediately recognize from a reading of *Henderson* why so many of our best critics consider him the most important American novelist of the postwar period. For one thing, it contains a wealth of comic passages that bear comparison with the wild, grotesque humor we find in some of Faulkner's stories, and for another it is endlessly fertile in invention and idea. Beyond that, however, this is by all odds the most brilliantly written novel to have come along in years. Mr. Bellow has finally been able to discipline the virtuosity that ran away with *Augie March,* and the result is a prose charged with all the vigor and vitality of colloquial speech and yet capable of the range, precision, and delicacy of a heightened, formal rhetoric.

Norman Podhoretz. *NYHT.* Feb. 22, 1959. p. 3

See *Dangling Man, The Victim, The Adventures of Augie March,* and *Henderson the Rain King* (novels); also *Seize the Day* (short stories).

See Supplement at end of text for additional material.

BENÉT, STEPHEN VINCENT (1898–1943)

John Brown's Body . . . is as good as knowledge, sincere personal feeling, and Mr. Benét's particular literary expertness, could make it. To argue that it is more than this, would be quite specially unjust. It is a popular patriotic epic of essentially the same order as Noyes's Elizabethan Odyssey; regarded as a grand historical poem like *The Dynasts,* it would be a heavy disappointment. All the virtues of readability, romantic charm, reminiscent pathos, it has in abundance; the higher virtues that one might expect of such a performance, it very definitely lacks. It lacks these partly because it is not organized and controlled, as such a poem would be, by a clear and sweeping philosophic vision; partly because it is not directed for all its competence, by a rigorous and corrective artistic purpose.

Newton Arvin. *NYHT.* Aug. 12, 1928. p. 2

John Brown's Body has been called among other things an epic and it has been compared, not unfavorably, to the *Iliad.* Mr. Benét himself has no such pretensions. . . . The poem is not in any sense an epic; neither is it a philosophical vision of the Civil War; it is a loose episodic narrative which unfolds a number of unrelated themes in motion picture flashes. In spite of some literary incompetence in the author and the lack of a controlling imagination, the story gathers suspense as it goes and often attains to power.

Allen Tate. *Nation.* Sept. 19, 1928. p. 274

Epic is too heroic a word, no doubt, to stand alone as descriptive of this poem (*John Brown's Body*); a word associated too loftily with Homer and Virgil, with Dante and Milton; suggestive of masterpieces of the past, whose royal rhythms carry mythical gods and heroes through magical exploits. Mr. Benét's poem is a kind of cinema epic, brilliantly flashing a hundred different aspects of American character and history on the silver screen of an unobtrusively fluent and responsive style.

Harriet Monroe. Poetry. Nov., 1928. p. 91

Stephen Benét has the true gift of poetry, and he has a scope and energy of ambition that is rare among poets in this practical age. . . . Even where Benét's poetry is not so fine, it is sustained by a fine sincerity— by the poet's own heart honestly feeling all that is felt—and it is adorned with interruptions of excellent lyrical song. All these virtues compel one to judge *John Brown's Body* by the standards of great art. And as a great work of art, I think the book fails. . . . It is a sophisticated book, an intellectual book, full of complicated, diverse and extremely up-to-date ideas. Only as a whole it lacks idea. It lacks attitude. It lacks the unity that is imparted by an intention.

Max Eastman. Bkm. Nov., 1928. p. 362

Mr. Benét keeps to the middle of the road in his verse as in his thinking. Neither an innovator nor an imitator, he is an able craftsman who draws upon sources both old and recent. With some lapses his poetry is interesting, perceptive, and in good taste. . . . He is the critical historian who shrinks from the half-truths and savageries of prophecy and partisanship; lacking the evidence for a final judgement, he is content to chronicle. As such he has his place and a not undistinguished one; for an honest chronicler who is also a skilful poet is better than a score of false prophets without art.

Philip Blair Rice. Nation. July 18, 1936. pp. 81–2

His verse is a survival of an abundant native line; it has become a virtual guide-book of native myth and folklore, their place-names, heroes, humours, and reverences. . . . Mr. Benét derived, through Lindsay, from the bardic romantics who held sway in American poetry for over a century. . . . In America this tradition, in its homeliest form, was the living authority of text-books and family anthologies all the way from Neihardt, Riley, and Markham, back through Hay, Harte, and Miller, to the bearded dynasties of Longfellow and Bryant—a succession hostile to eccentric talent or refined taste, scornful of modernity or exotic influence, once the pride of the burgeoning Republic, and now chiefly a source of cheerful embarrassment to teachers and blushing incredulity to their students. Mr. Benét has aspired from his school-days to a place in this old American line.

Morton Dauwen Zabel. Poetry. Aug., 1936. pp. 276

Mr. Benét, when not writing hundreds of pages of flat free verse, can be a poet, and can tell a first-rate story when not wrestling with attitudes towards history. I think posterity will treat him much like Stevenson. Some will ignore him; the young will treasure his adventure tales, especially *Spanish Bayonet;* and most people will like his ballads, love poems, and prose fantasies. At his unpretentious best he is a writer of sure skill and simple charm. But his efforts as interpreter of the American scene and the world crisis will be tactfully forgotten. No matter how fertile their imagination, little of worth results when writers who do not feel *prophetically* the power of ideas attempt to express social and historical truths.

Frank Jones. Nation. Sept. 12, 1942. p. 218

He was in sheer fact the poet so urgently called for by our last national poet, the first to chant songs for and of all America, Walt Whitman. And unlike Walt Whitman, whose prophetic symbolism could be read by the people only in single poems and passages, he broke through the ivory wall and was read (as Whitman prophesied some American would be) by the population at large. It seems probable that no writer of poetry in English has ever been read by so many in his lifetime—not even Longfellow—as was Stephen Benét. And while he was popular, he never wrote down to his public. He gave them his best, and it was good.

Henry Seidel Canby. SR. March 27, 1943. p. 14

His life was a model, I think, of what a poet's life should be—a model upon which young men of later generations might well form themselves. He was altogether without envy or vanity. He never considered appearance, or tried to present himself as anything but what he was, or paid the least attention to the prevalent notions of what a poet ought to be. Also, and more important, he was truly generous. . . . Moreover, his generosity was not a moral quality alone. It was an intellectual quality as well. . . . It was this warm and human concern with things seen, things felt beyond himself, which gave him his quality as a poet.

Archibald MacLeish. SR. March 27, 1943. p. 7

Stephen Vincent Benét's death was a particular loss because he added to the variety of American poetry. His contribution of the historical narrative was unique, since few practiced it and no other approached his success. It is important to define his effort. He was not interested in mouthing the word "America." . . . Benét's deep regard for the United States of America was based not on a feeling of blood and earth, but on an honest belief in this country as remarkably permitting human freedom. He knew the misery and corruption, and you'll find them in his books. But, stronger than any other motive, you will find Benét's fascination with the effort of these states to be a place where that reckless and distorted word "liberty" actually means individual right and intellectual exemption.

Paul Engle. Poetry. Dec., 1943. p. 160

Whatever may be the eventual position of Benét's work in the ranks of American letters, one suspects that it will persist, in a quiet way, pretty far forward, despite the cyclical clamor as advance guards change. . . . Stephen Vincent Benét had a faith and a delight in people and a belief that they could come to good ends. And it is precisely this faith and delight and belief that distinguish his work from that of most of his noisier contemporaries, that make his storied people stand out. . . . Benét's people exist in an older context . . . a context of accomplishment; of reaffirmation of the ancient and necessary faith that man not only can defeat his devils but can act with decency toward his fellows.

Robeson Bailey. SR. Jan. 4, 1947. p. 16

See *The Selected Works of Stephen Vincent Benét*.

BIERCE, AMBROSE (1842–1914?)

His stories are their own justification. We may not agree with the method that he has chosen to use, but we cannot escape the strange, haunting power of them, the grim, boding sense of their having happened—even the most weird, most supernatural, most grotesquely impossible of them—in precisely the way that he has told them. . . . Mr. Ambrose Bierce as a story teller can never achieve a wide popularity, at least among the Anglo-Saxon race. His writings have too much the flavour of the hospital and the morgue. There is a stale odour of mouldy cerements about them. But to the connoisseur of what is rare, unique, and very perfect in any branch of fiction he must appeal strongly as one entitled to hearty recognition as an enduring figure in American letters.

Frederic Taber Cooper. Bkm. July, 1911. pp. 478-80

He was as great a satirist as we have record of, and in his hands satire became a keen and terrible weapon. It has been deplored that he used his vast equipment of offense on small fry, but all the folk with whom he concerned himself satirically shared, in his estimation, a common insignificance, and he saw the great and famous of London and New York condemned in time to a like oblivion. . . . He was rich in anecdotes of lethal horrors, and neither the visible nor the unseen appanages of death seemed to hold any terrors for him. . . . For his exceeding power in invoking images and emotions of the uncanny and supernatural, we had dubbed him the Shadow Maker.

George Sterling. *AM*. Sept., 1925. pp. 15–8

Bierce was of imperial bearing, and cavalier beauty. His friends still speak of his deep blue steel-like eyes, his curly crown of tawny hair, his voice of haughty taciturnity. Almost six feet in height, his compact, well-knit figure gave the impression of clean-cut strength and restrained power. This appearance of rugged manhood Bierce never lost; when at the age of seventy-two he crossed the Rio Grande, he was as well preserved as an English country squire.

Leroy J. Nations. *SAQ*. July, 1926. p. 255

There was nothing of the milk of human kindness in old Ambrose; he did not get the nickname of Bitter Bierce for nothing. What delighted him most in life was the spectacle of human cowardice and folly. He put man, intellectually, somewhere between the sheep and the horned cattle, and as a hero somewhere below the rats. His war stories, even when they deal with the heroic, do not depict soldiers as heroes; they depict them as bewildered fools, doing things without sense, submitting to torture and outrage without resistance, dying at last like hogs in Chicago, the former literary capital of the United States. So far in this life, indeed, I have encountered no more thorough-going cynic than Bierce was.

H. L. Mencken. *Prejudices: Sixth Series* (Knopf).
1927. p. 261

With his air of a somewhat dandified Strindberg he combined what might be described as a temperament of the eighteenth century. It was natural to him to write in the manner of Pope: lucidity, precision, "correctness" were the qualities he adored. He was full of the pride of individuality; and the same man who spent so much of his energy "exploring the ways of hate" was, in his personal life, the serenest of stoics. The son of an Ohio farmer, he had no formal education. How did he acquire such firmness and clarity of mind? He was a natural aristocrat and he developed a rudimentary philosophy of aristocracy which, under happier circumstances, might have made him a great figure in the world of American thought. But the America of his day was too chaotic.

Van Wyck Brooks. *Emerson and Others* (Dutton).
1927. p. 152

In his stories . . . the events are narrated with restraint, the descriptions have no excessive details, for the various details are "constituents" of the atmosphere and nearly every word is necessary for the realization of the detail. As a rule, Bierce aims to obtain the total and enduring effect by means of atmosphere, and in many stories it would be unsafe to say that the narrative has greater importance than the impression or the conviction that he wishes to "flow" from the stories; in some instances, he allows us to view an action from several points of vantage. He has a delicate sense of the shades of meaning and of strength in words; therefore, he puts the right word in the right place. The style, in brief, is excellent.

Eric Partridge. *LM*. Oct., 1927. p. 637

Sense was in the balance with sensibility, for Bierce was in the very nature of the case a man of feeling. So on the aesthetic side he added the delicate perception of the portrait painter to the caustic judgements of the cartoonist. The attitude and utterance of the two are in complete contrast. The intellectual Bierce was always on the offensive; always ready to express himself in brilliant brevities. But the Bierce who wrote of the mysteries and the thrills of individual experience was receptive, deliberate, and deliberative, ready to surrender to a mood in a wise passiveness; willing to court in the shadows the shy thoughts that would not come out in the sunlight.

Percy H. Boynton. *More Contemporary Americans*
(Chicago). 1927. p. 89

The force which resided in Bierce and wrought through him was wit. The wit was coupled with, actuated by, a perversity which made it recoil even from itself, to the redoublement of both movements. And action and reaction, wit and recoil, coming into play as one impulse in one instant, as a lightning-stroke and a thunder-clap so near that no interval is detected—these determined the odd pattern of Bierce's thought and of his personal literary idiom.

Wilson Follett. *Bkm*. Nov., 1928. p. 284

If his names lives, it is within the range of probabilities that it will be as a tradition of wit, courage and decency. Whatever judgement may be passed on his work, it does not affect the important fact that Bierce was one of the most provocative figures of his generation. One cannot reflect on the facts of his life without coming to entertain an admiration for his splendid courage and indomitable spirit. To those of us in the West who have watched the fate of his reputation with a peculiar and personal interest, it has always been a source of satisfaction to realize that dead, absent or unknown, he has survived his critics and that he has even bettered his enemies who pursued him into Mexico, "to feast on his bones."

Carey McWilliams. *Ambrose Bierce* (Boni). 1929.
p. 335

The fame of Ambrose Bierce ultimately will rest upon his literary work as a whole. That his distinction as an author is not confined to his short-stories alone is apparent, for his fame as a writer was firmly established before any of them were written; they but extended his renown. To be sure, I hold these stories to be the greatest ever published in any language. . . . But Bierce was a great artist in all that he wrote; he was no better in one branch of literature than he was in another, poetry excepted—and his verse that was not poetry was yet the best of verse. So numerous were his literary activities, embracing so many classifications of literature—more classifications well done than any other author in all time achieved—that I find it impossible to isolate any one classification and say that his fame will endure mainly because of his contributions to that particular field.

Walter Neale. *Life of Ambrose Bierce* (Neale). 1929.
pp. 453–4

Rejecting violently the novel, realism, dialect, and all use of slang, humorous or otherwise, Bierce stood firmly for the short story, romance, and pure English produced through intense, self-conscious discipline. Bierce was first and foremost a disciplinarian. He placed great emphasis on the technique of fiction and verse. He was constantly eager to be correct, and to see that others were correct even in the details of punctuation. . . . He sought, like Poe, to make a single vivid impression upon the reader. To that end he eliminated all extraneous references. Furthermore, each story is a complete world in itself, controlled by the writer's logic, not by the illogicality of life. Since Bierce saw no point in reproducing the flat tones of ordinary life, he found an interesting topic only in the impingement of the extraordinary or the unreal on the normal course of events.

C. Hartley Grattan. *Bitter Bierce* (Doubleday). 1929.
pp. 118, 121–2

His stark simplicity, uniting beauty of diction with truth of presentation, arouses wonder, apprehension, curiosity and thrill, and the climax arrives with the reader pent-up with emotion. Then comes the startling *dénouement,* subtly simple, extremely plausible and pregnant with power. Bierce, the soldier, had lived dangerously. His stories of the American Civil War are among his best, realistic to a high degree, provocative of deep thought.

Clifford Bower-Shore. *BkmL*. August, 1930. p. 283

If it be objected that Poe's characters seldom seem lifelike, what must be our objection to Bierce? They have absolutely no relevant characteristics that strike us as human, save their outward description; it is never for the character's sake but always for the plot's sake that a Bierce story exists. Bierce was interested, even more than Brown, Poe, or Melville, in the *idea* of the story—seldom in the human significance of it. In fact some of the stories exist essentially for the whiplash ending, which in Bierce's handling antedated O. Henry. But the Bierce story can be reread with some profit for there is real evidence of a technician's hand.

George Snell. *AQ*. Summer, 1945. p. 51

It is fitting that someone should be born and live and die dedicated to the expression of bitterness. For bitterness is a mood that comes to all intelligent men, though, as they are intelligent, only intermittently. It is proper that there be at least one man able to give penetrating expression to that mood. Bierce is such a man—limited, wrong-headed, unbalanced, but in his own constricted way, an artist. He will remain one of the most interesting and eccentric figures in our literature, one of our great wits, one of our most uncompromising satirists, the perfecter of two or three new, if minor genres: a writer one cannot casually pass by.

Clifton Fadiman. *SR*. Oct. 12, 1946. p. 62

Along with Poe, Bierce was one of those rare birds in American literature—a Dandy in Baudelaire's sense of the term. The Dandy opposes to society, and to the human world generally, not some principles but himself, his temperament, his dreamed-of depths, his talent for shocking, hoaxing, and dizzying his readers. An aesthetic Enemy of the People, Bierce exploited whatever was most questionable in his personality, dramatizing his sense of guilt and perdition in theatrical horrors and a costume of malice. . . . Out there in his West Coast newspaper office Bierce was somehow seized by that hypnosis of evil and defiance that has inspired so much of modern literature from symbolism to Dada and Surrealism.

Harold Rosenberg. *Nation.* March 15, 1947. p. 312

There was never any danger that Bierce's stories would be forgotten. Now they are old-fashioned, creaky, melodramatic, but they are also art. . . . Throughout the writings runs a kind of fierce, disillusioned democracy, negative rather than positive—a warfare on all injustice and impiety. In Bierce's bitterness there is never a whine or whimper. You feel he had a relish for it. Or say he had a relish for the world, and finding it bitter he hated it with a whole heart.

Walter Havighurst. *SR.* Jan. 25, 1947. p. 16

See *The Collected Writings* (1947 edition).

BISHOP, ELIZABETH (1911–   )

Elizabeth Bishop is spectacular in being unspectacular. Why has no one ever thought of this, one asks oneself; why not be accurate and modest? Miss Bishop's mechanics of presentation with its underlying knowledge, moreover, reduce critical cold blood to cautious self-inquiry. . . . With poetry as with homiletics tentativeness can be more positive than positiveness; and in *North and South* a much instructed persuasiveness is emphasized by uninsistence. . . . At last we have someone who knows, who is not didactic.

Marianne Moore. *Nation.* Sept. 28, 1946. p. 354

The publication of Elizabeth Bishop's *North and South* . . . is a distinct literary event.

"The Map" introduces us to her strongly delineated, subtly colored world. Following it south, from "The Imaginary Iceberg" to "the state with the prettiest name" (Florida), we are exploring a style supple, versatile and idiomatic, brilliant without being shallow, profound without trying. . . . Without striving for novelty Elizabeth Bishop's poems make their appeal to the senses, the mind, the heart, and what goes beyond classification since it is, as in all original poetry, the reflection of a "light that never was, on sea or land."

Lloyd Frankenberg. *SR.* Oct. 12, 1946. p. 46

If the author of the thirty-two remarkable poems in this book used paint she would undoubtedly paint "abstractions." Yet so sure is her feeling for poetry that in building up her over-all water-color arrangements she never strays far from the concrete and the particular.

"The Fish" is a case in point. There has not been a poem like it, I think, since Richard Eberhart's "The Groundhog," but Miss Bishop approaches her symbol more impersonally and the diction is less mannered.

Selden Rodman. NYT. Oct. 27, 1946. p. 18

I find the same detached, deliberate, unmoved qualities in the new work as in her old. She is unhurried. The new poems represent two a year for the past nine years. . . . Miss Bishop is not interested in changing the language of poetry. She conserves good means. She is devoted to honest announcements of what she knows, to purity of the poem, to subtle changes in scope and intention. . . . Her work is as steady as prose, but it has its own poetic luminosity.

Richard Eberhart. NYT. July 17, 1955. p. 4

The augury of Miss Bishop's early poems has been fulfilled in a small body of work which is personal, possessed of wit and sensibility, technically expert and often moving.

The first collection of her poems brought together thirty poems and established Miss Bishop's reputation more soundly than is often achieved by a first book. One or another of a half dozen of the poems . . . have already become almost indispensable items in any anthology of modern poetry. . . . The poems of *A Cold Spring* offer not a further range but new poems which, at their best, have the same qualities which distinguish the most memorable of her previous work.

Coleman Rosenberger. NYHT. Sept. 4, 1955. p. 2

The distinction of the poetry . . . has been most often its insistence on the opacity and impenetrable presence of the object, whose surfaces will yield, to a pure attention, not sermons, but details. . . . The happiest consequence of this kind of work will be the refreshment it affords the language (which becomes impoverished by the moralizing of descriptive words) and the sense it gives of immense possibility opening; as if from playing checkers we now come to chess, we delightedly may foresee combinations endlessly intricate, and the happier for going beyond the range of conscious intention a good deal of the time. But there are consequences less cheerful as well: one of them is triviality, or you may call it the want of action, where the poem never becomes so much as the sum of its details and so, in two senses, fails to move; another closely related, is the inspired tendency to believe all things possible to a clever precision and a dry tone.

Howard Nemerov. Poetry. Dec., 1955. pp. 181–2

Miss Bishop's world is opulent, but in the most unexpected and most humble ways. As a poet, she gives order to this opulence. She enumerates it. She stabilizes the shudder, the nerve, the reflection, the pleasure and the irradiation. . . . In this poetic world there is nothing merely invented. There is no fantasy and no delirium. There are embellishments, in the best tradition, but what is embellished is always true. What is sanctioned is what has been found to be authentic. . . . Elizabeth Bishop is a partisan in the world.

Wallace Fowlie. Com. Feb. 15, 1957. p. 514

See *Poems: North and South and A Cold Spring.*

BISHOP, JOHN PEALE (1892–1944)

His tradition is quite evidently aristocratic. He prefers the fine, the delicate, the rare in character or in performance. Several of the poems have to do with the aristocracy of the South. I do not think, however, that one can accuse Mr. Bishop of snobbery. Through the poems runs the realization that, regardless of preference, the time has come when the fine flower of aristocracy is decadent, that terrible though this process may be, aristocracy must now be reinvigorated by contact with more primitive and ignorant classes. . . . He shrinks a little from the common herd, but he does not entirely deny them.

Eda Lou Walton. Nation. Feb. 7, 1934. pp. 162–3

There is, then, the contemporary preoccupation with styles (not simply style), with metrical forms, and with the structure of the line. But Bishop, of all the modern poets who take this approach, feels the least uneasiness about a proper subject matter. There is no one subject, no one scene, nor a single kind of imagery coming from a single subject or scene: every poem, as I say, is a new problem. And Bishop feels no inhibition in the presence of any kind of material.

Allen Tate. NR. Feb. 21, 1934. p. 52

One would surmise, even without the specific information, that his acquaintance with French poetry of the later nineteenth century is immediate, and not second-hand through Eliot and Pound. But it seems that Eliot, Pound, and Yeats have done something to define the precise use Bishop has made of these and other models. And it is not that Bishop has merely re-adapted current techniques; it is that he has written with the same attitudes from which those techniques were developed. The principle of unification to be detected in the attitudes behind the present poems is not so much the unification of a single personality or a philosophy or a fundamental theme, as it is the unification that a period affords its various fashions.

Robert Penn Warren. *Poetry*. March, 1934. p. 345

Mr. Bishop is one of the school of Eliot and Pound; he has the sense of an individual poem as being something as separately well made as a vase or a candlestick, a sense hardly to be found in Jeffers or Sandburg. . . . The range of Mr. Bishop's achievement is not great: a few detached observations sensitively recorded over a number of years; but he understands the meaning of craftsmanship. He knows that for words to take on the illusion of life there must be the precarious marriage between content and form.

F. O. Matthiessen. *YR*. Spring, 1934. p. 613

I believe that John Peale Bishop has written one of the few memorable novels of this decade (*Act of Darkness*). . . . Mr. Bishop has chosen his material with the same care that he devotes to the writing of a poem; and since he is a poet of unusual sensibility, one finds in his prose an admirable restraint in the use of the so-called "poetic" image and vocabulary. There is fine economy of words in his paragraphs; and by effective inversion of adjectives his prose cadence is of highly individual (but not spectacular) quality. I believe these matters were of concern to Mr. Bishop in the writing of his novel—and not whatever social implications it may contain. He had, however, something to say which was a record of experience, and the fact that he has said it well produced a narrative of continuously exciting revelation.

Horace Gregory. *NYHT*. March 10, 1935. p. 7

This sensitive re-creation of adolescence (*Act of Darkness*), poetic, obviously autobiographical, Proustian in conception although not in style, introduces a new Southern novelist. . . . If I have read the novel aright, it is this: That body and spirit are not one but two that move along parallel lines, supplementing each other to form a track. . . . *Act of Darkness* must by all means be set down as a superior book. There is power behind its sensitivity. And in its best passages this first novel achieves distinction.

Fred T. Marsh. *NYT*. March 17, 1935. p. 6

Mr. Bishop is one of the few men now writing in America or elsewhere who recognize the privileges, tests, and ordeals of the aesthetic discipline. . . . The unity in (his) poems derives from his effort to return, after widely eclectic experiences in art and the sophistication of New York and Paris, to his native roots and loyalties, his moral plight as an individual, and to the recovery of his local habitation and a name. . . . Mr. Bishop still respects the impersonal discipline and objective moral sense of his symbolist teachers. His work asks to be considered as poetry before it makes its appeal as a private history or an American document. . . . His work has everything that taste, finish, and conscience can give it.

Morton Dauwen Zabel. Nation. April 12, 1941.
pp. 447–8

It is difficult enough to describe Mr. Bishop's essential talent. It is a rather unusual combination of the scholar and the sensualist. The intellectual today likes his learning and the lyricist, of course, loves his love poems. There is a bad separation. Mr. Bishop thinks what he feels, he experiences actually what ideally he knows as a scholar, he can be at the same time serenely intellectual and terribly sensual. . . . He combines one's feeling with one's thinking.

Peter Monro Jack. NYT. Jan. 4, 1942. p. 5

Bishop's basic theme is the loss of form, the loss of myth, the loss of a pattern. . . . It is true that Bishop's poetry is often poetry about poetry, but then Bishop's conception of poetry is more profound than the man-in-the-street's essentially "literary" conception. The problems of writing poetry and the problems of a formless and chaotic age become at many points identical. . . . Certainly none of Mr. Bishop's problems would be solved by his abandoning his theme. . . . Or by giving up a concern for "form." Indeed, the most successful of Bishop's poems are precisely those which exploit his theme most thoroughly and which are most precisely "formal."

Cleanth Brooks. KR. Spring, 1942. pp. 244–5

One of Bishop's great merits was to have realized his limitations and, unlike so many other American writers, to have preferred perfect minor achievement to over-ambitious failure. In this way he turned a defect of destiny into an aesthetic virtue. He was that rare thing in American literature, a true type of the second-order writer who, though incapable of supreme creative achievement, keeps alive a sense for the highest values. It is this type of writer whom the French delight to honor, recognizing their importance for the continuance of a vital cultural tradition; and this is perhaps one reason why Bishop felt so powerful an attraction for French culture.

Joseph Frank. SwR. Winter, 1947. pp. 106–7

We have been used to hearing the West Virginian dismissed as *too* typical, i.e, too derivative on the one hand, too immersed in class consciousness (upper level) on the other; yet his essays and poems in their progress . . . amply display an original mind and reveal the generous, passionate, humane personality finally emerging from beneath the successive masks of the "provincial," the dandy, the snob, the ironist. . . . Toward the end, the romantic exile came home to his own idiom, and achieved in his poetry a density of meaning projected with classic purity of tone.

> Gerard Previn Meyer. *SR*. Oct. 2, 1948. p. 24

As a poet he is, perhaps, not obscure; his life was outwardly serene but it conceals a sensiblity that was courageously tortured; conditions that look identical seem simultaneously to have hamstrung his talents and set him free. He is infinitely discussable, for he raises (how forcibly I was not aware) the crucial problems of writing now, in America, as well as the adequacy of available solutions. He is more pertinent, both in achievement and mechanism, than, say, Kafka. The achievement matters but the torture is instructive, for it is the torture of the creative will, persistently willing to will, but the will being again and again dissipated, and reviving, being frittered or smashed, but always returning.

> William Arrowsmith. *HdR*. Spring, 1949. p. 118

See *Collected Poems, Collected Essays*, and *Act of Darkness* (novel).

BLACKMUR, RICHARD (1904–1965)

Poetry

Blackmur is preoccupied with pure poetry. . . . His metrics have the individuality of the classic composers of chamber music. . . . The joints of his moods with everyday are thin at times, and one must be alert with utter inner poise to hear or to heed him. A whole page of print, which yesterday opened vistas, today will seem blank until tomorrow it opens wider. Always the subject matter . . . illustrates human subterfuge from oblivion and ruse against the unavoidable futility of existence. . . . Even as he finds home Way Down East and in the Hub where landscape and men exhausted smile and move and speak with grace unknown to their past times of strength, so does he universally at once express and comment upon a cultural decadence.

> John Brooks Wheelwright. *NR*. July 21, 1937. p. 316

The writing . . . is nervous, extraordinarily complex in texture, and urgent with a kind of religious New England cantankerousness that one has scarcely heard in contemporary verse since the too early death of John Wheelwright—not that I mean to imply that Mr. Blackmur derives from Wheelwright (the debt, if it exists, must surely be reckoned the other way around), but that the vibrant originality of the one stirs memories of the other, *discordes concordantes.* . . . I am saying, in short, that Mr. Blackmur, extraordinarily difficult though he can be, is a poet *sui generis;* and the *genus* is rare and important.

Dudley Fitts. *SR.* March 20, 1948. p. 28

The poems . . . are nakedly of and about the human spirit, seriously concerned with the state of the individual caught in the enormous trap of a universe of things and theories.

It isn't easy to write poetry of a high metaphysical order. Blackmur avoids rhetorical bombast, occult mystification, overmodernized trimmings. . . . The fault of Blackmur is his deadly seriousness unlightened by even the grim humor of irony.

Oscar Williams. *Nation.* Oct. 10, 1942. p. 354

These are poems of the most extreme situations possible, of a constricted, turned-in-upon-itself, contorted, almost tetanic agony: the poet not only works against the grain of things, but the grain is all knots. . . . Sometimes the pain is too pure to be art at all, and one is watching the nightmare of a man sitting in the midst of his own entrails, knitting them all night into the tapestry which he unknits all day. But there is in the poems, none of that horrible relishing complacency with which so many existential thinkers insist upon the worst; the poems try desperately for any way out, either for the Comforter—*some* sort of comforter—or else for that coldest comfort, understanding.

Randall Jarrell. *Nation.* Apr. 24, 1948. p. 447

Criticism

Specifically and primarily, the method can be described as that of taking hold of the words of the poem and asking two very important questions: (1) Do these words represent a genuine fact, condition, or feeling? (2) Does the combining of these words result in "an access of knowledge"? Knowledge in the full sense, one must add, for something must be made known "publicly," "objectively," in terms which any intelligent reader, with the proper effort, can grasp; as distinct from terms and language used "privately," "personally," "subjectively." Now of the two questions, it is the first that Blackmur emphasizes and the second which he often neglects. The discrete parts—sentences, phrases, single words (which are sometimes counted)—are the main object of his attention. The way in which they combine is sometimes an afterthought (though this is less so in the more recent essays).

Delmore Schwartz. *Poetry*. Oct., 1938. p. 30

With a critic like Richard P. Blackmur, who tends to use on each work the special technique it seems to call for, and who at one time or another has used almost every type of criticism, the difficulty of placing any single way of operating as his "method" is obvious. What he has is not so much a unique method as a unique habit of mind, a capacity for painstaking investigation which is essential for contemporary criticism, and which might properly be isolated as his major contribution to the brew. . . . Blackmur is almost unique in his assumption that no demand for knowledge the poet makes on the serious reader (that is, the critic) is unreasonable, and that if he doesn't have the information he had better go and get it.

Stanley Edgar Hyman. *Poetry*. Feb., 1948.
pp. 259, 262

For Mr. Blackmur poetry is the supreme mode of the imagination and in his quest for the genuine in the mode he is nearly fanatical. He likes nothing better than breaking butterflies of poetry on the wheel of criticism, although it must be noted that almost every poet thus broken . . . emerges whole again and illuminated. What Blackmur does is focus attention and heighten awareness.

Milton Rugoff. *NYHT*. Dec. 28, 1952. p. 5

Again and again, until it touches a note of hysteria and one wonders at such insistence, Mr. Blackmur speaks out against his anathema—expressive language. He makes constantly an appeal to reason, which in poetry is objective form. . . . The fact is, Mr. Blackmur has been attempting as difficult a critical job as was ever conceived. . . . Perhaps Mr. Blackmur's fearful note is near to the cry of those who push analysis to the limit of reason. And perhaps, as I think, he has been pushed himself into statements that exceed his purpose, as when he says, for instance, that poetry is "language so twisted and posed in a form that it not only expresses the matter in hand but adds to the stock of reality." . . . Mr. Blackmur arrives, by way of the back stairs, at a sort of higher romanticism, where we children of his prior, or downstairs enlightenment are likely to feel timid or ill at ease.

Hayden Carruth. *Nation*. Jan. 10, 1953. p. 35

In recent years as a Professor of English at Princeton he has become the fountainhead of a distinctly personal and highly original school of criticism. His standards are high, his language fluent, though sparse, and on occasion recondite, and he pays extraordinary attention to minute detail; his work represents a constant searching of the mind for the highest amount of intellectual pressure and insight it will yield.

During these years Mr. Blackmur has, in reality, gone to the school of his own bold intelligence and allowed himself that free and full "response to experience" he deems to be the first duty of a critic.

Leon Edel. *NYT.* April 17, 1955. p. 4

The alienated artist is . . . ordinarily forced into one of two possible roles: that of the lonely prisoner in a personal "ivory tower," or that of a prophet without honor, a rather owlish Cassandra.

To some extent, perhaps, R. P. Blackmur fills both these roles. . . . While he has not abandoned the technique of "criticism of criticism" which is often regarded as a kind of hallmark of modern ivory-tower-ism, he is essentially engaged in a work of public persuasion, evangelical, almost apocalyptic. . . . Criticism should turn, Mr. Blackmur, believes, from poetry, which, as poetry, seems to him to have declined in value for us, to the novel, which he regards as the most significant literary form now and in the future. The ideal which he sets before the critic is thus a synthesis of Coleridge and Aristotle.

John F. Sullivan. *Com.* May 13, 1955. p. 159

See *From Jordan's Delight, The Second World,* and *The Good European* (poetry); *Language as Gesture* and *The Lion and the Honeycomb* (criticism).

BODENHEIM, MAXWELL (1893–1954)

He has humiliated nouns and adjectives, stripped them of their old despotisms and loyalties, and of the importance which ages of power as vehicles of broad emotions had given them over the minds of poets and men. He has given them the roles of impersonal figures tracing his mathematics of the soul. His words are sharp, neatly strung, with tapping consonants and brief unemotional vowels, like the chip of a fatal chisel. . . . Metaphysics is a man's choice of his own *mise en scene*—in Bodenheim's poems it is an arctic light in which his brilliant images accept their own insignificance as finalities, yet are animated by the macabre elation which has thrown them into relief.

Louis Grudin. *Poetry.* Nov., 1922. pp. 102–4

His verse is Chinese. It does not resemble Chinese poetry; it is not a direct and unfigured commentary on nature; quite the contrary. It is Chinese in etiquette rather, being stilted, conventional to its own conventions, and formally bandaged in red tape. It is a social gathering of words; they have ancestries and are over-bred; they know the precepts of the Law and take delight in breaking them. Meeting together they bow too deeply, make stiff patterns on paper or silk, relate their adventures in twisted metaphor and under an alias, sometimes jest pompously behind a fan. They discovered irony late in life.

Bodenheim is a master of their ceremony and arranges it with an agile fantasy which takes the place of imagination.

Malcolm Cowley. *Dial.* Oct., 1922. p. 446

Here is a ferocious anti-sentimentalist. I am not sure how much of a poet Mr. Bodenheim is. What I am sure of is that his work is honest—honest to the point of mocking at its own honesty—and that it never mistakes a state of sentiment for one of intense feeling. . . . Mr. Bodenheim is, as the stinging acidity of his style betrays, less concerned anyway with feeling than with thought. Life is to him a boundless paradox, an irony of defeat, a bitter act of treachery. Alike in his method of writing, his attitude to society at large, and his defiant individualism, he reveals the poet preoccupied with moral, rather than aesthetic, values.

John Gould Fletcher. *Fm.* Jan. 30, 1924. p. 502.

One has a picture of Bodenheim as ring master, cracking his savage whip over the heads of cowering adjectives and recalcitrant nouns, compelling them to leap in grotesque and unwilling pairs over the fantastically piled barriers of his imagination. It is a good show—particularly for those who have not seen it too often. . . . He is still—if I may take my metaphor out of the circus—the sardonic euphuist; his irony leaps, with fascinating transilience, from one image to another. . . . But, for all his intellectual alertness, the total effect is an acrobatic monotony: what started as a manner is degenerating into a mannerism.

Louis Untermeyer. *Bkm.* April, 1924. pp. 220–1

Though his sensitive feeling for words betrays him sometimes into preciosity, mostly he makes it serve his purpose. For his is an art of veiled and egoistic emotions, in which the immediate subject, be it a lady or a buttercup or the rear porch of an apartment building reflects, like an actor's practice-mirror, the poet's swiftly changing expressions and attitudes. . . . With Mr. Bodenheim it is the one all-engrossing phenomenon of the universe. Standing before the mirror, he is kindled to frozen fires of passion over the ever-changing aspects of his thought in its mortal sheath; he is intrigued—nay, moved to the white heat of ice by the subtle workings of his mind, trailing off from the central unreal reality there visible out to nebulous remote circumferences of an ego-starred philosophy.

Harriet Monroe. *Poetry*. March, 1925. pp. 322–3

His poems frequently testify to the fact that he has had, and that he is capable of emotion; but they are almost never a direct expression of emotions. Rather, they are an analytic recollection of such states of mind; and the effect, in the hands of the curious word-lover that Mr. Bodenheim is, is odd and individual and not infrequently pleasing. In his simpler and less pretentious things, when he merely indulges his fancy, as in "Chinese Gifts," he can be charming. Here the verbalist and the cerebralist momentarily surrender, hte colder processes are in abeyance, and the result is a poetry slight but fragrant. But for the rest, one finds Mr. Bodenheim a little bit wordy and prosy. One feels that he works too hard and plays too little; or that when he plays, he plays too solemnly and heavily.

Conrad Aiken. *NR*. June 1, 1927. p. 53

To consider Mr. Bodenheim at all is very much like considering a prickly pear; one never knows when he is going to get a thorn run through his finger. Still, like the prickly pear, once the combative surface is pierced an edible and tasty (albeit faintly acidulous) fruit is to be discovered. In other words, Mr. Bodenheim has his values, his poetical accomplishments (of no mean order, either), his impalpable connotations, and his savage satirical zest that is quite often salty enough to delight the victim. Together with his value he has drawbacks. Now these drawbacks are mainly on the surface, as the thorns of the prickly pear are. They are evidenced mainly in an undue suspiciousness of the world at large, in an instinctive gesture of defense that reveals itself in a consistent offensive, in an emphatic disgust for the commonplaces and courtesies of polite living and in a passion for cerebralism that sometimes goes to such lengths as to defeat its objective.

Herbert Gorman. *SR*. June 18, 1927. p. 912

Maxwell Bodenheim's book of poems (*Bringing Jazz*) might well be used as a starting point for a definition of jazz esthetics. First of all, it provides a particular kind of superlative entertainment that depends almost entirely upon the titillations of jazz rhythm and the impact of a brilliant, quickly assimilated image. . . . Next we see that Boden-heim's specific brand of irony which he has employed throughout his work, including the discovery of the American underworld in his novels, is converted into a jazz medium. . . . In spite of the many attempts to capture jazz rhythm with all its essentials intact and at the same time to create actual poetry, we have but two successful examples of this style, both significant because they display a like precision in technique: T. S. Eliot's "Fragments of an Agon: Wanna Go Home, Baby?" and a selection of three or four poems from *Bringing Jazz*.

Horace Gregory. *NR*. March 12, 1930. p. 107

Mr. Bodenheim is all personality. He has become a legendary figure of Bohemianism, a vague mixture of Greenwich Village orgies and soap-box oratory. Of course he is neither one nor the other. He is a poet entirely writing about himself and when he seems to be writing about the injustice of the world and the wretched social system of the world he is still writing about himself, as one might almost say, a willing and masochistic victim. He takes upon himself the whole burden of the worker's complaint against the capitalist's way of making his life. . . . His poems are largely a set of grievances, and they have their value. . . . Their value, in so far as it is a value, is in personality, not at all in communism or in religion but in one's self. . . . It is the quick, involved and rude life that Mr. Bodenheim writes of, his own life, not necessarily correlated with the life of our time.

Peter Monro Jack. *NYT*. March 29, 1942. p. 4

See *Selected Poems;* also *Blackguard, Georgie May, Crazy Man,* and *Sixty Seconds* (novels).

BOGAN, LOUISE (1897–   )

Under a diversity of forms Miss Bogan has expressed herself with an almost awful singleness. . . . One can be certain that experience of some ultimate sort is behind this writing, that something has been gone through with entirely and intensely, leaving the desolation of a field swept once for all by fire. But the desolation is not vacancy or lassi-tude. The charred grass is brilliantly black, and the scarred ground is fascinating in its deformity. There still is life, hidden and bitterly ur-gent.

Mark Van Doren. *Nation*. Oct. 31, 1923. p. 494

Miss Bogan's themes are the reasons of the heart that reason does not know, the eternal strangeness of time in its periods and its passage, the curious power of art. Her mood is oftenest a sombre one, relieved not by gaiety but by a sardonic wit. She is primarily a lyricist. . . . It is the spirit's song that Louise Bogan sings, even when her subject is the body. The texture of her verse is strong and fine, her images, though few, are fit, her cadences well-managed. . . . Implicit in her work is the opposition between a savage chaos and the world that the ordering imagination, whether directed by the intellect or the heart, controls.

Babette Deutsch. Poetry in Our Time (Holt). 1932.
pp. 238–9

There are bitter words. But they are not harassingly bitter. . . . There are paralleled series of antithetical thoughts, but the antithesis is never exaggerated. . . . There are passages that are just beautiful words rendering objects of beauty. . . . And there are passages of thought as static and as tranquil as a solitary candle-shaped flame of the black yew tree that you see against Italian skies. . . . There is, in fact, everything that goes to the making of one of those more pensive seventeenth century, usually ecclesiastical English poets who are the real glory of our two-fold lyre. Miss Bogan may—and probably will—stand somewhere in a quiet landscape that contains George Herbert, and Donne and Vaughan, and why not even Herrick?

Ford Madox Ford. Poetry. June, 1937. pp. 160–1

I hope she now decides to make some change in her theory and practice of the poet's art. Together they have been confining her to a somewhat narrow range of expression. Her new poems—meditative, witty, and sometimes really wise—suggest that she has more to say than can be crowded into any group of lyrics, and that perhaps she should give herself more space and less time. Most American poets write too much and too easily; Miss Bogan ought to write more, and more quickly, and even more carelessly. There are poems, sometimes very good ones, that have to be jotted down quickly or lost forever.

Malcolm Cowley. NR. Nov. 10, 1941. p. 625

Miss (Leonie) Adams and Miss Bogan were surely sisters in the same aesthetic current; and while I must confess that I have often wondered why that sisterhood insisted on wearing its chastity belt on the outside, poetry nevertheless remains wherever the spirit finds it.

But—speaking as one reader—if I admire objectively the poems of the first three (the earlier) sections of Miss Bogan's collection, with the poems of section four, I find myself forgetting the thee and me of it. . . . Miss Bogan began in beauty, but she has aged to magnificence, and I find myself thinking that the patina outshines the gold stain. . . . Miss Bogan sees into herself in the late poems—and not only into herself, but deeply enough into herself to find within her that jungle —call it the Jungian unconscious if you must—that everyone has in himself.

John Ciardi. *Nation*. May 22, 1954. pp. 445–6

Louise Bogan has always seemed to me a considerable problem. . . . At first you can see only the special hyperesthesia, the trance state so common in the poetesses of the first quarter of the century. . . . As you read on, you discover a fundamental, all-important difference. Louise Bogan really means what she says. . . . You have an honest, yet piercing awareness of life as fundamentally tragic. The hyperesthesia is there, but it is embroiled in life, it handles and judges life in real terms.

Kenneth Rexroth. *NYHT*. July 4, 1954. p. 5

The virtues of her writing which have been most often spoken of are, I should suppose, firmness of outline, prosodic accomplishment, chiefly in traditional metrics, purity of diction and tone, concision of phrase, and, what results in craft from all these, and at bottom from a way of seizing experience, concentrated singleness of effect. . . . A large part of their moral force derives from the refusal to be deluded or to be overborne. The learning of the unwanted lesson, the admission of the hard fact, a kind of exhilaration of rejection, whether of the scorned or the merely implausible, the theme appears in the earliest work. . . . It is an art of limits, the limit of the inner occasion and of the recognized mode.

Leonie Adams. *Poetry*. Dec., 1954. pp. 166–9

Women are not noted for terseness, but Louise Bogan's art is compactness compacted. Emotion with her, as she has said of certain fiction, is "itself form, the kernel which builds outward from inward intensity." She uses a kind of forged rhetoric that nevertheless seems inevitable. . . . One is struck by her restraint—an unusual courtesy in this day of bombast.

Marianne Moore. *Predilections* (Viking). 1955. p. 130

Miss Bogan's volume . . . is not the volume of a poet for whom verse is merely a pastime, a diversion; the care with which the details have been selected and ordered . . . is the care of devotion. . . . All this is fine and dandy, and it may properly lead—as it has led—to observations about the importance of cultivating a poetry of care in a careless world. . . . (Yet) some of the critics . . . have noted a coldness here, an overscrupulousness there, and a general absence of the warm rhetoric of persuasion in poems so strenuously dedicated to the "verbal discipline."

Reed Whittemore. *SwR*. Winter, 1955. p. 163

See *Collected Poems* and *Selected Criticism*.

BOWLES, PAUL (1910–   )

Much of this almost Gothic violence arises from the clash of the civilized with the primitive, but more basically it stems from the fact that Mr. Bowles's characters (both enlightened and native) are warped and morbid beings. They are all, if not mad, severely neurotic, hugging to themselves some quietly terrible frustration, some taint, some malevolent perverseness that finally can be no longer controlled and explodes with twisted fury.

John J. Maloney. *NYHT*. Dec. 3, 1950. p. 4

Paul Bowles is a man and author of exceptional latitude but he has, like nearly all serious artists, a dominant theme. That theme is the fearful isolation of the individual being. He is as preoccupied with this isolation as the collectivist writers of ten years ago were concerned with group membership and purposes. . . . Bowles is apparently the only American writer whose work reflects the extreme spiritual dislocation (and a philosophical adjustment to it) of our immediate times. He has "an organic continuity" with the present in a way that is commensurate with the great French trio of Camus, Gênet, and Sartre.

Tennessee Williams. *SR*. Dec. 23, 1950. p. 19

Mr. Bowles is one of the very few writers to depict the part Arab, part colonial-cosmopolitan life of North Africa without any trace of romanticization. He has a remarkable gift for evoking its atmosphere with graphic authenticity; and, at the same time, he externalizes in that atmosphere the inner drama he is unfolding—the drama of the Hollow Man, the man things are done to. . . . The weakness of both Bowles's novels is that a man as hollow as Nelson Dyar (and previously Port Moresby)—a man without purpose or will; a cipher—is not a hero whose fate can stir us deeply. If fiction is to have life it must see something more in life than a dreamlike drift from nullity to nothingness.

Charles J. Rolo. *At.* March, 1952. pp. 84–5

Paul Bowles stages his impressive novels in a climate of violence and pervading sentient awareness. The atmosphere in which his characters move and have their being is arid and parched, nourished by no springs of feeling or sentiment, relentless and neutral as the shifting yet eneluctable sands always just beyond the city. . . . The fruit of which Paul Bowles has eaten is, unfortunately, that which confers knowledge only of evil, not of good. But a writer with no awareness of this essential duality can never fully explore the country of horror into which he has ventured.

Richard Hayes. *Com.* March 7, 1952. p. 547

Mr. Bowles's stories and novels are the work of an exposed nerve. The pain is felt before the experience. There is a perennial dryness and irony in American literature of which Bowles is the latest and most sophisticated exponent; it has the air of premature cynicism, prolongs the moment when civilisation itself becomes entirely anxiety and disgust. . . . Bowles has been properly compared with D. H. Lawrence, for he has a marvelous eye for the foreign scene as it comes to the eye of the rich, rootless wanderer. He is also a brilliant collector of items of human isolation in its varying degrees of madness, and he is intellectually disapproving of both the isolated man and the man who has merely the apparent solidarity and gregariousness of the urban creature. . . . Where Bowles fails is that in reducing the Lawrence situations . . . to a kind of existentialist dimension, he has made them merely *chic*. The moral passion has vanished; even passion has gone.

V. S. Pritchett. *NSN.* July 12, 1952. p. 44

The Sheltering Sky

There is a curiously double level to this novel. The surface is enthralling as narrative. It is impressive as writing. . . . In its interior aspect, *The Sheltering Sky* is an allegory of the spiritual adventure of the fully conscious person into modern experience. . . . Actually this superior motive does not intrude in explicit form upon the story, certainly not in any form that will need to distract you from the great pleasure of being told a first-rate story of adventure by a really first-rate writer.

Tennessee Williams. *NYT.* Dec. 4, 1949. pp. 7, 38

It has been a number of years since a first novel by an American has contained as much literary persuasion and original interest as *The*

Sheltering Sky. . . . It is also the first time to my knowledge that an American novelist has met the French Existentialists on their ground and held them to a draw. . . . His characters are profoundly contemporary, out of a world that has neither God nor ethics. . . . Unlike other records of the same moral dilemma, this is not history, nor argument, nor description of moral paralysis. The cataclysm has occurred; the land is waste yet there are mirages; the water holes beckon. This is a carefully devised piece of fiction of unfaltering interest about some of those "ridiculous" mirages.

Florence Codman. Com. Dec. 30, 1949. p. 346

Let It Come Down

The metaphysical and imaginative dimensions of the pathological visions are impressive as created by Paul Bowles. They are quite unaccountable in the lay figure Dyar to whom they are attributed and who is totally uninteresting when he is not under narcosis. Yet it is clear that the action of the novel is intended to be taken as a philosophical and even spiritual quest for "reality" on Dyar's part. There is an uncomfortable suggestion that Dyar's murderous hashish dreams are the only possible equivalents in our time for the Platonic delight in beauty, even for the beatific vision, and that a masochistic torture dance is the only equivalent for the redeeming sacrifice of love. . . . The evidence is insufficient, especially when we have only the blank eyes of a Dyar to see it through.

What *Let It Come Down* does demonstrate is Paul Bowles's talent for dealing with the macabre, the dreamlike, the cruel and the perverse in a geninely imaginative way.

Robert Gorham Davis. NYT. March 2, 1952. pp. 1, 17

Once again, Mr. Bowles has written a frightening book. Only now there is an important difference. The *shock* is present, but is no longer a device. It is a conclusion justified by the hashish delirium that is the one possible resolution of Dyar's existentialist pilgrimage into the unknown interior of himself. If Mr. Bowles takes the chance of losing the *voyeurs* in his audience by this new discipline, he asks of others that he be judged more specifically on his merits.

These merits are considerable, but of a technical and exterior sort. Mr. Bowles, who is an accomplished composer, presents his characters contrapuntally. What each is doing at a particular moment is artfully disclosed. The theme of one is offered first and then followed by his antiphonal response to another whose theme has already been given. But only sensibility joins them, and a terrible rootlessness.

Leonard Amster. SR. March 15, 1952. p. 21

The Spider's House

The world and the people created by Mr. Bowles are completely convincing. *The Spider's House* is not a pleasant book, and its uncompromising portrayal of individual, group, and national wrongdoing will disturb the romantic or the squeamish reader. But this is the story of a mature writer who has freed himself from the excesses and eccentricities of his earlier fiction, who has something significant to say and who says it with authority, power, and frequently with beauty.

William Peden. *SR*. Nov. 5, 1955. p. 18

The Spider's House is richer than *The Sheltering Sky,* full of compassion and perceptive both intellectually and intuitively. As writing, it is powerful and moving. As reporting, it goes far beyond what the correspondents see or write. Few Americans have understood the forces at conflict in Morocco as well as Paul Bowles has done . . . or conveyed the spirit of the Arab world with such delicate nuance.

Ralph de Toledano. *NYHT*. Nov. 6, 1955. p. 4

See *The Sheltering Sky, Let It Come Down,* and *The Spider's House* (novels); also *The Delicate Prey* (short stories).

BOYLE, KAY (1903–   )

Anyone . . . whose standards of the short story are not the standards of the correspondence school will appreciate that the work of Miss Boyle, for simple craftsmanship, is superior to most of that which is crowned annually by our anthologies. Anyone with an ear for new verbal harmonies will appreciate that Miss Boyle is a stylist of unusual taste and sensibility. It is time, therefore, to cease to regard her as a mere lower case révoltée and to begin to accept her for what she is: more enterprising, more scrupulous, potentially more valuable than nine-tenths of our best-known authors.

Gerald Sykes. *Nation*. Dec. 24, 1930. p. 711

Gertrude Stein and James Joyce were and are the glories of their time and some very portentous talents have emerged from their shadows. Miss Boyle, one of the newest, I believe to be among the strongest. . . . She sums up the salient qualities of that movement: a fighting spirit, freshness of feeling, curiosity, the courage of her own attitude and idiom, a violently dedicated search for the meanings and methods

of art. . . . There are further positive virtues of the individual temperament: health of mind, wit and the sense of glory.

Katherine Anne Porter. NR. April 22, 1931. p. 279

Her short stories and her novels deal with the distress of human beings
reaching for love and for each other, under the cloud of disease, or the
foreknowledge of death. Her daring lies in an extravagance of metaphor, in roguishness, in ellipses. The short stories particularly revive
for us the painful brilliance of living. Here is poison—in the small
doses in which arsenic is prescribed for anaemia. . . . The author has
a deep distrust of the false clarities which destroy overtones and mystery, since actions are the solid but not too significant residues of what
goes on in heads and hearts.

Evelyn Harter. Bkm. June, 1932. pp. 250–3

Imagistic prose, stemming from the stream-of-consciousness, is a natural mode to people highly keyed to sensuous perception. But it varies
in kind. In Virginia Woolf, where the approach is intellectual as well as
sensuous, it is derived, an imagism of what the mind knows, a subtle
and sophisticated play. If the balance is decidedly in the other direction,
as in Waldo Frank, we have a feverish, almost physiological imagery.
In Kay Boyle, at her best, the balance is nice—emotional, but with
the perception swift and right. Where others clothe feeling in a bright
array of words, she gives it the exquisite body in which it lives.

Myra Marini. NR. July 13, 1932. p. 242

Somewhere on the church at Gisors there is a wanton efflorescence of
the latest Gothic which reaches its most intricate virtuosity only a
stone's length from the pure and simple lines of the earliest Renaissance.
In the tangle of the exquisite carving, figures of a brilliant precision are
half hidden in a lush overgrowth of tortured stone wreathing into meaningless shapes. The grace of a detail catches the breath, the whole is a
nullity, a confusion of motives eluding form.

Kay Boyle's writing is like that. . . . The carving hides the design,
the figures are blurred by it.

Henry Seidel Canby. SR. Nov. 4, 1933. p. 233

She is one of the most eloquent and one of the most prolific writers
among the expatriates; her work is always finished in the sense that
her phrases are nicely cadenced and her imagery often striking and
apt; her characters are almost always highly sensitized individuals who
are marooned or in flight in some foreign country, banded together in
small groups in which the antagonisms often seem intense beyond their

recognizable causes. . . . It is noteworthy how much Kay Boyle gets out of the casual coming together of her people, what untold dangers and mysterious excitement she finds in their first impressions of each other—out of the tormented relationships and the eventual flight.

Robert Cantwell. *NR*. Dec. 13, 1933. p. 136

Kay Boyle is Hemingway's successor, though she has not that piercing if patternless emotion which is what we remember of Hemingway at his best. It is significant that both writers received their literary training in Paris, as did Henry James, that they are familiar with deracinates and those casual sojourners in Paris whose search is for the exciting and the momentary. Each has the observational facility of the newspaperman, with the poet's power of meditating on life; their work stands out from any other type of fiction written in any other country, in both content and technique.

Mary M. Colum. *Forum*. Oct. 1938. p. 166

To my mind, the chief defect in Miss Boyle's equipment as an artist is to be traced to her lack of a subject which is organically her own; and by an organic subject I mean something more tangible than a fixed interest in certain abstract patterns of emotion and behavior. Being in possession of an elaborate technique and having developed disciplined habits of observation, Miss Boyle seems to be able to turn her hand to almost anything. As a result one feels all too often that she is not really involved with her themes, that she has not conceived but merely used them.

Philip Rahv. *Nation*. March 23, 1940. p. 396

Never in my life have I come across such descriptions of mountains. Never. . . . And I say this as a mountain-man. Her sentences about mountains go up and up to snow-peaked beauty almost unbearable, just as great mountains do, or swoop down like glaciers and snowfields, or are close and warming and exciting like snow in a village. Never have there been such descriptions of mountains.

Struthers Burt. *SR*. Jan. 15, 1944. p. 6

Kay Boyle . . . is one of the shrewdest stylists in the language and something of a mystic no matter what material she makes momentary use of. . . . The best thing she does is to transform the mundane detail and wring some spiritual essence from it; quite literally she can make (at her best) silk purses out of sows' ears, and you watch her writing as you would some marvelously deft machine performing this miracle, holding some scene or some person still while she outlines in space the nature of its, or his, meaning. And even when the miracle doesn't come off . . . even when the gears turn and the music soars, yet nothing is revealed but the fine hands of the operator, still the process is an exciting thing to behold. Miss Boyle can so compel us with symbols that we are lulled almost into accepting them as the stuff of life.

Nathan L. Rothman. SR. April 9, 1949. p. 13

She has written of love in all of its possible phases. . . . She has written of all people and of their virtues, their sins, their crimes, their loves. There is also a deep love of nature, of mountains, snow, and forests. Even in stories the theme of which may be marital maladjustment, the devotion to the country in which the drama is played exceeds the author's concern with the drama itself. A preponderant part of her writing is descriptive, although she does not conceive of scenery merely as background. In her character portrayals a kind of compassion permits Miss Boyle to enter into the life of others with an intensity as violent as if the life were her own. This compassion gives a moving quality to her skillful portrayals of the blight of Nazism and fascism in Europe.

Harry R. Warfel. American Novelists of Today
(ABC). 1951. p. 45

Miss Boyle achieves her characteristic force by showing us a vision of humanity in need of pity and understanding, a central idea that does not make for light reading but one which accounts for the realism and effectiveness we inescapably feel as we read through her work. While probably not the end result of a reasonable philosophy, it is a telling and significant attitude toward life that makes of her writing much more than a pretty toy or a tract. Miss Boyle is not simply *interested* in people; she is vitally *concerned* with people and profoundly moved to write about their struggle with themselves and with their dreams.

Richard C. Carpenter. EJ. Nov., 1953. p. 427

See *Plagued by the Nightingale, Year Before Last, Her Human Majesty, Death of a Man,* and *Monday Night* (novels); also *The Wedding Day* and *The White Horses of Vienna* (short stories)

BROOKS, CLEANTH (1906–)

Modern Poetry and the Tradition is sound without being sententious; it is suggestive yet precise; it avoids the temptation of sensationalism and the opposite extreme of stodginess. Mr. Brooks writes lucidly rather than brilliantly about the reach of the image . . . and goes to some length to explain the "difficulty" of modern poetry and the reader's resistance to it. . . . All in all, this is the work of a scholar who is sensitive to every nuance of feeling and every change of pitch. Mr. Brooks is a probing analyst, but he is not a pedant. His work, reflecting his subject, is allusive rather than simple and straightforward, complex but clear.

Louis Untermeyer. SR. Jan. 13, 1940. p. 17

One test of a critical theory is its range of enlightenment. Mr. Brooks is illuminating about Eliot and Yeats, but neglects certain poets altogether—D. H. Lawrence, for example, who is certainly witty, or Laura Riding who is certainly intellectual. He may say that they are not good poets—though I should disagree with him—but it is up to him to show why, and their omission makes me doubt if his theory is equipped with the necessary critical tools. . . . Admirable as far as it goes, his criticism of the propagandist view of art fails to account for its success not only among hack critics but quite good artists. In my opinion the social-significance heresy is a distortion of a true perception, namely, that the *Weltanschauung* of a poet is of importance in assessing his work, and that there is, after all, a relation, however obscure and misunderstood, between art and goodness.

W. H. Auden. NR. Feb. 5, 1940. p. 187

Poetry is assumed to rest within a sacred circle, from which historical and psychological considerations on the critic's part are exorcised as profane. To this illiberal outlook Brooks gives the name "humanism." A core of vigorous understanding is thus surrounded with inhibitions by no means always free from intellectual morbidity. Order becomes for Brooks almost an obsession. . . . Brooks is imprisoned in a cage. He suffers from the familiar limitations of narrow and dogmatic doctrines; yet within these limits he frequently writes with admirable discernment.

Henry W. Wells. SR. April 12, 1947. p. 50

Mr. Brooks suggests that poetry is great in proportion to its power to contain and reconcile whole systems of conflicting values. Truth in poetry is dramatic, determined by a right relation to its context. By studying the interior structure of poems it should be possible for criticism to discriminate the greatest poems from the less great and so to prepare the way for a new history of poetry based not on extraneous considerations but on solid observations of poems as poems.

Mr. Brooks's studies in the structure of poetry are masterly exercises in the kind of close critical explication that enriches our appreciation of the poems examined and confers a new dignity on the work of the poet.

George F. Whicher. *NYHT*. Apr. 20, 1947. p. 2

There was developed in the quarter-century between the wars both a system of criticism and a sensibility of poetry, the one fitting and predicting the other, which when they wanted a sanction invoked Donne and when they wanted a justification exhibited Eliot or Yeats. It is not surprising, therefore, that this criticism and this sensibility should bend backwards and try a testing hand on all the poetry that lay between Donne and Eliot. This is what Mr. Brooks tries for. . . . He reads the poems as if their problems were the same as those found in a new quartet by Eliot or a late poem of Yeats; and for his readings he uses the weapons of paradox, irony, ambiguity, attitude, tone, and belief.

R. P. Blackmur. *NYT*. June 8, 1947. p. 6

Either I imperfectly understand Mr. Brooks's theory of poetry . . . or there is nothing very new about it. A poem, I take it, cannot contain one thing only: out of several things it makes its single effect. Some of these, we learn, are *different* from others. In the laboring of this, "paradox" behaves like an acrobat. I share Mr. Brooks's interest in the history of English poetry and his resistance to the critical relativists, but to pinch the diversity of observable phenomena into a single set of terms or insist on anything resembling a unanimity of style seems to me to be indiscreet, or worse. Worse, because it will blind you.

John Berryman. *Nation*. June 28, 1947. p. 776

If there is one formulation which seems to him more suitable than others, for it recurs oftenest, it is that which asserts that the unity of poetic language has the form and status of a verbal paradox. He has always liked stand and marvel at paradox—"with its twin concomitants of irony and wonder"—while I think it is the sense of the sober community that paradox is less valid rather than more valid than another figure of speech, and that its status in logical discourse is that of a provisional way of speaking, therefore precarious. We do not rest in a paradox; we resolve it. . . . As a literary critic he has a hollow scorn for the procedures of logic, which he generally refers to as the procedures of "science"; and he advises the scientists in effect that they cannot understand poetry and had better leave it alone. But this is to underestimate the force of logic in our time and, for that matter, the great weight of the rational idea in western civilization.

John Crowe Ransom. *KR*. Summer, 1947. pp. 437–8

I do not question . . . that "irony," in Brooks's sense of the term, is a constant trait of all good poems, and I should have no quarrel with him had he been content to say so and to offer his analyses of texts as illustrations of one point, among others, in poetic theory. What troubles me is that, for Brooks, there are no other points. Irony, or paradox, is poetry, *tout simplement,* its form no less than its matter; or rather, in the critical system which he has constructed, there is no principle save that denoted by the words "irony" or "paradox" from which significant propositions concerning poems can be derived. It is the One in which the Many in his theory—and there are but few of these—are included as parts, the single source of all his predicates, the unique cause from which he generates all effect.

R. S. Crane. *MP*. May, 1948. pp. 226–7

It may be making virtues of natural limitations, but Brooks's style seems a deliberately plain, steady, utilitarian style. The critical commentary does not emulate but only serves the poem, assists it in the performance of its "miracle of communication," like the disciples distributing the bread and fish. . . . If one can avoid thinking of a critical essay as properly either a contest or an amorous exercise between the author and the reader, Brooks is perhaps simply trying very earnestly to be precise about what he is saying, and again, not saying. Further, he makes no pretensions. One perfectly good reason for putting it plainly might be that he thinks it is a plain thing he has to say.

John Edward Hardy. *HR*. Spring, 1953. pp. 160–1

See *Modern Poetry and the Tradition* and *The Well Wrought Urn* (criticism).

BROOKS, VAN WYCK (1886–1963)

He seems to wake up every morning and regard America, and everybody who ever wrote in America, or who signified anything in American life, with fresh, eager, and ever-interested eyes. His mind perpetually revolves around the idea of a national culture in America, and he pursues all sides of the subject with such a vividness of interest and vividness of language, that when you have read three or four of his books, you begin to believe that the creation of such a culture is one of the few causes left worthy of the devotion and self-sacrifice of men.

Mary M. Colum. *Dial*. Jan., 1924. p. 33

He, more than any one else, more even than Mr. H. L. Mencken, has created a certain prevalent taste in letters, a certain way of thinking about literature.

This eminence, though I feel it has been won through default, has been graced by estimable qualities of Mr. Brooks. He has scholarship which becomes imposing when applied to the waste land of American letters. . . . Happily, Mr. Brooks has a style at the service of his erudition and historical consciousness. . . . What is wrong with Mr. Brooks and what is wrong with nine-tenths of American critical writing is no less than a deficiency in the sense of proportion. . . . It lacks a standpoint which is high enough for the vision of contributory elements melting into a major and vital organism.

Gorham B. Munson. *Dial.* Jan., 1925. pp. 28–9, 42

He has been the most influential critic of the past twenty years. His early work was the principal factor in the erection of the lofty cultural standards that have encouraged the rise of a mature, serious, philosophical criticism. The effect of his later work was not so praiseworthy, for it led to the embittered subjectivity of Lewis Mumford's *Melville* and Matthew Josephson's *Portrait of the Artist as American.* . . . In any event, for good or bad, something of Brooks has seeped into almost every American critic under fifty (including even the Marxist, Granville Hicks). There is no better testimony to his fine mind, his exquisite taste, his integrity and unselfishness.

Bernard Smith. *NR.* Aug. 26, 1936. p. 72

When all is said and done, Mr. Brooks's achievement remains a prodigious one, conceived with audacity and carried out with extraordinary skill. In reading his literary history, one has a sense that Mr. Brooks has repeopled the American continent. On his benign Judgement Day, the dead arise from their graves, throw off their shrouds and become flesh and blood again, ready to take their place in eternity. The writer who in his youth called for a usable American past has, in the full tide of maturity, created that past for us; and has shown us that it was far richer, far sweeter, far more significant than we could, in our rebellious, dissident, adolescent days have dreamed of. To the writer who has accomplished this great feat, we owe unending admiration and gratitude.

Lewis Mumford. *SR.* Nov. 8, 1947. p. 13

Brooks has made so many switches in his forty years of writing and his nineteen books that it is difficult to perceive any consistent pattern. He has been an aesthete, a socialist, a Freudian, a manifesto-writer, a Jungian, a Tolstoyan book-burner, and finally a compiler of literary pastiche and travelogue for the Book-of-the-Month Club. He has moved from total arty rejection of America and its culture to total uncritical acceptance. He has occupied almost every political and philosophic position of our time, and called them all "socialism." Nevertheless, there is a consistent pattern to his work, from his first book to his last, but it is a method rather than a veiwpoint, the method of biographical criticism.

> Stanley Edgar Hyman. *The Armed Vision* (Knopf).
> 1948. pp. 106–7

It is always said that Mr. Brooks is "readable." This means that his style is pleasant and his anecdotes are delightful. Now Mr. Brooks's prose does have very agreeable manners, it has the air of well-tempered conversation. And his little stories are often charming. . . . We could wish for so civilized a "desire to please" in the writers of the humorless, perspiring little essays in some of American literary journals. But the chit-chat is too often without edge, where edge is needed: good form does not demand such a sacrifice. And the anecdotes come too close to being the whole of the book; so much so that for me they cease to be "readable," they are too dense on the page, they are so many acres of underbrush.

> Henry Rago. *Com.* March 28, 1952. p. 619

It is a complex personality, that of a cosmopolitan bent at all costs on being a glorious provincial. We can discuss all the high qualities, those that make him our one genuine "man of letters"—in the old-fashioned sense of the term—since the death of Howells. He has a style and manner, a sense of picturesque, a feeling for the anecdote as a work of art. He has a genuine relish for the idiosyncrasies and the *bizarréries* of literary bohemia and a tendency to suffuse with a pastel optimism even the dark moments in the lives of our great writers.

> Leon Edel. *NR.* March 22, 1954. p. 20

By his own account of childhood and youth Brooks is the heir of culture and breeding; in this sense he is perhaps the last great disciple of the genteel tradition in our letters. But what is heroic and admirable in all this is the rejection of his own tradition in favor of the new forces which have appeared in our society since the 1850's. And his affirmation of our central "Western" line of progressive or radical thought extends even to his praise of the "vulgarian immigrant" Dreiser. We know this vein of American thought is at present in eclipse, with both our literary critics and our politicians. When—or perhaps, in more desperate moments, *if*—our mood changes, Brooks will be seen as a major spokesman for our literature who is indifferent to leadership but who has never relinquished his "position." How could he? It is inside himself.

Maxwell Geismar. Nation. Apr. 3, 1954. p. 283

After *The Ordeal of Mark Twain*—and after "America's Coming-of-Age" and "Letters and Leadership," essays that Brooks wrote in the same period—there was a second renaissance, not so rich as the first in great personalities, perhaps not so rich in great works, but still vastly productive; it was a period when American writers once again were able to survive and flourish in their own country. The *Ordeal* and the essays had helped to make it possible. How much they had helped it would be hard to decide; one would have to know all the apprentice writers of the time who read them, and what the writers told their friends, and how the *Ordeal* in particular affected their ideals of the literary vocation. I can testify from experience, however, that the climate of literature seemed different after Brooks had spoken. He had given courage to at least a few writers, and courage is hardly less contagious than fear.

Malcolm Cowley. NR. June 20, 1955. p.18

See *The Ordeal of Mark Twain, The Flowering of New England, New England: Indian Summer, The World of Washington Irving, The Times of Melville and Whitman,* and *The Confident Years* (criticism).

BUCK, PEARL (1892–   )

There is a firm unity in her work which makes its component parts not easily distinguishable, . . . an identification with one's characters so complete and so well sustained is rare in fiction. . . . The language in which Mrs. Buck presents this material . . . is English—very plain, clear English; yet it gives the impression that one is reading the language native to the characters. . . . Mrs. Buck never, I think, uses a word for which a literal translation into Chinese could not be found. . . . Whether any novelist can be in the very first flight who depicts a civilization other than his own, I do not know. . . . But we may say at least that for the interest of her chosen material, the sustained high level of her technical skill and the frequent universality of her conceptions, Mrs. Buck is entitled to take rank as a considerable artist.

Phyllis Bentley. EJ. Dec., 1935. pp. 791–800

Throughout her writing life, Pearl Buck has been building bridges of understanding between an old and a new civilization, between one generation and another, between differing attitudes toward God and nationality and parenthood and love. Not all Miss Buck's bridges have withstood the weight of problems they were designed to bear. But *The Good Earth* will surely continue to span the abyss that divides East from West, so long as there are people to read it.

Virgilia Peterson. *NYT*. July 7, 1957. p. 4

The Good Earth

She is entitled to be counted as a first-rate novelist, without qualification for the exotic and unique material in which she works. . . . This is the elemental struggle of men with the soil.

The design is filled out with richness of detail and lyric beauty. If now and then there is a straining for effects of biblical poetry, more often there is poignancy in the simple narrative of simple, rude events. . . . Most of all there is verity.

Nathaniel Peffer. *NYHT*. March 1, 1931. p. 1

Such a novel as *The Good Earth* calls at once for comparison with other novels of the same general design—novels of the soil on the one hand and novels concerning Oriental life on the other. Any such comparison brings out the fact that despite Mrs. Buck's very good narrative style, despite her familiarity with her material, her work has a certain flatness of emotional tone. . . . Mrs. Buck is undoubtedly one of the best Occidental writers to treat of Chinese life, but *The Good Earth* lacks the imaginative intensity, the lyrical quality, which someone who had actually farmed Chinese soil might have been able to give it.

Eda Lou Walton. *Nation*. May 13, 1931. p. 534

It ought to be very moving to a Western reader. There is only one difficulty. Romantic love is a fake center of psychology to ascribe to the typical Oriental man or woman, reared in the traditional bondage to quite different ideals. Although romantic love is second nature to the Western woman, trained to it by the traditions of a thousand years, it would not even be understood by an old-fashioned Chinese wife. By placing the emphasis on romantic love, all Confucian society is reduced to a laughable pandemonium. . . . *The Good Earth,* though it has no humor or profound lyric passion, shows good technique and much artistic sincerity. Thus, it is discouraging to find that the novel works toward confusion, not clarification. . . . Mrs. Buck, the daughter of a missionary, refuses from the start of her book to admit that there is such a culture as Confucianism.

Younghill Kang. *NR*. July 1, 1931. p. 185

Mrs. Buck is clearly not the destined subject of a chapter in literary history, and would be the last to say so herself. . . . (But) *The Good Earth,* the first volume bearing that name, not the trilogy, is a unique book, and in all probability belongs among the permanent contributions to world literature of our times. . . . It was a document in human nature, in which questions of style—so long as the style was adequate, and of depth—so long as the surfaces were true and significant—were not important. It did not have to be as well written as it was, in order to be distinguished. . . . We do not wish to be unjust to Mrs. Buck. Her total achievement is remarkable even though it contains only one masterpiece.

Henry Seidel Canby. SR. Nov. 19, 1938. p. 8

Although *The Good Earth* was among the most popular books of the 1930's—ranking just after *Gone with the Wind* and *Anthony Adverse* —and although it has received more prizes and official honors than any other novel in our history, there are still literary circles in which it continues to be jeered at or neglected. . . . It is the story of Wang Lu, a poor farmer who becomes a wealthy landlord, but it is also a parable of the life of man, in his relation to the soil that sustains him. The plot, deliberately commonplace, is given a sort of legendary weight and dignity by being placed in an unfamiliar setting. The biblical style is appropriate to the subject and the characters.

Malcolm Cowley. NR. May 10, 1939. p. 24

It is a quarter of a century since Pearl Buck wrote a novel which, perhaps more than all earlier books combined, made the outside world China-conscious. In *The Good Earth* millions of Westerners first met the Chinese people as they really feel and think and behave. . . . Before 1930 many Americans pictured the Chinese as queer laundrymen, or clever merchants like Fu Manchu, or heathens sitting in outer darkness; few believed they could greatly influence our own fate. Since then historical events have taught us otherwise—and among those "events" Pearl Buck's book might well be included. Her more than two dozen novels, translations, and non-fiction books interpreting traditional and revolutionary Asia have fully justified the early award to her of the Nobel prize in literature.

Edgar Snow. Nation. Nov. 13, 1954. p. 426

See *The Good Earth, The Patriot,* and *Dragon Seed* (novels).

BURKE, KENNETH (1897–   )

Kenneth Burke is one of the few Americans who know what a success of good writing means—and some of the difficulties in the way of its achievement. . . . *The White Oxen* is a varied study, as any book where writing is the matter, must be. American beginnings—in the sense of the work of Gertrude Stein, difficult to understand, as against, say, the continuities of a De Maupassant. It is a group of short accounts, stories, more or less. They vary from true short stories to the ridiculousness of all short stories dissected out in readable pieces: writing gets the best of him, in the best of the book: "The Death of Tragedy" and "My Dear Mrs. Wurtlebach."

William Carlos Williams. Dial. Jan., 1929. pp. 6–7

Mr. Burke has a quick, assimilative, complicated mind, one not devoted to trivialities but not above them—the kind of mind which we stand to profit most from but which we do most to cramp in colleges. It is essentially a creative mind. Though devoted to criticism it is not less creative than the minds of most of the so-called "creative writers." It is especially creative in its ability to perceive connections between disparate entities. By choice he has worked mainly outside universities, as a critic among living writers rather than as a literary historian or philosopher among dead or classical writers.

Arthur E. DuBois. SwR. July, 1937. p. 345

Burke's approach to symbolism is not susceptible of verification, and depends for its convincing force on his ability to make the reader perceive immediately the author's intuitions. This is to say that the method is essentially a-scientific if not unscientific. A generation of readers brought up on the facile technique of popularized psychoanalysis will no doubt find this method acceptable. But even those who look with suspicion on the explosions of an imagination uncontrolled by a scientific governor must frequently adjudge Burke's intuitions to be happy hits indeed, often throwing a burst of light on the dark pockets of our social scene.

Eliseo Vivas. Nation. Dec. 25, 1937. p. 723

If he suffers from a restraint, I should think it a constitutional distaste against regarding poetic problems as philosophic ones. I suppose his feeling would be that poetry is something bright and dangerous, and philosophy is something laborious and arid, and you cannot talk about the one in terms of the other without a disproportion and breach of taste. . . . He has a whole arsenal of strategies, like the German general staff, who are said to have whistling bombs if they like, and whose campaigns rest upon a highly technical and sustained opportunism. . . . He is perspicuous and brilliantly original, and I would venture to quarrel with no positive finding that he makes, but only with his proportions, or his perspective.

John Crowe Ransom. KR. Spring, 1942. pp. 219, 237

Mr. Burke's distinction as a critic is twofold. First, he is a man of amazing learning, who knows how to use his learning unpedantically and, if necessary, with a dose of irony. Second, he is that very rare thing among critics: a man who examines creative manifestations without *parti pris,* who does not put his own intention before the intention of the poet but carefully scrutinizes the mind of the agent as embodied in the act. His erudition aids him in treating literature universally, i.e. each particular literary instance is brought into relation with the whole body of *Weltliteratur;* while his patient ingenuity manages to disengage the hidden cross-references and ambiguities of each work.

Francis C. Golffing. Poetry. March, 1946. p. 339

Fortunately, Mr. Burke's arduous argument and idiosyncratic use of key terms are made somewhat easier by a generous use of ranging illustrations. His focus fans out so extensively that only careful study can comprehend his system. He seeks to impose a pattern on all historical consciousness. He is more sympathetic to social thinkers than to rhetoricians, to anthropologists than to philologians. In essence, Mr. Burke writes a study on human relations. The psychological as well as the sociological cast leads the reader at last to suspect all motives, and to feel that in Mr. Burke's mind most idealisms are outmoded and should be treated as myths to be analyzed and dissected.

Donald A. Stauffer. NYT. June 11, 1950. p. 30

Mr. Burke's courage is not purely of the theoretical kind. He dares to translate his doctrines into very definite instances, although his purpose is not indoctrination. He is fighting for free thought and free speech at a time when these are denounced as un-American activities. . . . It is a great comfort to find one who, ignoring the stampede, dares to say: "So help me God, I cannot otherwise." There are enough clear-sighted and vigorous pronouncements in this book (*A Rhetoric of Motives*) to insure the wrath of Senator McCarthy; if the Senator could understand them.

Albert Guerard. NYHT. July 23, 1950. p. 8

He started from literary criticism (after writing two books of fiction); he has provided us with many brilliant examples of the critic's art; and yet the most brilliant of all the examples is possibly his essay on *Mein Kampf,* in which he explains Hitler's strategies of persuasion. In other words the quality of his intention does not depend on the literary greatness of his subject; and when his literary subject happens to be a great one, as in another brilliant essay, on *Venus and Adonis,* he may not even discuss the qualities that make it a masterpiece. He is more interested in mechanisms of appeal, as in the Hitler essay, and in the disguises of social attitudes, as in the *Venus and Adonis.* We could, however, go further and say that his real subject is man as a symbol-using animal.

Malcolm Cowley. *NR*. Sept. 14, 1953. p. 17

Is it unfair to suggest that Burke may be the prime example of the sophisticated mind ready, even eager, to embrace the naïve for its value as renewal? . . . This culture type continues, long after the Industrial Revolution, to be repelled by the city's artifacts. . . . This jump from sophistication to naïveté, coupled with a deeply-felt experience of the Depression, would account for a view of society that echoes the old socialist diatribes. . . . But truly, if his social protests posit any sort of political alignment, it's more a Thoreau-going party of one than the one-party state. . . . Burke is more the Old Bohemian than the Old Bolshevik—the last of the Bohemians, possibly, with a humor wry enough to go with his awry feeling.

Gerard Previn Meyer. *SR*. Sept. 3, 1955. p. 28

Burke's gift as a poet is . . . real. His word play is true mortal-fun, and his ear for a rhythm is rich and right. He does especially well in ending a poem on a kind of dissolving rhythm. Not with a bang but a whimper, perhaps, but the whimper sings. Above all, the poems, when put together, generate the sense of a real person—learned, bourbony, getting on to mortality as a bit of a hard case but still, and always, sweet on life. I like both the cantankerousness and the sweetness; one flavors the other. No one should have trouble believing that Kenneth Burke's despairs are humanly real.

John Ciardi. *Nation*. Oct. 8, 1955. pp. 307–8

See *A Grammar of Motives, A Rhetoric of Motives,* and *The Philosophy of Literary Form* (criticism); also *White Oxen and Other Stories* and *Book of Moments: Poems 1915-1954.*

BURNS, JOHN HORNE (1916–1953)

Each of (his) three books owes its degree of power to the author's ability to write exquisitely observed *mot*-filled prose which lends a stylish quality to every incident, even ones which might better have been omitted for reasons of taste. And common weaknesses stem mostly from the fact that Mr. Burns, the angry moralist, appears to be in conflict with Mr. Burns, the detached artist.

James Kelly. *NYT*. Sept. 7, 1952. p. 4

The Gallery

Mr. Burns writes unevenly, perhaps deliberately so, sometimes using the shock technique of photographic realism, sometimes employing a kind of stylized symbology, but always with telling effect. In this, his first novel, Mr. Burns shows a brilliant understanding of people, a compassion for their frailities and an urge to discover what inner strength or weaknesses may lie beneath the surface.

J. D. Ross. *NYHT*. June 8, 1947. p. 5

The appreciation of the Italian people grows occasionally into something like a sentimental idolatry. The bitterness against American crudity comes close in places to a youthful intolerance. And the steady stress upon sex . . . grows into what looks like an inadvertent concentration upon one aspect of human experience as if it were the sole aspect. The genuine love and understanding which marks much of this work are, indeed, in a real way, vitiated by what appears a far too simple, far too easy falling back upon both sexual activity and a kind of vague, wistful brotherliness.

Richard Sullivan. *NYT*. June 8, 1947. p. 25

In *The Gallery* John Horne Burns absorbs the soldier's idiom into a spacious narrative prose that modifies but does not dominate the language. It is an appropriate device, as the matter of the book is the mental confusion and emotional disruption of our American soldiers abroad. . . . On the one hand (Burns) is uneasy and guilty about the smug, provincial, materialist life in America, and shocked by the conduct of many American soldiers. . . . On the other hand, his sympathy with the Neapolitans is generous and ingratiating, and his affection for them is too specific and imaginative to be merely sentimental. . . . One regrets that he didn't employ his human insight and talent for social analysis to go beyond a just indignation and consider whether even American boorishness and immaturity couldn't be the reverse of certain substantial national virtues.

John Farrelly. NR. July 7, 1947. p. 28

It is not a book for little boys in any school, but for adults who recognize the truth and know good writing when they see it, and who do not object to blatant four-letter words. The author's place in American war fiction seems certain. Compared with *The Gallery . . . Three Soldiers,* the novel that started off the realistic fiction of the First World War, was a fragrant and tender lily.

Harrison Smith. SR. Feb. 14, 1948. p. 7

The Gallery is a hybrid book, made up of two kinds of material set in two different literary devices that are never fused. The affirmation of values in the "Promenades" is consistently thwarted by the negation of values in the "Portraits"; and the non-dramatic treatment of the one is in the end completely overcome by the tensely dramatic treatment of the other. There is one step that Burns might have taken to ensure his point. He might have disregarded altogether the innate potentialities of the material he put into the "Portraits" and twisted the action in such a way that the book would have been forced to end on an affirmative note . . . but it would have meant a deliberate falsification of the truth as he saw it, and Burns was too scrupulous an artist for that.

John W. Aldridge. After the Lost Generation
(McGraw). 1951. pp. 145–6

Lucifer with a Book

Mr. Burns was not far enough removed from his experiences to be capable of relating them without an excess acidity. Consequently his attack is not pointed as directly as it might have been. His book is too long, and a few of his most acute and penetrating observations are obscured by paragraphs of unleashed fury which become rather tedious.

Virginia Vaughan. Com. Apr. 29, 1949. p. 76

The central love affair of the novel, through which Guy Hudson finally realized the difference between sex and love, is not altogether convincing. What is apparent, however, just as in the English sophisticates, is the dominant sexuality of the novel, and a sexuality that finds expression in harsh and even violent terms. There is an inverted Puritanism in Mr. Burn's work, and a remarkably sophisticated sense of evil and malice.

Maxwell Geismar. SR. Apr. 2, 1949. p. 16.

John Horne Burns is one of those American writers who believe in shock treatment. To judge by *Lucifer with a Book* he is a satirical moralist rather than a novelist. He has much of Henry Miller's rich comic gift, a fluency which amounts at times to lallomania, a passion for scatological images and a strong tendency to preach. It is not always easy to discover, in this whirlwind of words, just what Mr. Burns is preaching about, but one thing seems to emerge clearly; nothing is so dangerous and destructive as virginity of mind and body and, until this impediment has been removed, preferably by rape, no one can begin to live.

Antonia White. NSN. Nov. 5, 1949. p. 520

See *The Gallery, Lucifer with a Book,* and *A Cry of Children* (novels).

CABELL, JAMES BRANCH (1879–1958)

That he says impeccably his say is indisputable; that he says it for only a few is undebatable. . . . He is . . . enjoyed only by those who possess a certain scholarship plus a but slightly secondary interest in fiction plus a mental kinship that recognizes the aptness of his means.

Blanche Williams. Our Short Story Writers (Moffat).
1920. p. 23

Mr. Cabell, by questioning the reality of reality, has been naturalized in the world of dreams till he moves about there without the scruples lasting over from another allegiance. Thus the beauty of his Poictesme is double-distilled. Those lovers of beauty who must now and then come down to earth for renewal will occasionally gasp in Poictesme, wishing the atmosphere would thicken and brilliant colors change. But always Poictesme hangs above the mortal clouds, suspended from the eternal sky, in the region where wit and beauty are joined in an everlasting kiss.

Carl Van Doren. James Branch Cabell (McBride).
1925. p. 83

Here at last is an American novelist with a culture and style of his own, a conscious artist and a man of letters. . . . Cabell . . . is an adept at artistic writing, the only prose writer in American fiction who cultivates style for its own sake. . . . He likes to call himself a classic, classic in style, though romantic in inspiration. . . . Cabell's ideal is harmony, clearness and grace. He moves within fiction as if it were a natural element and not as in a quarry where he is painfully hewing out stones.

Régis Michaud. *The American Novel Today* (Little).
1928. pp. 202–3

The high repute of the works of Mr. Cabell has not been attacked by critics, partly out of a faint snobbishness; partly for the amusing reason that those who were fit to criticize him found him almost impossible to read, and lastly because scholarship and love of good prose seemed too rare in America to be discredited on other grounds without a pang. His prose is, indeed, not only correct but constantly graceful in diction and liquid in rhythm. The trouble is that there is nothing in all these romances for the mind to grasp; one fumbles in a sunny mist; one hopes from page to page to come upon something either sharp or solid; that hope is soon abandoned and next it becomes clear that even the grace of this style is often falsely arch and knowing or effeminate and teasing. The style, in brief, is married to the matter and both are *articles de luxe,* like gorgeously enameled cigarette étuis diamond and ruby-studded, or riding crops with jeweled handles.

Ludwig Lewisohn. *Expression in America* (Harper).
1932. p. 531

This Virginian gentleman and genealogist could hardly be expected either to approve of life in the United States or to feel that he was under any obligation to improve it. Instead he has converted his petulant disgust into a melodramatic pessimism. . . . The artist has a function in this mad world, Mr. Cabell argues; it is to create beautiful illusions, which alone make life endurable. But, far from occupying himself with the dissemination of dynamic lies, Mr. Cabell has devoted all his talents to attacking man's illusions. He is, then, a fraud, for neither his romanticism nor his pessimism is genuine. He is a sleek, smug egoist, whose desire to be a gentleman of the old school breeds dissatisfaction with the existing order, but who has not enough imaginative vigor to create a robust world in which deeds of chivalry and gallantry are performed. Instead he has written mild little fantasies, carefully baited with delicate obscenities.

Granville Hicks. *The Great Tradition* (Macmillan).
1933. p. 221

His own style is indubitably established, consciously dependent on archaism, but dependent for relief on marked and homely modernisms. On the whole it is attractive, and sometimes it is charming. But it is pedantic in phrasing and in dispensable detail. Knowing that fancy is more important than fact in the tales, the reader is annoyed and distracted by circumstantial matters of chronology and genealogy that delay action and throw no light on motivation.

The notable fact about Cabell in the modern pageant has been his persistence in playing his own role until through ability and cooperation of the censors he achieved a wide hearing. He ought to be taken as seriously as he takes himself, which is not very seriously, for his tongue as a rule is ostentatiously in his cheek.

Percy H. Boynton. *Literature and American Life*
(Ginn). 1936. pp. 799–800

Critics have persisted in putting Cabell into the wrong category. They have repeatedly called him a romanticist, bent upon escape. They refuse to see that his extravanganzas of Poictesme are all allegories. He is as close to the modern pulse as the most intense realist, and as alarmed over it. He is a humorist, a wit, a satirist, an intellectual, a classicist. And he is a characteristic twentieth-century pessimist. He is right in the thick of life, and he is so disgusted with it that he can see nothing sensible to do except laugh. If he is a romanticist bent upon escape, then so were Aristophanes, Rabelais, Ben Jonson, Congreve, Voltaire, Mark Twain, and Anatole France.

Vernon Loggins. *I Hear America* (Crowell). 1937.
p. 287

Unlike that other artificer of the medieval, Thomas Chatterton, Cabell never persuaded himself; and he had no need to persuade his readers. They wanted just what he gave them: the touch of life bereft of life's prosaic sordidness; an easy road to wisdom; a masquerade of the soul in which, by mocking the daydreams of the great herd, one could liberate and enjoy one's own. Cabell did not pretend to be an "escapist"; he was a realist whose cynical appreciation of reality encouraged him to make it ridiculous. By dismissing the superficial world of the present, he illuminated its pathos lightly and fleetingly. . . . The critical Babbitts might think Cabell a satanic figure, but he was not even attempting to *épater le bourgeois;* he sought only to amuse him. Reading his books, good middle-class fathers and citizens, like good middle-class undergraduates, enjoyed the luxury of a depravity that was as synthetic as breakfast cereal, and as harmless.

Alfred Kazin. *On Native Grounds* (Reynal). 1942.
pp. 233–4

See *Domnei, Chivalry, The Rivet in Grandfather's Neck, The Cream of the Jest,* and *The Nightmare Has Triplets* (novels).

CALDWELL, ERSKINE (1903–   )

It is as difficult for an outsider as it is for Mr. Caldwell to find in his work any systematic, even any conscious doctrine. He has not shaped himself by reasoning and he does not make up stories to prove abstract points. . . . (His stories) somehow sound as if they had been invented a long time ago and cherished in the popular memory, waiting for the hand of art if it should chance upon them. Mr. Caldwell, handling these matters, partly goes back to a manner at least a hundred years old. Again and again he brings to mind the native humorists before Mark Twain, when American humor had not yet been sweetened but was still dry, blunt, and broad. . . . It is in Mr. Caldwell's choice of heroes and in the boldness with which he speaks of their love and religion that he goes beyond any of the older humorists.

Carl Van Doren. Nation. Oct. 18, 1933. p. 444

I have denied that Caldwell is a realist. In his tomfoolery he comes closer to the Dadaists; when his grotesqueness is serious, he is a Superrealist. We might compromise by calling him over all a Symbolist (if by Symbolist we mean a writer whose plots are more intelligible when interpreted as dreams). . . . I am not by any means satisfied by the psychoanalytic readings of such processes to date, though I do believe that in moralistic fantasies of the Caldwell type, where the dull characters become so strangely inspired at crucial moments, we are present at a poetic law court where judgements are passed upon kinds of transgression inaccessible to jurists, with such odd penalties as no *Code Napoléon* could ever schematize.

Kenneth Burke. NR. April 10, 1935. p. 234

Caldwell has lived among these Georgians, and has studied them with the enthusiastic attitude of young genius. He has a healthy masculine love for them. The record of his impressions of their way of living is fearlessly frank. Although brutal, his realism is genuine. These Georgia "Crackers" are as benighted as he makes them out to be. . . . He has decided where to lay the blame for the decadence of his chosen people. The cause of their plight is not a frowsy religion, nor false standards in education. It is poverty. These people were long ago downed in the economic fight. All initiative was ground out of them. So Caldwell sees them. He is passionate for the return of their initiative. He would kindle public feeling in their behalf. He would have them taught how to get up and begin fighting all over again. Not only is he one of the best of the contemporary regional writers; he is also the strongest of the proletarian writers.

Vernon Loggins. *I Hear America* (Crowell). 1937.

p. 222

Mr. Caldwell is said to think of himself as a realist with a sociological message to deliver. If that message exists I fail to find it very clearly expressed in the present play (*Journeyman*). . . . But there is no point discussing what a work of art means or whether or not it is "true to life" unless one is convinced that the work "exists"—that it has the power to attract and hold attention, to create either that belief or that suspension of disbelief without which its "message" cannot be heard and without which its factual truth is of no importance. And to me the incontrovertible fact is that both Mr. Caldwell's novels and the plays made from them do in this sense "exist" with an uncommon solidarity, that his race of curiously depraved and curiously juicy human grotesques are alive in his plays whether or not they, or things like them, were ever alive anywhere else.

Joseph Wood Krutch. *Nation*. Feb. 12, 1938. p. 190

His intention . . . seems to be that of arousing sympathy for Southern tenant farmers, black and white. I believe this intention is good and that nothing effective will be done to correct the bad conditions now prevailing throughout the South until the sympathy of the nation is aroused. At the same time, I am convinced that sympathy is not enough. There must be some real understanding, and the ideas in people's minds must have some correspondence with actual conditions as they exist. If the picture of tenant farmers and of poor people in the South generally, as rendered in *God's Little Acre* and *Tobacco Road* are authentic, then there is little which can be done by landlord or tenant, by government or God, unless, of course, Mr. Caldwell's writings should so arouse the interest of the Deity that he would then proceed to make tenant, landlord, and land over again.

W. T. Couch. *VQR*. Spring, 1938. p. 309

The chief theme of Caldwell's writing is the agony of the impoverished land, which has now so nearly reached a state of complete exhaustion in large sections of the old South that it is only a matter of time (he thinks) when the dust storms will cross the Mississippi and extend the desert to the east. This is the material basis for the social conditions which he sets forth in his stories. But, of course, it is the people who interest him as a student of human nature; and with the people, it is not so much their material sufferings as the moral degradation which follows steadily on the decline of their material well-being. It is the illiteracy passed on from generation to generation of those who cannot find time to go to school or have not clothes to wear to school. . . . It is the shiftlessness and irresponsibility wrought by habitual want of hope.

Joseph Warren Beach. *American Fiction 1920–1940* (Macmillan). 1941. p. 223

Erskine Caldwell is two writers, both good of their kind, and one a sort of genius in his own narrow field. They collaborate on most of his books, but with conflicting aims; and the result is that reading some of his novels . . . is like a week-end visit to a bickering household. "I am a social novelist," says the first Caldwell. . . . The second Caldwell does not talk about his aims, and in fact he isn't completely conscious of them; but sometimes, pushing his twin brother away from the typewriter, he begins pounding out impossible fancies and wild humor.

Malcolm Cowley. *NR.* Nov. 6, 1944. p. 599

Where Faulkner's supreme dimension is time, Caldwell's is space, and the whole quality of their art lies distinguished in these separate dimensions. Plot, being essentially a matter of space, becomes of necessity Caldwell's sphere of operations, and though his characters are seldom nuanced and the range of his emotions remains pretty narrow, he handles incident and action and spatial movement with a skill that holds the reader to attention. . . .

Yet the exigencies and narrowness of space landlock Caldwell's writing, and make it, despite its clearer and firmer outlines, more limited and less important than Faulkner's. It demonstrates that a mastery of plot linked to a cargo of social significance is not enough to establish a great reputation. Though Caldwell impresses his readers, he does not haunt them in the sense of lingering in their imaginations or compelling them to read him a second time.

Leo Gurko. *The Angry Decade* (Dodd). 1947. pp. 138–9

There is . . . no completely satisfactory attitude for the reader to assume toward these books. When we read them as comedies, Caldwell carefully and disconcertingly knocks the props from under the comic element; we look then for serious, socially-conscious reporting, and the comic element spoils our view; we resort, unwillingly, to taking them as exhibits of the picturesque, only to realize that Caldwell deserves better from his reader. So we come finally to the conclusion—for which we have been searching all along—that Caldwell's novels suffer from a multiplicity of meanings which are incompatible with one another. This is another way of saying that Caldwell's own attitude toward his material is ambiguous.

W. M. Frohock. *The Novel of Violence in America* (Southern Methodist). 1950. p. 143

Certainly the humor is gusty, uniquely gratifying, a largess, a bounty, for which one always thanks the giver. We cannot thank Caldwell too much or too often for giving us the robust and depraved and homely and vulgar tom-foolery as no one else has given us in our time. His literalities, equivalents, and approximations, particularly concerning the sex content in the lives of his people, come forth genuinely incorporated and derived from the traditional and popular mind-body of the rural South.

Robert Hazel in *Southern Renascence,* edited by Louis Rubin, Jr. (John Hopkins). 1953. p. 321

See *God's Little Acre, Trouble in July,* and *Tobacco Road* (novels).

CAPOTE, TRUMAN (1924–   )

"Get Capote"—at this moment the words are resounding on many a sixtieth floor, and "get him" of course means make him and break him, smother him with laurels and then vent on him the obscure hatred which is inherent in the notion of another's superiority.

Cyril Connolly. *Horizon.* Oct., 1947. p. 5

Capote's imagined world is as beautiful as a water moccasin, and as poisonous. A Freudian critic would call it a world of infantile regression; a sinister underwater universe populated by monstrous children, expressionistic automats, and zombie adults, all viewed obliquely through the bang-shaded eyes of a Louisiana Caligari-Hoffmann. . . . . There can be no doubt of Capote's evocative magic. . . . Only it is invariably black magic.

Charles A. Brady. *CW.* May, 1949. p. 156

Capote seems determined . . . to do nothing ordinary and therefore be memorable. This determination, plus an original sense for the macabre (exploited for all the sensationalism it is worth), a certain all too fallible delicacy and sensitivity, excellent powers of description and evocation, a genuine but unselective sense of humor, and an occasional sense for, and (rarely) the discipline of, poetry, sums up both his values and his equipment as a writer.

Alexander Klein. NR. July 4, 1949. p. 18

One thing about Truman Capote . . . that one notices right off is that he looks a little like a toy. That's what some people *say,* anyway. If he is a toy, he nevertheless has a mind that would turn those big thinking cybernetic machines green with envy. As a matter of fact, his mind has enough good steel in it to turn too many human beings the same violent color—and it has, no doubt about it. Mr. Capote's appearance is lamblike but all intellectual bullies are warned not to be deceived.

Harvey Breit. NYT. Feb. 24, 1952. p. 29

If the art of Truman Capote may be defined succinctly, it is highly-detailed perception by all the senses, in which nothing, however small, personal or languid escapes due attention, and which, by the time his fine-grained literary style has given it shape and perspective, has become an engaging tissue of story-telling. . . . Since this little world receives a precise accounting which inevitably suggests the whole-souled concentration of a precocious child, it for the moment becomes a much bigger world and one full of surprises and beauty.

Cyrus Durgin. Boston Globe. Dec. 15, 1958. p. 8

Other Voices, Other Rooms

Other Voices, Other Rooms abundantly justifies the critics and readers who first hailed Capote as a writer of exceptional gifts. . . . Capote's sensibility is as notable as his insight, and its range is impressive, for it enables him to describe elements of physical environment that would be scarcely perceptible to most of us; yet these elements, however unnoticed, are recognized by the reader as authentic, and indisputably present. But although his descriptive writing is masterly, it is his ability to create and interpret character—to increase both the scope and depth of our understanding of ourselves and others—that yields the major excellences of *Other Voices, Other Rooms*. . . . It is not only a work of unusual beauty, but a work of unusual intelligence. In it, readers will establish contact with one of the most accomplished American novelists to make his debut in many a season.

Lloyd Morris. NYHT. Jan. 16, 1948. p. 2

Even if Mr. Capote were ten or twenty years older than he is, his ability to bend language to his poetic moods, his ear for dialect and for the varied rhythms of speech would be remarkable. In one so young this much writing skill represents a kind of genius. On the other hand, I find myself deeply antipathetic to the whole artistic-moral purpose of Mr. Capote's novel. . . . For it seems to me to create a world of passive acceptance in which we are rendered incapable of thinking anybody responsible for his behavior in any department.

Diana Trilling. Nation. Jan. 31, 1948. pp. 133–4

Mr. Capote *does* have a remarkable facility with words; he can make perfectly normal horrors and shocks appear like enormities upon the senses. At times we can even hear a haunting funereal music behind Mr. Capote's wayward language. If he had selected his material more carefully, shown more restraint, and had been less concerned with terrifying us out of our wits, he might have easily made a real and tenderly appealing story out of the experiences of thirteen-year-old Joel Knox and the people he meets during that long and lonely summer of his approaching maturity.

Richard McLoughlin. SR. Feb. 14, 1948. p. 12.

Other Voices, Other Rooms is easily the most exciting novel to come from America this year. Though one of its chief characters is what is customarily referred to by reviewers as "decadent," both he and the rest of the characters in this emotional story of the South make the average character in contemporary American fiction seem perverted by comparison. For the only moral standard that literature knows is the truth, and it is the truthful intensity of Mr. Capote's book that makes it so remarkable. . . . He has dared to write of life in all its complex splendor and to tell of the human heart, and yet he has triumphed without sinking into romanticism or departing from any of the desired standards of taste and maturity. . . . But what ensures its success is the quality of Mr. Capote's writing, which is very high indeed, and original without being exhibitionist or obscure.

Robert Kee. Spec. Nov. 19, 1948. pp. 674–6

Tree of Night

Evidently concerned to a rare degree with the technique of writing itself, Mr. Capote in his style reveals a combination of eloquence and of simplicity. The perfectly apt, homely but unexpected adjective in a carefully limpid phrase: a familiar, plain, yet nowise banal vocabulary: a rare verb chosen rather than an elegant one—such are some of its more obvious characteristics. . . . Moreover, Mr. Capote's style serves, generally, as a flexible and vigorous instrument for the communication of truly remarkable gifts of observation, whether of gesture or atmosphere.

Iris Barry. NYHT. Feb. 27, 1949. p. 2

If the Mad Hatter and the Ugly Duchess had had a child, and the child had almost grown up, these are almost the kind of short stories he could be expected to write. . . . Who wants, really, to crawl back into the twilit cave and roll the papier-mâché stone over the doorway? Who would want to let Alice's wonderland serve as the myth around which he organized his adult life? . . . With these reservations, however, one must fairly assert for these stories a kind of triple power: a mind at times disciplined toward poetry, with a special skill at naming; a pleasant and only slightly grotesque humor, and an ability to suggest, as in the novel, the outlines of haunted personalities.

Carlos Baker. *NYT*. Feb. 27, 1949. p. 7

As a teller of tales he has a peculiar and remarkable talent. . . . In his hands the fairy tale and ghost story manage to assimilate the attitudes of twentieth-century psychology without losing their integrity, without demanding to be accepted as mere fantasy or explained as mere symbol. . . . In Capote's stories the fairy world, more serious than business or love, is forever closing in upon the skeptical secure world of grown-ups.

Leslie A. Fiedler. *Nation*. April 2, 1949. pp. 395–6

The Grass Harp

Mr. Capote's second novel, *The Grass Harp,* remains within the extreme limits of what we call Gothic, but it is a sunlit Gothic, an aberrant form with a personality, an agreeable personality, entirely its own. . . . Mr. Capote keeps his story beautifully under control. His story has elements of allegory, it expounds a rather simple, basic statement concerning the nature of love. . . . In the beginning of the novel one does catch whiffs of the well-known Southern decay, but the book is not concerned with morbidity. It is a light, skilful, delightful story.

Oliver La Farge. *SR*. Oct. 20, 1951. pp. 19–20

Within the slim compass of this work, Truman Capote has achieved a masterpiece of passionate simplicity, of direct intuitive observation. Without any loss of intensity, he has purified the clotted prose of *Other Voices, Other Rooms,* producing a luminous reflector for his unique visual sensibility. . . . He still deals in eccentricities but his characters are not wrenched out of their human context; in them, eccentricity becomes an extension, not a distortion of personality. Compassion, too—that abused quality—takes on a new depth here.

Richard Hayes. *Com*. Oct. 26, 1951. p. 74

Mr. Capote creates a world in which it seems perfectly natural for people to lodge in treetops; and equally natural for a retired judge to propose marriage to a dotty spinster while the two of them are perched on a branch. . . . Within its own terms, *The Grass Harp* comes pretty close, I should say, to being a complete success. It charms you into sharing the author's feeling that there is a special poetry—a spontaneity and wonder and delight—in lives untarnished by conformity and common sense.

Charles J. Rolo. *At.* Nov., 1951. pp. 89–90

See *Other Voices, Other Rooms* and *The Grass Harp* (novels); also *The Tree of Night* (short stories).

CATHER, WILLA (1873–1947)

Willa Cather's best work is satisfying because it is sincere. In her books, there is none of the sweet reek that pervades the pages of so many "lady novelists." Love, to her, is "not a simple state, like measles." Her treatment of sex is without either squeamishness or sensuality. She loves the west, and the arts, particularly music, and she has sought to express feelings and convictions on these subjects. She tried, failed, and kept on trying until she succeeded.

Latrobe Carroll. *Bkm.* May, 1921. p. 215

Miss Cather's mind is basically static and retrospective, rich in images of fixed contours. . . . The characteristic quality of her mind . . . is not its puritanism or its idealism, but something deeper in which these are rooted. She is preeminently an artist dominated by her sense of the past, seeking constantly, through widely differing symbolisms, to recapture her childhood and youth. A sort of reverence for her own early years goes, hand in hand, with her Vergilian ancestor-worship; and out of this has flowered her finest work.

Clifton Fadiman. *Nation.* Dec. 7, 1932. pp. 564–5

It is idle to try to classify her neatly as a realist, or a "novelist of character," or as one who went "beyond naturalism," as a satirist or a romanticist. She is all of these things. She is Willa Cather, mobile, capable, sometimes great, always clear-cut, and most of the time interesting, a social commentator whose pen is never sharp enough to hurt anybody, and whose vision is frequently inspiring. In her court the human race is acquitted of the most serious charges against it and given a character. It is very grateful for it, being in sore need.

Harlan Hatcher. *Creating the Modern American Novel* (Farrar and Rinehart). 1935. p. 59

Miss Cather's turn to the ideals of a vanished time is the weary response to weariness, to that devitalization of spirit which she so brilliantly describes in the story of Professor St. Peter. It is a weariness which comes not merely from defeat but from an exacerbated sense of personal isolation and from the narrowing of all life to the individual's sensitivities, with the resulting loss of the objectivity that can draw strength from seeking the causes of things. But it is exactly Miss Cather's point that the Lucretian *rerum naturae* means little; an admirer of Virgil, she is content with the *lacrimae rerum,* the tears of things.

> Lionel Trilling in *After the Genteel Tradition,* edited
> by Malcolm Cowley (Norton). 1937. pp. 61–2

Miss Cather's style, grave, flexible, a little austere, wonderfully transparent, everywhere economical, is wonderfully apt for her purposes. There are certain things, to be sure, it cannot do. It cannot register wit or amusement or even humor, save rarely; it never rises to passionate indignation; it lacks earthiness, despite Miss Cather's profound belief in a normal relation with the earth. Dialogue, as she reports it, is seldom more than adequate. But within its boundaries it is beautiful writing, liquid to the ear, lucent to the eye. . . . There are few to whom the adjective "classic" can be more truly applied, for beneath the quick sympathy there is a Roman gravity, a sense of the dignity of life which contemporary fiction . . . has mainly lost.

> Howard Mumford Jones. *SR.* Aug. 6, 1938. p. 16

Willa Cather's traditionalism was . . . anything but the arbitrary or patronizing opposition to contemporary ways which Irving Babbitt personified. It was a candid and philosophical nostalgia, a conviction and a standard possible only to a writer whose remembrance of the world of her childhood and the people in it was so overwhelming that everything after it seemed drab and more than a little cheap. Her distinction was not merely one of cultivation and sensibility; it was a kind of spiritual clarity possible only to those who suffer their loneliness as an act of the imagination and the will. . . . Later, as it seemed, she became merely sentimental, and her direct criticism of contemporary types and manners was often petulant and intolerant. But the very intensity of her nostalgia had from the first led her beyond nostalgia; it had given her the conviction that the values of the world she had lost were the primary values, and everything else merely their degradation.

> Alfred Kazin. *On Native Grounds* (Reynal). 1942.
>
> pp. 250–1

From beginning to end, the Cather novels are not stories of plot, but chronicles, given a depth and significance lacking in the merely historical chronicle by that "sympathy" which leads to a perfect interplay of environment and character.

Her art was essentially a representation of this reaction between the soul of man and its environment. That is why the best of her stories are told against the land. . . . Her own absorption in her people and her land creates the suspense that she herself has felt. . . . She is preservative, almost antiquarian, content with much space in little room —feminine in this, and in her passionate revelation of the values which conserve the life of the emotions.

Henry Seidel Canby. SR. May 10, 1947. pp. 23–4

From the whole range of Cather's values, standards, tastes, and prejudices, her tone is that of an inherent aristocrat in an equalitarian order, of an agrarian writer in an industrial order, of a defender of the spiritual graces in the midst of an increasingly materialistic culture. . . . Selecting and enhancing the most subtle effects of wealth, she has, rather like Sam Dodsworth's wife, either looked down upon or ignored the whole process of creating wealth. Writing so discreetly about the age when business was a personal adventure, she has neglected to mention the most typical forms of the adventure.

Maxwell Geismar. The Last of the Provincials
(Houghton). 1947. pp. 217–8

Mr. Maxwell Geismar wrote a book about her and some others called *The Last of the Provincials*. Not having read it I do not know his argument; but he has a case: she is a provincial; and I hope not the last. She was a good artist, and all true art is provincial in the most realistic sense: of the very time and place of its making, out of human beings who are so particularly limited by their situation, whose faces and names are real and whose lives begin each one at an individaul unique center. Indeed, Willa Cather was a provincial as Hawthorne or Flaubert or Turgenev, as little concerned with aesthetics and as much with morals as Tolstoy, as obstinately reserved as Melville. In fact she always reminds me of very good literary company. . . . She is a curiously immovable shape, monumental, virtue itself in her work and a symbol of virtue—like certain churches, in fact, or exemplary women, revered and neglected.

Katherine Anne Porter. The Days Before (Harcourt).
1952. pp. 72–3

Her vision is of essences. In her earlier novels the essential subject, a state of mind or feelings, was enveloped in the massiveness of the conventional realistic novel. It was there but it was muffled. Then she saw that if she abandoned the devices of massive realism, if she depended on picture and symbol and style, she could disengage her essential subject and make it tell upon the reader with a greater directness and power, help it to remain uncluttered in his mind. The things that pass, the things that merely adhere to states of mind and feeling, she began to use with a severe and rigid economy. Her fiction became a kind of symbolism, with the depths and suggestions that belong to symbolist art, and with the devotion to a music of style and structure for which the great symbolists strove, Pater and Moore and the later Henry James.

E. K. Brown. *Willa Cather* (Knopf). 1953. p. 340

My Antonia

In Antonia's contented domesticity Miss Cather offers a modern variation of an old theme. In the pages of Mrs. Stowe the latter stages of Antonia's career would have been treated as steps of abnegation, the surrender to a sense of duty in a home on earth which would be rewarded by a mansion prepared on high. By most contemporary novelists it would be treated as complete defeat, with no compensation here or hereafter. But Miss Cather with all her zest for studio life, has retained an imaginative regard for four walls and a hearthstone, and the vital experience of mothering a family.

Percy H. Boynton. *Some Contemporary Americans* (Chicago). 1924. pp. 169–70

In *My Antonia,* Antonia Shimerda . . . became the symbol of emotional fulfillment in motherhood on a Western farm. The thesis was arresting, appearing as it did in 1918 at the very moment when farm and village life were coming under the critical eyes of the novelists intent upon exposing its pollution. Without satire or bitterness and with only a little sentimentalism, Willa Cather pictured a strong character developing under severe difficulties which would crush a less heroic soul, surviving the most primitive hardships in a sod hut, toiling like an ox in the field with the men, enduring want, cut off from ordinary pleasures, withstanding betrayal and the cheap life as a hired girl in a village, and emerging at last after such desperate conditions to a triumphant serenity as mother to a healthy group of shy, awkward but happy and laughing boys who are content with their life on the farm.

Harlan Hatcher. *Creating the Modern American Novel* (Farrar and Rinehart). 1935. p. 66

A Lost Lady

A Lost Lady, Miss Cather's most explicit treatment of the passing of the old order, is the central work of her career. Far from being the delicate minor book it is so often called, it is probably her most muscular story, for it derives its power from the grandeur of its theme. Miss Cather shares the American belief in the tonic moral quality of the pioneer's life; with the passing of the frontier she conceives that a great source of fortitude has been lost.

Lionel Trilling in After the Genteel Tradition, edited
by Malcolm Cowley (Norton). 1937. p. 55

A Lost Lady reflects a curious "sunset of the pioneer"—a prismatic sunset, an almost mythical pioneer. Admirable as the story is with reference to its human relationships and emotional values, and remarkable for its creation of an atmosphere, it is still a kind of touching fairy tale of the more beneficent robber barons, or their second or third cousins. It is a reflection not of a society but of a point of view that, increasingly narrow, selective, and fanciful, is actually retreating further and further from society.

Maxwell Geismar. The Last of the Provincials
(Houghton). 1947. p. 183

Death Comes for the Archbishop

Death Comes for the Archbishop is a historical novel; it is also a regional novel and a deliberately picturesque novel, with natural description helping to set the emotional tone. . . . The ritual and beliefs of the Catholic Church, the heroic activity of missionary priests, and the vivid colors of the southwestern landscape combine to produce a new kind of warmth and vitality in her art. . . . Yet one wonders whether this lively creation of a golden world in which all ideals are realized is not fundamentally a "softer" piece of writing. . . . There is, it is true, a splendid sympathy in the treatment of the characters and a most genuine feeling for the period and natural setting in which the action is laid. But there is no indication here of an artist wrestling successfully with intractable material. The material is all too tractable, and the success, though it is real, seems too easy.

David Daiches. Willa Cather (Cornell). 1951. p. 105

See *O Pioneers!, My Antonia, A Lost Lady, The Professor's House, Death Comes for the Archbishop,* and *Shadows on the Rock* (novels).

CIARDI, JOHN (1916–   )

Evidently of immigrant family, Ciardi searches out for himself the meaning of America for his own generation. Undoubtedly he is well acquainted with the English poet, Auden. His technique, at best, stems from Auden. Weaker passages hint MacLeish. But, more important, he proves that for the young American poets as for the English, the personal themes of love, friendship and family relationships cannot be divorced from the social theme. . . . He can write . . . the symbolic lyric—and beautifully. But for his purposes—the precise representation of the American scene without utopian thinking, and of the growing psychology of general apprehension—his poetry of statement rather more than that of song or of violent image is successful.

Eda Lou Walton. *NYT*. Feb. 25, 1940. p. 5

The poems have a youthful ring which it is pleasant to come upon, and it is a tone not obscured by echoes. That Ciardi seems fresher than most poets is probably due to the fact that he is content with getting a scene down on paper, sometimes sprawlingly, but with care for the truth of it. He is not yet concerned to any great extent with interpretation.

Coleman Rosenberger. *NR*. July, 1940. p. 36

Unlike Eliot, who is only one of his "ancestors," Ciardi likes humanity well enough to satirize with warm wit, rather than with cold distaste. There is throughout his work a personality that expands to encompass the experiences of his fellows.

His considerable wit shows itself not only in the surprising juxtaposition of images, ideas, and language . . . but also in the rhythms and stanzaic forms. . . . But make no mistake—he deals in serious matters. His sense of the ironic gives him that authority (only the humorous should be allowed to be serious).

Gerard Previn Meyer. *SR*. Dec. 6, 1947. p. 60

John Ciardi is a poet of genuine if unequal gifts, whose best poetry has wit, perception and humanity. His greatest fault is lack of poetic liveliness, which derives not from any dullness of imagery or conventionality of vision but from rhythmic monotony. . . . But this fault Mr. Ciardi shares with many distinguished modern poets, including, in some degree, Eliot himself. His virtues are more individual and more interesting. . . . Ciardi produc(es) poetry both intelligible and mature, poetry which draws upon all the resources which the modern tradition has made available to the poet without losing touch with the reader.

David Daiches. *NYHT*. Jan. 1, 1950. p. 6

Mr. Ciardi's poetry depends on the world of his imagination as much as it does on the world in which he is living, and, they are not discrete but interdependent essences. Therefore, he writes a poetry that is psychologically sound as he exercises his wit, satire, and compassion with precise control. He may be acidulous, but he is genuinely humane.

I. L. Salomon. *SR*. Jan. 28, 1956. p. 24

The most notable thing about John Ciardi's *As If* is a kind of crude power. The hesitations, reticences, and inabilities of the poetic nature —for to be able to say what it does say is to be unable to say everything else—are unknown to natures of such ready force, natures more akin to those of born executives, men ripe for running things. This writer uses Stevens's, or Shapiro's, or half a dozen other poets' tricks and techniques as easily, and with as much justification as a salesman would use a competitor's sales-talk—it works, doesn't it? But he doesn't use the styles as delicately and helplessly as these poets used them— after all, he *can* help himself, has helped himself. . . . He is much at his best as a translator where his native force can put on a more sensitive and individual mask—his translation of the *Inferno* has more narrative power, strength of action, than any other I know.

Randall Jarrell. *YR*. Spring, 1956. p. 479

The one theme which stands out above others which could be cited in Mr. Ciardi's variously paced poetry is a concern with time, a concern which shows itself in the birthday poems, the elegies, the family poems . . . and those poems in which the poet mediates on the history and meaning of man. . . . Several of these poems which explore history and childhood are, at bottom, the signs of the poet's encounter with the hard old fact of death. The transiency of human life and all human things is a theme as old as poetry but Mr. Ciardi's version is so modern as to be almost fashionable. He faces time, death and change under the contemporary shadow of man's existential nothingness. . . . Yet the sweat of the engagement is real and is his own.

Ernest Sandeen. *Poetry*. July, 1956. p. 267

The best thing about John Ciardi is his personality. He is singularly unlike most American poets with their narrow lives and feuds. He is more like a very literate, gently appetitive, Italo-American airplane pilot, fond of deep simple things like his wife and kids, his friends and students, Dante's verse and good food and wine. The next best thing about John Ciardi is his poetry. It is truly refreshing. It is singularly free from the vices that beset most American poets nowadays, with their provincial imitations of English-Baroque verse and their trivial ambiguities. . . . These are good poems—clear, intimate and living.

Kenneth Rexroth. *NYT*. Aug. 3, 1958. p. 6

His poems show the same lack of subterfuge, perhaps even of nuance, as his editorial deeds. Everything is stated as it arises, with a curbed vigor rather than with mystery or subtlety. This poetry is the spectrum of a whole man who, however antic he may be in life, feels in his art no need to strike literary poses. . . . He is at times as good a phrase-maker as Dylan Thomas, but more sparing in his effects. . . . His phrases are the body, often the naked body, and not the clothing of his thought.

Dilys Laing. *Nation*. Sept. 13, 1958. p. 138

See *As If* and *I Marry You* (poetry).

CLARK, WALTER VAN TILBURG (1908–)

The tendency to explain, to probe, to analyze, is certainly more characteristic of the people of the eastern half of this country than it is of Westerners. Though born in the East, Walter Van Tilburg Clark is a Westerner in sympathy and spirit. Like the large landscapes with which the book is filled, his style is ample and spacious rather than compact. The reader whose life is not leisurely may find himself skipping paragraphs. . . . The dialogue is never false but it lacks the impact of character, and there is no humor.

William Maxwell. *SR*. June 2, 1945. p. 13

He is a storyteller before he is a moralist, a writer before he is a philosopher. . . . What makes him a serious writer, to my mind, is that he can write parables which are as absorbing for their telling as for their moral. . . . It may just be that Walter Van Tilburg Clark is a Young Lochinvar coming riding out of the West to the American novel's rescue.

Hilary H. Lyons. *Holiday*. Oct. 1949. p. 20

(*The Watchful Gods*) reinforces our awareness of that combination of personal integrity and artful concentration which, aside from his Western settings, is the trade-mark of Mr. Clark's talent. . . . The activities of the Western setting seem always to be under examination, as though the author recognized the challenge to investigate the relationship of the human being to an environment which has too often frustrated the attempts of the writer to subdue it.

Mr. Clark's nature is not the idyllic world of nineteenth-century romanticism; neither is it a world of irrational malevolence such as that portrayed by our literary naturalists. Nature represents, rather, a stage whereon man's actions of necessity become more clearly defined.

Ray B. West, Jr. SR. Sept. 30, 1950. pp. 17–8

The difficulty is not that Mr. Clark is too much preoccupied with man's relation to the forces of nature but rather that he is apparently so little interested in the relations that exist between men, except in those limited areas where people have differing conceptions of their connection with the natural world. . . . When in 306 pages of short stories (*The Watchful Gods*) perhaps only 15 contain any dialogue, aside from people talking to animals, one must inevitably consider the extent of their relevance to the human situation, and one must wonder whether the writer's horizons are not bounded on the one hand by the hawk and on the other by the boy with the twenty-two.

Harvey Swados. Nation. Oct. 7, 1950. p. 318

Clark's world is spiritually the world of the rural American, consisting of Nature, on the one hand, and Man on the other. . . . In all of Clark's fiction his exceptionally acute observations of outdoor sound, light, smell, mass, texture, and relationship are superior to his understanding of the human psyche in any but a decivilised area of operation. There is no living American writer of fiction who can type a richer page of landscape but no writer of equal talent is more endangered by the inability to enrich his human types.

Vernon Young. AQ. Summer, 1951. pp. 110–1

The Track of the Cat

The Track of the Cat deals with a great theme in American fiction, perhaps the greatest: the pursuit of an enemy in nature. . . . Clark localizes his theme in the attempt by a family of brothers to track down a great black panther during a mountain blizzard. His story is continuously and wonderfully exciting. He is able to bring before the reader with extraordinary vividness the clash of stubborn wills in the snow-bound ranchhouse, the unpopulated mountain landscape, the snow and cold, and above all, the hunt itself.

Paul Pickrel. YR. Autumn, 1949. pp. 190–1

There is an artistic unity and simplicity in *The Track of the Cat,* but there is also some of the looseness and apparent capriciousness of events which are in life. The actions have implications that go far beyond their limited context. . . . You can take *The Track of the Cat* as a symbolic, universal drama of Man against an implacable Evil Principle, forever stalking him, and you can ponder its implied question: If humility and violence meet the same end, is it a stalemate? Or you may enjoy it, without mysticism, as a stark story of man struggling with elemental antagonists in nature.

Edmund Fuller. SR. June 4, 1949. pp. 9–10

The Track of the Cat is one of the great American novels of "place." Something of its nobility should be suggested by the fact that one cannot bring to mind a similar novel of its kind that is quite worthy of comparison. One thinks of the best in the genre, even of such work as Elisabeth Madox Roberts' *The Tree of Man* and Willa Cather's *My Antonia,* and they come to seem, by comparison, more than ever like miniature studies of special manners, more than graceful surely, yet without grandeur. Mr. Clark's new novel likewise transcends his own earlier books. . . . *The Track of the Cat* may well be the achievement that twentieth-century American regionalism has needed to justify itself.

Mark Schorer. NYT. June 5, 1949. p. 1

See *The Ox-Bow Incident, The City of Trembling Leaves,* and *The Track of the Cat* (novels); also *The Watchful Gods* (short stories).

COWLEY, MALCOLM (1898–   )

Poetry

By an ill adjustment Malcolm Cowley is best known as a critic and translator, whereas his verse is by far his most important contribution. . . . Cowley is not to be labeled the poet exclusively of this or that. But the one note which appears most often is a kind of indefinite regret. Though willingly accepting this as the only possible of worlds, to the contemporary he supplies a Baudelairian corrective of nostalgia prior to the facts, a nostalgia which would prevail regardless of the environment. There is the frequent meditation upon death and upon that stagnation of the mind which may precede death by many years. There is the constant suggestion of a vague return. . . . There is the hankering after something native.

Kenneth Burke. NYHT. Aug. 18, 1929. p. 2

It would be difficult to find a single book of poems more symptomatic of the experiences of the post-war writers of America than Malcolm Cowley's. . . . *Blue Juniata* is important not only because it gives us the assembled verse of a new and definitely interesting poet, but because it sets itself up as a self-confessed logbook of literary youth in America during the ten years which followed the war. . . . Unlike many poets who at the present moment are being read and quoted with high favor, Mr. Cowley is not devising his tunes with gymnastic agility on a single string. He has obviously submitted to the charms of many influences, and he has managed to go through a period of high excitement in our cultural experience and yet realized a significance in the manifold distractions and vogues that crowded it.

Morton Dauwen Zabel. *Nation.* Aug. 21, 1929.
pp. 200–1

His mind is basically concrete and unspeculative; he brings to facts and observations an even emotional tone that is the mark of a genuine style; but in criticism Cowley's instinct for exact definition is not strong; and the necessity for a certain amount of abstraction only violates the even tone of his style. It is in poetry, at least for the present, that Mr. Cowley may be seen at his best.

And yet the long discipline of prose has given to his poetry much of its distinction of form. . . . There are no great moments in Cowley, and there are no disconcerting lapses. There is subdued emotion; there are exact feelings and images; and over all, a subtle vision of the startling qualities of common things.

Allen Tate. *NR.* Aug. 28, 1929. pp. 51–2

Mr. Cowley's consciousness is that of a young America which is both on terms of some familiarity with tradition in letters and with the life we see around us. . . . And if his poetry lacks something of traditional beauty and lyricism, it is because his mind has been formed under conditions only partly amenable to change through his own efforts. The poems of *Blue Juniata* are of an intellectual order, wholly disciplined, but the indigenous flavor has not been intellectualized, so to speak, out of them.

John Chamberlain. *NYT.* Sept. 8, 1929. p. 2

Criticism

"It was an easy, quick, adventurous age, good to be young in," Mr. Cowley remarks of the 1920's. That is the way in which some of us who shared the adventure he chronicles remember the era. It is evoking a revival of interest today, and it is being reconstructed with scholarly enthusiasm by young writers who were in their cradles when it passed. They have the right to their interpretation. But should you wish to know what it felt like to us who lived through it, read *Exile's Return*. Mr. Cowley has painted the classic picture, and it is not likely to be surpassed in authenticity, eloquence or beauty.

Lloyd Morris. *NYHT*. July 8, 1951. p. 10

Cowley has the sense of a lyric poet (which he is) for the unique value of the individual. . . . Yet because he also has the social historian's sense that each life, besides having a pattern of its own, is a part of the pattern of the age, he can make you see how all these lives fitted the pattern of alienation which led a whole generation of intellectuals into exile. . . . *Exile's Return* is far and away the best book about this generation (of the 1920's) by a participant, and this is a generation that was crucial not only for American literature but for the whole of American culture.

Arthur Mizener. *NYT*. June 10, 1951. p. 9

Calmly ignoring those austere critics who claim it is the literary work that should concern us and not the private life of the creator, Malcolm Cowley has put together a fascinating account of the American writer as a human being (in *The Literary Situation*). A critic, editor, and poet who brings to his interest in writers' lives an *avant-garde* background, Mr. Cowley transforms literary anecdotage and journalism into a valuable analysis of what makes the American writer run. His approach is like that of the Lynds to Middletown, U.S.A., except that his conclusions are based on personal observation and inquiry rather than statistics and questionnaires, and that some of the best things in the book are purely—and maliciously—subjective.

Milton Rugoff. *NYHT*. Oct. 24, 1954. p. 6.

His experience of active emotional participation in the literary life apparently came to an end with the period which he documented in *Exile's Return,* and of late years he has retreated more and more into seclusion; his point of view has grown increasingly elder statesmanish; and his tone has undergone a gradual change from the lyric to the avuncular. . . . After thinking back over Cowley's critical career and setting aside those fine and definitive essays on writers like Hemingway and Faulkner which he has occasionally been able to do, one is forced to conclude that he has suffered increasingly from the effect of trying to simplify his ideas for the benefit of what he obviously considers a simple-minded reading public.

John W. Aldridge. *Nation.* Feb. 19, 1955. pp. 162–4

See *Blue Juniata* (poems); also *The Lost Generation, Exile's Return,* and *The Literary Situation* (criticism).

COZZENS, JAMES GOULD (1903–   )

He wrote three rather tropical and violent stories of Cuba and other southern latitudes in *Confusion, Cockpit,* and *Son of Perdition,* in which he derived something from Joseph Hergesheimer and maybe something from Nick Carter. He wrote one atrocious Elizabethan yarn, *Michael Scarlett.* He followed Conrad profitably in *S. S. San Pedro;* the result did no discredit to the model. Perhaps he is not committed to the hard-boiled school beyond the present offering (*The Last Adam*). It will be exceedingly interesting to see what he will do next. For it is more than likely he has something of his own to say.

Isabel Paterson. *NYHT.* Jan. 8, 1933. p. 6

There is no question but that Cozzens's work, except in regard to his larger dramatic frames, shows a steady progress toward greater mastery of his craft, increased consciousness of his effects, and constantly augmented scope. Except for *Castaway,* however, he has given us every ingredient of first-rate novels except the novels themselves. His faults, the prejudices and blockages that make his treatment of race and sex so unsatisfactory, and his constant dissipating of tragedy into irony and melodrama, seem to be the obverse of his virtues: his enormously representative quality and his uncompromising honesty. When Cozzens can write novels with the breadth and depth of *The Just and the Unjust* or *Guard of Honor* in as taut and satisfactory a dramatic frame as *Castaway* has, when he learns to combine the realism of his later work with the symbolism of his middle period and deepen both in the process, he should be a novelist to rank with the best America has produced.

Stanley Edgar Hyman. *NMQ.* Winter, 1949. p. 497

He is a professional. . . . The professional as novelist is a man who has subdued himself to what he works in, who holds himself humbly in relation to fiction but holds fiction to be the most important thing in the world, whose deepest shame it would be not to write his novel wholly in the terms which the novel itself sets. He is also a man who has mastered his job and substitutes skill for literary pretensions and affectations. In his novels form and content are so welded together that they have become inseparable; they are the same thing. Morover, each of his novels is a handful of novels made one; it is packed tight with life; any of its parts or characters and many of its mere parentheses would make a novel for a smaller man.

Bernard De Voto. *Harper*. Feb., 1949. p. 73

He has nothing less than a passion for detachment.

This passionate detachment of his is closely associated with his great technical skill. I do not mean that he has acquired that skill merely by virtue of being detached, for obviously he has worked hard for it, but the basis on which his craftsmanship has developed is his objectivity. Deliberately standing apart from his material, he strives to see clearly and to render with perfect accuracy what he sees. His writing is always careful and never more careful than in the avoidance of pretentiousness.

Granville Hicks. *EJ*. Jan., 1950. p. 4

Mr. Cozzens's grasp of American life is not based upon long familiarity with a single region, . . . but upon his wisdom in the ways of the upper middle class, which is very much the same all over the country. He has profound respect for the responsible citizens who actually make our civilization work. Ibsen called them "pillars of society," and made the very term imply hypocrisy. Mr. Cozzens, on the other hand, likes to portray this class from the point of view of a member of one of the great professions, Law; the Church, Medicine, and by that means he brings out the humane values he sees in *his* pillars of society.

Francis Fergusson. *Per*. Winter, 1954. pp. 36–7

I know of no modern novelist who commands such a range of idiom, allusion, cadence, rhetorical radiation and vocabulary. It is a muscular, virile style with certain strong affinities to seventeenth-century prose—Cozzens is fond of Bunyan, Milton, Defoe, among others. Yet one does not get the feeling of reading a literary novel. The ironic view alone prevents this. . . . In Cozzens's novels the world of types explored by Dickens and by Shaw and by Ben Jonson comes before us again in its unfamiliar shape—the shape of the local, urban, and workaday, qualities too trivial to most novelists in recent years to seem worthy of their attention. Cozzens forces our attention, concentrates it, makes us inescapably aware of the density of the lives we live.

Louis O. Coxe. *AL*. May, 1955. pp. 163, 168–9

Cozzens is not Thackeray. He is more judicial, less sentimental and he lacks Thackeray's magic. But he deals as Thackeray did with man in society, with related man. And it is impossible to believe that Cozzens did not remember Colonel Newcome's "Adsum," when he wrote Winner's "I am here" (in *By Love Possessed*). Thackeray's passage has been in the anthologies for a hundred years. Far more moving, because it is a way of living instead of dying, is Winner's "I am here."

Jessamyn West. NYHT. Aug. 25, 1957. p. 1

Cozzens would no more deform a character to meet the demands of his plot than he would steal from his Delaware Valley neighbors. Nevertheless, it *is* a pattern, almost a formula, and it has reappeared in one of his novels after another.

There is a lawyer, young or old, or a staff officer in the Air Force, or a clergyman deeply involved in the lives of his parishioners. There is a climax in his career, a period of two or three days during which hell breaks loose; men die in accidents, women commit suicide, friends of his family are charged with sexual crimes, his closest associates betray him through irresponsibility; and meanwhile the hero tries to do his best for everyone, succeeding in some cases, failing lamentably in others, yet somehow surviving by force of character.

Malcolm Cowley. NYT. Aug. 25, 1957. p. 1

The essential difference between Cozzens and his contemporaries lies in the character of his work. Here he is the complete nonconformist: a classic man, operating in a romantic period. This, I suspect, is the basic reason why he has missed both popular and critical appreciation. He puzzles ordinary readers whose palates have been dulled by the Gothic extravagance of most fiction; and he offends critics whose professional mission has been to exalt the romantic novel which has been in high fashion for the last thirty years. . . . Cozzens may, indeed, signal the turning of the tide. In his salad days, he too flirted with the romantic technique, but in his mature novels he has moved steadily away from it. Instead he has been attempting something far more difficult: to write an engrossing story about ordinary people, living ordinary lives, in ordinary circumstances.

John Fischer. Harper. Sept., 1957. pp. 15–8

Cozzens's heroes are becoming steadily richer and more Protestant, while his upstarts—Catholics, Jews, or reformers—are something like caricatures and invariably obnoxious. (His Negroes now, because of spotless subservience, fare somewhat better. They *like* to take communion last.) He has, of course, like any author, the right to choose the class he will deal with—Jane Austen did as much—but this kind of limitation is doubled because of Cozzens's obvious distaste for the people into whose minds he will not choose or deign to enter. . . . His sympathy is husbanded too narrowly, and he lacks what Henry James called "the sacred rage." He walks away from us cool, disenchanted, a little superior, pleased to have kept his distance.

Richard Ellmann. *Reporter*. Oct. 3, 1957. pp. 43–4

Like most of Mr. Cozzens's novels (making some exceptions for *Castaway*) *By Love Possessed* suffers from a want of essential drama: though all the great rites of tragedy are prepared and invoked, the demonstration remains at last unmade; as though the author had some reservations—possibly about "real life" and "the way things really work out"—which protect his major actors from their ends. I cannot help thinking that the book, in this respect, functions as a kind of secular apologetics, the defense of an image of life, much idealized, which is regarded with so much reverence and nostalgia that its exemplars may not and must not be brought down from their high places. . . . The mere acknowledgement of the possibility will do instead, so that in the end honor, wealth, position, are saved at the expense of honesty, on the stated ground that considerations higher than honesty (charity, compassion, expedience) are involved, a shift of justifications not without its Jesuitical quality.

Howard Nemerov. *Nation*. Nov. 2, 1957. p. 308

Cozzens's work is defined not by these technical devices, the compression of dramatic time and the interpenetration of various actions, but also by certain pervading themes, the need for experience and the discrepancy between the ideal and the actual. . . . Because Cozzens does not write about the man in the gray flannel suit many readers will miss the fact that Cozzens is a contemporary writer in the deepest sense of the term. His subject is the limited world in which man is enmeshed in a congerie of forces which radiates far beyond his personal control. Cozzens's heroes are professional men, themselves an instance of a specialized society, and his subjects are various; but his theme is the complex world in which man, in his already limited estate, is further limited.

John W. Ward. *AS*. Winter, 1957. pp. 93, 99

In his previous works there has always been a certain absence of primary feeling; he is a cold writer who has needed a recharge, say, of human sympathy. To a certain degree *By Love Possessed* is probably the attempt to get at just this issue in his own work and career—but an attempt which, rather than enlarging the writer's capacity to feel, simply confirms his prejudice against feeling. It is a treatise on the different kinds of love—parental, oedipal, sibling, self-love or vanity, religious, sexual. But why is it that all these types of love are only destructive and never even momentarily rewarding? . . . What Mr. Cozzens does not seem to understand for all his classical lore, is that the Goddess of Love, whatever her cruel demands on her afflicted subjects, is also the Goddess of Life.

Maxwell Geismar. American Moderns (Hill and
Wang). 1958. pp. 148–50

He should not be ignored because he is unfashionable nor should he be disparaged because John Fischer nominated him for the Nobel Prize. He has been writing for a long time now, and he has shown a greater capacity for growth than the majority of his contemporaries. He clings tenaciously to his own point of view, and it yields him a vision of human experience that the reader has to respect even when he doesn't like it. We don't have to belittle other writers to appreciate Cozzens, although some critics . . . act as if we did. We can never have too much excellence, and if it takes different forms, so much the better.

Granville Hicks. SR. Aug. 8, 1959. p. 12

He is writing about the individual in society, about the obligations, the hazards, the rebellious and painful accommodation of human beings to the way things—not *are* (this has been misunderstood)—but *work:* the way things work, the functioning of the world. His heroes are men who understand these functions, live with them, interpret them for others and in some part keep the machinery running. Able, responsible men, more burdened by duty than eager for power, learning in maturity that one never really knows enough, stoically bearing the weight of the world—these are the men Cozzens sets up as admirable. They are admirable. But they are also the Ruling Class, if only on the provincial level.

This being so, it is easy to see why he has been attacked for supporting the status quo and writing "Novels of Resignation."

Elizabeth Janeway. NYT. Aug. 9, 1959. p. 1

See *The Last Adam, Castaway, S. S. San Pedro, The Just and the Unjust, Men and Brethren, Guard of Honor,* and *By Love Possessed* (novels).

CRANE, HART (1899–1932)

Mr. Crane has a most remarkable style, a style which is strikingly original—almost something like a great style, if there could be such a thing as a great style which was, not merely not applied to a great subject, but not, so far as one can see, applied to any subject at all. . . . One does not demand of poetry nowadays that it shall provide us with logical metaphors or with intelligible sequences of ideas. Rimbaud is inconsecutive and confused. Yet, with Rimbaud, whom Mr. Crane somewhat resembles, we experience intense emotional excitement and artistic satisfaction; we are dazzled by the eruption of his images, but we divine what it is that he is saying. But, with Mr. Crane, though he sometimes moves us, it is in a way curiously vague.

Edmund Wilson. *NR*. May 11, 1927. p. 320

What is divine about the poetry of Crane is the energy which fills it, that intense, dionysian, exalted energy that by sheer pressure lifts him to heights unattainable by less titanic poets. . . . One cay say this: at sixteen he was writing at a level that Amy Lowell never rose from and at twenty-eight he is writing on a level that scarcely any other living American poet ever reaches.

Gorham Munson. *Destinations* (Sears). 1928.

pp. 162–4

It is in single grand passages, rather than whole poems, that Crane reveals the power and sweep of his concentric vision. One cannot condone the obscurities in toto, nor entirely subscribe to a style which is often more grandiose than a given occasion demands.

Alfred Kreymborg. *Our Singing Strength* (Coward-McCann). 1929. p. 604

Crane labored to perfect both the strategy and the tactics of language so as to animate and maneuver his perceptions—and then fought the wrong war and against an enemy that displayed, to his weapons, no vulnerable target. He wrote in a language of which it was the virtue to accrete, modify, and interrelate moments of emotional vision—moments at which the sense of being gains its greatest access—moments at which, by the felt nature of the knowledge, the revealed thing is its own meaning; and he attempted to apply his language, in his major effort, to a theme that required a sweeping, discrete, indicative, anecdotal language, a language in which, by force of movement, mere cataloging can replace and often surpass representation. He used the private lyric to write the cultural epic.

R. P. Blackmur. *The Double Agent* (Arrow). 1935.

p. 126

His world has no center, and the compensatory action that he took is responsible for the fragmentary quality of his most ambitious work. This action took two forms, the blind assertion of the will; and the blind desire for self-destruction. The poet did not face his first problem, which is to define the limits of his personality and to objectify its moral implications in an appropriate symbolism. Crane could only assert a quality of will against the world, and at each successive failure of the will he turned upon himself. . . . By attempting an extreme solution of the romantic problem, Crane proved that it cannot be solved.

Allen Tate. *Reactionary Essays* (Scribner). 1936.

pp. 40–2. Courtesy of Alan Swallow

Although Pound and Eliot had been largely responsible for reviving an interest in the poetry of the sixteenth and seventeenth centuries, they were themselves temperamentally incapable of doing more than adapting, imitating, and assimilating certain of its characteristics. . . . It remained for Crane, unschooled, unspoiled by scholastic nostalgia and self-consciousness, to use the medium in a completely modern way, easily and naturally combining in it rhetoric, conversation, and discursive thought, and sounding afresh the grand note so rarely heard in modern times. . . . In the process of renovating blank verse Crane also revivified the poetic language of his time. He was able to discover words, and use them, almost as things in themselves, prized their colors, sounds, and shapes as more meaningful than their strict definitions.

Philip Horton. *Hart Crane* (Norton). 1937.

pp. 309–10

Crane's poems often have a hypnotic power about them which marks them out as among the most extraordinary performances with language to be found in American poetry. One may call it genius or one may say that he had a wholly exceptional mediumistic power to set on paper the contents of the subconscious carrying with them still a kind of inhuman quality.

Amos N. Wilder. *The Spiritual Aspects of Poetry*
(Harper). 1940. p. 124

Crane was incapable of a sustained irony, which might have produced an inclusive attitude harmonizing his vision of actuality, his romantic transcendentalism and his personal neuroses. His natural power of poetic expression was prodigious, but its effectiveness was defeated by his uncertainty of technical control. This accounts for his essential "patchiness," his exasperating combination of the meritorious and the meretricious. . . . His most extraordinary stirring and kindling power with words is most manifest in scattered lines which shoot suddenly like a rocket from dark surroundings.

Elizabeth Drew. *Directions in Modern Poetry* (Holt).
1941. pp. 69–70

Crane . . . had the absolute seriousness that goes with genius and with sanctity; one might describe him as a saint of the wrong religion. He had not the critical intelligence to see what was wrong with his doctrine, but he had the courage of his convictions, the virtue of integrity, and he deserves our respect. He has the value of a thorough-going demonstration. He embodies perfectly the concepts which for nearly a century have been generating some of the most cherished principles of our literature, our education, our politics, and our personal morals. . . . We shall scarcely get anything better unless we change our principles.

Yvor Winters. *In Defense of Reason* (Morrow).
1947. pp. 602–3. Courtesy of Alan Swallow

His efforts to create an artistic "shorthand," to rid poetry of the rigidity of logical sequence and make his language the equivalent of a state of consciousness and immediate experience, led him to employ the methods of displacement familiar among contemporary artists in music and painting. . . . The unit was the word, and, like the spot of color in pointillism, that word could be altered in various ways by the other words placed around it.

Barbara Herman. *SwR*. Jan., 1950. p. 61.

Essentially Crane was a poet of ecstasy or frenzy or intoxication; you can choose your own word depending on how much you like his work. Essentially he was using rhyme and meter and fantastic images to convey the emotional states that were induced in him by alcohol, jazz, machinery, laughter, intellectual stimulation, the shape and sound of words and the madness of New York in the late Coolidge era. At their worst his poems are ineffective unless read in something approximating the same atmosphere, with a drink at your elbow, the phonograph blaring and somebody shouting into your ear, "Isn't that great!" At their best, however, the poems do their work unaided except by their proper glitter and violence.

Malcolm Cowley. *Exile's Return* (Viking). 1951.
pp. 230–1

The Bridge

The late Hart Crane was not a learned man; he was not trained in or given to nice distinctions. . . . Now life was too proddingly real for him to concede the impossibility of giving it meaning. He might be said to be the only modern poet sufficiently *blind* to give his concepts the force of convictions *felt,* not cerebrally, and perhaps timorously, posited. That (*The Bridge*) is the product of desire rather than of fulfillment must mitigate, in the eliminating process of time, its claims as a successful epic. Its convictions are frenziedly positive; one's reactions are mixedly negative.

Howard Blake. *SwR.* Spring, 1935. pp. 193–4

The fifteen parts of *The Bridge* taken as one poem suffer from the lack of a coherent structure, whether symbolistic or narrative: the coherence of the work consists in the personal quality of the writing—in mood, feeling, and tone. In the best passages Crane has a perfect mastery over the qualities of his style; but it lacks an objective pattern of ideas elaborate enough to carry it through an epic or heroic work. The single symbolistic image, in which the whole poem centers, is at one moment the actual Brooklyn Bridge; at another, it is any bridge or "connection"; at still another, it is a philosophical pun, and becomes the basis of a series of analogies. . . . Alternately he asserts the symbol of the bridge and abandons it, because fundamentally he does not understand it. The idea of bridgeship is an elaborate blur leaving the inner structure of the poem confused.

Yet some of the best poetry of our times is in *The Bridge.* Its inner confusion is a phase of the inner cross-purposes of the time. Crane was one of those men whom every age seems to select as the spokesmen of its spiritual life; they give the age away.

Allen Tate. *Reactionary Essays* (Scribner). 1936.
pp. 32–8. Courtesy of Alan Swallow

The Bridge is a noble and basically impersonal poem of epic vision fulfilling its author's boldest claims as a monument to America. In fits of drunkenness Crane declared that he was a reincarnation of Christopher Marlowe. In one sense there is sober justice in the vaunt. The youthful and ecstatic Crane is at least as successful a poetic spokesman for modern America as the youthful and ecstatic Marlowe for Elizabethan

England. The American public has as yet scarcely appreciated the contribution of *The Bridge* to a distinctively national literature.

> Henry W. Wells. *The American Way of Poetry*
> (Twayne). 1943. p. 204

We may ask whether the bridge, the metaphorical strength of which, obviously, is its power to unite one part with another, is as powerful a symbol as Crane thought. The bridge, over and above its metaphor value, does have ready associations for an industrialized world. But a more basic consideration is this: Can any amount of arbitrary spanning or bridging on the part of the poet—Crane bridges the agrarian and industrial worlds; the Tunnel and the final vision of hopefulness—create a unity in the minds of a society that normally sees the parts in isolation or in opposition? It would seem that the bridge symbol, which would have been remarkably appropriate to the medieval world, is an ironic one for ours.

> William Van O'Connor. *Sense and Sensibility in*
> *Modern Poetry* (Chicago). 1948. p. 23

In the tension set up between an oversimplified vision and a tortured awareness of realistic circumstance, the poem demonstrates the very mood of experiment in the literature of the 1920's: its complexities, its untraditional modes of approach to the uses of poetry, its attempts to force a new idiom and to utilize a new range of subject matter, and above all, its moral concern over the special value and function of poetry itself. The poet of *The Bridge* is a man alienated from his community because of (and in the very act of) his search for an acceptable, believable synthesis of that community.

> Frederick J. Hoffmann. *The Twenties* (Viking). 1955.
> p. 239

See *The Bridge, Collected Poems,* and *Letters.*

CRANE, STEPHEN (1871–1900)

He sang, but his voice erred up and down the scale, with occasional flashes of brilliant melody, which could not redeem the errors. New York was essentially his inspiration, the New York of suffering and baffled and beaten life, of inarticulate or blasphemous life; and away from it he was not at home, with any theme, or any sort of character. It was the pity of his fate that he must quit New York, first as a theme, and then as a habitat; for he rested nowhere else, and wrought with nothing else as with the lurid depths which he gave proof of knowing better than anyone else.

William Dean Howells. *NAR*. Dec., 1902. p. 771

In his art he is unique. Its certainty, its justness, its peculiar perfection of power arrived at its birth, or at least at that precise moment in its birth when other artists—and great artists too—were preparing themselves for the long and difficult conquest of their art. I cannot remember a parallel case in the literary history of fiction. . . . His art is just in itself, rhythmical, self-poising as is the art of a perfect dancer. There are no false steps, no excesses. And, of course, his art is strictly limited. We would define him by saying he is the perfect artist and interpreter of the surfaces of life. And that explains why he so swiftly attained his peculiar power and what is the realm his art commands and his limitations.

Edward Garnett. *Friday Nights* (Knopf). 1922. p. 205

He had a quiet smile that charmed and frightened one. It made you pause by something revelatory it cast over his whole physiognomy, not like a ray but like a shadow. . . . Contempt and indignation never broke the surface of his moderation simply because he had no surface. He was all through the same material, incapable of affectation of any kind, of any pitiful failure of generosity for the sake of personal advantage, or even from sheer exasperation which must find its relief. . . . Though the word is discredited now and may sound pretentious, I will say that there was in Crane a strain of chivalry which made him safe to trust with one's life.

Joseph Conrad. Introduction to Thomas Beer's
Stephen Crane (Knopf). 1923. pp. 5, 7, 9–10

He is American literature's "marvelous boy." Like the Bowery, he was elemental and vital. He would sleep in a flop house to taste the bitter of experience. He loved living. And adventure enough was crowded into his eight sick years of manhood. He looked at life clearly and boldly, knew its irony, felt its mystery and beauty, and wrote about it with a sincerity and confidence that spring only from genius.

Vernon Loggins. *I Hear America* (Crowell). 1937.
p. 23

Crane left on me an impression of supernaturalness that I still have. It was perhaps the aura of that youth that never deserted him—perhaps because of his aspect of fraility. He seemed to shine—and perhaps the November sun really did come out and cast on his figure, in the gloom of my entry, a ray of light. At any rate, there he stands . . . radiating brightness. But it was perhaps more than anything the avenging quality of his brows and the resentful frown of his dark blue eyes. He saw, that is to say, the folly and malignity of humanity—not in the individual but in committees.

Ford Madox Ford. Portraits from Life (Houghton).
1937. p. 24

For all its beauty, Crane's best work was curiously thin and, in one sense, even corrupt. His desperation exhausted him too quickly; his unique sense of tragedy was a monotone. No one in America had written like him before; but though his books precipitately gave the whole aesthetic movement of the nineties a sudden direction and a fresher impulse, he could contribute no more than the intensity of his spirit. Half of him was a consummate workman; the other half was not a writer at all. . . . His gift was a furious one, but barren; writing much, he repeated himself so joylessly that in the end he seemed to be mocking himself with the same quiet viciousness with which, even as a boy, he had mocked the universe.

Alfred Kazin. On Native Grounds (Reynal). 1942.
pp. 71–2

Crane was one of the first post-impressionists. . . . He began it before the French painters began it or at least as early as the first of them. He simply knew from the beginning how to handle detail. He estimated it at its true worth—made it serve his purposes and felt no further responsibility about it. I doubt whether he ever spent a laborious half-hour in doing his duty by detail—in enumerating, like an honest, grubby auctioneer. If he saw one thing that engaged him in a room, he mentioned it. If he saw one thing in a landscape that thrilled him, he put it on paper, but he never tried to make a faithful report of everything else within his field of vision, as if he were a conscientious salesman making out an expense account.

Willa Cather. On Writing (Knopf). 1949. pp. 69–70

Maggie

Maggie is not a story *about* people; it is primitive human nature itself set down with perfect spontaneity and grace of handling. For pure aesthetic beauty and truth no Russian, not Tchekhov himself, could have bettered this study which, as Howells remarks, has the quality of Greek tragedy.

Edward Garnett. Friday Nights (Knopf). 1922.
pp. 214–5

It is short, a novelette. Yet it suggests more life than any American contemporary of Crane could have depicted in a thousand pages. In its every crowded phrase and metaphor it is reality. The little book breaks all traditions of fiction. Crane has no model for it—except possibly the page or two he had read from Zola. But it is not Zolaesque. Critics like to call it the first specimen of genuine realism produced by an American.-Perhaps it is that. But it should be judged as a thing unique—just a faithful and vivid projection of the grim degradation and sordid beauty of the Bowery.

Vernon Loggins. *I Hear America* (Crowell). 1937.

p. 25

The Red Badge of Courage

The deep artistic unity of *The Red Badge of Courage* is fused in its flaming, spiritual intensity, in the fiery ardour with which the shock of the Federal and Confederate armies is imaged. The torrential force and impetus, the check, sullen recoil and reforming of shattered regiments, and the renewed onslaught and obstinate resistance of brigades and divisions are visualized with extraordinary force and color. If the sordid grimness of carnage is partially screened, the feeling of war's cumulative rapacity, of its breaking pressure and fluctuating tension is caught with wonderful fervour and freshness of style.

Edward Garnett. *Friday Nights* (Knopf). 1922.

pp. 212–3

Intense, brutal, bloody, *The Red Badge of Courage* vitalizes the smoke, noise, stench, dread, terror, agony, and death of the battlefield. Thrust into the horror, the reader identifies himself with Henry Fleming and feels with him the trepidation of fear and heroism. How a boy of twenty-two conceived the story and within a few days got it down on paper with such truthfulness to detail that no veteran soldier has ever been able to question its authenticity is one of the mysteries of artistic creation.

Vernon Loggins. *I Hear America* (Crowell). 1937.

p. 26

Suddenly there was *The Red Badge of Courage* showing us, to our absolute conviction, how the normal, absolutely undistinguished, essentially civilian man from the street had behaved in a terrible and prolonged war—without distinction, without military qualities, without special courage, without even any profound apprehension of, or passion as to, the causes of the struggle in which, almost without will, he was engaged. . . . With *The Red Badge of Courage* in the nineties, we were provided with a map showing us our own hearts. If before that date we had been asked how we should behave in a war, we should no doubt have answered that we should behave like demigods, with all the marmoreal attributes of war memorials. But, a minute after peeping into *The Red Badge* we knew that, at best, we should behave doggedly but with a weary non-comprehension, flinging away our chassepot rifles, our haversacks, and fleeing into the swamps of Shiloh.

Ford Madox Ford. *Portraits from Life* (Houghton).
1937. pp. 22–3

Crane's hero is Everyman, the symbol made flesh upon which war plays its havoc and it is the deliberation of that intention which explains why the novel is so extraordinarily lacking, as H. L. Mencken puts it, in small talk. Scene follows scene in an accelerating rhythm of excitement, the hero becomes the ubiquitous man to whom, as Wyndham Lewis once wrote of the Hemingway man, things happen. With that cold, stricken fury that was so characteristic of Crane—all through the self-conscious deliberation of his work one can almost hear his nerves quiver—he impaled his hero on the ultimate issue, the ultimate pain and humiliation of war, where the whole universe, leering through the blindness and smoke of battle, became the incarnation of pure agony. The foreground was a series of commonplaces; the background was cosmological.

Alfred Kazin. *On Native Grounds* (Reynal). 1942.
pp. 71–2

See *Maggie, The Red Badge of Courage,* and *The Monster* (short novels); also *Twenty Stories* and *The Collected Poems.*

CULLEN, COUNTEE (1903–1946)

There are numerous things which Mr. Cullen as a poet has not yet begun to do, and there are some which he will never do, but in this first volume (*Color*) he makes it clear that he has mastered a tune. Few recent books of poems have been so tuneful—at least so tuneful in the execution of significant themes. . . . Mr. Cullen's skill appears in the clarity and the certainty of his song. . . . If Mr. Cullen faces any danger it is this—that he shall call facility a virtue rather than the aspect of a virtue.

Mark Van Doren. *NYHT.* Jan. 10, 1926. p. 3

This first volume of musical verses (*Color*) offers promise of distinction for its author, shows him to be a young poet of uncommon earnestness and diligence. Serious purpose and careful work are apparent in all of his poems. One feels that he will cultivate his fine talent with intelligence, and reap its full harvest. He has already developed a lyric idiom which is not, perhaps, very unusual or striking in itself, but which he has learned to employ with considerable virtuosity.

George H. Dillon. *Poetry*. April, 1926. p. 50

With Countee Cullen's *Color* we have the first volume of the most promising of the younger Negro poets. There is no point in measuring him merely beside Dunbar, Alberry A. Whitman, and other Negro poets of the past and present: he must stand or fall beside Shakespeare and Keats and Masefield, Whitman and Poe and Robinson. The volume has much promise, some achievement, and a long advertisement of its author's excessive youth and metrical conservatism. . . . That Cullen is a poet is clear; if he can attune himself to the negative merit of avoiding "the stock poetical touches," and build from that, he may grow to commanding stature.

Clement Wood. *YR*. July, 1926. p. 824

Cullen is, it seems to me, just a little too much the product of our American colleges. His earlier work was more his own. This is true not only because his earlier poems had to do, often, with the emotions of the Negro race, but because they were more direct statements of the poet's own sensitivity. If the earlier poems were less perfect technically, they had more complete sincerity. Sincerity is not necessarily art, of course, but while a poet speaks his own language, however crudely, there is hope that he may develop the necessary skill of the true artist. When he speaks too often in literary phrase and image, he ceases to be significant. These last lyrics and sonnets of Cullen's have this defect.

Eda Lou Walton. *NYHT*. Sept. 15, 1935. p. 17

Where Oxford dons have so often failed, an American Negro writer has succeeded. Mr. Cullen has rendered Euripides's best known tragedy (*The Medea*) into living and utterable English. He has made little attempt to convey the poetry of the original, preferring to concentrate on dramatic situation and realistic portrayal of character. The result is a very forceful and poignant re-creation of the story of the barbarian sorcerer. . . . Mr. Cullen's version is admirably suited to the exigencies of the contemporary stage. For an adaptation which does not pretend to be a literal translation, it follows the original closely, giving English equivalents for all but a few of the speeches in the Greek.

Philip Blair Rice. *Nation*. Sept. 18, 1935. p. 336

One feels he is happiest in his sonnets to Keats and in his variations of the "made ballad." . . . At his best . . . Cullen shows a real gift for the neat, sensitive, and immediate lyric. When the observation contained in the poem is direct and personal, dealing immediately with people seen and events that really occurred, the poems emerge movingly.

Too often, however, the treatment is marred by a taint of "artiness" that is too obviously derivative. . . . It is for the one poem in ten that emerges whole that Countee Cullen will be remembered.

John Ciardi. *At*. March, 1946. p. 145

As one rereads Mr. Cullen's verses, deploring the pity that so real a talent should have been lost in early death, one is bothered by various doubts. Would his talent have matured if he had lived? Was it ever more than a skill at echoing, at assuming the poetic attitudes of the late Victorian and the Georgian past? Is not this verse pretty thoroughly undergraduate—smooth metric, pretty imagery, college Lit. diction? Mr. Cullen wrote like all of one's favorite poets of the traditional order.

Dudley Fitts. *NYT*. Feb. 23, 1947. p. 26

Cullen's verses skip; those by Hughes glide. But in life Hughes is the merry one. Cullen was a worrier. . . . Equally evident . . . was Cullen's tendency to get his inspiration, his rhythms and patterns as well as much of his substance from books and the world's lore of scholarship. . . . Cullen was in many ways an old-fashioned poet. . . . About half of his "best poems" were written while he was a student of New York University, and it was during these years that he first came up for consideration as an authentic American writer, the goal to which he aspired. . . . Cullen did not live to see another springtime resurgence of his own creative powers comparable with the impulse that produced his first three books of poetry, the books which give his selected poems most of their lilt and brightness.

Arna Bontemps. *SR*. March 22, 1947. pp. 12–3, 44

Probably no one can tell just how or why Cullen's promise faded into mediocre fulfillment, but it is possible to suggest some of the reasons. Cullen neither accepted nor developed a comprehensive world-view. As a consequence, his poems seem to result from occasional impulse rather than from direction by an integrated individual. . . . He was, in other words, an able and perplexed intelligence and a sensitive and confused heart.

Harvey Curtis Webster. Poetry. July, 1947. p. 222

As we read Cullen's racial poetry today, our feelings are mixed. Even though we understand and appreciate the larger implications of the alien-and-exile theme, we recognize its basic fallacy just as Cullen himself seemed to recognize it in The Black Christ. We also recognize that protest poetry of every type has lost much of its former popularity. We realize too that in the age of "new criticism" and intellectual verse, Cullen's style and general approach to poetry are dated; the Pre-Raphaelite delicacy of his lyrics is lost upon a generation which can find value only in "metaphysical" poetry. And yet in spite of these drawbacks, I believe that Cullen's racial poems will live. They will live first of all because they are a record of and a monument to the New Negro Movement, and as such they will always be important to the literary historian. Second, they will live for the social historian because they have made articulate the agony of racial oppression during a dark period in our continuing struggle for democracy. And most important of all, a few of them will live because they are good poems— good enough to survive the ravages of time and changing taste.

Arthur P. Davis. Phylon. Sept., 1953. p. 400

See On These I Stand (poetry).

CUMMINGS, EDWARD ESTLIN   (1894–1962)

The poet always seems to be having a glorious time with himself and his world even when the reader loses his breath in the effort to share it. He is as agile and outrageous as a faun, and as full of delight over the beauties and monstrosities of this brilliant and grimy old planet. There is a grand gusto in him.

Harriet Monroe. Poetry. Jan., 1924. pp. 213–4

Since the highbrows have taken to vaudeville, Cummings is their favorite Touchstone. At times, he overplays the clown; at others he has the instinct of the perfect comedian. When he is perfect, no poet is more dazzling; when he plays the bad boy too many times, one has an itch for spanking and shooing him to bed.

Alfred Kreymborg. Our Singing Strength
(Coward-McCann). 1929. p. 519

I have heard two personal friends of E. E. Cummings debating as to whether his prosodical and punctuational gymnastics have not been a joke at the expense of the critics of poetry. One of them thinks Cummings will some day come out and announce that he has been joking; the other insists with fervent and faithful admiration that he is really as crazy as he seems.

Max Eastman. *The Literary Mind* (Scribner). 1932.
p. 103

What Mr. Cummings likes or admires, what he holds dear in life, he very commonly calls flowers, or dolls, or candy—terms with which he is astonishingly generous; as if he thought by making his terms general enough their vagueness could not matter, and never noticed that the words so used enervate themselves in a kind of hardened instinct.

R. P. Blackmur. *The Double Agent* (Arrow). 1935.
p. 20

No American poet of the twentieth century has ever shown so much implied respect for the conventions of his milieu through conscious blasphemy as E. E. Cummings. If Cummings's verse seemed "revolutionary" and radical (which it was in the sense that its wit was concerned with the roots of syntax and grammar) it was because its life was and still is so completely surrounded by conventions. . . . The entire question of Cummings's maturity in the writing of his poetry has been and still remains a private matter. In the light of Cummings's accomplishments and in the recognition of the boundaries or limits that they have circumscribed, it is very nearly an impertinence for anyone to tell him to "grow up," for one must not forget that he is one of the finest lyric poets of all time.

Horace Gregory and Marya Zaturenska. *History of American Poetry* (Harcourt). 1947. pp. 337–47

If Cummings is undistinguished as a thinker, he is always surprising as a creative craftsman. He is simultaneously the skillful draftsman, the leg-pulling clown, the sensitive commentator and the ornery boy. The nose-thumbing satirist is continually interrupted by the singer of brazenly tender lyrics. A modern of the moderns, he displays a seventeenth century obsession with desire and death; part Cavalier, part metaphysician, he is a shrewd manipulator of language, and his style —gracefully erotic or downright indecent—is strictly his own.

Louis Untermeyer. *Modern American Poetry*
(Harcourt). 1950. p. 509

In an age when language tends to become platitudinous and anemic, it is a splendid thing to have a poet take the most colourless words of all —the necessary anonymous neuter robots that ordinarily do their jobs without asking for wages of recognition—and suddenly give them character and responsibility. It's as if an albino sparrow were suddenly to grow red and blue feathers, or the little switch engine in the round-house were shown that it could draw the Sante Fe Chief.

Theodore Spencer. Modern American Poetry, edited
by B. Rajan (Roy). 1952. p. 122

Some of Cummings's early lyrics have an Elizabethan decorativeness. His later poems make words as abstract as "am," "if," "because," do duty for seemingly more solid nouns. By this very process, however, he restores life to dying concepts. "Am" implies being at its most responsive, "if" generally means the creeping timidity that kills responsiveness, and "because" the logic of the categorizing mind that destroys what it dissects. Here is a new vocabulary, a kind of imageless metaphor.

Babette Deutsch. Poetry in Our Time (Holt). 1952.
p. 113

At his worst, Cummings can achieve an almost Guestian bathos. At his best, he creates a pure poetry in which a venerable tradition meets the modern idioms. In these latter poems, e. e. resembles some of Lyonel Feininger's paintings: at first you see only non-representation, cubes and cones, but then, behind the very contemporary style, the shapes of familiar cities come before you.

Michael Harrington. Com. Dec. 10, 1954. p. 295

Are briskly vibrating sound and verbal paradox enough? . . . He is still a poet who is considerably more talked about than he deserves to be, a man who has made his vogue out of a large amount of—at best —casually semi-private writing.

Carl Bode. Poetry. Sept., 1955. pp. 362–3

(Cummings's poetry) has come . . . to assert, remonstrate, and define rather than simply to present, as it once predominantly did. Cummings's gift of impressionistic evocation, though it could not be said to have departed entirely . . . is sinking into desuetude together with his impulse toward typographical experimenting. . . . Regardless of the quality of change, one thing does not change: the unique Cummings voice. Or if it might be said to change, it is only in the direction of a still profounder individuality.

Rudolph Von Abele. PMLA. Dec., 1955. pp. 932–3

We see him ever as an individual, liking and respecting other individuals, but hating the masses as masses, hating governments, hating war, hating propaganda (ours or anybody else's), hating machinery, hating science. Willing to settle for nothing less than perfection, he is a great hater, although he is also a great lover, perhaps the most ardent or at any rate the most convincing poet of love in our day. Whom and what he loves he loves deeply, but for him the existence of love demands the expression of anger, contempt, disgust for what is unworthy of love. That is what he is and what he has been since coming of age, though practice has refined him in the art of being nobody-but-himself.

Granville Hicks. *SR*. Nov. 22, 1958. p. 14

Love Lyrics

Cummings's Paganism is as much a reaction against New England Puritanism as it is a passionate embrace of the earth and its ladies. Behind his beautiful gamboling, one hears the heartbeats, subtle and exquisite, of a poet steeped in sentiment. He is the love poet of the radical era.

Alfred Kreymborg. *Our Singing Strength* (Coward-
McCann). 1929. p. 516

Cummings wrote excellent love lyrics, lyrics which contained all the compliments that a young woman would like to hear, and such compliments also enhanced the figure of a perennially youthful lover who would go to war against any and all of the conventions that were outside of or that threatened to impede or divert the course of courtly love.
. . . All these were written (so it seems) in the same spirit that graced the songs and speeches of the *commedia dell'arte,* which traveled up from Italy in the sixteenth century to entertain the peoples of the rest of Europe.

Horace Gregory and Marya Zaturenska. *History of
American Poetry* (Harcourt). 1947. pp. 338–45

This is courtly love, full of *thee*'s and *thou*'s and ballads to "my lady," and elaborate conceits which would be cloying were it not for the freshness of Cummings's rhetoric. These tender songs, delicate in grace, ethereal in mood, are founded on emotion, the realness of the feeling of this man for this woman. For all their delicacy they are resilient and durable; he is a love-lyricist of timeless appeal.

David Burns. *SR*. Dec. 18, 1954. p. 11

Satiric Poems

Leave him alone, and he will play in a corner for hours, with his fragilities, his colors, and his delight in the bright shapes of all the things he sees. . . . The important point about E. E. Cummings is, however, that he was not left alone. He was dumped out into the uninnocent and unlyrical world. . . . His lyricism, shy enough at best, ran completely for cover, and he turned upon the nightmare worlds of reality, partly with the assumed callousness and defensive self-mockery of the very sensitive, and partly with the white and terrible anger of the excessively shy.

S. I. Hayakawa. Poetry. Aug., 1938. pp. 285–6

He has a nose for decay wherever it shows itself. It may be in verse that caters to the stock responses of flyspecked sensibilities. It may be in "the Cambridge ladies who live in furnished souls," those afflicted with the occupational diseases of gentility: blindness and deafness to the natural world. It may be the "notalive undead" who make up a "peopleshaped toomany-ness." He recognizes the fixed grin of death in the insane cheerfulness of the brotherhood of advertisers and high-pressure salesmen. His sales resistance to them is complete, whether their products be red shirts, brown shirts, white shirts with Arrow collars, or shrouds.

Babette Deutsch. Poetry in Our Time (Holt). 1952.
p. 115

He challenges in a lyric version of civil disobedience the entire framework of our soi-disant civilization till the whole structure and its inhabitants threaten to fall down about his head.

Cummings has satirized . . . extinction of personality in some of the most virulent philippics to grace literature since mad Dean Swift.

David Burns, SR. Dec. 18, 1954. p. 11

The Enormous Room

The book has few dead phrases in it—it lives, if somewhat with the horrible life of a centipede. It has fire, now smoldering, now for a bit blazing into unhealthy violet and mustard-colored flame. There is precious metal in it, but Mr. Cummings has brought up from his agonized and subterranean digging along with some nuggets of character and description all manner of sweepings, cobwebs, and twisted iron.

Robert Littell. NR. May 10, 1922. p. 321

Butt of a great white joke, Cummings observed with awe and fascination the perfectly unreasonable geometry of cosmic antics. . . . A new, crisp, brindled style had presented itself for birth. The prose forming Cummings's vision of the illogical will of things and the unsuspected affinities between pain and delight, leads one out among advertising, skyscrapers, and movies. The verbal integument affirms ultimate values, since it remains organic and subtle; and still it does not contradict the style of life existing in American streets and assembly places. . . . And shrilly pitched, caricatural, even more in tempo than in tendency, taut of rhythm, Cummings's prose relates rebellious matters, never before associated, with exquisite smoothness of modulation. It juxtaposes ancient elegances and brutalities of expression, sensitively employed traditional idiom and gamiest crudities of the vernacular.

Paul Rosenfeld. *Men Seen* (Dial). 1925. pp. 192–5

The Enormous Room has the effect of making all but a very few comparable books that came out of the War look shoddy and worn. It has been possible to re-read it, as I have done . . . and always to find it undiminished. . . . Cummings . . . encountered, in that huge barracks at La Ferté-Macé which he calls the Enormous Room, a sad assortment of men. They from being his companions in misery become, whether they speak or not—and the most eloquent are those who have the smallest command of words—his counsellors in compassion. . . . The mind provides no answer to the problem of suffering. . . . The answer, even for a poet, is not in words. . . . For what can oppose the poverty of the spirit, but the pride of the body? . . . And in Cummings there is from now on, in all he writes, an exaltation of the lowly and lively. He is himself, and he accepts his common lot.

John Peale Bishop. *Collected Essays* (Scribner). 1948.

pp. 89–91

See *Poems, 1923-1954;* also *i: six nonlectures* (memoirs), *him* (play), and *The Enormous Room* (novel).

DICKINSON, EMILY (1830–1886)

I heard an extremely faint and pattering footstep like that of a child, in the hall, and in glided, almost noiselessly, a plain shy little person, the face without a single good feature, but with eyes, as she herself said, "like the sherry the guest leaves in the glass," and with smooth bands of reddish chestnut hair. She had a quaint and nun-like look, as if she might be a German canoness of some religious order, whose prescribed garb was white pique, with a blue net worsted shawl. She came toward me with two day-lilies, which she put in a child-like way into my hand, saying softly, under her breath, "These are my introduction," and adding, also under her breath, in child-like fashion, "Forgive me if I am frightened; I never see strangers, and hardly know what to say."

Thomas Wentworth Higginson. Carlyle's Laugh
(Houghton). 1909. p. 272

Emily Dickinson, New England spinster of the nineteenth century, was an unconscious and uncataloged *Imagiste*. She had the visual imagination, the love of economy of line and epithet, the rigorous austerity of style, and the individual subtlety of rhythm demanded by the code of the contemporary poets who group themselves under that title. Born a Puritan, her shy soul brooded upon the abstract, but her wildly pagan imagination at once transmuted the abstract into the concrete, gave it form and color.

Harriet Monroe. Poetry. Dec., 1914. pp. 138–9

The advance and retreat of her thought, her transition from arch to demure, from elfin to angelic, from soaring to drowning, her inescapable sense of tragedy, her inimitable perception of comedy, her breathless reverence and unabashed invasion upon the intimate affairs of Deity and hearsay of the Bible, made her a comrade to mettle inspiration and dazzle rivalry. . . . She revelled in the wings of her mind,—I had almost said the fins too,—so universal was her identification with every form of life and element of being.

Martha Dickinson Bianchi. Preface to Emily
Dickinson's The Single Hound (Little). 1914. p. xiv

Saint and imp sported in her, toying with the tricks of the Deity, taking them now with extreme profundity, then tossing them about like irresistible toys with an incomparable triviality. She has traced upon the page with celestial indelibility that fine line from her soul, which is like a fine prismatic light separating one bright sphere from another, one planet from another planet; and the edge of separation is but faintly perceptible. . . . Who has had her celestial attachedness—or must we call it detachedness?—and her sublime impertinent playfulness, which make her images dance before one like offspring of the great round sun?

Marsden Hartley. Dial. Aug. 15, 1918. p. 96

In her mode of life she carried the doctrine of self-sufficient individualism farther than Thoreau carried it, or the naïve zealots of Brook Farm. In her poetry she carried it, with its complement of passionate moral mysticism, farther than Emerson: which is to say that as a poet she had more genius than he. Like Emerson . . . she was from the outset, and remained all her life, a singular mixture of Puritan and free thinker. The problems of good and evil, of life and death, obsessed her.

Conrad Aiken. *Dial.* April, 1924. p. 305

Emily Dickinson is often abstract, sometimes even verbal, but she is always saved from the merely allusive cleverness of our cerebralists by the passion which runs through all her poetry like a consuming flame. . . . Her spiritual passion is all the more a thing of wonder because it so steadfastly refused to identify itself with any of our accepted faiths and symbols. . . . In short, Emily Dickinson's poetry leads straight to the conception of an intuitively felt spirit which can be subordinated neither to any of its experienced forms nor to any kind of absolute standing without.

Edward Sapir. *Poetry.* May, 1925. pp. 102–3

If the voice of heavenly vision alone had spoken in Emily, she would have been a mystic poet. She is not a mystic poet. She constantly corrects vision by another faculty. Vision is not her truth. What is her truth? She named it "fact"—the truth perceived and then anatomized. The real mystic's experience is an ecstasy, and his invariable report is that life is single and divine; he abhors a double. Against her primary impulse, which is something akin to the mystic intuition, Emily constantly placed her correcting fact.

Genevieve Taggard. *The Life and Mind of Emily Dickinson* (Knopf). 1930. p. 320

It is a tough and poetry-resisting soul which does not eventually succumb to her rhetoric, irregularities and all. Her vivacity covers self-consciousness and carries off her self-contradictions; her swift condensations—surpassed by no writer of any age—win the most reluctant. One gasps at the way she packs huge ideas into an explosive quatrain. . . . She may annoy us by her self-indulgent waywardness, but illumination is never far off; out of a smooth, even sentimental sky comes a crackling telegram from God.

Louis Untermeyer. *SR.* July 5, 1930. p. 1171

Emily Dickinson was reason's pupil but her technique was intuitive, and in that matter she was "wayward." Study which she bestowed on her poems related only to a choice of words that would sharpen the meaning, we are told. . . . A certain buoyancy that creates an effect of inconsequent bravado—a sense of drama with which we may not be quite at home—was for her a part of that expansion of breath necessary to existence, and unless it is conceited for the hummingbird or the osprey to not behave like a chicken, one does not find her conceited.

Marianne Moore. *Poetry*. Jan., 1933. pp. 223–5

I think it is a fact that the failure and success of Emily Dickinson's poetry were uniformly accidental largely because of the private and eccentric nature of her relation to the business of poetry. She was neither a professional poet nor an amateur; she was a private poet who wrote indefatigably as some women cook or knit. . . . She came, as Mr. Tate says, at the right time for one kind of poetry: the poetry of sophisticated, eccentric vision. That is what makes her good—in a few poems and many passages representatively great. But she never undertook the great profession of controlling the means of objective expression.

R. P. Blackmur. *SoR*. Autumn, 1937. pp. 346–7

The fragmentary nature of many of the poems, their irregularity of form, the grammatical aberrations which occur at times, the elaborate conceits and occasional mixed metaphors cannot dispel the unusual power of the imagery, the most salient characteristics of which are vividness, boldness of conception, interplay of the concrete and the abstract, variety of sense appeals, drama, freshness and surprise. On the other hand, the most abstruse and cryptic of her "versicles" and those most likely to be neglected are the ones lacking in imagery.

Ruth Flanders McNaughton. *The Imagery of Emily Dickinson* (Nebraska). 1949. pp. vii–viii

The most intelligible mode of relationship or tension within the poetry of Emily Dickinson is a relationship of the rococo and the sublime. There is hardly a poem in the whole canon which does not in some way exhibit both orders of experience. . . . In her best poems the rococo principle has been forced by the exigencies of the poem's structure to yield nothing but what is most admirable in it, its immediacy of pathos and its delicacy of form—the qualities with which, in these poems, the sublime must and does invest itself. This sustained imbalance constitutes the economy of Emily Dickinson's verse.

Richard Chase. *Emily Dickinson* (Sloane). 1951.
pp. 236–7

Feelings for her took the place of ideas, but feelings so clearly contemplated, so disciplined, and so wittily clear-cut, that they became the equivalent, in precision and in penetration of thought. . . . To read her letters is to be in a world that combines Kate Greenaway's elegant nostalgia, something of Beatrice Potter's innocent fantasy of a world of rabbits with blue jackets and housekeeping field-mice, and that American *timor mortis* that Emily Dickinson has in common with Edgar Allen Poe. What makes her a poet is her delicate precision of image, deliberately finite, as with Marianne Moore; and her wren's note of pure lyricism.

Kathleen Raine. *NSN*. April 19, 1952. p. 472

See the Modern Library's *Poems of Emily Dickinson* for first readings, Thomas H. Johnson's three-volume edition for the definitive text.

DOOLITTLE, HILDA (H.D.) (1886–1961)

The word *temperamental* qualifies the whole manner and substance of her verse, and the degree of the reader's appreciation will depend on the amount of natural sympathy with which he temperamentally can approach it. . . . The affinity of her art to the radical characteristics of her own time is to be found . . . not in choice of subject but in the following characteristics: She has rejected the traditional forms of English poetry in favour of a more personal rhythm which derives its impulse from such rules as her own temperament may dictate. Poetry is to her an art to be cultivated, not an inspired message to be conveyed. Bulk of production is of no importance to her as compared with excellence of finish.

Harold Monro. *Some Contemporary Poets* (Parsons).
1920. pp. 103–4

The poems of H.D. do not lend themselves to convenient classification, as Poems of Passion and Emotion, Poems of Reflection, Poems of the Imagination, and Poems Descriptive, and so on. In all of them, passion, emotion, reflection, and the image, the sharp, vivid image that does the work of description, are fused together in the burning unity of beauty. . . . H.D. invariably presents her subtlest, most metaphysical idea under some living sensuous image solid enough to carry the emotion. The air we are given to breathe may be rarefied to the last degree, yet we are moving always in a world of clear colours and clear forms.

May Sinclair. *Dial*. Feb., 1922. p. 203

It has been said of H.D.'s earlier poetry that it was perfectly wrought but cold and passionless, and that it was concerned rather with the loveliness of a perished age than with the modern world of everyday emotions. . ; . Perfectly wrought the poems are: the rhythms swoop in and out of the head as birds perch and flutter in and out of apple-branches. Lines haunt the ears as the sound of rain in the South. The use of some simple but unexpected syllable brings all the fragrance into a mood that Ionian roses suddenly awaken after some swift storm. But they are not cold, they are not passionless; and apart from the color of some Attic names how are these songs anything but the expression of the emotions and desires of an extremely present age?

Winifred Bryher. *Poetry*. March, 1922. pp. 334–5

It had better be said that H.D.'s scope (at least, her characteristic scope) is narrow. At the same time it may be retorted that her poetry is of a kind to which scope has uniquely slight application. With other poets of modern life, we are compelled to go on asking for a wider apprehension, a broader spiritual awareness more fundamentally expressed. But H.D. implies what the others do not, that she is asserting no spiritual attitude of her own; but building upon traditional assumptions. She assumes that what may be called the moral factor in our reception will demand of beauty what the Greeks were content to demand.

H. P. Collins. *Modern Poetry* (Cape). 1925. p. 157

To one who is as extreme a classicist as H.D., a knowledge of the machinery of verse is of as much moment as the material selected, and as regards her early work one might say both discreetly and truthfully that it is not so much the matter as the manner that is important. The emotion resulting from such a synthesis is one that H.D. calls "intellectual ecstasy"; a curious condition in which intensity of emotion is quite dependent upon the perfection and definiteness of the artificial form: the passion of a sea-gull in a bright steel cage.

Frank A. Doggett. *SwR*. Jan., 1929. p. 1

H.D.'s thoughts were not often concerned with the world she lived in; another one, to her far more desirable, filled her mental vision almost completely. . . . She often sat with us, chatting of everyday things, when I am sure her spirit was somewhere near the shores of the Aegean. . . . I think a large part of her peculiar charm lay in the fact that she was always coming back to us; and she never came back reluctantly. . . . We had . . . the idea that she found us satisfying in our way and that her preoccupation with an ancient world only made her the more pleased with her own when she was in it. Her sudden entries into our talk and her effortless domination of it filled us with elation because she brought with her such disarming enthusiasms and delivered herself with such amazing speed and clarity on any subject that might be uppermost.

James Whitall. *English Years* (Harcourt). 1935.
pp. 55–6

There was about her that which is found in wild animals at times, a breathless impatience, almost a silly unwillingness to come to the point. She had a young girl's giggle and shrug which somehow in one so tall and angular seemed a little absurd. She fascinated me, not for her beauty, which was unquestioned if bizarre to my sense, but for a provocative indifference to rule and order which I liked. She dressed indifferently, almost sloppily and looked to a young man, not inviting—she had nothing of that—but irritating, with a smile.

William Carlos Williams. *Autobiography* (Random).
1951. pp. 67–8

Her special form of the mode of Imagism—cold, "Greek," fast, and enclosed—has become one of the ordinary resources of the poetic language; it is a regular means of putting down words so that they will keep; and readers are mistaken who confuse familiarity with flatness or who think facile imitation of the form emulates the perception that goes with the mode. She has herself made sharply varied use of her mode, but she has not exhausted it; she has only—for present changing purposes of a changing mind—partly broken it down into the older, perhaps primary mode of the distich. The relatively long uncoiling of a single spring of image, unpredictable in its completeness, now receives a regular series of impulses and arrests, of alternations and couplings.

R. P. Blackmur. *Language as Gesture* (Harcourt).
1952. p. 352

H.D. has herself abandoned the "Imagist" effects of her early poems, the best of which suggest the clean line of Greek vase-paintings and, for all the passion they assert, have a lapidary quality about them. In her later work the old vehemence, if subdued, is present, and the phrasing recalls the familiar cadences. Yet it differs from what went before in carrying a far heavier weight of symbolic meaning and in being overtly subjective. . . . Again and again, turning the pages of this quondam Imagist, the reader hears a melody not only in the lines themselves but suggested by them, as it were, hovering just beyond the expressed sounds for some musician, not a maker of verse, to capture and realize.

Babette Deutsch. *NYT*. Sept. 22, 1957. p. 37

"Invisible," "most proud," in love: these are the strength of the poet throughout the work of H.D. Ardent and clear, her lyrics show us that an everpresent devotion to the art of the poem sustains passion. The strength of the poem lies in her command of words so that they call up sensual immediacies (as images) and are themselves sensual immediacies (as elements of a most skilled tonal structure), and, increasingly in the later work, in her knowledge of words, their roots and histories, their lore and powers. Her trilogy written during the Second World War (*The Walls Do Not Fall, Tribute to Angels,* and *The Flowering of the Rod*) stands with Ezra Pound's *Cantos,* Eliot's *Four Quartets,* and William Carlos Williams' *Paterson* as a major work of the Imagist genius in its full.

Robert Duncan. *Poetry.* Jan., 1958. p. 256

She gives us the best glimpse we have today of classic poetry, an English poetry so nearly Greek in concept and execution as to be remarkable. She gives us that stasis in the poem which keeps a perfect tension between emotion and reason, between fact and idea, between sensitized perception and elegant restraint, between the brute world and art. . . . She gives us, in rare poems, the early poems, a glimpse and capture of an ideal world of eternal poetic values, crystal-bright, hard and pure, clean and fine. H.D. has the impersonal height from which streams a radiant purity.

Richard Eberhart. *Poetry.* Jan., 1958. p. 265

H.D. in her perceptions of timelessness, and in her search for the "real," has always seemed to be writing in advance of her times. In that respect the present generation might well regard her as "a poets' poet."

To be "a poets' poet" has few tangible rewards, for this means that the poet who holds that title must often wait upon the future for true recognition. Yet the poems of H.D. have acquired a life, a being of their own; at this date one need not argue that they should be read. Of contemporary poets H.D. is among the few whose writings are likely to endure.

Horace Gregory. *Com.* April 18, 1958. p. 83

See *Selected Poems* (1957 edition).

DOS PASSOS, JOHN   (1896–   )

Dos Passos *may* be, more than Dreiser, Cather, Hergesheimer, Cabell, or Anderson the father of humanized and living fiction . . . not merely for America but for the world.

Just to rub it in, I regard *Manhattan Transfer* as more important in every way than anything by Gertrude Stein or Marcel Proust or even the great white boar, Mr. Joyce's *Ulysses*. For Mr. Dos Passos can use and deftly does use, all their experimental psychology and style, all their revolt against the molds of classic fiction. But the difference! Dos Passos is *interesting!*

Sinclair Lewis. SR. Dec. 5, 1925. p. 361

If we compare Dos Passos with other of our leading novelists, we find no one who is his superior in range of awareness of American life. In his tone, he most nearly approaches Hemingway. He can be as "hard-boiled" as the latter, particularly when he is dealing with hard-boiled characters; his freedom of language is, if anything, greater; his viewpoint, also, is nearly as external and behavioristic. But he has a greater range of sympathy. . . . And his social sympathies, one might almost say his class passions, give a drive to his work that Hemingway's, with its comparatively sterile point of view lacks. In its social implications Dos Passos' work is more nearly akin to that of Dreiser and Sinclair Lewis, and still more to that of Upton Sinclair. But where Sinclair's people are wax dummies, Dos Passos' are alive and convincing.

Henry Hazlitt. Nation. March 23, 1932. p. 344

We can say now that the Harvard aesthete in Dos Passos is almost dead. The spiritual malady of tourism no longer drains his powers. He has entered the real world. He has definitely broken with capitalism and knows it is but a walking corpse. He wars upon it, and records its degeneration. But he has not yet found the faith of Walt Whitman in the American masses. He cannot believe that they have within them the creative force for a new world. This is still his dilemma; a hangover from his aristocratic past; yet this man grows like corn in the Iowa sun; his education proceeds; the future will find his vast talents, his gift of epic poetry, his observation, his daring experimentalism, and personal courage enlisted completely in the service of co-operative society.

Michael Gold. EJ. Feb. 1933. p. 97

Dos Passos will perhaps be remembered more as the inventor or at least the early practitioner of a technique in fiction than for the lasting significance of his novels. . . . Dos Passos attempts to catch in fiction the inventions of the day, the camera eye, the movie, the newspaper headline. He conveys dates and the background by flashes of contemporary events. The effect on the unity of the novels is confusing but the representation of confusion is evidently one of the author's chief aims. The "hero" of the novels is the contemporary scene rather than any individual. He attempts to crowd an era, a whole cross-section of a city or a period of economic development into a novel.

> Halford E. Luccock. *Contemporary American Literature and Religion* (Willett). 1934. p. 148.
> Courtesy of Harper and Brothers

Dos Passos owes to Joyce the conception of a novel devoted to the life of a city (for *Ulysses* is more concerned with Dublin than Mr. Bloom), to Proust the use of significant detail and careful documentation, to Stein (of the *Three Lives* period) the notions of the importance of the simple lives of obscure people and the effectiveness of bald narration. But he added to his borrowing a great deal of his own: a feeling for the common man which led him to picture all the strata of life, a knowledge of life on the great majority of these levels, a sense of the universality of the evils that he found, a lyrical spirit, and some technical devices which are remarkable for their success—and for their failure, in the main, to put off the traditional reader.

> Mason Wade. *NAR*. Winter, 1937. p. 356

He has again and again hazarded bold and enlightening solutions to problems of both content and structure that few traditional novelists have even recognized and fewer still have dealt with. Paramount has been his attempt to get a sense of the whole complex social panorama, and, as corollary, a sense of the flux, of the simultaneity of lives and events, and the passage of time in terms of the entire culture as well as individuals. Equally significant have been his attempts to integrate the individual with the period, to leave us everywhere conscious of how the age has moulded the man, made him one of its peculiar products.

> Milton Rugoff. *SwR*. Oct. 1941. pp. 467–8

Certainly he is not a Tolstoy or even a Zola, to mention two masters of the panoramic form. In America today he ranks below Hemingway and Faulkner for many reasons, but principally because he seldom feels his way deeply into his characters. As a novelist—and in life, too —he is always moving, always hurrying off to catch a taxi, a bus, a train, a plane or a transatlantic steamer; and he tells us as much about people as a sensitive and observing man can learn in a short visit. That leads to his writing a special type of novel, broad and wind-scarred into intricate patterns like the Aral Sea, not deep like Lake Baikal, that gash in the mountains which is said to contain more water than all the Great Lakes together.

There is, however, a converse to this statement. To achieve breadth in a novel is a difficult art in itself and it is one in which no other American writer—not even Frank Norris—has ever approached Dos Passos.

Malcolm Cowley. *NR*. Feb. 28, 1949. p. 21

Nothing is deeper in the man than his fear of power. To begin with, he feared the power of the military, as he had experienced it in the first World War, and the power of men of wealth. The hatred of war and exploitation grew so acute that he accepted for a time the tempting radical doctrine that only power can destroy power. But what he saw of communism in Russia, in Spain, and at home convinced him that the destroying power could be more dangerous than the power it overcame. . . . His sympathies are wholly with the people who get pushed around, whether it is Big Business or Big Government that does the pushing. His trouble is simply that he has not found the "better than that," the alternative to both bignesses, and hence his growing fear of government can only be accompanied by a growing toleration of business. . . . He has allowed himself to be forced into choosing one horn of the dilemma, and he is nicely impaled.

Granville Hicks. *AnR*. Spring, 1950. pp. 95–8

Dos Passos' libertarianism is generally anarchist in character. That is to say, Dos Passos believes in absolute or primitive liberty, the supreme good of the anarchist creed. With Lord Acton, he believes that power always corrupts because by its very nature it exercises restraints. All social wrongs are therefore rooted in family, government or state authority; and the remedy lies in the curbing of this oppressive power. Each individual must live as he wishes and must not permit anyone to rule over his fellows, for each is a sovereign power.

Martin Kallich. *AnR*. Spring, 1950. p. 100

Chronic remorse, most moralists agree, is an unsalutary sentiment—the sinner who has genuinely repented does not become any the cleaner by rolling interminably in the mud; and chronic remorse is peculiarly disastrous where novelists are concerned. The novelist obsessed with the errors of the past—John Dos Passos is a case in point, since his political switch from far left to far right—is irresistibly drawn to revenge himself on his past by rewriting it, by showing that what he found good was disgusting. And the literary results of such an enterprise are apt to resemble a dredging operation: the principal yield is mud.

Charles J. Rolo. *At.* Oct. 1954. p. 98

Dos Passos' hate, despair and lofty contempt are real. But that is precisely why his world is not real; it is a created object. I know of none —not even Faulkner's or Kafka's—in which the art is greater or better hidden. I know of none that is more precious, more touching or closer to us. This is because he takes his material from our world. And yet, there is no stranger or more distant world. Dos Passos has invented only one thing, an art of story-telling. But that is enough to create a universe. . . . Dos Passos' world—like those of Faulkner, Kafka, and Stendhal—is impossible because it is contradictory. But therein lies its beauty. Beauty is a veiled contradiction. I regard Dos Passos as the greatest writer of our time.

Jean-Paul Sartre. *Literary and Philosophical Essays*
(Criterion). 1955. pp. 89, 96

In retrospect, the work of Dos Passos falls into three periods. There is first the expression of the lonely dissident, the esthetic recluse. . . . Almost alone among the high individualists of the 1920's, those gifted expatriates and exiles, Dos Passos had, by the end of the decade, found a cultural base for his literary work.

This base was a theoretical rather than strictly political Marxism. The product of the second period included *Manhattan Transfer* in 1925 and the major trilogy, *U.S.A.,* published from 1930 to 1936. These are still the core of Dos Passos' fiction; they are persuasive and penetrating novels; and their description of American civilization, which hardly applied in the 1930's, may seem all too prophetic in the 1950's. But the crux of the Dos Passos problem is right here, too. The collapse of his belief in the Russian Revolution, the disillusionment with the methods of the Communist Party, led not only to a major revision of his thinking, but, apparently, to a complete cessation of his creative energy and his human emotions. There was a psychic wound that has never stopped bleeding.

Maxwell Geismar. *Nation.* April 14, 1956. p. 305

U.S.A.

In Dos Passos . . . there is a beautiful imaginative sympathy which permits him to get under the skin of his characters, but there is no imagination, and no Don Quixote. Dos Passos testifies to all this by his use of newsreels, just as he seeks the full sensibility in the impressions of the camera eye and the heroic character in the biographies; but in his central narrative the standpoint is always narrowed to what the character himself knows as the quality of his existence, life as it appears to him. And this leveling drags with it and tends to make rather crude and sometimes commonplace the sensibility shown in the other panels. . . . The whole truth of experience (if past literature is not wholly nonsense) is more than the quality of most lives. One is sure that Dos Passos knows this, since it is the reason for his four forms and his discontinuity. His novel is perhaps the greatest monument of naturalism because it betrays so fully the poverty and disintegration inherent in that method. Dos Passos is the gifted victim of his own extraordinary grasp of the truth. He is a victim of the truth and the whole truth.

Delmore Schwartz. SoR. Autumn, 1938. pp. 364–7

U.S.A. demonstrates Dos Passos' extraordinary capacity for observation; his "scholarship" in this respect is amazing; the sheer bulk and variety of his reading as reflected in both the biographies and the fictional sections have been tremendous. The work as a whole is one of the most impressive performances in contemporary writing. Yet one cannot say, "Here is the essence of American life." One can say rather that here in parallel columns is a pretty complete report of the human and social elements of American life from which the essence might be distilled. Eventually, however, the reading of parallel columns becomes monotonous.

Margaret Marshall. Nation. Jan. 6, 1940. p. 17

The philosophy of *U.S.A:* was taut, as the book itself was taut. Everything in it echoed its mass rumble, and the far-reaching tactile success of the book came out of that massed power, the heaping together of so many lives in symmetrical patterns of disaster. Dos Passos' effects have always depended on a violence of pace, on the quick flickering of the reel, the sudden climaxes where every fresh word drives the wedge in. No scene can be held too long; no voice can be heard too clearly. Everything must come at us from a distance and bear its short ironic wail; the machine must get going again; nothing can wait.

Alfred Kazin. NR. March 15, 1943. p. 353

In his trilogy Dos Passos looked backward to the optimistic American faith of 1900 from the vantage point of the collapse of prosperity in 1929 and drew a savage indictment of those forces in our society which had frustrated its immense promise. Could that promise be reinstated with some chance of fulfillment? The poet in Dos Passos reached beyond indictment and social criticism into prophecy and the first two volumes of his trilogy implied the answer to this question. Nothing less than an overturn of the existing order would restore the promise of American life, he surmised; and he pledged his faith to a future social revolution. But before the third volume of his trilogy appeared, this faith had deserted him. The work that had begun as an epic closed as an elegy, and on a note of despair.

Lloyd Morris. *NYHT*. Jan. 2, 1949. p. 3

Dos Passos . . . knows the everyday world of the ordinary apprehension—in which the essential Dos Passos appears to be so self-consciously not at home—as the movement of whole groups and classes and the clash of group prejudices. He is so preoccupied with representing these movements by newspaper headlines, historical figures, and, above all, by type characters that he reduces the movement of awareness in his characters to the simplified pattern we ascribe to the imaginary average man. You do not know his people except as you know the journalist's average businessman, Vassar girl, or labor leader; nor can you believe that the drama of their lives represents Dos Passos' full awareness of experience; the stifling personal and sensory awareness of the "Camera Eye," so completely isolated from any larger context, is the Dos Passos who is omitted from the narrative: it is his Mallarmé, as the narrative is his Lenin.

Arthur Mizener. *KR*. Winter, 1950. pp. 16–7

See *Three Soldiers, Manhattan Transfer,* and *U.S.A.* (novels).

DREISER, THEODORE   (1871–1945)

In his muddled way, held back by the manacles of his race and time, and his steps made uncertain by a guiding theory which too often eludes his own comprehension, he yet manages to produce works of art of unquestionable beauty and authority, and to interpret life in a manner that is poignant and illuminating. There is vastly more intuition in him than intellectualism; his talent is essentially feminine, as Conrad's is masculine; his ideas always seem to be deduced from his feelings. . . . He gets his effects, one might almost say, not by designing them, but by living them.

But whatever the process, the power of the image evoked is not to be gainsaid. It is not only brilliant on the surface, but mysterious and appealing in its depths. One swiftly forgets his intolerable writing, his mirthless, sedulous, repellent manner, in the face of the Athenian tragedy he instills in his seduced and soul-sick servant girls, his barbaric pirates of finance, his conquered and hamstrung supermen, his wives who sit and wait.

H. L. Mencken. *A Book of Prefaces* (Knopf). 1917.
pp. 95–6

Theodore Dreiser is one of those who are utterly incapable of swallowing the world as a young cuckoo swallows the grub that its wagtail mother has brought to it. He must look under every leaf, turn over every stone. His great, lumbering imagination, full of a divine curiosity, goes roaring through the prairie-lands of the Cosmos with the restless heavy-shouldered force of an old bull *wildebeest*. Whenever I am with him and can watch his cumbersome intellect at work upon any one of the manifold subjects like "the trickiness of women," the breeding of pigeons, the reasoning power of a spider he studied once in his bed-chamber, or the electronic basis of the Universe, I never fail to feel awe at the struggles of this ungainly giant, whose limbs are still half-buried in clay.

Llewelyn Powys. *The Verdict of Bridlegoose*
(Harcourt). 1926. p. 64

It must not be supposed, of course, as has now and then been done, that the writings of a man of his stature can be without artistic virtue. Far from it. He possesses the central artistic virtues, though he lacks the peripheral ones. . . . Dreiser has the root of the matter in him, which is detachment and transcendence during the creative process. He can keep his eye on the object, only and solely and entirely on the object. . . . He can take the clay and mold men; he can create the relations between them. . . . What counts against him is . . . the heavy, amorphous verbiage, which will seem duller as time goes on, the unrestrained meticulousness in the delineation of the trivial, the increasing grittiness of his texture.

Ludwig Lewisohn. *Expression in America* (Harper).
1932. pp. 481–2

It is a prime refreshment in the works of Theodore Dreiser that he is free of the mysterious sense of degradation, of filth and discomfort into which most Americans and many Europeans have translated one of the three elements of desire. Life then in his books is free to assert its own volume, where the huge desire to live, the wild desire to love, the insane desire to excel, variously mingled, produce various actions.

And they disclose the special chasms that have come about because in some hidden way we have sacrificed the second to the first and third of these angles. But without dogma: "They can't put me down as a liberal or free thinker," he insists. "I don't know, I wouldn't say I know. I know nothing."

Dorothy Dudley. *Forgotten Frontiers* (H. Smith). 1932. p. 481

I admired the things which he could do in writing which nobody else could do—the simple and poignant truths of life; and I thought his philosophic notions bosh and his historical truths mere uneducated ignorance. I found that he did not agree with those critics who praised him for the immense amount of bricks and mortar that were visible in his towering structure of fiction—the multiplicity of details which such critics called "realism." He was not especially interested in the details, but was using them, and perhaps over-using them, earnestly in trying to achieve beauty. He once told me with honest tears in his eyes that a novel had no excuse for existence unless it was beautiful. And by beautiful I knew that he meant true to the deep emotions of the human heart, not to the mere visible surface aspects of life.

Floyd Dell. *Homecoming* (Farrar and Rinehart). 1933. p. 268

It is because he has spoken for Americans with an emotion equivalent to their own emotion, in a speech as broken and blindingly searching as common speech, that we have responded to him with the dawning realization that he is stronger than all the others of his time, and at the same time more poignant; greater than the world he has described, but as significant as the people in it. To have accepted America as he has accepted it, to immerse oneself in something one can neither escape nor relinquish, to yield to what has been true and to yearn over what has seemed inexorable, has been Dreiser's fate and the secret of his victory.

Alfred Kazin. *On Native Grounds* (Reynal). 1942. pp. 89–90

Theodore Dreiser . . . suggested to me some large creature of the prime wandering on the marshy plains of a human foreworld. A prognathous man with an eye askew and a paleolithic face, he put me in mind of Polyphemus . . . a Rodinesque figure only half out from the block; and yet a remark that someone made caused him to blush even up to the roots of his thin grey hair. Dreiser was hypersensitive, strangely as one might have thought,—he was a living paradox in more than one way; but a lonelier man there never was.

Van Wyck Brooks. Days of the Phoenix (Dutton).
1957. p. 20

Dreiser's true form has revealed itself with time, and has nothing to do with our relative sympathy for the characters or any conventional suavity of construction, but a great deal to do with the intensity of the process and the "representation" resulting from it. . . . In the kind of organic plotting for which Dreiser . . . deserve(s) to be famous, intuition and intelligence work together to supersede the type of novel in which action flows more directly from character and character is more opaque and compact. . . . Dreiser uses such conventional devices as the trial, often quite ineptly, for terminal suspense; but the common refusal to grant him tragic status comes from a failure to see the *emotional* unity of his plot. . . . Dreiser's success made him *the* great American novelist of his time and place (no competition with James implied), the one in whom we feel the most sustaining and exhilarating press of life.

R. W. Flint. Nation. April 27, 1957. p. 372

There is little question that Theodore Dreiser is the most distinguished member of the whole group of modern American novelists. . . . He was a realist. . . . Yes, he, partly through his own innocence, perhaps, and early origins, told the truth about life when he could discover it. Probably no one else in our literature has had such a direct and intimate feeling for the common forms of experience, pleasant or disgraceful. But he was also, like Balzac, who is the closest European counterpart, one of the high romantics of literature.

What gave his work its remarkable texture, its glamour, really, was his simple sense of the variety and mystery of life on all its levels.

Maxwell Geismar. American Moderns (Hill and
Wang). 1958. p. 50

He was not, by and large, an attractive figure, and the letters present his unattractive qualities more relentlessly than the books that have been written about him have done. One notes, for instance, his dependence on other persons, particularly women, and his offhand acceptance of their services to him. One notes his arrogance and his greed. But at the same time one feels in the letters, as in the novels, that this was a man who was utterly faithful to his own vision of life.

As he wrote Mencken, he was born with a bias, a bias not so much in favor of the common man as a bias in favor of men and women as victims—of the economic system, of their own impulses, of life itself.

This bias led him into ridiculous contradictions, but it also gave him insights that have made his novels, with all their many faults, a permanent part of our literature.

Granville Hicks. SR. April 4, 1959. p. 16

Dreiser was willing to risk being wrong; and he had great wrong-looking juts to his character. He was a stiff-armer, an elbower who never gave ground outside his novels or in them. And though outside the books he could be so obtuse and unjust, inside them his passion for justice rang true. At the height of his success, when he had settled old scores and could easily have become the smiling public man, he chose instead to rip the whole fabric of American civilization straight down the middle, from its economy to its morality. It was the country that had to give ground.

Nelson Algren. Nation. May 16, 1959. p. 459

An American Tragedy

In its larger features the construction of *An American Tragedy* is as solid as a bank building. It is very long, to be sure, but there is little in it which is not functional, not a part of Mr. Dreiser's ponderous design. I was very nervous for fear that the roof would fall during a couple of sagging chapters early in the second volume; but, no, he slowly swung his heavy timbers into place, restored his tension and retained it to the end. The structure of a novel he has mastered. It is the structure of a sentence which has remained a mystery to him. Often he plunges into a sentence head foremost, "trusting to God Almighty to get him out of it"; and is vouchsafed no divine aid. And yet the work as a whole is massively impressive. I do not know where else in American fiction one can find the situation here presented dealt with so fearlessly, so intelligently, so exhaustively, and *therefore* with such unexceptionable moral effect.

Stuart Sherman. The Main Stream (Scribner). 1927.
p. 144

His difficulty is that his mechanistic naturalism compels him so to select and manipulate facts of experience as to deny, through his narrative, that human life has any meaning or value. The attempt is suicidal, and the more consistently it is carried out the more completely is Mr. Dreiser forced to divest his creatures and their actions of any distinctively human quality and meaning. The more successful he is the more insignificant his work becomes. *An American Tragedy* . . . is more skilfully, faithfully, and consistently executed on the naturalistic level than any of its author's earlier novels, and precisely for this reason it contains no single element of tragedy in any legitimate sense of the word, and it impresses thoughtful readers as a mere sensational newspaper story long drawn out.

Robert Shafer in *Humanism and America,* edited
by Norman Foerster (Farrar and Rinehart). 1930.
pp. 165–6

The best of Theodore Dreiser is in this book. It is an epic of one important aspect of American life, its crass materialism, its indifference to all that is not glitter and show, its irresponsibility for the youth, its condemnations instead of understanding, its thirst for punishment instead of prevention, its hypocrisy, its ruthless savagery, and the ferocity of its mobs and courts of prosecution. There is less naturalistic detachment and more of the fire and brooding pity for men who live with such impoverished ideals. It is an indictment without malice.

Harlan Hatcher. *Creating the Modern American
Novel* (Farrar and Rinehart). 1935. p. 55

The great advantage of *An American Tragedy* (over Dreiser's other novels) was that it was dramatized rather than reported in events. For the first time and the only time in Dreiser's career he had a subject that could be presented dramatically for at least three-fourths of its length. As a result, this novel, despite its tremendous size (840 closely printed pages), has much the best integrated dramatic structure of any Dreiser novel. . . . Basically the story is without novelty; in fact, at first glance it even appears unpromising. But in the hands of a writer of Dreiser's sympathies and tragic sense, it becomes a great one. He explored every possible mutation of his theme; he probed more deeply and developed greater significance from the simple human story than had been done by any American who handled a similar theme before him.

George Snell. *The Shapers of American Fiction*
(Dutton). 1947. pp. 244–5

See *Sister Carrie, Jennie Gerhardt, The Financier, The Titan, The Genius, An American Tragedy,* and *The Bulwark* (novels); also *A Book about Myself* and *Dawn* (autobiographies).

EBERHART, RICHARD (1904–   )

Richard Eberhart insists on the immaculate Ego. He allows himself contaminating identification with no system of ideas, while his tradition is that of the traditionless. Writing under the more primitive compulsions of the heart, he makes his way through an emotional and intellectual labyrinth whose relation to the real world is, at best, a verbal accident. . . . His finest poems . . . express with economy and intellectual beauty the sovereign individual. Convention drops away and the reader feels the immediate record of free sensibility. . . . Such exaltation, however, illuminates but the barest handful of his poems. For the most part, it appears in disassociated examples momentarily, like vistas opened by lightning.

John Malcolm Brinnin. Poetry. Dec., 1942. pp. 508–9

Mr. Eberhart, either because his ear is defective or because he is over-anxious to avoid the merely smooth, makes the not uncommon mistake of establishing violence and perversity as his norm, with the inevitable result that where everything shrieks and clashes, the uproar at last cancels itself out, and it is as if nothing had been heard at all. This is a great pity, for he has a wonderful energy of vision, together with a fine gusto in phrase and an enviable muscular capacity for compressed statement: if he could only be severe with himself, and canalize his gifts, instead of simply going hell-for-leather at his Idea, with capitals, he could be one of the very best of contemporary poets, as he is already one of the most exciting.

Conrad Aiken. NR. Apr. 2, 1945. p. 452

In the manufacture of malt whiskey the barley is soaked, then dried, and then the malt thus obtained is brewed into a beer-like liquid. This liquid, when distilled, produces the raw whiskey. It has to lie mellowing a long time in sherry casks. Mr. Eberhart is always a good brewer but he does not always bother with the further processes of distilling and maturing—or rather, he often matures without distilling. Let him distil his poetry more often: the finer, subtler, stronger and more profound flavor of pot-stilled malt whiskey (now almost unobtainable, alas) is more exciting to the discriminating palate than the pleasantest of beers.

David Daiches. Poetry. May, 1945. p. 95

His trouble has always been that his faults are very obvious and easy to feel superior to, because they are as unmodish as it is possible for faults to be; they are Victorian faults. That Mr. Eberhart has also the Victorian virtues is easy to overlook. . . . When Mr. Eberhart succeeds, he achieves a kind of direct rightness of feeling towards central experiences which is about the rarest thing there is in contemporary verse; and·he does it in a language as simple and perfect for its purpose as you could ask.

Arthur Mizener. *Poetry*. Jan., 1949. pp. 226–7

To be a poet, he has taken greater risks than most of his contemporaries. That is there is rather little intellectual content in his verse. . . . But the open mind or heart is just as hobbled as the closed one. It is not enough for a man simply to keep his head clear or his nose clean. He needs to dance between these opposites like the angels. And Mr. Eberhart's great quality is that he can put up a show of violence behind the heartfeltness and the vision—just as Blake could, of course. All the same he is a man with a definite and tragic sense of the small use of his kind of experience in the world of busyness, with a feeling (not especially contemporary) of having been cornered; a man much given to backward-looking. He is obsessed with childhood and death and union with earth; he has a hatred of fuss and affairs, and a liking for subtlety, harmony, oddness, and the natural.

Pete Duvall Smith. *NSN*. July 21, 1951. p. 78

What . . . must be said for him . . . is the compassion, the sad and gentle and terribly exact understanding he has of his own and of all human experience. This is his "bias toward the spiritual," and it comes near greatness. It was in "The Groundhog," the war poems, and the many contemplations of death, and in the short unforgettable "The Full of Joy" and "Cover Me Over." Wisdom and compassion permeate the poetry.

John Holmes. *NYT*. Aug. 19, 1951. p. 14

Oddly, though he has a very recognizable poetic personality, Mr. Eberhart has never acquired a distinctive "style" of his own. . . . Perhaps a "style" is sometimes a mere crystallizing of stereotyped responses. Though the unevenness and imperfection of much of his work is a heavy price to pay for this, Mr. Eberhart has a quality which is very rare indeed in contemporary poets. He does not feel himself bound by what the last stanza of a poem is going to be like while he is grappling with the first stanza. There is nothing preconceived or ready-made in his work.

G. S. Fraser. *NSN*. Nov. 21, 1953. p. 647

Richard Eberhart without ever raising his voice, using for the most part the forms that are supposed to be worn out, is a natural poet, and, happily, one who just keeps getting better and better. . . . For all his intellectual preoccupation with death, there is a sunny disposition, an even temper, a healthy optimism, a muscular goodwill in Eberhart that stamps his writing as peculiarly American.

Selden Rodman. *NYT*. Nov. 22, 1953. p. 5

In the romantic mode, Eberhart's individualism is naked and un-ashamed; and in contrast to the tormented, metamorphic victims of our age, it rings adventurous and cheerful. It is almost as if the great age of the individual were beginning all over again, instead of fighting for its life. . . . Because his style is governed so much by the extreme in-dividualism of the unconscious, Eberhart's use of reckless imagery sometimes involves him (and his reader) in blind-alley surrealism. . . . More often, though, he achieves an opaque magnificence, how-ever arbitrary the tropes.

Gerard Previn Meyer. *SR*.. May 22, 1954. p. 22

Eberhart's lyric gives us almost always the diction of a single speaker who is arguing a relation between appearance and reality. The language differs from the seventeenth-century poet chiefly in its determination to avoid the elaborate or extended figure of speech, or conceit. During his career, Eberhart has developed through, and out of, some aspects of this influence partly through a progression of subjects—from an early concern with mortality, through an intermediate concern with the problem of human knowledge, into a later concern with God and nature. . . . His direction has been from the sharply lyrical toward the more free-handed narrative and satiric forms and from them, by a leap, into verse dialogue and drama.

Reuel Denney. *Poetry*. Nov., 1954. p. 103

His mysticism is self-aware and a little humorous. He writes in a good grainy language that puts him squarely in the most attractive tradition of American verse, and he reveals, in some of his poems at least, a marvelous control of stress and pitch, the play of the spoken language within poetic forms. Moreover, like Emily Dickinson, he possesses the ability to hit sometimes upon the absolutely perfect image, startling and simple, lustrous against the setting of the poems.

Hayden Carruth. *Poetry*. Oct., 1957. pp. 55–6

Whatever it is that makes a "true" poet, in the old Platonic or the new subliminal sense, Richard Eberhart has it. When the god's hand is on him, the language pours forth, powerfully channeled, alive without bombast, rhetorically true. . . . Too many of his poems do begin in brilliant fashion, then fade into some forced paradoxical turn, or into the thick, guttered out language of a conventional and semi-mystical piety, or even into tautology. . . . But though we should not quite forgive him his failures of self-criticism, it is quite likely that Eberhart needs to work as he does; that if he allowed himself certain kinds of "doubts," the greater successes, those poems in which we sense the god's presence at every moment would be impossible.

M. L. Rosenthal. *Nation*. Dec. 21, 1957. p. 480

See *Selected Poems, Undercliff,* and *Great Praises* (poetry).

EDMONDS, WALTER (1903–   )

Rome Haul would be a notable book in any season. As the first novel of a man born in 1903 it is extraordinary. There are men and women here, of course. But not one of them bulks so large, in the completed tapestry, as the Erie Canal on which they live. . . . Mr. Edmonds undoubtedly set forth to make this a chronicle of the Erie Canal. In this he has succeeded most admirably. . . . Great deeds were done and great lives lived along the canal. *Rome Haul* is a fitting, if somewhat belated, monument.

William Vogt. *NYHT*. Feb. 17, 1929. p. 5

One need hardly say more than that *Erie Water* is as good an historical novel as was Mr. Edmonds's first, *Rome Haul*. It is full of accurate detail and incidents recreated with all the stress and drama of the moment. The conversations, the expletives, in fact, the complete scene of that period and region are utilized with a mastery which points to the author's special study and love of his subject. The romance with which he flavours his story has not the virtue of originality, but its sincere emotion and suspense adequately serve the purpose of narrative interest.

Archer Winster. *Bkm*. March, 1933. pp. 295–6

Whether the mood is light or dark, you will find in these stories (*Mostly Canallers*) a freshness of characterization which goes far to explain their eminent readableness, and which itself calls for some explanation. It seems to be founded not merely on quick imagination and the shrewd sense of where one man differs from another but in the author's solid admiration for these rough people of his, on the humor and sympathy with which he draws them out. . . . He has . . . given them an idiom and a relation to environment which give them individuality as a group. When they are lounging or storming about in their own peculiar attitudes they are honest-to-God, and very satisfying to know.

Otis C. Ferguson. *NYHT*. Feb. 25, 1934. p. 2

Drums Along the Mohawk is crowded with people and with incidents. And they all . . . are convincing. Mr. Edmonds is obviously not a born novelist. He cannot create clearly individualized characters who dominate a book and walk away with the reader's emotions. But he can do very well in painting a society, a countryside full of people. He did it expertly enough in his stories of the building of the Erie Canal; he has done it still more expertly and vigorously in this full book of the Valley in the days of Tories and hostile armies.

Allan Nevins. *SR*. Aug. 1, 1936. p. 5

Because he is primarily an artist, the work of Walter D. Edmonds goes beyond a local realism. Beneath his faithful use of local color he attempts to express the essential truths of human experience. His novels and stories have been compared to the folk literature of a region, for he treats innocence, courage, the home, as the ancestral virtues of our national birthright. . . . In style as a device for literary experiment he is not at all interested; he holds firmly to the story-telling tradition of the Anglo-Saxon novel. He has a story to tell as well as characters to present, and from characters against a definite background come the outlines of plot.

Dayton Kohler. *EJ*. Jan., 1938. pp. 10–1

Mr. Edmonds does not content himself with going up into the attic and fetching down a beaver hat and a hoop skirt. He fetches in a whole lost age and makes it so natural that soon one is living in it. He is almost as much at home in Northern New York in the Eighteen Thirties as Mark Twain was with life on the Mississippi. He catches the incidental things. . . . The reader need not look for social significance (in *Chad Hanna*), for this is a yarn of local color, romance, and adventure. . . . This book is a vacation. It is an escape book. It pictures a land and time in which one would like to be for a change, and experiences not too painful to live through—and certainly not too dull!

R. L. Duffus. *NYT*. April 7, 1940. p. 1

His outlook is almost exclusively masculine; his best portraits of women are those of women who might as well have been men, and he shows little delicacy of insight regarding the other sex. Against this objection if it is one, we may set the fact that he has great delicacy of perception regarding natural beauty, animals of all sorts, and children. He has not yet exhibited the highest type of constructive imagination, and his invention is in general short-breathed. But on the other hand few writers can excel him in straight story-telling or in the brilliancy with which he can flash a scene. His historical perspective has seldom achieved grandeur and his portrayal of the past lacks both latitude and altitude. He has, however, chosen to cultivate a restricted field intensively and he may have no ambition to extend it.

Robert M. Gay. At. May, 1940. p. 658

Mr. Edmonds is a romantic realist, he enjoys spinning a yarn for the yarn's sake, but he likes people for themselves rather than—as is the way of so many yarn-spinners—for the function they may be made to perform in the unfolding of the story. So his characters, whom one gets to know slowly, and likes better and better as one knows them, are a refreshingly genuine collection of characters from an America that is gone.

The words that Mr. Edwards puts into their mouths are particularly admirable. This, one says to oneself, is the way Americans must have talked in those days.

Robert Littell. YR. Summer, 1940. pp. vi–viii

Like all Mr. Edmonds's historical novels, *In the Hands of the Senecas* plays tricks with your calendar. It projects a more dangerous, headier age plump in your living room, and for a few hours you find yourself battling flames and hostile savages with no aid available from fire department or police; none, either, from your immediate neighbors, for in all likelihood you have none. You have become a rugged individualist, not from choice but in order to survive. . . . Mr. Edmonds takes advantage of every opportunity offered by his material and often creates breathless suspense by such devices as escapes, pursuits, and the like. But a different, more organic type of suspense also pervades the story, one's natural anxiety to know what will happen next to a group of always believable characters.

Jennings Rice. NYHT. Jan. 26, 1947. p. 8

See *Rome Haul, Erie Water, Chad Hanna,* and *In the Hands of the Senecas* (novels); also *Mostly Canallers* (short stories).

ELIOT, T. S. (1888–1965)

Eliot's own opinions are not merely related to his poetry. They qualify his whole critical attitude, and they make him to some extent a preacher.

His aim as a writer has been to be a traditionalist: the tradition which he has adopted, being derived from the Church, has also sociological and educative implications. It is his object to show that the application of these principles in social life is as just as it is correct to apply them to literature. He seems to feel that unless he can prove this, he is, in his work, an individualist: not a traditionalist radically connected with the historic process: but isolated, original, personal, in the sense that he is writing about his own beliefs which are "home-made," and so make him eccentric and different from the people around him.

Stephen Spender. *The Destructive Element*
(Houghton). 1936. pp. 164–5

If there is a metaphysical distinction between the poetry and the prose of T. S. Eliot, it is this: that in the former he is sceptical of his own knowledge of truth, and in the latter he is indicating the path along which he hopes to find it. In the poetry he sees things through a glass darkly; in the prose he is proclaiming the truth that will make us free. Both these activities, however, are offshoots of a unified intelligence, of a man who is singularly whole in his conception of the dignity and importance of his art. There is no real divergence between his theory and practice, no matter how lucid he may contrive to make his criticism, or how obscure his poetry.

A. C. Patridge. *T. S. Eliot* (Pretoria). 1937. p. 3

It is to him, together with Ezra Pound, that we can trace the awareness of the urban scene, the employment of anti-poetic imagery, conversational rhythms, cinematic transitions and close-ups, which make contemporary verse deserve the adjective. And even the most vigorous and provocative of the younger men have not shown an "auditory imagination" equal to Eliot's. . . . What his "feeling for syllable and rhythm" has brought back, in its curious workings, has been chiefly a sense of disorder, of frustration and waste, an intimate and horrifying vision of death.

Babette Deutsch. *AS*. Winter, 1939. p. 30

Eliot, in brief, has surrendered to the acedia which Baudelaire was able to judge; Eliot suffers from the delusion that he is judging it when he is merely exhibiting it. He has loosely thrown together a collection of disparate and fragmentary principles which fall roughly into two contradictory groups, the romantic on the one hand and on the other the classical and Christian; and being unaware of his own contradictions, he is able to make a virtue of what appears to be private

spiritual laziness; he is able to enjoy at one and the same time the
pleasure of indulgence and the dignity of disapproval.

Yvor Winters. KR. Spring, 1941. p. 238

Eliot seldom involves himself steadily with the world about him. Instead he makes brief and startling sallies into the world and hence his
poetry sometimes strikes us either as a discontinuous anthology of
images or as an imitation of involuted psychological or biological processes which remain purely verbal. . . . Another result of this nervous
intermittence is that Eliot's criticism of other poets—such as Donne,
Marvell, or Dryden—makes the excellence of their poetry depend too
much on their surprising success in image-making and too little on their
steady sense of life. Eliot tends to give us what is occasional and spas-
modic in a poet, rather than the poet's normal excellence.

Richard Chase. KR. Spring, 1945. pp. 220–1

The reconciliation of opposites is as fundamental to Eliot as it was to
Heraclitus. Only thus can he envisage a resolution of man's whole being. The "heart of light" that he glimpsed in the opening movement of
"Burnt Norton" is at the opposite pole from the <i>Heart of Darkness</i>
from which he took the epigraph for "The Hollow Men." Essential
evil still constitutes more of Eliot's subject matter than essential good,
but the magnificent orchestration of his themes has prepared for that
paradisal glimpse at the close, and thereby makes it no decorative
allusion, but an integrated climax to the content no less than to the
form. Such spiritual release and reconciliation are the chief reality for
which he strives in a world that has seemed to him increasingly threatened
with new dark ages.

F. O. Matthiessen. The Achievement of T. S. Eliot
(Oxford). 1947. p. 195

Eliot's mind, let us say, is a mind of contrasts which sharpen rather
than soften the longer they are weighed. It is the last mind which, in
this century, one would have expected to enter the Church in a lay
capacity. The worldliness of its prose weapons, its security of posture,
its wit, its ability for penetrating doubt and destructive definition, its
eye for startling fact and talent for nailing it down in flight, hardly go
with what we think of today as English or American religious feeling.
. . . However that may be, within the Church or not, Mr. Eliot's
mind has preserved its worldly qualities. His prose reflections remain
elegant, hard (and in a sense easy—as in manners), controlled, urbane

(without the dissimulation associated with ecclesiastical urbanity), and fool-proof.

R. P. Blackmur. *Language as Gesture* (Harcourt). 1952. pp. 176–7

Poetry

By technique we . . . mean one thing: the alert hatred of normality which, through the lips of a tactile and cohesive adventure, asserts that nobody in general and some one in particular is incorrigibly and actually alive. This some one is, it would seem, the extremely great artist: or, he who prefers above everything the unique dimension of intensity, which it amuses him to substitute in us for the comforting and comfortable furniture of reality. If we examine the means through which this substitution is allowed by Mr. Eliot to happen in his reader, we find that they include: a vocabulary almost brutally tuned to attain distinction; an extraordinarily tight orchestration of the shapes of sound; the delicate and careful murderings—almost invariably interpreted, internally as well as terminally, through near-rhyme and rhyme—of established tempos by oral rhythms.

E. E. Cummings. *Dial.* June, 1920. p. 783

It is true his poems seem the products of a constricted emotional experience and that he appears to have drawn rather heavily on books for the heat he could not derive from life. There is a certain grudging margin, to be sure, about all that Mr. Eliot writes—as if he were compensating himself for his limitations by a peevish assumption of superiority. But it is the very acuteness of his suffering from this starvation which gives such poignancy to his art. And, as I say, Mr. Eliot is a poet—that is, he feels intensely and with distinction and speaks naturally in beautiful verse—so that, no matter within what walls he lives, he belongs to the divine company. . . . These drops, though they be wrung from flint, are none the less authentic crystals.

Edmund Wilson. *Dial.* Dec., 1922. p. 615

The writer of "The Waste Land" and the other poems of that period appeals to us as one struck to the heart by the confusion and purposelessness and wastefulness of the world about him. . . . And to that world his verse will be held up as a ruthlessly faithful mirror. The confusion of life will be reflected in the disorganized flux of images; its lack of clear meaning in the obscurity of language. . . . And now against this lyric prophet of chaos must be set the critic who will judge the world from the creed of the classicist, the royalist, and the Anglo-Catholic.

. . . I think . . . that a sensitive mind cannot read "Ash Wednesday" without an uneasy perception of something fundamentally amiss in employing for an experience born of Anglo-Catholic faith a metrical form and a freakishness of punctuation suitable for the presentation of life regarded as without form and void. . . . He is a leader and a very influential leader. Our difficulty is that he seems to be leading us in two directions at once.

Paul Elmer More. *SR*. Nov. 12, 1932. p. 235

When Eliot stood isolated and dispossessed amid the ruins of a familiar universe, every nerve and sensation quivered with its own life. The antennae of his intelligence were alive with nervous vitality. This resulted in images and allegories of great focal sharpness. In more recent years, approaching a stranger territory, this grip on identity is no longer held, and with its relaxation the nervous sensibility of his diction and cadence has lessened. He writes either a more relaxed and speculative verse, or a sort of argument which attempts to extend his intellectual problems beyond their own limits. He has become a poet of more public qualities, of religious responsibilities, and even (in *The Rock*) of social concerns. These have entailed a change from a style of cryptic historical reference and erudition to one of dialectic lucidity, or even of popular simplification.

Morton Dauwen Zabel. *SoR*. Summer, 1936. p. 170

The rich store of childhood treasure which is contained within Eliot's poetry, and more particularly, within his imagery, is obvious to any reader. The repetition of the same small group of images in poem after poem, from the early Jamesian ironies to the time of the later "Quartets," the recurrence of the curling smoke of evening, of stairs and windows and doors, of the hidden bird and the pool, the children's voices and the garden, the music and the thunder: these things by themselves argue that such images have a personal origin and a deep personal significance. It is this habitual use of optical "constants," of material which could be described as in a sense "obsessive," that imparts to Eliot's work its characteristic quality of seeming to be less a collection of single pieces than one continuing poem in permanent process of revision.

S. Musgrove. *T. S. Eliot and Walt Whitman* (New Zealand). 1952. p. 11

More than one critic has remarked that in Eliot the over-all organization of the poem as a whole is not lyrical in any recognizable and traditional way; nor is the poem organized in terms of narrative; nor is it dramatic in the literal theatrical sense; and it is certainly not logical, argumentative, or expository. . . . Where poets in the past would have used a logical, emotional, dramatic, or narrative basis for the transition from part to part, Eliot uses some one of these kinds of transition freely and alternatively and without committing himself to any one of them or to any systematic succession of them; or he omits the connection between one passage and the next, one part and the part which succeeds it. . . . The characteristic over-all organization of the poem—of which "The Waste Land" is the vividest example—can be called, for the lack of a better phrase, that of sibylline (or subliminal) listening.

Delmore Schwartz. Poetry. Jan., 1955. pp. 236–7

Drama

He will soon make ordinary drama look cheap because of its lack of metaphysical interest, just as he had part in making the ordinary shallow poetry of twenty years ago look the same way, and for the same reason. . . . On the realistic level Mr. Eliot is superb in his mastery of characterization (both the satiric and the sympathetic), handling of plot sequence, exposition of background through dialogue, and, I imagine, such other techniques as belong to an oral form like drama. It is comforting to think that an intellectualist, so strict and unconceding that he has been accused of living in a tower, has picked up without any fuss the knack for the close structural effects of drama.

John Crowe Ransom. Poetry. Aug., 1939. pp. 264–6

What is it that marks these plays off from the commercial drama, and from previous plays in verse or even in prose, and forces us to classify them as poetic drama? There is, first, their mixture of high seriousness in poetry and human colloquial speech, both in prose and verse. There is the tone of liveliness and intensity. There is the action on more than one level, the perpetual parable or allegory, and there is, finally, the startling variety of elements derived from every conceivable theatrical activity past and present. In short, there is a wider theatrical equipment harnessed to a deeper poetical purpose.

J. Isaacs. An Assessment of Twentieth-Century
Literature (Secker). 1951. pp. 142–3

What most critics of Mr. Eliot's plays seem to ignore is that he is writing a new kind of drama. Whereas most plays appeal to the passions —pity, terror, the glamor of love—or to the intellect, or would stir our zeal for political reform, his plays are based on an appeal to the conscience, or the consciousness of self. Here is this person, he says in effect, guilty of this or that; how far are you, dear spectator, in the like case? Our response comes from a different center. That is why some people do not applaud his plays; nobody likes to be made to think about his weakness, his failures, or his sins. Not that many of us have committed crimes: but then crimes, as we are told in this play (*The Elder States-man*) are in relation to the law, sins in relation to the sinner. . . . In all the plays about conscience, from Sophocles to Ibsen, we are de-tached spectators. . . . Here, however, we are forced to ask ourselves: "Have I never run away from myself? Have I never tried to blot out in-cidents from my past?"

Bonamy Dobrée. SwR. Winter, 1959. pp. 109–10

Criticism

Eliot not only follows the classical dogma because he cherishes classi-cism; he follows it also because he cherishes dogma. . . . He loses much by being fastidious. He loses much by having no humor whatever, but he is capable of something else by having splendid wit. And the presence of wit and the absence of humor in Eliot argue his possession of great intellect and egoism, his lack of humanity, his lack of modesty and unself-consciousness. He rests with those men who have chosen to see life distantly, from a single vantage-point; and had he, in the absence of warmth and sinew, a great intensity, he might possess permanent value for us. . . . But he is not intense, he is merely correct.

Louis Kronenberger. Nation. Apr. 17, 1935. p. 453

In spite of everything, Eliot *has,* in his critical essays, said many of the things that most needed to be said in our time. He has documented with appropriate *dicta* the final ebb of the romantic movement, the reversal of the trend which saw poetry as the expression of the poet's unique per-sonality, the rediscovery of the glories of the metaphysical poets, and the parallel reintroduction into English and American poetry of wit *and* passion. In some of his best essays—those on Dante, for example— he is often rearranging (as Mario Praz has shown) the ideas of Ezra Pound or others; in some of his worst, he is merely perverse or pig-headed or exhibitionistic. But his critical ideas are in themselves full of interest and excitement, and have become part of the intellectual at-mosphere of our time.

David Daiches. YR. Spring, 1949. pp. 466–7

To my notion T. S. Eliot is the greatest of all literary critics. . . . Eliot's merit lies almost equally in his ability to raise the pertinent prob-lems and in the fineness of his taste. He gave himself a rule of cogency early on and has had the strength of mind to obey it without evasion. This is the first critic of whom we can feel sure that the most important question will always be answered—namely, how successful *as art* is the work of art in hand? Eliot is no philosopher of aesthetics or criticism; he is both more and less than that: his critical practice demonstrates the right principles in action and we recognize them by their fruits rather than their definition.

Clement Greenberg. Nation. Dec. 9, 1950. p. 531

See *Complete Poems and Plays* and *Selected Essays;* also *The Elder Statesman* (play).

ELLISON, RALPH (1914–   )

Many Negro writers of real distinction have emerged in our century. . . . But none of them except, sometimes, Richard Wright has been able to transcend the bitter way of life they are still (though diminishingly) condemned to, or to master patiently the intricacies of craftsmanship so that they become the peers of the best white writers of our day. Mr. Ellison has achieved this difficult transcendence. *Invisible Man* is not a great Negro novel; it is a work of art any contemporary writer could point to with pride.

Harvey Curtis Webster. SR. April 12, 1952. p. 23

The reader who is familiar with the traumatic phase of the black man's rage in America, will find something more in Mr. Ellison's report. He will find the long anguished step toward its mastery. The author sells no phony forgiveness. He asks none himself. It is a resolutely honest, tormented, profoundly American book. . . . With this book the author maps a course from the underground world into the light. *Invisible Man* belongs on the shelf with the classical efforts man has made to chart the river Lethe from its mouth to its source.

Wright Morris. NYT. April 13, 1952. p. 5

Ellison has an abundance of that primary talent without which neither craft nor intelligence can save a novelist; he is richly, wildly inventive; his scenes rise and dip with tension, his people bleed, his language stings. No other writer has captured so much of the confusion and agony, the hidden gloom and surface gaiety of Negro life. His ear for Negro speech is magnificent. . . . The rhythm of the prose is harsh

and tensed, like a beat of harried alertness. The observation is expert.
. . . For all his self-involvement, he is capable of extending himself
toward his people, of accepting them as they are, in their blindness and
hope.

Irving Howe. Nation. May 10, 1952. p. 454.

Unquestionably, Ellison's book is a work of extraordinary intensity—
powerfully imagined and written with a savage, wryly humorous gusto.
It contains many scenes which are brought off with great *brio* and a
striking felicity of detail. To my mind, however, it has faults which cannot simply be shrugged off—occasional overwriting, stretches of fuzzy
thinking, and a tendency to waver, confusingly, between realism and
surrealism.

Charles J. Rolo. At. July, 1952. p. 84

Ralph Ellison's *Invisible Man* is a basically comic work in the picaresque tradition, influenced by the novels of Louis-Ferdinand Céline.
The hero of *Invisible Man* just happens to be a Negro, and everything
he is and does includes ultimately the experience of all modern men.
But this is not accomplished by abstraction; Mr. Ellison has managed
to realize the fact of his hero's being a Negro in exactly the same way
as nineteenth-century novelists realized their characters being French or
Russian or middle-class: by making it the chief fact of their lives,
something they take for granted and would not think of denying. Mr.
Ellison displays an unapologetic relish for the concrete richness of Negro living—the tremendous variety of its speech, its music, its food,
even its perversities.

Steven Marcus. Cmty. Nov., 1953. p. 458

Many may find that *Invisible Man,* complex in its novelistic structure,
many-sided in its interpretation of the race problem, is not fully satisfying either as narrative or as ideology. Unlike the novel which depends
for its appeal chiefly on the staple elements of love or sex, suspense and
the dynamics of action, *Invisible Man* dispenses with the individualized
hero and his erotic involvements, the working out of his personal destiny. Here we have, subtly and sensitively presented, what amounts to
an allegory of the pilgrimage of a people. . . . By means of the revealing master symbol of vision, Ralph Ellison has presented an aesthetically distanced and memorably vivid image of the life of the American Negro.

Charles I. Glicksberg. SWR. Summer, 1954. pp. 264–5

See *Invisible Man* (novel).

FARRELL, JAMES THOMAS   (1904–   )

Like Proust, Farrell seems to have endured certain personal experiences for the sole purpose of recording them; but he also desired to avenge them, and he charged his works with so unflagging a hatred of the characters in them, and wrote at so shrill a pitch, that their ferocity seemed almost an incidental representation of his own. Like Caldwell, he wrote with his hands and feet and any bludgeon within reach; but where Caldwell's grossness seemed merely ingenuous or slick, Farrell wrote under the pressure of certain moral compulsives that were part of the very design of his work and gave it a kind of dreary grandeur.

Alfred Kazin. On Native Ground (Reynal). 1942.
p. 380

In Farrell's view, the people of his stories—whether of the exploiting or exploited class—were the natural products of a competitive social order in which material acquisition represented the highest good. Their human failure, to the degree that they were brutalized and rendered both spiritually and socially sterile, flowed inevitably from the culture which an acquisitive society had imposed on them. As a novelist, Farrell reported the mores of an economic jungle. . . . For him, the "dark realities" and the "pervasive spiritual poverty" of American society could not be eliminated within the present social order. For regeneration, for restoration of genuine social function, only the Marxian revolution would suffice.

Lloyd Morris. Postscript to Yesterday (Random).
1947. p. 166

Farrell has exploited the documentary novel very ably. He should be judged as a documentary novelist. It is quite true that even when viewed in this light he does not loom as large as a Dos Passos or a Wolfe, but neither does he look the blithering incompetent that some of his reviewers have represented him to be. . . . The importance of Faulkner is his private vision, whereas the importance of the documentary, and of the novel of James Farrell to the extent that it succeeds in achieving documentary status, is that the vision is completely public.

W. M. Frohock. The Novel of Violence in America
(Southern Methodist). 1950. pp. 69, 71

The accurate ear and the retentive memory of such a writer as James T. Farrell constitutes a kind of literary field-telephone, a two-party line possessing the double advantage of getting a message down straight without getting smacked in the teeth with a hatful of slops. A method based on the judicious non-com's understanding that if you can keep from getting hit by anything long enough you'll still be around when the war is won.

Where the field-telephone school, of which Farrell is the most prolific protagonist, succeeds is in its photographic fidelity. Where it fails is in affording that convulsive sense of life we discover in a Conrad, a Poe, a Stephen Crane, or a Scott Fitzgerald.

Nelson Algren. SR. Nov. 14, 1953. p. 29

Farrell the moralist is all-of-a-piece with Farrell the fiction writer. The one reflects upon the experience the other records. The fiction writer composes canvases depicting frustrated petty hopes and mean defeats, prolix obituaries of the spiritually impoverished, of greenhorns and other outsiders, the anonymous integers that go only to swell the population figures, the devalued people of his time whose fruitless dignity and courage (when these they have) are eternally betrayed by what Thomas Hardy called "circumstances". . . . The writer of fiction may leave us with the impression that his vision is of the drabness and tawdriness of life; and Farrell has indeed been beaten over the head innumerable times for precisely that crime, but the moralist takes a different tack and from the same data draws the conclusion that these things need not be.

C. Hartley Grattan. Harper. Oct., 1954. p. 93

Anderson and Dreiser taught him integrity; they took him aside and patted him on the head and told him always to speak the truth, my son, and no harm will ever come to you. They helped to develop in him the one quality for which today we rightly do him honor. But then Farrell stopped learning. . . . The integrity that became an obsession, the integrity that made him an honest writer, has held fast to its truth, and the truth now holds Farrell fast, blocking his ascent into the greatness that might have been his. It has forced him, instead, deeper and deeper into his pedantry, his thick, almost scholastic preoccupation with every last physical detail of his world.

John W. Aldridge. Nation. April 2, 1955. p. 291

Mr. Farrell has always had two important qualities that make it impossible to dismiss him. He is relentlessly honest and in the face of a fact he is artistically humble. These very virtues, perhaps, are responsible for the stylistic deficiencies. . . . His limited vision is honestly passed along and, however limited, it is vision. He sees not deeply but he sees clearly and what he sees is a part of the American experience.

While he is not to everyone's taste, it would be a shame to miss him because of fastidious feelings about syntax.

Frank Getlein. *Com.* Jan. 27, 1956. pp. 436–7

Twenty years ago a validating conjunction of the time and the circumstances enabled us to forgive the heedless ineptitudes of the Studs Lonigan and Danny O'Neill books, allowing us in fact to accept them with pride (others may have the style and the art, but what are those; these have the power and the truth). Much writing of the thirties got by because of a misunderstanding of what literature is, through a misconception of the term "naturalism." But now, when we are no longer confused by quasi-literary doctrine, we are no longer willing to forgive bad writing, or a vision which is never superior to that of the least of us.

Saul Maloff. *Nation.* Feb. 11, 1956. p. 124

Mr. Farrell's stories are painful, awful and wonderful.

How can he commute so easily between such extremes? I think the answer proceeds from the fact that Mr. Farrell dispenses with art as well as with artifice. . . . Mr. Farrell is innocent of all the invisible but complicated apparatus now fashionable with the short-story writer— the subtleties of form, the casual but cunning clues for motivation, the deployment of symbol and the planned ambiguities. His language is humble, but never studiedly so. He doesn't make an *outré* elegance out of plainness, as Hemingway sometimes does, or Steinbeck in his portraits of the primitive. Mr. Farrell's simplicity is helpless and genuine. . . . Yet who is better—the slide-rule fictioneer of our day, who frequently refines his short story into a weary and well-tailored void, or Jim Farrell, who reaches out with a rough hand and comes up, quite often, with an authentic fistful of human truth?

Frederic Morton. *NYT.* Feb. 10, 1957. p. 30

Studs Lonigan

This is not only Farrell's best book . . . it is also a distinguished and outstanding contemporary novel. To the American reader, who whether bored or amused, is not self-conscious about seeing in print the kind of talk that would be bandied about in the Greek's poolroom by the Fifty-eighth Street gang, who doesn't have to swallow his naturalism as though he were taking a dose of castor oil, who doesn't feel called upon to write or talk apologetically about it, *The Young Manhood of Studs Lonigan* is recommended as an absorbing novel, a book of significance, a great piece of American realism. One pushes through it with accelerating speed, unable to drop it. And it leaves one shaken.

Fred Marsh. *NR.* March 21, 1934. p. 166

See *Studs Lonigan, The Face of Time,* and *Bernard Clare* (novels).

FAST, HOWARD (1914–   )

Place in the City is an astonishing novel for a boy of twenty three to have written; but it is astonishing not because it is so good, for most of it is not good at all, but because it is so exasperatingly soft. . . . Despite the superficial toughness the book is really a study in innocence, full of garlands and tears and sighs, and there are passages, in fact, where it reads like a cross between Fannie Hurst and Sherwood Anderson. . . . Mr. Fast has talent and that talent bubbles in this book; but he has not learned that second-hand pathos is the easy refuge of second-hand thoughts.

Alfred Kazin. NYT. Aug. 8, 1937. p. 7

Mr. Fast . . . has a certain pretentiousness in his asides and betrays his immaturity in many of his Causes and Reasons, but he tells his tale so swiftly and glibly that it doesn't make much difference whether the Causes fit or not. He writes easily, probably too easily.

Paul Love. Nation. Aug. 14, 1937. p. 177

Mr. Fast writes with a catch in his breath and sometimes brings tears to his own eyes instead of the readers'. Sometimes his words are less an echo of history than they are of Hemingway. . . . Sometimes he takes his characters from the same casting agencies that are used by other historical novelists. . . . If his book does not belong to the history of American literature, at least it will be important in the history of the popular mind.

Malcolm Cowley. NR. Aug. 17, 1942. p. 203

Once again Howard Fast has taken a figure out of American history and by the intensity of his emotional sympathy and intellectual respect had made him into a living man. Just as in *The Unvanquished* George Washington became under Mr. Fast's austerely glowing art an individual of flesh and blood, beset by doubts and fears of personal inadequacy in the role he had to play, so does Thomas Paine in the novel *Citizen Tom Paine* become a creature known and knowable in his moments of grandeur and his moments of degradation. . . . Mr. Fast's story of this unique character in history is a brilliant piece of fictional biography.

Rose Feld. NYHT. April 25, 1943. p. 3

When a writer of historical fiction is in top form he somehow can suggest that he does not merely re-create the past but rather that he lives there and is reporting on the life around him. Sometimes the author of

Citizen Tom Paine and *Freedom Road* does this . . . when he is writing well and effectively, in a minor key, and you follow along with him and belong to the world he evokes. . . . His gift in his best work is for a certain reticence—and this is no negative virtue in the historical school, many of whose practitioners would dazzle you by piling up of theatrical "props" and are concerned with character only secondarily, if at all.

John K. Hutchens. *NYT*. Apr. 8, 1945. p. 6

In half a dozen novels this popular author has dealt with various critical periods in the American past and the last three of his books—*Citizen Tom Paine, Freedom Road,* and now *The American*—fit the same pattern. A society full of class tyranny, economic exploitation and political corruption; a proletariat, dumb, yearning, struggling, that plainly waits for a great leader; a hero who rises to struggle against the entrenched forces of Mammon and the dead weight of middle-class complacency; a defeat that gloriously points the way to future victories—this is the general scheme that Mr. Fast uses.

Allan Nevins. *NYT*. July 21, 1946. p. 4

In the writing career of Howard Fast we trace the unusually rapid decline of a pleasant fictional talent into dull political servitude. . . . His eye (has) been ever more tightly shutting itself to the kind of truth with which fiction is properly concerned, his heart increasingly hardening under the strain of pumping such a steady stream of practical benevolences until now . . . all that remains of any original creative gift is some kind of crude energy of intention, a shallow but complex urge to pedagogic power. Mr. Fast has come of literary age in a period in which to be a radical or even a liberal is to feel no need to smile when one says patriotism.

Diana Trilling. *Nation*. Aug. 3, 1946. p. 134

Howard Fast is a historical novelist with a difference. He has always shunned the standard ingredients of that art—sex, saber, and swashbuckling—and he has never permitted the drama on the stage to be obscured by the opulence of the setting. Nor has he tried to retell our history or ancient legends with our modern vision, pouring in (as Thomas Mann has done in the Joseph cycle) the intellectual resources of the twentieth century. Rather has he always been fascinated by the spectacle of those who either singly or in groups gave their powers and their lives for a cause, for the extension of human dignity and for what is perhaps the greatest of all rights, the right to be let alone.

Thomas Lask. *NYT*. Oct. 10, 1948. p. 4

Fast was long considered to be a diabolical Communist, hardly even human; now, as he presents himself as a disillusioned idealist, he seems sincere and very human. If we trust his motive and listen to what he has to say, we must grant his idealism and humanity even while a Communist. . . . It is far better when a man like Fast leaves his party for the reasons he did than because of fear or other opportunistic reasons.

> Paul Knopf. *NYT mag.* June 30, 1957. p. 2

See *The Last Frontier, The Unvanquished,* and *Citizen Tom Paine* (novels).

FAULKNER, WILLIAM   (1897–1962)

Faulkner seems to me to be melodramatic, distinctly. All the skies are inky black. He deals in horror as in a cherished material. Coincidence, what he would call "fate," does not stand on ceremony, or seek to cover itself in any fussy "realistic" plausibility, with him. . . . A man like William Faulkner discovers fatalism, or whatever you like to call it: it at once gives his characters something to live for—namely a great deal of undeserved tribulation culminating in *a violent death.* That simplifies the plot enormously—it is, in fact, the great "classical" simplification, banishing expectation.

> Wyndham Lewis. *Men Without Art* (Cassell). 1934.
> pp. 54–5

Not since Swift's conclusion to *Gulliver's Travels* (with the possible exception of some of the pages of Aldous Huxley) has humanity in all walks of life been pictured as such contemptible vermin. Nor has anyone probed with greater power into the volcanic fury, the corruption, the depravity in the black hearts of men who are only incidentally dwellers in the South, or written of such matters in more brilliant prose, or with finer control of mood and suggestion and careful spacing of atrocities. . . . It is the natural and ultimate extension of the materials and the moods clearly to be discerned in the literature of the contemporary period.

> Harlan Hatcher. *Creating the Modern American*
> *Novel* (Farrar and Rinehart). 1935. p. 240

As a thinker, as a participant in the communal myth of the South's tradition and decline, Faulkner was curiously dull, furiously commonplace, and often meaningless, suggesting some ambiguous irresponsibility and exasperated sullenness of mind, some distant atrophy of indifference. Technically he soon proved himself almost inordinately subtle and ambitious, the one modern American novelist whose devotion to form has earned him a place among the great experimentalists in modern poetry. Yet this remarkable imaginative energy, so lividly and almost painfully impressed upon all his work, did not spring from a conscious and procreative criticism of society or conduct or tradition, from some absolute knowledge; it was the expression of that psychic tension in Faulkner ˸ . . which, as his almost monstrous overwriting proves, was a psychological tic, a need to invest everything he wrote with a wild, exhilarated, and disproportionate intensity—an intensity that was brilliant and devastatingly inconclusive in its energy, but seemed to come from nowhere.

Alfred Kazin. *On Native Grounds* (Reynal). 1942.
pp. 456–7

Certain features of Faulkner's work suggested that it originated in a profound need to account, to himself, for the retarded condition of culture and civilization in the South. To some extent, therefore, his books recorded an exploration, a sustained and consistent effort to arrive at a coherent explanation of the nature of his environment in his own time. His exploration was imaginative rather than purely historical. His purpose was to understand events in terms of the human experiences which had produced them; the ambitions, the needs, the attitudes of mind and heart that had shaped destiny. The result was a series of volumes which, collectively, formed a single saga.

Lloyd Morris. *Postscripts to Yesterday* (Random).
1947. pp. 160–1

Inside this amazing, convolute and inimitable saga is everything that Poe was able to suggest in his macabre tales, much that Brown and Melville and Hawthorne foreshadowed, plus not only Faulkner's own incredibly fecund conjurations of the terrible and phantasmal, but also a very definite and real world of social significances and broad slapstick humor, which is outside the domain of any apocalyptic writer, any Gothic novelist of any time or place.

George Snell. *The Shapers of American Fiction*
(Dutton). 1947. p. 88

In addition to being a fatalist, Faulkner is also an idealist, more strongly so than any other American writer of our time. The idealist disguises itself as its own opposite, but that is because he is deeply impressed by and tends to exaggerate the contrast between the life around him and the ideal picture in his mind . . . of how the land and the people should be—a picture of painted, many-windowed houses, fenced fields, overflowing barns, eyes lighting up with recognition. . . . And both pictures are not only physical but moral; for always in the background of his novels is a sense of moral standards and a feeling of outrage at their being violated or simply brushed aside. Seeing little hope in the future, he turns to the past, where he hopes to discover a legendary and recurrent pattern that will illuminate and lend dignity to the world about him.

Malcolm Cowley in *A Southern Vanguard,* edited by
Allen Tate (Prentice). 1947. pp. 26–7

The quality of Faulkner's vision, his fundamental way of seeing people, seems to me to approach the Euripidean. . . . If we read him as though he were a tragic poet, many difficulties disappear. It becomes natural now that he should withhold much that the reader wants immediately to know, in order to prepare the recognition scene; that he should abandon the traditional time manipulation of the novel for one which turns the fullest, whitest light possible upon the moment of crisis . . . that personal relations among the characters should be determined by their sense of the inevitability of the evil yet to come upon them; and that Faulkner's effort should go into showing how the world looks to his characters rather than how it should look to them.

W. H. Frohock. *The Novel of Violence in America*
(Harvard). 1950. pp. 123–4

Faulkner believes that individual responsibility is the most important goal for man. Here is his positive answer to his own negative despair. . . . Thoreau based his personal individualism upon his tremendous love of nature. In Faulkner the love of nature is replaced by the love of the land. How much one would want to distinguish between land and nature I don't know. Basically the only difference is . . . the transcendental ideas in Thoreau's concept of nature. . . . Instead of having Thoreau's leaven of transcendentalism, he has Hawthorne's leaven of the brotherhood of man. Man must love the land that God has supplied to him for his well-being. Through the intimate association with the land, man acquires a sense of loyalty to his family, his immediate social environment, and the all-encompassing land itself. Loyalties, as with so much of man's activities, are governed by what is inherited from the past. By accepting these loyalties and the force of the past, man develops his individuality—the end for which all the other things of man's existence are means.

Ward L. Miner. *The World of William Faulkner*
(Duke). 1952. pp. 153–4

Faulkner's style and content have been the subject of endless scholarly analysis. The best as well as the shortest analysis may well be that contained in an interchange between him and his cousin Sallie Murray Williams. She asked, "Bill, when you write those things, are you drinkin'?" and he answered, "Not always."

Robert Coughlan. *The Private World of William Faulkner* (Harper). 1954. p. 125

Faulkner's post of observation usually lies with some individual who, out of his need for self-knowledge, even salvation from those complications of the human scene which "outrage," tells the story and, in telling it, resolves it, not solves it which only God can do. But in the resolution there is usually a fuller knowledge which rescues the protagonist from the accidents of his own situation, or allows him to see it in a larger context of meaning, by means of which he can "endure"; or his plight in the end illumines by its shock some disaster of epical proportions implicit in the enveloping action. Or else the point of view roves from individual to individual, each of whom discloses differing insights and revelations of the complication. But whatever, the point of view is essentially bardic, with the difference that the bard himself is crucially involved.

Andrew Lytle. *SwR*. Summer, 1957. p. 475

The Sound and the Fury

It is as merciless as anything I know which has come out of Russia. I find myself wishing for someone with whom to compare William Faulkner, but to compare this writer from Mississippi with James Joyce or Marcel Proust or Chekov or Dostoevsky gets one nowhere, for Faulkner is definitely American. . . . If Faulkner is mad, then James Joyce is equally so; if Faulkner is obsessed with futility and insanity, so is Fyodor Dostoevsky. It is true that *The Sound and the Fury* is insane and monstrous and terrible, but so is the life that it mirrors. . . . I believe simply and sincerely that this is a great book.

Lyle Saxon. *NYHT*. Oct. 13, 1929. p. 3

Certainly the craft of *The Sound and the Fury* is brilliantly planned. Once the central structure is arrived at, every detail falls into its place with a sort of astounding precision. Like the opening of a safe, given the combination, we can hear all the bolts clicking into place; and we may suspect that Faulkner has added a few extra bolts just for the satisfaction of making them click. . . . Very often the use of these details at once so mathematical and dramatic is justified. . . . For in *The Sound and the Fury* the technique of the novel, and its pyrotechnics, are after all subordinated to a meaning—to the history of the degenerating Compsons.

Maxwell Geismar. *Writers in Crisis* (Houghton).
1942. pp. 157–8

To speak of greatness with regard to one's contemporaries is dangerous. But if there are any American novels of the present century which may be called great, which bear comparison—serious if not favorable —with the achievements of twentieth-century European literature, then surely *The Sound and the Fury* is among them. It is one of the three or four American works of prose fiction written since the turn of the century in which the impact of tragedy is felt and sustained. Seized by his materials, Faulkner keeps, for once, within his esthetic means, rarely trying to say more than he can or needs to. *The Sound and the Fury* is the one novel in which his vision and technique are almost in complete harmony, and the vision itself whole and major. Whether taken as a study of the potential for human self-destruction, or as a rendering of the social disorder particular to our time, the novel projects a radical image of man against the wall. Embodied and justified, this is an image of great writing.

Irving Howe. *William Faulkner* (Random). 1952.
pp. 126–7

See *Sartoris, The Sound and the Fury, As I Lay Dying, Light in August, Absalom, Absalom!, The Hamlet, The Town* and *The Mansion* (novels).

See Supplement at end of text for additional material.

FEARING, KENNETH   (1902–1961)

The world of Fearing is nothing if not metropolitan. He is as involved in, and fascinated by, metropolitan existence (with its "touch of vomit-gas in the evening air") as Frost with his New England landscape, decorated with commonplaces, and Jeffers with his prop boulders and gulls. . . . Held by this life in futile ambivalence that has persisted for fifteen years, Fearing's mood appears to have changed little . . . although the tone has become increasingly harsh. In the ticker tape, the radio, the tabloid, the pulp magazine and the advertisement he has found an objective correlative that has never deserted him.

Weldon Kees. *Poetry.* Jan., 1941. p. 265

He wants as many people as possible to react with immediate horror or delight; consequently he has dramatized the most ordinary sights and happenings of everyday living. What, then, is added to make it poetry and not mere reporting? Principally, it is Fearing's imaginative viewpoint. He has the double vision of the poet who sees the object we all see and sees at the same time its universal shadow.

Ruth Stephan. Poetry. Dec., 1943. p. 164

Mr. Fearing is a poet who can compete in excitement with the journalists and surpass them in that his words have a speed equal to his impressions. He at times seems too closely in competition with them, so rapidly does he pass from a personal anguish to a cold impersonal dismay. What saves him is that, in his approach to what he sees, "hatred and pity are exactly mixed." He is a product of the depression and somewhat limited to its mood. In his America is more despair than hope, and even hope is ominous. But it is a country in which, while he disclaims his ability to bring miracles to pass, he knows that miracles still occur.

John Peale Bishop. Collected Essays (Scribner).
1948. pp. 319–20

Kenneth Fearing has sought and found his permanent level in the range of modern verse, and . . . it lies somewhere between Auden and Ogden Nash, with something of the former's surrealist imagination and a good deal of the latter's urban ability to pillory suburban mediocrity. Fearing does not, of course, derive his style from either. His style (it is a very good one, and by this time wholly his own) originated in Walt Whitman's long and casual line.

Selden Rodman. NYT. Oct. 24, 1948. p. 18

Kenneth Fearing's poems are less prosy, more formal, than their appearance on the page would indicate. The long line, the irregular, or not particularly anything stanza pattern invite the risk of sagging; Mr. Fearing is a master of not letting the line down, and he can, with a very slight and deft touch indeed, point up his ironic effects with a brief parenthesis, an apparent afterthought, a single adverb or adjective. . . . Mr. Fearing does what he does so very well that it is all a little exasperating; you wish that he would be a bit more venturesome, inventive, experimental.

Rolfe Humphries. Nation. Nov. 13, 1948. p. 557

As a practiced writer, Mr. Fearing can do a great deal with repeated words that would sound like material for nursery rhymes were it not for the grown-up ideas of change and decay that accompany them. It is readable, often brilliant writing of innuendo, of things seen out of the corner of his eye, of fears and doubts and strange characters in the background.

Eugene Davidson, *YR*. Summer, 1949. pp. 725–6

I don't think a poet can be much more American, in the psychological if not the Fourth-of-July sense, than Kenneth Fearing. He talks the lingo straight, simple, and sardonic and knows the native panic at being lost in the shuffle which has created it. . . . In Fearing's writing, the "enemy" gradually becomes the Mob, official and unofficial, that thrives on the regimentation of individual thought and feeling through ever-greater control of the avenues of communication. . . . Fearing is an original, a canny Quixote and—more to the point—a kind of melancholy Jacques of the age, whose writing has often a topical surface that belies its depth of wry compassion and its stylistic purity. Edward Dahlberg once compared him with Corbière, and the comparison was apt. But there are also American comparisons: He is one of the harder-bitten sons of Walt Whitman, a more mordant Masters or Sandburg, a poetic Lardner of wider scope.

M. L. Rosenthal. *Nation*. Jan. 19, 1957. pp. 64–5

It is a fighting poetry, thank God, a poetry of angry conviction, few manners and no winsome graces. It is stubborn in its Old Guard attitude, stubborn in its technique: so unfashionable, indeed, in its resistance to the prevalent obsession with metrical vacuity, that a well-bred young neo-classicist might regard it as almost theatrically conservative.

Dudley Fitts. *NYT*. Feb. 17, 1957. p. 4

His tone, for the most part, remains ironic. If he is a revolutionary poet, out of the proletarian tradition of the Thirties, and the best survivor of that tradition, he is one without a revolution to propose. . . . His art of brilliant surfaces and quick contemporaneity seemed more daring once, as a poetic configuration, than it does today, though the best poems keep their early lustre.

Stanley Kunitz. *SR*. June 29, 1957. pp. 25–6

The irony sometimes seems dated and callow, despite its honesty and technically accomplished presentation. It is as if Fearing's habitual irony only permitted him to see things by the gross or in generalities (as conventional as the "finny tribes" of earlier mannerists). Often, the consequence is too insufficient a discrimination to see a world behind the old stereotypes. For thirty years Fearing has fought the dragons of commercialism and conformity; the effects of the struggle on his poetry have not been altogether good. But there are those poems like "Five

A. M.," "Continuous Performance," and "The Face in the Bar Room Mirror" that transcend the struggle and comment on it with the ominous and witty power Fearing can achieve at his best.

Leonard Nathan. *Poetry.* Aug., 1957. p. 328.

See *New and Selected Poems*

FISHER, DOROTHY CANFIELD   (1879–1958)

Miss Canfield wants the whole of the psychic life to be carried on under the spot-light of the attention. It follows that she is opposed to the creation of instinct; that she desires, in fact, that the psyche should be like a country that refers all its business to a central government. That is a system that leads in the end to a tyrannous and inefficient bureaucracy and the decay of provincial life. . . . The fact is that Miss Canfield's mind is a stranger to the idea of "the thing in itself"; and that makes her very little of a poet and rather less of a moralist.

Rebecca West. *NSN.* July 28, 1921. p. 444

To satisfy . . . worried, but conscientious souls, and perhaps to satisfy herself, Dorothy Canfield has written an earnest and serious vindication of marriage. . . . She has evidently tried to be honest. . . . Dorothy Canfield makes marriage a real thing—a thing of substance and color—but she makes its alternative weak and pitiful. . . . If Dorothy Canfield would face the intensity of love and the lure of freedom as willingly as she faces the reality and depths of family life, she could make a memorable contribution to current thought.

Freda Kirchwey. *Nation.* Dec. 7, 1921. pp. 676–7

Mrs. Fisher has taken issue with the indictment of the American scene which has colored the writing of many of our most significant contemporary novelists. Her loyalties are the old ones of the New England school; she finds neither malice nor stagnation nor dullness in the village. Her New Hampshire landscape glows with the veritable color of the hills; her village folk are kindly and simple and human; for her rural life still has the atmosphere of contentment and of a large peace. These contacts are notable because, in a sense, they place her definitely among the conservative in her outlook on life.

Lloyd Morris. *NYT.* Oct. 15, 1922. p. 25

Dorothy Canfield's sense of humor is keen but she has not wit. Neither does she indulge in epigram. She has done very effective scenes but she

is not a quotable novelist. It comes back, I should say, to the fact that with her the story is the thing. Very earnest people are seldom witty. . . . Dorothy Canfield is concerned with ideas and with people. She has chapters of passion and beauty, but you must take them as a whole.
Dorothea Lawrence Mann. *Bkm*. Aug., 1927. p. 700

Her stories seem to be verifiably true, because they are never written with scorn or with the endeavor to prove anything; unless it be to prove that ordinary day-by-day life may be filled with excitement, that love may grow in the intimacy of marriage stronger instead of weaker; that there are just as many Main Streets in Europe as in America; that the society of one's own children is more diverting than the average crowd at a Night Club. . . . I sometimes think that Dorothy Canfield, who has a deservedly international reputation, would be even a greater novelist if she did not possess so much common sense. She knows actual life so well, her ideas are so rational, so sound, and so sensible that her love of truth and reality may actually stand in the way of her reaching the highest altitudes.
William Lyon Phelps. *SR*. Oct. 11, 1930. p. 199

Despite an imperfect mastery of the art of compression and terseness, Dorothy Canfield is foremost today among those novelists who stand for sane perspective rather than sensationalism, for verity rather than realism, for selection of facts focused upon an indwelling universal law rather than a chaos of facts-for-facts'-sake, for limited free will rather than complete determinism. Thus, amidst the stultifying and stale conventions of naturalism, Dorothy Canfield is radiantly and dynamically unconventional.
H. H. Clark. *Bkm*. Nov., 1930. p. 300

Because she has been popular from the beginning of her career, because her shrewd common sense and understanding of the conditions of everyday life, even more than her emotional power, make her the "favourite author" of enormous numbers of unanalytical women who find in every story some illumination for their own lives, she has never had the recognition which her work deserves. She is journalistic to the extent that she produces constantly. She is unliterary partly because she is completely unself-conscious. If she achieves a beautiful passage it is because the words and sentences express what she has to say, and not because she is interested in beautiful writing except as a tool.
Elizabeth Wyckoff. *Bkm*. Sept., 1931. p. 44

Like Miss Cather, her wide knowledge at first hand of many sections of the United States and of some of Europe, prevented her from making those superficial generalizations which weaken the work of the satirists like Lewis, Dreiser, and Sinclair, and her knowledge of adolescence gained through her experience as a teacher, spared her from the errors of those novelists like Anderson who picture youth as a quagmire of evil. If her material seems at times to overwhelm her power of artistic assimilation and expression, her best fiction has an acuteness of insight which will keep her place secure.

> Arthur Hobson Quinn. *American Fiction* (Appleton-Century) 1936. p. 714

It's always illuminating to see Dorothy in process of stabilizing all she writes by her constant re-pinning it fast to the common lot, to generic human experience. Her greatest achievement, to my way of thinking, lies in her power to stand firmly on this realistic ground, while at the same time she pulls a possible future through the present. It's a thing teachers sometimes do, but they seldom know how they do it, and I'm fairly sure Dorothy doesn't know how she does it. Teachers do it for individual children, whom they know fairly well; Dorothy does it for an unknown multitude. . . . Nobody could single out the influences strongly affecting American life for the first quarter of this century without including Dorothy's novels. They seize the reader by an intimate hand and take him at once on an incursion and an excursion.

> Sarah N. Cleghorn. *Threescore* (H. Smith). 1936.
>
> pp. 132–3

Miss Canfield has had an accumulated mass of experience and anecdote from which to build her tales, and a birthright understanding of the persons of whom she writes. . . . Miss Canfield writes from the inside, looking out. . . . It is the ageless and universal striving of the human spirit of which she writes, and the material she has chosen is less noteworthy than the way she uses it.

All of us who are still learning to write should mark and envy the transparent simplicity, the quiet fluency of these tales. . . . Even more than these inestimables, warm tenderness that doesn't grow mawkish and sentiment that never sugars-off into sentimentality make the pretty everyday raw substances of Miss Canfield's tales beautiful and memorable.

> Frederic F. Van de Water. *NYT*. Oct. 23, 1949. p. 4

See *The Bent Twig, The Brimming Cup, The Deepening Stream,* and *Seasoned Timber* (novels).

FISHER, VARDIS (1895–   )

Mr. Fisher has written strikingly of a great subject, of the appalling and beautiful Wilderness and of the men and women who conquered it. He has remembered them, the way they talked and moved, the loneliness in their faces as winter came on, their astonishing adaptability in difficulty, the grim laconic quality of their heroism, their coarseness and lewdness and wildness. . . . *In Tragic Life* . . . ranks with the best work of our young writers. It is strong and vital and holds forth great promise for its sequels.

John Bronson. Bkm. Jan., 1933. p. 91

The novels of Vardis Fisher, emerging from the last stronghold of the American frontier tradition, the Rocky Mountain West, belong in the main stream of American letters. These are not mere regional novels. In their courage and rigorous honesty they are kin to the great works of confessional literature which know no national boundaries. But just as surely they grow out of the heroic, tragic, building and destroying conquests and aspirations of the pioneers—the fruits of which are now visited on the sons unto the third and fourth generation. . . . Vardis Fisher, single-handed, as he sees it, is conducting a revolution against the pioneer tradition. . . . Like Rousseau, he is intent on showing, without modesty, his hero's courage and nobility; and, without shame, his hero's sins and silliness, ineptitudes and secret mortifications.

Fred T. Marsh. NYT. Jan. 20, 1935. p. 4

A tetralogy concerned with present-day life in the United States, which remains to the end a puzzling combination of obvious talent for fiction, extreme egocentricity, an honest search for the meaning of life and loose thinking, comes to an end with Vardis Fisher's *No Villain Need Be.* Like its three predecessors, *In Tragic Life, Passions Spin the Plot,* and *We Are Betrayed,* it takes its title from a poem of George Meredith's. . . . There is no justification whatever for the loose and scattered ending of the work. . . . Nothing could be more fatal to an author's attempt to communicate his meaning to others than this deliberate failure to take into account the obligation to give his work as much coherence as possible, to use form as a means of communication, and not to deceive himself into thinking that he is being more honest than anybody else merely by discarding the conventions of the novel.

Herschel Brickell. NAR. June, 1936. pp. 358–9

With all its faults—its sprawling formlessness, its monotony of tone, its occasional pomposity, and the didacticism and loss of story interest consequent upon the eventual absorption of Vridar Hunter in Mr. Fisher himself—the tetralogy had moments of power and passion. The naked spectacle of the awful secret agonies of childhood and adolescence dominated by terror and shame compelled emotional response; and there was conviction and trenchancy in the unsparing portrayal of the pettiness and pusillaminity of certain aspects of academic life.

Lucy Ingram Morgan. *CF*. April, 1937. p. 30

A novelist can make no more serious demand on his art than that it tell us this: Granted such and such circumstances—and they will probably be those which the unsought experience of his own life has led him to consider—how shall a man conduct himself so that his soul may not sicken and die? It is because Vardis Fisher makes this demand that he commends himself to our interest. His resources as an artist are limited, his taste is uncertain, and his sense of form is not strong enough to allow him with impunity to discard the common conventions of the novel. But no one could doubt the earnestness of his moral purpose. His effort has been extreme to set down his conclusions honestly.

John Peale Bishop. *SoR*. Oct., 1937. p. 350

Placing Vardis Fisher is one of the sharpest problems offered by recent American fiction. Fisher's sincerity is so marked and his refusal to be beaten down is so gamely stubborn that he may seem at times to be a more significant novelist than he really is. . . . It is not a pleasant duty to list the faults of an author with so much talent and honesty and sense of human justice. . . . Perhaps Fisher could probe deeper into the current evasions if he also had a social scalpel, and his work might be given a logic and balance it now lacks. But the whole situation isn't so simple. Because Fisher has fallen into the trap of writing novelese, part of the answer to his problem would have to be technical.

Harry T. Moore. *NR*. July 27, 1938. p. 342

Vardis Fisher has chosen for his very considerable literary talents a very considerable fictional task. He has decided to write a family saga encompassing the history of man, beginning with prehistoric nomads and ending with whatever is left of contemporary humanity after the present military engagement. . . . It is his contention that the great discoveries which modern science has made concerning the origin and early experiences of man are locked away from the average citizen in text books and technical studies. Pondering this, he concluded that if such knowledge were put into the most popular form of literature, i.e., the novel, it would reach a general audience, and be absorbed into the national consciousness, where it might do some good by giving the voters in a democracy better knowledge of themselves and their problems.

Thomas Sugrue. *SR*. March 27, 1943. p. 22

(He) is, in part, fascinating, in part tedious and, throughout, plethoric. . . . No one can quarrel with (him) for being a novelist and wanting to be an anthropologist. One can only wish that he would keep his ambivalences to himself and be one or the other, for what emerges from his efforts is certainly not a novel and even less a reliable source-book. It is, rather, a kind of cross-pollination of the two and the resulting hybrid, defying classification, tends unpleasantly to baffle the reader.

R. J. Bender. *CS*. Aug. 10, 1947. p. 6

In Fisher's case (as opposed to that of Erskine Caldwell) we have none of (the) sense of removal; he insists that we identify ourselves with his people. His characters' ignoble patterns of thought and pretenses of superiority are presented as the norm for humanity. Our self-love is affronted, and we read insults into these books. That is exactly the trouble: we feel that this is precisely how Fisher wants us to react. It is as if he has a perverse wish to outrage us, as if in his desire to publish discoveries of our common frailty he stands in the position of prosecutor and accuses us of crimes.

George Snell. *Shapers of American Fiction* (Dutton).
1947. p. 278

In each of the first four volumes (of the *Testament of Man* series) he has examined the deep motives and the major contrivings of early men and women, adroitly deployed in the various fateful circumstances of the misty dawn of humanity. Each book is self-sufficient, an engrossing story of male and female, of man and the gods he dreamed, of the pains of man's writhing emergence from all that he once was. . . . Touching as it does the most tender sensitivities of our self-consciousness, it will enlighten, disturb and delight its readers in all the ways that their own age-old symbolic conditionings will allow and necessitate.

Wendell Johnson. *NYT*. Sept. 19, 1948. p. 21

Mr. Fisher's interpretations of man's development are naturally personal and conjectural. It is easy to see that there is more of modern psychology than anthropology in his approach, and it is possible to feel that his ancient men and women, only just out of the caves, have a strangely modern quality of subtlety in their thinking. Nevertheless, Mr. Fisher is creating his continuous fabric of man's mental history with considerable success and is bringing to bear upon it a powerful poetic imagination.

Nathan L. Rothman. SR. Oct. 2, 1948. p. 30

See *In Tragic Life, Children of God, Darkness and the Deep,* and *The Valley of Vision* (novels).

FITZGERALD, F. SCOTT (1896–1940)

The world of his subject matter is still too much within Fitzgerald himself for him to see it sustainedly against the universe. Its values obtain too strongly over him, and for that reason he cannot set them against those of high civilization and calmly judge them so. Hence, wanting philosophy, and a little overeager like the rest of America to arrive without having fully sweated, he falls victim to the favorite delusions of the society of which he is a part, tends to indulge it in its dreams of grandeur, and misses the fine flower of pathos. He seems to set out writing under the compulsion of vague feelings, and when his wonderfully revelatory passages appear, they come rather like volcanic islands thrown to the surface of a sea of fantasy. . . . He has seen his material from its own point of view, and he has seen it completely from without. But he has never done what the artist does: seen it simultaneously from within and without; and loved it and judged it too.

Paul Rosenfeld. Men Seen (Dial). 1925. pp. 222–3

I think of all you did
And all you might have done, before undone
By death, but for the undoing of despair. . . .
None had such promise then, and none
Your scapegrace wit or your disarming grace; . . .
And there was none when you were young, not one,
So prompt in the reflecting shield to trace
The glittering aspect of a Gorgon age.

John Peale Bishop. NR. March 3, 1941. p. 313

And now it seems almost too contrived that Scott should have chosen this year in which to die. For it is altogether fitting that Scott's career should begin where one world war ends and end where another begins. He spoke for a new generation that was shell-shocked without ever going to the front. He was one of our better historians of the no-man's-time between wars. He was not meant, temperamentally, to be a cynic, in the same way that beggars who must wander through the cold night were not born to freeze. But Scott made cynicism beautiful, po-etic, almost an ideal.

Budd Schulberg. NR. March 3, 1941. p. 312

His style keeps reminding you, particularly in his earlier stuff, of his own sense of the enormous beauty of which life, suitably ornamented, is capable; and at the same time of his judgement as to the worthless-ness of the ornament and the corruptibility of the beauty. The irony of regret lies deep in the individual contour of phrase and assortment of words; if the felicity of its expression is no doubt not to be explained, it is still, it seems to me, the key to the consistency of the peculiar Fitz-gerald tone.

Andrew Wanning. PR. Sept., 1943. pp. 547–8

Fitzgerald, as writer, wanted above all, he said, to achieve a wise and tragic sense of life. There are places enough in his books where he seems to do this beautifully and so it does not sound funny or whimsical when he jots down: "My sometimes reading my own books for advice. How much I know sometimes—how little at others." But the conclusion which forces itself out is that he was finally less wise than tragic. It is probably not possible for a writer to be as wise as he was tragic. Only saints come that size.

J. F. Powers. Com. Aug. 10, 1945. p. 410

There are novelists who find their material almost entirely outside themselves, and there are others who find it almost entirely within themselves. Scott Fitzgerald's talent lay in an unusual combination of these two modes. The basis of his work was self-scrutiny, but the actual product was an eloquent comment on the world. He was that rare kind of writer, a genuine microcosm with a real gift of objectivity. The com-bination explains his success. It is the reason that the force of his best work always transcends its subject matter.

Mark Schorer. YR. Autumn, 1945. p. 187

Fitzgerald's great accomplishment is to have realized in completely American terms the developed romantic attitude, in the end at least in the most responsible form in which all the romantic's sensuous and emo-tional responses are disciplined by his awareness of the goodness and evilness of human experience. He had a kind of instinct for the tragic view of life. . . . He had, moreover, with all its weakness and strength and in a time when the undivided understanding was rare, an almost exclusively creative kind of intelligence, the kind that understands things, not abstractly, but only concretely, in terms of people and situations and events.

Arthur Mizener. SwR. Jan., 1946. pp. 66–7

Horror and compassion were what Fitzgerald quickly came to feel for the segments of American society he chose to explore. These segments were as narrow as those claimed by Henry James and Mrs. Wharton, but they were equally representative. They exhibited the way of life deliberately adopted by those who were absolutely free to choose. And, while they represented the reality of only a very few, they also represented the aspiration of many. Almost from the first, Fitzgerald had been pretty aware that living wasn't the reckless, careless business these people thought. And, in even his earliest tales, unnoticed by most readers, there was always a touch of disaster.

Lloyd Morris. Postscript to Yesterday (Random).
1947. p. 151

The root of Fitzgerald's heroism is to be found, as it sometimes is in tragic heroes, in his power to love. Fitzgerald wrote much about love, he was preoccupied with it as between man and woman, but it is not merely where he is being explicit about it that his power appears. It is to be seen where eventually all a writer's qualities have their truest existence, in his style. Even in Fitzgerald's early, cruder books, or even in his commercial stories, and even when his style is careless, there is a tone and pitch to the sentences which suggest his warmth and tenderness, and, what is rare nowadays and not likely to be admired, his gentleness without softness.

Lionel Trilling. The Liberal Imagination (Viking).
1950. p. 244

The odd, the haunting thing about F. Scott Fitzgerald himself is how close he always was to being a "fringe writer." Or a marginal writer, perhaps, always treading the edge of the abyss, following a narrow ledge between achievement and disaster. And perhaps it was this artist's original confusion about fame (or popularity or cash) and art which led him so swiftly to catastrophe. In any case Fitzgerald's work is split down the middle, between the "objective" novels like The Great Gatsby, which lacked somewhere a solid center, and the "confessional" novels like The Beautiful and the Damned which lacked a solid form.

Maxwell Geismar. SR. April 26, 1958. p. 17

The Great Gatsby

The novel is one that refuses to be ignored. I finished it in an evening and had to. Its spirited tempo, the motley of its figures, the suppressed under-surface tension of its dramatic moments, held me to the page. It is not a book which might, under any interpretation, fall into the category of those doomed to investigation by a vice commission, and yet it is a shocking book—one that reveals incredible grossness, thoughtlessness, polite corruption, without leaving the reader with a sense of depression, without being insidiously provocative.

Walter Yust. *LR*. May 2, 1925. p. 3

Let us mean by (a masterpiece) a work of the literary imagination which is consistent, engaging, and dramatic, in exceptional degrees; which exhibits largely mastered a human subject of the first importance; and which seems in retrospect to illuminate the whole physical and spiritual situation of which it was, by the strange paturition of art, an accidental product. One easy test will be the rapidity with which, in the imagination of the good judge, other works of the period and kind will faint away under any suggested comparison with it. Now a small work may satisfy these demands as readily as a large one, and *The Great Gatsby* satisfies them, I believe, better than any other American work of fiction since *The Golden Bowl*.

John Berryman. *KR*. Winter, 1946. pp. 103–4

In contrast to the grace of Daisy's world Gatsby's fantastic mansion, his incredible car, his absurd clothes . . . all appear ludicrous. But in contrast to the corruption which underlies Daisy's world, Gatsby's essential incorruptibility is heroic. Because of the skilful construction of *The Great Gatsby* the eloquence and invention with which Fitzgerald gradually reveals this heroism are given a concentration and therefore a power he was never able to achieve again. The art of this book is nearly perfect.

Arthur Mizener. *The Far Side of Paradise*
(Houghton). 1951. p. 177

He is so familiar with the characters and their background, so absorbed in their fate, that the book has an admirable unity of texture; we can open it to any page and find another of the touches that illuminate the story. We end by feeling that *Gatsby* has a double virtue. Except for *The Sun Also Rises* it is the best picture we possess of the age in which it was written and it also achieves a sort of moral permanence. Fitzgerald's story of the innocent murdered suitor for wealth is a com-

pendious fable of the 1920's that will survive as a legend for other times.
Malcolm Cowley. Introduction to *The Great Gatsby*
(Scribner). 1953. p. xx

See *This Side of Paradise, The Beautiful and the Damned, The Great Gatsby,
Tender Is the Night,* and *The Last Tycoon* (novels); also *Tales of the Jazz
Age* (short stories).

FITZGERALD, ROBERT (1910–   )

Robert Fitzgerald is one of the many young poets who have learned
a great deal from the school of Eliot. His poetry is obviously influenced
in technique and in philosophy by those figures in poetry who since
1925 have dominated the scene. This is both good and bad. He writes
exceedingly well, with a fine command of form, of phrase and with a
careful selection of imagery. He understands the use of the heightened
statement. But he has not, as yet, a great deal to say that has not already
been said.

Eda Lou Walton. *NYHT*. Jan. 26, 1936. p. 4

"Craftsman" is by a shade too earthy a word for Mr. Fitzgerald; "artificer," which suggests the silver-smith, the lace-maker, and the illusion-
ist, is better. His first volume reveals a technique that is not equaled in
subtlety and polish by any other of our younger poets. The magic of
these poems springs from precision in the descriptive use of language,
brilliance and intricacy of metaphor, and a mastery of elaborate patterns of sound. . . . This poetry has both the merits and the limitations
of a mind that seems to be an isolated and a highly introspective one.

Philip Blair Rice. *Nation*. Feb. 19, 1936. pp. 227–8

A follower of Eliot and Pound, Mr. Fitzgerald is at present notable
chiefly for the intelligent use he has made of his models and for his
scrupulous craftsmanship. There is here little of the uncertainty or
crudity of statement common to first books of verse—even when most
derivative, these poems evince a skillful manipulation of cadence and
phrasing that must command our respect.

In absorbing the stylistic virtues of his masters, however, this poet
seems to have been obliged also to accept their philosophic and emotional attitudes. Loneliness, nostalgia, despair and bitter resignation are
ghosts Mr. Fitzgerald seems unable to rout from his pages.

T. C. Wilson. *NR*. June 10, 1936. p. 138

At every turn Fitzgerald gives the impression of knowing what he is doing and where he is going. He has devoted himself to a definite method with an admirable but perhaps needlessly exclusive single-mindedness. . . . Here is none of the nibbling at many uncongenial stylistic foods, none of the purblind groping that goes so far to damage most initial efforts. Here, instead, is the work of a man who is sensitively aware of his method and of his own temperament and who speaks with the tone of authority that is characteristic of the practiced.

C. A. Millspaugh. *Poetry*. June, 1936. p. 166

How good it is to read a book of poems not frantic with a message, not fancy with frilly fashions, using words gravely, for music's sake, or brightly, for that of image; literate without pedantry or affectation; sensitive without being neurotic or too full of nostalgia; moved but not excited; if not quite up to a pitch of high and joyous serenity, yet contemplative and calm, without complacence! How good, how rare; but these blessings are vouchsafed to us in Robert Fitzgerald's collection of poems, entitled *A Wreath for the Sea*.

Rolfe Humphries. *NR*. March 6, 1944. p. 324

Today we are more ready (than in 1936) to appreciate his remarkable modulation and poise. The absence of trickiness, fever and "drama" is a relief. The poems have color and vigor, a spry, confident intelligence constantly at work fusing picture, metaphor, emotion, reflection into deeply satisfying utterance. At times there is a touch of artificiality or super-refinement, but not often.

Kerker Quinn. *NYHT*. April 30, 1944. p. 10

Beyond any poet of my own generation, Fitzgerald seems to me to command the magic of evocative poetry; now in a phrase or line, now in a stanza, sometimes in an entire poem, scene and emotion are called up with a swiftness, an exactness, a poignancy so sharp and lovely and strong, that one is lifted past response to participation. . . . Fitzgerald seems to me a descendent of imagism, yet almost unrecognizably so since remarkably crossed with classicism. . . . It is the balance of emotion and intellect which so distinguishes these poems.

Winfield Townley Scott. *Poetry*. May, 1944. pp. 111–2

The poetry, the lyric gifts of Robert Fitzgerald are probably best known in the fine translations, with Dudley Fitts as his collaborator, of *Oedipus Rex* and *The Antigone* of Sophocles. As reinterpreters of Greek drama in terms of twentieth-century poetry and wit, Fitts and Fitzgerald made a rare, an almost priceless combination. The wit of Dudley

Fitts counter-balanced Fitzgerald's lyricism—and the brilliance of their collaboration has already withstood the test of time. . . . It would seem that for some undiscovered cause behind the poems Fitzgerald is at his best in his translations from the Greek. There is no question of his seriousness, or his fine temper; yet a paradox remains: he is most at liberty, and most profoundly his "own man" behind the mask of Sophocles.

Horace Gregory. NYT. Feb. 17, 1957. p. 5

Fitzgerald's material ranges through graceful lyrics to long, autobiographical recitatives, taking in translations from the Latin on the way. Among the most amiable qualities of Fitzgerald's writing are calm and lucidity. . . . Fitzgerald's lines are clean; and despite their often personal character, cooly objective. . . . Here is none of the pseudo-elegance of dependence on superficialities of form, like wearing borrowed clothes, but an authentic grace implicit in the nature of the poems. It is a genuine poetry developing from an inner organic need which, after all, is the hallmark of good things at all times. Its classic qualities geometrically balance form and content, the realities of existence with poetic imagination.

Byron Vazakis. SR. April 13, 1957. p. 20

While he has been little favored by the popular anthologists and curiously neglected by the critics, the new volume of selected poems by Robert Fitzgerald makes it clear that he has never belonged anywhere but in the first rank of contemporary poetry. There is so much to commend in his book, that, in fear of shading work that deserves only praise, one hesitates to make a preference or lay an emphasis. Here is a poet, rare in the era of the one-shot chance and the jazzy push to "make it," who begins in a spirit of apprenticeship to form, and to a twenty-five hundred year old heritage which, in his case, is assumed as lightly as though it were a personal endowment. Under hard taskmasters—the Greek and Latin poets and the English poets of the seventeenth century—he proceeds at his own pace toward refinement of technique and attitude the outcome of which must either be self-determination or self-exemption.

John Malcolm Brinnin. YR. Spring, 1957. p. 455

See In the Rose of Time (poetry); also translations of Sophocles' Oedipus Rex and The Antigone (with Dudley Fitts).

FLETCHER, JOHN GOULD   (1886–1950)

In the idea of a series of symphonies in which the sole unity was to be a harmony of color, in which form and emotional tone could follow the lead of coloristic word-associations no matter how far afield, Mr. Fletcher discovered an "Open Sesame!" so ideal to his nature, and so powerful as to not merely open the door, but at one stroke to lay bare his treasure entire. . . . The result was, naturally, the most brilliant and powerful work which Mr. Fletcher has yet given us—a poetry of detached waver and brilliance, a beautiful flowering of language alone, a parthenogenesis, as if language were fertilized by itself rather than by thought or feeling.

Conrad Aiken. Dial. Feb. 22, 1919. p. 190

He has yet to learn the restraint of the Greeks, whose exuberance was always proportioned and controlled. But since the first naïve blossoming of Imagism he has grown steadily. He has thought and felt deeply and sincerely. . . . Even when Mr. Fletcher describes what is dead or dying, he keeps his own vitality; even when he presents the grotesque, he sees it in relation to beauty. . . . He has not accepted the doom of an echoing discipleship. He realizes that to go alone is to arrive.

Marguerite Wilkinson. NYT. March 13, 1921. p. 6

What Mr. Fletcher has not is patent enough; he has no instinct for telling a story, he employs neither wit nor satire, he is dramatic only in the large. What he has are his own unique perceptions and impressions, great knowledge, love of colour, form, and significance, and understanding to interpret the forces behind the actions of men.

Amy Lowell. LR. April 16, 1921. p. 1

It is a question how far deliberation is creative. One rarely feels in Mr. Fletcher's art the true lyric rapture, the emotion that seizes the singer and carries him away. But one does feel something only a little less impassioned—the absorption of the contemplative spirit in its object, the self uplifted, and transcended into ecstasy. This latter mood or method, while more conscious than the other, while invoked rather than inspired, is but a little less authoritative in all the arts. It implies an imagination sensitive and worshipful, keen to accept and reflect all of this world's varied manifestations of beauty.

Harriet Monroe. Poetry. Jan., 1926. p. 206

His work would be important, if for no other reason, on account of the extension of rhythmical possibilities of the language and the peculiar care bestowed upon the richness and variety of verse texture. In the verse of both Swinburne and Hopkins there is a great intricacy and richness of texture, but a certain monotony. In his "highly-orchestrated and colored words" Fletcher has exploited surprise and resolution in a fashion not dissimilar to the verse of "Ash Wednesday". . . . And Fletcher was the first, or one of the first, to develop in English a type of imagery which Edith Sitwell has since erected into something like an oblique technique of vision.

Robert Penn Warren. Poetry. May, 1932. pp. 106–7

His imagery, curiously delicate, pale-tinted, often vague, is now accompanied by an echo of formal music, as though it were something made precious by distance and imperfect hearing. Like Shelley, like Whitman, his verse contains air-pockets: there is a frequent decline into soft, blurred phrasing, but at this point we must recall again that Fletcher's work also retains the imprint of the lesser Symbolists, whose poetry reveals the flaws as well as the sensibilities of their master, Paul Verlaine.

Horace Gregory. NYHT. Dec. 29, 1935. p. 6

There is nothing to burrow in to find and feel the meaning out. There is more meaning immediately, at first glance, than can ever be found on subsequent intimacy; that is because the general intent, not the specific datum, is viable. You do not anywhere weigh these poems: you run through them. If you run through a lot of them, you will get quite a lot of Mr. Fletcher himself, a generous, brilliant, prodigal lot. . . . Mr. Fletcher is a personal poet in that it is the prevalent sense of his personality that animates his poems and alone gives them form.

R. P. Blackmur. Poetry. March, 1936. pp. 346–7

I think it is fair to say that Mr. Fletcher's noticeable defects as a poet have been these: his sense of humor sometimes fails to come to his rescue, he often seems to lack a real centre, whether geographical or emotional or both, he has diffused his effort into much experimentation, and his disillusionment, though understandable, is tiresome because it seems to have no beginning, no middle and no end. But these faults are occasional, and even if he had not outgrown them he would still be one of the three or four greatest living American poets.

Baucum Fulkerson. SwR. July, 1938. pp. 286–7

The early work of John Gould Fletcher illustrates the weaknesses intrinsic in a strict application of the Imagist creed. The most memorable parts of his early poetry are the eleven color-symphonies in *Goblins and Pagodas*. These remarkable sequences of beautiful images are a practical demonstration of the inability of the human mind to live by images alone. It is not enough to string bright images on the thread of a single color; the reader demands the dynamic allurements of emotion or thought or action. But Imagism was merely a stage in Fletcher's complex development; in succeeding volumes, emotion and thought were not absent.

Fred B. Millett. Contemporary American Authors
(Harcourt). 1940. p. 142

Although he shared in many group enterprises, he was never truly of any group or coterie, never had the support of any claque or organization, cultural, commercial, or political, never was the darling of any publisher, never enjoyed a real popular success. He is an extraordinary, almost unique example of the isolated artist. Independent to the last degree, outspoken and frank, uncompromising where his principles were involved, yet wholly without guile, he won all that he won by the test of merit alone. . . . He gave his strength to the cause of art and to those who were enlisted in that cause. To Fletcher, this was a chivalric pursuit, the only chivalric pursuit left to modern man to cherish. For this, and for much more, he will be remembered and honored.

Donald Davidson. Poetry. Dec., 1950. pp. 160–1

When he is compared with his contemporaries, his stature is not lessened. His range is greater than that of Frost; he takes into account nations and not alone individuals. His literary background is as rich as that of Amy Lowell, and his sympathies are broader. He is as philosophic as Robinson, and though he lacks the Maine poet's sense of narrative, his verse has greater clarity and equal lyric dexterity. . . . Through his residence abroad, his Americanism was thrown into sharper relief. Because of his prolific output, his technical abilities, his breadth of sympathy and experience, he may eventually come to be considered the poet most representative of his generation.

Norreys Jephson O'Conor. SWR. Summer, 1953.
p. 243

See *Selected Poems* and *Burning Mountain* (poems).

FOWLIE, WALLACE   (1908–   )

There is something lofty, elegant and austere in the style Wallace Fowlie has made his own. Capable of tremendous absorption, condensation, sifting and synthesis, he imparts his profound erudition lightly. He is at home amidst the most antagonistic elements, directing his frail bark with the skill of a born mariner. . . . His certitude is never arrogant or pedantic. Woven into his skill, his grace, his dexterity there is always the element of risk, of daring, known alike by the acrobat and the poet. His moments of suspense are those same moments known to the performer and the man of solitude—when he takes flight with his whole being and emerges from the experience a new man, a man dedicated to still greater flights of daring, whether in the air or in the mind.

Henry Miller. Chimera. Autumn, 1944. pp. 47–8

Repeatedly he insists that "all great poetry is knowledge of the occult." But Dante's poem, to which greatness cannot be denied, offers the knowledge that comes of a journey through the moral universe, which is not quite the same thing as "knowledge of the occult," and Homer's epics, even when they take us in the realms of the dead, are wonderfully lacking in mystery, except that mystery to which all being is inescapably knit. There are more kinds of poetry than the kind that Rimbaud wrote, and to take cognizance of their value is not to destroy or impair his greatness. One wishes that Mr. Fowlie had shown his appreciation of this fact. . . . His hierophantic air detracts from his most acceptable pronouncements.

Babette Deutsch. NYHT. Oct. 27, 1946. p. 30

Two outstanding gifts distinguish Wallace Fowlie as a critic. First, in the Bergsonian sense he understands "duration," the curve which is both art and philosophy and which marks a configuration in time. . . . His second gift is his reduction of multiple details to key symbols and categories. Fowlie's successors will be his debtors. They will borrow and debate his key signs. . . . Maritain characterizes Thomas Aquinas as a theocentric humanist. Fowlie extends the terms to Maritain. It is also applicable to Fowlie himself. His range of vision saves him many stumbles.

Jeremy Ingalls. SR. Sept. 20, 1947. p. 34

The author fell in love with the French language at school. He mastered the language as well as any American ever has, wrote several books of criticism . . . and became one of the most inspired teachers in the country. . . . Some of the sketches (in *Pantomime*) . . . are drawn with a delicate pen and reveal a sensibility which rarely coexists with scholarly knowledge or survives an academic career. . . . Behind the delicate and discreet touch of the author one gradually perceives a tragic obsession with the problem of the artist in the world and especially in America.

Henri Peyre. *NYT*. June 3, 1951. p. 5

He considers himself a spectator, a person playing different parts throughout life. He feels himself strongly attracted to the clown, "unashamedly awkward, exalted by the noblest dreams, and always tricked in some way before touching his dream."

And his reminiscences, like his interpretation of the clown, completely lack irresponsible spontaneity, a healthy sense of malice, and a reassuring arrogance: traits indispensable to the true clown. If Mr. Fowlie were the least bit fairer or more poised and gentle, he would be dull.

Serge Hughes. *Com.* July 13, 1951. p. 338

Fowlie can write with equal ease about people and places and ideas, he can be intimate and general, poetic and grave: and yet one has the feeling that it is all of a piece. It might be added, too, that this writing is in the French tradition of the journal; and this is not at all surprising coming from one who has so thoroughly adopted his beloved country that his work has sometimes been more generally appreciated abroad than at home. . . . Fowlie—in making his own the great French tradition—has brought to his prose-writing something of the penetration and sweep which he had found in his French masters.

Robert Heywood. *Ren.* Autumn, 1951. p. 110

Before visiting a foreign city or foreign country, we often avoid dull Baedekers and consult friends who have been there. . . . In dealing with the foreign domain of contemporary French letters, Wallace Fowlie offers just such informal advice to the prospective traveler. His *causeries* are lively, personal, and stimulating. . . . If Mr. Fowlie frequently remains superficial and spends space in anecdotes, this is inherent in his conversational manner which is at the opposite extreme from the academic monograph.

Justin O'Brien. *NYT*. Nov. 17, 1957. p. 56

See *Clowns and Angels, Rimbaud, Age of Surrealism,* and *Mallarmé* (criticism); also *Pantomime* (autobiography).

FROST, ROBERT   (1875–1963)

Mr. Frost's book (*A Boy's Will*) is a little raw, and has in it a number of infelicities; underneath them it has the tang of the New Hampshire woods, and it has just this utter sincerity. It is not post-Miltonic or post-Swinburnian or post-Kiplonian. This man has the good sense to speak naturally and to paint the thing, the thing as he sees it. And to do this is a very different matter from gunning about for the circumplectious polysyllable. . . . One reads the book for the "tone," which is homely, by intent, and pleasing, never doubting that it comes direct from his own life, and that no two lives are the same.

Ezra Pound. Poetry. May, 1913. pp. 72–4

"Yankees is what they always were," sings Mr. Frost. His New England is the same old New England of the pilgrim fathers—a harsh, austere, velvet-coated-granite earth. . . . To present this earth, these people, the poet employs usually a blank verse as massive as they, as stript of all apologies and adornments. His poetry is sparing, austere, even a bit crabbed at times; but now and then it lights up with a sudden and intimate beauty; a beauty springing from life-long love and intuition.

Harriet Monroe. Poetry. Jan., 1917. pp. 203–4

The Frostian humour is peculiarly important for America. No other of our poets has shown a mood at once so individual and so neighborly. Moreover, the comparative thinness of American literature, its lack of full social body and flavor, is due to the extraordinary interval between our artistry and our national life. Our nation is widespreading and unformed, tangled in raw freedom and archaic conventionalities. Our poetry, now responding to and now reacting from our national life, tends to be rather banal, or rather esoteric—in either case, thin. Mr. Frost's work is notably free from that double and wasting tendency. His own ambiguity is vital: it comes from artistic integrity in rare union with fluent sympathy. His poetic humour is on the highway toward the richer American poetry of the future, if that is to be.

G. R. Elliott. VQR. July, 1925. pp. 214–5

He is a poet of the customary in man and nature, not the exploiter of the remarkably arresting and wonderful. Nor does his feeling for decorous proportion require argument beyond saying that he does not commit the mistake of the neo-classicists who have been properly accused by Professor Babbitt of confusing the language of the nobility with the nobility of language. Frost's people are humble, but they speak a language and utter feelings appropriate to them: they are restrained by conventions which are inherently worthy of respect, and the result is decorum in the true sense.

Gorham B. Munson. *Robert Frost* (Doran). 1927.
pp. 108–9

Robert Frost is as near English "as makes no difference." So English is he, in fact, that if one had to name the poet whose work is most like his, one would inevitably instance that most English of all English poets, the late Edward Thomas. The likeness between their poetry is quite extraordinary; and it is no wonder that Frost counted Thomas among his best friends and dedicated to his memory the *Selected Poems* which appeared in America some two years ago. Both loved the same things in life; and (by one of those miracles that unite men over seas and centuries) both found much the same way of expressing in poetry their delight.

C. Henry Warren. *BkmL*. Jan., 1931. p. 242

Upon the eve of Robinson's fame, some spoke of Frost in the same breath; and now Robinson is dead, Frost is our leading poet. His fame shall rest upon a firmer basis. Robinson, like MacLeish, can be judged not so much by his work as by why people like it, whereas with Frost the audience counts less than the good work. He has never been able to be as boring as Robinson's most boring; his best is beyond Robinson's best.

John Wheelwright. *Poetry*. Oct., 1936. pp. 45–6

Mr. Frost's poetry was first awarded critical approval because it was thought to be in revolt against something at a time when poetry must be in revolt. . . . Poetry must now not be anything like Imagism and must not even revolt, but must be the kind of poetry that Mr. Pound or, more purely and quintessentially, Mr. Eliot wrote. . . . It is quite true that Frost does not write like Eliot, Pound, Auden, or Spender. Fools may conclude that he is therefore a bad or an unimportant poet, but intelligent people look at the poetry he has written. When you do that, unless your nerves are sealed with wax, you immediately and overwhelmingly perceive that it is the work of an individual and integrated poet, a poet who is like no one else, a major poet not only in regard to this age but in regard to our whole literature, a great American poet.

Bernard De Voto. *SR*. Jan. 1, 1938. pp. 4, 14

If he does not strike far inward, neither does he follow the great American tradition (extending from Whitman through Dos Passos) of standing on a height to observe the panorama of nature and society. Let us say that he is a poet neither of the mountains nor of the woods, although he lives among both, but rather of the hill pastures, the intervales, the dooryard in autumn with the leaves swirling, the closed house shaking in the winter storms (and who else has described these scenes more accurately, in more lasting colors?). In the same way, he is not the poet of New England in its great days, or in its late-nineteenth-century decline (except in some of his earlier poems); he is rather a poet who celebrates the diminished but prosperous and self-respecting New England of the tourist home and the antique shop in the abandoned gristmill. And the praise heaped on Frost in recent years is somehow connected in one's mind with the search for ancestors and authentic old furniture.

Malcolm Cowley. *NR*. Sept. 18, 1944. pp. 346–7

Frost . . . may be described as a good poet in so far as he may be said to exist, but a dangerous influence in so far as his existence is incomplete. He is in no sense a great poet, but he is at times a distinguished and valuable poet. . . . He is the nearest thing we have to a poet laureate, a national poet; and this fact is evidence of the community of thought and feeling between Frost and a very large part of the American literary public. . . . The principles which have hampered Frost's development, the principles of Emersonian and Thoreauistic Romanticism, are the principles which he has openly espoused, and they are widespread in our culture. Until we abandon them in favor of better, we are unlikely to produce many poets greater than Frost.

Yvor Winters. *SwR*. Autumn, 1948. p. 596

Creatively, there are at least three Frosts—the actual artist, the legendary public character, posed and professed, and the latent, potential poet that might have been. . . . Frost himself all through his work, more or less, offers clues as to the kind of thing he might have done, the line of a frightful and fascinating interest that he almost dared to follow. The road not taken. . . . One wishes he had been a little less fearful of evil tidings, less scared of his own desert places. One wishes he had wasted less time being sane and wholesome, and gone really all out, farther than he did beyond the boundaries of New England's quaintness into its areas of violence, madness, murder, rape, and incest. . . . It is this night side of life and nature that Frost's art has, I think, scamped reporting, and not because he did not know it; no American poet, nor Poe in his stories, has come closer to Baudelaire.

Rolfe Humphries. *Nation*. July 23, 1949. pp. 92–3

The controlled development of his talent, and the finality and grace of statement in his best poems, are of moral no less than artistic value, exemplary for all who practice this art. . . . His vein of romantic triviality and perversity is not hard to distinguish, and it may be indulged.

That stern critic, Yvor Winters, considers Frost an Emersonian and therefore untrustworthy sage; but he would probably concede that on occasion Frost has had a harder edge and eye than Emerson, more humor, and more of the fear of God. It would be going too far to think of him as a religious poet, but his work tends towards wholeness, and thus towards a catholicism of the heart.

Robert Fitzgerald. NR. Aug. 8, 1949. p. 18

His cheerfulness is the direct opposite of Mr. Babbitt's or even of Mr. Pickwick's. It is a Greek cheerfulness. And the apparent blandness of the Greeks was, as Nietzsche showed in his *Birth of Tragedy* the result of their having looked so deeply into life's tragic meaning that they had to protect themselves by cultivating a deliberately superficial jolliness in order to bear the unbearable. Frost's benign calm, the comic mask of a whittling rustic, is designed for gazing—without dizziness—into a tragic abyss of desperation. . . . In the case of this great New England tragic poet, the desperation is no less real for being a quiet one, as befits a master of overwhelming understatements.

Peter Viereck. At. Oct., 1949. p. 68

Frost is that rare thing, a complete or representative poet, and not one of the brilliant partial poets who do justice, far more than justice, to a portion of reality, and leave the rest of things forlorn. When you know Frost's poems you know surprisingly well how the world seemed to one man, and what it was to seem that way: the great Gestalt that each of us makes from himself and all that isn't himself is very clear, very complicated, very contradictory in the poetry. The grimness and awfulness and untouchable sadness of things, both in the world and in the self, have justice done to them in the poems, but no more justice than is done to the tenderness and love and delight; and everything in between is represented somewhere too, some things willingly and often and other things only as much—in Marianne Moore's delicate phrase —"as one's natural reticence will allow."

Randall Jarrell. KR. Autumn, 1952. pp. 560–1

Mirth has always been attendant on his moral. He will not, for earnest half-truths, stay completely reverent. He has to keep the door ajar for the other half of the truth. Even in his caperings that irk the solemn

and embarrass the earnest, wisdom is usually implicit. Trifling is pertinent, though often it seems pesky, when dealing with inflated trifles.
And even with God, the fear of not pleasing whom is the beginning of
wisdom, Robert Frost sets his soft hat on one side of his head and looks
Him in the eye.

Sidney Cox. *A Swinger of Birches* (NYU). 1957.

pp. 2–3

See *Complete Poems.*

See Supplement at end of text for additional material.

GARLAND, HAMLIN (1860–1940)

In Hamlin Garland we meet an earnest man—one who believes in his
own work so thoroughly that he cannot fail to impress others. His
characters are real men and women. He has lived with them, toiled
with them, suffered and resented wrong with them. It would be impossible for him to write anything else than those dreary, hopeless
stories of life upon Western ranches.

Edwin Markham, 1893 in mss. quoted in *AL*. May,

1945. p. 153

Mr. Garland's books seem to me as indigenous in the true sense as any
our country has produced. They are western American, it is true, but
America is mostly western now. . . . I like being in the company
of men who believe so cordially in man's perfectibility; who believe
that wrongs can really be righted, and that even in our depraved conditions, which imply selfishness as the greatest personal good, teach
that generosity and honesty and duty are wiser and better things. I like
stirring adventure without bloodshed, as I find it so often in his pages; I
like love which is sweet and pure, chivalry which is in its senses, honor
for women which recognizes that while all women ultimately are good
and beautiful some women are better and beautifuller than others.

William Dean Howells. *NAR*. Oct., 1912. p. 526

American criticism, which always mistakes a poignant document for
esthetic form and organization, greeted these moral volumes as works
of art, and so Garland found himself an accepted artist. No more grotesque miscasting of a diligent and worthy man is recorded in profane
history. He had no more feeling for the intrinsic dignity of beauty, no
more comprehension of it as a thing in itself, than a policeman. He was
a moralist endeavoring ineptly to translate his messianic passion into

esthetic terms, and always failing. *A Son of the Middle Border,* undoubtedly the best of all his books, projects his failure brilliantly. It is, in substance, a document of considerable value—a naïve and often illuminating contribution to the history of American peasantry. It is, in form, a thoroughly third-rate piece of writing—amateurish, flat, banal, repellent. Garland got facts into it; he got a sort of evangelical passion. But he couldn't get any charm. He couldn't get any beauty.

H. L. Mencken. *Prejudices: First Series* (Knopf).
1919. pp. 134–5

Mr. Garland told his early stories in the strong, level, ominous language of a man who had observed much but chose to write little. Not his words, but the overtones vibrating through them cry out that the earth and the fruits of the earth belong to all men and yet a few of them have turned tiger or dog or jackal and snatched what is precious for themselves while their fellows starve and freeze. Insoluble as are the dilemmas he propounded and tense and unrelieved as his accusations were, he stood in his methods nearer, say, to the humane Millet than to the angry Zola.

Carl Van Doren. *Nation.* Nov. 23, 1921. p. 596

To us of the Middle Border the Hamlin Garland books are epic. Their unashamed provincialism is their glory. Here is the perfection of the willingly provincial—not on the defensive, not in any challenge, never by a breath apologetic. But completely articulate. . . . Not only to one who knows the land and the people, but to anyone who finds inestimably worth while an honest record of any section of national life —of world life—the Border books are almost intolerably precious. They are the record of that rarest of creatures, the provincial who goes into the world and makes it his own without seeking to "change front" —and then tells the whole progress with power.

Zona Gale. *YR.* July, 1922. p. 852

Hamlin Garland has been called a realist; he might with better reason be called a romanticist. Like lads romantic, he paused, tired to the bone from plowing, to read of dukes and duchesses and of people with charmed lives. . . . Although he pictures his boyhood as hard, still the book probably considered his masterpiece, *A Son of the Middle Border,* tells of a bright world vanished, a landscape so beautiful that it hurt him to have some parts of it revealed to aliens. At every step, in his description of the terrible toil of his people, the beauty of the natural scene remains.

Ruth M. Raw. *SwR.* April, 1928. p. 202

What, one wonders, would have happened if he had kept his loyalty to the humble, hapless farmers of (his) early stories? What if he had extended that loyalty so that it embraced urban as well as rural laborers? He might have avoided the whole period of unhappy experimentation in romanticism, and he might have ended, not as a complacent and garrulous chronicler of past glories, but as the great novelist he once gave promise of becoming.

Granville Hicks. *Nation*. Oct. 21, 1931. p. 436

Garland's "middle border" had been little treated in literature before, as deliberately chosen subject matter. Here it appeared, simple, humble —oh, so humble!—but with a certain candor, a direct view of life, that was to be its hallmark, and a new note in American culture. The country boy born in Wisconsin, who had declaimed the standard pieces of eloquence in a two-by-four academy in Iowa, who had seen what the pioneer was up against on the burning plains of Dakota, and who in good time had the chance to orient himself amidst the world's store of knowledge in Boston, swore to tell what he knew, without dressing or palliation. Young Garland in the first fresh tide of self-consciousness is almost the very type of intellectual young America, so eager, so serious, so full of his new truth.

Ferner Nuhn. *The Wind Blew from the East*
(Harper). 1942. p. 80

The movement, nurtured by Howells, found its major spokesman in Hamlin Garland. . . . When he came to Boston and found the example and personal encouragement of Howells, he wrote his only substantial work of fiction: *Main-Travelled Roads,* the book that almost singlehandedly exploded the myth of the West as the Garden of America, the happy lair of noble primitives surrounded by the soft beneficence of a friendly nature. It was a work, Howells saw immediately, which expressed the sad spirit of the rural Northwest from the experiences of one who had been part of what he saw. Following Howells' precepts, Garland wrote out of his own experience and about the region that he knew best, and for the particular brand of realism which dealt explicitly with the provincial environment out of which an author came, he coined the word "veritism."

Everett Carter. *Howells and the Age of Realism*
(Lippincott). 1954. pp. 120–1

See *Main-Travelled Roads* (short stories), *Rose of Dutcher's Coolly* (novel), and *A Son of the Middle Border* (autobiography).

GARRIGUE, JEAN (1914–   )

Using such symbols as the forest, the zoo, the statue and the centaur, Jean Garrigue explores the loves, loneliness and anxieties of modern man, crystallizing them in poems that have the sensuous immediacy of actual experience. The effect is achieved in an idiom that is always fresh and meaningful, capable of analysis and with a music that has just the right amount of dissonance to identify it as contemporary. Miss Garrigue has passion and intellect and fine technical equipment with which to give them embodiment.

Stephen Stepanchev. NYHT. Sept. 28, 1947. p. 18

Jean Garrigue is a very resourceful young American poet, and *The Ego and the Centaur* is a rich and full record—if rather too much so—of her self-exploration. It leaves little doubt of her ability to range in any one of several directions and to learn from a number of people without losing her own identity. But the general effect of this book is one's feeling that Miss Garrigue finds it easier to try out the same idea in a number of different poems, all of them more or less unfinished, than to stake all her possibilities in one definitive poem and let it stand. The poetry is all over the book instead of being a number of poems in the book and the ink sometimes seems to run.

Henry Rago. Com. Jan. 16, 1948. p. 353

Miss Garrigue's first book of poems is notable for two qualities: an acute introspective sensibility, at its best in such delicate probings of mood and motive as "Letter for Vadya," and an unusual accuracy of physical observation, especially when she is dealing with animals. The verse is relentlessly honest, stripped of tricks—too stripped, perhaps—, alive at every point. . . . Unhappily . . . the greater part of the poems, for all their vitality, are marred by a sloppiness that seems to be the result less of obtuseness than of impatience. There is *brio* enough here, and to spare; but there is a tendency to sag, to go unkempt.

Dudley Fitts. SR. June 19, 1948. p. 26

This poet, whose first poems ten years ago were in a metaphysical-imagist vein and showed the influence of John Crowe Ransom and Marianne Moore, now steps forward with a very personal style of her own. When this style . . . is used to convey a lyrical ecstasy or a sensory nostalgia, it is effective. When it is used for straight description, it can be magnificent. . . . Unfortunately Miss Garrigue is not partial to

. . . simplicity. Like Ransom, but without that poet's saving wit, she prefers the oblique, metaphysical, verbally affected and syntactically confused.

Selden Rodman. NYT. Nov. 8, 1953. p. 30

It takes but a few lines of Jean Garrigue's second volume (<i>The Monument Rose</i>) to hear a really significant voice sing out with deep internal drama and verbal excitement. . . . Being inventive, sensual, and lyrical—word-inventive—her language is often just as startling as her imagery and her original phrasing, the essential elements if poetry is to remain alive and not become just a sentimental sewer. Even originality is not enough if it is merely sensational or extravagant; but when originality is allied to a critical intelligence and is embedded in the systematic values of poetry, then poetry renews itself and the reader, adding another page to literature's uncertain history. Jean Garrigue has done that, if modestly, with a dignified attitude and an exciting air.

Harry Roskolenko. Poetry. Dec., 1953. pp. 177–9

Her poetry is at once lush and cryptic, extravagant and concise. It is elaborate with color and imagery, rich with alliteration and a frequent Elizabethan elegance. . . . There are occasional overtones of Hopkins and Dylan Thomas in her work, but she is undeniably original and individual as an artist and a craftsman in complete command of her medium. . . . The poetic intensity, the wealth of light and color, and the real distinction of Miss Garrigue's work cannot fail to impress the perceptive and careful reader.

Sara Henderson Hay. SR. Jan. 16, 1954. pp. 19–20

The world of <i>The Monument Rose</i> is romantic in its richness and strangeness and curious elaboration of detail. . . . Most of all, though, and for all the elegance in particular words, the character of this poetry is just where it belongs, in the play between rhythms and syntax, the wave-motion so to say, which makes the identity of passage after passage and makes all one and most fine. This thing, the weaving and stitching, is the most neglected part of poetry at present, but attention to it is a mark of mastery, and the gift for it, the melodiousness which is, as Coleridge claimed, the final and distinguishing sign of a poet, is something Miss Garrigue wonderfully has.

Howard Nemerov. SwR. Spring, 1954. p. 317

See <i>The Ego and the Centaur</i> and <i>The Monument Rose</i> (poetry).

GINSBERG, ALLEN (1926–   )

This poetry is not "rational discourse" such as we find in almost all other American literature of dissidence. Nor is it that flaccid sort of negation, too easy and too glib, that so often reduces the charge in the writing of Patchen and others. . . . It is the fury of the soul-injured lover or child, and its dynamic lies in the way it spews up undigested the elementary need for freedom of sympathy, for generous exploration of thought, for the open response of man to man so long repressed by the smooth machinery of intellectual distortion. . . . Despite his many faults and despite the danger that he will screech himself mute any moment now, is he the real thing?

What we can say, I think, is that he has brought a terrible psychological reality to the surface with enough originality to blast American verse a hair's-breadth forward in the process.

M. L. Rosenthal. *Nation*. Feb. 23, 1957. p. 162

Among the literary radicals of the West Coast, Allen Ginsberg and his poem "Howl" have acquired a succès d'estime remarkable in both its proportions and its manifestations. The poem so clearly intends to document—and celebrate—several types of modern social and psychological ills that the question of its literary merit seems to me almost irrelevant. . . . Walt Whitman is the poet's chief master. . . . But the virulence of Ginsberg's revolt against modern society comes—if these things really have any literary antecedents—from the verse of the Great Depression: Fearing, Patchen, Richard Wright, et al. . . . It's a very shaggy book, the shaggiest I've ever seen.

Frederick Eckman. *Poetry*. Sept., 1957. pp. 391–3

Ginsberg gets away with it because he is frankly justifying himself (in "Howl"), because his assault on America is a personal cry that rings true, because his hysteria is tempered with humor, and because the dope-addicts, perverts, and maniacs he celebrates are not finally glamorized. . . . (But) no new territory is being staked out by these writers—Ginsberg's return to Whitman is a shift in fashion, not the mark of a revolutionary sensibility. . . . The fact is that it takes more than a feeling of "disengagement" from the contemporary world to provide the materials for a genuine avant garde revolt.

Norman Podhoretz. *NR*. Sept. 16, 1957. p. 20

He does have a rhythm, and he does have a feeling for the value of words; but despite these great advantages he still hasn't managed to write a poem which can stand up to any but an excessively sympathetic examination. . . . The poem "Howl" . . . has won more notice than any other work of the "San Francisco school." . . . The poem tries to be what the title proclaims: a howl of rage and defiance, in long Whitmanesque lines. . . . Apparently for many readers it is Mr. Ginsberg's very frenzy and incoherence that are to be valued, as a defiant assertion of the individual spirit in an ugly time. . . . I must say, so far from finding "Howl" defiant and anarchic . . . , "Howl" struck me as being pathetically dependent on a concurrent movement of literary opinion, on the *Zeitgeist* as familiar ally, on the anxious support of those who make it their business to jump as the "generation" jumps.

Dan Jacobson. *Cmty.* Dec., 1957. pp. 476–7

The thing that strikes me most forcefully about "Howl" is that it is worded in what appears to be a contemporary tradition, one that did not cause me any particular consternation in reading, a tradition most evident in the modern period following the First World War, a tradition that resembles European literary tradition and is defined as "Dada," a kind of art of furious negation. By the intensity of its negation it seems to be both resurrective in quality and ultimately a sort of paean of possible hope. I wouldn't say that the chances for redemption or chances for salvation in a work of this kind are deemed to be very extensively possible but, nonetheless, the vision is not a total vision of despair.

Herbert Blau. *ER.* Vol. 1, no. 4. pp. 154–5

The simplest term for such writing is prophetic, it is easier to call it that than anything else because we have a large body of prophetic writing to refer to. There are the prophets of the Bible, which it greatly resembles in purpose and in language and in subject matter. . . . The theme is the denunciation of evil and a pointing of the way out, so to speak. . . . And "Footnote to Howl," of course, is Biblical in reference. The reference is to the Benedicite, which says over and over again, "Blessed is the fire, Blessed is the light, Blessed are the trees, and Blessed is this and Blessed is that," and he is saying, "Everything that is human is Holy to me," and that the possibility of salvation in this terrible situation which he reveals is through love and through the love of everything Holy in man.

Kenneth Rexroth. *ER.* Vol. 1, no. 4. p. 154

See *Howl and Other Poems.*

GLASGOW, ELLEN   (1874–1945)

There is much of Mercutio about Miss Glasgow herself. She is gallant and she is a philosopher. She is brave. . . . There is moreover a gaiety, a wit, a joy of living, along with the relentless iron hand in the velvet glove. . . . ¯She possesses a passionate pervasive love of life but she shears away with that sharp rapier of her irony the false traditions, amiable humbugs, even the smaller tricks of behavior and opinion which obscure what is fine and vigorous.

Dorothea Lawrance Mann. Bkm. Nov., 1926. p. 265

In all her novels one is aware of an attendant keenly observant ethical spirit. Her morality is her own, tolerant of nature, intolerant of cant and humbug, but her consciousness is as unmistakably ethical as that of George Eliot. She likes to see the wheel come full circle. She builds her stories with a view to showing Time bringing in revenges.

Her style is firm, lucid, and if I were not afraid of giving offense, I should add, it has a masculine rhythm. It has wit and beauty. At its best it has a proud and impressive reserve, and goes over depths with the tension and moving stillness of deep rivers.

Stuart Sherman. Critical Woodcuts (Scribner). 1926.
pp. 79–80

In reality, Ellen Glasgow has invariably been as much preoccupied with form as with subject matter; almost instinctively, when she proclaimed a discordant truth she stated it in sonorous prose, a prose that somehow disguised the fact that it was harsh and anathema. In her brilliantly epigrammatic style many of her most acidulous commentaries have had a universal rather than a personal challenge. Whether she meant it to be so or not, the way she expressed a thing, rather than the thing itself, is what impressed her audience and, however inverted or contraverted, this is a Victorianism certainly.

Sara Haardt. Bkm. April, 1929. p. 134

Ellen Glasgow has shown a remarkable receptivity to new ideas. She began to publish when the idealistic treatment of the romantic material of Southern life had reached its climax of popular appeal. She did not break sharply with the traditions of that school, but she took the best lessons it had to teach, and turned them into a new achievement. Through her the Puritan strain, always present in Virginia, which had animated Bacon's rebellion in the seventeenth century and had reached

its height in the iron tenacity of Stonewall Jackson, came into its proper
place in the panorama of fiction.

Arthur Hobson Quinn. *American Fiction* (Appleton-
Century). 1936. p. 681

When others have cheapened their manners, their speech, and their
style to fit ears accustomed to be flattered by such accomodations, she
has preserved her dignity and her charm without becoming quaint. At a
time when the Southern Lady is reverenced as a tradition or exploded
as a myth, Ellen Glasgow, as a novelist no less than as a person, is an
authentic example of her at her best—vivid, witty, sharp when necessary and, (lovely trait of womanhood!) on occasion, without necessity,
tender.

James Southall Wilson. *VQR*. Jan., 1939. p. 124

Miss Glasgow has refused to consider herself less than an artist. She
has not written of Virginian life but of human life in Virginia. She has
taken two or three years to perfect a book, not because she wanted to
be sociologically accurate but because she wanted to be artistically mature, and this sense of pace and dignity, this tacit assumption that the
novel is a major work of art—these are the qualities she has brought to
her interpretation of immediate environment.

Howard Mumford Jones. *SR*. Oct. 16, 1943. p. 20

Her face was like a camellia, one of those tight-petaled camellias of
old Southern gardens, that risk and often defy the February frosts, and
retain a virginal freshness even when time has touched them. . . .
She talked constantly of the technique of writing, but always it was of
her own, except her brilliant sallies at successful contemporaries whom
she regarded as incompetent artists or able charlatans. . . . It was not
vanity which made her talk of her own books in that meticulous voice
of the deaf, with its precise articulation and its slight crackle. It was
her desire that her total purpose should not be missed.

Henry Seidel Canby. *SR*. Dec. 22, 1945. p. 13

You have in the work of Ellen Glasgow something very like a complete
social chronicle of the Piedmont section of the State of Virginia since
the War Between the States, as this chronicle has been put together by
a witty and observant woman, a poet in grain, who was not at any moment in her writing quite devoid of malice, nor of an all-understanding
lyric tenderness either; and who was not ever, through any tiniest half-
moment, deficient in craftsmanship. You have likewise that which, to

my first finding, seemed a complete natural history of the Virginian gentlewoman throughout the last half-century, with all the attendant features of her lair and of her general habitat most accurately rendered. But reflection shows the matter to be a great deal more pregnant than I thought at outset; for the main theme of Ellen Glasgow, the theme which in her writing figures always, if not exactly as a Frankenstein's monster, at least as a sort of ideational King Charles's head, I now take to be The Tragedy of Everywoman, As It Was Lately Enacted in the Commonwealth of Virginia.

James Branch Cabell. *Let Me Lie* (Farrar, Straus).
1947. p. 243

In the end . . . Miss Glasgow found strength where before she had seen only weakness, inspiration where before she had detected insincerity. She had come out of the deep past, and it was to the deep past that she returned, in the end, for she learned that the past had not only adorned a tale but pointed a moral. She who had been the historian of change became its elegist, her novels exercises not in irony, but in nostalgia.

Henry Steele Commager. *NC*. Nov., 1949. pp. 315–16

In her comedies as in her serious novels, Ellen Glasgow significantly advances but a single thesis, that man is the enemy of woman. The comedies rout him with ridicule and edged contempt; the serious novels display his dead body as proof of love's futility. . . . In no major work from the publication of *Virginia* which may be reckoned as the author's first demonstration of mature powers, does a man of questing virility appear but to dupe or otherwise humilate a woman spiritually his superior. . . . Nor is one villainous hero to be confused with the other; such are the author's gifts that each betrayer remains sharply individualized. By multiplying particularized instances, Miss Glasgow seeks to establish the general truth of her proposition, that men, until winnowed by the years, bring only rue in their wake. Rue, that is, to women; for Ellen Glasgow presents masculine character primarily as it subserves feminine.

Josephine Lurie Jessup. *The Faith of Our Feminists*
(H. Smith). 1950. pp. 52–3

Ellen Glasgow was a literary rebel in the first half of her career, a literary ancestor in the second half, but her work has never had the full recognition it deserves. One of our top three women writers, she has been eclipsed by the glow of Willa Cather's lovely fairy tales and by the cool glitter of Edith Wharton's social snobbery. Yet as a literary figure Miss

Glasgow was superior to these ladies in many respects, and her best novels are of equal interest and importance with theirs.

Maxwell Geismar. *Nation*. Nov. 13, 1954. p. 425

See *Barren Ground, The Romantic Comedians,* and *Vein of Iron* (novels); also *A Certain Measure* (criticism) and *The Woman Within* (autobiography).

GOLD, HERBERT (1924–   )

If it is true that Mr. Gold's novel (*Birth of a Hero*) has a special importance because it represents a turning point in the intellectual's attitude toward the middle class . . . , it must not be overlooked that Mr. Gold writes with charm and talent. He understands the phenomena at which he is smiling, and he communicates adroitly his delighted recognition of the significance of such neglected rituals as the office party and the commuter's daily journey. If we are really at the beginning of a new era of conservatism, we can only hope that the writers who will choose to celebrate the heroic virtues of the middle-aged and the comfortably placed will be able to do so with at least a portion of Mr. Gold's benevolent wit, radical perception, and intellectual vigor.

Harvey Swados. *Nation*. Oct. 6, 1951. p. 284

Like Flaubert, Herbert Gold hangs his effects on a faithful reporting of sensations recorded by the five senses. . . . Scenes are strung together necklace-style and motivation is not always clear or credible. Characters have labels and are stuck to them. It's a cerebral performance with a tangle of long, long thoughts, most of them entertainingly presented in colorful, runaway language. A high fidelity ear and eye are at work here.

James Kelly. *NYT*. Feb. 14, 1954. p. 5

The Man Who Was Not With It is itself a carnival, bringing the reader into a strange and fascinating tent. The novel is a spectacular linguistic performance. Herbert Gold's writing is sometimes flashy and full of sideshow guile, but much more often his story is beautifully told, with tough and tender humor. . . . Herbert Gold is no longer a novelist to be watched in the future—his performance is here, and well worth watching right now.

Alan Harrington. *Nation*. June 23, 1956. p. 535

Herbert Gold's *The Man Who Was Not With It* belongs to (a) tradition, that of the picaresque, which Mr. Gold has fitted with the existentialist idea of the tragedy of "engagement," in a novel that is exciting both as language and as figuration of destiny. . . . Mr. Gold's story has as its human substance the awful risk inherent in adult faith between men. The picaresque design of the book lies in the adventures of a kid who travels with a carnival. . . . To be "with it and of it" is the carnival lingo for the ultimate loyalty to the strange, spiritually islanded life of the carnival.

Dorothy Van Ghent. YR. Summer, 1956. p. 632

Gold's intelligence is the brightness of skill, exuberance, and his prized risk-taking. It is the sheer vitality of a talented writer. . . . Herbert Gold . . . seems to have found, evolved, or perhaps been born with, a Baroque style that is exciting and controlled; but he has yet to find a theme thick and heavy enough with significance or rooted deeply enough in the universals of "human nature" . . . to be worthy of this style. . . . The only resonance is that of the word-music; and though rich and various, it sometimes seems like pleasant ornamentation, or fireworks and exhibitionism, and occasionally it reminds me of Parmigianino's mannerist portraits of the long-necked Madonna: exceedingly beautiful, except that a little of such beauty goes a long way.

Melvin Seiden. Nation. April 25, 1959. pp. 389–90

There are no writers under forty—and there are few of any age—for whom I have more admiration than I have for Herbert Gold. His first novel, *Birth of a Hero,* published while he was still in his twenties, was an extraordinarily perceptive study of love in middle age. He followed it with a dramatic and vivid novel of city life and race conflict, *The Prospect Before Us,* and then came his novel of carnival ways, the drug habit, and young love, rich in carnie talk, *The Man Who Was Not With It.* He has also written several first-rate short stories and some vigorous criticism. In less than ten years he has produced a body of work that establishes him as a central figure in today's literature.

Granville Hicks. SR. April 25, 1959. p. 12

See *Birth of a Hero, The Prospect Before Us, The Man Who Was Not With It,* and *The Optimist* (novels)

See Supplement at end of text for additional material.

GOYEN, WILLIAM (1918–   )

Here are the most extravagant feelings, the most absurd recklessness of revealment, at times there is real danger of the fatal drop into over-

pathos, over-saying: a boyish tearfulness over some very dubious at-
tachments. . . . To balance this fault, the writing as a whole is disciplined on a high plane, and there are long passages of the best writing,
the fullest and richest and most expressive, that I have read in a very
long time—complex in form, and beautifully organized, shapely as a
good tree, as alive and as substantial.

Katherine Anne Porter. *NYT*. Aug. 20, 1950. p. 17

William Goyen's prose is as sonorously emotional and lushly spangled
as the previous generation's was muted and bare. *The House of
Breath* is in effect a prose poem, an incantation which conjures up the
narrator's small home town in Texas . . . in the years of his childhood and adolescence. . . . The novel abounds in passages that have
a poetically original sheen; in strong feeling sensitively recaptured. But
Goyen has neglected to pay his dues to the sage dictum of Buffon which
included sound thinking in the trinity of values essential to good writing.

Charles J. Rolo. *At.* Sept., 1950. p. 81

A sober and often inspired effort to force prose into a new rhapsodic
form and the use of sharp, fresh imagery are the most salient characteristics of this first book by a young Texan writer. . . . Some of the influences which preponderate as yet in Mr. Goyen's mannered, highly
individual, writing seem to be Whitman as well as Joyce with Melville
more dominant than either. . . . It is in writing about the external
world of nature, rather than about people, that he most succeeds in the
difficult, highly poetic prose style which he has used here.

Iris Barry. *NYHT*. Sept. 10, 1950. p. 5

There is about these people something of the Greek: fresh, unspoiled,
immemorial, a little larger than life. Each, also, is buttressed by a world
of symbolism, some as ancient as the earliest myths. . . . Yet it is not
the Greek but the Christian concept that finally compels them. . . .
For its brilliant evocation of a world, for its poetic and disciplined use
of language, and for its subtle discernment of character and purpose,
The House of Breath stands a major achievement and William Goyen a
young writer to be reckoned with.

Ruth Chapin. *CSM*. Sept. 16, 1950. p. 11

William Goyen set out to re-create a sensuous and physical world of
memory in his first novel, and he has done so. Narrative is not so important to this re-creation, but texture is. So are rhythm, tone, the right
and evocative detail. . . . It is the tone of the approach to memory

that matters, and this tone, a semi-Biblical, semi-folksy rant of grieving, sometimes achieving a pathos just short of theatrical, is made to rise at times to heights operatic, you might say, in rhetorical effect. . . . Prose wants to do here what poetry does. And it succeeds.

Jean Garrigue. NR. Dec. 25, 1950. p. 20

He has the poet's ear for the spoken word and he knows how to use the regionalist's best tools. All of these tales (in *Ghost and Flesh*) but one are set in the dusty country of east Texas, and even in that single exception a young man in a San Francisco hotel room recalls those landscapes, though he has abandoned them. Mr. Goyen knows how these people blending South and West in their inheritance, talk and move and how they dress and what they raise in their gardens and what churches they go to, and his writing takes on strength and richness from that familiarity. He can tell stories in dialect that is fresh and unforced; and he has noted the figures of speech used by country people.

Sylvia Stallings. NYHT. Feb. 10, 1952. p. 5

William Goyen's short stories exhibit the same qualities which made his recent literary debut an exciting one: intelligence and sensitivity, an intense and sometimes florid imagination, and an extreme preoccupation with form and language. At their best these stories possess a magical quality rare in contemporary American fiction which marks this Texan as one of the strikingly talented young writers of the last decade. . . . The author examines the problem of the nature of reality in terms of a never-ceasing conflict between the present and the past, between the visible and the invisible.

William Peden. SR. March 22, 1952. p. 17

It would be foolish to venture an analysis of this novel (*The House of Breath*). One does not analyse a poem. And even in prose, one does not analyse a confession or a prayer. There is all that in *The House of Breath,* and more besides. If it were necessary to complain of the book, it would have to be of its excess of riches which often renders it indigestible to a Cartesian spirit. Is this a sin of youth—or of adolescence— which will pass with maturity? . . . The young "hopefuls" of American literature have given us so far a reflection of their anguish in a world where they feel lost, alone, orphans without a possible refuge, without a "mother." But, if their work is to last, it seems they must pass through this stage of pure destruction. What is necessary for them is to reach the age of reason.

Raymond Las Vergnas (trans. by Editor). Hommes
et Mondes. Feb., 1955. p. 453

In a captivating fantasy called *In a Farther Country* William Goyen continues to fabricate the fragile world of super-reality which characterized *The House of Breath* . . . and . . . *Ghost and Flesh*. . . . Events in the story grow not out of rationally plausible circumstance, but occur simply because the author exercising the fiat of a fairy tale, waves his wand and bids them happen. All seem on the verge of vanishing momentarily if removed from the sustaining medium of Mr. Goyen's evocative prose style. That they do not vanish until the end, when the dream is broken, attests to the efficacy of that style and to the talent of a strangely gifted writer.

Jerome Stone. *SR*. July 23, 1955. p. 27

Evidently the desire to say great things has caused Mr. Goyen to discard the conventions of fiction. He discards even that rule which all the great innovators, Joyce and all the rest, respected: the message must be embodied in a story. Mr. Goyen has decided that the story is to be embedded in a message and he devotes his formidable gifts—his strength of imagery, his rhythmic sense, his glyptic phrasemaking, the intelligence that he showed in *Ghost and Flesh* and *House of Breath*—to making his message passionate, copious, and sibylline.

Donald Barr. *NYT*. July 24, 1955. p. 17

See *The House of Breath* and *In a Farther Country* (novels); also *Ghost and Flesh* (short stories).

GREGORY, HORACE (1898–   )

Chelsea Rooming House is an extraordinary book; a fresh poetic vision and an individual talent here are loosed to express a great fear and a deep tenderness concerning human life. Mr. Gregory as poet interprets unintellectual humanity hurling itself at doors to which it has no key. . . . Although Mr. Gregory's poems spring from a strong feeling about social conditions they never become propaganda. The poet is far too intellectual to allow that. Instinctively and rightly he connects the past with the future, throwing a vision of life backwards and forwards along its right plane. The pattern of life is different in each age, but the feeling for life is universal.

Eda Lou Walton. *Nation*. Dec. 17, 1930. p. 680

Gregory is grouped among writers of social revolution, where he is remarkable for adding the authority of a poet to the authorization, whatever it may be worth, of official orthodoxy. But this destination is incidental to his fundamental qualities. The sincerity and art that have gone into his books should be major assets to any cause, but they are too substantial to need or allow partisan coercion. What is important is that their authority exists before and after the specific issues of subject matter are faced. This is equivalent to saying that Gregory, as a poet, dignifies his beliefs by bringing to them the highest integrity of which the intelligence, socially or practically directed, is capable.

Morton D. Zabel. *NR*. June 19, 1935. p. 173

The agrarian pattern is that of the "Eternal Now." It brings the past to us, not as if of antiquarian interest, as a collection of curios in a museum, but as another version of the present. The events of today (and Gregory can note them as concretely as does any barrister's indictment before a Grand Jury) are at the same time fused with a sense of the long perspective, whereby the poet is *close-to* and *remote-from* simultaneously. In his case, a specific intimate event, existing in its particularities but once, is reported with an overtone of migrations and historic sweeps. The poet observes through a screen of myth, so that what he sees bears the markings of this screen upon it.

Kenneth Burke. *Poetry*. July, 1935. pp. 228–9

His technique is particularly interesting. Like Eliot, he is fond of the dissonant chord and unresolved suspense; like Hart Crane, he crowds image upon image to increase sensation and suggest new perspective. But he does not share Eliot's disillusion nor Crane's disorganization. There is constant control as well as positive belief in Gregory's poetry; his faith is a social faith. His method and manner created a new tone, half-ruminative, half-lyrical, superficially descriptive yet somehow integrated.

Louis Untermeyer. *SR*. April 12, 1941. p. 15

By temperament Gregory seems happiest as an elegiac poet, celebrating, with his grieving rhetoric, the lost places, the lost persons, the lost world of his inheritance. . . . Gregory is not and never will be a casual writer. To be sure, he has a strong sense of the contemporary, in both its historic and its idiomatic aspects, but to use the contemporary breezily, *au naturel,* is not his talent: he must work on it imaginatively and break it down into the deep, grave rhythms of his reflective spirit.

Stanley J. Kunitz. *Poetry*. June, 1941. p. 155

Gregory is no less a craftsman than MacNeice. But his material is so much more substantial and it is given such a solid poetic integration that the mechanics of his writing are less assertive than those of MacNeice. Gregory is primarily a dramatic poet with the command of lyric which, in our poetic tradition, has always accompanied true dramatic expression. . . . Human experience is his material, but he does not patronize or poeticize it. He simply extracts its essence, adding nothing which might artificially dignify it. The inherent dignity of the essential is the beauty of Gregory's poetry.

John L. Sweeney. *YR*. Summer, 1941. p. 821

It is Mr. Gregory's intention, and high distinction, to be conscientiously contemporary, deriving his imagery from what is most recent in our surroundings. . . . Yet his effectiveness as a poet of the present depends, paradoxically, on an allegiance felt rather than declared to the past. . . . Other poets who have shared this doubleness of vision have often yielded to the urge to use it with satiric malice. Mr. Gregory is free of that. One feels behind his sharp awareness of what is about him a depth of terror and a depth of tenderness for the human lot.

George F. Whicher. *NYHT*. May 4, 1941. p. 2

Mr. Gregory is a stubborn formalist. His project is before him and he sticks to it; he foresees and numbers the details that must be attended to in its careful execution, and like a good general he always has a firm thumb on the map. This makes, let us admit it, for a certain rigidity. It is a little as if the resultant poetry were too much done to formula. The right ingredients are there—imagination, tenderness, humor, irony, the pathos of distance, the pathos of the contemporary-ephemeral, the convenient stairway that always leads from the finite to the infinite—but one has the feeling that Mr. Gregory has somehow got them there by a clever and cultivated sort of sleight-of-mind, a trained and studious dexterity.

Conrad Aiken. *NR*. Sept. 15, 1941. p. 346

Most of Mr. Gregory's poems do not have regular meters, line lengths, or stanzas; any poet knows how hard it is really to organize a poem without these. But his feeling for speech and tone, his real selectivity, . . . do manage to hold his poems together surprisingly often. . . . He belongs more to the conversational-colloquial half of modern poetry than to the rhetorical-obscure half; his textures often have the particularity and precision and bareness of successful prose. He is an accomplished, sensitive, and complicated poet; honest, too: he never fools his readers without fooling himself.

Randall Jarrell. *Nation*. Sept. 20, 1941. p. 258

We who have known Gregory's poetry over the last ten years know that a great deal of its force and depth have arisen from an acute perception of the past as being still alive and working in the present day. Gregory is inferior to no poet living; but he has learned to trace out, carefully, just where in the past, both of the strains that made up our present actually got started.

John Gould Fletcher. NYT. April 16, 1944. p. 3

It may seem a long jump from an early poem called "Salvos for Randolph Bourne" to a late one called "Homage to Circe," but if you examine them side by side you find a similar delicacy of texture, a similar unerringness of choice of detail, and in the later poem a further growth of an ear so intricately modulated it has few rivals this side of Eliot.

Without brains, such facility could be mere dulcet tone. It never is. . . . Horace Gregory has always moved the mind. Now he has ways of twitching at one's nerves also, and latterly, at his best, moving the heart.

Winfield Townley Scott. NYHT. Aug. 19, 1951. p. 3

Each of the poems of this collection (<i>Selected Poems</i>) represents a degree of formal attainment, of formal success.

Yet Mr. Gregory is striving for much more. The myths he evokes are in a constant state of flux and as a poet he seeks to integrate himself therein. . . . Each of the poems is some form of question on the essential mystery of man, and some form of lament over the poet's consciousness engaged in a life which limits the consciousness. Mr. Gregory revindicates one of the oldest functions of poetry, envisaged as the reservoir of human unhappiness, and also as the means, the noblest means perhaps, to transcend the unhappiness, to make of it a way of contemplation, a way of understanding.

Wallace Fowlie. NYT. Aug. 19, 1951. pp. 5, 20

See <i>Selected Poems</i>.

GUTHRIE, A. B., JR. (1901–   )

We shall never know exactly how the mountain men talked; they had no literal reporters. We shall never know as much as we should like about their psychology; they told little of themselves and wrote almost nothing. We do not even know as much as we should just how they dressed, fed. . . . All this has to be patiently reconstructed with historical research, first-hand knowledge of the Western scene, and above all imagination. Mr. Guthrie has not written a great novel (in <i>The Big Sky</i>), but he used imagination and study to do an impressive work of reconstruction.

Allan Nevins. SR. May 3, 1947. p. 10

The Big Sky is an authentic and exciting novel about the mountain men and their lonely country. Mr. Guthrie, a former Montanan now living in Kentucky, has poured into his book all of the Westerner's fierce fondness for sun and sky and space; and he has succeeded in explaining (perhaps for the first time in fiction) what motivated the wilderness wanderers of a century ago, the rough and ruthless men who dreamed of freedom under the big sky.

Joseph Kinsey Howard. *NYT*. May 4, 1947. p. 1

(On *The Big Sky*) A monument of a book! One of those monuments made out of rough boulders, native to the spot, rolled together to serve as a pedestal for a towering bronze figure of epic size. The first monument raised to the men who in the wild emptiness of those middle plains and beyond, in the mountains which are the spine of our country, preceded the home-making pioneer, a monument to the "mountain man."

Dorothy Canfield Fisher. *NYHT*. May 4, 1947. p. 1

I can't help feeling that Mr. Guthrie has applied the realistic technique to material of which the reality cannot be captured by the documentary method. This method serves him well in one respect. The brutality and the plain squalor of life in the early West come through. On the other hand, one suspects that its rather solemn and pedestrian compulsions inhibit him in another respect. Though a few tall tales are spun around campfires, he makes very little use of the humorous myth-making which was and still is a constant and indigenous American way of coping with the overwhelming presence. . . . Mr. Guthrie's mountain men would be more believable if they were more legendary—by which I do not mean romantic.

Margaret Marshall. *Nation*. May 24, 1947. p. 632

Even more successfully than its predecessor, *The Big Sky,* Mr. Guthrie's second novel (*The Way West*) repossessses the past and gives a sense, not of fiction, but of the Western experience itself as it was totally known a hundred years ago by the men who underwent it, who chose it, and who were re-created by it as Western Americans. Mr. Guthrie writes with modest but sure art, especially in his feeling for the idiom of Western talk and for the narrative style proper to it.

Robert Gorham Davis. *NYT*. Oct. 9, 1949. p. 5

Recollection falters at the attempt to number the troops of fictional tales spawned of Parkman's *Oregon Trail* and the library of overland emigrants' journals. Just as Emerson Hough's *Covered Wagon* was the best of the lot when it appeared, now *The Way West* tops them all; indeed it is another kind of book. They were adventure stories. This is a novel. It is not an action story for action's tumultuous sake, but a story of people.

Elrick B. Davis. *NYHT*. Oct. 9, 1949. p. 3

What emerges above all from a consideration of *These Thousand Hills,* and a glance back at *The Big Sky* and *The Way West,* is the fact that Mr. Guthrie is moved by a fictional purpose as high and valid as his historical purpose is big, and that the two are soundly related, that he is writing, out of the real events of a real world, something like a spiritual epic of the Northwest.

Walter Van Tilburg Clark. *NYT*. Nov. 18, 1956.
p. 54

One of the wonderful things about A. B. Guthrie's novels . . . is that they grow out of a great popular literary tradition—the "Western." . . . We see how a sort of folk literature, become sterile and puerile to the point of absurdity, can be lifted up. And I think its roots have everything to do with its artistry. There's only a slight difference between it and the better tales in the conventional manner. But that slight difference takes this novel out of the rut to a point where it can take its place beside other superior novels growing out of other traditions the world over. It will hold its own.

Fred T. Marsh. *NYHT*. Nov. 18, 1956. p. 3

See *The Big Sky, The Way West,* and *These Thousand Hills* (novels).

HAYES, ALFRED (1911–   )

Poetry

His poems are socially conscious, all about the movies, bars, dance halls, sex, the big time in the big city, no concealed sneering at the poor for being poor. Hayes's structure is lacking in form; his technical equipment is insufficient for a focused presentation of his emotional matter. However, the emotion is pure and forceful and his book, *The Big Time,* is an American document of importance.

Oscar Williams. *NR*. April 24, 1944. p. 582

He uses the less flagrant rhythms between good prose and good poetry to interpret realistically what many will call the seamy side of city life.

It is the side of life which fascinated such great draughtsmen as Daumier and Forain, and it is not too much to say that in his own field, with workmanship that never degenerates into the slovenly, Mr. Hayes meets their eyes across the years. His work has drama, sophistication, and bite. It is full of real irony.

William Rose Benét. *SR*. April 29, 1944. p. 24

All my . . . praise has been only for his content—its interest, its authenticity—and not for his form. . . . His favorite meter is the enormously long line of Whitman and Jeffers, except that he prefers to rhyme it.

This device becomes monotonous and diffuse; it is rarely crammed with the intensity of Whitman or Jeffers. Yet despite the narrow range and occasional brassiness of his musical instrument, it twangs forth some magnificent psychological truths about human beings.

Peter Viereck. *NYT*. April 16, 1950. p. 6

Hayes is not a "natural" poet in the sense of Blake, Hopkins, or Dylan Thomas; that is, there does not seem to be any compulsive music or verbal preoccupation through which poetic thought seeks expression. Rather one has the impression of a sensitive individual with a social conscience and a vivid historical sense who has chosen verse for his deepest reflections because of its succinctness and the opportunity it offers for dramatic contrast and suggestive paradox. In this genre, with his long, loose line and his violent mastery, he takes his place in the modern tradition that begins with Browning and includes among contemporaries such various figures as Jeffers, Fearing, Rukeyser and MacNeice.

Selden Rodman. *NYHT*. April 16, 1950. p. 4

Welcome to the Castle is harsh and tender, clear and profound, beautifully composed. . . . The language is freshly minted, the handling of long free lines supple, the occasional rhymes barely heard, and the undulating movement not only haunting but faithful to plots and characters in the story. . . . In my humble opinion, *Welcome to the Castle* places Alfred Hayes in the front rank of young American authors, whether prosemen or poets. He is an artist of the first order, an order and understanding we need.

Alfred Kreymborg. *SR*. May 20, 1950. p. 19

Novels

Mr. Hayes, a former soldier and poet turned novelist, has written a tough, tired, and blunt-spoken book (*All Thy Conquests*) about the cynical corruption, indifference, and despair of Rome shortly after its conquest-liberation. His book is as tensely emotional, sensitive and imaginative as only a poet could make it. Unusually adept at dialogue, expert in the use of stream-of-consciousness technique, Mr. Hayes has produced a work of real distinction. . . . Here are excellent portrait sketches, haunting suggestions of the fetid atmosphere of Rome, where hunger and poverty were less serious than hysteria and corruption, savage glimpses of Americans in victory. Mr. Hayes has no sermon to preach, no whipping boy to punish. He has been content to paint an impressionistic picture of a situation and to do it extremely well.

Orville Prescott. *YR*. Winter, 1947. pp. 381–2

There are passages in *The Girl on the Via Flaminia* that come a little too close to Hemingway, although this fault appears less in the dialogue than in the expository writing. . . . The best of the lessons that Hayes has learned from the older novelist are beyond mere tricks of style. They are the habits of writing under pressure, with painstaking accuracy and of never saying too much. What sets him apart from most of our younger novelists is his feeling for words and his sense of how to make them count. *The Girl on the Via Flaminia* is one of the very few war books of which one can prophesy that it will seem as true and effective in twenty or thirty years as it does today.

Malcolm Cowley. *NYT*. March 20, 1949. p. 3

The Girl on the Via Flaminia manages to impart much by implication and poetic indirection only, for the characters and the scenes are by no means fully realized. It is as a mood piece, a study in wistfulness and melancholy, that this book is memorable. Mr. Hayes effectively uses images of wind, cold, and loneliness, and emphasizes significant details to give the illusion of completeness. With more substance and intensity, *The Girl on the Via Flaminia* conceivably could have been this war's *A Farewell to Arms,* but in his own manner Alfred Hayes does make his every note ring clear and true.

Siegfried Mandel. *SR*. April 2, 1949. p. 32

Those who may have wondered if the findings of Dr. Kinsey will make stale and unprofitable the theme that has long proved most popular in fiction, should feel reassurance in Alfred Hayes's new novel, entitled in artful artlessness *In Love*. . . . Mr. Hayes writes with a rolling momentum that hides his quest of the uncannily right word. The Jamesian clauses, terraced with qualifications and parentheses, occasionally get out of hand . . . but in the main the reader is won over and the convoluted style seems justified by its success in conveying the utmost intricacies of self analysis. *In Love,* indeed, is a brilliant piece of dissection—a post-mortem in which even the corpse comes alive.

James Hilton. *NYHT.* Sept. 20, 1953. p. 3

Alfred Hayes has given us a powerful and disturbing novel of morality. It should also be said—and quickly too—that *My Face for the World to See* is an exciting, engrossing work, written with beautiful economy and the sure skill of an artist who knows what he is doing. . . . Choosing the lowest common denominator—an adulterous love affair between a wretched psychopathic Hollywood hopeful and a freelance screen writer—Mr. Hayes tells the story of two people, each reaching to find a reflection of himself in a mirror that produces shattering pieces. . . . Mr. Hayes has created characters that are the essence of human hopes and frailty.

Lenard Kaufman. *NYT.* Feb. 2, 1958. p. 24

See *Welcome to the Castle* (poetry); also *All Thy Conquests, The Girl on the Via Flaminia, In Love,* and *My Face for the World to See* (novels).

HEARN, LAFCADIO (1850–1904)

He stands and proclaims his mysteries at the meeting of three ways. To the religious instinct of India,—Buddhism in particular,—which history has engrafted on the aesthetic sense of Japan, Mr. Hearn brings the interpreting spirit of Occidental science; and these three traditions are fused by the peculiar sympathies of his mind into one rich and novel compound—a compound so rare as to have introduced into literature a psychological sensation unknown before. More than any other living author he has added a new thrill to our intellectual experience.

Paul Elmer More. *At.* Feb., 1903. p. 205

If, as some hold, the problem of modern romantic literary art is to portray the human spirit caught in a magic web of necessity, "penetrating us with a network subtler than our subtlest nerves"; to marry strangeness with beauty; to accomplish this in a style as express and gleaming as goldsmith's work; then few writers have solved it more brilliantly than Lafcadio Hearn. In this, rather than in his elaborate interpretation of Japan, may lie his enduring achievement.

Ferris Greenslet. *At.* Feb., 1907. p. 272

Théophile Gautier remains his model from the beginning to the end, and the warmth of colour of Latin literature the thing he wishes to put into "the stone-grey and somewhat chilly style of latter-day English or American romance." In this he had some considerable success, and his style, though it may not always be quite "sound" from the severest Anglo-Saxon point of view, nevertheless has merits which compel attention. His real value, however, was behind the style, in the restless, sensitive, curious soul, which could bring back to more sluggish, stay-at-home imaginations the lovely loot of strange countries across the seas.

Harrison Rhodes. *Bkm*. March, 1907. p. 75

Hearn's irrepressible craving to create a style impelled him to seek ideas; and as Time—its eras, its epochs, its aeons—cast the greatest spell on his imagination, we find him irresistibly attracted to those facts and speculations which called up the past, and yet emphasized its distance. He is lured away . . . by an old song, a folk story, and every tradition and habit that gathers about a race. . . . The search for style is the search for the phrase that will reveal the deepest of these varied feelings to one's self and so perhaps to others.

Herbert Vaughan Abbott. *SAQ*. April, 1907.
pp. 192–3, 197

As to literary aim, Hearn distinctly and repeatedly confessed to me that his ideal was, in his own words, to give his reader "a ghostly shudder," a sense of the closeness of the unseen about us, as if eyes we saw not were watching us, as if long-dead spirits and weird powers were haunting the very air about our ears, were sitting hid in our heart of hearts. It was a pleasing task to him to make us hear the moans and croonings of disincarnate griefs and old pulseless pains, begging piteously, but always, softly, gently, for our love and comforting. But it should not be unrecognized that no allurement of his art can hide from view the deeper pathos of a horrid and iron fatalism which to his mind moved the worlds of nature or of life, throttled freedom, steeled the heart, iced the emotions, and dictated the essential automatism of our being and of these sad dead millions which crowd the dimly seen dreams of Hearn's mind.

George M. Gould. *Concerning Lafcadio Hearn*
(Jacobs). 1908. pp. 174–5

An intrepid soldier in the ranks of literature was Lafcadio Hearn. His work was not merely literary material turned out of his brain, completed by his industrious hand; to him it was more serious than life. He is, indeed, one of the most extraordinary examples of the strange and persistent power of genius, "ever advancing," as he himself expresses it, "by seeking to attain ideals beyond his reach, by the Divine Temptation of the Impossible!" . . . From the earliest years of his literary career, his delight in composition was the pure delight of intellectual activity, rather than delight in the result, a pleasure, not in the work but in the working.

Nina H. Kennard. *Lafcadio Hearn* (Appleton).
1912. pp. 348–9

Hearn knew many things. He had dabbled in all the out-of-the-way corners of literature, particularly those obscure byways that contained exotic or macabre studies. . . . He began with a vivid and sometimes violent creation of atmosphere, an intense visual reaction to the abnormalities of existence. But as time passed he began to speculate more and more about the hidden side of things. . . . He remained to the last a painter in prose, a man who handled words as an artist handles pigments, but his subjects ceased to be highly colored exteriors.

Herbert S. Gorman. *NYT*. Oct. 19, 1924. p. 11

Hearn was a romanticist who found his double impulse in a distrust of the theology under which he was brought up, and the sordid life into which he was thrust, his philosophical support in the teachings of Herbert Spencer, and his release in a lifelong search for beauty.

Percy H. Boynton. *VQR*. July, 1927. p. 421

The same words might be spoken of him that he used in talking of William Blake: "In eighteenth century literature Blake blossoms like a strange wildflower of unfamiliar colour and yet more unfamiliar perfume." Even so, in our own literary annals does Lafcadio Hearn's work glow, with the spiced and honied beauty of an unknown bloom. For he wrote of gold-eyed falcons poised on crests of pine, and slim fawns feeding under maple shadows, of wild ducks in snow and herons flying and iris flowers blooming, and of long-armed monkeys clutching at the face of the moon in water.

Jean Temple. *Blue Ghost* (Cape). 1931. pp. 5–6

Hearn was a minor artist and his work will never occupy a very large place in the history of American literature. Yet the place may be larger than critics are now willing to grant and it is likely to be permanent. What he could do on his limited scale, he did supremely well. . . . He had a gift, almost a genius, for retelling legends, and when all his Japanese ghost and fairy stories are collected into a single volume we may find that he is the only writer in the English language who can be compared with Hans Christian Andersen and the brothers Grimm.

Malcolm Cowley. *NR*. April 18, 1949. p. 24

His work, which includes newspaper pieces, essays, translations, interpretations of oriental cultures, fairy tales and a considerable correspondence, is colored by his exotic, romantic outlook, his faculty for probing luminously into the mores of other peoples. In his leaning toward both the macabre and the romantic, his place in the stream of literature is as assured as that of Poe, or in lighter moments, of Lamb.

Harry E. Wedek. *NYT*. Nov. 13, 1949. p. 9

Though he accepted evolution, he recoiled at the brutality, the ugliness, and the seeming immorality of it all. He found no prospect that pleased him long except Spencer's far-off golden realm. The romantic ideal of perfectibility was both his comfort and his despair. . . . Hearn's *Japan* can best be read with the awareness that Hearn, in spite of such labels as folk-artist, decadent, impressionist, and the like, was a Victorian, with some of the same problems of the so-called "solid" Victorians on the other side of the world.

Allen E. Tuttle. *NR*. Oct. 24, 1955. p. 18

See *Selected Writings* (which includes *Kwaidan, Some Chinese Ghosts*, and *Chita*); also *Kokoro* and *Kotto* (essays and stories) and *Japan: An Attempt at Interpretation*.

HELLMAN, LILLIAN (1905–   )

Miss Hellman is not a specialist in abnormal psychology and not a specialist in the Marxian interpetation of society. She is a specialist in hate and frustration, a student of helpless rage, an articulator of inarticulate loathings. Ibsen and also Chekhov have been mentioned in connection with her plays. Strindberg would be nearer, though perhaps still far enough from the mark. . . . She is fascinated by her own hatred of something.

Joseph Wood Krutch. *Nation*. Dec. 26, 1936.
pp. 769–70

Watch on the Rhine . . . binds the attention of the audience to the stage, and very often binds it tight. A great deal of this is due to the expert stage craft of the melodrama itself. But a great deal, also, comes from the author's remarkable gift for character, the way in which she can lay out a group of characters that are not crudely differentiated one from another or hammered at in the writing or thrown at each other's heads for the sake of contrasts and variety. They are observed with much pains as to the exact kind of detail that will convince us of their actual existence and difference.

Stark Young. *NR*. April 14, 1941. p. 499

Lillian Hellman, her friends say, has a "masculine mind." Physically, she is small and curvilinear, and she dresses trimly in suits and furs. Her bearing suggests a quiet, under-the-surface dynamic force and a strong singleness of purpose. She answers questions quickly and simply, with a precise choice of words, and apparently is used to making up her mind about things without dawdling.

Charlotte Hughes. *NYT mag*. May 4, 1941. p. 10

However different the story, and the place and the people, the theme of Miss Hellman's play is always the same, the struggle between good and active evil, between evil and good that are sometimes ignorant of themselves, sometimes in full knowledge of what they are. It takes creative skill and technical equipment to approach a single goal from many angles and still to keep each separate line of approach clear, each story vivid. The single-minded devotion to her own idea of what is important today and her ability to translate the idea into play form over and over again with an increasing power and persuasion are Lillian Hellman's distinctive achievement.

Edith J. R. Isaacs. *TA*. Jan., 1944. pp. 22–3

The author is just with her characters; she sees them with a certain smiling asperity, an astringent, almost cruel, clarity. But she is unable to reveal in their weakness that which makes them part of what is blessed and great in life. The blunderers in Chekhov are brothers in our nobility even as in our abjectness. The characters in *The Autumn Garden* are our equals only in what we do not respect about ourselves. Miss Hellman refuses to be "metaphysical," poetic or soft. She will not embrace her people; she does not believe they deserve her (or our) love. Love is present only through the ache of its absence. Miss Hellman is a fine artist; she will be a finer one when she melts.

Harold Clurman. *NR*. March 26, 1951. p. 21

Even in her most loyal Ibsenite days Miss Hellman was never a copyist. Far from it. She had found her own way of making her own comment upon the American scene. She was a progressive who was old-fashioned only in the sense that in a period of slovenly workmanship she continued to write "well-made plays." Her pride as a craftsman was clear. She excelled at contrivances, at big scenes, and sulphurous melodramatics. Although sometimes misled into overcomplicating her plots, she wrote with fervor as a person to whom ideas and causes came naturally.

The protest in her voice was strong. It was as characteristic of her as the energy of her attack or the neatness of her planning.

John Mason Brown. *SR*. March 31, 1951. p. 27

Stern moralist as always, our hanging-judge of the American theatre, Lillian Hellman presented the hard doctrine (in *The Autumn Garden*) that the little weaknesses we allow ourselves over the years pile up like calcium in the body and end in a bursitis of character. She made her points deftly and surely. At the same time, she found a way of relieving the sour taste of a stage prosecution with variety of characterization and some leavening of humor and pathos. . . . Like the old-fashioned preacher, she was against sin; specifically, the sin of personal laxness or "accidia." But what was she *for?*

John Gassner. *TA*. Sept., 1951. pp. 17, 73

The Autumn Garden marks a step forward in psychology for Lillian Hellman, enlarging her grasp of unconscious motivation beyond the sado-masochism which permeated the Hubbard plays (*The Little Foxes* and *Another Part of the Forest*). The theme of latent inversion, too, is suggested in a number of her plays. The task of bringing together in one play the complex and deeply perceived motives of *The Autumn Garden* and the superbly structural theatrical tension of *The Little Foxes* remains the task which Miss Hellman's talents give promise of fulfilling.

W. David Sievers. *Freud on Broadway* (Hermitage).
1955. p. 289

See *The Children's Hour, Watch on the Rhine, The Little Foxes, Another Part of the Forest,* and *The Autumn Garden* (plays).

HEMINGWAY, ERNEST (1898–1961)

Hemingway is the hero thrown up by the American ferment, as, in a different way and on a profounder level, D. H. Lawrence was thrown up by the industrial ferment of England. Hemingway is the modern primitive, who makes as fresh a start with the emotions as his forefathers did with the soil. He is the frontiersman of the loins, heart, and biceps, the stoic Red Indian minus traditions, scornful of the past, bare of sentimentality, catching the muscular life in a plain and muscular prose. He is the hero who distrusts heroism; he is the prophet of those who are without faith.

Clifton Fadiman. *Nation*. Jan. 18, 1933. pp. 63–4

It may be too late, in view of the misinformation that has been circulated about Hemingway for years, to say that he is a shy and diffident man, eager for appreciation and constructive criticism, not at all sure of himself, a gay companion, and a loyal friend. It is true that he is a good boxer, an expert fisherman, and an accomplished tennis player, but like most men who know how to handle themselves, he is not at all belligerent, never ostentatious, in fact, conspicuously gentle and considerate.

Elliot Paul. *SR*. Nov. 6, 1937. p. 3

Hemingway is, among his contemporaries, incomparably conscious of the art of prose. He seems to have known throughout what he had to do; and that was, as he discovered on the bed in Verlaine's old room, to find out in any given incident what really had happened. It is the mark of the true novelist that in searching the meaning of his own unsought experience, he comes on the moral history of his time. It is a hard task, and one that requires great scrupulousness; it is not one that can be generously undertaken while serving a cause.

Hemingway's accomplishment will, I think, stand. It has an historical, as it has a literary importance. . . . It was given to Hawthorne to dramatize the human soul. In our time, Hemingway wrote the drama of its disappearance.

John Peale Bishop. *VQR*. Winter, 1937. p. 118

Hemingway has expressed with genius the terrors of the modern man at the danger of losing control of his world, and he has also, within his scope, provided his own kind of antidote. This antidote, paradoxically, is almost entirely moral. Despite his preoccupation with physical contests, his heroes are almost always defeated physically, nervously, practically: their victories are moral ones. He himself, when he trained himself stubbornly in his unconventional, unmarketable art in a Paris which had other fashions, gave the prime example of such a victory; and if he has sometimes, under the menace of the general panic, seemed on the point of going to pieces as an artist, he has always pulled himself together the next moment.

Edmund Wilson. *At*. July, 1939. p. 46

His writing was exciting and possessed of an extraordinary power of suggestiveness; it won over the reader to the feeling that he was actually participating in the lives of very real men and women. His use of dialogue helped enormously to create this impression. Others, notably Ring Lardner, preceded Hemingway in exploring and revealing the literary possibilities of the use of American vernacular, but he used it

with amazing skill and originality. Both his suggestiveness in conveying a sense of life and his use of dialogue tended to turn the attention
of youth toward common American experiences and to the speech expressing them on city streets and farms.

James Farrell. *NYT*. Aug. 1, 1943. p. 6

From the beginning the thing that stirred him most was violence, and
the emotions of which he wrote were those stimulated by pain and killing—war, and bull-fighting, and big game-hunting, and fishing to kill
rather than for sport, and love conceived as something in itself very akin
to violence. Purposely he chose a material which was stronger stuff
that that of Frank Norris, and wrote about it as Sherwood Anderson
might have written, if Anderson, who was a great story-teller but a
lazy artist, had not sloughed the job whenever a specific emotion was
involved. The places where Anderson dodged, saying "that's another
thing" or "but let that pass," are the ones in which by instinct Hemingway saw his major goal.

W. M. Frohock. *SWR*. Spring, 1947. p. 91

Why do they all (the critics) hate him so?

I believe the truth is that they have detected in him something they
find quite unforgiveable—Decent Feeling. Behind all the bluster and
cursing and fisticuffs he has an elementary sense of chivalry—respect
for women, pity for the weak, love of honor—which keeps breaking in.
There is a form of high, supercilious caddishness which is all the rage
nowadays in literary circles. That is what the critics seek in vain . . .
and that is why their complaints are so loud and confident.

Evelyn Waugh. *Com*. Nov. 3, 1950. p. 98

To Hemingway, as to others at the moment, only the primitive was
real, the plane to which men were reduced if they were to survive, if
they were to endure the monstrous conditions of life at the front and
accept as normal the perpetual presence of death. The four-letter word
played a necessary part, like drunkenness and lust, where sensitive
men had to live like men of the Stone Age and where they could only
adjust themselves to a life that was so perilous and harsh by violently
reducing their complexities to the rudimentary level. For Hemingway,
who was deeply in tune with this war-induced frame of mind, whatever was not primitive and simple was verbose and false.

Van Wyck Brooks. *SR*. Dec. 1, 1951. p. 52

What Hemingway has attempted throughout his mature career is his
own synthesis. Sometimes he has brought it off wholly; sometimes
he has failed to bring it off except in part. What he has attempted

to do—it is a metaphysical rather than an aesthetic aim, because it is related to his fundamental attitude toward all of life—is to fuse under a sustained pressure the opposite elements of experience and vision, of prosaic event and dramatic or poetic insight. Say it how you will, in his continuous, exacting, and independent operations in prose, Hemingway has attempted to annihilate that shadow which, according to T. S. Eliot, falls between the idea and the reality, between the essence and the descent.

Harvey Breit. *Nation.* Sept. 6, 1952. p. 194

Over the last quarter of a century Hemingway's influence on prose fiction has been so great that it is scarcely possible to measure it. For a while it looked as if practically no one had escaped it, at least in this country, and there are any number of modern American writers who could be called on to say that they all imitated him at one time or another. Nor have other countries failed to feel the stimulus of his style. Malcolm Cowley has claimed that these things have extended even to the Russians. Mario Praz gives personal testimony of their prevalence in Italy, first on the novelist Vittorini, and then on just about everyone. . . . Very likely there is no country in which American books are read whose literature has been entirely unaffected by Hemingway's work.

Philip Young. *Ernest Hemingway* (Rinehart). 1952.

p. 171

For many years Hemingway has been the literary personification of Natural Man. All kinds of widely differing people looked to him as the writer who best expressed their own longings. The only thing they had in common was a dislike of restraint, though frequently only in one field, remaining perfectly conventional in others. Young men who enjoyed the idea of free love and constant drinking could find their type-heroes in Hemingway. Other men who felt that the real test of manhood was a refusal to be squeamish found that attitude plainly expressed by Hemingway. Hemingway managed to amalgamate the attitudes of people who in other ways were congenitally antagonistic. It is another way of saying that Hemingway is the best modern example of a writer who pleases critics and entertains the general reading public.

John Atkins. *The Art of Ernest Hemingway* (Roy).

1953. p. 2

Naturalism does not respond to life; it adds nothing and subtracts only because selection is unavoidable. It reproduces, copies, as best it can. But it does not respond. Hemingway's writing, on the other hand, has from the beginning . . . been an active response, a gallant response. In this gallantry, however disguised, we find the most vital of Hemingway's own vital juices, and the key to all the characters he admires. His heroes and heroines are men and women who, seeing clearly what they are up against as actors in the human drama, are able not only to "take it," but to take it in a certain way—gallantly. They and their creator have translated *noblesse oblige* into *soi-même oblige*. It is the motto by which they live, however far their applications of it may depart from orthodox morality.

Ben Ray Redman. *SR*. June 6, 1953. p. 18

He is essentially a poet, and a high romantic individualist, alienated from the world, and charting a dangerous course between glamour and despair. He is a poet of youth, unable to face the complexities, or even the advent of maturity. The drab circumstances of common experience are, so to speak, suburban; what he has always sought has been the exotic. Beneath a somewhat tenuous realism that extends only from climax to climax, never from day to day, he is the chronicler of intense emotional states that are deeply felt, beautifully projected, and never quite understood.

Maxwell Geismar. *SR*. Nov. 13, 1954. p. 24

The Sun Also Rises

The Sun Also Rises jerked Hemingway in a few weeks from the obscurity of a White Hope to the notoriety of a moderate best-seller. . . . *The Sun Also Rises* won the *succès de scandale* of a *roman à clef* floated on *vin ordinaire*. Lots of people took it instead of a trip abroad. It was dull in spots, consciously so. Sometimes this very dullness was successful and became exciting. The New Note in American Literature has been Struck.

Robert Littell. *NR*. Aug. 10, 1927. pp. 303–4

The Sun Also Rises is usually considered in terms of the futility of the life it portrays. Its importance lies in Hemingway's method of portrayal. He dwells on no emotions. He shies away from introspective thought. He concerns himself mainly with the speech and actions of his characters. Sense impressions of every kind fill the book. . . . Hemingway has been content to sketch with startling clarity and gusto the real feelings of his livelier contemporaries toward active experiences.

Arthur Dewing. *NAR*. Oct., 1931. pp. 366–7

The Sun Also Rises is . . . Hemingway's *Waste Land*, and Jake is Hemingway's Fisher King. This may be just coincidence, though the novelist had read the poem, but once again here is the protagonist gone impotent, and his land gone sterile. Eliot's London is Hemingway's Paris, where spiritual life in general, and Jake's sexual life in particular, are alike impoverished. Prayer breaks down and fails, a knowledge of traditional distinctions between good and evil is largely lost, copulation is morally neutral and, cut off from the past chiefly by the spiritual disaster of the war, life has become almost meaningless. "What shall we do?" is the constant question, to which the answer must be, again, "Nothing."

Philip Young. Ernest Hemingway (Rinehart). 1952.
pp. 59–60

The critical question (in both senses of the word) is why The Sun Also Rises has lasted and by what hidden art and artifice its survival is more or less permanently guaranteed. Four parts of an answer can be readily given. First its language, having been pruned of the temporary, the faddist, and the adventitious, is still in daily use among us. Age cannot wither the possible variations of which this clean, clear, denotative diction is capable. Second is the devotion to fact, that debt—as Conrad's wisest preface observed—which the writer always owes to the physical universe. Third, and a corollary of the second, is the skill in the evocation and manipulation of emotional atmospheres. Such a skill is possible only to one for whom the moral and aesthetic apprehensions of human situations—their truth and falsehood, their beauty and their ugliness—has the immediate force of a blow to the midriff, or of the quiet leap and stir of the pleasurably astonished heart. Fourth is the symbolic landscape which in company with the diction, the recorded fact and the deeply implied emotion, sustains and strengthens The Sun Also Rises from underneath, like the foundation of a public monument.

Carlos Baker. SR. July 4, 1953. p. 13

See The Sun Also Rises, A Farewell to Arms, For Whom the Bell Tolls, and The Old Man and the Sea (novels); also In Our Time (short stories).

See Supplement at end of text for additional material.

HERSEY, JOHN (1914–   )

Mr. Hersey, it so happens, is a realistically minded young man, who up to the present, at least, has found some ground for belief in the existence of occasional good-will among his fellows. There is already evident in his writing that basic quality which a front-rank novelist must have

—a consuming interest in men and women and a genuine love for them. Good novels have been written by men who had a great interest in humankind but no great love for individual members of their species; the great novelist must have both.

> J. Donald Adams. *The Shape of Books to Come*
> (Viking). 1944. p. 186

(*Hiroshima's*) stark simplicity has brought home to hundreds of thousands of persons what it meant to drop an atomic bomb on a great city. . . . Even at this moment, when the topical interest of John Hersey's story overshadows all else, *Hiroshima* is important on other counts. It is a capsule of Japanese life, and it tells more about our ex-enemy Japan than many learned books.

> Ruth Benedict. *Nation*. Dec. 7, 1946. p. 656

Only a true novelist could breathe warmth, compassion, humor, into what a historian would necessarily have pictured as a stark, hopeless, tragic series of events. Only a sensitive novelist could compel us to embark upon such a fearful adventure as this and remain until the end; you do not "read" *The Wall*—you live it—and if the experience is shattering it is infinitely rewarding.

> Quentin Reynolds. *NYT*. Feb. 26, 1950. p. 1

One feels after reading *The Wall* that (Hersey) has, at the age of thirty-five, leapt, overnight so to speak, to the forefront of our creative writers. For this book is a monumental product of an overpowering imagination. And whereas many of our "promising" young writers . . . have been handicapped by a lack of discipline which led to awkward groping toward form and structure in their novels, Mr. Hersey emerges suddenly not only as a novelist of remarkable scope and depth and power but as a superb craftsman whose work has that polished, finished quality of, say, Flaubert. It is something, so far as I know, unique among contemporary American novelists, at least among those who have something to say.

> William Shirer. *NYHT*. Feb. 26, 1950. p. 1

Mr. Hersey can't quite bring himself to describe the full extent of the Nazi terror. This was surely a nightmare world from its inception to the flaming inferno of its finale, and what *The Wall* lacks is just this final sense of horror and evil. Its tone is almost too rational, fluid, delicate, and tender. Nevertheless, it is an urgent and remarkable novel on a grand scale, and one which seizes upon our minds and hearts.

> Maxwell Geismar. *SR*. March 4, 1950. p. 16

Two things about John Hersey that contribute the most to his stature as an important American writer (are) first, his conviction that human values, human feelings, and human experiences are the basic building blocks of writing—no matter how sweeping or seemingly abstract the event written about may be. This holds for fiction and non-fiction both. The second is a deep sense of purpose in his writing—the feeling that history-in-the-making calls for the most painstaking care and research.

Norman Cousins. *SR*. March 4, 1950. p. 15

The Wall is a journalistic narrative that far outshines its predecessors in diligence, compassion, and virtuosity. . . . To call it a great novel . . . is to invite comparisons that *The Wall* is not constructed to meet. . . . He (Hershey) is a man who attends catastrophes to observe how people act in an extreme situation. It is the shattering event that sets him in motion and the pattern of his narrative does not arise from his actors; it is imposed upon them. His talent rests in finding out precisely what happened and conveying the information in terms that enlist the reader's respect and warm allegiance. No one writing today can match Hersey's appreciation of man under stress; he is a witness for humanity in a time of terror.

Robert Hatch. *NR*. Apr. 3, 1950. p. 18

Mr. Hersey obviously has carefully studied many of the available documents (for *The Wall*), and has also acquainted himself with Jewish legends, customs, language, and literature. . . . His profound sympathy with what the Jews suffered is clear, so is his intense admiration for the heroism of many individual Jews. . . . The book as a whole, however, . . . fails to impress. . . . Mr. Hersey's Jews are not only non-representative; they have no reality as Jews or as people. . . . He never gets very deeply into what Noach Levinson (in *The Wall*) . . . calls "inner Jewishness."

Charles Angoff. *AM*. May, 1950. pp. 626–30

The Wall lays all doubt concerning Hersey's mastery of his favorite mode but it does not quite allay the suspicion, bred by his earlier work, that his gifts and modes are not those of the Dostoyevskys, the Jameses, or the Hardys. Even in such historical novels as *War and Peace* and *A Tale of Two Cities* we feel that the author is interested first of all in men and women and then in their relationship to the historic moment; Hersey becomes interested in the historic moment—Bataan, Hiroshima, the Warsaw ghetto—and then seems to seek out or reconstruct characters that typify the effects of that moment.

Milton Rugoff. *NYHT*. Aug. 20, 1950. p. 3

Mr. Hersey's concern with current affairs has given way increasingly to an interest which can only be called mystical. And in continuation of this movement, his new novel is a quasi-religious document, the embodiment in simple fable of certain mystic truths. . . . The real deficiency of *A Single Pebble* is the vagueness of its ideas. If Mr. Hersey is seriously repudiating Western rationality in favor of mysticism and non-thought, as he seems to be doing, he must deal with the question more thoroughly than he does here.

R. T. Horchler. *Com.* June 29, 1956. pp. 329–30

Were Mr. Hersey's attempt more modest, his bland and pleasant narrative might do, but it is tragedy that is missing here, the story flounders on a blandness so pervasive—in the characters, in the limpness of perception and the leached ideas, in the stricken fuzziness of his tragic sense and the flatfooted march of his prose—that little more than a husk of tragedy survives. If, at first, we respond, it is to the intimation of the tragic, the feel of a generous and large intent; but, in the end, if it is tragedy and not dying falls we require, *A Single Pebble* must seem a disappointing book.

William Arrowsmith. *NR.* Aug. 13, 1956. p. 19

This writer, who is a master in a very high form of journalistic fiction (as in *Hiroshima*), who is really so intelligent, civilized, and "right" in his moral values, has a curious deficiency in the area of pure fiction. He is admirable also in his most recent tales, but not memorable. He belongs perhaps with those novelists of sensibility who are masters of illusion, but not of life. One may suspect that there is a whole psychic area roped off from Hersey's consciousness, and that he sees people in terms of a situation—or a crisis—rather than in and for themselves.

Maxwell Geismar. *American Moderns* (Hill and
Wang). 1958. pp. 185–6

See *The Wall* and *The War Lover* (novels) and *Hiroshima* (long essay).

HOWARD, SIDNEY (1891–1939)

He has attempted nothing alarmingly "experimental" in the way of dramatizing so far.

Yet within the boundaries he has marked out for himself, he has written at least three plays that are so much more than competent that it would be understating the case to call them merely that. Mr. Howard is as skilful a dramatic wizard as is living in the United States today. One is continually aware of his theatrical proficiency. . . . But, to change the tune, Mr. Howard has given us nothing as tremendously moving and suggestive as *The Hairy Ape*. . . . His sympathy is with people more normal, happy, reasonable and amusing. He nurses no social indignation, no flaming grudges. He has no strong appetite for tragedy, and either side-steps it or softens it when it obtrudes itself into his plays.

Charles M. Prager. NYEP. March 5, 1927. p. 11

Although both *Ned McCobb's Daughter* and *The Silver Cord* are in every sense of the word acting plays they also have a stylistic distinction of their own which grants them an independent literary life. Their pages smell of grease paint but they are not smeared with it, and hence it is that they do not have to fear the cold light of print. They hold their own in type not only because of Sidney Howard's *flair* for plotting and characterization, but also because of the vigorous and vivid style which stamps his dialogue.

John Mason Brown. SR. July 2, 1927. p. 940

Sidney Howard ranks easily among the first three playwrights of America. Eugene O'Neill probably comes first. . . . Either Sidney Howard or Elmer Rice might easily pass O'Neill in the race, but neither has done so as yet. Howard, I think, has the greatest native dramatic ability of the trio and the greatest versatility, but suffers too frequently from acute self-consciousness. . . . Sidney Howard is essentially a poet who has disciplined himself too self-consciously into becoming a vigorous, hard-hitting theatrical writer. He has a great tenderness which he is afraid of showing, and a decent sentimentality which he is always trying to hide.

Richard Dana Skinner. Com. March 15, 1933. p. 553

To witness one of his plays is to experience the same sort of exhilarating pleasure that one gets from the society of an active man with quick and vigorous perceptions. One in plunged at once into a series of happenings and made to share the wholehearted interest of a writer who throws himself into everything with an unreserved enthusiasm. The characters are observed with extraordinary intentness and set down in sharp bold strokes. Something of the author's own decisiveness is communicated to them, and the dialogue has something of the crisp clarity of his own speech. Subtlety of a kind is by no means absent and poetry of a kind is also present. But the subtlety does not exhibit itself as hair-splitting and the poetry is never rhapsodical nor dreamy.

The men and women are plain people with their feet on the ground; the scene, some very definite corner of our particular America.

Joseph Wood Krutch. *Nation*. Sept. 13, 1933. p. 295

A curious dualism runs through the work of Sidney Howard. Undoubtedly his forte is character portrayal. His finest creations along this line are the simpler types—sterling, vivid, individual, and solidly human—which people our heterogeneous American scene. . . . Yet the creator of such distinctive American types has devoted a large portion of his energies as a playwright to the adaptation of superficial Continental comedies of the type of *Ode to Liberty*. This is due to two things: first, to Howard's undoubted mastery of stagecraft, in which he runs second only to George S. Kaufman and which makes him greatly in demand among theatrical producers for work that requires such mechanical deftness and inventiveness; second, and more important to his work as a whole, to a superficiality of mind. . . . For while Sidney Howard is gifted with genuine insight into human character, he persistently ignores the conditions under which human character is obliged to exist and function. Thus he never probes the essentials of any dramatic situation.

Eleanor Flexner. *American Playwrights 1918–1938*
(Simon). 1938. pp. 30–1

I am fortunate in having known many fine talkers. But Sidney Howard's conversation was of a special character. It was terse almost to the point of abruptness, and it was always energetic and intense with belief. It had a yea and a nay in it, remarkably satisfactory by comparison with the graceful equivocations of so many persons who enjoy a reputation for talking well. One was pleased by his frank condemnation and commendation, because it is impossible to resist the simplicity of the genuine.

Leonard Bacon. *SR*. Sept. 2, 1939. p. 8

I think he was the most completely alive man, the most multitudinous and abounding person with whom I ever had anything to do. That tall figure of his, usually clothed in heavy gray tweeds, the broad shoulders, the giant strides that gave the impression of someone treading on air; his air of bursting into a room as if he had just descended from the clouds, and his wholly unconscious and deferential way of gettings things done in a hurry—they all come back to me whenever I think of Sidney Howard. . . . His work, his many associations with people, his exulting enthusiasm for the visible world about

him, and children, as a sign of healthy and normal living in the present
—these were the overwhelming realities in his life.

Barrett H. Clark. *TA*. April, 1949. pp. 27, 30

A situation that a decade or so earlier in America, in 1910, would
have been a romantic triangle tragedy, and that would have been a
Sacha Guitry boulevard farce across the Atlantic, was canalized into a
drama of human relations (*They Knew What They Wanted*) neither
jejeunely romantic nor sophisticated. The play belongs to an intermediate genre, which if not overwhelmingly successful because tragicomedy
is never entirely successful, has the ring of truth. It is funny but also
truthful, it is of the theatre but also of life. It is, indeed, quite remarkable in this respect, tragicomedy being normally evasive of the
truth and dishonest by any yardstick other than mere or, shall we say
sheer, theatricality.

John Gassner. *Forum*. May, 1949. p. 288

Howard, like almost every contemporary, felt to some extent the influence of Shaw, although he was always as far from being a doctrinaire
as Shaw was inveterately a preacher. . . . His weakest plays, I think,
are those in which he allows himself to become involved in what looks
like a thesis—*Yellow Jack,* for instance, and the better but still not best
The Silver Cord. Next to *They Knew What They Wanted* is, I think,
Ned McCobb's Daughter, and that is not a discussion of bootleggers as
a social phenomenon but simply a *story* about bootleggers and, especially, about the very interesting character that Alfred Lunt interpreted with such wonderful humor.

Joseph Wood Krutch. *TA*. Feb. 1957. p. 92

See *They Knew What They Wanted* and *The Silver Cord* (plays).

HOWELLS, WILLIAM DEAN (1837–1920)

He has interested his readers from the start in scenes and characters
near at hand. Detaching individuals from the multitudes who pass us
unnoticed or without significance, he has by some magic been able
to transform them, making them typical and absorbing. They were
common before, seen (if at all) at an indifferent angle, they are *uncommon* when transferred to his books, and deeply significant. They
were all "average facts" on the street; but in this new light, transformed

by the wonderful alchemy of his art and his gracious personality, they have become humorous, beautiful, far-reaching.

> Hamlin Garland. *NAR*. March, 1903. pp. 337–8

I do not think any one else can play with humorous fancies so gracefully and delicately and deliciously as he does, nor has so many to play with, nor can come so near making them look as if they were doing the playing themselves and he was not aware they were at it. For they are unobtrusive and quiet in their ways and well conducted. His is a humor which flows softly all around about and over and through the mesh of the page, pervasive, refreshing, health-giving.

> Mark Twain. *Harper*. July, 1906. pp. 224–5

A miracle of the literary art of Howells is achieved time and again in his use of what to an inexperienced critic might seem the hackneyed. Howells never consents to go beyond the facts of human experience for his material. His art rests upon life as we Americans live it. He has no adventitious aids in the form of artificial plots, gods out of machines, climaxes. The scene is commonplace. The conversation is that which we all overhear. They types are familiar. The effect is invariably beautiful.

> Alexander Harvey. *William Dean Howells* (Huebsch-
> Viking). 1917. p. 31

In its maturity his style, in essay or in story, has been charmingly modulated to the tone of conversation—partly for companionable intimacy of communications, but chiefly as indicating the modesty and tolerance generated by profound and pervasive human sympathy. Out of his heart, truly, are the issues of his life; and his feeling of life is so real as to exclude sentimentality and romanticism, though neither sentiment nor romance.

> Henry Mills Alden. *Bkm*. July, 1919. p. 554

His life was the daily working of his mind. To record its operations was his task and his pleasure. It was a smooth-flowing life, but that was because he was so orderly a man, and found his vocation so early and was so happy in it, and pursued it with such undistracted diligence. . . . He was a wise man and knew how to live, and he was admirably self-governed and hated "irregularities."

> Edward S. Martin. *Harper*. July, 1920. pp. 265–6

He will presently be established in the critical consciousness as a literary leader, as a social historian, and as an unrivalled technician. In the mind of the student of letters, he will emerge from the great artistic evolution that was consciously forming the world literature of his time—the realistic movement, as we loosely style it—the most conspicuous figure on this side of the Atlantic. Many of less exclusive interests will look at him, with astonishment at the accuracy of his methods and at the length and singleness of his devotion, as an indispensable recorder of the national life. And his perfection in all that relates to literary handling ought to become a still more compelling source of refreshment and renewal to fellows of his craft.

Delmar Gross Cooke. William Dean Howells
(Dutton). 1922. p. 1

In the work of William Dean Howells, realism came into its own. His creative achievement was so preeminent for a quarter of a century that he became in a sense a standard rather than a competitor. As Clyde Fitch truly said, "It was the Howells Age." For while others were discussing the qualities that should belong to "the great American novel," he had quietly written it, and he had supplemented his creative achievement by a criticism that rivalled that of Poe in analysis and that of Lowell in constructive quality.

Arthur Hobson Quinn. American Fiction (Appleton-
Century). 1936. p. 257

It is clear enough to the critical sense of this decade that, with all his deficiences, Howells is one of the decisive figures in the development of our literary culture. The meaning of his career it is no longer possible to neglect or to belittle: he was the first of our important imaginative writers thoughtfully to consider and intelligently to comprehend what was happening to the form and quality of American life as it moved away from the simplicity, the social fluidity, the relative freedoms, of the mid-century toward the ugly disharmonies of monopolism and empire. He was the author of the first realistic novels of permanent interest in which the effects of that development are represented dramatically with any fullness or clarity.

Newton Arvin. NR. June 30, 1937. p. 227

If Howells thought it salutary to confine his novels to those aspects of life which, as "the more smiling ones," seemed to him "the more American," we have only recently begun to see the value of his work in proper perspective. Even though he was more courageous in his criticism and his appreciation than in his own creative work, there is much more awareness now than there was even ten years ago that restricted though they were, the novels of William Dean Howells brought something both solid and illuminating to the depiction of American life.

His title to fame as a pioneering American realist (with self-imposed reservations), and an artist of delicate rather than powerful perceptions, will one day stand unquestioned.

> J. Donald Adams. *The Shape of Books to Come*
> (Viking). 1944. pp. 27–8

·Three decades after his death, Americans, if they could be persuaded to read his books, might find that Howells still had something to say to them. In his later work, he spoke from an anxiety no less acute than their own. . . . Yet Howells faced the problems of his time with honest realism, had faced them also with courage and had achieved serenity. His books counseled Americans not to ignore their problems and not to despair because of them. He suggested a ground for hope in "the fruitful fields of our common life"; a ground for faith in the energy of the American will and the vitality of the American conscience.

> Lloyd Morris. *AS*. Sept., 1949. p. 416

As the first American writer to attack in serious fiction the problem of ethics in a society of competitive industrialism (*The Rise of Silas Lapham*) and that of divorce in a society of disintegrating standards of conduct (*A Modern Instance*), he prepared the way for more daring followers; but these novels deserve to be read for themselves even today. They are excellent stories, told with supreme vividness and delight; they are sharp studies of human character; and they are accurate documents for a phase of American social development.

> Robert E. Spiller. *SR*. Sept. 2, 1950. p. 11

Howells, for all his geniality, was discriminating too, with a virtually unerring eye for important new talents. He missed scarcely one in forty years. . . . He was the mirror of American society for thousands of sympathetic minds, and, thanks to his unique experience and training, in the West and in Europe, in Boston and New York, he had no American compeer as a living man of letters. In part through his attacks on Dickens and Thackeray, he had destroyed, in America, the ascendency of the English Victorian novel, endeavoring to sever American fiction from the tradition of England and bring it into the main stream of the fiction of the world. This cause he assisted in the critical essays on French, Spanish, Russian, and Norwegian authors he had either written or published as an editor in Boston; for as a literary cross-fertilizer between Europe and American he anticipated James Huneker and others who were appearing in the nineties.

> Van Wyck Brooks. *The Confident Years* (Dutton).
> 1952. p. 143

Howells was trapped by his infatuation with normality, by his excessive concern, as Vernon L. Parrington remarked, with "the usual." He did not realize how normal abnormality is. He did not sufficiently grasp the fact that even the most naturalistic novels are full of fantasy, grotesquerie, and symbolic distortions. I do not mean to complain that he didn't pursue his vein to its depths. . . . Nor is it my point that Howells wasn't as great a writer as Tolstoy; it is rather, as Henry James put it, that he lacked "the really *grasping* vision." He was too easily content.

> Irving Howe. *SR*. Oct. 23, 1954. pp. 28–9

Howells felt that a simple act of goodness is the highest artistic action that can be taken, for it is a part of conduct which is the "beautiful-lest" thing of all. Feeling this, he set art below humanity; but, having set it there, he spoke up for the right of the artist to serve human needs in whatever way his talents took him. In his own honest, sensible, con-sistent work, he kept alive and growing a major American tradition of an intuitive reverence for the homely and native, showed us how this intuition could be part of an age of science, and prepared the grounds for much that we find in subsequent American literature.

> Everett Carter. *Howells and the Age of Realism*
> (Lippincott). 1954. p. 275

See *A Modern Instance, The Rise of Silas Lapham,* and *A Hazard of New Fortunes* (novels); also *Criticism and Fiction* (essays).

HUGHES, LANGSTON (1902–   )

Langston Hughes, although only twenty-four years old, is already con-spicuous in the group of Negro intellectuals who are dignifying Harlem with a genuine art life. . . . It is, however, as an individual poet, not as a member of a new and interesting literary group, or as spokesman for a race, that Langston Hughes must stand or fall, and in the numerous poems in *The Weary Blues* that give poignant moods and vivid glimpses of seas and lands caught by the young poet in his wanderings I find an exceptional endowment. Always intensely subjective, passionate, keenly sensitive to beauty and possessed of an unfaltering musical sense, Langston Hughes has given us a "first book" that marks the opening of a career well worth watching.

> Du Bose Heyward. *NYHT*. Aug. 1, 1926. pp. 4–5

Fine clothes may not make either the poet or the gentleman, but they certainly help; and it is a rare genius that can strip life to the buff and still poeticize it. This, however, Langston Hughes has done, in a volume (*Fine Clothes to the Jew*) that is even more starkly realistic and colloquial than his first,—*The Weary Blues*. It is a current ambition in American poetry to take the common clay of life and fashion it to living beauty, but very few have succeeded, even Masters and Sandburg not invariably. They got their effects, but often at the expense of poetry. Here, on the contrary, there is scarcely a prosaic note or a spiritual sag in spite of the fact that never has cruder colloquialism or more sordid life been put into the substance of poetry.

Alain Locke. *SR*. April 9, 1927. p. 712

Langston Hughes . . . interprets the emotions of primitive types of American Negroes. . . . He has done this without pretension or regard for conventional forms. Stark, fierce, tragic bits of life fall into simple words which keep up an insistent rhythmic beating, beating. No matter what the mood is each one of these poems has that definite swing, or cadence, which is the sign of an unfailing musical sense. . . . Tragic cries and questions, prayers and hallelujahs are turned into poetry with an art and skill that makes them available for the enjoyment and experience of all human beings, regardless of color or race.

Julia Peterkin. *Poetry*. Oct., 1927. pp. 44–5

Langston Hughes, whose search for a native substance does not run along lines of any known English or American convention, can make free-verse rhythms sound inevitable—the true test for such verse. The primitive blues resemble nothing so much as caterwauling when they are reduced to spoken words or the printed page. . . , but Hughes can take the monotonous basic structure of the blues and elaborate upon it until he has a poem that concentrates a number of racial aspects and sings in print. The rhythm of life, to Mr. Hughes, is a jazz rhythm, and he gets it in his verse as no one else can.

John Chamberlain. *Bkm*. Feb., 1930. p. 611

The double role that Langston Hughes has played in the rise of a realistic literature among the Negro people resembles in one phase the role that Theodore Dreiser played in freeing American literary expression from the restrictions of Puritanism. Not that Negro literature was ever Puritanical, but it was timid and vaguely lyrical and folkish. Hughes's early poems, *The Weary Blues* and *Fine Clothes to the Jew*, full of irony and urban imagery, were greeted by a large section of the Negro reading public with suspicion and shock when they first appeared in the middle twenties. Since then the realistic position assumed by Hughes has become the dominant outlook of all those Negro writers who have something to say.

The other phase of Hughes's role has been, for the lack of a better term, that of a cultural ambassador.

Richard Wright. *NR*. Oct. 28, 1940. p. 600

Langston Hughes's poetry is what, in terms of the art of the motion picture, would be called documentary. His concern is to document the moods and problems of the American Negro, to set side by side in simple and lively form pictures and impressions which will add up to a presentation of the American Negro's present situation. This kind of writing is worlds apart from the subtle distillation of meaning aimed at by other serious contemporary poets. For Mr. Hughes, the idiom of poetry is valuable only to the degree that it pins down a situation and draws it to the attention of his readers. The ultimate meaning, the subtler vision of reality, the oblique insight into man's personality and man's fate are not for him; he has a more urgent and immediate problem, to project the living American Negro onto the page. And he does so, on the whole, with success.

David Daiches. *NYHT*. Jan. 9, 1949. p. 4

Few people have enjoyed being Negro as much as Langston Hughes. . . . He would not have missed the experience of being what he is for the world. . . . Langston Hughes has practised the craft of the short story no more than he has practised the forms of poetry. His is a spontaneous art which stands or falls by the sureness of his intuition, his mother wit. His stories like his poems, are for readers who will judge them with their hearts as well as their heads. By that standard he has always measured well.

Arna Bontemps. *SR*. April 5, 1952. p. 17

Hughes writes a lucid, conversational style intimate as a personal letter and casual as a feature column. However the apparently effortless, facile prose contains undercurrents of sly humor, quiet bitterness and social consciousness that echo in the mind. It is the sort of lean, compact writing that implies as much as it states; an active, rhythmical prose without excess literary fat.

Stanley Cooperman. *NR*. May 5, 1952. p. 21

See *The Langston Hughes Reader* (poetry and prose).

INGE, WILLIAM (1913–   )

Come Back, Little Sheba (is) a mean tragedy in which the aftermath of a youthful sin is shown with merciless precision and a Belascan realism which includes a succession of assorted snacks, a prominent garbage pail, dirty dishes and water left running in a sink to the shocked murmurs of the audience.

Euphemia Van Rensselaer Wyatt. *CW*. April, 1950.
p. 67

It is the supreme distinction of Mr. William Inge's world to exist solidly as an imaginative fact, with more energy and vitality than that of any American dramatist of his generation. Neither deliquescent as is that of Tennessee Williams, nor shaped by Arthur Miller's blunt polemic rage, it is a world existing solely by virtue of its perceived manners. . . . The poetry, in Mr. Inge's plays, is all in the pity; he gives us the hard naturalistic surface, but with a kind of interior candescence.

Richard Hayes. *Com*. March 20, 1953. p. 603

He is probably not a great playwright (at least I doubt that anything he has done thus far will be included in the archives of our century), but he is an acute, compassionate, and amused observer who has trained himself to write approximately perfect theater. Like all good craftsmen, he makes it look as easy as instinct.

Robert Hatch. *Nation*. March 19, 1955. p. 245

As much as one admires and enjoys *Bus Stop,* one feels that Mr. Inge has done not much more than interweave a trio of not very startling sketches. True, they all deal with the conflict between insecurity produced by selfishness and true love, but what happens in any one sketch doesn't have much effect on what happens in any other. The play's chief distinction lies in the way Mr. Inge has served up banal characters with most of their sentimental fat trimmed off. On the other hand, he avoids rich dialogue, colorful eccentricities, and the theatrical exploitation of dramatic situations. While this makes his comedy an honest etching of life, one sometimes wishes that Mr. Inge might more completely free himself from the demands of the commonplace.

Henry Hewes. *SR*. March 19, 1955. p. 24

Prior to the Freudian revolution, men and women discovered sex through love. Nowadays love is discovered through sex. This theme has come to obsess William Inge, and he ought to realize the essential limitations of this theme before it dissipates one of our most promising dramatic talents. In *Come Back, Little Sheba,* his most moving play, the idea of love through sex was a minor motif. In *Picnic,* although sex was more rampant, it was still only one thread in a larger pattern. In *Bus Stop* the noble savages are the predominant and, in fact, the only point of the story. Inge is fascinated by the problem of two healthy animals of the opposite sex lusting after each other. It is perhaps an indication of my debility that I find this problem one of the less significant issues of our times.

Maurice Zolotow. *TA.* May, 1955. p. 22

Picnic illustrates the most mature level of the American drama in the fifties, able to draw upon Freudian insights without succumbing to the obvious or the trite, able to extract ever fresh and original patterns of human relationship from contemporary life and to view with psychological as well as aesthetic perception the life around us.

W. David Sievers. *Freud on Broadway* (Hermitage).
1955. pp. 355–6

The mark of Inge's method is its modesty. He never goes beyond his depth, he never promises more than he can fulfill, he ventures only into what he can master. He writes sparsely, almost laconically, but his choice of words and of situations is so shrewd that he makes them go a long way in creating a stage life far more potent than the written page may indicate. His work is very telling for us, too, because it is peculiarly American—in its setting and characters, in its sadness and humour, in its folksiness and in its Freudianism which is never pressed to the point of declamatory "revelation," but is tempered by a certain cautious optimism.

Harold Clurman. *Nation.* Dec. 21, 1957. p. 483

Mr. Inge is a writer of literate soap opera. . . . This is in no way intended to deprecate Mr. Inge's work, for his soap is of the best French-milled quality. His writing is adult. He is incapable of schmaltz. His characters are funny when he wants them to be funny, sad when he wants them to be sad, and always touching and understandable.

Patrick Dennis. *NR.* Dec. 30, 1957. p. 21

William Inge . . . is now contributing his fourth smash hit to Broadway. It is certainly his best play since *Come Back, Little Sheba;* and because its scope is broader than that of the first play, and its attitudes even warmer, the new one doubtless may be said to be the best of the lot. . . . Mr. Inge's "dark at the top of the stairs" represents the terrors of growing up, the unknown fears which taking adult responsibility entails. Primarily he has tried to show us that dark through the eyes of children, but the original thing he has to say is that even grownups still face that dark and must wrestle with its fears.

Tom F. Driver. *CC*. Jan. 1, 1958. pp. 17–8

See *Come Back, Little Sheba, Picnic, Bus Stop*, and *The Dark at the Top of the Stairs* (plays).

JACKSON, SHIRLEY (1919–   )

The middle-class emotion of embarrassment has been substituted for many of the human passions and passion itself is very often treated in such a way that the reader is only embarrassed by it. The mixture of the macabre and the familiar—hell yawning beneath the commonplaces of life—and especially the combination of cruelty and the childlike is a standard theme, which Miss Jackson treats, not as a source of macabre humor, as Saki treated it, but as a source of macabre embarrassment.

Donald Barr. *NYT*. April 17, 1949. p. 4

She sees life, in her own style, as devastatingly as Dali paints it, and like Dali also, she has a sound technique in her own art. There is a beguilingness in the way she leads her readers to the precise point at which the crucial shock can be administered.

The stories are of varying length and quality, but there is in nearly all of them a single note of alarm which reminds one of the elemental terrors of childhood—as when the pages of a book are unsuspectingly turned upon a frightening picture, or a shadow moves into sudden shape upon a wall.

James Hilton. *NYHT*. May 1, 1949. p. 4

The short stories of Shirley Jackson . . . seem to fall into three groups. There are the slight sketches like *genre* paintings, dealing with episodes which by means of her precise, sensitive, and sharply focussed style become luminous with meaning. . . . In these she is completely successful. . . . The second group comprise her social-problem sketches. . . . Here she has, in addition to an enlightened point of view, a penetrating understanding of the subtle ways . . . prejudices operate. . . . Her final group deals with fantasy ranging from humorous whimsey to horrifying shock. Her method is to establish with meticulous detail a concretely realistic setting, and then to allow the story to crumble . . . into unreality.

Robert Halsband. *SR*. May 7, 1949. p. 19

Magic is the word that has been woven around the literary personality of Shirley Jackson, the latest to join the select corps of triumphant women short-story writers who apparently flourish in America. Of the stories that make up her surprisingly high-selling collection—entitled *The Lottery*—critics have said they signalled a return to the era of witchcraft and magic, the supernatural and some sort of devil worship. . . . True, Miss Jackson believes in magic. She says it works for her, both the black and white varieties. But she also says it's a silly thing to talk about. Obviously, Miss Jackson was able to be natural even about the supernatural.

Harvey Breit. *NYT*. June 26, 1949. p. 15

There is, throughout *The Lottery,* a ghostly teasing resemblance to the work of people like Aubrey Beardsley and Algernon Blackwood —there is the same air of the fantastic, the improbable, the cruel and the evil, all overlaid by a veneer of the commonplace, but the final impression is that even this surface shines, not with the sheen of polish, but with the iridescence of decay, so that one is left believing that even the commonplace is fantastic. This is, of course, the modern romantic belief that nothing is ever right or happy or genuine.

E. G. Langdale. *CF*. July, 1949. p. 94

The collected short stories, *The Lottery* . . . left little doubt anywhere of the distinctive order of Shirley Jackson's talent. Even so, it is a rarity when a novel by a writer as young as Miss Jackson (she is just 30) turns out to be a work of artistic maturity; a novel within its own brief, but not shallow limits, of courage, integrity and persuasion. Such, happily, is the case with *Hangsaman*.

The language of *Hangsaman* . . . is alive, complex and clear. Its perceptions are piercing beyond the ordinary. The characters are true to themselves (and to life) with every breath they draw; the situations are true to the characters and, in turn, subtly affect and alter them. One cannot doubt a word Miss Jackson writes.

Alice S. Morris. *NYT*. April 22, 1951. p. 5

Having delighted untold thousands with her recent account of life among the savages in Bennington, Vermont, Shirley Jackson the housewife and mother has once more yielded to Shirley Jackson the literary necromancer, who writes novels not much like any others since the form was invented. . . . Sinister, sardonic, and satirical by turns *The Bird's Nest* is what one might expect from the author of those frightening stories in *The Lottery*. And yet, as the book races from one astonishment to the next, we come to feel that the other Miss Jackson must have had a hand in it, too. The drama repeatedly turns into farcical comedy, and under the comedy lies pathos. . . . And the climax of the story and its conclusions are curiously moving.

Dan Wickenden. *NYHT*. June 20, 1954. p. 1

Miss Jackson shocks her readers into instant attention by the effective juxtaposition of startling incident and unusual characters. . . . In addition to being a first-class story-teller, she has always been concerned with the conflict between good and evil in a world deplorably deficient in common sense, kindness, and magnanimity in the Aristotelian sense.

William Peden. *SR*. March 8, 1958. p. 18

See *The Lottery* (short stories); also *Hangsaman* and *The Bird's Nest* (novels).

JAMES, HENRY (1843–1916)

I am tired of hearing pettiness talked about Henry James's style. The subject has been discussed enough in all conscience, along with the minor James. Yet I have heard no word of the major James, of the hater of tyranny; book after early book against oppression, against all the sordid petty personal crushing oppression, the domination of modern life; not worked out in the diagrams of Greek tragedy, not labelled "epos" or "Aeschylus." The outbursts in *The Tragic Muse,* the whole of *The Turn of the Screw,* human liberty, personal liberty, the rights of the individual against all sorts of intangible bondage! The passion of it, the continual passion of it in this man who, fools said, didn't "feel." I have never yet found a man of emotion against whom idiots didn't raise this cry.

Ezra Pound. *LtR*. August, 1918. p. 7

He was a critic who preyed not upon ideas, but upon living beings. It is criticism which is in a very high sense creative. The characters, the best of them, are each a distinct success of creation. . . . The general scheme is not one character, nor a group of characters in a plot or merely in a crowd. The focus is a situation, a relation, an atmosphere, to which the characters pay tribute, but being allowed to give only what the writer wants. The real hero, in any of James's stories, is a social entity of which men and women are constituents. . . . James's critical genius comes out most tellingly in his mastery over, his baffling escape from Ideas; a mastery and an escape which are perhaps the last test of a superior intelligence. He had a mind so fine that no idea could violate it.

T. S. Eliot. *LtR*. August, 1918. pp. 45–6

His themes were intimately thrilling; then there was the method, subtle yet not over-subtle, lucid yet profound, still waters really running deep, the preparation and the involution, the return upon itself; and for "showing" of all this, there was the diction and the manner, beautiful and lustrous—pages that shone and shimmered and sparkled, that spread and spilt and built before our eyes the grass and flowers and trees and streams and brooks. . . . You found yourself in an enchanted place and never knew how you got there. Was it better than the "real" place? You often thought it was, and people told you you were decadent, that that was decadence—to find the words about it better than the thing itself. You said you didn't care; if this were decadence you were glad to be a decadent. It was a time, believe me, worth the living in, when Henry James was in his middle period.

Ethel Coburn Mayne. *LtR*. August, 1918. p. 2

The Wings of the Dove, The Ambassadors, and *The Golden Bowl* are like the faintly audible tread of destiny behind the arras of life. The reverberations are almost microphonic; it is spiritual string-music, with the crescendo and the climax not absent. We must go to other novelists for the roast beef and ale. The Jacobean cuisine is for cultured palates, and most precious is the bouquet of his wine. But characterization and the power of narration inform his every book. To use his own expression, he "never saved for the next book."

James Gibbons Huneker. *Bkm*. May, 1920. p. 367

The tiny movement that is the last expression of an act or a fact carries within it the history of all it has passed through on the way—a treasure of interest that the act, the fact in itself, has not possessed. And so in the social scene, wherever its crude beginnings have been left furthest behind, wherever its forms have been most rubbed and toned by the hands of succeeding generations, there he found, not an obliteration of sharp character, but a positive enhancement of it, with the whole of its past crowded into its bosom. The kind of life, therefore, that might have been thought too trifling to bear the weight of his grave and powerful scrutiny was exactly the life that he pursued for its expressive value.

Percy Lubbock. Introduction to *The Letters of Henry James* (Scribner). 1920. pp. xxiv–v

His outward appearance developed in accordance with his moral and intellectual expansion. I have said that in early life Henry James was not "impressive"; as time went on his appearance became, on the contrary, excessively noticeable and arresting. He removed the beard which had long disguised his face, and so revealed the strong lines of mouth and chin, which responded to the majesty of the skull. In the breadth and smoothness of the head—Henry James became almost wholly bald early in life—there was at length something sacerdotal. As time went on, he grew less and less Anglo-Saxon in appearance and more Latin.

Edmund Gosse. *Aspects and Impressions* (Cassell).
1922. p. 41

The extreme and almost tantalizing charm of his talk lay not only in his quick transitions, his exquisite touches of humour and irony, the width and force of his sympathy, the range of his intelligence, but in the fact that the whole process of his thought, the qualifications, the resumptions, the interlineations, were laid bare. The beautiful sentences, so finished, so deliberate, shaped themselves audibly upon the air. It was like being present at the actual construction of a little palace of thought, of improvised yet perfect design. The manner was not difficult to imitate: the slow accumulation of detail, the widening sweep, the interjection of grotesque and emphatic images, the studied exaggerations; but what could not be copied was the firmness of the whole conception.

Arthur Christopher Benson. *Memories and Friends*
(Putnam). 1924. pp. 218–19

He had emerged as an impassioned geometer—or, shall we say, some vast arachnid of art, pouncing upon the tiny, air-blown particle and wrapping it round and round. And now a new prodigy had appeared, a style, the style that was the man Henry James had become. He had eschewed the thin, the sharp, the meagre; he had desired the rich, the round, the resonant, and all these things had been added unto him; everything that he had thought and felt and tasted and touched, the fabrics upon which his eyes had feasted, the colors that he had loved, the soft sounds, the delicate scents, had left their stamp upon the house of his spirit. . . . Metaphors bloomed there like tropical air-plants, throwing out branches and flowers; and every sound was muted and every motion vague.

> Van Wyck Brooks. *The Pilgrimage of Henry James*
> (Dutton). 1925. pp. 130–1

To James's intimates, (his) elaborate hesitancies, far from being an obstacle, were like a cobweb bridge flung from his mind to theirs, an invisible passage over which one knew that silver-footed ironies, veiled jokes, tiptoe malices, were stealing to explode a huge laugh at one's feet. This moment of suspense, in which there was time to watch the forces of malice and merriment assembling over the mobile landscape of his face, was perhaps the rarest of all in the unique experience of talk with Henry James.

> Edith Wharton. *A Backward Glance* (Appleton-
> Century). 1934. pp. 178–9

No man of letters, I suppose, ever had a more disarming smile than his, and smiles, as I have been told, are a subject about which I can speak with authority. It was worth losing a train (and sometimes you had to do that) while he rummaged for the right word. During the search the smile was playing about his face, a smile with which he was on such good terms that it was a part of him chuckling at the other parts of him.

> J. M. Barrie. *The Greenwood Hat* (Scribner). 1938.
> p. 241

In most writers their works exemplify their ambitions; Henry's were about his ambition, as they were, in one sense, only his ambition written large. Just as William (James)'s vision always came back to a loose sea of empiricism in which man could hold on only to his own plurality, so Henry's was to decline and to fill out the moral history of composition. His theory of art was not preparatory to a manipulation of experience. . . . The story of Henry James was the story of Henry James writing his novels.

> Alfred Kazin. *NR*. Feb. 15, 1943. p. 217

That James's sensibility was essentially moral is made clear at once if we set his work beside that of, say, Proust. James was concerned with moral issues as they emerged in social behavior, while Proust's interest was in social behavior as such, a purely psychological interest in social mannerisms. Both writers, however, were novelists of sensibility: what interested them in human affairs was determined not by any public standard but by a sense of values peculiar to themselves for the communication of which they depended on technique—on style, on pattern, on the way emphasis was distributed throughout the narrative. And the "story" did not in any real sense exist apart from the technique.

David Daiches. *KR*. Autumn, 1943. pp. 572–3

Loyalty to the pledged word, kindness as against cruelty, honor as against expedience—these are not the only specific values with which James concerns himself in his books; but they are basic to his vision of the world; and it is in his clear apprehension of what these values mean in a world in which intelligence is usually the tool of a self-assertive or sometimes merely meddlesome, but always immoral, will, that the quick of his interest lay.

Eliseo Vivas. *KR*. Autumn, 1943. p. 585

James did not deal with etiquette detached from deep feeling. . . . Most of his novels and tales deal with middling people pursuing the two simplest objects of human concern—love and money. . . . It is true that James's mind is engrossed by the complexities and refinements to which passion and greed give rise in a world of elaborate laws and subtle modes of communication. But even in the course of inventing and unmasking the numberless disguises which these passions can assume, James holds to a simple view of their meaning: in acting out their feelings, people turn out either good or evil—a moral attitude which, taken with James's addiction to violent plots, leads me to say that he is a writer of melodrama.

Jacques Barzun. *KR*. Autumn, 1943. p. 509

James perceived what was lacking in his father's world. His father's concern with what was universal rather than with what was individual had diffused itself so widely that it ended by losing the image of any actual man. Hence James was impelled to believe that the primary obligation for the artist was to start with the tangible, with what he had seen for himself. And if his image of man is restricted, if it has little of the radiant aura of his father's or of Emerson's aspirations, it possesses the indispensable quality of mature art: it is compellingly concrete. Therefore, although James did not advance the empirical attitude with the simple vigor of his brother, the world portrayed in his novels is of substantial value to us in recharting our own world, if only by providing us with a target to shoot against.

F. O. Matthiessen. *Henry James: The Major Phase*
(Oxford). 1944. p. 150

No one of his books has the survival value, in and by itself, of the great masters of life in representative portrayal—Dickens, Shakespeare, and in his limited field, Twain. But James did create a cult which gives his books a significance outweighing sometimes even their interest. It was not, as his enemies said, a cult of difficulty and obscurity. Difficulty was his personal choice. Obscurity is the fault of the reader who lacks, as James complained, the faculty of attention. . . . The true cult that Henry James founded was the cult of awareness. . . . James has educated his readers in *seeing* much as the psychologists and psychiatrists have educated us in *explaining,* new aspects of behavior.

Henry Seidel Canby. *Turn West, Turn East*
(Houghton). 1951. p. 296

Henry James stands astride two centuries and reaches backward to a third; with him the American novel, in a single leap, attained a precocious maturity it has never surpassed. And it is now recognized that with Henry James the novel in English achieved its greatest perfection. By some queer irony, a writer from the New World—in an era when Americans were preoccupied with ever-widening frontiers and material things—arrived upon the scene of the Old World to set the house of fiction in order. To this Henry James dedicated the whole of his life. He became, in his time—and reaching over into ours—the first great theorist and scholar in the art which he himself practiced with such distinction.

Leon Edel. *Henry James: The Untried Years*
(Lippincott). 1953. pp. 10–1

The extremes with which Henry James was obsessed had largely to do with the personal human relations and almost nothing at all to do with public relations except as they conditioned, marred, or made private relations. It may be said that James wooed into being—by seeing what was there and then going on to create what might be there in consciousness and conscience—a whole territory of human relations hitherto untouched or unarticulated. So excessive is this reach into relation, there is no escape possible for the creature caught in it except by a deepening or thickening of that relation until, since it cannot be kept up, it must be sacrificed. That is to say, its ideal force becomes so great that its mere actual shade becomes intolerable.

R. P. Blackmur. *The Lion and the Honeycomb*
(Harcourt). 1955. p. 281

During the last third of the century James was engaged in doing something so different, so quintessently American rather than European, that we have no terms in which to describe it. He was engaged in celebrating a triumph, the triumph of the vision of the moral life founded on personal freedom and unsupported by institutional props which the generation of his father and Emerson had elaborated. In this respect he was very nearly the contemporary of Hawthorne, Whitman, and Melville, each of whom, like himself, had worked out a version of tradition, a more or less complete apologetic, which, incorporated in their works, had served to define the very criteria by which they wished to be judged.

Quentin Anderson. The American Henry James
(Rutgers). 1957. p. 7

See *The Portable Henry James* (for selected short stories, criticism, and letters); also *The American, The Europeans, Portrait of a Lady, Washington Square, The Bostonians, The Princess Casamassima, The Tragic Muse, The Spoils of Poynton, The Wings of the Dove, The Ambassadors,* and *The Golden Bowl* (novels).

JARRELL, RANDALL (1914–   )

Poetry

He has great promise, he has a sense of form, he has emotional power, he has music, and unlike many young contemporaries he is not long-winded. . . . It is something to be able to take such an out of the way form as the sestina . . . and fill it with the modern mood and a sort of lost loneliness that is characteristic of our time.

Mary M. Colum. NYT. Nov. 1, 1942. p. 8

In a way Jarrell represents . . . an ideal toward which many younger poets are striving. It is for this reason that we cannot help asking whether a New Sentimentality is not arising, even more deadly than that of the nineteenth century because clad in the technical efficiency which is our dazzling legacy from Pound and Eliot.

M. L. Rosenthal. NYHT. Nov. 28, 1948. p. 18

Randall Jarrell is our most talented poet under 40, and one whose wit, pathos and grace reminds us more of Pope or Matthew Arnold than of any of his contemporaries. . . . Monstrously knowing and monstrously innocent—one does not know just where to find him . . . a Wordsworth with the obsessions of Lewis Carroll. . . . Jarrell has gone far enough to be compared with his peers, the best lyric poets of the past: he has the same finesse and originality that they have, and his faults, a certain idiosyncratic willfulness and eclectic timidity, are only faults in this context.

Robert Lowell. NYT. Oct. 7, 1951. pp. 7, 41

His unflinching grasp of brutal events is dictated by a great compassion. He is like one who, in order to cut off the dragon's head, must grasp his sword below the hilt, and does so. . . . Along with such obvious victims as the Jews and the soldiers and their kin, his compassion includes the enemy, not only German children, but PW's. His work sometimes seems obsessively repetitive, and no single piece is as brilliant as his criticism, but nearly all are redeemed by a tender incisiveness.

Babette Deutsch. Poetry in Our Time (Holt). 1952.
pp. 376-7

The poems are packed with a kind of brilliant melancholy, a genial atrabiliousness which provides an excellent setting for the grave dignity and compassionate exuberance of his thought. Here the poetry is not a plume worn to distinguish its creator from the common man. It is rather the grammar of his reason, built up out of his understanding of man and his study of man's works.

Raymond Holden. SR. July 3, 1954. p. 26

Jarrell's verse . . . was promising. But it seems to me that the flaws in his early poems have become the mannerisms of his later work: a conscious sentimentality—flung, evidently, in the face of sophistication —and a conscious carelessness, a deliberate disregard of the means of control, whether in "free" or "regular" verse. His war poems have done the most to give him the reputation he now possesses, but it is difficult to understand why these particular verses have been so celebrated; perhaps they seem more realistic, concentrating as they do on the more obvious horrors. Bathos and sentimentality is what they contain for me.

Donald Hall. NWW #7. 1955. p. 238

His recurring themes are childhood, war and literature. The world of the child is his chief area of symbolism—Jarrell is practically the only living poet who insists on this world—and his almost obsessive return to the great childhood myths is sometimes as painful as a psychoanalysis. . . . In some of Jarrell's writing, criticism and fiction as well as poetry, there is a tendency toward sentimentality and cruelty, but in the major part—and the major part is certainly the poetry—there is a breadth of spirit which is wholly admirable and exemplary.

Karl Shapiro. NYT. March 13, 1955. p. 4

Criticism

He is a man of letters in the European sense, with real verve, imagination, and uniqueness. Even his dogmatism is more wild and personal
than we are accustomed to, completely unspoiled by the hedging
"equanimity" that weakens the style and temperament of so many of
our serious writers. His murderous intuitive phrases are famous; but
at the same time his mind is essentially conservative and takes as
much joy in rescuing the reputation of a sleeping good writer as in
chloroforming a mediocre one.

Robert Lowell. *NYT*. Oct. 7, 1951. p. 7

It has been clear for some time that Randall Jarrell is one of the most
gifted poets and critics of his generation. . . . Jarrell goes beyond
the standards and the discriminations of T. S. Eliot, which have dominated the criticism of poetry for the past twenty-five years, and he
does so by including and assimilating Eliot's views. . . . He succeeds
in being joyous, angry, contemptuous and gay as well as lucid, direct
and colloquial with complete genuineness and ease. And when he is
amusing as he often is, he is at the same time and unerringly illuminating.

Delmore Schwartz. *NYT*. Aug. 16, 1953. p. 1

Mr. Jarrell's riches are of the mind; they consist in his passion for
understanding and particularly for the understanding poetry embodies.
. . . He makes fine wry jokes . . . which recognize both his painful awareness of undemocratic superiority and his discomfort at the
maldistribution of intelligence which causes it. . . . But some of the
time he is no better than the rest of us, failing to keep himself suspended between his two truths. . . . In these moods he alternates
between oversimplified invectives against comic books and television
sets . . . and exaggerations of the badness of literary criticism which
would make you think—did you not know better—that all the critics in
the country show up regularly at New York cocktail parties in order
to make it clear that they never read any book not recommended by
The Partisan Review.

Arthur Mizener. *SwR*. July, 1954. pp. 504–7

Jarrell is an eclectic, an urbane, and a generous and deeply human
critic of other poets' poetry. His concern is . . . with the growing and
embittered isolation of the poet in our age. . . . Randall Jarrell ex-
aggerates but little, and always with gentle humor. . . . He is right in
asserting that the duty of the critic is to chart new lands, . . . to stick

his neck out, as the artist did; and to feel intensely and, if possible, write finely, and with simplicity.

Henri Peyre. *YR*. Winter, 1954. pp. 294–5

Pictures from an Institution

Mr. Jarrell is on the side of the angels. His is a divine meanness. . . . The language is pure and inventive; the "seething of metaphors" reaches points of considerable beauty. . . . He is a brilliant satirist . . . a genuinely witty man.

Francis Steegmuller. *NYT*. May 2, 1954. p. 4

Mr. Jarrell . . . makes in his pages a sustained exhibition of wit in the great tradition. It is seldom that he falters or strains and he is often immensely funny and very devastatingly shrewd. . . . Mr. Jarrell's quiet comedy of ideas and people is a welcome gift. While it laughs at much of our intellectual pride and pomposity, it also develops a breadth of warm sympathy for the angelic touch that may visit the most foolish of us.

Edmund Fuller. *SR*. May 8, 1954. p. 15

Mr. Jarrell doesn't miss a trick. There, one begins to think, the trouble lies; he misses and leaves out—nothing, at least nothing that can make his people and their world of Benton grotesque, heartless, inhuman. . . . Humanly, the book troubles the heart. Why all the apparatus brought to bear on these odious vermin? . . . Under the wit we feel a void aching away for substance to fill it, and neither the devastating portraiture nor the wide spread of allusion can fill it, for the picture is indeed *la vie morte*.

Louis O. Coxe. *NR*. May 10, 1954. p. 20

See *Selected Poems, Poetry and the Age* (criticism), and *Pictures from an Institution* (novel).

JEFFERS, ROBINSON (1887–1962)

He has glorious imagination; his dithyrambs have the range and movement of the tides he worships; his people throb and bleed with reality; the Californian background is Olympian. But the artist backstage lacks the hard integrity of his Greek masters. His fingers "had the art to make stone love stone," but not the art to make every word love every word. His love of language makes speech run in torrents; his contempt of language fails to control the streams and guide them seaward. Two men, two wrestlers, two serpents, are at odds in the poet: the lover and the hater, the human and the hermit, the man and the superman.

Alfred Kreymborg. Our Singing Strength
(Coward-McCann). 1929. p. 626

Mr. Jeffers . . . has abandoned narrative logic with the theory of ethics, and he has never achieved . . . a close and masterly style. His writing is loose, turgid, and careless; like most anti-intellectual-ists, he relies on his feelings alone and has no standard of criticism for them outside of themselves. There are occasional good flashes in his poems . . . but they are very few, are very limited in their range of feeling and in their subject matter, and they are very far between.

Yvor Winters. Poetry. Feb., 1930. p. 283

Jeffers is a great word artist and he is vastly important in that he goes on pointing out the horrors and dangers of introversion, personal and social; as an introvert erupting out of his introversion he is deeply representative of vast mobs of introverts and, as such, worthy of the closest study. He is magnificent poetically, which is strange—for philosophically, with all his "terribleness," he is more the self-con-scious worm under a lowering heel about to crush him, than, say, a raindrop which does not resign itself to despair even if it happens to fall on a rotting carcass and sinks therein.

Louis Adamic. My America (Harper). 1938. p. 476

Jeffers is an important poet because of the exalted range and dignity of his thought. There is in all of his work a strain of nobility which is no more than a reflection of his own character. He has suffered (and does), and as a result some of his verse is too tortured and painful to endure. There are those who are shocked by his frank use of sexual themes; others disagree with his philosophy and values; some find his unorthodox faith to be sinful. But none can deny the simple forth-right honesty and passion for truth implicit in everything Robinson Jeffers has written.

Lawrence Clark Powell. Robinson Jeffers
(San Pasqual). 1940. p. 210

One must, somehow, separate the idea and its expression, remembering that the poem transcends the experience and the personality that prompted it. Between Jeffers the philosopher and Jeffers the poet there is a significant dichotomy. The philosophy is negative, repetitive, dismal. The poetry, even when bitterest, is positive as any creative expression must be. It is varied in movement and color; it vibrates with a reckless fecundity; it is constantly breaking through its own pattern to dangerous and unfathomed depths. . . . Here is a full-throated poetry, remarkable in sheer drive and harrowing drama, a poetry we may never love but which we cannot forget.

Louis Untermeyer. *Modern American Poetry*
(Harcourt). 1950. p. 378

We stand tongue-tied before the poetry of Jeffers, not merely in awe of its primitive strength, but in bewilderment: what is one to think of these anachronisms? In an age that has forsworn prophecy, especially in art, Jeffers speaks always in the accents of Isaiah and Jeremiah, albeit invoking no deity. In a time of multiple meanings and ambiguous tropes, Jeffers speaks directly, with no mistaking his meaning. In a period of harmonic subtleties, he employs only the whole tone scale. . . . Jeffers, with a contempt for artistry that is as pervasive as his contempt for man, delivers his parables of violence and his hymns to hopelessness with a one-dimensional straightforwardness that is almost Homeric. And the similes he uses, if not Homeric, are as primitively American as the flintlock and the Maypole.

Selden Rodman. *Poetry*. July, 1954. pp. 226–7

Carmel narratives

Primitive instincts still ruling humanity in the twentieth century are the source of the tragic events in Jeffers's longer poems. He believes with Plato that "madness like vice must be known but not practiced or imitated." To avoid hard realities, to save ourselves through illusion, to try to be happy in deluding ourselves, or in considering evil only as "bad dreams" is not Jeffers's gospel.

Rudolph Gilbert. *Shine, Perishing Republic*
(Humphries). 1936. pp. 94–5

The unerring psychic unity of a story is one of his capital achievements. In addition he has to an unusual degree mastery of the narrative form and an uncanny ability to impart life. . . . His themes are ve-hemence, intense and frequently frustrated passion, perversion, bitter introspection; and sex being consummated repeatedly, for the gesture is nearly as common in his dramas as *attitude* and *arabesque* in Russian choreography.

Hildegarde Flanner. *NR*. Jan. 27, 1937. p. 379

In the field of narrative poetry he has given new versions of classical and Biblical themes, but his greatest work in this genre are the tragic folk-tales of the Carmel region. These poems relate the violent ends which befall human beings tormented by desire and pain. They are studies in morbid psychology, dream-ridden. . . . Their setting is the great panorama of nature, conceived by the poet with imaginative fidelity. Nature dwarfs their protagonists, but also dignifies them.

Lawrence Clark Powell. *Robinson Jeffers*
(San Pasqual). 1940. p. 208

(*Hungerfield*) Here, once more, is Jeffers's approximation of Greek tragedy, transferred to the melodramatic coast of California. Here, concentrated misanthropy is extended into a narrative of angry love and driving hatred. . . . A Jeffers reader will be prepared for all this. But, although, he will no longer be either shocked or surprised, he will not fail to be roused. Jeffers has not lost the gift of biting language and the ability to communicate the phantasmagoria of terror.

Louis Untermeyer. *SR*. Jan., 16, 1954. p. 17

Adaptations of Greek tragedies

In *The Tower Beyond Tragedy*, Jeffers's greatest work, he imitates the Greek drama. . . . Not since Swinburne's *Erechtheus* and *Atalanta* has a tragic poem of such height, depth, and power been written.

Rudolph Gilbert. *Shine, Perishing Republic*
(Humphries). 1936. pp. 102–4

Although *The Tower Beyond Tragedy* has been hailed by some as this poet's chef d'oevre, it is, in my opinion, one of the poorest poems he has written. Loaded with twentieth-century philosophy, the old Greek plays are further encumbered with unrelieved excessive emotions and bombastic speeches. The inspired prophetic utterances which Jeffers puts in the mouth of Cassandra do not make up for the absence of the chorus, which in Aeschylus, by its commonsense remarks, serves to balance the towering emotions of the drama.

Lawrence Clark Powell. *Robinson Jeffers*
(San Pasqual). 1940. p. 56

Mr. Jeffers's alterations are . . . distortions of the *dynamis,* the central drive, of the play itself. And the trouble lies in his language. With few exceptions, a heightening of the dramatic tension of a situation is the signal for the shouting to begin; and the shouting, like noises heard in delirium, drowns out the meaning of the poem. The passion of Euripedes becomes the Californian violence of Mr. Jeffers, and I must further particularize that violence as Hollywoodian. . . . (In

Medea) he gives us a Grand-Guignol version of an oriental Hedda Gabler with the diction of Termagant and the manners of a fishwife.

Dudley Fitts in Kenyon Critics, edited by John Crowe
Ransom (World). 1951. pp. 309–11

The best introduction to the writings of Jeffers is the Modern Library edition of *Roan Stallion* or *Selected Poems;* also see "The Women at Point Sur," "Cawdor," and *Medea.*

JONES, JAMES (1921–   )

For the nonsqueamish adult *From Here to Eternity* is the best picture of Army life ever written by an American, a book of beauty and power despite its unevenness, a book full of the promise of great things to come. . . . The background of Prewitt's experience is saturated with the class struggle in America and the deeds of its martyrs. In that, as in his style, Jones is like Dreiser. Prewitt, like his creator, is a man of utter honesty. And Jones, like Prewitt, has been there. When we have read him we have been there, too, and have been shaken and chastened by what he has made us feel. This is proof that, in spite of imperfections, *From Here to Eternity* is a work of genius.

Ned Calmer. SR. Feb. 24, 1951. pp. 11–2

From Here to Eternity is the work of a major new American novelist. To anyone who reads this immensely long and deeply convincing story of life in the peacetime army, it will be apparent that in James Jones an original and utterly honest talent has restored American realism to a pre-eminent place in world literature. . . . There have been more subtly written books about the American soldier, and books with more finished conscious technique, but none that has been written with more integrity, or with a surer grasp of its material.

David Dempsey. NYT. Feb. 25, 1951. p. 5

James Jones has taken no less than life itself for his theme, and he has written of it in the strongest tradition of realism, seeking truth, sparing nothing. He has transcended the graphic and explicit; he has permitted himself neither ornament nor nicety; he has produced a book entirely adult. . . . The reader who surrenders . . . to the cumulative power of this novel, to its complexity and brutality so close to living experience, will discover here a wealth of human feeling and compassion and a belief in the constructive possibility of human existence.

Gene Baro. NYHT. Feb 25, 1951. p. 7

The book is a remarkable achievement in somewhat the same way that *Studs Lonigan* or *The Naked and the Dead* are remarkable achievements: it is big, it is very serious (and sometimes very funny), it is least convincing when ideas get the upper hand over feelings, it makes a kind of fetish of "honesty" (i.e., insistence on the more sordid details of life), and yet the intensity of its emotions welds these details into a whole. And there are some passages, such as a description of a bugler playing taps, that are very movingly written.

Paul Pickrel. *YR*. Spring, 1951. pp. 573–4

James Jones uses the Army as the symbol of an abstract, dehumanized, soul-crushing institution which subjugates the individual by imposing the fear of authority. . . . The value of a novel like *From Here to Eternity,* that is large in scope as well as in bulk, is that it operates on many levels at the same time. That is to say, it gives us shifting, kaleidoscopic pictures of different aspects of reality, some of which conflict, some of which are complementary, but all of which are fused and integrated to serve as a symphonic interpretation of American life. . . . (Yet) Prewitt's love for Lorena, a glorified prostitute, smacks of fake romanticism, and is as unconvincing as the author's attempt to define democracy in terms of the hero's attachment to the underdog.

Charles I. Glicksberg. *Phylon*. No. 4, 1953. pp. 384–8

From Here to Eternity is a big, solid, and formidable novel; and only upon reading it a second or third time, maybe, do we begin to realize the brilliance of its craft. . . . *Eternity* is a definitive novel of the American peacetime Army. Despite the blasphemy of its content, the poetic obscenity of its speech (which becomes contagious), and its open description of certain sexual values which have not been prominent in our literature, it is both a heroic and an epic novel. Yes, and it upholds those "eternal verities" that are shared by novels of this class, and which the conservatives can never find in modern literature. Only the previous mold of thought has been broken here, and the new expression is momentarily surprising or shocking.

Maxwell Geismar. *American Moderns* (Hill and
Wang). 1958. pp. 225–6

In James Jones's first novel, sheer intensity of feeling triumphed over crudity of style and mind. . . . In his new novel (*Some Came Running*) Jones is no longer working with materials as fresh or as highly charged. . . . The savage passion which energized *From Here to Eternity* is muffled, and there remains the yammer of self-pity, to which is now added the earnest drone of portentous banalities. Out of the author's hope chest of ideas come tumbling all the fuzzy bits and pieces of thought solemnly cherished by an essentially primitive mind. . . . There are enough forcefully realized episodes or scenes to suggest that Jones might do a lot better if he were to conquer his thousand-page-or-more complex. As it stands, however, his novel represents the dubious victory of six years' perspiration over lack of inspiration.

Charles Rolo. *At.* Jan., 1958. pp. 78–9

One can . . . recall that literary history is lined with figures of giants who have gained eternal life despite the tediousness of their prose, while the corpses of their niggling critics now lie happily nameless and forgotten. These are the writers who succeed in making us forget their clumsiness by the grandeur of their conceptions, the depth of their insights, the persistent "living quality" of their characters. It is a matter of . . . profound regret that none of these attributes are present in any measureable degree (that is, in any degree capable of competing for our attention with the wretchedness of the prose) in Mr. Jones's new novel.

Harvey Swados. *NR.* Jan. 27, 1958. p. 16

With *Some Came Running,* Mrs. (Lowney) Handy has her teacher's dream fulfilled. Her student has written a book about her, acknowledging his indebtedness to her in a note calling the book a "collective enterprise". . . . Mrs. Handy's philosophy served Jones well in *Eternity.* Her faith in the tragic consequences of what we might loosely term sin (straying from commandments) was convincing when punishment also proceeded from bucking the U. S. Army. When it is nothing but an extension of her belief that sex ruins the artist, readers less religiously inclined are likely to be left perplexed, seeing such events as Dave's death as mere contrivances.

David Ray. *Nation.* Feb. 8, 1958. p. 124

Does *The Pistol* indicate a change of heart, or did Jones write it just to show that he can be a disciplined writer if he sets out to be? So far as the book itself is concerned, his motives don't matter: for whatever reasons Jones wrote it, it is a good book, certainly a better book than either of its predecessors. But when one considers the future, one would be glad to know how Jones feels about what he has done. . . . The notion that a man can be a writer without knowing it or without having written, a notion that Wolfe's example has often and unhappily fostered, has been Jones's curse. He does have talents, and *The Pistol* proves that he can learn a lesson or two if he tried. But one wonders if he has yet outgrown the absurd notion of the born writer.

Granville Hicks. *SR*. Jan. 10, 1959. p. 12

See *From Here to Eternity* and *The Pistol* (novels).

KANTOR, MACKINLAY (1904–   )

There is no book ever written which creates, so well as this (*Long Remember*) the look and smell of battle, the gathering of two armies, the clash, and the sullen separation. *The Red Badge of Courage* as a work of art is superior to *Long Remember,* but it is a study in the psychology of courage, not a spectacle. Mr. Kantor contrives to give us the movement of the whole spectacle in a series of sharply drawn scenes. We get glimpses of the great leaders done so naturally and unobtrusively that they are wholly credible. The appearance of Lee riding along his lines on Seminary Ridge is perfect.

Allen Tate. *NYHT*. April 8, 1934. p. 2

Mr. Kantor's merit (in *Long Remember*) is his realistic treatment of a historical moment: the thing might have happened yesterday. No doubt the literature of the last war has helped to balance the mood and style. There is a sheer understanding of the horror of war and at the same time a sense that it happened so, inevitably, in spite of Bale's passionate protest; and the realism of his acceptance of the fighting, while still protesting against it, is the measure of his sanity. A soldier can understand the business of war, a civilian can only hope to stand it, and it is this long suspense of despair and discouragement of action that makes the character of Bale and makes the book.

Peter Monro Jack. *NYT*. April 15, 1934. p. 6

Both in verse and prose, both in his monumental novel, *Long Remember,* and in his collection of ballads, *Turkey in the Straw,* MacKinlay Kantor has already given us much that is memorable concerning the American Civil War. Now he has well-nigh achieved a masterpiece in a short story . . . *The Voice of Bugle Ann*. . . . So far as atmosphere goes, the tale of this fabulous foxhound *is* a masterpiece. . . . The narrative ability of Mr. Kantor is greatly above the average. Here's a thoroughly American writer who deserves your salute.

William Rose Benét. *SR*. August 31, 1935. p. 4

MacKinlay Kantor, in *Happy Land,* takes us into an average small-town home, bereaved of its son in this war. It is a short book, yet into its few pages it packs the feeling and substance of several generations of simple, decent people. . . . *Happy Land* has been called sentimental. . . . And so perhaps it is, if sentimentality in a writer means abetting his readers' emotions in sneaking up on them. Perhaps Mr. Kantor strums the heartstrings a little too deliberately, though he does it with imagination and restraint. But *Happy Land* remains a book for which one has respect and affection.

Robert Littell. YR. Spring, 1943. pp. vi–viii

Of the established popular writers of our time—the writers, that is, whose main contributions are to the big magazines and to the movies—MacKinlay Kantor is surely one of the most attractive. Never pretending to be more than he is—a gifted and practiced story-teller—he has knowingly produced his full share of that artful blend of sentiment and melodrama which makes up the large part of our popular fiction. Yet he has also managed to bring forth on occasion work of genuine dignity and value. In a few of his short stories, and in at least one of his short novels, there is rich and memorable writing, unmarked by either contrivance or concession.

Richard Sullivan. NYT. Feb. 9, 1947. p. 7

Twenty years ago, in *Long Remember,* MacKinlay Kantor gave us a moving picture of the impact of battle on the little town of Gettysburg. Even before he wrote that book his imagination had been stirred by the possibilities of a story that mirrored the whole of the Civil War, and *Andersonville* . . . is the product of a quarter-century of study and writing. Onto the warp of history Mr. Kantor has woven with the stuff of imagination an immense and terrible pattern, a pattern which finally emerges as a gigantic panorama of the war itself, and of the nation that tore itself to pieces in war. Out of fragmentary and incoherent records, Mr. Kantor has wrought the greatest of our Civil War novels.

Henry Steele Commager. NYT. Oct. 30, 1955. p. 1

In 1934 a new writer, MacKinlay Kantor, seized our attention with his intense, compassionate story of Gettysburg, *Long Remember.* . . .

The Civil War was and is his first love. . . . I think it likely that the revulsion against the concentration camps of our time was the final imperative which compelled him to write his new long, heartfelt novel, *Andersonville.* . . . The novelist employs a thousand different episodes to bring the war within the focus of the prison, and there are times when his power of invention leads him too far afield. But in his pictures of tenacity, endurance, and cleansing mercy he has written with truth and power.

Edward Weeks. At. Nov., 1955. p. 88

Andersonville is a most impressive performance. This is obviously a book that Kantor dreamed of doing all his life. And he has turned in a stirring work, shaped of forty years of delving in Civil War material, a profound sense of identity with the American past, and a craft which, if not inventive or fresh, has been well sharpened over twenty-eight antecedent books. Both in its techniques and its situation this novel is a cross between John Hersey's *The Wall* and Norman Mailer's *The Naked and the Dead*.

Sidney Alexander. *Reporter*. Jan. 12, 1956. p. 40

See *Long Remember, Voice of Bugle Ann,* and *Andersonville* (novels).

KEROUAC, JACK (1922–   )

The extravagant vitality both of his materials and his presentation of them verges often on the uncouth. He is almost always unmistakably sincere and in earnest. He writes with an untrained eloquence that carries one briskly along over some pretty hobbledehoy passages, a few definite boners and many solecisms. But what of that? . . . In this, his first novel (*The Town and the City*), Mr. Kerouac provides the most enlightening and persuasive over-all account of the motives and ways of the currently young generation it has been my good fortune to come upon.

Florence Haxton Bullock. *NYHT*. March 5, 1950. p. 7

Like Wolfe, to whom he seems to owe much, Mr. Kerouac tends to overwrite. Admirably, however, he avoids imposing a false thematic framework on his material, pinning everything by force to "lostness" or "loneliness." His is the kind of novel that lets life lead where it will. More often than not, the depth and breadth of his vision triumph decisively over his technical weaknesses.

John Brooks. *NYT*. March 5, 1950. p. 6

On the Road contains a good deal of excellent writing. Mr. Kerouac has a distinctive style, part severe simplicity, part hep-cat jargon. He uses each of these elements with a sure touch, works innumerable combinations and contrasts with them, and never slackens the speed of his narrative, which proceeds like Dean (Moriarty) at the wheel, at a steady hundred and ten miles an hour.

The book is most readable. It disappoints because it constantly promises a revelation or a conclusion of real importance and general applicability, and cannot deliver any such conclusion because Dean is more convincing as an eccentric than as a representative of any segment of humanity.

Phoebe Adams. *At.* Oct., 1957. p. 180

Some of the writing (in *On the Road*) is immediately attractive; but what is attractive about it is not its "wildness" or its "desperation," but a certain unmistakable simplicity and openness of mind. . . . When Mr. Kerouac says "Wow!" he can convey a certain sense of wonder and innocence that is affecting. As the narrator hitchhikes or drives back and forth across the American continent, and never for any good reason, he meets fellow tramps and travelers, sees towns and cities that he approaches and lives in and leaves again, and the plains and mountains between—and to these he can respond with an engaging candor.

Dan Jacobson. *Cmty.* Dec., 1957. p. 478

This wolf . . . ravens down the raw streets of America, taking gladness in the fact that the Mississippi has lived up to its advance notice in Mark Twain, describing one haunt after another as "storied," literary as literary can be, raised on the great books, as aren't we all? Where Thomas Wolfe broke his head butting against the world of intellectual highlife, Jack Kerouac is butting but unbroken against the world of hipsters. . . . Despite its drag race of words and gestures, *On the Road* does nothing, thinks nothing, acts nothing, but yet manages to be a book after all—a loving portrait of hip Dean Moriarty and his beat, cool friends as they run a hundred and ten miles an hour in order to stand still. It's a frantic book, and for that reason there is hope for Jack Kerouac.

Herbert Gold. *Nation.* Nov. 16, 1957. p. 355

The central character in Jack Kerouac's *On the Road* is no hipster, even if the literary critics may call him one. That is, he is no hipster in the jazz musician sense. But he is a hipster in the Broyardian sense of trying to get somewhere. His motivation is the same and it carries with it the identification with jazz. The entire book is, on more than one level, the account of postwar youth trying madly to get somewhere somehow. . . . His book assumes a knowledge of the language and litany of jazz. . . . The jazz generation is marking time, being cool, waiting, disengaged, if you must, looking for somewhere to be. Meanwhile, writers like Kerouac and music like jazz are its voice.

Ralph Gleason. *SR.* Jan. 11, 1958. p. 75

The most noteworthy quality of *The Subterraneans* is its coalescence of theme and style. The tumult in one is made comprehensible, and bearable, by the tumult in the other. Kerouac calls himself a jazz poet. There is no doubt about his great sensitivity to language. His sentences frequently move in tempestuous sweeps and whorls and sometimes they have something of the rich music of Gerard Manley Hopkins or Dylan Thomas.

Clyde S. Kilby. *NYHT*. Feb. 23, 1958. p. 4

Kerouac can describe a simple supper of pea soup and wild mushrooms, or even a spartan repast prepared from those little plastic bags of dried food carried by seasoned mountaineers, in a way to make your mouth water. He is at his very best in describing the smells, sounds, sights and general feeling of walking a Western trail.

In his often brilliant descriptions of nature one is aware of exhilarating power and originality, and again when he creates the atmosphere of lively gatherings for drinking, talking, and horsing around in those simple but highly stylized dwellings of his Pacific Coast friends.

Nancy Wilson Ross. *NYT*. Oct. 5, 1958. p. 14

Despite its unlikely subject, *The Dharma Bums* belongs in every fiction collection for the following reasons. Its prose is pure American of the sort William Carlos Williams has been asking for all these years; its philosophy, its anti-organization-man-ism is a precious and also radically American stand. Kerouac can see the panorama of American land- and city-scapes in broad, bright flashes and can say what he sees (some of his nature writing recalls Muir and Thoreau) and, at the very least, his book is a close sociological study of contemporary phenomena. Sometimes Kerouac seems a little foolish, often he is extreme, but he is genuine, he is alive, and he is native.

Dorothy Nyren. *LJ*. Sept. 15, 1958. p. 2441

See *The Town and the City, On the Road, The Subterraneans, The Dharma Bums,* and *Doctor Sax.* (novels).

KINGSLEY, SIDNEY (1906–   )

Men in White is what might be called . . . a masculine play. That is to say it deals not so wholly with women, their interests, exaltations, and claims as it does with the male line of life, as centered in a profession, a pursuit, a ruling passion and the fellowship of men with men. The story involves love enough, with one betrothal and promised chance of marriage and one abortion and death. But love, nevertheless, is in this play one of the sources of life that feed the whole. If you did not feel so moved and satisfied by *Men in White,* you would feel somewhat complimented by it for taking you thus as a full human being in the midst of a living world. All through the three acts of *Men in White* the distribution of the stresses is admirable, the progression of the interest, almost a suspense, is unbroken, and good images are found for the dramatic expression of the points to be made.

Stark Young. *NR*. Oct. 11, 1933. p. 241

Sidney Kingsley had the imagination to transfer an aspect of modern science into dramatic terms so vividly and so rightly that the meaning is clear to all and thrilling to all. If he does it with steam sterilizers and bichloride and white robes and rubber gloves, in symbols of the eye rather than words for the ear, he is no less a dramatist and no less to be praised. . . . On the whole, *Men in White* captures reality with almost a passion of sincerity and breathes a spirit of idealism—the idealism of the medical profession at its best, which is probably one of the reasons for its great popular success.

Walter Prichard Eaton. *NYHT*. April 1, 1934. p. 17

Mr. Kingsley's plays have always been completely devoid of what we call "literary quality," and for that reason there is a kind of seriousness with which they cannot possibly be taken. Indeed, it is that fact rather that the undue prevalence of mere external violence which makes "melodrama" the inevitable label to apply to them. But I know no contemporary American who can take a topic—slum children in *Dead End* or doctors and nurses in *Men in White*—and then turn out a more stage-worthy piece, full of shrewd if not too profound observation crisply and humorously embodied in recognizable types.

Joseph Wood Krutch. *Nation*. April 9, 1949. pp. 424–5

In a world behind the footlights Mr. Kingsley's ingenuity is not to be underestimated. He is a technician of outstanding abilities. His instinct for the stage is keen, his mastery of its means genuine. He happens to be a realist of the most painstaking sort. Everyone who saw *Men in White, Dead End,* or *Detective Story* must remember his inclination to hold the pier glass rather than the hand mirror up to nature. His fondness for the gadgets of realism remains undisguised even in *Darkness at Noon.*

John Mason Brown. *SR*. Feb. 3, 1951. pp. 23–4

Kingsley has a gift for making theatre out of local color and documentation in such dramatic milieus as hospitals, off-center neighborhoods, detective bureaus. Being a man of the thirties, Kingsley has also a penchant for liberal social preachment. He has, however, no psychological insight, no poetic eloquence, no capacity to convey the quality of any inner state.

Harold Clurman. NR. Feb. 5, 1951. p. 23

Mr. Sidney Kingsley's *Lunatics and Lovers* is all raw and garish surfaces; the dramatic equivalent of the magenta neon sign which shines relentlessly over this raffish cage in the moral zoo of Broadway. . . . The generous, comfortable bawdry to which it aspires never coalesces; the wit is as metallic and rasping as the chromium decor of the setting. . . . Mr. Kingsley, nothing if not ambitious, has privately invoked in support of *Lunatics and Lovers* the shades of Moliere and Rabelais, Schopenhauer and Shakespeare, but no such distinguished presence seemed to me to haunt the play: what I caught was the stale whiff of a herring from Damon Runyan's net, a little gamy from over-exposure among the cardboard guys and dolls of this particular asphalt jungle.

Richard Hayes. Com. Jan. 14, 1955. pp. 407–8

See *Men in White* and *Dead End* (plays).

KREYMBORG, ALFRED   (1883–   )

He trips about cheerfully among life's little incongruities; laughs at you and me and progress and prejudice and dreams; says "I told you so!" with an air, as if after a double somersault in the circus ring; grows wistful, even tender, with emotion always genuine even though not too deep for momentary tears. And always, whatever his mood, whatever his subject or purpose, he is, as becomes the harlequin-philosopher, entertaining. . . . I do not mean that Mr. Kreymborg is always a satirist. Even in his most serious moods, however, he keeps his light touch-and-go manner and his telegraphic, almost telescopic, style.

Harriet Monroe. Poetry. Oct., 1916. pp. 51–3

He chooses words with an apparently naive simplicity, only to combine them subtly into repetitions which form delicate rhythms not unlike the patterns of a fugue. With each repetition the theme develops, the harmonies deepen. He gains his effect as directly, as mysteriously as does music; there is indeed a kinship between Kreymborg's style and Bach's. I can think of no other musician combining his cerebral quality, economy of ornament and architectural sense of form. . . . Mr. Kreymborg, who is a thoroughly educated musician, has drawn upon the technique of counterpoint and melody in a wholly original manner, thereby greatly enriching his style, and introducing a new element into American verse.

Marjorie Allen Seiffert. Poetry. Jan., 1919. pp. 226–7

Almost all of his plays possess that direct appeal to children, although they are often too abstruse or fantastical for older audiences. To enjoy them completely one must have an open mind, unprejudiced by stage conventions. The whole volume (Plays for Merry Andrews), with its delightful caricatures, with its humors, with its tongue-in-the-cheek bombast, is very reminiscent of Dickens.

Malcolm Cowley. NYEP. Dec. 31, 1920. p. 5

Mr. Kreymborg's simplicity appears to be guileless, but there is always the suggestion under his naive surfaces. His rhythms and images are easy to imitate, but not his charm and his humor; and to capture his agile handling of suggestion is a challenge—the quiet glance with a keen edge back of it which points up to a dart and shoots through so deftly that we are unaware of its awareness.

Laura Sherry. Poetry. July, 1921. p. 219

Alfred Kreymborg deserves more than he has received of his country. An original craftsman in the aesthetic of the drama, he has been neglected by the American theatre of which he has more claim to be called a founder than Eugene O'Neill. A free, felicitous, versatile adventurer in the forms of the lyric, he has warmed up a public to smile upon such poets as E. E. Cummings. . . . A land which finds no use for the sensibilities of this fantastic lover, and provides him neither with satisfactory comrades in his isolation nor in sufficient nurture in himself to do without, is either a pathetic or a tragic land. Much as the social hunger of Mr. Kreymborg capering so featly before a dropped lead curtain of inertia and indifference affects one, the imperviousness of our land behind the curtain is more moving.

Waldo Frank. Dial. July, 1925. pp. 72–4

The whimsical in poetry has had in the work of Mr. Alfred Kreymborg its most entertaining contemporary expression. His work, first circulated through Others, encountered, inexplicably enough, a great deal of amazed ridicule. . . . The literate public supposed that Mr. Kreymborg and his confreres were trying to be profound. The public was wrong. . . . For the universe and the cosmic inflow and outflow of esoteric emotion have not visibly interested him. He has been said to express himself too indirectly; his poems have been charged with obscurity. This, too, is a mistake. He is casual, simple, direct.

Allen Tate. NYHT. July 18, 1926. p. 3

It is easy to admit that Alfred Kreymborg's poetry has many short-comings, and still turn to it with interest and relief. Granted that one must be in just the right mood and of the right temperament to enjoy the strange blend of intellect, intuition and childishness, and that this mood cannot be summoned at will; granted that apart from the appeal of their whimsicality only a half-dozen poems can hold one's admiration when read six weeks later, and that none of these plays the delicate bells of poetic ecstasy; granted that at their worst the poems are irritatingly unclear, and disappointingly anti-climactic—still after all they are never banal and if they are affected it is at least never a saccharine or over-esthetic affectation.

Margery Swett Mansfield. *Poetry*. Jan., 1927. p. 226

Mr. Kreymborg prefers the theatrical variety show and the stage effects rather than the inner play and subtlety of an art form. . . . Action or movement, combined with the public address, become the fulcrum of Mr. Kreymborg's early drive. A kind of simplified statement studded in a riot of nature and stars, with personalized items, is the usual background. . . . His themes . . . remain in 1944 what they were in 1912. The same light touch and free-style movement of words and phrases, and a dependence on sensory as well as surface awareness prevail.

Harry Roskolenko. *NYT*. April 22, 1945. p. 44

No one can deny that the simple and essentially modest man who inhabits Mr. Kreymborg's physical shape has accomplished a body of work which—if compared with the more sporadic efforts of poets much more frequently discussed—is impressive. Alfred Kreymborg has been, for thirty years at least, an intensely active force in the accomplishment of whatever achievement poetry in the United States may be credited with by literary historians. If he has never exactly stood at the center, the focus of any of the various currents of interest, Imagistic, regional, neo-classic, metaphysical, cosmopolitan, satiric, that have moved through American verse since he first began to write, he has never been removed from any—he has always remained aware of what was going on, and able to find an attitude of his own with which to meet it.

John Gould Fletcher. *Poetry*. July, 1945. p. 216

In our poetry Kreymborg has been at his best as acrobat and juggler, in a variant of the Pagliacci, *He Who Gets Slapped,* and *Laugh, Clown, Laugh* tradition. And he has created a troubadour personality for himself which is engaging and bears credentials to the Court of the Muses; he is a man with a big heart and a fantastic mind, in poetry a puppet-showman whose barbs (to mix metaphors) directed at the shams of society are always feathered.

William Rose Benét. *SR*. July 20, 1946. pp. 13–4

See *The Selected Poems, Plays for Merry Andrews*, and *Troubadour* (autobiography).

KUNITZ, STANLEY (1905–   )

One feels in his poetry none of the awkward one-sidedness that one feels in nearly all of even the most brilliant poetry this side of Mr. Robinson. The experience in which Mr. Kunitz deals is normal, rich and complex; he is firm on his feet, and, now and again, quick on them. He has experimented with a syntactic instrument which, when he controls it, enables him to achieve tremendously vigorous synthesis. . . . Even at his second best, Mr. Kunitz will bear a great deal of careful reading.

Yvor Winters. *NR*. June 4, 1930. p. 78

He is a graceful writer of very feminine tone, perhaps almost over-delicate in gesture and accent; he is nevertheless beautifully in command of his medium and of his own subtle shadings through language and rhythm. . . . He strikes no profound note. His is the art of creating poetry for poetry's sake. Mr. Kunitz gives the reader always the impression of the romantic image of delight seen through the fragile lens of the mind, no impact against the flesh, but, nevertheless, a wistful, remote eagerness. His unique quality is the perfection with which he accomplishes this, and his waving, scarflike rhythm.

Eda Lou Walton. *Nation*. June 18, 1930. p. 709

Enough of the probing seriousness and curiosity of a keen poetic intelligence is exhibited in this first volume (*Intellectual Things*) to warrant a considerable confidence in the talents of the author, and in his future work. . . . Mr. Kunitz shares his faults with a large company of his contemporaries. . . . These weaknesses grow from an effort at stylization not always justified by the results. . . . The reader's patience, however, finds its reward in the best poems. . . . Mr. Kunitz possesses what in a musician would be called a melodic gift —a special ability to define and sustain fluently the verbal and tonal pattern upon which his poem is built. The presentation of such patterns necessarily involves a good deal of creative courage, and Mr. Kunitz plunges into his elaborate imagery, conceits, and phraseology with none of the hesitation that detains the poet stricter in matters of form and logic.

                                Morton Dauwen Zabel. *Poetry*. July, 1930. pp. 218–20

From the beginning he was a "metaphysical" poet in the triple sense that he was interested in the analysis of, not the mere submission to experience; that that analysis was made by means of imagery predominantly intellectual in its manipulation; and that the images were drawn from every corner of the poet's experience. But he was also "metaphysical" in the less satisfactory sense that he echoed, quite directly, certain seventeenth-century poets. . . . Now the "metaphysical" style has become entirely his own, and he writes with terse, fresh imagery at nearly every point. . . . Kunitz has now (it would seem) every instrument necessary to the poetic analysis of modern experience.

                                Mark Schorer. *NYT*. March 26, 1944. p. 21

Very catholic in his tastes, many of these poems of Kunitz's exhibit that by now not curious synthesis of the new and the old which one finds in the earlier paintings of Picasso and Matisse, a synthesis to which modern painting, so-called, seems to be returning, and which involves freshness of image and perception but no essential distortion, rather a stressing and renewing of the careful craftsmanship of the older painters.

Thus in many of the poems one encounters subject matter that is strongly or partly surrealistic, but interpreted in forms as classic as those of Frost, Millay or Keats.

                                Harry Sylvester. *Com*. April 21, 1944. p. 20

Passport to the Wars is a sincere and sound achievement. It is the work of a talented craftsman, with a sharp and elegant mind, and it concerns itself with the most significant problem of the modern world—the murderous and efficient mechanization of our environment that has invaded and corrupted the mind itself. This problem is implicit everywhere in Mr. Kunitz's poems, where under the pressure of our failure, energies that might have been concentrated upon the service of humanity or the love of God are dissipated in frustration and hysteria. . . . "In the destructive element immerse" has been the practical wisdom forced upon this poet, but the method, which has the virtues of necessity and honesty, has also its nullifying weaknesses.

                                A.J.M. Smith. *Poetry*. June, 1944. p. 165

How sweetly the usual word slips fresh into the line (in "Deciduous Branch") and how sweetly the rhythm sways the thought alive! Such lines are not only in the purest lyric tradition of English poetry, but do honor to that tradition. To be sure Kunitz is not always that immediately clear. He is a poet of intellectual passions. The point is that the labor will not be in vain. Kunitz is certainly the most neglected good poet of the last quarter-century.

John Ciardi. *SR*. Sept. 27, 1958. p. 18

Stanley Kunitz has a rich lyrical style; sometimes a redundancy of it. Rock-faults of feeling, however, thrust their way up through the smooth surface; and, as he confesses, he looses "a gang of personal devils" and makes them "clank their jigging bones as public evils." The devils are brought to heel formally—Kunitz does not let them run away with his poems—but they are in evidence. . . . Though the heavy Baudelairean sense of secular damnation and all-pervasive ennui does not altogether dominate Kunitz's work it has marked it indelibly.

M. L. Rosenthal. *Nation*. Oct. 11, 1958. p. 214

In mood and subject, the poems range widely but perhaps not as widely as some could wish. Kunitz moves from the forceful lyric to the tour de force, but always with clenched fists. Although his ear is delicate, he seldom allows that part of his gift to predominate. This seems to me unfortunate because his obviously flexible technical skill might be put to singing simply, a task it would perform beautifully. . . . But these matters lose almost all their importance in the face of the achievement the book represents: imagination functioning repeatedly at the highest pitch.

David Wagoner. *Poetry*. Dec., 1958. pp. 176–7

Well over a third of *Selected Poems* is new . . . and I happily report that many of the new poems give evidence of a poetic personality that is growing both broader and deeper. The tension in the poetry has not slackened, but much of the strain (or straining) has disappeared. . . . Kunitz's imagery may often be far-fetched, but it is never obscure; it reveals rather than shrouds the subjects of the new poems. Like several of the greatest modern poets, Kunitz speaks more directly to us—and more richly, too—as he grows older. If the quantity of his output catches up with its quality, we may yet learn to rank him among the great American poets of this century.

Vivian Mercier. *Com*. Feb. 13, 1959. p. 524

Consider the love poems. Kunitz's way of contending with this subject is to take careful strategic precautions, lest the savagery and blood which are at the very source of the experience of love should escape into the multitudinous alleyways which we all contrive. In case my description should make Kunitz sound like another professional sensationalist, another flinger of blood-and-guts in the manner of Rafael Sabatini and George Barker, I hasten to point out that the ultimate achievement of the love poems in *Selected Poems* is tenderness. The delicacy of feeling which the poems record can exist *in the poems* only if the author has already run the whole course of love's experience, with its hatreds, its suicidal impulses. . . . To love is to effect an overwhelmingly difficult act of self-knowledge, and the reader can like it or lump it. In the hands of this poet, the subject flinches and wails. It is not pretty. It has grandeur.

James Wright. *SwR*. Spring, 1959. pp. 332–3

See *Selected Poems: 1928–1958*.

LARDNER, RING   (1885–1933)

For one thing, he has a ready invention—which most American realists have not; and for another thing—which is even rarer—he has a special personal accent which represents a special personal way of looking at things. . . . Lardner has imitated nobody else and nobody else could reproduce his essence: . . . there is scarcely a single paragraph of Lardner which, in its blending of freshness with irony, does not convey the sense of a distinguished intelligence and an interesting temperament.

Edmund Wilson. *Dial*. July, 1924. pp. 70–1

His remarkable eyes . . . were startling in an expression that I am in a dilemma to describe, wondering if I should use the word "hypnotic," or if, on the contrary, they appeared instead to be hypnotized. Very large and dark, they dominate his other vigorous features; nearly the entire iris is visible at all times, and were it not for the gentle mildness of manner and expression they, with their black brows soaring in vigorous arcs above them, could rival those of *Svengali*. Instead, they give an effect similar to those of the haunting Russian ladies of Chauve-Souris.

Walter Tittle. *Century*. July, 1925. p. 313

His studies, to be sure, are never very profound; he makes no attempt to get at the primary springs of human motive; all his people share the same amiable stupidity, the same transparent vanity, the same shallow swinishness; they are all human Fords in bad repair, and alike at bottom. But if he thus confines himself to the surface, it yet remains a fact that his investigations on that surface are extraordinarily alert, ingenious and brilliant—that the character he finally sets before us, however roughly articulated as to bones, is so astoundingly realistic as to epidermis that the effect is indistinguishable from that of life itself.

H. L. Mencken. *Prejudices, Fifth Series* (Knopf).
1926. pp. 51–2

Somewhat to my surprise, after I had finished reading consecutively six volumes of his work, I wasn't thinking of Lardner as a mirth-maker but as a sardonic satirist with a grip on his characters cruelly hard. This picturesque, garrulous, slovenly speech which he imputes to most of his persons is not a mere transcription of the vulgar tongue, it is an artful selection from the popular speech, craftily employed in the business of evisceration. . . . It is a whip of small cords to scourge American roughnecks, whether on the ball field, in the prize ring, on the golf links, or at the bridge table.

Stuart Sherman. *The Main Stream* (Scribner). 1927.
pp. 170–1

He is about six feet in height, perhaps a little over. His complexion is swarthy and he looks like the classical type of American Indian, except for his eyes, which are very large and round and shaded by long black lashes. . . . When Lardner talks, which he does very slowly and quietly, he throws his head back, raises his eyebrows, blinks, sways his chin a little from side to side, stares at you for a brief instant and then stares away from you. His comments are brief and mostly sardonic.

Burton Rascoe. *A Bookman's Daybook* (Liveright).
1929. pp. 248–9

Somewhere Lardner refers to "this special police dog" which "was like the most of them and hated everybody." Lardner himself is the police dog of American fiction, except that his hatred is not the product of mere crabbedness but of an eye that sees too deep for comfort. As a whole his work is devoted to tearing down the stucco facade of certain familiar American types. He takes some recognized national trait which is ordinarily treated with good-natured humor and reduces it to its basic viciousness. . . . What Lardner . . . is interested in getting at is the core of egotism from which even our apparently most impeccable virtues spring.

Clifton Fadiman. *Nation*. March 22, 1933. p. 316

Proud, shy, solemn, shrewd, polite, brave, kind, merciful, honorable—
with the affection these qualities aroused he created in addition a certain awe in people. His intentions, his will, once in motion were formidable factors in dealing with him—he always did every single thing he
said he would do. Frequently he was the melancholy Jacques, and sad
company indeed, but under any conditions a noble dignity flowed from
him, so that time in his company always seemed well spent.

F. Scott Fitzgerald. *NR*. Oct. 11, 1933. p. 255

There will be many to talk of his bitter hatred of the human race's
selfishness and stupidity, but he was filled with a mighty compassion for
the possessors of these qualities. But his loathing for pretentiousness
and leering obscentiy was uncompromising. And . . . he had a great
effect upon journalism, for he, more than anybody else, made it possible for reporters to write, and to have printed, the words that people
said instead of a lot of high sounding, mealy-mouthed phrases and
sentiments.

Franklin P. Adams. *The Diary of Our Own Samuel
Pepys* (Simon). 1935. p. 1174

In his light moments Lardner was . . . our greatest comic personality,
in his serious work an incomparable artist, and for his new American
literature Lardner fashioned a new American language. After him
refined English can never be quite so respectable. Lardner the puritan
scoffed at one immaculate conception: he deflowered the virgin word.
As a Joyce is elaborating a new vocabulary from the top of our knowledge up, onward, beyond the esoteric, Lardner made one from the
bottom, from the talk of the people, from the genuine base, and not the
theoretical one, of our society.

Maxwell Geismar. *Writers in Crisis* (Houghton).
1942. pp. 27–8

Others have written satire with more pretension, or with a greater surface scope; but to my mind no other American writer has achieved
Lardner's mastery of satire. His knife was sharper; it cut more deeply
—so deeply, in fact, that these people who seem so dreary, so banal, so
self-centered, often emerge for us as yearning, unhappy creatures who
are lost, deprived and vaguely unsatisfied.

James T. Farrell. *League of Frightened Philistines*
(Vanguard) 1945. p. 35

There are times in reading Lardner when you feel his total sympathy
with Swift's terrible verdict on humanity—that we are the most odious

little race of vermin that ever inhabited the planet; you feel his sympathy with the half-hidden sardonic side of Mark Twain's temperament. He takes less pleasure in the accidents of human behavior than Twain did and is not so thoughtful as Swift; but like both of these, Lardner has the habit of catching human beings when they think no one is looking at them; and he touches them with tiny drops of acid to see what they do and how they react.

Gilbert Seldes. Introduction to *The Portable Ring Lardner* (Viking) 1946. pp. 1–2

Mr. Lardner does not waste a moment when he writes in thinking whether he is using American slang or Shakespeare's English; whether he is remembering Fielding; whether he is proud of being American or ashamed of not being Japanese; all his mind is on the story. . . . It is no coincidence that the best of Mr. Lardner's stories are about games, for one may guess that Mr. Lardner's interest in games has solved one of the most difficult problems of the American writer; it has given him a clue, a centre, a meeting place for the divers activities of people whom a vast continent isolates, whom no tradition controls. Games give him what society gives his English brother. Whatever the precise reason, Mr. Lardner at any rate provides something unique in its kind, something indigenous to the soil, which the traveler may carry off as a trophy to prove to the incredulous that he has actually been in America and found it a foreign land.

Virginia Woolf. *The Moment and Other Essays* (Harcourt). 1948. pp. 122–3

Actually sport provides Ring with a serviceable framework within which he could examine quite a range of human behavior. In Ring's fiction baseball is an ordered world with definite rules of conduct; it demands skill and integrity and it has a code of honor. . . . His preoccupation with sport reflected a longing for an ideal world where the rules, if observed, guaranteed the triumph of merit; it also reflected his acute sense of the disparity between the way people were supposed to behave and the way they did. Sport provided Ring with a useful and significant scale for measuring his characters. Moreover the criteria of sport were especially valuable because everyone knew exactly what they were.

Donald Elder. *Ring Lardner* (Doubleday). 1956. pp. 205–6

Lardner had tremendous talent. Though he left behind no large work and he often fooled away his gifts on trifles, the sardonic brilliance of his comic imagination at its best is unsurpassed in American letters; though he is little noticed in contemporary criticism, he is still a vital influence on some of our best young writers—J. D. Salinger, for instance. His manipulation of language would have entitled him to the company of the foremost experimental writers of his time; his dazzling nonsense plays are among the earliest and best surrealistic literature produced in this country.

Paul Pickrel. *Harper.* July, 1956. p. 92

Lardner's hypersensitivity to language was a hypersensitivity to human suffering, a fact which becomes clear only when his fiction is related to his humor. His acute sense of the disparity between the way people should behave and the way they do is very often expressed in his stories by translations from the Mastoid, the use of English that dramatizes the disparity between the way English ought to be used and the way it is used. Since the comic style of his humor is identical with the narrative method of his fiction, where the characters often damn themselves by their own account of human behavior, it is natural enough to overlook the depth of satirical meaning that characterizes his fiction and a good deal of his humor also.

Delmore Schwartz. *Reporter.* Aug. 9, 1956. p. 52

See *The Portable Ring Lardner.*

LEVIN, MEYER (1905–   )

The Old Bunch . . . is one of the most ambitious novels yet attempted by any fiction writer of his generation, a work which demands a discipline and intelligence that are as yet unmatched by most novelists of his age. . . . Mr. Levin's treatment must be extensive rather than intensive. The novel is written in a series of brief episodes, the greater proportion of them from half a page to two pages. He switches from character to character, from tendency to tendency. . . . *The Old Bunch* impresses me as being one of the most ambitious novels yet produced by the current generation of American novelists.

James T. Farrell. *SR.* March 13, 1937. p. 5

The "bunch" were probably men and women with whom Mr. Levin grew up; he thinks of them tenderly, he pities the ones he saw fall, he has a neighborly admiration for those who succeeded. . . . There is a legend to the effect that all Jews are cousins; Mr. Levin often writes as if he thought that happily true. The novel is friendly and gay. . . .

Mr. Levin has not written the definitive novel of the contemporary generation of American Jews, he has not written a powerful novel. . . . But he has written a supple novel that furnishes swift and enjoyable reading.

Alfred Kazin. *NYHT*. March 14, 1937. p. 5

The Old Bunch is a landmark in the development of the realistic novel. . . . Meyer Levin does for a group of Chicago Jews what James Farrell did for the Chicago Irish. But while Farrell got inside of the mind of Studs Lonigan and stayed there for three volumes, Meyer Levin looks at the world through the eyes of "the bunch," eleven boys and eleven girls who went to school together and lived in the same neighborhood in Chicago. . . . It is a loose galaxy of experience, mirroring in its form the form of the bunch. . . . Although *The Old Bunch* must be called plotless, nevertheless, incident by incident it makes vivid and exciting reading.

Harold Strauss. *NYT*. March 28, 1937. p. 6

Intrinsically this (*The Old Bunch*) is the classic American story of defeat and frustration so often presented in American literature by novelists like Dreiser, Farrell, and Dos Passos. Mr. Levin's particular distinction lies in having discerned and recreated this story within the Jewish American milieu, of which scarcely a detail of background or development escapes him. And, ironically enough, it is through showing the failure that they share with their American hosts that Mr. Levin naturalizes his Jews within their new homeland.

Philip Rahv. *Nation*. April 3, 1937. p. 385

(*The Old Bunch*) is a collective novel with the group as hero . . . and it tells the whole story of the spiritual and financial plunder of Chicago. *The Old Bunch* is written in good, hard-driving colloquial prose, and is full of sharp characterizations, though the cinematic shuttling of the technique makes it hard to establish character in the round. The book suffers from defects most collective novels have suffered from, chiefly in its lack of psychological depth. . . . But on the whole it is a very fine novel, with the speed and lustiness and brawling of the world's fourth largest city.

Harry T. Moore. *NR*. April 7, 1937. p. 273

As a writer, as American, as Jew, he seeks his seminal culture and his place in a world that, he thinks, regards him suspiciously and without full understanding. . . . Among Americans writing of Jews he is preeminent. His novel, *The Old Bunch,* while not quite the literary landmark we may have thought it during the Thirties, remains a very significant benchmark to those surveying that decade's fiction. He has produced two remarkable motion pictures on Israel's magnetism and its fulfillments for European Jewry. He has tracked down the indescribably terrible saga of Europe's Jewish survivors.

Peter R. Levin. *SR*. July 8, 1950. p. 14

Levin has a swift, economical and unpretentious style, but he also has the inner eye which relates the outer event to the psychic demands of a devouring heart. . . . There is no question that Levin was "oversensitive" to his Jewishness, whether in flight or in militancy, but it's exactly this over-sensitivity that makes the material of literature.

Max Lerner. *NR*. July 24, 1950. p. 19

He was among the first of the young American-born intellectuals to go to Palestine. . . . And long before the rise of Israel made Zionism fashionable, he was personally involved in its struggles. It is therefore natural that he proved to be one of the most effective reporters of contemporary Jewish history from Dachau to Israel. . . . Despite an unpretentious, almost haphazard style, Levin succeeds in conveying the scope of the events that he describes. This unfailing sense of perspective constitutes the difference between journalism and history.

Marie Syrkin. *Nation*. Aug. 12, 1950. p. 152

Levin retells the Leopold and Loeb story to recapture a sickness that is part of our times; retells this tale of murder and depravity to tell us about ourselves. . . . Levin has slapped together a strong indictment of our ignorance, our malice, our inhumanity; but he has done so in what is often painfully awkward stumbling prose. . . . (Yet) in his concern for his story, and in his understanding of the importance of the crime and the trial, Levin is writing his way to the truth. He has given us an important novel.

Charles Shapiro. *Nation*. Dec. 1, 1956. pp. 483–4

Compulsion can take its place with Dreiser's *American Tragedy*. To its telling Levin brings a compelling creative power rooted both in subjectivity and objectivity. As a campus contemporary of the two criminals . . . he writes with the immediacy and intimacy of first-hand knowledge of the principals in the case. To this he adds the maturity of a man and novelist who probes the influences, the motives and compulsion, the psychological forces, that led to the monstrous crime.

Rose Feld. *NYHT*. Oct. 28, 1956. p. 5

See *The Old Bunch* and *Compulsion* (novels); also *In Search* (autobiography).

LEWIS, SINCLAIR   (1885–1951)

The texture of the prose written by Mr. Lewis gives one but faint joy and one cannot escape the conviction that for some reason Lewis has himself found but little joy, either in life among us or in his own effort to channel his reactions to our life into prose. There can be no doubt that this man, with his sharp journalistic nose for news of the outer surface of our lives, has found out a lot of things about us and the way we live in our towns and cities, but I am very sure that in the life of every man, woman, and child in the country there are forces at work that seem to have escaped the notice of Mr. Lewis.

Sherwood Anderson. *NR*. Oct. 11, 1922. p. 172

Sinclair Lewis is the drummer of ideas, the sales executive of the new American literature. He has made the Revolt of the Younger Genera-tion a paying proposition, operating an exclusive territory on a royalty basis, and presenting an unusual household speciality, burlesque made up to look like satire. Every home a prospect; its simplicity sells it. If you are interested in building a repeat business for the future, Mr. Sinclair Lewis can demonstrate his product; attractive book combina-tions that get orders; unlimited possibilities, with large royalties.

Ernest Boyd. *Portraits: Real and Imaginary* (Doran).
1924. pp. 183–4

Besides his mastery of the realistic approach, Mr. Lewis has other literary virtues which have helped to establish his eminence among modern novelists. He has a keen, if rather sardonic, sense of humor, he has notable insight into the confused emotions of the ordinary man and woman; and he has brilliant descriptive powers. . . . And in ad-dition to all these virtues Mr. Lewis has still one more—the virtue of having boldly chosen the whole of American civilization as the subject of his novels.

Edgar Holt. *BkmL*. Jan., 1931. p. 234

The pastels, the chiaroscuro of personality are quite beyond him. He has made his way through the American scene with a naïveté, a sim-plicity of point of view, a limpidity, and even a shallowness which it is now time to pronounce invincible. And yet these qualities have en-hanced his satire. Simplicity enables him to concentrate his super-human energy; insensitiveness to chiaroscuro prevents the doubt that would be fatal. He becomes a flaming hate, and out of that hate he has written the most vigorous sociological fiction of our times, in America or anywhere else.

Bernard De Voto. SR. Jan. 28, 1933. p. 398

The style is the story, the story's well-paved road, the story's rapid vehicle. It runs but does not fly. It is precise but not exquisite, sensitive but not fastidious, direct but seldom breath-taking, rich in its fullness not in its adornment. Its best music is plain-song, without complicating harmony. . . . The poetry of the style appears almost wholly as exuberance. Above the essential irony of the actions there is a continuous play of laughter, pointing at whatever calls for ridicule or sympathy.

Carl Van Doren. Sinclair Lewis (Doubleday). 1933.
pp. 65–6

Sinclair Lewis does love the essential humanness of people. He can be savagely against the ideas they may hold; just as he can scourge and has scourged America, for many things. But when he said, as he did recently, that he loved this country, he said the truth. He is fundamentally an American. No other soil could have grown him. And he is a better thing than a humanist, he is a human-beingist.

William Rose Benét. SR. Jan. 30, 1934. p. 422

He is more aware of the monstrous extent of the stables that must be cleaned than he is of the possibility of any Hercules ever cleaning them; and when he pictures people who are pitted against their environments he usually shows them struggling without much hope of victory, without allies, and often with ingrown doubts as to whether or not they are on the right side. . . . For Lewis is the historian of America's catastrophic going-to-pieces—or at least of the going-to-pieces of her middle class—with no remedy to offer for the decline that he records; and he has dramatized the process of disintegration, as well as his own dilemma, in the outlines of his novels, in the progress of his characters, and sometimes, and most painfully, in the lapses of taste and precision that periodically weaken the structure of his prose.

Robert Cantwell. NR. Oct. 21, 1936. p. 301

A tolerable and beautiful life for everyone was the old American dream. . . . Beginning with Main Street, Sinclair Lewis' most important novels were to expose with savage humor those facets of American society which contradicted this ideal. But his moral scorn often obscured for readers the fact that their pitiless indictment of failure was dictated by passionate faith. He believed in the genuine possibility of a

personal kinghood, an education in brotherhood and responsible nobility. He became, as it were, a nostalgic gadfly tormenting the nation
—himself tormented by its repudiation of his exalted youthful ideals.

Lloyd Morris. *Postscript to Yesterday* (Random).
1947. p. 137

"Good Lord," I thought, "here's a revivalist minister on the loose." I
stayed silent in awe and admiration. For the first time in my life I was
aware that I was listening to a man who violently and passionately
cared about the same kind of things that had been vaguely concerning
me, that here was a man dangerously aroused, brilliant. Part of my
own awakening had come from reading Bernard Shaw and H. G.
Wells. I thought of Lewis as a beardless, younger Shaw, or another
Wells perhaps, and suddenly I knew that I had met my first genius. I
had never liked to use that banal word, but then and later I attached it
in my mind without embarrassment to Sinclair Lewis.

Harrison Smith. *SR*. Jan. 27, 1951. p. 8

Where Sinclair Lewis will eventually stand in the hierarchy of American letters is not for this generation to decide, but there is no doubt that
Main Street, Babbitt, and, I think, *Arrowsmith* will survive, if only as
genre pictures. It is my own belief that future generations will find in
them a good deal more, but that may be a prejudiced view because I
believe that the American philosophy of life is going to have a long run.
We are not ready for quietism. We still believe that when something is
wrong, something can be done about it; and a raucous voice bawling out
the wrong is not yet for us mere sound and fury, but a trumpet blast
summoning the mighty men of valor to stand to their arms.

Gerald W. Johnson. *NR*. Jan. 29, 1951. p. 15

Though Lewis had to a remarkable degree mastered his method, that
method is a good deal like the one so successfully employed in the
writing of many present-day best-sellers—the method, I mean, which
produces books that are not so much naturalistic novels as "docu-
mentaries," pseudo-fiction in which everything is recognizable as true
but with the fidelity of a waxwork and no suggestion of any sort of
autonomous life. . . . The literary gift that he developed to an extraordinary degree was, of course, the gift for mimicry which is as
definitely something more than mere naturalistic reproduction as it is
definitely something less than imaginative recreation. . . . The typical
fact or the typical gesture is one step above the merely authentic. But
it is also one step below the symbolic.

Joseph Wood Krutch. *Nation*. Feb. 24, 1951. p. 180

Lewis was a born story-teller. When he had no memorable story to tell, he told one that wasn't memorable. The urge to tell some kind of story was so strong that it kept him always at work. In this he differed sharply from American writers of his day who were far more self-consciously artists and had far more to say, as the expression is. Lewis, with his unappeasable itch to tell stories and his conviction that the most important characteristic of a writer was the ability to apply the seat of the pants to the seat of a chair, went right along pouring out stories when a writer of a different cast of mind would have brooded and hesitated and struggled with thought and form.

C. Hartley Grattan. *NR*. Apr. 2, 1951. p. 19

I think one of the most tragic facets of his nature was his disbelief in his own capacity to evoke love from others. He hurt others, very often out of this frustration. He was unquestionably one of the most "difficult" human beings who ever lived. But it was impossible ever to be really angry with him, in his case, the old parental saw was really true, "this hurts me more than it does you."

He *was* incorruptible!

Dorothy Thompson. *At*. June 1951. p. 73

What Lewis loved so passionately about America was its potentiality for and constant expression of a wide, casually human freedom, the individual life lived in honest and perhaps eccentric effort (all the better), the social life lived in a spirit that first of all tolerates variety. And what he hated about America, what made him scold it, sometimes so shrilly, was everything that militated against such a free life: social timidity, economic system, intellectual rigidity, theological dogma, legal repression, class convention. These two, the individual impulse to freedom and the social impulse to restrict it, provide the bases of his plots.

Mark Schorer. *NR*. Apr. 6, 1953. p. 19

He was as lean and as tough-looking as a long string of jerked beef and . . . he had long talon-ended pale hands and a high-doming forehead and quick though cracked lips and swift eyes that seemed to notice everything. . . . My eyes fastened on his face. And the face I saw was a face to haunt one in dreams. It was a face that looked as if it were being slowly ravaged by a fire, by an emotional fire, by a fire that was already fading a little and that was leaving a slowly contracting lump of gray-red cinder.

Frederick F. Manfred. *AS*. Spring, 1954. pp. 165–6

It is interesting that the cultural lag in Lewis's work should be so marked. Just as the real social forces of his time are placed for the most part quite outside of his literary scene, so the real social changes of his time are reflected cursorily and late. The ordinary mark of a first-rank author is that his writing is generally in some degree ahead of its time. The typical characteristic of Lewis's writing is that it is generally, to a marked degree, behind its time. Very likely this is the final key to Lewis's achievement—the key which opens the secret chamber in this otherwise absolutely uninspiring middle-class mansion.

For it would appear that Lewis's whole literary world . . . *is* in the end haunted by the sense of its own unreality.

Maxwell Geismar. *American Moderns* (Hill and
Wang). 1958. pp. 113–4

See *Main Street, Babbitt,* and *Arrowsmith* (novels).

LEWISOHN, LUDWIG   (1882–1956)

To us newer Americans, *Up Stream* is not merely a book. It is vision, revelation. It is our struggles, our hopes, our aspirations and our failures made articulate. It is the cry of young America to old America not to confine literature, education and thought to the formula of a small group. *Up Stream* is a dynamic protest against the sanctification of a priestcraft in education, a revolt against the existence of an Anglo-Saxon intellectual aristocracy in a country that is the gathering together of a people from every corner of the earth.

Anzia Yezierska. *NYT*. April 23, 1922. p. 22

The author is a thoroughgoing individualist. He urges, as the true end and aim of life, the happiness of an unfettered emotional and aesthetic self-expression in the here and now. . . . He would have us seek what he calls Life, the life of the finer senses, the more delicate emotions, the life of this present world at its best and richest, and seek it through an unashamed self-expression; through art and poetry and passion and feeling and beauty; yes, through a behaviorism in which yellow beer, free love, and birth-control play a not inconspicuous part.

Charles E. Park. *At.* June, 1922. p. 12 (sup.)

Nature is abominably undemocratic, and has made him an intellectual aristocrat. He is endowed with the power of competently appreciating the masterpieces created by the spirit of man in literature, music, and the plastic arts. The price invariably exacted for this is precisely that excessive sensitiveness to commonplaceness and ugliness which America has so often tortured in him. In no land and at no time could he have escaped the exasperating sense of the gulf between himself and the large majority, which denied by nature his power of appreciation, his subtle and versatile intellect, can never understand or adapt themselves to the feelings of those who possess them.

Horace James Bridges. *The God of Fundamentalism*
(Covici). 1925. p. 282

There is probably no distinguished writer in our time for whom the life of the mind is so much an affair of the passions, for whom the intellectual life is a love affair, which the reader is made to share. There is also no writer who is so frankly, sometimes so embarrassingly, and on occasion so annoyingly intimate in his self-revelation. . . . Mr. Lewisohn is a romantic German as well as a passionate Jew.

Irwin Edman. *Nation.* June 5, 1929. p. 674

It is a mistake to describe Lewisohn as either a propagandist or a special pleader. He is rather a prophet for his people who makes use of parable, in Biblical fashion, for the emphasizing of his message. He has become somewhat too much the prophet to be a true novelist.

F. L. Robbins. *Outlook.* Jan. 14, 1931. p. 67

He knows literature because he has loved it, and he is fascinated by the great figures because of his concern with what they have to say. Hence he treats the best of them as though they were his contemporaries, and he is really concerned only with that part of them which is still living in the sense that it still raises living issues. . . . Mr. Lewisohn's mind happens to be . . . a mind both born and trained to respond to the appeal of literature. The language of literature is his language in a sense by no means always true of those who are concerned primarily with its substance, and because of that fact he escapes the usual limitations of the doctrinaire as well as the usual limitations of the academician.

Joseph Wood Krutch. *NYHT.* March 13, 1932. p. 1

There lurks behind the caustic discernment of Mr. Lewisohn's critical and prophetic genius a sort of compassion for the author of anything, be it what it may. Loving literature as he does, he can never be entirely harsh with its sources; loving humanity as he must, he can never be entirely heartless toward his fellow-man who is his brother-in-literature, after all.

Minnie Hite Moody. *SwR.* Oct., 1932. p. 507

At his most exalted Mr. Lewisohn is a curious and sharply memorable figure. Few writers command so superb a dignity. He startles majestically, he arraigns loftily, he draws centuries of learning and spiritual experience together in flashing, bitter, or tenderly wise generalizations.

At such moments his characters breathe the air of mountain tops; they sense divinity in the atmosphere, they feel themselves drawn to greater and perhaps not insurmountable heights. They possess a rather wonderful humanity; one is a bit disconcerted by so deep an immersion in selflessness, but one respects so unusual a nobility and so intense an effort.

Alfred Kazin. NYHT. May 2, 1937. p. 2

Though Mr. Lewisohn is a notable figure in both contemporary American literature and in certain Zionist circles, he shows not a trace of the humor of either Josh Billings and Mark Twain or of Mendele Mocher Seforim and Sholem Aleichem. He always maintains the humorless and rigid self-importance that is so often found in his native Prussia. And I venture the opinion that no one who has not laughed at himself and at pompous human ignorance generally is a safe leader for members of the genus *homo sapiens*.

Morris Cohen. Reflections of a Wondering Jew
(Free). 1950. p. 123

Mr. Lewisohn doesn't care much for modern intellectual poetry. . . . Lewisohn's attitude toward poetry in general is affirmative and spiritual. His poets must be prophets with a sense of public obligation, never doubters of the ultimate high destiny of mankind. His style produces effective epithet and a resonant oratory.

A. M. Sullivan. SR. May 20, 1950. p. 40

Lewisohn is a scholar, a creative critic, a scrupulous craftsman whose work is informed with high seriousness and moral passion. His books, he maintains, are not the expression of purely literary opinions but personal confessions rendered in more or less objective terms, weapons used in the unending struggle of life. . . . Lewisohn endeavors to communicate what he considers unimpeachable and eternal truths; his mission, he feels, is to redeem and preserve those immemorial virtues of freedom and justice which constitute the good life.

Charles I. Glicksberg. American Literary Criticism
(Hendricks). 1952. pp. 198–200

See *Up Stream* (autobiography); also *Expression in America* (criticism) and *The Case of Mr. Crump, Don Juan*, and *The Island Within* (novels).

LINDSAY, VACHEL (1879–1931)

He has crude gestures, this emerging poet of Illinois. He has intonations of the preacher and fancifulness of the infant wearing a paternal silk hat. He finds it hard to forget Hathor, the Rose of Sharon and ambrosial nouns. He forces his note. But to say these things is not to reach the kernel. Where else in this country of emergence is there in combination nationalism so free and swinging, religion so vigorous, human contact so unprejudiced, beauty so adored?

Francis Hackett. Horizons (Huebsch-Viking). 1919.
p. 295

Mr. Lindsay . . . can whoop like a whale. He is a poet in search of superlatives beyond the superlatives. He cannot find them, but he at least articulates new sounds. As one reads him, one is reminded at times of a child in a railway-train singing and shouting against the noise of the engine and the wheels. The world affects Mr. Lindsay as the railway-train affects some children. He is intoxicated by the rhythm of the machinery.

Robert Lynd. Books and Authors (Putnam). 1923. p. 243

He is a reformer, an evangelist. He lifts his standard for all who gather round it; he spreads his arms to all who will come to them. His business is not, as that of a different poet might be, to find only the purest gold or the clearest gems. It is rather to spade up new sod and see what unexpected flowers will spring from it; to peer into dusky corners and see that nothing precious has been hidden there; to explore the outer boundaries of the regions of poetry and see if they cannot be extended to include virgin territories hitherto unoccupied.

Carl Van Doren. Many Minds (Knopf). 1924. pp. 164–5

The good black earth of Springfield, Illinois, seeped into his bones, and all the prejudices and idealisms of the "valley of democracy" went into the formation of his mind and philosophic temper. William Jennings Bryan was the product of the same locality, and he and Lindsay had striking points of similarity. Both were ardent democrats and champions of the commoners. Both burned with fervent idealism, both earnestly desired that all men be happy and virtuous, both had unbounded faith in the efficacy of political and moral evangelism, and both interpreted politics, economics, and diplomacy in terms of middle-western morality.

Russell Blankenship. American Literature (Holt).
1931. pp. 594–5

With his belligerant assertion of the noisier and cruder phases of the American inheritance Lindsay seems a throwback to some of the earlier comedians of the last century. He is often oratorical, theatrical, evangelical. But when he began to write, about 1910, that fundamental past had receded farther away than the Revolution; bringing this into view, he may be counted one of those writers who sustain a tradition and in large measure re-create it, for at his best he succeeds in writing a fresh poetry.

Constance Rourke. *American Humor* (Harcourt).
1931. p. 275

That Vachel was primarily an evangelist is obvious not only from his program but from his performance. . . . He combined, in his poetry as well as his personality, the free improvising of the minstrel with the fervor of the missionary. He never ceased to be a propagandist for the preservation of the spirit. Just as he believed that every slum might become a part of a holy city, so he insisted that every person housed a poet.

Louis Untermeyer. *SR*. Dec. 12, 1931. p. 368

Lindsay's rebelliousness . . . was the rebelliousness of a Christian finding himself in a pagan country. And it was also the rebelliousness of an artist who finds that people expect him to live in an ivory tower and who refuses to do so. Lindsay's fundamental attitude is that of a natural piety—Christian in him, to be sure, but of the sort which we associate with classical antiquity: a piety towards ancestors and one's hearth and city, as well as toward the Gods. . . . For Lindsay the essence of religion was this personal continuity: something you have inherited by tradition and even by blood.

Llewellyn Jones. *CC*. Dec. 23, 1931. p. 1619

Poetry for him was still a chant, and his sonorous, slightly nasal chanting, with upraised face and dropped eyelids, like a blind Illinois Homer, still lingers in our memories. His rhythms sought the rhythms of native speech, but unlike the cool and humorous colloquialism of Robert Frost, it was an excited speech, like the shouts at camp meetings, or the boasts of oxmen and boatmen. Listening to him one was carried backward not forward, back of the American folk history now being so extensively written, back of Walt Whitman . . . back into an authentic minstrelsy.

Henry Seidel Canby. *SR*. Jan. 9, 1932. p. 1

Readers and critics have always misunderstood him, even thought him humorous or grotesque. But the truth is that his passion for rhythm led him into seemingly ludicrous situations, inspiring him to write literary monstrosities which in reality were not in the least funny to their author, but were only his sincere effort to express in words the rhythms which he heard so clearly. . . . Life, to him, was rhythm, and the passion of his soul was to pass this on to others.

A. Longfellow Fiske. Com. Feb. 10, 1932. p. 410

How little of the scholar he was, the man of conscious artistry, the precious jeweler of verse! How much the man who believed, who loved, who felt, whose character and moral fervor were his style, that style in truth which cannot be learned, but is bestowed at birth by the good fairy, even upon lame boys! His style was his love of America, and this was his wonderland too. But above that were his dreams of America and his city. . . . The land he sang can be lost, because in so many fundamental, even phenomenal senses, it never existed. But the song he sang, and by which he created a land and a State, belongs at least to the history of literature.

Edgar Lee Masters, Vachel Lindsay (Scribner). 1935.
pp. 374–5

Like Whitman and every true American, Lindsay believed that the good things of life were meant to be shared, and that without sharing they ceased to be good. His poetry was therefore communal, emotional and scarcely ever intellectual. It was written, like the purple patches of Elizabethan dramatists, to arouse the feelings of crowded, popular audiences: it deliberately appealed to the groundlings.

Arthur Bryant. The American Ideal (Longmans).
1936. p. 261

No one loved adulation more than did Vachel Lindsay, and no artist has ever seen more clearly that he was being ruined by it. He lived for his audience; he loved reciting his poetry, he loved the applause that he always got, and yet he knew that applause was his poetic destruction. Unable to deny himself the temporary pleasure, he saw his stream of inspiration dwindle, die, while helplessly he bemoaned the conflict within him. No one has seen more clearly the necessity for discontent, an ideal and the quietness in which to pursue it.

C. P. Lee. SR. Aug. 10, 1940. p. 7

Vachel Lindsay has long been out of fashion. His reputation began to decline during his not very long lifetime, and it has never been revived. No poetry could differ more from that which is currently esteemed than his. He was exuberant and open, whereas the moderns are disciplined and intricate. He was a preacher, and though it was often difficult to say what he was preaching, there was no mistaking his fervor. He was enthusiastic and hopeful; the moderns are secretive and dark. . . .

Lindsay speaks to us out of the innocence of the years before the First World War, but there is, as W. B. Yeats observed on the occasion of their first meeting, a strangeness in his poetry that lifts it above provincialism.

Granville Hicks. *SR*. Nov. 21, 1959. p. 39

See *Collected Poems*.

LONDON, JACK (1876–1916)

If this youthful California writer makes a study of literary style, it is not apparent, so simply and unaffectedly does he relate a story. There is, indeed, small showing of that painstaking polish so dear to the academic mind; this young man of twenty-four has something more virile to offer than finish. Crude as is his diction, he has learned the ways out of prescribed literature into a spontaneity and freedom that charm and invigorate. One sees no straining after effect, no circumlocution; he reaches the humanity of his readers by direct course.

Ninetta Eames. *OM*. May, 1900. p. 424

Whether human or canine, the heroes of Jack London's purely literary works are, to use one of his favourite phrases, "rampant individualists". . . . Whence comes it, then, that the author of such forceful and even ferocious types should be himself an advocate of socialism? In part, no doubt, the explanation may be found in the fact that a vigorous, opposition-loving person can most easily get all of the latter he wants by taking up the championship of some radical social doctrine.

Robert C. Brooks. *Bkm*. Sept., 1905. pp. 61–2

Form or subject that he happens to choose to write in or about matters little. It is the same vivid, virile personality pouring itself out in a wealth of words that mean warmth and strength or pitiless cold and pitiless cruelty—extreme in either case; exaggerated, but alive, always alive. This is Jack London, and it is of very little importance whether he is writing a story about a man or a dog, about a wolf or a whaler; whether he gives us a sociological treatise on the city slums or a love story in letters. We enjoy it all because it is Jack London, not because it is whatever it happens to be in outer form.

Grace Isabel Colbron. *Bkm*. Feb., 1907. pp. 599–600

Ordinarily one takes a febrile over-excitement and love of excessive violence to be signs of weakness; but in Jack London they were not—

he really did have strength. So likewise in his writing: his fury of language and intemperance of emotion have led some critics to deny that
he possesses genuine vigor and power. But to do so is surely an error;
those who are not too offended by his excesses can hardly fail to feel his
force. Only, in his books as in his own life and character, the strength
he had is turned, as if he could realize it only in fighting, coercion, and
destruction, not to creation, but to violence.

T. K. Whipple. *SR*. Sept. 24, 1938. p. 4

Jack London had been one of the three young pioneers who at the turn
of the century had blazed the literary trails into modern American
literature. Although a few predecessors had shown the way, Stephen
Crane, Frank Norris, and Jack London had vigorously insisted upon
introducing themes, characters, and styles of writing previously unheard of in American literature, but already large and vital in American life. All three died young, but Jack London lived longer in the
twentieth century. All were timely, catching unerringly the drumbeats
of the new day, which was to develop swiftly into a day of struggle,
but Jack London was a Socialist, and with conscious social perspective
he had inquired into history for pattern or lack of pattern. Before he
fell victim to the competitive spirit and commercialism of the times, he
had described more boldly and with more fundamental insight than
Frank Norris the real protagonists in that struggle and its causes and
had forseen its end.

Joan London. *Jack London and His Times*
(Doubleday). 1939. p. 377

He needed action to live up to his reputation of being a man of action.
But there was something more. Even when he wrote stories of action so
well that the whole world wondered, it wasn't enough. The internal
drive to the unattainable was superhuman. His tragedy lay in that. It
was the tragedy of frustration. It was always what he had to fight people
for that gave him satisfaction. In the end, as in the beginning, he was
always hungry for something not on the bill of fare. Not once in his
forty-one years did Jack look on life with quiet eyes, nor did he ever
know the meaning of quiet happiness.

Joseph Noel. *Footloose in Arcadia* (Lippincott).
1940. p. 270

He remains one of America's most significant writers because he concerned himself with the vital problems of his age. Of working class
origin, he was the first American writer to portray his class sym-
pathetically and one of the few to use literature for building the

foundations of a future society. He was not educated in the formal sense, but his comprehension was so great that he rose above educated men in ability and power to portray in his writings the fundamental issues of our times. The spirit of the common people of America, heroic, fiery, and adventurous will live forever in the pages of his rebel stories, novels, and essays.

Philip S. Foner. Jack London, American Rebel
(Citadel). 1947. p. 130

In the literature of protest in America from John Woolman to Richard Wright, the writings of Jack London must occupy a place very near the top. To London the brotherhood of man was no mere exercise in economic adjustment but a passionate gospel and he preached it with an intensity and dialectical skill that made his books virtual manuals among Socialist readers of his day. Although the number of his readers has diminished from the time he was known as the "Kipling of Alaska," the vigor and energy of his narrative, and his tender and exact portraits of the poor in his autobiographical writings are insurance that these readers will never entirely disappear.

Thomas Lask. NYT. Jan. 18, 1948. p. 24

I think part of the reason for London's popularity in Europe is that he is a very intense writer at his best, and the great élan and vigor that are properly associated with this country and its people emerge often from his pages. To a Europe drained dry of such faculties, it is understandable that London's people, their concerns and their virtues, should have a nostalgic appeal, that Europeans might even read of them as other more credulous generations read of such heroic figures as Roland and Hector.

Harry Sylvester. NYT. Aug. 19, 1951. p. 18

Jack London always insisted that his books were not mere adventure stories; they had a meaning. Theoretically, he was a materialist, Socialist, Darwinian, Nietzschean—all in one; and many of his admirers have trustingly envisioned him as perched upon the backs of all these horses, even when they were galloping furiously in different directions. Temperamentally he was closest to Nietzsche, as his supermen and superdogs attest.

Edward Wagenknecht. Cavalcade of the American
Novel (Holt). 1952. p. 224

A subhuman world of instinctual emotion and, in its purest expression, of complete animal identification was the one in which he moved so easily and so instinctively himself. And the dominant mood was of primitive fear or, at its best, of brief and still terror-haunted and transient pleasure amidst all the horrors of the jungle.

Maxwell Geismar. *Rebels and Ancestors*
(Houghton). 1953. p. 185

London's instinct was to feel life as chaos and battle and to exult in the strength which produced both, but his intelligence, which was not of of the most acute, tried to rationalize instinct, to fit jagged pieces into a design, and so he found laws operating in the vast spaces of the far North: the law of natural selection, the law of Eskimo and Indian whereby iron sank in water and women obeyed men, and the law of the white man, enforced by stalwart Mounted Police. Since London's eye was not single, since he could not decide whether he was a disciple of Nietzsche or of Marx, he compromised a narrative gift originally distinguished by vigor, freshness, and dramatic proficiency, and eventually wrote some of the poorest novels of the day.

Grant C. Knight. *The Strenuous Age in American
Literature* (North Carolina). 1954. pp. 222–3

See *The Call of the Wild, The Sea Wolf, Martin Eden,* and *The Iron Heel* (novels).

LOWELL, AMY (1874–1925)

Amy Lowell . . . is perhaps the least formula-bound poet now writing. She is an Imagist, but she does not see the world exclusively in the terms of Imagism; she feels, and makes the reader feel, its enormous variety. Her historical sense does not permit her to despise the past, nor to fear the future because it lies around a bend in the road. So she writes freely and flexibly and experimentally, as a poet should who springs from a free, flexible, and experimental people. . . . It is not enough to say that she is a realist, it is scarcely half the truth. She is rather a veritist, and a romantic veritist at that, not seeking to relate the fact to the phantom, but to incorporate the phantom with the fact. She accomplishes this by bringing to bear upon the fact, civilized, conventional, artificial as it must be in her accepted world, senses as acute and unsophisticated as those of a savage.

Helen Buller Kizer. *NAR.* May, 1918. pp. 739, 742

The style she has chosen to use, whether regarded with a view to rhythm or to colour-distribution is essentially pointillistic. Now Miss

Lowell should have known that the pointillistic style is, in literature, suited only to very brief movements. A short poem based on this method may be brilliantly successful; Miss Lowell has herself proved it. A long poem based on this method, even though sustained brilliantly and perhaps in direct ratio to its brilliance, almost inevitably becomes dull. . . . This style, obviously, is ideal for a moment of rapid action or extreme emotional intensity. But its effect when used *passim* is not only fatiguing, it is actually irritating.

> Conrad Aiken. *Scepticisms* (Knopf). 1919. pp. 121–2

She has camouflaged an inherent feminine sensibility, so that it appears aggressive, and masculine. *Au fond* she is soft and gentle like Francis Jammes, who excites her profound admiration. Somewhat unfairly to her frank generosity and sensitive appreciation, she will go to remarkable lengths at times to convince us that she is insensitive to the feelings of others, contemptuous of their convictions, disdainful of their beliefs. She has the aggressiveness of Samuel Johnson, the daring of George Borrow and the tenacity of John Bunyan.

> Joseph Collins. *Taking the Literary Pulse* (Doran).
> 1924. p. 61

Miss Lowell . . . comes on things full-face. She walks around them and looks at them. She recognizes them. She knows their names. They belong in her world and she in theirs, and it is a sane, balanced, homogenous world. . . . Miss Lowell is one of the great personalities of our time and one of the great aristocrats of literature. No one who has heard her talk will ever forget it. But . . . Miss Lowell's great achievement as a poet lies in precisely the fact that her poems are the most important things about her. She has succeeded in creating poems which owe her nothing but their creation, poems which are not the publications of her heart nor the revelations of her philosophy, but finalities, entities, existences.

> Archibald MacLeish. *NAR*. March, 1925. pp. 509–10

That Amy Lowell's creative spirit occupied a large and unwieldly body is important because the triumph lay with the spirit. Her handsome head, unflinching in its carriage, had much to reckon with. First, perhaps, a passionate and untrammeled heart. Next, physical illness, disability and a kind of fleshly discomfort that no woman could bear in youth without suffering self-consciousness, and the sense of a lost paradise. Yet I doubt if I have known a maturity as full-flavoured and wholly sustaining as Amy Lowell's. Every twisted strand, every quirk in her destiny which earlier challenged normality and happiness, became woven into the warp and woof of a noble and dedicated career.

Elizabeth Shepley Sergeant. *Fire Under the Andes*
(Knopf). 1927. p. 11

The lack of personal emotion in Miss Lowell's verse is due in part to two elements in her nature, her aristocratic ancestry and her great intellectual power. Her inherent pride keeps her from opening her heart too wide in public, and emotion is always somewhat alien to people of marked intellectuality. Emotion Miss Lowell had in plenty, but it was the emotion of the critic and controversialist, not the emotion of the creative artist. Her brilliant mind and her wide reading gave her an immense amount of material for her poetry, so much that it would have tended to crowd out personal experience, if she had been inclined to use it, and her fine critical powers made her labor on the surface of her poetry until it shone like burnished metal.

Russell Blankenship. *American Literature* (Holt).
1931. p. 618

She got away completely from her predecessor's doleful egoism, effeminacy, and conventional moralizings, by recording life as one knows it, not as former poets had written of it. Her flowers came from the gardens of Sevenels, or the fields of Dublin, not from the limited *hortus siccus* of the literary past. Her five senses ranged freely in her search for sharper and more inclusive perceptions of reality. . . . Amy Lowell was the first of our poets to take full advantage of the civilizations across both the Atlantic and Pacific, and yet remain thoroughly American.

S. Foster Damon. *Amy Lowell* (Houghton). 1935. p. 724

I like you in your poetry. . . . Why don't you always be yourself. Why go to France or anywhere else for your inspiration. If it doesn't come out of your heart, real Amy Lowell, it is no good, however many colors it may have. I wish one saw more of your genuine strong, sound self . . . full of common sense and kindness and the restrained, almost bitter, Puritan passion. Why do you deny the bitterness in your nature, when you write poetry? Why do you take a pose? . . . When you are full of your own strong gusto of things, real old English strong gusto it is, . . . then I like you very much.

D. H. Lawrence. In S. Foster Damon's *Amy Lowell*
(Houghton) 1935. p. 278

No poet writing today, I think, save Thomas Hardy, saw and heard with more acute perception, or saw and heard and felt so many shades and tones and shapes of things—brilliant and subtle and fugitive and firm. And joined with this quick sensitiveness to physical impressions was an intellectual honesty as sensitive—a passion for truth which never knowingly falsified the report of what was seen. And that alert and vivid sense of beauty, restless with a poet's craving for expression, yet in expression lucidly exact, has schooled us, skeptical and reluctant scholars, to a quickened vision of strange loveliness in familiar things.

John Livingston Lowes. Essays in Appreciation
(Houghton). 1936. p. 162

She remained a challenging and interesting figure of many and various talents, but not essentially a great writer, if one classifies only those writers as great who are able to extract out of the common and universally human themes of birth, love, loss, death, struggle, achievement, and failure, new meanings of universal import and new notes of perpetual poignancy. She was, and is, a writer well worth reading from every point of technical interest; but it was only towards the very end of her life that she began to use her technique on themes of universally human import. . . . That she had the capacity to do so is abundantly proven. She did not care to exert it often; and this was not so much her own fault as the fault of the public and the critics, who demanded only too often from her a showy brilliance of surface at all costs.

John Gould Fletcher. Life Is My Song (Farrar and
Rinehart). 1937. p. 208

The rakish cigar and the abnormal stoutness were forgotten five minutes after she had seated herself. One noticed only the marvellous neatness, the fine hands and delicate ankles, the small mobile mouth, the coolly modulated voice, the quick-appraising but not unkind eyes, the fine features and almost transparent skin. One saw a woman who was not only intelligent but—there is no other word for it—pretty.

Louis Untermeyer. Harper. Aug., 1939. p. 266

The central figure of the poetic life of the twenties, though not of its literature in general, was Amy Lowell. Yet not so much as a poet as a dynamo, sending impulses of energy wherever interest and excitement were needed. A good poet, an erudite and sometimes insolent critic, a rich and aggressive personality, she would have become a renowned bluestocking in any age. . . . Invalid in body, often moving with difficulty, I have seen her sitting at home like a chained eagle, lunging at what she called the pedantries of Harvard, of which her brother was president, or crushing with one claw some reviewer who lacked scholarship and a gentleman's education.

Henry Seidel Canby. American Memoir (Houghton).
1947. pp. 313–4

She touched a fuse wherever she went, and fire-works rose in the air; and there were no set-pieces more brilliant than hers, no Catherine-wheels or girandoles or fountains. There was no still, small voice in Amy Lowell. Her bombs exploded with a bang and came down in a shower of stars; and she whizzed and she whirred, and she rustled and rumbled, and she glistened and sparkled and blazed and blared.

Van Wyck Brooks. A Chilmark Miscellany
(Dutton). 1948. p. 265

See Complete Poetical Works.

LOWELL, ROBERT (1917–   )

The prime virtue of Lowell's writing is lack of slickness. . . . (His) awkward recalcitrarinesses seem to me marks of integrity. . . . The poems are conscientiously written rather than urbane; less witty and ironic than earnest.

Austin Warren. Poetry. Aug., 1947. pp. 263–4

On the whole . . . Lowell is probably the most interesting of all the recent young American poets. Above everything else, he has control, conciseness, a rare sense of form. . . . There seems, generally, a disparity between intent and performance, a solemnity that does not quite come off. . . . Lowell is walking an invisible tightrope; his poetic salvation is to be found, not in prayer, but in the rich obscurity of his unconsciousness, and in release from himself, as in love.

William Elton. Poetry. Dec., 1947. pp. 138–40

Robert Lowell's conviction cannot readily be named as the usual grip of the Catholic convert. He has not merely put on a faith like a new overcoat when the weather of the century chills. He has created his own terms of belief and his own locality and planted in it his own gnarled tree. . . . Based on a world of opposites and of contrasts, the poems are taut with the strain of linking contraries together. There is fury in the lines, and that has made the lines furious in sound. There is the feeling that Lowell has not wrestled with an angel but with Christ himself. In the course of that struggle the hand that had touched the immaculate body has taken on a radiance which it transfers to the words of the poems. . . . A man has stared at dread and street and vision and has put them all into coiled and striking poetry.

Paul Engle. EJ. Feb., 1949. pp. 60–4

It is immediately apparent that Robert Lowell's poetry does not make for easy reading; the images are so congested, the allusions so complex that the uninitiated reader is likely to be confused. But it is also apparent that this is a poetry of deep passion and fierce tension; the impact is violent, the intensity of a traditional Protestant turned Catholic. Beneath the surface formalism of the verse, there is a deep protest against what New England has become, against the commercialism of the age and degeneration of the community. . . . His is a tortured outcry against the corruption of the times; a grim need to find a faith in a world torn between frivolity and failure.

Louis Untermeyer. *Modern American Poetry*
(Harcourt). 1950. p. 693

One might call the poems studies in the instability of memory and desire; they are all charged in some degree with mystery, with the unpredictable association and the vivid but wild allusion. . . . They all have a flushed air that makes us feel that we are watching the poet talk to himself before he has come to write the poem. But perhaps some such effect was intended.

David Daiches. *YR*. Sept., 1951. p. 157

His poems are shaken with the cold reverberant roll of the north Atlantic. He hears it with the ears of a familiar of the Nantucket coast. But what, louder than sea water, batters at his mind is the memory of the old whalers and of the meaning that Melville read in their bloody work, and the sound of the guns thundering for the new Leviathan. . . . Lowell is under no illusion about the power and the terror of the sea and, with the possible exception of Eliot, who has enlarged its significance symbolically, no living poet can realize it more terribly.

Babette Deutsch. *Poetry in Our Time* (Holt). 1952.
pp. 368–9

Lowell's violence and individuality come almost as much from prosody as from imagery and idea. Though his syllable regularity is extreme, his licenses within the control of syllables are numerous. He is fond of the eccentric caesura; time and again he ends a sentence after the ninth syllable, and begins a new one with the rhyme word. He is also fond of medial inversion, and his enjambement, often coupled with early or late caesura, is more extreme than any other syllabic English poet. His assonances abound. . . . Harsh and consonantal monosyllables . . . also serve to clot the line and slow its pace. Initial inversion occurs in about twenty percent of the lines, a relatively huge proportion. . . . The master of variation within rigidity, he can make his lines rush, slow,

hurtle, and come to a quiet halt, always fully under his control. . . .
One might say that Lowell forces the Law upon himself in his syllabic
strictness, and within this rigidity, this self-created confinement, hurls
himself like an animal at the bars, achieving the definition of an emotion in the struggle of interior opposites.

Donald Hall. NWW 7. 1955. pp. 234–5

Mr. Lowell has a completely unscientific but thoroughly historical
mind. It is literary and traditional as well; he can use the past so effectively because he thinks so much as it did. He seems to be condemned
both to read history and to repeat it. His present contains the past—
especially Rome, the late Middle Ages, and a couple of centuries of
New England—as an operative skeleton just under the skin. . . . He
does not present themes or generalizations but a world; the differences
and similarities between it and ours bring home to us themes, generalizations, and the poet himself.

Randall Jarrell. Poetry and the Age (Knopf). 1955
pp. 192–5

Lowell . . . continually dwells upon scenes of death and burial. . . .
To Lowell, man is clearly evil and a descendant of Cain and Abel is the
eternal forgotten victim, hustled away from sight and consciousness.
. . . These are the themes. . . . Lowell does not state them so much
as present himself in the act of experiencing their weight. It is impossible to read his poems without sharing his desperation.

Louise Bogan. Selected Criticism (Noonday). 1955.
p. 391

Robert Lowell is an outstanding pioneer extending the frontiers of
language, making notable conquests of material which often seems too
eccentric for poetry and consolidating it in very strong and compact
form. . . . He has taken a lot of facts, observed or remembered
(each of them strikingly separate as brittle shape or anecdote), and
made from them his own truth. This truth is obstinate, moving and
sometimes even tragic. . . . What these poems point out is the possibility of a humanist kind of poetry, in which disparate experiences are
bound up within the sensibility of a poet who has himself an immense
compassion combined with clearness and hardness. Tension is supplied
by the reconciliation of very opposite personal qualities of the poet
within his poem.

Stephen Spender. NR. June 8, 1959. p. 17

See *Land of Unlikeness, Lord Weary's Castle, The Mill of the Kavanaughs,*
and *Life Studies* (poetry). See Supplement at end of text.

McCARTHY, MARY (1912–   )

Miss McCarthy has learned the difficult art of setting down everything as it might have happened, without telling a single self-protective lie and without even failing, in the midst of a seduction, to mention the safety pin that holds up the heroine's badly mended underwear. *The Company She Keeps* is not a likable book, nor is it very well put together, but it has the still unusual quality of having been lived.

Malcolm Cowley. NR. May 25, 1942. p. 737

What is delightful about *The Oasis* is the infectious energy and enthusiasm of Miss McCarthy, who plunges gallantly into the thick of so many complicated ideas and problems with a rebarbative gusto.

There is a violence in this writer which is both exhilarating and amusing. . . . Miss McCarthy's mind has what people are accustomed to calling a masculine width or range. She sees people in terms of moralities—both civic and personal. But it is even more her feeling for words and her talent for epigram which emerges at the end of the book as her particular gift.

Julia Strachey. NSN. Feb. 26, 1949. pp. 211–2

The McCarthy pictures have horror in them, and all her characters live in hell, but there is nothing depressing about reading her stories. Her style has such verve and swiftness, is so compelling, that the reader follows after her, on the scavenger hunt for the revealing incident, the ultimate perception that will give away another person and deliver him, naked and quivering, into his understanding. There is an intellectual satisfaction to be found here, gratification in a style that is so perfect a tool for its purpose.

Lorine Pruette. NYHT. Sept. 24, 1950. p. 8

Her highly sophisticated and intellectualized prose leads her into fascinating digressions which make her sound like an essayist *manqué;* it also leads her into frequent epigrams, but instead of the shallow verbal sparkle of drawing room comedy, hers have the psychological penetration of La Rochefoucauld. . . . Like Joyce she has been deeply affected by her early religious training even when fleeing from it. Although she has stepped out of the confessional booth to lie down on the analyst's couch she is still on the same quest for the essential, the quintessential self. Her brief incisive pieces are etched with corrosive acid, it is true; but they still have a savage honesty, a bristling sensibility, and at bottom a pitiless humility.

Robert Halsband. SR. Oct. 7, 1950. p. 23

It is the anguished urban sensibility that Miss McCarthy's prose writh-
ingly plots. The people in her stories all seem uncontrollably involved
in endless showdowns with the people around them, or as often as not
just with themselves; and nobody, unfortunately, ever seems to win.
But this is the deadly pattern of relationships among "thinking" people.

Miss McCarthy's attitude toward the people in her stories is one of
contempt and outrage, but it is not just a shallow, critical attitude. It
originates in a deep and almost continually disappointed moralism.
She wants people with intelligence to be good and decent and productive, and that they are not arouses the furious broken-hearted chastiser
in her.

Chandler Brossard. *AM*. Feb., 1951. pp. 232–3

The most important thing in fiction is binding connection, that which
makes the characters adhere to one another, as it were of their own
affinity, through all the situations the novelist invents. This is love. It
cannot be derived from the satirical connection. . . . Yet it is this
which Miss McCarthy vainly tries to do in her last two novels (*The
Oasis* and *The Groves of Academe*). . . ; she would have satire do
the work of love. Apparently she cannot prevent the substitution, because satire has become for her more than a genre; a virtual ontology
which throws up a world of ridiculous objects, even when she herself
belongs to that world and berates it only because she is unable to break
her dependence on it.

Isaac Rosenfeld. *NR*. March 3, 1952. p. 21

The major distinction Miss McCarthy makes with regard to people,
the only distinction that has force and reality to her, is between the intelligent and the stupid. . . . A Mary McCarthy heroine examines
her soul with the scrupulous, unashamed persistence of a professional
model looking herself over in the vanity-table mirror. . . . In general,
it might be said they dramatize the disjunction—or rather, the hostility
—between Reason and Impulse. This is Miss McCarthy's true subject,
a theme which underlies her satirical castigations, which calls forth all
her famous brilliance, which gives point to her acerbity and depths to
her apparently gratuitous bitterness.

Norman Podhoretz. *Cmty*. March, 1956. p. 272

Unlike other notable hatchet-women (Dorothy Parker, for instance),
Miss McCarthy is not a Sophisticate but an Intellectual. . . . And
though time and circumstance cast her in with the young radicals for
whom Marxian criticism of "the system" furnished that rationalization
of their discontents which the previous generation had found in the

war against "provinciality," she never committed herself wholeheartedly to that either. In fact, if she ever discovered what she believed, admired, or wanted she never devoted much time to praising or expounding it. But she can justify her contempt for what she does not like— and that is almost everything including other intellectuals—with telling thrusts and shrewd analysis.

Joseph Wood Krutch. *SR*. May 26, 1956. p. 20

Memories of a Catholic Girlhood, Mary McCarthy's account of her childhood and adolescence, has made clearer to me the traits which make her the particular sort of artist she is. They are, I believe, perfectionism, a fanatical striving for honesty, and a fierce sense of hierarchy—a combination calculated to produce a thoroughly disturbing vision of life. For to the perfectionist, things-as-they-are appear for the most part lamentably worse than they ought to be; the cult of honesty makes it a duty to portray this state of affairs as unsparingly as possible; and in a hierarchical order, it is always easy to disgrace oneself but almost impossible to behave so well as to transcend one's station. . . . The portraiture of her recollections is more tolerant of human frailties than in her fiction and therefore more attractive and richer in vitality.

Charles J. Rolo. *At*. June, 1957. pp. 90–1

What she has written so far has been of the fashionably acid and shocking kind: it is concerned on the whole, even to the point of ruthlessness, with the discrepancy in an urban and aggressive society between moral jargon and the inanity of pretentious action, with the atrophy of feeling and the protective surrogate of sentimentality and middle-class convention. These defects in our life she has represented with an unmerciful eye for weakness and vulgarity. *Memories of a Catholic Girlhood* is no less skeptical toward the world of the past half-century in which she grew up, but it is more perceptive, more critical of her own resources of understanding, and therefore, more mature, than any of her previous fiction.

Victor Lange. *NR*. June 24, 1957. p. 18

See *Memories of a Catholic Girlhood* (autobiography); also *The Company She Keeps* and *Cast a Cold Eye* (fiction).

McCULLERS, CARSON (1917–   )

Maturity does not cover the quality of her work. It is something beyond that, something more akin to the vocation of pain to which a great poet is born. Reading her, one feels this girl is wrapped in knowledge which has roots beyond the span of her life and her experience. How else can she so surely plumb the hearts of characters as strange and, under the force of her creative shaping, as real as she presents. . . . Carson McCullers is a full-fledged novelist whatever her age. She writes with a sweep and certainty that are overwhelming.

Rose Feld. *NYT*. June 16, 1940. p. 6

Miss McCuller's picture of loneliness, death, accident, insanity, fear, mob violence and terror is perhaps the most desolate that has so far come from the South. Her quality of despair is unique and individual; and it seems to me more natural and authentic than that of Faulkner. Her groping characters live in a world more completely lost than any Sherwood Anderson ever dreamed of. And she recounts incidents of death and attitudes of stoicism in sentences whose neutrality makes Hemingway's terse prose warm and partisan by comparison.

Richard Wright. *NR*. Aug. 5, 1940. p. 195

No one could say . . . that Miss McCullers has not succeeded in making her genuine talent felt, a talent which is less of subtlety than of infant-terrible insight expressed with quite grown-up precision, as yet unmellowed and unhallowed. It should not be forced in order to take advantage of a passing vogue, for it will surely crack up in the hurly-burly of competition. It is a brave talent; but not, I think, a very sturdy plant. It calls for gentle handling and careful cultivation.

Fred T. Marsh. *NYT*. March 2, 1941. p. 6

She is a suggestive rather than an eloquent writer, and often seems to present us less with a meaning than with a hint. And yet the lines of her work are clear and firm. . . . Though she has an acute observation, she does not use it to make rounded people. . . . Carson McCullers's work has always seemed to me to be a form of self-dramatization. . . . She does not dramatize herself in the sense that she is merely autobiographical; but she does dramatize herself in the sense that she seems to invest the various sides of her personality with attributes skilfully collected from the outside world.

George Dangerfield. *SR*. March 30, 1946. p. 15

Her gifts are limited—as Virginia Woolf's were limited, or Glenway Wescott's.

I do not mention these writers casually, or because I am unfamiliar with them. Like them both, Mrs. McCullers, though operating in a narrow field, ploughs deep furrows. Like them both, if I may pursue the metaphor, she engages in what Southerners used to call intensive cultivation. The trick about intensive cultivation . . . is that the earth runs sterile. Such, surely, was the fate of Mrs. Woolf and Mr. Wescott. Up to the moment Mrs. McCullers has not thus been cursed. She does not, of course, write the kind of gleaming, perfect prose Mrs. Woolf was capable of. But hers is beautifully fitted to her purposes, and that, I suppose, is what good writing means.

Francis Downing. Com. May 24, 1946. p. 148

The art of Carson McCullers has been called "Gothic." Perhaps it is—superficially. Certainly her day-to-day world, her little Southern towns, are haunted by far more masterful horrors than were ever conjured up in the dreary castles of a Horace Walpole. It seems to me, however, that the "Gothic" label misses the essential point. Because Carson McCullers is ultimately the artist functioning at the very loftiest symbolic level, and if one must look for labels, I should prefer to call her work "metaphysical." Behind the strange and horrible in her world there are played out the most sombre tragedies of the human spirit; her mutes, her hunchbacks, speak of complexities and frustrations which are so native to man that they can only be recognized, perhaps, in the shock which comes from seeing them dressed in the robes of grotesques. They pass upon the street everyday but we only notice them when they drag a foot as they go by.

William P. Clancey. Com. June 15, 1951. p. 243

Since all her novels represent some kind of variation on the one theme of human loneliness, a knowledge of her treatment of this theme is necessary to understand the purpose and cast of her writing. We should not take it for granted, however, that her work is in any way systematic or mechanical. Her way is not the course of allegory . . . but the way of myth. She is, after all, a novelist haunted by the elusive nature of human truth, and her underlying theme gives coherence to the variety and surprises she has found in the world about her.

Dayton Kohler. EJ. Oct. 1951. pp. 421–2

The same fundamental pattern exists in all Mrs. McCullers's major prose works. The pattern is more elaborate in <i>The Ballad of the Sad Café</i> than elsewhere, but the beginnings of it are recognizable in her first novel and its evolution has occupied the whole of her literary career. It is a closed pattern, and one which many readers will view with a reluctance which is a measure of their suspicion that it is, after all, authentic. . . . But it is a pattern with a strange vision of life which Carson McCullers has attained in <i>The Ballad of the Sad Café;</i> an eternal flaw exists in the machinery of love which alone has the power to liberate man from his fate of spiritual isolation.

Oliver Evans. NWW 1. April, 1952. p. 310

The Heart Is a Lonely Hunter

With subtlety and power, with suggestions and forthright statements, by means of well realized characters and revealing episodes, Mrs. McCullers circles her theme, coming closer and closer to its core, until she has encompassed and exposed its meaning. The task she set herself called for more than mere narrative skill, more than effective dramatic technique, and she has met its requirements with remarkable success. But narrative skill and dramatic episodes speed the reader on his way, while sudden, surprising insights illumine it. The author is never commonplace: used props, stock characters, and worn literary counters have no place in her writing.

Ben Ray Redman. *SR.* June 8, 1940. p. 6

It is always exciting to discover a new, real talent in writing. Or a new, real talent for characterization. Or a new and genuine gift of understanding. Twenty-two-year-old Carson McCullers has all three. She has written a novel that is baffling in a way. *The Heart Is a Lonely Hunter* is not the kind of novel you expect a young woman to write; it is a story of pitiful people told without any touch of sentimentality, giving each one the dignity that is his in his own eyes. . . . One wonders how any young person could know so much about the lonely hearts of men, women, and children too.

Lorine Pruette. *NYHT.* June 9, 1940. p. 4

See *The Heart Is a Lonely Hunter, A Member of the Wedding, Reflections in a Golden Eye,* and *The Ballad of the Sad Café* (novels).

MacLEISH, ARCHIBALD (1892–   )

The Hamlet of A. MacLeish is frequently fiercely subjective and therefore romantic; but from time to time, at the close particularly, it broadens into universal utterance, becomes in a way selfless, classical in its dignified acceptance of the burden laid upon man by life. That there are flaws in the poem I should not deny: here and there ill-chosen words, now and then a too facile line. But the conception of the poem is lofty, the design pure, the accent moving and true, the vocabulary rich and poetical. It will betray nobody's taste to affirm Mr. MacLeish a poet of true distinction, and, incidentally, the finest craftsman in verse now writing in English.

Lewis Galantiere. *Nation.* April 17, 1929. p. 472

Through all (his) books the poet's philosophy of life—or perhaps one should say the instinctive feeling about life which becomes the underlying motive of his art—is less hard in texture and brazen in tone than most of the Parisian-American group could sympathize with; there is room for human pity in it, and even for human love—that love of the race which, implying the merging of the individual in the mass, may be the democratic, or at least the communistic ideal—an ideal difficult, perhaps inaccessible to the poet, who is always by instinct an individualist. . . . I have much faith in the ability of this poet to interpret his age. . . . There is perhaps only one fundamental doubt—it would take gusto to express this age, a shout of driving rage and laughter, a rush of god-like or demoniac power. . . . Can MacLeish, shy, sheltered, melancholy by temperament, compass all this?

Harriet Monroe. *Poetry*. June, 1931. pp. 154–5

MacLeish's nostalgia is less dramatic than Eliot's, in a sense less passionate. It is not the fatuous and repetitive daydreaming of Aiken. In his general attitude toward life MacLeish . . . resembles Pound of the many lyric poems. To the general feeling of defeat prevalent among these poets of the past he has contributed only one idea—that the American poet *must* return to his own land, cannot remain an exile. . . . MacLeish states that he speaks to his own lost generation and wishes to speak to no one else. Certainly he sums up the feelings of that generation. . . . MacLeish's strongest passion is a sense of irrevocable loss.

Eda Lou Walton. *Nation*. Jan. 10, 1934. p. 48

The point of departure, one might say, is the nostalgic, the note of self-pity, the "pathos of distance," which everywhere cries and rings in these poems—so much so that one eventually thinks of them as all one repetition of the same theme. . . . It is like somebody speaking to himself in a mirror. . . . Mr. MacLeish can do better than this—he has already proved it. He has the means, he only lacks the aim. Already a poet to make us all envious, if he could only break this glass and walk inward on himself or outward to the world, he could perhaps say what no other contemporary poet could say.

Conrad Aiken. *NR*. Jan. 17, 1934. pp. 287–8

MacLeish is a superb craftsman. The musical and pictorial qualities of his verse deserve the highest praise. And he also won his growing audience through the mood of his poetry: a tragic disdain of life, even of love, of sex; a devotion to death, bone, stone, and all; an adoration of nature, as opposed to man; an adoration of past heroes, as opposed to the human worms who infest the contemporary planet. . . . The best of MacLeish will survive contemporary arguments. It seems to me, nonetheless, that the poet in search of heroes . . . need not return to the past for his sole inspiration.

Alfred Kreymborg. *SR*. Jan. 27, 1934. p. 435

From the start his technical labor had been sensitive and passionately sincere; but both his sensibility and sincerity come to their supreme test in the solution of an inner, specifically personal problem. To externalize them in the interests of a general depersonalization of the human consciousness is to strike at their very life. This may be done by social propagandists in the cause of public reform or revolution. Or it may be done, as he has done it, in the interests of a more abstract sense of universals, the poet sinking his moral personality in the total consciousness of humanity, and in what is conceived to lie behind it—the unconscious life of nature and the universe.

Morton D. Zabel. *Poetry*. June, 1934. pp. 153–4

Clear realization of the necessity of living up to one's ideas emotionally has led MacLeish, in a kind of desperation to value deeply his own beliefs. . . . MacLeish's career, considered in terms of the ideas he has held, has the appearance of being a series of unconnected allegiances. . . . (But) continuity of fundamental feeling is one of the great rewards of MacLeish's approach to the world. His sensibility may develop —it has done so continuously up to the present—but there is never any sharp break. . . . There is an organic and continuing relationship in MacLeish's poetry because he has so very rarely been false to what he felt, no matter what the cost.

Arthur Mizener. *SwR*. Dec., 1938. pp. 511–8

Two currents of poetic attitude can be traced through the poetry of Archibald MacLeish: his sense of the past and his deep loyalty and passion for the American land. . . . Although he disdains classicism as a formal motive of art, MacLeish is a traditional poet in the same way that Eliot and Pound are also in the stream of tradition. That is to say, he is not lacking in the historical sense which links his work with the literature of the past. . . . For MacLeish himself the problem of man's fate depends upon the preservation of a national tradition. His Americanism is as far removed as possible from the easy nationalism of a Walt Whitman or a Paul Engle, and his poetry makes evident the fact that his choice was deliberate and difficult.

Dayton Kohler. *SAQ*. Oct., 1939. pp. 420–1

Mr. MacLeish . . . fail(ed) in his attempts to write affirmative public poems, patriotic poems, poems inspired by liberal enthusiasms. He succeeded, it is true, much better than many other poets who, during the depression years, were trying to do the same thing, but still he failed. . . . Mr. MacLeish's short lyrics are his best poems. . . . The love poems, and there are many of them, written during every phase of the poet's career and in every aspect of feeling, are all excellent; they are composed with a restraint and an exactness of language that make them songlike, Elizabethan. Among the latest poems are several that challenge with vigor, bitterness, and yet with good taste the cheapness and stupidity of public life today.

Hayden Carruth. Nation. Jan. 31, 1953. p. 103

I believe that MacLeish has written a number of lyrics . . . which must certainly endure as long as poetry is read and the cadences of American and English speech are valued. . . . It must certainly be significant to the theory of poetry as Public Speech, that none of these successes are "message" poems. . . . One can agree with the Public Speech poems, but one is never quite convinced that they exist.

Then, at the very moment when all seems lost, the miracle happens back. MacLeish stops saving the world and saves himself. I do not mean to imply that he has lost his social concern as a citizen, but the evidence of the new poems is indisputable that whatever the citizen gives to duty, the poet is more universe in himself than all the world combined.

John Ciardi. At. May, 1953. pp. 67–8

Though fashion made it pleasant to note that MacLeish's preoccupation with extending the audience for poetry had led to a great waste of his talents, I didn't believe this. In the first place waste was what MacLeish had, I thought very properly, noted among those contemporaries of his who were contemptuous of his audiences. . . . And in the second place MacLeish's preoccupation with his audience seemed to me to have had one tremendously important effect upon his writing which was not a bad effect, not wasteful. It had made him write with the intent of persuasion. What he attempted to persuade people of was not, in some cases, to my liking, but what he tried to do rhetorically when he undertook persuasion seemed to me to be elementary and admirable.

Reed Whittemore. SwR. Autumn, 1953. pp. 706–7

A first reading of Archibald MacLeish's new play, J. B., makes one thing quite certain: it is a signal contribution to the small body of modern poetic drama, and it may well turn out to be an enduring one. The impact of its finest passages is instantaneously exciting, and the power remains, deepening in the memory long after the initial delight has passed. A passionate work, composed with great art; a philosophical poem, but also a play that cries out for the physical stage—here is an answer, in terms of the contemporary theatre, to the prophets of enervation who see drama as a dead end.

Dudley Fitts. NYT. March 23, 1958. p. 3

If we count T. S. Eliot as English, then it can be said that among American poets Archibald MacLeish has been the most serious in his efforts to write verse drama and that *J. B.,* his adaptation of the Book of Job, is probably the best American verse drama so far. . . . The constant shifting from the play through the play-within-the-play to the reality within the play is first-rate theater as are the sudden interpositions of Biblical language. . . . It is a sign of how good *J. B.* is that in reading it one keeps visualizing it on the stage and wishing to see it there.

Robert Langbaum. NYHT. May 11, 1958. p. 31

See *Collected Poems, 1917–1952;* also *J. B.* (play).

MAILER, NORMAN (1923–   )

Mailer's concern is with the individual and the way of life that formed him. He uses the shocks and tensions of wars as a corrosive agent which bites through to the hard core of truth about men. *The Naked and the Dead* is vastly more mature, intellectually, than the war novels of the twenties, with their romanticization of chronic mutiny. Artistically, it ranks comparison with the best of them. . . . It is a work of remarkable power, of amazing penetration, both into people and the determining forces of American life. Mailer has made his start with one of the most exciting American novels published since the end of the twenties. . . . *The Naked and the Dead* is not just a good book, it's almost a great book.

Charles J. Rolo. At. June, 1948. p. 114

What he tells us is scarcely news, but it has the value of the authentic inflection, the undeniably accurate feel and shape of what happened, and not the echo of other books about other wars. . . . But Mailer has his own borrowings and his own conventions—Dos Passos and Farrell seem to be his chief literary influences—and by and large these stand in the way of his native ability to tell a story and depict a character. His main error was to cast his novel in the mass-novel form. . . . Actually . . . his novel deals with as close a group of characters as *Wuthering Heights,* and suffers from the added machinery of choruses and flashbacks.

Raymond Rosenthal. Cmty. July, 1948. p. 92

Among the war novels, Norman Mailer's *The Naked and the Dead* remains a monument to destructiveness and to man's inhumanity to men. No book with its range of characters, its emotional impact, its fierce contempt for human beings, its anarchical conception of any noble cause, its disparagement of any virtue, whether of honor, or kindness, or love, or justice, has been published for many a year. This long novel of the assault and capture of the small Pacific island of Ano-popei was grimly ironical, but it had no humor; it was savage without the ameliorating touch of satire; its three hundred thousand words were so many bullets fired into the reader's mind; and yet for months it headed the best-seller lists everywhere.

Harrison Smith. *SR*. Feb. 12, 1949. p. 9

Norman Mailer's new novel (*Barbary Shore*) . . . is genuinely comic and bawdy, and yet succeeds in capturing the flavor of a New York summer with a careful attention to the psychological complexities of metropolitan people strongly reminiscent of Saul Bellow's *The Victim*. But Mailer's story, like Bellow's, is a parable of our time. Layer is on layer. . . . Mailer's prose is plain and powerful, but the complexities of his theme will unavoidably make portions of the book obscure to even the most patient readers. . . . We must pay him honor for spurning the easy success that could so obviously have been his, in order that he might dare to fail, grappling with questions of man's fate as a serious writer.

Harvey Swados. *NR*. June 18, 1951. pp. 20–1

In *The Deer Park* Mailer has made a real advance over *The Naked and the Dead,* which must have been a comparatively simple novel to write. Given its grandly simple theme—the war in miniature, or the conquest of a single island—and given the decision to include every element in the picture, from the commanding general down to the private in a rifle squad, the rest depended chiefly on patience and understanding. In *The Deer Park* the characters are treated more in depth, the structure of the novel is more complicated, and the author had to make up his own rules as he went along. He has taken risks and made mistakes, but not cheap or shameful ones. . . . The book leaves us with the feeling that Norman Mailer, though not a finished novelist, is one of the two or three most talented writers of his generation.

Malcolm Cowley. *NYHT*. Oct. 23, 1955. p. 5

Once one has niched *The Deer Park*—as a cross between naturalism and symbolism—one perceives the inadequacy of the categorization, for it is in the nearly perfect blending of these two styles—the complex,

artful, almost ritualistic plan, and the naturalistic manner of its execution—that the fame of *The Deer Park* will reside. Mailer has developed
a meticulous concern for structure and a brilliant flair for characterization; he seldom slops over the confines of the narrative; and although
he will never be a frugal writer, he has acquired among much else, a
respect for the value of economy. . . . In addition to his furious energy and true ear, Norman Mailer is *simpatico* with humanity, and
gives evidence of a preoccupation with all its affairs on a level rare in
American fiction.

Dachine Rainer. *NR*. Oct. 31, 1955. p. 25

The Deer Park is being promoted as a sensational sex book. But Mr.
Mailer is not a panderer; he is a vengeful moralist. His story involves a
good deal of sex perversion, and the point of it all is to tell us how admirable true love is by contrast. . . . This is neither a cheap nor a
simple book. There is a lot wrong with it, but more that is right. Mr.
Mailer simply is not the kind of writer who produces books which can
be judged successful or unsuccessful. He piles up enormously talented
stuff, some of it incongruous, some of it boozy and pretentious, and it
is both successful and unsuccessful, good and bad, but it is serious and
worth the respect of serious readers.

William Pfaff. *Com*. Dec. 2, 1955. p. 230

The general similarity between the narrators in *Barbary Shore* and *The
Deer Park* suggests that Mailer, as should be clear anyway, is a highly
self-conscious, though often wild-swinging novelist. He seems to have
taken up a convention practiced so far with much greater success by
Europeans than by Americans—that of projecting oneself into one's
novels as an emerging novelist. . . . One cannot say that he has
brought off the difficult trick, or even that it is necessarily desirable that
he should. Still, he is making a serious attempt at one of the accomplishments that have to be included in a complete art of the novel.
The least one can say in general about *The Deer Park* is that it is written
by a novelist who is still very obviously going places.

Richard Chase. *Cmty*. Dec., 1955. pp. 582–3

Mailer's novels, at least for me, personify the dilemma of novelists who
are deeply concerned with history but dangerously oversimplify it; if
they seem consumed by their interest in sex it is because they are always seeking some solution for "the times." In many ways Mailer
seems to me the most forceful and oddly objective novelist of his age,
objective in the sense that he is most capable of imagining objects to
which a reader can give himself. . . . Yet Mailer's interest in the ex-

ternal world has dwindled to the point where the theme of sexual power and delight—which Mailer feels to be a lost secret in contemporary life—has become a labyrinthian world in itself. Mailer now seems bent on becoming the American Marquis de Sade, where once he seemed to be another Dos Passos.

Alfred Kazin. Harper. Oct., 1959. p. 130

See *The Naked and the Dead* and *The Deer Park* (novels); also *Advertisements for Myself* (selections).

See Supplement at end of text for additional material.

MALAMUD, BERNARD (1914–   )

The Natural is an unusually fine novel . . . although I don't know how the professionals are going to take it. For Bernard Malamud's interests go far beyond baseball. What he has done is to contrive a sustained and elaborate allegory in which the "natural" player—who operates with ease and the greatest skill, without having been taught—is equated with the natural man. . . . In his telling and always deliberate use of the vernacular alternated with passages evocative and almost lyrical, in his almost entirely successful relation of baseball in detail to the culture which elaborated it, Malamud has made a brilliant and unusual book.

Harry Sylvester. NYT. Aug. 24, 1952. p. 5

The appearance of an intelligent novelist who finds it possible to say something about a popular—"mass"—phenomenon through the medium of a popular literary form is a very healthy sign. Bernard Malamud's *The Natural* is the first serious novel we have had (after Ring Lardner's *You Know Me Al*) about a baseball player. . . . Mr. Malamud suggests that baseball is the American way of providing for needs which our culture generally refuses to satisfy. . . . But the ball park in itself is not enough for the writer. . . . *The Natural* is loaded with Homeric parallels and suggestion of myth—overloaded in fact. . . . The habit of symbolizing everything, from baseball bats to men and women, and of multiplying allusions to the point where they begin to crowd out reality altogether, is one of the more unfortunate legacies bequeathed by Joyce and Eliot to contemporary writers.

Norman Podhoretz. Cmty. March, 1953. pp. 321–3

His unrelenting pity for straining souls reminds us of Dostoevsky—if we can imagine Dostoevsky tempered by Chagall's lyric nostalgia for a lost Jewish past. Chagall too makes extensive formal use of dreams. . . .

The Assistant is almost perfect as far as it goes. In his work to come, it will be important for Malamud to take some chances on the wit and the love of life which he gives us so far in a minor key. This book and his stories are lyric marvels, and they make us want more—the headlong architectural daring of a great novelist.

Herbert Gold. *Nation*. April 20, 1957. p. 350

It is a commonplace that a writer of true talent will take commonplace material and produce through it in the reader a sense of utterly fresh discovery of human qualities. This, Bernard Malamud has achieved in his new novel, *The Assistant*. He has succeeded also in individualizing his people to a point where one feels able to continue conversation with them outside the book, and yet he has kept for each of them a symbolic role, so that the tale has moral echoes, indeed almost a runic quality; it is essentially a parable. . . . Malamud creates an amazing tension in his story of the growth of conscience. . . . He is a writer who certainly will count amongst the literary figures of our day.

Meyer Levin. *SR*. June 15, 1957. p. 21

Malamud is naturally a fantasist of the ordinary, the commonplace, the average. He writes, a little, the way Chagall paints—except that the natural course of Malamud's imagination is not to seek the open and the lyrical but symbols of the highly involuted personal life of Jews. He loves what he himself calls "violins and candles" in the sky, old-clothes-men who masquerade something sinister yet unnameable; he has a natural sense for the humdrum transposed to the extreme, of the symbolic and the highly colored. He tends to the bizarre, the contorted, the verge of things that makes you shiver, not laugh.

Alfred Kazin. *Cmty*. July, 1957. p. 90

There is a kind of crystalline hardness over the tautly lyrical descriptions of people and scenes; there is never a literariness or any intrusion of philosophic values in Mr. Malamud's world. . . . Mr. Malamud's people are memorable and real as rock, and there is not one gesture of sentimentality or theatrics to render them so. He knows his people and keeps them free with the kind of writer's control that one does not find often enough in the myriad novels about simple people.

William Goyen. *NYT*. April 28, 1957. p. 4

Man or woman, intellectual or artisan, young or old, Mr. Malamud's characters are dogged by a grief, which is centuries old yet at the same time as fresh as the searing memories of concentration camp and gas chamber that torment the attractive youthful heroine of one story. . . . This atavistic identification with grief permeates all these moving stories.

Yet Mr. Malamud's fiction bubbles with life. Although his people may wear their sorrows like a garment, they also refuse to give up. . . . Out of the antithesis of humor and pathos, the starkly realistic and the bizarre, Mr. Malamud has created a world which seems to have about it the inevitable, irrevocable ring of truth. Here are my people, he seems to say. God help them, and me.

William Peden. *NYT*. May 11, 1958. p. 5

Set principally in the New York slums, dealing mostly with Jewish and other immigrants, *The Magic Barrel* is a collection of short stories unified by a tone of resigned and humorous wisdom and an unsentimental central compassion. . . . The responsibility of being, first of all, a man and then a Jew, involves all these characters. They are simple people, of basic integrity. They commit unpremeditated acts of faith or perversity, and when they are caught up in the results, their grief is more than personal: it is the mourning of a whole people. This gives a depth to the writing that is missed when the Jewish element is lacking. Depth, but not darkness; for even hopelessness, in Mr. Malamud's hands, is infused with a kind of New World vitality.

Ruth Chapin Blackman. *CSM*. May 15, 1958. p. 13

In *The Assistant,* which seems to me one of the important novels of the postwar period, Jewish experience is used as a way of approaching the deepest, broadest problems of love and fear, of communion and isolation in human life. So, too, in *The Magic Barrel:* the more faithfully Malamud renders Jewish life, the wider his meanings are.

Malamud's stories often have a legendary quality whether his method is realistic, as "The First Seven Years," or fantastic, as in "Angel Levine". . . . The question Malamud asks more often than any other is: what are the limits of human responsibility?

Granville Hicks. *SR*. May 17, 1958. p. 16

Like the so-called Magic Realists in painting, he is master of an alchemy whereby the grossest reality is converted to the most imaginative uses. He transcribes everyday life and yet the result glows with lights never seen on land or sea. His creatures are often grubby, pathetic or even mean, but they reveal longings, passions, weaknesses, capacities for sacrifice or faith that transfigure them. In his hands the line between the cruel and the kind, the holy and the profane, the grotesque and the beautiful is redrawn in a dozen inspired ways.

Milton Rugoff. *NYHT*. May 25, 1958. p. 3

There is nothing poetic about Malamud's prose and yet he achieves lyricism through the wide-ranging play of his imagination, the richness of his emotion, the intricacy of his perceptions. . . . Malamud has no interest in character as such. His response is not to the individual but to the tragedy of the human condition in its most general aspects. He has humor but, springing out of a sorrow too great to be contained, it verges on hysteria.

                                    Gordon Merrick. *NR*. July 21, 1958. pp. 20–1

See *The Natural* and *The Assistant* (novels) and *The Magic Barrel* (short stories).   See Supplement at end of text for additional material.

MARCH, WILLIAM (1893–1954)

The outstanding virtues of Mr. March's work are those of complete absence of sentimentality and routine romanticism, of a dramatic gift constantly heightened and sharpened by the eloquence of understatement. Your first impression is that of the ultimate "low-down". . . . A second, less favorable impression follows, not unnaturally, from the very advantage just mentioned. The author's freedom, that is to say, to pile horror on horror, cynicism on cynicism, ends by leaving one with a sense of that "too much" which defeats itself. . . . The continuous heaping up of bitterness and irony . . . results in a sort of reverse-romanticism.

                                    Arthur Ruhl. *SR*. Jan. 28, 1933. p. 399

"The Little Wife" . . . seems to be particularly illustrative of March's gift for opening the window of the universal upon the individual instance, for concealing extreme technical skill in an absence of conscious technique and for establishing almost unbearably close communication with his reader. . . . Mr. March's collected tales make a disturbing book. It possesses a unity that has nothing to do with locale, for though the author has largely confined himself to the boundaries of Mississippi his characters fill their beings with a common air that is not the malarial breath of the deep South but the deadlier and less indigenous one of frustration.

                                    Elizabeth Hart. *NYHT*. Feb. 10, 1935. p. 3

His special gift as a story-teller is his faculty of catching on the wing some bit of penetration into human life, and creating about it a slight tale, a short narrative, an episode, a piece of realistic description, by way of elucidation.

   These are superior stories; lacking the sensational qualities necessary for a journalistic success, they are sound to the core. . . . They are slight in surface compared to the best American short stories being written (and they are to be compared with the best) but they have intelligence, depth and quality.

Fred T. Marsh. NYT. Feb. 17, 1935. p. 2

Not since Hardy died have we been given the same sense of the President of the Immortals having his sport with mortals. . . . I have had occasion to note before . . . William March's remarkable power in drawing psychopathic characters, characters driven beyond themselves by frustration, by feelings of inadequacy, by the complexity of life. The realists who copy life or caricature it can never give the illusion of a living world as can a writer of this kind, who has so few of the tricks of realism but who can take human passions, human longings for happiness and love and beauty and make a world for them.

Mary M. Colum. Forum. Jan. 1937. p. 35

William March is making a considerable reputation for himself, particularly as a writer of short stories. Apparently simple as these are, quite uncompromising and often more than a little bitter, they are quite unforgettable—sometimes uncomfortably so. . . . Above all, he never errs in saying too much or in pointing a moral: it is the reader who is forced into indignation, or pity, out of his own response to what is set forth with such seeming artlessness. In the world of this author the sun shines with a peculiarly revealing and sometimes cruel light on the just and the unjust alike but, if there are no bad people, there are some totally unbearable circumstances.

Iris Barry. NYHT. April 2, 1939. p. 5

March, in the great tradition, is centrally concerned with the theme of guilt and expiation. . . . March seems to believe that all men must live in loneliness and isolation, their only possible communication "lies," but that the threads of their lives are nevertheless inseparably bound together. He tends to see all people as either mentally or psychologically deformed, and all relationships between them, particularly close family relationships, as only endless variants of sadism and masochism, hatred and answering love, murder and expiation. His books may be lower-keyed than Faulkner's, but they are quite as lively.

Stanly Edgar Hyman. NR. Feb. 8, 1943. p. 188

Mr. March, unlike Ernest Hemingway and John Dos Passos, never escapes the defeatism of the war years of his young manhood. If one reads slowly through these stories, the growing power of their negative quality, however, becomes apparent. . . . From the start, he has been one of the finest technicians writing the short story in English. . . . His later stories show a gathering force and economy of method and also a stronger and clearer statement of his ideas. It seems to me entirely clear . . . that William March is one of our most flexible and most powerful writers.

John Farrar. *SR*. Oct. 13, 1945. p. 44

March's writing is classic in its undistracted realism, its bareness, its freedom from salable amenities. . . . We have a prose style rather old-fashioned in its grave, consequential way, describing in unhurried serenity life as he has known it since the late 1890's. Most of his characters, considered as historical types, appear to be Southerners of the years before and during the First World War. . . . His best work . . . reflects the alternate play of two qualities that Anatole France perceived in fiction that is to be classic: pity and irony.

Alistair Cooke. *NR*. Dec. 3, 1945. pp. 756–8

When I asked David Mynders Smythe . . . what (March) looked like David replied that he looked like a preacher with wicked eyes.

It was rather a neat description. I met a man of medium height, of slim physique and erect carriage, with a thick crop of wavy, graying hair. He looked much younger than what I knew his age to be, and his whole appearance was mild; his voice was soft, his manner gentle. Only his eyes were different. They gleamed from behind his glasses, probing, studying everyone in the room, and, as I became conscious of what the quiet voice was saying, I discovered it was a highly barbed monologue that was pouring out at us, witty, mischievous, brilliant.

Robert Tallant. *SR*. July 17, 1954. p. 33

In the late Nineteen Twenties he had achieved a complete and mature view of life, while some of the more famous chroniclers of the day now seem young and shallow, eloquent but narrow. During the social turbulence of the Nineteen Thirties, moreover, he went on writing quiet short stories, tragedies and comedies of Southern life. . . . It is difficult to do justice to the complex texture of these stories—indignant and ironic, witty, melancholy and resigned.

Maxwell Geismar. *NYT*. Feb. 26, 1956. p. 5

Even in his comparative failures, there was that profound respect for the materials with which he dealt, and that faith in his chosen method of approaching them. In his best stories, I should say, he was closer to the Sherwood Anderson of *Winesburg, Ohio* than to any other contemporary. But there never was a time when he seemed to imitate any one at all.

He would not fake, or "heighten," or pile on local color. He was a true writer who had mastered the simple declarative sentence. And it would be good to think that, by a happier irony than some of those he experienced in his lifetime, his deep, straight stories will outlive the showier writing that has tended to shade his own.

John K. Hutchens. *NYHT*. March 4, 1956. p. 2

See *A William March Omnibus* (which includes *Company K* and some short stories); also see *October Island, The Looking Glass,* and *The Bad Seed* (novels) and *The Little Wife* and *Trial Balance* (collections of short stories).

MARKHAM, EDWIN   (1852–1940)

Mr. Markham is democracy's greatest living poet. His stately lines not only conform to the canons of art and are rich in melody, but they ring true at every point; they are instinct with the virility of democracy; they are vibrant with the spirit of justice and fraternity; they represent all that is best, truest and finest in the new social awakening which is battling against the rising tide of reaction, imperialism and class-rule based on privileged interest and acquired wealth.

B. O. Flower. *Arena*. Feb., 1906. p. 143

The idea of making a newspaper sensation out of a serious piece of blank verse ("The Man with a Hoe") was probably the wildest that any journalist ever had; but, thanks to the swing of Markham's lines, I actually succeeded in doing that impossible thing, and soon it was speeding all over the land. California is, I believe, the only place in this country where such a sensation could have had its genesis. . . . Markham's mouth-filling words were soon being read aloud in nearly every house on the coast, ministers were preaching sermons on it, lawyers were quoting it in court arguments, and every orator and elocutionist in a land of countless spellbinders were spouting it from the platform. The labour unions became very much excited over the poem, and applauded it to the echo whenever it was read at meetings.

Bailey Millard. *Bkm.* May, 1908. p. 267

Markham with all his defects of platitudinous idealism, puritanical sex-prudence, sentimental metaphysics and dedication flap-doodle, is steeped in the ecstasy of eternals. There is a touch of crazy beauty in him, too. And he has caught the wild music of the Angel Israfel. But he is hopelessly of America, with its paste humanitarianism, its paste optimism, its paste culture.

He is productive but uncreative. He sticks to the old forms, the old metaphors, the old lilts, the old griefs, with suddenly a line or simile of mirific magic leaping forth from the page like a dazzling dragon-fly out of a New England mince-pie.

Benjamin De Casseres. *AM*. Dec., 1926. pp. 398–9

Edwin Markham has continued to write as he always wrote, as his great predecessors wrote, particularly as Bryant on the one hand and Poe on the other, wrote. So it is not easy to do him justice, yet it would surely be exhibiting a merely fashionable mind to deprecate his work by a term so illegitimate in real criticism as "old-fashioned". . . . The most telling count that could ever be charged against him has been that his work is highly rhetorical. Much of it can be called "rhymed rhetoric." But, so often, what gorgeous, thrilling, powerful rhetoric!

Shaemas O'Sheel. *Com*. June 29, 1932. p. 251

Today Mr. Markham's poetry seems, in its rhetoric and in its romanticism, almost another language from that spoken by most of the troubled and disillusioned modern poets. . . . Although the whole tradition of modern poetry has, seemingly, passed, we find this poet of eighty years still voicing his desire toward loveliness, the imperishable, still exuberant in a faith in mankind, still youthful and eager, clad in all of the old illusions which were the subjects for poetry so many years ago.

Eda Lou Walton. *NYHT*. July 31, 1932. p. 2

His was the first authentic American voice in our time to be raised against the injustice that is in the world; and his most famous poem, "The Man with the Hoe," swept through our land, and ultimately, in translation, reached the whole world. The power and pity of it have not diminished with the years. . . . He stood for nobility of character, for everything that is great in the American spirit.

Charles Hanson Towne. *Poetry*. April, 1940. pp. 30–1

No poem was ever better timed (than "The Man with the Hoe"). The social conscience was just enough awake to respond to it, but had not been awake long enough and was still not wide enough awake to have heard any comparable clarion call. It was better than a thousand sermons on the "social gospel." This poem was no mere trick of versification, and no exploitation of a popular idea. The idea was not yet popular, and Markham really meant it with a prophet's intensity of conviction.

W. E. Garrison. *CC*. May 17, 1950. p. 618

Edwin Markham lived and died the bard. He was a prophet of his people, a poet in the tribal and traditional sense. No ivory tower could contain him. His ideas, his songs, his passion came from his association with people. He never asked adulation as the pet of society; all he wanted was an audience and he applied all of the techniques of the evangelist and humanist to gain the ear of the people. Let other people whisper or speak conumdrums. He shouted and was heard.

A. M. Sullivan. *SR*. July 22, 1950. p. 21

See *Poems* (1950 edition).

MARQUAND, JOHN P. (1893–1961)

He was a master of graceful satire that is at once healthy and humanely uncorrosive. In all technical matters relating to plot structure, economy of developing character, artistic control over every detail of the movement, however minute, and over the pace, the dialogue, the big scenes and the crises, Marquand was expert. And he had attained complete dominance over the method of narrating a story in the first person from the point of view of an observer or active participant in the action without straining the credulity or breaking the illusion, apparently subordinating him to his role as narrator but at the same time making him one of the most important characters in the dramatis personae.

Harlan Hatcher. *EJ*. Sept. 1939. p. 514

He is entirely and unmistakably honest, about his work, about himself. The honesty is neither forced nor obtrusive but an essential part of the man. And with it—and with the protective coloration—goes an eye as mild as can be, and as deadly accurate as a very fine rifle. Agreeable, well-mannered, polite, he can bring down a Bo-jo-Brown at 3,000 yards and stuff him afterwards with neatness and dispatch.

Stephen Vincent and Rosemary Benét. *NYHT*.
March 16, 1941. p. 5

It is clear that intellectually New York is admirable to Mr. Marquand and Boston reprehensible and foolish, but there is an emotional difficulty: Mr. Marquand still likes Boston better than New York. The curious combination of satire and apologia which characterizes Mr. Marquand's tales of two cities, and which makes them so richly rewarding to the reader who knows both cities, is the result of this unresolved conflict of intellect and emotion. And since Boston has left an indelible mark on American life and New York is leaving a still more indelible one, Mr. Marquand is not to be dismissed summarily as a minor novelist or his Boston books as mere entertainment.

Thayer Donovan Bisbee. SR. July 5, 1941. p. 14

It is because Marquand is so acutely conscious of the changes time brings not merely to people but also to their values that all of his major novels move back and forth between present and past. . . . His sense of time is even more precise than his sense of place or his sense of class. He knows the past thirty-five years—on the social planes and in the places with which he is concerned—as unerringly as one of Mark Twain's pilots knew the Mississippi River. A serious anachronism in one of his books is almost unthinkable, not because he is a pedantic researcher but because his feeling for time approaches infallibility.

Granville Hicks. Harper. April, 1950. p. 106

On the face of it, J. P. Marquand possesses all the attributes of a great novelist. He has a fine sense of milieu, technical skill to spare, and an acute insight into his main characters. . . . To the talents with which he was by nature endowed, to the blessings of worldly success, he has added a toughness of will, never permitting himself the luxury of happy endings or allowing his characters easy ways out of their dilemmas. They enjoy in fact no outs at all. . . . Yet among so many virtues, Marquand's novels are almost exactly alike. They deal with a fixed problem, and pass through three identical stages in the course of working it out. . . . Here is the restricting element that has kept Marquand —and will probably always keep him—from reaching the level of his great predecessors.

Leo Gurko. AS. Autumn 1952. pp. 444–5

As a writer Marquand is somewhat short on talent, imagination, brute ability, but is long on care, observation, directed curiosity, and is longest of all on personal involvement, subjective compulsion. Most of his books, under their veneer of patiently observed objective detail, seem versions of the same subjective fable, one designed to say to him and also to us: "You were right to do as you did; or if not right, still, you had no choice; or if you had a choice, still, it's the choice all of us necessarily make wrong. . . ." The fable is told in a series of flashbacks, of sighs as elegiac, nostalgic, and wistfully submissive—as mannered and unvarying—as a Puccini opera.

Randall Jarrell. Harper. Nov. 1954. p. 96

He has been for most of his life a respectable member of the upper middle class and he has seen no reason hotly to renounce all its values merely because that was for a time the modish thing to do. Instead he has set himself to understand, without indulgence but also without aversion, the curious tragicomedy of that class. The circumstance that its tragicomedy is, though only partially, his own infuses into his best works a certain melancholy that gives them depth. . . . Of all the writers I can think of he most resembles Thackeray. He has Thackeray's fruitfully ambivalent attitude toward his own class, his irony, his good manners, his self-doubts and much of his humor.

Clifton Fadiman. Introduction to Thirty Years by
John P. Marquand (Little). 1954. pp. x–xi

John Marquand is that rare kind of writer, a really good novelist of manners. He knows what only the best novelists of this kind do, how to make the reader see the customs and habits of large areas of a society through the realized life of the people who generate them and give them vitality. . . . Mr. Marquand's knowledge never exists apart from his perceptions of people—of the particular gesture, the precise expression, the exact phrase; and that is what makes his novels so good and makes us feel that even when he is not at his absolute best . . . he is much better than most of our novelists.

Arthur Mizener. NYT. Feb. 27, 1955. p. 1

John P. Marquand as a critic of American society is something like a newspaper when its own political party is in office: he may be gently reproved, but his disapprobation is not harsh enough to occasion doubts among the faithful or to alienate any subscribers. . . . Mr. Marquand probably has at his disposal more information about American society than any other novelist now writing. He particularly excels in the kind of information sociologists are fond of—the size of people's income, the kind of cars they drive, the clubs they join, and so on—and he can fill many a not uninteresting page with this kind of detail.

Paul Pickrel. YR. Spring, 1955. pp. 476–7

Mr. Marquand is by now an old pro. . . . The old pros know all the tricks and they know them well enough to keep them out of sight. . . . Mr. Marquand has something of a reputation as a satirist, though only a gentle one, and it is with satire that the old pros tend to get soft. . . . The machinery is no less efficient, the movement as effortless, but that pleasant tang of irony which made the journey so exhilarating is on the way out; instead there is a cosiness that is on the stuffy side, an indulgence that is distinctly cloying.

Richard Lister. NSN. Dec. 24, 1955. p. 864

See *The Late George Apley, Wickford Point, H. M. Pulham, Esquire,* and *Sincerely, Willis Wayde* (novels).

MASTERS, EDGAR LEE (1868–1950)

It is apparently not yet agreed what Mr. Masters's book is,—except that it is "free verse." Convinced that it is certainly not poetry, and horrified by its content and structure, the aesthetic Calvinists have exhorted Mr. Masters to be still, in the spirit of the command of the immortal ship-captain to his mate: "What I wants of you, Mr. Coffin, is SILENCE, and damn little of that." But Mr. Masters is unlikely to oblige. It is extremely doubtful if silence is his long suit. Certainly it is not a conspicuous characteristic of his *Spoon River Anthology,* which is nothing if not articulate and alive and what we have a fancy to call psychically reverberatory. In this village *comédie humaine* are assembled the life histories of the inhabitants of Spoon River, and the overtones of the jangling music of these spent lives reverberate from page to page, clash and re-echo, attaining at times a poignancy which we do not quite know how to regard or appraise.

Lawrence Gilman. NAR. Aug., 1915. pp. 271–2

It is appropriate, no doubt, that Masters should be less selective than Frost—the West is less reserved than New England. . . . This is the prairie's exuberant way—one must look at this poet, not in close detail, but in the mass. Thus one may get from him, as from the prairies themselves, a sense of space and richness. One feels in him too the idealistic vision of a man accustomed to far horizons—that impatience with things near, things more or less faithless to the imminent beauty, and that relief in the contemplation of things remote, beauty's survivals or prophecies. This chaotic half-baked civilization, growing up out of these broad and fruitful plains into dull little towns and mad great cities all fitfully, inadequately spiritualized—this one feels in Mr. Masters's books.

Harriet Monroe. Poetry. Jan., 1917. p. 205

Whitman had his eye continually upon broad expanses and far distances, the land of his quest. Masters, too often perhaps, sees nothing but enclosing walls. Whitman is the romanticist. . . . Masters is the scientist, a sworn devotee of facts, confessing no *a priori* theories, I say confessing, because I suspect Mr. Masters of being almost as predisposed to pessimism as was Walt Whitman to optimism. . . . Masters is predisposed to see the weakness that is in human nature and the tragedy that pursues it, and he finds, of course, plenty of both. . . . To

Whitman the world was a pageant, to be enjoyed; to Masters it is a drama, to be analyzed, and the motif is one of tragedy.

Julius W. Pratt. SAQ. April, 1917. pp. 157–8

Like Jonathon Swift, Mr. Masters is consumed with hatred for insincerity in art and insincerity in life; in the laudable desire to force the truth upon his readers, he emphasizes the ugly, the brutal, the treacherous elements which exist, not only in Spoon River, but in every man born of woman. The result, viewed calmly, is that we have an impressive collection of vices. . . . I therefore regard *Spoon River Anthology* not as a brilliant revelation of human nature, but as a masterpiece of cynicism.

William Lyon Phelps. Bkm. May, 1918. pp. 265–6

Mr. Masters's *Spoon River Anthology* in the first years after its publication was altogether the most read and talked-of volume of poetry that had ever been written in America. . . . People who really knew poetry were interested and amused at their combination of a very old Greek form with the doings of an Illinois town. People who were allured but disappointed by the glitter and the hollowness of the new poetry were refreshed by the grim substance of this book.

Percy Boynton. Some Contemporary Americans
(Chicago). 1924. p. 52

Spoon River Anthology remains in the face of all detractions the most original work—with the exception of Theodore Dreiser's novels—that American genius has produced since the death of Henry James. Nor could it have become what it is if its author had not in his own nature combined a deep Rabelaisian zest for the freer aspects of this gross village life with an infinite loathing of its cramped limitations. In the contrasted intensity of his love and his hate for this America of his, Mr. Masters's mind is an almost perfect medium for the precise enterprise that blind chance or his tutelary genius set him upon undertaking.

John Cowper Powys. Bkm. Aug., 1929. p. 650

The Fate of the Jury carries on the Masters tradition of a writer more lawyer, psychologist, and story-teller than poet. A disciple of Browning, Masters has been using the dramatic monologue, and *Domesday Book* was patterned on *The Ring and the Book*. In *The Fate of the Jury* we have the story continued. . . . *The Fate of the Jury* is interesting reading, an intricate weaving of tale into tale, an account of lesbianism, masochism, and duplicity such as Jeffers himself might, very differently, have used. The blank verse is the best Masters has ever written, and he has denied himself the long passages of personal philosophy which weighted his earlier stories.

Eda Lou Walton. *Nation*. July 17, 1929. p. 72

Man as a social being; man as a sexual being. These are the subjects of Masters as well as of Dreiser and Anderson. The treatment and the conclusion of all three may be as outmoded now as a foreign bond. Aesthetic considerations aside, however, it seems to me that Masters deserves as much praise for his stand as Anderson or Dreiser or anyone else of the younger radicals now in their sixties. He helped set the intellectual tone of the post-War period. He realizes that most things accepted by most people as true and just are in reality false and unjust, and that in these matters it is usually best to be a radical.

Herbert Ellsworth Childs. *SwR*. July, 1933. p. 342

Judged as poetry and not as sociology or any other variety of doctrine, *Invisible Landscapes* is Mr. Masters's finest book. The best pieces in it have a lyrical quality which he has achieved hitherto in only a few scattered lines. . . . Along with the late flowering of the lyrical gift, and perhaps in part as its cause, these poems breathe a serenity of mind. The crusty old fighter has found peace in nature and in contemplation of the past of the race. . . . I am not sure that Mr. Masters has found the most desirable type of serenity; there is much weariness in it, an undertone of defeat, and a resignation which to younger men will seem premature. . . . Mr. Masters will probably be continued to be remembered for his Spoon River books, which despite their stylistic flaws and crudities of perception had the stuff of life in them. *Invisible Landscapes* is nevertheless a memorable volume.

Philip Blair Rice. *Nation*. Oct. 16, 1935. p. 445

He seems at home anywhere in American history, whether he is writing of Martin Van Buren or Daniel Boone or the Battle of Gettysburg. . . . One reads the later Masters more for the matter than the manner. . . . Masters has read enormously and experienced a great deal of life. His comments upon the past and present are therefore of more than usual interest. My own view of his technique is that it is inclined to be slipshod. He is rather the philosopher musing and moralizing than the artist trying to shape out of resistant material a work beautiful in its contours and elements, as well as full of meaning. . . . He appears willing to recede into his memories, and to be rather remote from the world of today. He cherishes his nostalgias.

William Rose Benet. *SR*. Sept. 12, 1936. p. 20

Edgar Lee Masters is very much like the mountain being chiseled by Mr. Borglum. He has left sharp nuances throughout the hard past of American life and letters, and as a poet has contributed along with some few others the sense of history which has been accepted and molded into a tradition. What Robert Frost and Robinson did for New England's folk essence and experience, Masters wrote into the plains of the Middle West, into the rivers, the valleys. Whitman had initiated the impulse . . . and Masters, along with Lindsay and Sandburg—for they were the folk singers—continued and spread the pattern.

Harry Roskolenko. *Poetry*. Jan., 1940. p. 211

Masters in his flouting of tradition, with his scorn for hypocrisy, with his sympathetic appreciation of the eternal problems of the artist as well as the eternal frustrations imposed by a materialistic culture, found himself the poetic voice of the age to much the same degree that Sinclair Lewis and F. Scott Fitzgerald were the fictional voices. Today we can still admire the skill and finish of the Spoon River portraits even though we turn increasingly to poetry with greater intellectual subtlety and a richer use of language.

John T. Flanagan. *SWR*. Summer, 1953. p. 236

See *Spoon River Anthology, Domesday Book, The Fate of the Jury,* and *Invisible Landscapes* (poetry).

MENCKEN, H. L. (1880–1950)

Like Max Beerbohm, Mencken's work is inevitably distinguished. But now and then one wonders—granted that, solidly, book by book, he has built up a literary reputation most to be envied of any American, granted also that he has done more for the national letters than any man alive, one is yet inclined to regret a success so complete. What will he do now? The very writers to the press about the blue Sabbath hurl the bricks of the building he has demolished into the still smoking ruins. He is say, forty; how of the next twenty years? Will he find new gods to dethrone, some eternal "yokelry" still callous enough to pose as intelligentsia before the Menckenian pen fingers? Or will he strut among the ruins, a man beaten by his own success, as futile, in the end, as one of those Conrad characters that so tremendously enthrall him?

F. Scott Fitzgerald. *Bkm*. March, 1921. p. 81

Mencken, in spite of all his protestations of realistic resignation, is actually a militant idealist. Most Americans—even of fine standards—

have long ago resigned themselves to the cheapness and ugliness of America, but Mencken has never resigned himself. He has never ceased to regard his native country with wounded and outraged eyes. The shabby politics, the childish books, the factories turning out wooden nutmegs have never lost their power to offend him. At this late date, he is, I suppose, almost the only man in the country who still expects American novelists to be artists and politicians gentlemen.

Edmund Wilson. *NR*. June 1, 1921. pp. 11–12

What he really is, is a social critic, and besides that, a humorist of a very high order. Literature he may look upon as an escape and a refuge from life, and "extra-aesthetic valuations" he may regard with odium; but there is nothing anaemic or effete in his own comment on the life of man, or on the life of the society he moves in. As to the promptness of his results, at least, we have had almost no critic in this generation who has written with greater relevance or rightness, or who has been a greater sanative force. . . . He has been a gadfly to the state, a voice crying in the wilderness, a mouthpiece of the Lord. . . . His style, as a style, is a medium of efficiency; it is vibrant, athletic, vascular. He should take rank among our first-rate prosateurs.

Newton Arvin. *Fm*. Dec. 27, 1922. p. 382

Mr. Mencken is so effective . . . because his appeal is not from mind to mind but from viscera to viscera. If you analyze his arguments you destroy their effect. You cannot take them in detail and examine their implications. You have to judge him totally, roughly, approximately, without definition, as you would a barrage of artillery, for the general destruction rather than for the accuracy of the individual shots. He presents an experience, and if he gets you, he gets you not by reasoned conviction, but by a conversion which you may or may not be able to dress up later as a philosophy. If he succeeds with you, he implants in you a sense of sin, and then he revives you with grace, and disposes you to a new pride in excellence and in a non-gregarious excellence.

Walter Lippmann. *SR*. Dec. 11, 1926. p. 414

Mencken is in a Berserk rage against stupidity, dullness, and sham; he is a whole army, horse, foot, artillery, aviation and general staff all in one, mobilized in a war upon his enemies. He has a spy bureau all over the country, which collects for him illustrations of the absurdities of democracy. . . . If you ask Mencken what is the remedy for these horrors, he will tell you they are the natural and inevitable manifestations of the boobus Americanus. If you ask him why then labor so monstrously, he will say that it is for his own enjoyment, he is so constituted

that he finds his recreation in laughing at his fellow boobs. But watch
him a while, and you will see the light of hilarity die out of his eyes
. . . and you will realize that he is lying to himself and to you; he is a
new-style crusader, a Christian Anti-Christ, a tireless propagandist of
no-propaganda.

Upton Sinclair. *Bkm.* Nov., 1927. p. 255

Courageous and independent he began early to fight against cant and
stupidity, shams and hypocrisy, intolerance and reaction, and he fought
against great odds and many enemies—and won. In the fight circumstances and expediency have doubtless thrown him off repeatedly from
the high resolves he once had, and so, like Valentino, he has felt sadly
that he has never done quite all that it was in his power to do. . . . A
poet of a peculiar order, who uses all the license of fact that a poet is entitled to, Mencken has been and is a personality, he has meant and
means something in the life and thought of this country, he is a symbol; and as a symbol he must also be and mean something—again like
Valentino—that is foreign to his wishes and more than a little distaste-
ful to him. *Hinc lacrimae rerum.*

Burton Rascoe. *Bkm.* Feb., 1928. p. 676

There can be no denying that, at first, there was a delightful charm in
his hilariously impish maneuvers and his agreeable jargon. It must have
been a rare pleasure for many of his nature, who lacked his ability and
fearlessness, to watch him as he went through life making faces at everything most people were afraid to make faces at. But today that old
charm of Mr. Mencken is dead, or at least fast dying. . . . His *Prejudices* have been admirably named in order to protect anything written
therein, but in the handling of his subjects he does not seem to remember that he is actually prejudiced; and he makes the mistake of taking
himself very seriously, which is probably the only thing he does take
seriously. . . . It is too bad that Mr. Mencken is intolerant for that is
as much a sin as cruelty.

William Saroyan. *OM.* March, 1929. pp. 77–8

In the thick of his blistering charges against American life in general,
Mencken somehow contrived to make the individual reader feel exempt
from the indictment, an *âme bien née* who belonged on the side of
Mencken and the angels. Thus the situation, from the outset, was ironical. Mencken, exposing the ghastly inadequacies of all matters of public interest, encouraged his readers to be too snobbish to give a damn
about them. He insisted he could offer no remedy and was amused
that he should be expected to. Those whom he influenced at once ac-

cepted his conclusions, turned their backs on the national plight and set up as a civilized minority. . . . Mencken, far from leading America out of the wilderness, merely bade the elect, from some secure elevation, watch their less enlightened brethren wriggle and squirm.

Louis Kronenberger. NR. Oct. 7, 1936. pp. 243–4

His value . . . lies as much in his profound and unwilling reflection of a period as in his brilliant reporting of it. If he helped to mold the spirit of the post-war epoch, he also betrayed its underlying pressures. . . . And if he undervalued the resources of our democratic social arrangement—exaggerating in this as in so much else, he could hardly exaggerate the blind consuming power as well as the blind fertility of our industrial machine. For, otherwise, knowing as well as we do now the distorted sources of the Menckenian imagery whose goatish prancing drew into such a macabre dance of death—still, why do these recurrent omens and portents of disaster, those acrid visions of dissolution and the whole unlovely prophetic end of what had been in its day the world's last best hope: why does all this linger so uncomfortably in our minds?

Maxwell Geismar. The Last of the Provincials
(Houghton). 1947. pp. 65–6

He was a social critic and a literary showman who had taken lessons from Macauley, as well as from Nietzsche, Huneker and Bierce, and he fought with all his masculine force against the elements in American society that impeded the creative life and stifled its growth. A transatlantic Attila, with his own Teutonic fury, a coarse mind that had undertaken a literary spadesman's work, he accomplished a task that only a coarse mind could do. . . . After the jazz age passed, when he had become an institution, Mencken's limitations and faults were more generally apparent. It was evident that he had the vaguest of literary standards.

Van Wyck Brooks. AS. Autumn, 1951. pp. 414–6

In private one might make bold to esteem him both as a literary and social critic more than often wrong—or childish even, or it might be just slightly pig-headed—in his estimate of this or of the other affair or person. But the magnificent verve and gusto with which always the man presented his chosen point of view, no matter what might be his theme, resulted almost always in a work of dramatic art that you savored with enjoyment.

Think what you might, whether before or after the performance, there was at the moment no denying this H. L. Mencken was putting on a rousing good show. So that temporarily his aesthetic or political or social rightness or wrongness did not seem, to me at least, to be of weight.

James Branch Cabell. *Nation*. Sept. 12, 1953. p. 213

As a thinker Mencken probably had only a temporary vogue, for his fund of knowledge was limited and his ideas . . . were few and largely dubious. But as a journalist, his influence was immense. Indeed, he was one of the greatest editors in all our history. . . . He was a man of contradictions and obscurities, and puerilities and even cheapness, but he was a great editor, and his *Mercury* was, all in all, a great magazine.

Charles Angoff. *NR*. Sept. 13, 1954. pp. 19–22

Looking over the whole range of his work today we can see that, if he was overrated in his day as a thinker (though not more so than his victims), he was vastly underrated as a humorist with one deadly sensible eye on the behavior of the human animal. He helped along this misconception by constantly reminding people that he was a critic of ideas, which was true only as the ideas were made flesh. He was, in fact, a humorist by instinct and a superb craftsman by temperament. So that when all his private admirations were aped and exhausted there emerged the style of H. L. Mencken, purified and mellowed in later years, a style flexible, fancy-free, ribald, and always beautifully lucid: a native product unlike any other style in the language.

Alistair Cooke. *SR*. Sept. 10, 1955. p. 64

It has become a commonplace of literary history that Mencken was an emancipator who helped free American writing from gentility and American manners from provinciality; and this is true or at least true enough to be worth saying. But it is also true that whenever we fall back upon a writer's "historical importance" and try to assert his value in terms of what was peculiarly local to his time, it is probably due to an uneasy awareness that his voice no longer reaches us. In the recent efforts to "revive" Mencken it has been customary to speak of the need for a similar figure in our time. To be sure, nothing could be more useful than a cultural leader who would outrage our genteel and conformist literary world. But the whole point is that Mencken, even at his best, would no longer be adequate . . . for . . . it is unlikely that we can again respond to the carnival Nietzscheanism that was the essence of his thought.

Irving Howe. *NR*. May 21, 1956. p. 17

Of course, it is hardly news to say that Mencken had his serious weaknesses. . . . There are those who deplore (the) resurgence (of interest in Mencken) and it is not hard to sympathize with them. After all, Mencken was a reactionary in many of his ideas about social, economic and foreign affairs, behind the times in the Twenties and Thirties and certainly offering no specific program that fits the Fifties. But the deeper essence of Menckenism—that non-ideological ridicule of cant— may have its high uses today. . . . Perhaps before we are going to get any really fresh thinking we need the catharsis of mocking laughter.

Eric F. Goldman. *SR*. Oct. 20, 1956. p. 222

See *Prejudices* and *The American Language*.

MILLAY, EDNA ST. VINCENT (1892–1950)

One would have to go back a long way in literary history to find a young lyric poet singing so freely and so musically in such a big world. Almost we hear a thrush at dawn, discovering the ever-renewing splendor of the morning. . . . The surprise of youth over the universe, the emotion of youth at encountering inexplicable infinities—that is expressed . . . and it is a big thing to express.

Harriet Monroe. *Poetry*. Dec., 1918. p. 167

Her appearance in no way disappointed me. She was dainty with a daintiness of Queen Anne's lace or with the daintiness of a spider-web gossamer such as I have seen decorating the leaves of dahlia flowers on a September morning. It is true that I did detect in her look an April shadow of vanity, but below this self-conscious protection was a living representation of the divine spirit of poetry, uncontaminated as the spirit of Catullus, gay as the spirit of John Suckling. I never became disillusioned; the more I saw of this young and most beautiful girl, the more I came to appreciate the rash quality of her nature, heedless and lovely as a fieldfare rising from the wintry ground. She might disguise herself in all the pretty frippery that she could buy . . . and yet below her laces and ribbons there will always remain a barefoot poet, doomed yet redeemed, under the shadow of Eternity.

Llewelyn Powys. *The Verdict of Bridlegoose*
(Harcourt). 1926. pp. 37–8

A sensitive spirit on a romantic pilgrimage through an over-sophisticated civilization from which most of its romance has been robbed— this is the keynote of her work, as it is the keynote of many other modern poets not so finely tempered or so feverishly alert. . . . Sensitively, and with swift strokes, she has set down, if not the Odyssey of a heart, at least a record of all its poignant moments, its strange terrors, its little absurdities, and much, too, of its mocking emptiness.

John Hyde Preston. VQR. July, 1927. p. 343

Taking the vocabulary of nineteenth-century poetry as pure as you will find it in Christina Rossetti, and drawing upon the stock of conventional symbolism accumulated from Drayton to Patmore, she has created, out of shopworn materials, a distinguished personal idiom: she has been able to use the language of the preceding generation to convey an emotion peculiar to her own. . . . There are those who will have no minor poets; these Miss Millay does not move. The others, her not too enthusiastic but perhaps misguided partisans, have seen too much of their own personalities in her verse to care whether it is great poetry or not; so they call it great. . . . Miss Millay is one of our most distinguished poets, and one that we should do well to misunderstand as little as possible.

Allan Tate. NR. May 6, 1931. pp. 335–6

Her reciting voice had a loveliness that was sometimes heartbreakingly poignant. I fell in love with her voice at once; and with her spirit, when I came to know it, so full of indomitable courage. But there was in her something of which one stood in awe—she seemed, as a poet, no mere mortal, but a goddess; and, though one could not but love her, one loved her hopelessly, as a goddess must be loved.

Floyd Dell. Homecoming (Farrar and Rinehart).
1933. pp. 301–2

Her work is not rich enough in overtones and in contrapuntal cross-references to be great musical verse; not sufficiently marmoreal for great plastic verse; nor of such comprehensive ordering power as to be great poetry of ideas. At its best, it falls just short of that intensity which is found in the highest moments even of some contemporary poetry. There is a word slightly in the way or else the image lacks the needle point. It never quite to use E. E. Cumming's phrase, "lifts the top of your head off."

Philip Blair Rice. Nation. Nov. 14, 1934. p. 570

Millay may be happy or unhappy or angry or loving or perplexed; she may be in any one of a hundred different moods; but when she is writing a poem she is never debilitated or unconscious. Whatever her mood, she is intensely alive in every one of her five senses, and all her senses are fused in a single controlling mood and purpose. Her poems represent only those moments in her life when she has succeeded in becoming utterly at one with herself and intensely aware of the world.

Elizabeth Atkins. *Edna St. Vincent Millay and Her Times* (Chicago). 1936. p. 148

In Edna Millay's high lyrical talent, the Yankee note, which one felt from the first, increased in depth and clarity as time went on, as the flippancy of her earlier verse,—its conscious naïveté mingled with wonder,—yielded to profundity of feeling. She had begun with fairy-tale fancies and travesties of nursery-rhymes, in which she turned the moral inside out; but this mood of an infantile mischief-maker had always been half-rapturous and the rapture grew, together with her force of passion. An accomplished and disciplined craftsman, Miss Millay was a learned poet, with the Yankee love of Virgil, Catullus, Chaucer, and especially the Elizabethans whose vein she recaptured in her tragic sense of youth and the brevity of life.

Van Wyck Brooks. *New England: Indian Summer* (Dutton). 1940. p. 540.

A writer must be judged by his best. Edna Millay's best came at a time when many needed her excitement. Whether her capture of that audience was a good or a bad thing for the course of poetry one cannot say with any conviction. Certainly her intimate treatment of the frankly sensuous was some part of an age's contribution toward broadening the range of subjects permissible to poetry. That much is surely good. . . . But neither merit nor lack of merit defined her position in the poetry of the Twenties. It was not as a craftsman nor as an influence, but as the creator of her own legend that she was most alive to us. Her success was as a figure of passionate living.

John Ciardi. *SR*. Nov. 11, 1950. p. 77

She wrote some bad verse when she was young and some worse verse when she was older, as who has not. . . . She could be silly, cute, arch, hysterical; she could commit ghastly errors of taste. She also could and did, write so memorably that her language was on every tongue. . . . She was a fine lyric poet, also in the classical sense, a fine elegiac poet. . . . She expressed a great deal more than the spirit of a tinsel age: there was the silver of an individual voice, the legal tender of no base emotion.

Rolfe Humphries. *Nation*. Dec. 30, 1950. p. 704

Edna Millay . . . had not sufficient education to allow her to use effectively her poetic endowment. . . . This inadequacy of artistic education also injured her self-criticism: in spite of her interest in ideas, she could not cope with them in writing.

Mary Colum. NR. March 12, 1951. p. 17

Let me register this unfashionable opinion here, and explain that Edna Millay seems to me one of the few poets writing in English in our time who have attained to anything like the stature of great literary figures in an age in which prose has predominated. It is hard to know how to compare her to Eliot or Auden or Yeats—it would be even harder to compare her to Ezra Pound. There is always a certain incommensurability between men and women writers. But she does have it in common with the first three of these that, in giving supreme expression to profoundly felt personal experience, she was able to identify herself with more general human experience and stand forth as a spokesman for the human spirit, announcing its predicaments, its vicissitudes, but, as a master of human expression, by the splendor of expression itself, putting herself beyond common embarrassments, common oppressions, and panics.

Edmund Wilson. Nation. April 19, 1952. p. 372

It was her anxiety (I feel) that an intellectual passion keep pace with an emotional passion which so increasingly troubled and labored her mature work. She was essentially a lyric and emotional poet, and her art, which belonged to that side of her nature, suffered in the attempt to express her maturer convictions, and under the weight of an active social consciousness.

And it is her own poetic vitality, her immense capacity for delight in the world of nature which she observed so lovingly and accurately and so unforgettably made plain, the intensity of her relationships, her responsiveness, her vulnerability, and above all else her unshaken dedication to her art, which made her, in the face of what she feared but never capitulated to, and under the bludgeoning of ill-health and an encroaching neuroticism, the truly great lyric poet which she was.

Sara Henderson Hay. SR. June 5, 1954. p. 20

See Collected Poems.

MILLER, ARTHUR   (1915–   )

All My Sons is a serious drama, on its technical side in the Ibsen tradition, I suppose we may say, though that is intended to indicate only the general school rather than any imitation. It has a genuine story, a good moral basis in the theme, a good variety of characters, well drawn,

and offers an unusually rewarding vehicle for the acting and the directing. . . . The writing in many of the situations in *All My Sons* has
real feeling and an admirable, and often moving, realization of the
dramatist's motivations, or themes.

Stark Young. *NR*. Feb. 10, 1947. p. 42

Arthur Miller has attempted and delivered (in *All My Sons*) a tragedy:
time—now; place—a suburban backyard in an American town. . . .
The play is good because it does solve itself. If what is thrown in our
laps at the final curtain, in spite of the resolution of all interior action,
is questions rather than answers, this will be because these are the big
inescapable questions and their statement and reiteration in terms of
theater is the current point. Mr. Miller has dared and done.

Kappo Phelan. *Com*. Feb. 14, 1947. pp. 445–6

Arthur Miller is a moralist. His talent is for a kind of humanistic
jurisprudence: he sticks to the facts of the case. For this reason his
play (*Death of a Salesman*) is clearer than those of other American
playwright with similar insight whose lyric gifts tend to reflect the more
elusive and imponderable aspects of the same situation. There is poetry
in *Death of a Salesman*—not the poetry of the senses or of the soul,
but of ethical conscience. It might have been graven on stone—like
tablets of law. *Death of a Salesman* stirs us by its truth, the ineluctabil-
ity of its evidence and judgement which permits no soft evasion. Though
the play's environment is one we associate with a grubby realism, its
style is like clean accounting on the books of an understanding but
severe sage. We cry before it like children being chastised by an occasionally humorous, not unkindly but unswervingly just father.

Harold Clurman. *NR*. Feb. 28, 1949. p. 27

Let's have no doubts or frets about young Arthur Miller's drama,
Death of a Salesman: it is a fine thing, finely done, vastly well delivered.
The mere seeing and hearing of it—and the consequent assault and
battery it will perpetrate upon your feelings—make for an unforgettable experience. There is more than that there, however: there are the
American language, the American scene, the Brooklyn accent, the
Bronx cheer, all the muck and melancholy joke of our petty-class life
taken, shaken, rearranged, revitalized and somehow rehallowed into
the stuff of a compelling, surging quasi-poetry, or a widespread pity,
a great-hearted dream.

Gilbert W. Gabriel. *TA*. April, 1949. p. 15

In *Death of a Salesman* . . . Miller has managed to rise above the
ordinary flat lands of moralization and thesis drama. His play is a con-

summation of virtually everything attempted by that part of the theatre which has specialized in awareness and criticism of social realities. It is a culmination of all efforts since the 1930's to observe the American scene and trace, as well as evaluate, its effect on character and personal life. . . . Miller's achievement lies in successfully bridging the gap between a social situation and human drama. The two elements in *Death of a Salesman* are, indeed, so well fused that the one is the other. . . . Undoubtedly *Death of a Salesman* is one of the triumphs of the mundane American stage. It moves its audience tremendously, it comes close to their experience or observation, it awakens their consciousness, and it may even rouse them to self-criticism.

John Gassner. *Forum*. April, 1949. pp. 219–21

Death of a Salesman is a great American tragedy, shattering to the audience, overwhelming in its implications, cutting to the root of the poisonous fruits of the success rule of life. . . . This is the tragedy of the poor man, not ruthless like the rich man, but sinning against his sons to the same degree. Written with relentless truth, with no eye on curtain lines or sure-fire scenes, Miller's play hits at the heart of the audience with the dull pain of a sledge hammer.

Euphemia Van Rensselaer Wyatt. *CW*. April, 1949.
pp. 62–3

It is the biting truth of Arthur Miller's insight into the rotten moral base of our selling society that gives the play *Death of a Salesman* its power. . . . Arthur Miller casts a score of darts—at advertising, credit selling, the family automobile; at the petty larceny and the subversive attitude toward sex characteristic of our time. But his main attack is against the view that a man is a fool if he does not get something— as much as possible—for nothing more than a smile, being a good fellow and having good connections.

In the very act of striking a blow at the immorality of our commercial civilization, and the salesman mentality it has engendered, Arthur Miller has raised a shout for the individual and his right to his own soul.

Albert A. Shea. *CF*. July, 1949. pp. 86–7

The form of his play (*Death of a Salesman*) is not that of "flashback" technique, though it has been classified as such. It is rather the same technique as that of *Hamlet:* the technique of psychic projection, of hallucination, of the guilty expression of forbidden wishes dramatized. . . . It is visualized psychoanalytic interpretation woven into reality. . . . The entire play has the aura of a dream, a wish of prehistoric proportion, its strength lying in its adroit social rationalization, in its superlative disguise of the role of the younger son Hap. . . . *Death of a Salesman* is an enduring play. It will be performed over and over for many years, because of its author's masterful exposition of the unconscious motivations in our lives. . . . It is one of the most concentrated expressions of aggression and pity ever to be put on the stage.

Daniel E. Schneider. *TA*. Oct., 1949. pp. 18–21

The Crucible does not, I confess, seem to me a work of such potential tragic force as the playwright's earlier *Death of a Salesman;* it is the product of theatrical dexterity and a young man's moral passion rather than of a fruitful and reverberating imagination. But it has, in a theatre of the small success and the tidy achievement, power, the passionate line—an urgent boldness which does not shrink from the implications of a large and formidable design. . . . His characteristic theme is integrity, and its obverse, compromise. . . . In *The Crucible* . . . he has stated his theme again with a wholly admirable concision and force.

Richard Hayes. *Com.* Feb. 20, 1953. p. 498

If *The Crucible* is a drama of 1953, as well as of 1692, it does not follow that it is a simple parable. On the contrary it is self-contained rather than contained by time of place. It is the terrible and tragic situation that provides the real setting. . . . The situation is convincing to the last irrational detail. The conflict emerges in subtly differentiated forms and shadings. . . . Beginning slowly, with a prologue somewhat diffuse and confusing, the play gathers momentum and power with each act. The final scene, just before the hanging, is immensely moving, summarizing the theme of the play with an eloquence that carries the audience . . . out of the theatre in a mood of resolve rather than despair.

Freda Kirchwey. *Nation.* Feb. 7, 1953. pp. 131–2

Arthur Miller is a writer who in his own words is "becoming" a playwright rather than one who has arrived. He is not a "celebrity," with such skill, sureness, and style that his next work is only a matter of varying the place, plot, and names of the characters. Mr. Miller is also a man who has revealed an extraordinary ear for the language of the working man, and an ability to regard his crumpling under the pressure of malignant social forces as tragedy. . . . He is concerned with how our society fits into the mosaic of world civilizations. . . . Mr. Miller might also be said to have an interest in such questions as the relation of written law to natural law . . . the precedence material conditions must take over romantic illusions . . . (and) the supreme importance of a man's self-respect.

Henry Hewes. SR. Oct. 15, 1955. pp. 25–6

He is, basically, a political or "socially conscious" writer. He is a distinguished survivor of the thirties, and his values derive mostly from that decade. He is not much of a hand at exploring or exploiting his own consciousness. He is not inward. He writes at times with what may be a matchless power in the American theatre today, but not with a style of his own, and those who see his plays can leave them with little or no sense of the author as a character. He is not, in fact, much concerned with individuality of any sort. This is not an adverse judgement; it is a distinction, or an attempt at one. What interests Miller and what he can often convey with force is the crushing impact of society upon its members.

Richard H. Rovere. NR. June 17, 1957. p. 13

See *All My Sons, Death of a Salesman, The Crucible,* and *A View from the Bridge* (plays).

MILLER, HENRY (1891–   )

Miller has something in common with Lawrence and Joyce; in his detestation of the abstract, depersonalized life of his time he is on the side of Lawrence, and he is like Joyce in that all his work is a confession. But it is undertaken in a very different temper from Joyce's; it completely dispenses with dignity and is all the better for it. . . . He pours out everything, getting over his shame by a sort of braggadocio, as Rabelais did; not so completely as Rabelais, but more completely than Joyce.

Edwin Muir. The Present Age from 1914 (Cresset).
1939. p. 149

Miller invokes food and sex as heroic sentiments and even generalizes them into principles. For the man who is down and out has eyes only for that which he misses most frequently; his condition makes him a natural anarchist, rendering irrelevant all conventions, moral codes or any attempt to order the process of experience according to some value-pattern. The problem is to keep alive, and to that end all means are permissible. . . . Miller's claims as a guide to life and letters or a prophet of doom can be easily discounted. . . . He is remarkable, however, as the biographer of the hobo-intellectual and as the poet of

those people at the bottom of society in whom some unforeseen or sur-
reptitious contact with art and literature has aroused a latent antago-
nism to ordinary living, a resolve to escape the treadmill even at the
cost of hunger and degradation.

Philip Rahv. *NR*. April 21, 1941. pp. 557–9

I don't know any other writer who has succeeded in completely hu-
manizing the writer as a character, stripping him of any special prestige, making of him a true Everyman who wins his laurels, if any, only
in actual competition with other individuals for the possession of human
qualities and for the enjoyment of whatever there is to be enjoyed in
life. The exhilarating quality of Miller's best things comes precisely
from the fact that he has succeeded in making of writing a natural
way of existing, and also in making of the reader a companion in the
material and moral odyssey, the dejection, the hunger, the shame, and
the very real pitfalls which have to be experienced by an individual
in order to have that kind of existence.

Nicola Chiaromonte. *NR*. Dec. 4, 1944. pp. 751–4

Miller is part of the anti-intellectual spirit of our times, which stems
back to the emotionalists and humanitarians (all tender-minded) of the
French Revolution. He is a primitivist with the kick of a mule. He is
an anarchist more dangerous than Emerson and Nietzsche rolled into
one . . . Miller, with an intense fusion of the conscious and subconscious, tells all and spares no one, least of all himself. He is the mighty
I AM in literature as in life. . . . He is as elemental as a thunder-
storm or a Himalayan avalanche. Along with other mystics he appears
to be half sinner, half saint, and sometimes both simultaneously.

Herbert Faulkner West. *The Mind on the Wing*
(Coward). 1947. pp. 116–7

Around (Kenneth Rexroth), as around Miller, there collected a group
of young intellectuals and writers. . . . In this particular group around
Rexroth, the Henry Miller kind of anarchism is held to be irresponsible,
for Miller goes so far on the lonely, individualistic trail as to sneer at
even anarchist organization. To the outside observer, however, the
difference between the Miller adherents and the Rexroth followers are
more than outweighed by their similarities. They both reject rational-
ism, espouse mysticism, and belong to the select few who are orgastic-
ally potent.

Mildred Edie Brady. *Harper*. April, 1947. pp. 319–20

He has always been a martyr in his idolators' minds and it must be said
that Henry Miller has done nothing to remove the opinion that he is

a genius who can expect nothing but contempt and more martyrdom from his countrymen. It may well be that he is one of the truly great writers of his time, as his admirers believe; it may be that the strain of willingly suffering indignities, plus an ego as large as all outdoors, will prevent the fulfillment of his genius.

Harrison Smith. *SR*. Aug. 16, 1947. p. 18

Both (Gertrude Stein and Henry Miller) are tremendously good Americans, because they are wholly concerned. America is the background of all their thinking and writing. . . . And in spite of continual disillusionment (and how Miller can describe the etiolated, emasculated blotting-paper Americans call bread! And how he can suggest the anonymity, the forlornness, the tastelessness of Main Street!) Miller yet has a faith Walt Whitman would have envied. . . . So, at the end, these two great expatriates do not have to come home, because they never went away. With lancet and probe for armor, these are valiant Americans, because they have suffered to discover what America is, and why, and to relate America with Europe, with the world, and with the Creator of the world.

Anne Fremantle. *Com*. Dec. 12, 1947. pp. 229–30

He spruces up words conventionally regarded as vulgar and taboo and brings them out on parade, thus achieving an effect of daring originality, what Kenneth Burke calls perspective through incongruity. The solemn he treats with ribald mockery and iconoclastic disdain, the sublime with profane levity; the erotic, the sensual, the luridly carnal— forbidden themes—he honors with lyrical fanfares, almost mystical exaltation. Since the time of the Greeks, sex has been proscribed by Western civilization; Henry Miller considers it his mission to redress the balance, to restore sex to its position of primacy.

Charles I. Glicksberg. *SWR*. Summer, 1948. p. 289

You don't walk beside Henry, you are conveyed, practically levitated. His relish of the miraculous outburst of nature that is Big Sur seems to hoist you into a sultan's howdah beside him. Like a potentate greeting his subjects, he bows left and right to the Big Sur flora and fauna. Cars pass unnoticed; a roar of planes overhead will not divert his attention from an interesting bug. I constantly had the feeling that he was on leave of absence from ancient Greece or China, pledged to observe in our day only those things that had eternal currency.

Harold Maine. *AQ*. Autumn, 1951. p. 201

For most writers, "I" is an ambiguous protean affair upon which many claims are staked—by God, the family, or the state, but none of the embarrassment of the personal pronoun clings to Miller. In anecdote, he has the tactical advantage of an invisible man or a messenger from Mars (who unaccountably wears a Western Union uniform). When he tries to deal in general ideas, the boot is on the other foot: Miller is all too plainly visible, but he can see nothing. It is only when he writes, not from within his isolation but about its origins . . . that he is able to touch others.

Alwyn Lee. NWW 2. Nov. 1952. p. 342

Here in my opinion is the only imaginative prose-writer of the slightest value who has appeared among the English-speaking races for some years past. Even if that is objected to as an overstatement, it will probably be admitted that Miller is a writer out of the ordinary, worth more than a single glance; and after all, he is a completely negative, unconstructive, amoral writer, a mere Jonah, a passive acceptor of evil, a sort of Whitman among the corpses. . . . It is a demonstration of the impossibility of any major literature until the world has shaken itself into its new shape.

George Orwell. Such, Such Were the Joys
(Harcourt). 1953. p. 199

Henry Miller is a really popular writer, a writer of, for, and by real people. In other countries he is read, not just by highbrows, or by the wider public that reads novels, but by the people who, in the United States, read comic books. In the United States he has been kept away from a popular public and his great novels have been banned. Only highbrows who could import him from France have read him. . . . I should say he has become part of the standard repertory of reading matter everywhere but in England and in the United States. If you have read Balzac, or Baudelaire, or Goethe, you are also expected to have read Miller.

Kenneth Rexroth. Nation. Nov. 5, 1955. p. 385

As a creative spirit, Miller has to be accepted like a live volcano—with all the ever-latent dangers of eruptions. The volcano does not erupt because it wants to, but because it must. Miller pours himself out like hot lava; his vision is often blurred, not by misjudgements—for he judges rarely—but by contradictory feelings, fantastic appetites, erratic ideas, generous prejudices, bizarre nostalgias, sacrificial self-offerings. . . . His raw material is formlessness and chaos, but under his hand the formlessness turns into life, the chaos into the world we live in.

Alfred Perlès. My Friend Henry Miller (Day). 1956.
p. 186

It would not be amiss, I think, to say that he emerges . . . the Billy Graham of the bohemian Left. In his present state of modified beatitude, he may indeed be *the* spokesman of the Diverted Revolution in America—a movement without banners, individualistic and "personalist," mystically inclined toward a creed something like Schweitzer's "reverence for life" but rather more self-indulgent, nihilistic and averse to the concept of Duty. . . . Of course, Miller's claims as a spiritual influence remain open to hilarious question. . . . Yet the things that annoy us in Miller are frequently things true of ourselves also—and of a sort which shame and "self-respect" hardly permit us to admit to ourselves, let alone to the world. His freedom in communicating such matters is one of his true distinctions.

M. L. Rosenthal. Nation. June 8, 1957. p. 502

Even in books like the two *Tropics* where Miller was piling sordidness upon sordidness to get the effect of reality, the thing (on rereading) does not come off as real, especially if you compare him with writers in the same genre like Céline and Beckett. The excitement of the books as good sexual pornography has also considerably worn off; partly perhaps because we have got used to those things from other sources, but chiefly because Miller's own interest in sex (as a writer, of course, not in life) is not fully authentic, but here again seems a little forced. It is not the genuine interest in sex as a thesis, as in Lawrence, or in sex as sensuality, as in Colette; it is not the experience of sex itself that is important to Miller but the symbol of it—symbol of the violent quest for experience that flung Miller out of an ordinary office job and a bourgeois career into the stews of Paris. As a writer Miller has never dealt with experience as such but with himself having the miraculous adventure of having experience. He is an innocent abroad—he is even now the innocent abroad in California.

William Barrett. SR. Aug. 3, 1957. p. 10

See *Tropic of Cancer* and *Tropic of Capricorn* (novels); also *Books in My Life* (essays).   See Supplement at end of text for additional material.

MOODY, WILLIAM VAUGHAN (1869–1910)

No other new poet of the past score of years, either in America or in England, has displayed a finer promise upon the occasion of his first appearance, or has been deserving of more respectful consideration. . . . We wish to say, furthermore, that we have not for many years been so strongly tempted to cast aside critical restraints and indulge in "the noble pleasure of praising". . . . Nor do we hesitate to add that, with the possible exception of what has been done by Professor Woodberry, no such note of high and serious song has been sounded in our recent American poetry as is now sounded in *The Masque of Judgement* and the *Poems* of Mr. Moody.

William Morton Payne. *Dial.* June 1, 1901. p. 365

The Masque of Judgement is not . . . a defiance of the Almighty. It is a reverent, but tremendous, protest against the doctrine of eternal punishment; and, as a work of constructive imagination, it ranks with the great masterpieces.

And the workmanship is worthy of the grandeur of the prodigious scheme. Professor Moody's verse has the "large utterance" of great poetry and those rhythms that haunt the chambers of the memory like music. . . . Such poetry will never be popular. . . . But it is great poetry none the less. . . . We must thank him for demonstrating that American poetry can grapple with the greatest problems, and handle them with masterly vigor.

G. B. Rose. *SwR.* July, 1901. pp. 333–6

His quality is opulence, a certain gorgeousness that is never barbaric, owing to his power of classic restraint. His sweetness is crystal, never luscious or impure. . . . In one sense Mr. Moody's genius is not dramatic, not impersonal; he sees all things, all persons, suffused with his own imagination. . . . He has found, like Mr. Swinburne, his masters in the Greek tragedians. The compassion is obvious, but no poet since Shelley has united such masterly metrical plasticity, such exuberance of sensuous imagery with so vast a sweep of metaphysical imagination. . . . He has the Euripidean color and mobility, the Euripidean sweetness, the Euripidean pathos.

May Sinclair. *At.* Sept. 1906. pp. 328–9

Much of Moody's work, like that of the Symbolists, was intricate analysis of emotion. What men do was of less interest to him than what men feel. But the feeling that fills his poetry is commonly the great feeling that is stirred by great issues, not the sentimentality of mere temperament. True, he is alive to the beauty of delicate sensations. . . . But he was a man of too much intellectual power, and also of too critical humor, ever to be mawkish or trivial in his imaginings. . . . It is indeed one of the remarkable things about Moody that, with all his subtle emotions and subtle imaginings, he is almost free from over-elaboration and from frigid excess of heat.

Charlton M. Lewis. *YR.* July, 1913. pp. 701–2

The ability to think profoundly and yet to express his thoughts in vivid concreteness of poetic images, distinguishes Moody from the mere versifier who turns out ethical and aesthetic commonplaces. Moody never succumbed to the desire to please the *Musa Meretrix,* and his greatness as a poet is due to his dogged tenacity and persistence in attempting to express a coherent, centered interpretation of man's spiritual destiny in a world of glowing beauty and appeal. His singleness of aim, his steadily increasing insight, his fastidious self-criticism kept him from rapid and vapid composition. Consequently we have not a large body of poetry from his pen, but what we do possess is most carefully wrought.

Martha Hale Shackford. *SwR*. Oct., 1918. p. 408

That his present popularity is in no way commensurate with his achievement is due partly to the lack of public interest in poetry during his lifetime, partly to the poetic revolution instigated by the Imagists immediately after his death. . . . Some of the objectives declared by the Imagists Moody had already achieved; towards others he was clearly progressing. . . . Moody passed from the realm ruled by Tennyson and Browning, Rossetti and Swinburne, to that in which he was akin to Maeterlinck, Francis Thompson and Ernest Dowson. Like the latter, he confronted the eternal problem of the dualism of flesh and spirit and the inevitable union, although his solution was different.

Robert Morse Lovett. *At*. March, 1931. pp. 392–3

Moody was constantly growing in poetic power. Primarily a scholar, with the tendency to derive his themes from literature rather than from life, his life ended just at the time when he might reasonably have been expected to put forth his most significant and individual work; which is not to say that he did not leave us poems of distinctive craftsmanship and spirited nobility. . . . Moody attempted greatly. Certain phrases in his rhetoric ring like old counters now, but the exercise of his imagination was a daring one, and again and again he snared the precise epithet, the distinguished expression of exalted feeling. . . . In a day when poetry was, or seemed to be, of but the very slightest interest to American readers, he persevered as one of the elect to perfect his own gift, driven by his genuine daemon.

William Rose Benét. *SR*. May 2, 1931. p. 802

One finds . . . traces of the Greek dramatists, of Shakespeare, of Shelley and of Milton, but one finds even more evident the sweet gravity of Tennyson and Matthew Arnold and the lyric vigor of Kipling. One finds too seldom the precision and intensity which were the battle cry and the goal of Moody's immediate successors. . . . If he was concerned with major themes, his philosophy was not sufficiently considered or perhaps not expressed clearly enough to be convincing; his music, if sounding, was too often reminiscent, and his imagery, though often fine, was also too often literary. He was rooted in the great tradition but did not rise above it.

Babette Deutsch. *NR.* July 29, 1931. pp. 293–4

Here was a poet who, according to the enthusiasm of his own generation, wrote out of great promise a considerable achievement, and exerted upon his contemporaries and upon those a little younger, a wide and liberal influence. We must be indebted, gladly or not, for the influence, without knowing precisely what it was. Perhaps it was the influence of a man writing verse of a large order without intellectual or spiritual constriction; the influence of example; the influence of a man taking poetry seriously and naturally at a time when poetry was commonly taken either uncouthly or artificially. . . . But on the whole, Moody's verse is only the poetry of a man with a good deal of feeling. The poetry depends on the man who wrote it and not on itself.

R. P. Blackmur. *Poetry.* Sept., 1931. pp. 331–3

The subtlety of his music, the richness of background, the carefully wrought imagery, the depth of thought, the extensive allusions, the use of the academic and the remote, the strong suggestion of ethical authority—these are features which do not endear a poet to the mass of readers and which are perceived in full appreciation only by the poet, or the student and lover of poetry. . . . As an artist, he endorsed a fundamental tenet of contemporary workmanship—freedom of manner and thought. In his repudiation of conventional thinking, in his candor and frankness, in his analysis of emotion and his emphasis upon psychological interpretation, Moody linked his poetry to modern taste.

David D. Henry. *William Vaughan Moody*
(Humphries). 1934. pp. 221–2

See *Selected Poems* and *The Great Divide* and *The Faith Healer* (plays).

MOORE, MARIANNE (1887–   )

The grim and haughty humor of this lady strikes deep, so deep as to absorb her dreams and possess her soul. She feels immense incongruities, and the incongruity of her little ego among them moves her art not to grandeur but to scorn. As a satirist she is at times almost sublime—what contrary devil balks even at those moments, tempting her art to its most inscrutable perversities?

Harriet Monroe. Poetry. Jan., 1922. p. 215

This volume is the study of a Marco Polo detained at home. It is the fretting of a wish against a wish until the self is drawn, not into a world of air and adventure, but into a narrower self, patient, dutiful, and precise. . . . Miss Moore has preferred, to date, to express simply the pictorial aspect of the universe, and she has fulfilled perfectly each self-imposed task.

Winifred Bryher. Poetry. Jan., 1922. pp. 209–10

This exacting moralist, who enforces with such intricate resonance the profound convictions of her ethical and emotional fastidiousness, has dumfounded most of those readers whom she has not completely sub-jugated. . . . (She is) a poet whose style, at once intensely cultivated and painstakingly honest, never fails to charm me and whose mastery of phrase and cadence overwhelms me.

Yvor Winters. Poetry. April, 1925. pp. 39, 44

I suspect that the motive which forces upon Miss Moore an esoteric style, that restricts her choice of materials, and makes her cling to Victorian proprieties in attitude, is by no means purely aesthetic. It may be something much less rational, something indeed that looks like self-protectiveness. . . . Behind the elaborate inconsequence of her stylistic behavior . . . there peers at moments simplicity, humble and timid, immature and shy, disliking sophistication. . . . But to reach the elements that compose this simplicity, through what labyrinths one must work, what traps for the inattentive one must evade!

Gorham Munson. Destinations (Sears). 1928. pp. 93–4

Her style combines the frigid objectivity of the laboratory with the zeal of naive discovery; it mixes the statistics of newspapers with the casual hints and cross-references of a mind constructed like a card catalogue. This is not a perversity of erudition, not of ironic parody. It is a picture of the problem of the modern intelligence. . . . Hers is a poetry of superimposed meanings, and her object is to lift the layers of convention, habit, prejudice, and jargon that mask the essential and irreducible truth.

Morton D. Zabel. Literary Opinion in America
(Harper). 1937. pp. 427–8

She is difficult because she will not buy triumph at "horrifying sacrifice of stringency"; she refuses to descend to the level of those to whom "the illustration is nothing without the application"; and she demands of her readers that their minds shall follow hers in leaping by fifths and sevenths from point to point like the jerboa in her poem. She has affinities of spirit with Henry James—the same thoroughness and elegant restraint, the same astute detection of minute differences, the same gradual foliate disclosure and sharp clarity of definition. But all these qualities are condensed into the "contractibility" of verse. Her subtlety of ear and delicacy of rhythmic perception, the variations in her use of full, light, vowel, end, and internal rhymes, and her ingenious designs of syllabic divisions, are all functional parts of the setting in which she arranges her brilliant "jewelry of sense."

Elizabeth Drew. *Directions in Modern Poetry*
(Norton). 1940. p. 68

Only Marianne Moore could write a poem about the mind and fill it with thoughts that glow like buried treasure just brought to light. . . . Literally and figuratively, light is the source of her enchantment. What she sees provides symbols for the unseen, the inner vision. . . . Her poetry dreams with its eyes wide open and weaves its spell out of the visible, the tangible, the intelligible; a wide-awake magic; proof that a passionate intelligence can be haunting. . . . In her poetry the appearance of things—the way they greet the eyes and ears; what they feel like to the touch; their characteristic impact—come to us in a blaze of reincarnation. . . . Through art such as this, with its demand upon the attention of the whole person, we are restored not to a state of nature, but to that totality of experience which is a sign of organic development.

Lloyd Frankenberg. *Pleasure Dome* (Houghton).
1949. pp. 121–3, 133

Miss Moore has great limitations—her work is one long triumph of them; but it was sad, for so many years, to see them and nothing else insisted upon, and Miss Moore neglected for poets who ought not be allowed to throw elegies in her grave. I have read that several people think So-and-So the greatest living woman poet; anybody would dislike applying so clumsy a phrase to Miss Moore—but surely she is. Her poems, at their unlikely best, seem already immortal, objects that have endured their probative millennia in barrows; she has herself taken from them what time could take away, and left a skeleton the years can only harden.

Randall Jarrell. *Poetry and the Age* (Knopf) 1953.
pp. 183–4

Philosphically, she might have been a bore, had she not been rescued by erudition. One unique quality of her work is that she has made learning more lively than any poet save Dame Edith Sitwell. Pound and Eliot have convinced us that immense knowledge is valid equipment for poets, but they have not the winsome finesse with which Miss Moore and Dame Edith display the emeralds and rubies that the mind alone collects.

Bette Richart. Com. Dec. 28, 1956. p. 338

It has been remarked, but not sufficiently, that there is a strong streak of didacticism in Miss Moore's poetry. Acute observation is severe limitation, the way in which it is reported is the measure of its significance. So I suggest, further, that Miss Moore's work is most lastingly interesting where it widens into moral statement.

Winfield Townley Scott. SR. Feb. 2, 1957. p. 17

See *Collected Poems; Predilections* (essays).

MOORE, MERRILL (1903–1957)

Many of the poems show a fine perception of the apparently trivial and incidental things which can illuminate a character or a situation. This perception is a gift usually associated with a dramatist, or more especially with a certain sort of novelist, rather than with a sonneteer, but Mr. Moore has this gift, and his dramas and novels are precisely fourteen lines long. The fact proves how well he has learned to use his formal curb, for in the best examples there is exactitude and an unusual impression of the circumstantial: in some matters at least his facility is subject to an extraordinary compression.

Robert Penn Warren. NR. Jan. 29, 1930. p. 280

Mr. Ransom, in his introduction to Mr. Moore's poems, has said that Mr. Moore has always found it easier to write a new poem than to revise an old one; this is, I imagine, true of all of us. Mr. Moore's poems are obviously unrevised; the meters are a kind of rhymed and butchered prose, and the diction is for the most part very, very approximate, to speak as charitably as possible. The fact that Mr. Moore has written badly with a deliberate intention and consistent effect does not alter the fact that he has written badly. The reviewers who find "originality" in this sort of thing are deluding themselves.

Yvor Winters. Poetry. May, 1930. pp. 104–5

He may well be pioneering in a variety of the form (sonnet) as native as Petrarch's arrangement was Italian and Shakespeare's was English.

There is something distinct and, I believe, autocthonous in the loosened, speech-inflected rhythms; in the heightened tempo of the lines; in the substitution of a set of unpredictable, sometimes jagged, and even syncopated rhymes, instead of well-regulated rhyme-schemes; in the refusal of the poem to split neatly into traditional octave and sestet, and dividing itself anywhere with what seems sheer perversity—all held somehow within the prescribed, though no longer formal fourteen lines.

But these sonnets are American in the broader sense. They are not, I must add, braggart; they do not celebrate any particular section of the country; there is none of the loud spread-eagle affirmation which is a not unnatural reaction to the contempt and weariness of a negative "lost" generation. This poetry is American in attitude as well as in subject-matter—in its insatiable appetite and unsated curiosity, in its combination of naive egotism and astounding detachment, in its excesses of awe and flippancy, of puzzled insecurity, a nonchalance and eagerness "to match with Destiny for beers."

Louis Untermeyer. SwR. Jan., 1935. pp. 60–1

He has a fine ear, but too often it is intrigued by seeming contrapuntal effects; by internal rhymes and near-rhymes, and by puns. . . . Too often he strives. His difficulty is that one word suggests another and leads him off the track. He dilates; he flows; but he does not get any place.

However, in a journalistic style, Merrill Moore has produced a few fine poems. . . . He has a sharp gift of characterization in a civilized manner like that of La Bruyère. He has an undoubted eye for color, an ear for words; a smooth and running formlessness which is in itself a new form when it is successful. He has a vivid imagination and an occasional adroit turn for whimsey.

Cyrus L. Sulzberger, II. NYT. June 16, 1935. p. 8

These fourteen-line poems are not, in the first place, sonnets. Their rhymes, the inner rhythms, their pauses are not those of the true sonnet at all. . . . Nor is there in these lines any of the fusion or intensity of true poetry. They are rather a kind of rapid-fire comment on life—original, sometimes startling, sometimes quite sensitive representations of people, actions, disease, emotions. If one disregards their claim to being poetry, one finds them very interesting.

Eda Lou Walton. Nation. Aug. 7, 1935. pp. 166–7

I do not know of any contemporary poetry of consequence that yields so many points of adverse criticism. It invites attacks of every kind.

. . . We cannot refute that criticism which meets the poems on their own ground and convicts them of loose diction, imprecise imagery, and, all too often, inconsequence of subject and treatment. There is scarcely a poem . . . that is not in some detail exceptionable. . . . And we may add, for what it is worth, that the author reveals no political, social, or philosophical tendencies: he belongs to no school, he fights for no significant "cause."

Yet these objections do not dispose of Merrill Moore. They do not touch the real meaning of his work, the passionate humanity of these records of daily life. He is something of an earth-force, like Gertrude Stein. He compels our attention.

Dudley Fitts. SwR. April, 1939. pp. 292–3

Some (of the poems) are simply pretty, some are very flat, and some ramble like an epigram in a fourteen-line uniform. A few bring the full promise of an opening line straight home, and ring a bell like a cash register. In others, even when they get lost on the way, and the bell doesn't ring, there is a sense left that you can cash in on them because the register drawer is still open from preceding ones that did ring. What is surprising in so many poems is their cleanness, their immediacy, their lightness and speed. The idiom is contemporary, supple, and like good talk, doesn't nag. There are rarely any inversions to force a rhyme, and the emphatic word seems mostly to be the substantive rather than the modifier or verb. Even when the lines are padded, as so many perhaps must be, the padding is made up of the common debris of living speech, not of dead archaisms.

Edwin Honig. Poetry. April, 1952. p. 59

Several circumstances make some of his verse appear to superficial view lighter in tone than is actually the case. His colloquial idiom, swift, multi-syllabic foot, habitual reliance on implication, on understatement, and on mystery, if not mystification, readily cast into some minds doubts as to the seriousness of the man and artist. . . . His amused smile is no indication of a want of robust humor, his emotional control, no mark of lack of emotion. In each case he appears not only a superior artist but a faithful physician to mankind and in a peculiar degree the modern urbane man and thinker.

Henry W. Wells. Poet and Psychiatrist (Twayne).
1955. pp. 289, 296

See *Clinical Sonnets, M,* and *Illegitimate Sonnets* (poetry).

MORRIS, WRIGHT (1910–   )

Few authors would be foolhardy enough to buttress their rustic rhapsody with photographs of the same scenes that they attempt to describe in restrained epic fashion. The fact that Wright Morris in his photographs seems to produce an indecent invasion of the privacy of his text is a tribute to his accurate and selective descriptive powers. It is the nearest thing to a documentary film that today's publishing has found. Mr. Morris' talent may be unique. Certainly it should be fostered.

> William Germain Dooley. *NYT*. July 18, 1948, p. 5

Mr. Morris writes a crisp, simple prose. His is almost basic English, but he doesn't get affected about it and uses two- or three-syllable words on occasions when needed. . . . Professional writers . . . would be sunk in the funk of frustration by the startling example of the crystal prose of (this) man who rose to national prominence as a photographer before he took a pen in hand to show us all that prose need not be muddled and verbose, that it could even be made to say something if not allowed to talk itself to death.

> Carl Victor Little. *SR*. June 2, 1951. p. 13

I should say that he has demonstrated by now that he is unrivalled as an interpreter of those tangents of the American scene where the funny and the pathetic collide, and that there is wanting only the warm narrative flow that has been mastered by lesser novelists, to make his writings transcendently powerful and important. . . . Mr. Morris moves relentlessly from the particular to the general, naming everything that the eye can see, superficially in the manner of the naturalistic novelists but actually in the service of a wider frame of reference, of a brilliantly defined reality that gradually takes on the characteristics of a singular myth akin to Chaplin's.

> Harvey Swados. *Nation*. June 1, 1952. pp. 587–8

His writing is simple but his method is as complex as his subject matter, so he uses the multiple flashbacks, the melting of past into present. He is also obsessed with certain themes and images—in his work birds take the place of Thurber's dogs, railroads at night fascinate him as do hotel lobbies and Mid-Western towns, and a father's hesitant love for his children is depicted recurrently although since happiness is denied most men the sons generally die.

> Eleanor M. Scott. *NYHT*. Sept. 13, 1953. p. 2

Lately a new and healthier sinister note has crept into Mr. Morris' novels. . . . His charmingly native types, his average husbands and wives, have grown slightly monstrous; his homely domestic circles have come to resemble the lairs of predatory female animals strewn with the carcasses of men. What was once warming to the heart is now chilling; and with the change Mr. Morris has acquired new meaning and stature as a novelist.-Henceforth we will have to reckon with him seriously, no longer as one of an order of rustic, neo-frontier humorists, but as a member of that select company of haunted and bitterly obsessive American writers, the analysts of our spiritual and moral disease, of whom perhaps the best recent example was the incomparable Nathanael West.

John W. Aldridge. *NYT*. Sept. 13, 1953. pp. 4–5

Mr. Morris' writing is occasionally obscure but always absorbing. He does not, like so many authors, hover omnisciently over his characters. He prefers to project himself into their innermost and very human thoughts and emotions, leaving the reader to draw his own conclusions. His characters understand as much about each other as most of us about the members of our own family and no more. Mr. Morris writes with wit, taste, and refreshing originality.

William Murray. *SR*. Sept. 19, 1953. p. 16

Mr. Morris . . . makes you see and feel as well as think. He always has; and one wonders why he is not more generally recognized as one of America's leading novelists. Each of his seven novels, excepting perhaps *The Works of Love,* marks a distinct advance in his ability to convey his original and remarkable insights. I hope that *The Huge Season* will have such success that it will send readers and critics back to such excellent novels as *Man and Boy* and *The Deep Sleep,* for Mr. Morris is a major writer and a major writer can be understood fully only when he is read entire.

Harvey Curtis Webster. *SR*. Oct. 2, 1954. p. 29

In his last three novels (*The Huge Season, The Deep Sleep,* and *The Works of Love*) he has strongly suggested Sherwood Anderson at his best—an Anderson without wooliness, without loose language and looser feelings, without all the mumbling and rumbling and bumbling that one associates with much of Anderson's prose; rather the "dry" Anderson who could present, with perfect directness, the American "grotesque." Morris is the only American who now seems to write in the full spirit of Constance Rourke's *American Humor.* . . . A master of the comic and deeply sensitive to the most inarticulate of American sorrows, Morris' work is moving as only truly original work can be.

Mark Schorer. *NYT.* Oct. 3, 1954. p. 4

For one thing—but it is basic to his work—Morris is so simply and naturally an American novelist. Aside from contemporaries who don't much use the home place we have some who use it a shade too thoughtfully: their bones of theory show through. Not Morris—he is marvelously observant, and he knows the look of American towns and people as he knows his own skin. He can by one detail take you instantly where he wants you.

Winfield Townley Scott. *SR.* Oct. 6, 1956. p. 24

For the reader willing to accord the inner world of action a significance equal to that of the outerworld, there are universes upon universes to explore under Mr. Morris' skilled guidance. The characters (in *The Field of Vision*), thus viewed from within, build up to uncanny vividness, and most of them, no matter how pitiful they may appear from without, have the persistent dignity of men and women somehow made restless and homeless by a vision which lures and more often than not eludes them. Mr. Morris has published close to a dozen books since his debut with *My Uncle Dudley* in 1942. The present work should do much to consolidate his position as an original and powerful talent.

Chad Walsh. *NYHT.* Oct. 7, 1956. p. 6

Mr. Morris, who was born in Nebraska, wrote once that his work bears "the stamp of the plains". . . . But the plains are not bountiful seas of wheat rolling under a yellow sky. The eye moves across the illimitable grayness of Mr. Morris's plains, fixing eagerly on the relief of windmill, water tank, or clapboard house. "Objects what few there are on the plains," Mr. Morris added, "acquire a dense symbolical significance."

Jack Patterson. *Com.* Nov. 9, 1956. p. 156

See *The Home Place, Man and Boy, The Deep Sleep, The Huge Season, The Field of Vision,* and *Love Among the Cannibals* (novels).

See Supplement at end of text for additional material.

NIN, ANAIS (1903–   )

One feels the effort of truth in the face of curious reticences and obscurities. The vast congeries of prose is lyrically expressive of certain feminine, in instances almost imperceptible, feelings connected with an aesthetic world mainly that of decadent Paris; expressive even more of a feminine self-consciousness strangely enamored of the very state of feeling, yet singularly perceptive of the subliminal and marvelous. The element of the irrational, germane to all lyricism, is included in the style: it is prevalently surrealistic. Audaciously it exploits the connotative power of language while presenting the unseen through wild, often far-flung analogies.

Paul Rosenfeld. *Nation.* Sept. 26, 1942. p. 276

The virtue of Miss Nin's writing, in a time of "human winter," is that by its exclusive preoccupation with the intimate problems of feminine psychology, it is concerned with an aspect of human values as such. Her style, moreover, in its use of fairly broad emotive language and in the expression it gives to feeling and sentiment, possesses a certain *Innerlichkeit,* an air of immediate reality, for lack of which so much of modern American writing is dying such a hideous, choking death. But Miss Nin approaches the human by way of psychoanalysis. . . . The task she assigns to literature seems to be no more than to present and amplify the insights of psychoanalysis.

Isaac Rosenfeld. *NR.* Dec. 17, 1945. pp. 844–5

She is fascinated in a simplified psychoanalytic way with waking fantasies, with ego-ideals, and our pictures of ourselves as they affect our relations with others. Except for occasional flashes into the past, she does not work out articulated case histories. She omits what can be directly observed and objectively reported. She does not look at scenes and faces like a photographer or even a painter. . . . What Miss Nin records are subjective states, configurations of character, the fields of electric tension, movement and resistance in human relationships. She defines these with elegance and insight in apothegmatic general statements of a sometimes pretentious sort. . . . The result is an abstract, psychic music, a dance of generalities and types, charming and suggestive in a narrowly romantic way.

Robert Gorham Davis. *NYT.* Nov. 23, 1947. p. 36

Miss Nin's flavorful words are as piquant and stimulating to one's mental taste as exotic, highly seasoned foods to one's palate. Her constant psychoanalyzing of characters never lags. In these two characteristics lie the fascination of her writing. The present book (*The Four-Chambered Heart*) considered man's dual nature, i.e., of construction and destruction as brought out by the two women in his life. The characterizations are fuller, less impressionistic and less sketchy than in her previous writings. The story is closer knit, attaining a wholeness, an entity absent from Miss Nin's other books. There is the same swiftness of rhythm and fluidity of movement—Miss Nin's artistic label.

Elizabeth P. Nichols. LJ. Dec. 1, 1949. p. 1818

To Miss Nin external events form only one side of true reality, in which two realms—the inward and the outward, the world of dream and of waking—are united.

Miss Nin has the gift of communicating directly. External action is deepened by being converted to inward experience; the visionary and hallucinatory become integral parts of reality. The River Seine and the flowing Seine of the psyche are thus presented as one stream of life.

Rene Fulop-Miller. NYT. Jan. 29, 1950. p. 4

Anais Nin is, as Edmund Wilson has said, "a world of feminine perception and feminine fancy"; a world, too, in which the iron curtain between the ego and the unconscious is continually pierced. . . . The effects achieved by Miss Nin's writing—poetic prose of singular vitality and beauty—reminded me, rather strongly, of the dance. *The Four-Chambered Heart* evokes the grace-in-motion and the elegant patterns, the emotional directness and dreamlike aura of a classical ballet.

Charles J. Rolo. At. Feb., 1950. p. 87

A Spy in the House of Love is . . . a sensitive and discerning fable of a woman's love life, which manages to compress within a very brief compass some of the rewards and almost too many of the anguishes of passion for its own sake. . . . We begin to realize that Miss Nin is one of the few women writers in our literary tradition to affirm the centrality of the biological impulses for her own sex, and on the same terms as for men.

The point is also that she is prepared to describe these emotions from the feminine point of view with the same ruthless honesty that marked a D. H. Lawrence or a Dreiser.

Maxwell Geismar. Nation. July 24, 1954. pp. 75–6

See *Children of the Albatross, The Four-Chambered Heart,* and *A Spy in the House of Love* (novels).

NORRIS, FRANK (1870–1902)

Personally, the young novelist gave one the impression of strength and courage that would hold out to all lengths. Health was in him always. . . . I never met him but he made me feel that he could do it, the thing he meant to do, and do it robustly and quietly. . . . Norris heard nothing, or seemed to hear nothing, but the full music of his own aspiration, the rich diapason of purposes securely shaping themselves in performance.

William Dean Howells. *NAR*. Dec., 1902. p. 777

There is no need of apology in dealing with *McTeague*. In it is some of the best work Norris ever did. . . . It is inexorable in its unrelenting lifelikeness. . . . It is gray, gray and cold, in tone. . . . Norris's interest was not that of the ethical teacher, the reformer who turns on the light. He rejoiced in McTeague and Trina as terms in a literary theorem. Their suffering leads to no conclusions. They are in the book because they appealed to his dramatic sense, his love for character. This book is without direct prototype. You may say it reminds you of Flaubert in treatment, or of Zola in theme, but in reality it is without fellow. Its originality is unquestionable.

Hamlin Garland. *Critic*. March, 1903. p. 216

To him fiction-writing was a branch of reporting. In this may be found the genesis of his peculiarly perverse attitude and the origin of many of his weaknesses. Norris did not have the analytical intelligence of an iconoclast. His rebelliousness was emotional and disorderly. He did not possess the faculty of concentrating his intelligence with piercing, destructive consistency upon his enmities. Instead, he shouted his blasphemies and trusted to the emotional force of his assertions to win him adherents.

C. Hartley Grattan. *Bkm*. July, 1929. p. 506

Here is what makes Frank Norris such a fascinating problem: the weakest side of his work is, in a way, the strongest side of the man. His moral passion, his idealism, his desire to make fiction contribute somehow to the good of his country and the needs of men—all this was intimately bound up with what we may call his journalism. . . . He had the exuberant temper of romanticism; he had been profoundly moved by the ideals of Zola; he admired the chastened, decorous realism of William Dean Howells; and on the weak, immature, journalistic side of him, he suffered a bad attack of Richard Harding Davis! Is it any wonder that he was not able to resolve all these elements and to bring them to a harmonious adjustment by the time he was thirty-two?

Edward Wagenknecht. *VQR*. April, 1930. pp. 314, 317

Life for him was an adventure in which fiction-writing was his greatest pleasure. He wrote as he lived: with zest, with enthusiasm, with

gusto. His successes as well as his failures were due to his intense affirmation of the creed of youth. It was his fortune to see, as few people
see, at the beginning of an epoch; to impress his name ineffaceably on
American fiction at a time of flux when old patterns were melting
away and a new literature was taking form. This he did because he
affirmed rather than denied, because he lived rather than meditated,
because he saw with clarity and wrote with enthusiasm.

Franklin Walker. *Frank Norris* (Doubleday). 1932.
pp. 3–4

Without in the least impairing his capacity for minute observation, he
was enamored of vastness, of all things large, powerful, and excessive;
enormous, tremendous, colossal, gigantic, titanic, immense, mammoth,
inordinate—these words form the backbone of his vocabulary. Crowds,
great cities, even inanimate nature in its larger features—mountains,
forests, deserts, seas—these have for him an independent life of their
own; they breathe, and the sound of that breathing, composed of innumerable smaller sounds, manifests itself to the ear attuned to catch
it in the form of a ceaseless, profound, all-pervading monotone. This
almost mystical sense of an exhaustless life reaching down into the
very roots of being stirs and excites him; it is almost an obsession.

Ernest Marchand. *Frank Norris* (Stanford). 1942.
pp. 177–8

It is easy now to see the faults of his work. He was a borrower of
literary effects; he took those he needed wherever he found them, in
Kipling, Stevenson or Tolstoy, as well as Zola. He depended on instinct
rather than intelligence for his choice of borrowings, since he thought
viscerally, with his heart and bowels instead of his brain. . . . His
great virtues were . . . freshness, narrative vigor, a marvelous eye for
the life around him and courage to portray it in its drama and violence,
besides the ability to construct his novels, like Zola's, in massive blocks.

Malcolm Cowley. *NR*. May 5, 1947. p. 33

Beneath the delicate and skilful texture of Norris's prose at its best, and
the very often attractive tone of what was essentially a leisure class
temperament and view of experience, there were, to be sure, other
elements of feeling not far from the morbid. As in the case of Scott
Fitzgerald, it was this strain which gave to Norris's work—work based
on his own sense of life rather than on literary programs or social
polemics—an underlying tension and interior dynamics different from
the facade of virility and action which he stressed. . . . And wasn't it
after all the presence of the "Brute" in Frank Norris himself—that is

to say, his awareness of the sensual drives even in terms of morbid sin or "evil," and his own sense of a certain isolation and exile because of this—which enabled him to break through the restrictions of his craft to the degree that he did? . . . The wound was also the source of his power; the animal instincts were the origins of his most human insights; and even the tormented rites of reversionary emotions became a path of liberation in the works of art.

Maxwell Geismar. Rebels and Ancestors (Houghton).
1953. pp. 51–2, 66

He did not completely master the art of the novel. When he was successful it was the success of vividness and vitalism, of realistic scenes and intense, violent emotions, of poetic though not always fully realized characters. When he failed it was a failure to achieve a balanced tension between conflicting but reconcilable methods of approach. His novels as a whole do not indicate a steady development as an artist, but they do reflect consistently the tenets of his responsibility as a novelist as he saw it: a realistic fidelity to life in all its variety and color and mystery, a sincerity of purpose, and a seriousness and complexity of theme, character, and content.

Charles G. Hoffman. SAQ. Oct., 1955. p. 515

See McTeague, The Octopus, and Vandover and the Brute (novels).

O'CONNOR, FLANNERY (1926–1964)

There is in Flannery O'Connor a fierceness of literary gesture, an angriness of observation, a faculty for catching, as an animal eye in the wilderness, cunningly and at one sharp glance, the shape and detail and animal intention of enemy and foe. The world of Wise Blood is one of clashing in a wilderness. . . . Miss O'Connor's style is tight to choking and as direct and uncompounded as the order to a firing squad to shoot a man against a wall. One cannot take this book lightly or lightly turn away from it, because it is inflicted upon one in the same way its people take their lives: like an indefensible blow delivered in the dark.

William Goyen. NYT. May 18, 1952. p. 4

Wise Blood is the first novel of a twenty-six-year-old Georgia woman. It is a reasonably accomplished, remarkably precocious beginning. Written in a taut, dry, economical and objective prose, it is an important addition to the grotesque literature of Southern decadence. It

is also a kind of Southern Baptist version of "The Hound of Heaven."
. . . The stifling world which emerges from these pages is an animal-istic world. The author's predilection for zoological symbolism is more than a trick of style. . . . Nobody here is redeemed because there is no one to redeem.

John H. Simons. *Com*. June 27, 1952. pp. 297–8

The theme of *Wise Blood* is Christ the Pursuer, the Ineluctable, with a satire on Protestantism thrown in. . . . It is quite clear what Miss O'Connor means to say . . . is . . . there is no escaping Christ. But the author's style, in my opinion, is inconsistent with this statement. Everything she says through image and metaphor has the meaning only of degeneration, and she writes of an insane world, peopled by mon-sters and submen. . . . Let me say of *Wise Blood* that it does deal with one of the themes, and shows a variety of sensibility, out of which the kind of fiction that matters can be made.

Isaac Rosenfeld. *NR*. July 7, 1952. pp. 19–20

Miss O'Connor is a regionalist in the best sense of the word; that is, she understands her country and its people so well that in her hands they become all humanity. The stories in *A Good Man Is Hard to Find* take place in Georgia, but they are moving for their inescapable reality and not because of picturesque and local color. Such things, we recognize, could happen anywhere; some are grotesque and some terrible but we dare not say of any, "This only took place in the writer's imagination."
    For she lays hold of the significant detail; her poetic awareness is constantly receiving, selecting the illustration which gives us a man or a woman or a certain kind of hot summer evening living and whole.

Sylvia Stallings. *NYHT*. June 5, 1955. p. 1

Miss O'Connor's works like Maupassant's, are characterized by preci-sion, density and an almost alarming circumspection. There are few landscapes in her stories. Her characters seem to move in the hard, white glare of a searchlight—or perhaps it is more as if the author viewed her subjects through the knot-hole in a fence or wall. . . . Miss O'Connor for all her apparent preoccupation with the visible scene, is also fiercely concerned with moral, even theological prob-lems. In these stories the rural South is, for the first time, viewed by a writer whose orthodoxy matches her talent. The results are revolu-tionary.

Caroline Gordon. *NYT*. June 12, 1955. p. 5

Scarcely thirty years old, and a Georgian by birth and chance, Flannery O'Connor is not easily fitted into any identifiable group of Southern

writers. She stands among, but is not of them. To be sure, her characters have certain traits linking them with the Southern tradition in
fiction: for the most part they are poor and rural folk dominated by
the old ancestral fears—of death, the unknown, the foreign, and all
the shadows of evil. But they are strangers to despair, and this is their
distinction. They hold their fears at bay with a rustic religiosity that is
as functional as their speech or dress.

> James Greene. *Com*. July 22, 1955. p. 404

A Good Man Is Hard to Find certainly presents an abundance of
victims of grotesque fate and weird villains. . . . Beyond the grotes-
query and the symbolism, this reviewer finds in these diamond-hard,
diamond-brilliant stories a fiery rejection of Bible Beltism, of small,
mean minds and small, mean ways. Interestingly enough, the critical
touchstone is Catholicism.

> Riley Hughes. *CW*. Oct., 1955. pp. 66–7

Something about Miss O'Connor's work is reminiscent of the best work
of another Georgia writer, Erskine Caldwell. Perhaps it is subject matter most of all. Though in no sense concerned with the pornography
and lasciviousness to which Caldwell often resorts, she too goes in for
the miseries of the poor whites. . . . Perhaps the similarities are en-
hanced, too, by the style of Miss O'Connor's stories—realistic, plain,
literal. . . . Where Miss O'Connor's art differs—profoundly—from
Caldwell's is not in language and subject matter as much as in the attitude
of the author. Caldwell is the naturalist, out to make a social point. . . .
More kin to the Bundrens of *As I Lay Dying,* her people confront
spiritual and moral problems, not economics. There is in her characters
a dignity, a human worthiness, that shows the real respect Miss O'Connor has for them.

> Louis D. Rubin, Jr. *SwR*. Autumn, 1955. pp. 678–9

See *Wise Blood* and *The Violent Bear It Away* (novels) and *A Good Man Is
Hard to Find* (short stories).

ODETS, CLIFFORD (1906–1963)

Awake and Sing . . . reveals as interesting a new talent as I have
seen in the theatre for a long time. To say that it deals with the humor and the tragedy of a Jewish family domiciled in the Bronx, that it
recreates from shrewd observation the minds and manners of a stubborn and struggling family, is by no means to say enough. . . . Ob-

servation is there in full measure but so, too, is something else—enthusiasm, passion, and the same almost painful intensity of feeling that distinguishes the characters. . . . Emotionally he is still close to the people he is writing about, and he understands them from the inside out. . . . The subject of the play is . . . the persistent and many-sided rebellion of human nature against everything which thwarts it.

Joseph Wood Krutch. Nation. March 13, 1935. p. 314

It seems to me the first thing about Mr. Odets's new play (Golden Boy) that we should mention is a certain quality in the dialogue. . . . Where his theatrical gift most appears is in the dialogue's avoidance of the explicit. The explicit, always to be found in poor writers trying for the serious, is the surest sign of lack of talent. To write in terms of what is not said, of combinations elusive and in detail, perhaps, insignificant, of a hidden stream of sequences, and a resulting air of spontaneity and true pressure—that is quite another matter. In this respect Mr. Odets is the most promising writer our theatre can show.

Stark Young. NR. Nov. 17, 1937. p. 45

What has been impressive in Mr. Odets's plays has not been their ideas, which are usually pretty confused, or their structure, which has been pretty melodramatic, but the fact that the characterizations and the dialogue have a bite and an originality of turn which set them apart from the somewhat pallid characters and dialogues of most modern plays. . . . Mr. Odets's people are at once primitive and intelligent, and it is this antinomy which imparts to them their color and variety. Neither of these qualities are hurt by the fact that their emotion is not strong enough to conquer their intelligence nor their intelligence deep or keen enough to kill their emotion. It is this struggle of emotion with intelligence which is the basis of much of the great drama of the world, and it is this struggle which is abundantly evident in the half-Americanized Jews of Mr. Odets.

Glenville Vernon. Com. Dec. 16, 1938. p. 215

Each of Odets's faults has almost its counterpart in creative quality. Against his extreme subjectiveness can be placed his wise desire to express the nature and the problems of the people that he knows. Against his errors of cause and effect, his intention to give his plays a social background and to make them purposeful enough to carry the burden of their content. Against the fact that he himself does most of the talking in his plays, there is the fact that the talk is exceptionally alive and theatrical, speech for an actor's tongue. Against the fact that the majority of his characters are clichés, the recognition that in almost every play there is at least one that is a real creation, sometimes only a subordinate character, sometimes a leading figure, but recurrently one that has three dimensions and a soul.

Edith J. R. Isaacs. *TA*. April, 1939. p. 261

Clifford Odets can do just about what he wants to, because he has the right eye—what he has seen makes a storehouse of vivid people and things and action from the immediate world—and because he has theatrical genius. He is a poet too, of course, and along with Shaw, Kober, Weidman he has tapped a source of homely poetry in Jewish family life. But better poets have written god-awful plays. And very few playwrights have so constantly managed the explosive comment, the juxtaposition of varied types, the rising expectation, the unexpected in a flash, which give even his sermonizings theatre motion. He simply has the gift: his imagination goes in all directions at once, and his selective dramatic sense tells him which of the ways can be brought together to the most effective cross purpose.

Otis Ferguson. *NR*. Sept. 27, 1939. p. 216

By a considerable margin, the most important achievement in the literature of the American Jews is that of Clifford Odets. No one else has been able to maintain that degree of confidence in the value of the exact truth which made his best work possible. His social understanding is limited, but he has been able to keep his eyes on reality and to set down his observations with great imagination and remarkable detachment. Jews are never commonplace to him—but neither are they prodigies, either of absurdity or of pathos or of evil. He has perceived that they are human beings living the life which happens to be possible to them.

Robert S. Warshaw. *Cmty*. May, 1946. p. 17

The Big Knife proved that Odets had lost none of his theatrical vigor and that no one writing realistic drama, not excluding the Arthur Miller of *Death of a Salesman,* can surpass his power to write with an explosive force and with a wild and swirling poetry of torment and bedevilment. . . . If *The Big Knife* is not a successfully realized play, it is not because Odets still writes some embarrassingly callow lines of dialogue and has himself under imperfect control. It is because Odets, a product of the agitated left-wing theatre of the 1930's, is heir to its major faults —to the tendency to put too much of the blame on society and too little on the individual.

John Gassner. *Forum*. May, 1949. pp. 286–7

Although *The Country Wife* is not Mr. Odets's best play, it has some of his best writing in it. Moreover, it discloses a new and unexpected Odets. This in itself is reassuring and welcome. Mr. Odets has usually been associated with dramas of social significance if not social protest. . . . It is interesting to see in *The Country Wife* that Mr. Odets can write from affection with the same intensity and insight with which he first wrote with indignation. . . . His scenes race forward with the drive of his earliest works. His gift for deriving tension from small things is as effective as it used to be in developing large climaxes.

John Mason Brown. *SR*. Dec. 9, 1950. pp. 26–7

Night Music is a lyric improvisation (a sort of dramatic *suite*) on the basic homelessness of the little man in the big city. It is charmingly sentimental, comically poetic, airy and wholly unpretentious. It's characters are as simple as those of a commedia dell'arte scenario, and its cutely obstreperous hero is a twentieth-century Pierrot—weeping, sighing, cursing and deeply tender and funny withal. . . . In it Odets takes for granted that we all recognize our homelessness, that we all believe the rootlessness and disorientation of his hero to be typical, that we all know that most of the slogans of our society are without substance in terms of our true emotions. In *Night Music* Odets is far more wistful than angry.

Harold Clurman. *NR*. April 30, 1951. p. 22

Clifford Odets wrote *Golden Boy* at the height of his powers as an angry, moralizing neo-realist, and it remains his most successful play. Where the earlier *Awake and Sing,* for all its skill in infusing a surface realism with the natural poetry of Jewish-American speech, still moved loosly about the stage in the accepted Chekovian manner, *Golden Boy* pulled the dramatic reins tight and shocked its way through the evening like a series of body-blows. Without loosing rhythm or imagery, the speech of the play adapted itself to the lean and hard-driving urgency of a thoroughly theatrical structure; the language remained richer than what we had been getting under the guise of keyhole naturalism, and the play moved like lightning besides.

Walter Kerr. *Com*. March 28, 1952. p. 614

I think that one of the reasons for Odets's importance to the American theatre is that his work reflects so strikingly certain American national characteristics: rebelliousness, virility and violence coupled with tenderness, sentiment, and humor. Perhaps this is the very reason Odets has been so successful in England, where other important American playwrights seemingly have not been understood. The English probably find some fascination—perhaps it is a repulsive fascination—in this simple, robust, naked emotion of his, so directly in contrast with their polite expression.

It is interesting to me that Odets's earlier works, sometimes charged with being limited by their topicality, all possess the same underlying general theme—the need and the search for responsibility and self-respect that can help generate the finest nature in man.

Robert Whitehead. TA. Oct., 1954. p. 25

Waiting for Lefty, Golden Boy, and *Rocket to the Moon* did not attempt to speak *for* America. They spoke of America, of its indestructible good nature. They infused the white-collared, pale-fleshed middle class with the spirit of the expanding West. The shipping clerk could feel like Paul Bunyan. His nature was wedded to Walt Whitman. . . . Odets's audiences listened and heard their inner voices echoing in his expostulation. His protest was an articulation of theirs. His dreams were their yearnings. His testament was that the human being not be nullified. . . . Odets was a member of the family, a friend and relation to all who paid the price of admission.

Barry Hyams. TA. April, 1955. p. 70

See *Waiting for Lefty, Awake and Sing, Golden Boy, Night Music,* and *The Country Wife* (plays).

O'NEILL, EUGENE (1888–1953)

The Hairy Ape is not a perfect play. Felicity of any kind is not a characteristic of Mr. O'Neill. He is strong and feeble. No touch of beauty or charm ever hides the moments of failure in his work. In *The Hairy Ape* those moments are few. The drama is momentous in its vision, strength, and truth. There is something hard in its quality, but it is the hardness of the earth's rocks; there is something of violence, but it is the violence of an intolerable suffering.

Ludwig Lewisohn. Nation. March 22, 1922. p. 350

Mr. O'Neill reveals the first burst of his emotions in powerful clean-cut pictures that seem almost like simple ballads in our complex world. . . . His first acts impress me as being the strongest; while the last, I shall not say go to pieces but, undoubtedly, are very much weaker than the others. The close of *The Hairy Ape,* as well as that of *The Emperor Jones,* seems to me to be too direct, too simple, too expected; it is a little disappointing to a European with his complex background, to see the arrow strike the target toward which he had watched it speeding all the while.

Hugo von Hofmansthal. *Fm.* March 21, 1923. p. 41

The two gifts that Eugene O'Neill up to now has displayed are for feeling and for dramatic image. His plays have often conveyed a poignancy that is unique in the modern drama. You felt that whatever was put down was at the dramatist's own expense; he paid out of himself as he went. His great theatre gift has been in the creation of images that speak for themselves. . . . In *Mourning Becomes Electra* Mr. O'Neill comes now into the full stretch of clear narrative design. He discovers that in expressive pattern lies the possibility of all that parallels life, a form in which fall infinite shadings and details, as the light with its inexhaustible nuances and elements appears on a wall. He has come to what is so rare in Northern art, an understanding of repetition and variation on the same design, as contrasted with matter that is less deep or subtle, though expressed with lively surprise, variety, or novelty.

Stark Young. *NR.* Nov. 11, 1931. pp. 354–5

Of character as O'Neill portrayed it the touchstone is the stark reality of human suffering, faintly illuminated at best by an aspiration that is groping and dumb. In the true sense of the word it is passion and that is a thing which was . . . lamentably absent from American drama before O'Neill. . . . To develop such passion in the theatre requires dramatic instinct and a dramatic technique as simple as they are strong. For the "situations" and the "great scenes" of his predecessors O'Neill had as little use as for their comedic laughs and their saccharine tears. No contrivance was visible in his plays, no effort of any sort; yet the human heart somehow revealing itself, caught in the meshes of that most tragic fate which is character—what one essentially is and must remain.

John Corbin. *SR.* April 30, 1932. p. 694

In the case of Eugene O'Neill, it is very plain that the changing conditions of American life from the 'nineties to the present have largely conditioned his choice of both plot and theme. . . . The struggle of the 'nineties between a general smug complacency and a limited but intense idealism and devotion to beauty and art; the philosophic unrest and discontent of the succeeding decade with its intellectual pride; the defeat of scientific materialism . . . all of these national currents of mind and soul have influenced profoundly his consciousness of special forms of human struggle. But as a poet in the larger sense, he has also in his successive handling of these problems, reflected the inner development in his own soul of the universal poet's quest.

Richard Dana Skinner. *NAR*. June, 1935. p. 66

Not only has O'Neill tried to encompass more of life than most American writers of his time but, almost alone among them, he has persistently tried to solve it. . . . Not the minutiae of life, not its feel and color and smell, not its nuance and humor, but the "great inscrutable forces" are his interest. He is always moving toward the finality which philosophy sometimes, and religion always, promises. Life and death, good and evil, spirit and flesh, male and female, the all and the one, Anthony and Dionysius—O'Neill's is a world of these antithetical absolutes such as religion rather than philosophy conceives, a world of pluses and minuses; and his literary effort is an algebraic attempt to solve the equations.

Lionell Trilling. *NR*. Sept. 23, 1936. pp. 176–7

Into the modern theatre, the theatre of individual character study or Shavian reform, came Eugene O'Neill, a man deeply troubled by the ancient riddle of good and evil, vexed by the problem of Man's place in the universe, his mixed inheritance, his evil deeds, his capacity for struggle. . . . O'Neill has been intent on writing about life; and because life is profound and perplexing and filled with dark things of evil and pitiful frustrations of the human spirit and because these things have troubled him O'Neill has constantly tended to make his characters subservient to some tragic end far larger than they. . . . In his aloofness from realism, his reflections on life rather than individuals, and his passionate sympathy with the unconquerable aspirations of the human spirit, immersed in evil howsoever deep it be, he is certainly Greek enough to be a strange and compelling figure in our modern playhouse.

Walter Prichard Eaton. *AS*. Summer, 1937. pp. 307, 312

He has always gone his own austere, fierce, usually frowning way, ignoring the cheap whims of showshops and making the theatre do what he wanted rather than doing what its timid souls thought would be popular.

No dramatist has ever been a more dauntless experimenter or a more fearless innovator. He has dared in play after play to change his pattern, even when successful, and reach for what for him (and usually for the stage) was the untried. With varying degrees of success, ranging from pretentiousness and the preposterous to the very threshold of greatness, he has worked as a naturalist, a realist, an expressionist, a Freudian, a mystic, a symbolist, or as a poet whose poetry was deader than the feeblest prose even when his prose as spoken has burned with the fires of poetry.

> John Mason Brown. *SR*. Oct. 19, 1946. p. 26

That he is the foremost dramatist in the American theatre is . . . generally granted. His eminence is predicated on the fact that no other has anywhere near his ability to delve into and appraise character, his depth of knowledge of his fellow man, his sweep and pulse and high resolve, his command of a theatre stage and all its manifold workings, and his mastery of the intricacies of dramaturgy. His plays at their best have in them a real universality. His characters are not specific, individual and isolated types but active symbols of mankind in general, with mankind's virtues and faults, gropings and findings, momentary triumphs and doomed defeats. He writes not for a single theatre but for all theatres of the world.

> George Jean Nathan. *AM*. Dec., 1946. p. 718

Other men have conceived tragic situations, and other men have made full use of the resources of the modern stage. Few, however, have achieved a balanced combination of the two with the consistency of Eugene O'Neill. O'Neill has a unique combination of skill and vision. . . . In his non-realistic as well as his realistic plays, O'Neill demonstrates the acute sense of organic form which was to make him a leader of American expressionism. The structure of the play, the pattern of the action, even the shaping of the dialogue always follows a strict design, usually one devised for that particular play.

> Alan S. Downer. *TA*. Feb., 1951. pp. 22–3

At one time he performed a historic function, that of helping the American theatre grow up. In all his plays an earnest attempt is made to interpret life; this fact in itself places O'Neill above his predecessors in American drama and beside his colleagues in the novel and poetry. He was a good playwright insofar as he kept within the somewhat narrow range of his own sensibility. When he stays close to a fairly simple reality and when, by way of technique, he uses fairly simple forms of realism or fairly simple patterns of melodrama, he can render the bite and tang of reality or, alternatively, he can startle and stir us with his effects. . . . But the more he attempts, the less he succeeds. *Lazarus Laughed* and *The Great God Brown* and *Days Without End* are inferior to *The Emperor Jones* and *Anna Christie* and *Ah, Wilderness!*

> Eric Bentley. *KR*. Summer, 1952. p. 488

O'Neill brought ordinary life into the theater, and it turned out to be full of bizarre fantasies; but that is what ordinary life is like. . . . All his ducks are wild. Yet O'Neill was no Ibsen. He had not Shaw's power to provoke thought. He strove after but could not reach Strindberg's intensity. But these are the names he invokes. Whatever else he was not, O'Neill was large. What we have to acknowledge finally is the scale and energy of his fantasy in the theater.

Montagu Slater. *Nation*. Feb. 27, 1954. p. 175

Many of us . . . have been irritated by O'Neill for various reasons. We find him gloomy and morbid, certainly not "sunny" in the manner of typical Broadway. . . . We find his "thinking" fuzzy and his "eloquence" windy and his "poetry" at times embarrassing. Yet we admit that a theater which has no place for the tragic view of life is only a childish toy. O'Neill's earnestness, intensity, and courage were the qualities our drama needed. And if other playwrights now dare to write seriously of human terror and pity—and find production and an audience—we must be grateful to O'Neill for having shown the way.

N. Bryllion Fagin. *AnR*. Spring, 1954. p. 25

O'Neill was a faulty craftsman; he was not a sound thinker. . . . Yet to dwell on these shortcomings . . . is to confess one's own inadequate and bloodless response to the world we live in. . . . O'Neill not only lived intensely but attempted with perilous honesty to contemplate, absorb and digest the meaning of his life and ours. He possessed an uncompromising devotion to the task he set himself: to present and interpret in stage terms what he had lived through and thought about —a devotion unique in our theatre. . . . O'Neill's work is more than realism. And if it is stammering—it is still the most eloquent and significant stammer of the American theatre. We have not yet developed a cultivated speech that is either superior to it or as good.

Harold Clurman. *Nation*. March 3, 1956. pp. 182–3

O'Neill can be deeply involved in genuine passion because he is not merely playing a game to exhibit his skill. He can be black enough at times and on occasion fall a victim to the nihilism against which he perpetually struggled. But there may be "more faith in honest doubt" if "honest doubt" is not "complacent doubt." And O'Neill is never complacent, never other than deeply involved.

Man emerges from the bludgeonings he receives in O'Neill's plays with his essential dignity intact. He is still a creative being worthy of respect. That can hardly be said of either Tennessee Williams or Anouilh. And it may be that the present generation has found O'Neill stimulating for precisely that reason.

Joseph Wood Krutch. *NYT*. Sept. 22, 1957. p. 42

See *Anna Christie, The Emperor Jones, The Hairy Ape, Mourning Becomes Electra, The Iceman Cometh,* and *A Long Day's Journey into Night* (plays).

PARKER, DOROTHY (1893–   )

Dorothy Parker runs her little show as if it were a circus; she cracks her whip and the big elephant joke pounds his four legs in glee and the pink ladies of fantastic behavior begin to float in the air like lozenges. . . . Mrs. Parker has begun in the thoroughly familiar Millay manner and worked into something quite her own. . . . Miss Millay remains lyrically, of course, far superior to Mrs. Parker. . . . But there are moods when Dorothy Parker is more acceptable, whiskey straight, not champagne.

Genevieve Taggard. *NYHT*. March 27, 1927. p. 7

Here is poetry that is "smart" in the fashion designer's sense of the word. Mrs. Parker need not hide her head in shame, as the average poet must, when she admits the authorship of this book. For in its lightness, its cynicism, its pose, she has done the right thing; she is in a class with the Prince of Wales, the Theatre Guild, Gramercy Park, and H. L. Mencken. And these somewhat facetious remarks are not intended as disparagement. It is high time that a poet with a monocle looked at the populace, instead of the populace looking at the poet through a lorgnette.

Marie Luhrs. *Poetry*. April, 1927. p. 52

In verse of a Horatian lightness, with an exquisite certainty of technique, which, like the lustre on a Persian bowl, is proof that civilization is itself a philosophy, Dorothy Parker is writing poetry deserving high praise. . . . I suspect that one should quote Latin rather than English to parallel the edged fineness of Dorothy Parker's verse. This belle dame sans merci has the ruthlessness of the great tragic lyricists whose work was allegorized in the fable of the nightingale singing with her breast against a thorn. It is disillusion recollected in tranquillity where the imagination has at last controlled the emotions. It comes out clear, and with the authentic sparkle of a great vintage.

Henry Seidel Canby. *SR*. June 13, 1931. p. 891

More certain than either death or taxes is the high and shining art of Dorothy Parker. . . . Bitterness, humor, wit, yearning for beauty and love, and a foreknowledge of their futility—with rue her heart is laden, but her lads are gold-plated—these, you might say, are the elements of the Parkerian formula; these, and the divine talent to find the right word and reject the wrong one. The result is a simplicity that almost startles.

Franklin P. Adams. NYHT. June 14, 1931. p. 7

To say that Mrs. Parker writes well is as fatuous, I'm afraid, as proclaiming that Cellini was clever with his hands. But it's fun to see the lamented English language rise from the Parisian boneyard and race out front with the right jockey in the saddle, and I cannot help attempting to communicate to others my pleasure in the performance. . . . The trick about her writing is the trick about Ring Lardner's writing or Ernest Hemingway's writing. It isn't a trick.

Ogden Nash. SR. Nov. 4, 1933. p. 231

Drunk or sober, angry or affectionate, stupid or inspired, these people of Mrs. Parker's speak with an accent we immediately recognize and relish. Mrs. Parker has listened to her contemporaries with as sharp a pair of ears as anyone has had in the present century, unless, to be sure, Lardner is to be considered, as he probably is, without a rival in this field. Mrs. Parker is more limited than Lardner; she is expert only with sophisticates. . . . But she does her lesser job quite perfectly, achieving as she does it a tone half-way between sympathy and satire. . . . Again it is only Ring Lardner who can be compared with her in the matter of hatred for stupidity, cruelty, and weakness.

Mark Van Doren. EJ. Sept., 1934. pp. 541–2

One comes back to Mrs. Parker's light verse with the greatest pleasure; with its sharp wit, its clean bite, its perfectly conscious—and hence delightful—archness, it stands re-reading amply. Here her high technical polish has great virtue. . . . But what, of course, is more important is the sense of personality that converts what might otherwise be merely a witty idea into a dramatic, however cockeyed, situation; a sense of personality that gives us not cynicism in the abstract but laughter applied to an objective. There is no one else in Mrs. Parker's special field who can do half as much.

Louis Kronenberger. NYT. Dec. 13, 1936. p. 28

Men have liked her poems because of the half-bitter, half-wistful tribute to their indispensability and their irresistible, fatal charms. A different kind of lover, the lover of light verse, has admired her extraordinary technical competence and the way in which her verse constantly veers over into the domain of genuinely lyric poetry. The wits of the town have been delighted to see a Sappho who could combine a heart-break with a wisecrack.

Irwin Edman. *Nation*. Dec. 19, 1936. p. 737

The urbanity of these stories is that of a worldly, witty person with a place in a complex and highly-developed society, their ruthlessness that of an expert critical intelligence, about which there is something clinical, something of the probing adroitness of a dentist: the fine-pointed instrument unerringly discovers the carious cavity behind the smile. . . . Mrs. Parker may appear amused, but it is plain that she is really horrified. Her bantering revelations are inspired by a respect for decency, and her pity and sympathy are ready when needed.

William Plomer. *Spec*. Nov. 17, 1939. p. 708

Mrs. Parker's published work does not bulk large. But most of it has been pure gold and the five winnowed volumes of her shelf—three of poetry, two of prose—are so potent a distillation of nectar and wormwood, of ambrosia and deadly nightshade, as might suggest to the rest of us that we all write far too much. Even though I am one who does not profess to be privy to the intentions of posterity, I do suspect that another generation will not share the confusion into which Mrs. Parker's poetry throws so many of her contemporaries, who, seeing that much of it is witty, dismiss it patronizingly as "light" verse, and do not see that some of it is thrilling poetry of a piercing and rueful beauty.

Alexander Woollcott. *The Portable Woollcott*
(Viking). 1946. pp. 181–2

See *The Portable Dorothy Parker* (poetry and prose).

PATCHEN, KENNETH (1911–   )

At their worst his poems are like the dream compositions of a leftist editorial writer, repeating class sentiments with a strange syntactical or structural distortion. . . . Patchen's word-pour may be praised as creative vitality or condemned as artistic debauchery, but in either case it is more wearisome than interesting.

Robert Fitzgerald. *Poetry*. Sept., 1936. p. 342

Mr. Patchen has the high scorn of a certain type of young man, and the determination to use certain words that poetry has eschewed. This does not make his poetry any better. Neither does certain snarling and scrambled invective. But you have to give the man his head, because he can write desperately and movingly at times, and his era is responsible for him. Mr. Patchen is trying to talk as the tough-minded talk in the street and at the same time write poetry. It is not an easy assignment.

William Rose Benét. *SR.* Nov. 25, 1939. p. 16

Beyond any book of poems I have encountered *First Will and Testament* gives a lively sense of what it is to be a young man in America in a time when, for more of the young than we like to think, living and dying have lost all meaning. Kenneth Patchen is sure of his vocation as a poet, somewhat less sure of his craft. But he is able and eloquent, witty and strong. And what he is trying to do in this book is through poetry to recover meaning. . . . His poetic speech is contemporary and close to the streets; but he has held to nothing he has heard in the streets unless it has its own vigor to recommend it.

John Peale Bishop. *Nation.* Dec. 2, 1939. p. 620

Whatever the ideology of the earlier poems was, the poems themselves had a hard beauty, an imaginative frenzy abstracted out of reality, a moving sad terror. And there was a quality of bewilderment that got into the poems. In his new book (*The Dark Kingdom*) all of those qualities seem to be there, but they are there only as masquerades, larger, vaster in scope, but with less weight. . . . I believe Patchen to be one of the finest talents in America today. He has depth, imagination, and resourcefulness. He is "endowed" lyrically, but he appears a little contemptuous of it.

Harvey Breit. *Poetry.* June, 1942. pp. 160, 162

Here (in *The Dark Kingdom*) is proof, if proof is needed, that Mr. Patchen is a poet. But he is also a seer, and there seems to be some danger that the seer will eat up the poet. It is possible that the seer has already taken a chunk out of the poet. What is left is, however, interesting enough. . . . There is a wealth of exciting images and sharp phrases, sometimes splendid, sometimes horrible, always violent and apocalyptic. . . . He affirms his world too vehemently, too wholeheartedly. The seer cannot wait on the slow process of poetic exploration. And this means that though there is poetry in the book there are few poems with a recognizable structure.

Robert Penn Warren. *Nation.* July 4, 1942. p. 17

Mr. Patchen has and habitually uses the naive vision of life. . . . But to have the naive vision and nothing else is to be a child. . . . It must be granted that Mr. Patchen knows this; the signs of his departure from the childlike approach are manifold, and include the elaborate and evasive technique of the drawing-and-type poem . . . along with other practices. . . . And these devices are to an extent successful, for they generate interesting and even brilliant effects to which the naivete then becomes contributory. Finally, however, I feel that the poems . . . do not "satisfy"; and I trace this dissatisfaction to the poet's lack of a body of sharp and empirically genuine ideas—of perhaps a political and psychological nature.

E. S. Forgotson. *Poetry*. Feb., 1944. p. 280

A representative chunk of Patchen will contain references to immortality, God and death of the gods (à la Nietzsche), capitalism, anarchism, and pacificism, sex, murder, and blood-guilt, and any number of generally unacknowledged leanings toward and derivations from psychoanalysis. . . . The fact that the tradition in which Patchen writes depends to such a large extent on surrealistic maneuvers deprives it of a good deal of the power and wisdom it claims for itself. It has staked all on a sleight-of-hand, a trick of symbolism that actually throws out the deeper human context that it is supposed to provide for literature. Patchen's politics, for example, a kind of anarcho-pacificism, uncompromisingly opposed to capitalism and war, is the nearest thing to an escape from politics that can be contrived in political language.

Isaac Rosenfeld. *NR*. Dec. 3, 1945. pp. 773–4

Faced with the problems of our complex and chaotic world, Mr. Patchen, in regarding them, is not serene in the knowledge of invisible realities, nor does he project a better world of the imagination, neither has he a program of revolt; he goes to pieces. . . . There is but one remedy—to hide his face on the breast of his beloved. . . . While he may, as his admirers claim, possess a real spark of genius, his talent is inadequate, thus far, consistently to catch this spark and blow it to a flame.

Jean Starr Untermeyer. *SR*. March 22, 1947. pp. 15–6

There is no denying the compelling power of his poetry at its best . . . nor the tremendous vitality of the personality from whence it flows. Moreover the coupling of his name with Whitman is in a way inevitable, since the compulsion which drove Whitman to utter his "barbaric yawp" in non-metrical verse is the same which urges Patchen to the audacities of his own free technique; and what transpires from the poetry of both is the sense of a "fullness of being" too ebullient to be confined to the sophisticated and severely disciplined modalism of regular versification.

But while Whitman in spite of his "barbarism" achieved a kind of Olympian dignity, there is about Patchen a faint aura of darkness which betrays him as a sort of minor chthonian deity, at the same time a little above and a little below the merely human.

Frajam Taylor. *Poetry*. Aug., 1947. pp. 270–1

Kenneth Patchen writes with much more violence (than William Carlos Williams), with a Celtic turbulence and humor, and passion for and against. . . . His descriptions are accurate, sharp with color, sounds, and tastes; and his anger can be cool and the passion turn to a love song of surprising delicacy. . . . There is much of death and graves in the poetry, the rollicking dead under beer cans, the dead of history and legend, all of them envious of those alive, however evil their lot may be.

Eugene Davidson. *YR*. Summer, 1949. p. 725

Much of Patchen's work is conceived in the limbo of nightmare, in a world where the humor is worse than the horror. Frenzy rules here; phantasmagoria triumphs in slapstick satire, casual killings, and sinister obscenity. But there is more to Patchen than his power to evoke ugliness, violence, and nonchalant treachery. . . . The tone is savage disillusionment, but not apathy; it is rebellious and ribald, indignant and desperate, but clean-cut even in its fury.

Louis Untermeyer. *Modern American Poetry*
(Harcourt). 1950. p. 642

It is Patchen who extends the vision of (Henry) Miller and Céline to the farthest stretches of sanity and by the agility and poetry of his language brings their wail to full throat. Patchen, whose basic message, after all the variations, is no more than this:

WE BELIEVE IN YOU. THERE IS NO DANGER. IT IS NOT GETTING DARK.
WE LOVE YOU.

He tells you again and again: "I must tell you what I have said is not true. This is all a damn lie." But we still remember what we wanted to see, what we wanted to hear. We must milk dry the doubt he provides us with. It is all he leaves us to combat the terrors he has made rise in us. But one senses, in a stunned way, that it is a very valuable thing to have.

Hugh McGovern. *NMQ*. Summer, 1951. p. 195

See *First Will and Testament, The Dark Kingdom,* and *Red Wine and Yellow Hair* (poetry); also *The Journal of Albion Moonlight* (novel).

PORTER, KATHERINE ANNE (1894–   )

Miss Porter's mind is one of those highly civilized instruments of perception that seems to have come out of old societies, where the "social trend" is fixed and assumed. The individual character as the product of such a background also has a certain constancy of behavior which permits the writer to ignore the now common practice of relating individual conduct to some abstract social or psychological law; the character is taken as a fixed and inviolable entity, predictable only in so far as a familiarity may be said to make him so, and finally unique as the center of inexhaustible depths of feeling and action. In this manner Miss Porter approaches her characters, and it is this that probably underlies many of the very specific virtues of her writing.

> Allen Tate. *Nation.* Oct. 1, 1930. pp. 352–3

It is to Miss Porter's high credit that, having fixed upon the exceptional background and event, she has not yielded, in her treatment of them, to queerness and forced originality of form. . . . Miss Porter has a range of effects, but each comes through in its place, and only at the demand of her material. She rejects the exclamatory tricks that wind up style to a spurious intensity, and trusts for the most part, to straightforward writing, to patience in detail and to a thorough imaginative grasp on cause and character.

> Louise Bogan. *NR.* Oct. 22, 1930. p. 277

Katherine Anne Porter moves in the illustrious company headed by Hawthorne, Flaubert, and Henry James. It is the company of story-tellers whose fiction possesses distinct esthetic quality, whose feelings have attained harmonious expression in the work. . . . Each of the narratives maintains its own tone—in the sense of effects of color and modulation and accents appropriate to the expression of its individual sentiment. And each of the poignant little dramas represented by them unfolds continually and unpredictably, never betraying its ultimate turns, which arrive as shocks and surprises. Ideal beauty, a fugitive poetry, again and again flashes through the substance of the narrative. But the tone, too, invariably is unemphatic and quiet.

> Paul Rosenfeld. *SR.* April 1, 1939. p. 7

Emphasis on her style should not obscure the fact that Miss Porter has other attributes of a good fiction writer. At her best she has mastered narrative pace and narrative construction; her dialogue is colloquial and at the same time graceful and dignified: she has observed with minuteness a variety of locales and ways of living; her people are speaking likenesses; she has wit; and there is a shrewd modern intelligence, if not an extremely original or forceful one, dominating the story from some little distance.

Philip Blair Rice. *Nation*. April 15, 1939. p. 442

Miss Porter has no genius but much talent. Her average level is high, and she doesn't let you down. She is more fundamentally serious than Katherine Mansfield, less neurotic, closer to the earth. She is dry-eyed, even in tragedy: when she jokes, she does not smile. You feel you can trust her. . . . Having praised so much, I pause and wonder just what it is that prevents me from uttering the final, whole-hearted hurrah. . . . She is grave, she is delicate, she is just—but she lacks altogether, for me personally, the vulgar appeal. I cannot imagine that she would ever make me cry, or laugh aloud.

Christopher Isherwood. *NR*. April 19, 1929. pp. 312–3

Among her Southern contemporaries in short prose fiction Miss Porter has few peers. She lacks the social emphasis of Mr. Erskine Caldwell, but she also lacks his sensationalism. She has nothing of Mr. William Faulkner's hypnotic quality, his violent power, or his flair for abnormal psychology; but neither has she any of his obliquity. At her best she is superior as a craftsman to both. At any point in her art she is one of the most talented of living American writers.

Lodwick Hartley. *SwR*. April, 1940. p. 216

Both in conception and execution her work seems to me to bear the relation to prose that the lyric bears to poetry. Her intelligence is extraordinary, but it is akin to that of a poet rather than that, say, of a novelist like Henry James, who was also interested in the thumb-print but had both the strong desire and the capacity for broad formulation which the long flight requires.

Margaret Marshall. *Nation*. April 13, 1940. p. 474

The exquisite rightness of this author's art has been commented upon by many; and these sketches and tales reveal to the vague tribe, the discriminating reader, what fundamental brainwork goes into the creating of episodes that, on the surface, seem hastily thrown together. To be sure, this deftness is bought at a price, and the careful casualness of Miss Porter's approach sometimes reminds one of a cat stalking its prey with unnecessary caution. If some of these narratives were told in the straightforward narrative manner formerly characteristic of the short story, they might not lose in delicacy and might gain in dramatic power.

Howard Mumford Jones. *SR*. Sept. 30, 1944. p. 15

Miss Porter's thematic statements are given their extraordinary power through a rich and complex characterization. Four or five outstanding personality traits are usually boldly established, and these are used as reference points from which to thrust with the quick image and the loaded phrase into the spaces of modifying qualification. The qualification made, she retires for a moment to the centre, waits calmly, and then stabs again—this time either farther in the same direction or in a new direction. In the end, though the characters are typical, recognizable types, they are also particular flesh and bones—somewhat fluid, unpredictable, elusive, contradictory.

> Charles Allen. *AQ*. Summer, 1946. p. 93

The important thing to notice is that in all cases Katherine Anne Porter's characters possess qualities which have some point of similarity with her own experience. If they are Irish or Mexican, they are also Roman Catholic—or they are political liberals. They are usually Southerners. I don't mean to suggest this as a serious limitation, but it may help to account for the consistently high level which her work represents, a level probably unsurpassed by any writer of her time.

> Ray B. West, Jr. *HR*. Fall, 1952. p. 19

See *Flowering Judas, The Leaning Tower* and *Pale Horse, Pale Rider* (short stories); also *The Days Before* (essays).

> See Supplement at end of text for additional material.

POUND, EZRA (1885–   )

He is like a man who goes hunting hedgehogs with bare feet—and finds his prey all prickles; to vary and mix the metaphor, he sits on his little hill in Kensington as if it were Olympian, casting forth winged words which, like boomerangs, are returned unto him an hundred-fold! In the melee his work is disloyally attacked, his least errors are exposed with a malignant triumph; his sensitiveness, which hides under a cover of bluster, is denounced as conceit; his fineness of perception is misunderstood as triviality. His scholarship, with its rather overwhelming pretension, is suspect; his polemics verge on hysteria. His fault is that he is an anachronism. With the enthusiasm of a Renaissance scholar, one of those whose fine devotion but faulty learning revealed to the fifteenth-century world the civilization of Greece, he lives in an age which looks at literature as a hobby, a freak, a branch of education; but never as a life study, a burning passion.

> Richard Aldington. *Poetry*. July, 1920. p. 214

Given a mind that is not averse to labouring, provided that a kernel lies beneath the hard shells, you can reach the purpose of these poems. They contain the subconscious matter deposited by years of reading and observation in one man's mind, and in their residence in this sub-conscious state they have blended into the man's mental and emotional prejudices and undergone a metamorphosis, in which they become his visualization and interpretation of past men's events. Legendary heroes, kings, dukes, queens, soldiers, slaves, they live again as this man would have them live, and speak words that are partly his and partly their own, in the manner of ubermarionettes. Their fragmentary and often tangled existence—quick appearances and vanishings—is a distinctive feature of the subconscious state that enclosed them before they were extracted from the poet.

Maxwell Bodenheim. *Dial.* Jan., 1922. p. 91

When a man has written poetry as good as the best of Pound, it is impossible to dismiss him, however much the conservative mind may so desire. It is there now and poetry-lovers will be sure to find it. Its qualities are individual and they are compact of color, brilliant and flashing phrasing, and the subtle marriage of mood and manner. These things, I should say, are its distinguishing characteristics. There is always the creation of an atmosphere, always the melody of phrasing, always the quick ear for the shy felicities of beautiful words, always the varying of form to suit the emotional content.

Herbert S. Gorman. *NAR.* June, 1924. pp. 864–5

There are many so-called educators in our over-instructed world, but few inspired teachers. Ezra Pound is one of the few. . . . His method has been fiercely destructive of rooted prejudices, but magically encouraging to every green shoot of new growth. His mind, being imaginatively creative, presented examples as well as precept, offered beautiful poems to the world. . . . Whether or not he ever offers us more songs, his best work has already the completeness of adequate beauty. As a leader, a revolutionist in the art, he will have a place in literary history; as a poet he will sing into the hearts and minds of all free-singing spirits in the next age—and perhaps in the ages beyond much of our prophecy.

Harriet Monroe. *Poetry.* May, 1925. pp. 94–7

Pound talks like no one else. His is almost a wholly original accent, the base of American mingled with a dozen assorted "English society" and Cockney accents inserted in mockery, French, Spanish, and Greek exclamations, strange cries and catcalls, the whole very oddly inflected, with dramatic pauses and *diminuendos.* It takes time to get used to it,

especially as the lively and audacious mind of Pound packs his speech
—as well as his writing—with undertones and allusions.

Iris Barry. *Bkm*. Oct., 1931. p. 159

Some would say the facing in many directions of a quadriga drawn by
centaurs, that we meet in the Cantos, puts strain on bipedal understanding; there is love of risk; but the experienced grafting of literature
upon music is very remarkable—the resonance of color, allusions,
tongues, sounding each through the other as in symphonic instrumenta-
tion. Even if one understood nothing, one would enjoy the musicianly
manipulation. . . . Mr. Pound, in the prose that he writes, has formulated his own commentary upon the Cantos. They are as an armorial
coat of attitudes of things that have happened in books and in life; they
are not a shield but a coat worn by a man, as in the days when heraldry
was beginning.

Marianne Moore. *Poetry*. Oct., 1931. pp. 48–50

The cantos are a sort of *Golden Ass*. There is a likeness, but there is no
parallel beyond the mere historical one: both books are the production of worlds without convictions and given over to a hard secular program. Here the similarity ends. For Mr. Pound is a powerful reactionary, a faithful mind devoted to those ages when the myths were not
merely pretty, but true. And there is a cloud of melancholy irony hanging over the cantos. He is persuaded that the myths are only beautiful,
and he drops them after a glimpse, but he is not reconciled to this aestheticism: he ironically puts the myths against the ugly specimens of
modern life that have defeated them. . . . He understands poetry and
how to write it. This is enough for one man to know. And the thirty
cantos are enough to occupy a loving and ceaseless study—say a canto a
year for thirty years, all thirty to be read every few weeks just for tone.

Allen Tate. *Nation*. June 10, 1931. pp. 633–4

When we consider this devotion to literature, we come upon the essential characteristic of the Cantos: their philological discussions, their
translations, their textual references, their peculiar and unceasing interest in how things are said, not to speak of the various dialects and slangs
which are introduced, and the habitual quotation of letters, codices,
and other documents. . . . Pound has been the pure literary man, the
complete man of letters; the concern with literary things, with the very
look of print upon the page, is at the center, the source of his writings.
. . . Pound fits one of his own categories: he has been a great inventor
in verse, and we know how few can be supposed to know the satisfaction of fulfilling their own canons of excellence.

Delmore Schwartz. *Poetry*. March, 1938. pp. 326–39

But what is Pound's class, and how can it be described without contemptuousness in the description and without giving the effect of anything contemptible in the class; for it is an admirable class and ought to be spoken of with admiration. Essentially it is the class of those who have a care for the purity of the tongue as it is spoken and as it sounds and as it changes in speech and sound, and who know that that purity can only exist in the movement of continuous alternation between the "fawn's flesh and the saint's vision," and who know, so, that the movement, not the alternatives themselves, is the movement of music. . . . Poets like Pound are the executive artists for their generation; he does not provide a new way of looking . . . but he provides the *means* of many ways of looking.

R. P. Blackmur. *Poetry*. Sept., 1946. pp. 344–5

The opinion has been voiced that Pound's eventual reputation will rest upon his criticism and not upon his poetry. (I have been paid the same compliment myself.) I disagree. It is on his total work for literature that he must be judged: on his poetry, *and* his criticism, *and* his influence on men and on events at a turning point in literature. In any case, his criticism takes its significance from the fact that it is the writing of a poet about poetry: it must be read in the light of his own poetry, as well as of poetry by other men whom he championed. . . . Pound's great contribution to the work of other poets (if they choose to accept what he offers) is his insistence upon the immensity of the amount of *conscious* labor to be performed by the poet. . . . He . . . provides an example of devotion to "the art of poetry" which I can only parallel in our time by the example of Valéry.

T. S. Eliot. *Poetry*. Sept., 1946. pp. 331–8

Pound's cantos are the words of a man for whom the thing given has, in general, the upper hand over deliberation, a man whose long isolation in Rapallo and unfretful assurance as to his own technical power have allowed unusual freedom in moving here or there, up or down, forward or backward (like a swimmer in clear water) among verbal or substantial intimations and seizing them, putting them down, when a more hesitant—or sluggish—artist would have left them in the air. . . . In perception or vision he would mount to a *paradisio* as his master, Dante did. . . . Well, the moral universe of the *Divine Comedy* was orthodox, graded, and public, firmly conceived to its uttermost corner; and this of Pound's is quite a different thing. But at their least valuation I submit that these cantos in which light and air—and song—move so freely are more exhilarating poetic sketch-books, *Notes from the Upper Air,* than can be found elsewhere in our literature.

Robert Fitzgerald. *NR*. Aug. 16, 1948. pp. 21–3

The Cantos are like a tremendous tapestry in which certain designs predominate, or like a great fugue with recurring motifs, or like a modern
Commedia, with the stenches from hell more often than not climbing up
to smother purgatory and hover cloudily on the sill of paradise. . . .
Pound uses . . . stories, some legendary, some apocryphal, some true,
to symbolize or exemplify the cruelties of usury, and to point up his fury
with those "who set money lust before the pleasures of the senses,"
those responsible for the mutilation of men and of art. In his rage he
sometimes gets out no more than a stuttered curse or lashes blindly at
the innocent, but I do not think even Dante has more powerfully set
down the hideousness of corruption, and the fewest lyricists have
equaled Pound's gift for evoking particulars of breath-taking delicacy
and luster.

Babette Deutsch. NYHT. Aug. 22, 1948. p. 7

Pound was one of the most opinionated and unselfish men who ever
lived, and he made friends and enemies everywhere by the simple exercise of the classic American constitutional right of free speech. His
speech was free to outrageous license. He was completely reckless about
making enemies. His so-called anti-Semitism was, hardly anyone has
noted, only equaled by his anti-Christianism. It is true he hated most in
the Catholic faith the elements of Judaism. It comes down squarely to
anti-monotheism. . . . Pound felt himself to be in the direct line of
Mediterranean civilization, rooted in Greece. . . . He was a lover of
the sublime, and a seeker after perfection, a true poet, of the kind born
in a hair shirt—a God-sent disturber of the peace in the arts, the one
department of human life where peace is fatal.

Katherine Anne Porter. NYT. Oct. 29, 1950. p. 4

I could never take him as a steady diet. Never. He was often brilliant
but an ass. But I never (so long as I kept away) got tired of him, or, for a
fact, ceased to love him. He had to be loved, even if he kicked you in
the teeth for it (but that he never did); he looked as if he might, but he
was, at heart, much too gentle, much too good a friend for that. And
he had, at bottom, an inexhaustible patience, an infinite depth of human
imagination and sympathy. Viscious, catty at times, neglectful, if he
trusted you not to mind, but warm and devoted—funny, too, as I have
said. We hunted, to some extent at least, together, and not each other.

William Carlos Williams. Autobiography (Random).
1951. p. 58

Because the poet is still there one cannot pity Pound—he has retained
an integrity as a poet which can be admired without reluctance. It is

clear that he will go on now to the end of the Cantos regardless of what is done for him or about him, in Saint Elizabeth's because he happens to be there, but with equal vigor in prison, or back at Rapallo, or anywhere else. He will go on blasting usury and preaching Social Credit, praising Mussolini and damning Roosevelt, as long as he has a voice and a listener. And however wrong-minded we may think all this is in a citizen of a democracy, we must, I think, admire it, however grudgingly, in the uncompromising poet.

Sam Hynes. *Com.* Dec. 9, 1955. p. 254

Certainly Ezra Pound can be read and understood in depth only with a detailed explication of his references in the other hand. . . . Yet the fact remains that even a reader who drives through these Cantos at full gallop will see that the poem is epic in intent, that its subject is the history of modern man's consciousness, and that the telling occurs in a kind of perpetual present, a sort of reverie of the racial consciousness. . . . A book, I propose, becomes a good book when it creates a world one can enter credibly in imagination and a perception of a life one can live vicariously. A good book becomes a great book when that world achieves a magnitude and that life-perception a depth that not only satisfies the imagination but enlarges it beyond all expectation. The final measure of the Cantos lies, I believe, in the fact that they do offer such an enlargement to a willing reader.

John Ciardi. *NYT.* June 24, 1956. pp. 4–5

Pound should be credited with having weighed the perils of the method he elected. It pays the reader the supreme compliment of supposing that he is seriously interested: interested, among other things, in learning how to deploy his curiosity without being a dilettante. . . . His utility enters its second phase when disparate materials acquire, if only by way of his personality, a unity of tone which makes them accessible to one another. . . . In his third phase of utility . . . the poet instigates curiosity: how many people in the last thirty years have read the *Odyssey* on account of Joyce, or Donne at the encouragement of Mr. Eliot, or Dante and Confucius thanks to Pound? . . . And he would consider that he was performing his maximum service for the fourth kind of reader, the one with the patience to learn and observe, within the poem, how exactly everything fits together and what exactly, page by page and canto by canto, the fitting together enunciates.

Hugh Kenner. *Poetry.* July, 1957. pp. 240–1

See *Personae, The Cantos, Section: Rock Drill* and *Selected Poems;* also *Collected Letters.*

RANSOM, JOHN CROWE (1888–   )

Poetry

I suppose that if I were set to fill in a literary passport to send Ransom to Parnassus, I should include in a summary of his Ransomness first, a humorous turn of speech, including a sweetening scepticism; second, a muscular quality of both metre and thought, and third, the periodic detonation of most unlikely and effective phrases.

Robert Graves. SR. Dec. 27, 1924. p. 412

The poet cannot solve his problem (the relation of the artist to the ordered, or disordered society in which he happens to live) by an act of will, but he can attempt to work out some sort of equilibrium that may permit him, even though at odds with himself, to continue the practice of his art without violating his own honesty. Analysis will show that most of Ransom's poems are objectifications of this little interior drama. . . . These poems are not mere commentary, however witty, on the nature and conduct of the external world.

Robert Penn Warren. Poetry. May, 1930. p. 111

No pavilioned clipper ships appear on his horizon; no peculiarities, human or zoological, except the actors in an occasional allegory; no flashing tropical color nor tinkling lilt of harlequinade enter his theater. He reflects sombrely on the inexorable duality of things, the gulf between the senses and the intellect, the body and head; between the life of actuality and the life of contemplation; between scientific knowledge and imaginative vision; between the joys of childhood and adult self-torment. His irony is the most important single element in his poetry. It dictates the subdued key which is so much more susceptible of subtle economics of tone-change than a larger volume would be. It restricts his language to the simple, lucid forms which take on a special sheen and sharpness when an oddity is dropped in their midst or a film of archaism passed over them. It infuses humor into his philosophic reflections and tempers his occasional solemnities.

Elizabeth Drew. Directions in Modern Poetry
(Norton). 1940. pp. 77–8

Without making a fetish of the Old South, Ransom is the last notable poet to express its more enduring and engaging qualities. . . . Ransom is quite capable of sympathy with the modern world, yet above all is heir of the best spirit of a fatherland dearer to its sons because of its heroic distrusts, so that a delicate irony pervades his verses. . . . The many parallels between the wit and irony in Ransom's verse and in the Elizabethans are again due to the history and mental climate of the South.

Henry W. Wells. *The American Way of Poetry*
(Columbia). 1945. pp. 161, 171

To be a Ransom in Tennessee is something more precious than it is easy to say. . . . Mr. Ransom's poems are composed of Tennessee. . . . He drew a picture of it, many pictures of it, in his book. The greater the value he set on it, the dearer it became, the more closely he sought out its precise line and look, the more it became a legend of things as they are when they are as we want them to be, without any of the pastiche of which the presence vulgarizes so many legends and possibly everything legendary in things, not as they are, but as we should like them to be.

Wallace Stevens. *SwR*. Summer, 1948. pp. 367–9

Ransom's production is small—his selected poems take up only seventy-four pages. . . . It is the work of a lifetime. When I reread it, I marveled at its weight—few English poets have written so many lyrics that one wants to read over and over again. . . . There is the language; it's a curious mixture of elaboration and bluntness; courtesy and rudeness. . . . To appreciate the language in Ransom's poems, you must realize that it is the language of one of the best talkers that has ever lived in the United States. . . . There is the unusual structural clarity, the rightness of tone and rhythm, the brisk and effective ingenuity, the rhetorical fire-works of expository description and dialogue; but even more: the sticking to concrete human subjects—the hardest; and a balance, control, matureness, nimbleness, toughness, and gentleness of temperament.

Robert Lowell. *SwR*. Summer, 1948. pp. 374–6

To my mind the most striking thing about John Crowe Ransom's poems is their elegance. . . . Elegance, in this connection, is a means to a precision of statement, more especially a means to the control of tone: it implies manners, or style. . . . The attitude I seek to distinguish has much to do with irony. . . . The emphasis of the poems is for the most part clearly on intellect and brilliance; the vocabulary is more than usually exotic, the rhymes are witty and boldly slanted, the poet's attitude and stance are in the main remote, often amused.

Howard Nemerov. *SwR*. Summer, 1948. pp. 417–422

Instead of listening to him through the hands, with closed eyes, as one is sucked deeper and deeper into the maelstrom, one listens with one's eyes wide open and one's head working about as well as it usually works. Most writers become over-rhetorical when they are insisting on more emotion than they actually feel or need to feel; Ransom is just the opposite. He is perpetually insisting, by his detached, mock-pedantic, wittily complicated tone, that he is not feeling much at all, not half as much as he really should be feeling.

Randall Jarrell. *Poetry and the Age* (Knopf). 1953.
pp. 98–9

Criticism

His chief criterion of literary excellence is metaphysical poetry. According to him it is the best poetry of the past, and poetry like it should be the poetry of the present. It is the finest way to express that concentration on the particular moment of experience which is the business of art as opposed to the less human, less adult business of science, which concentrates on the abstract.

Theodore Spencer. *NR*. Aug. 10, 1938. p. 27

Mr. Ransom . . . comes through as a kind of enlightened reactionary. He is too well-informed to be lumped with the ivory-tower school and too cynical to be lumped with any liberal one. . . . He has qualities of acumen and wit to which not very many critics of today can lay claim. But the problem of poetry today can hardly not be linked to the problem of human culture, which is plainly being menaced.

Louis Kronenberger. *Nation*. Aug. 13, 1938. pp. 161–2

He began by excoriating naturalism and positivism, yet ended by affirming that the analysis of the "structural properties" of poems were the main business of criticism. . . . This new criticism, based on a vicarious orthodoxy and textual analysis of advanced poetry, seemed . . . the only answer to the havoc of the times. . . . What one saw in the work of critics like Ransom and Tate, Blackmur and Yvor Winters, was the use of form as a mysterious ultimate value, form as a touchstone, a kind of apotheosis in a void.

Alfred Kazin. *On Native Grounds* (Reynal). 1942.
pp. 429–31

His major contribution to American criticism has been made through the *Kenyon Review,* which he has edited since 1939. . . . It is as a critic that Ransom is best known and most influential. He is the founder and leader of the Kenyon School—literally a school where the most distinguished critics have come to teach and lecture, and, less literally, that phase of contemporary criticism, usually designated as the "New

Criticism," which seeks to study poetry in terms of its structure (the logic of the poem) and its texture (the detail of the poem), quite apart from its historical and social contexts.

> Stanley J. Kunitz. *Twentieth Century Authors.*
> *First Supplement* (Wilson). 1955. p. 814

See *Selected Poems* and *The World's Body* (criticism).

REXROTH, KENNETH (1905–   )

At his best, he is a simple-minded man, with a liking for outdoors, in particular the high Sierra, and a decent reverence for nature and the stars. Of these he writes well; his observation is direct and immediate, leading him to the true line—"The stone is clean as light, the light steady as stone." . . . Mr. Rexroth's other aspect, the erudite indoor ponderer over many and difficult texts is less deserving of encouragement. . . . For his poetry's sake he would be well advised . . . to beat out of his head the idea that . . . abstractions, whether simple or involute, are the serviceable material of poetic art.

> Rolfe Humphries. *NR.* Aug. 12, 1940. p. 221

Rexroth owes a great deal to the early Ezra Pound. Imagism, D. H. Lawrence . . . and the Chino-Japanese lyricists are other discernible influences. . . . Which is not to say that Rexroth is not Rexroth. He has made a style, and an instantly recognizable one, out of the most tenuous elements. But its classicism, the rather self-conscious sensuality expressed in an equally self-conscious avoidance of rhetoric, is not what makes the poetry come to life. This spark is provided by observation, the delight in what used to be called Nature, and the choice of the appropriate word to express that delight.

> Selden Rodman. *NYHT.* May 7, 1950. p. 22

Rexroth is one of the leading craftsmen of the day. There is in him no compromise with the decayed line of past experience. His work is cleanly straightforward. The reek of polluted Shakespeare just isn't in it, or him. . . . As verse, reading them through, the plays (in *Beyond the Mountain*) are a delight to me for the very flow of words themselves. The pith is there, don't mistake me, and there with a jolt to it (in the very line, I want to make it clear) that goes well below the surface. But the way of the writing itself is the primary attraction. It palls, at times, I acknowledge it, but that is the defect of the method. It does not falsify. It is a feat of no mean proportions to raise the colloquial tone to lines of tragic significance.

William Carlos Williams. NYT. Jan. 28, 1951. p. 5

Anything Kenneth Rexroth writes is worth reading. He has a directness, a virile imaginative power, a seeming self-sufficiency rare among contemporary poets. As it does upon all men so the law of compensation operates upon him, and Rexroth's virtues as poet are liable also to exhibit overdoses of flat prosiness, traces of immature exhibitionism in the virile power, and occasional slapdash carelessness in the self-sufficiency. But take him by and large, he is one of our contemporary poets whose work is always interesting to read. (If that sounds like mild praise, such is not my intention: consider how seldom one can apply it.)

Winfield Townley Scott. NYHT. Feb. 1, 1953. p. 8

It is as though in Rexroth we had a Mark Twain who had grown up; who, without yielding an iota of his sense of the absurd and the pitiful, had discarded the clown's motley for the darker dress of the comic philosopher; and who had miraculously been endowed with the power of making poetry. This account (The Dragon and the Unicorn) of Rexroth's travels in England, Wales, France, Italy, and so on operates on many levels of which the surface one—narrative, anecdote, description—though the most entertaining, is the least ponderable. It is an indictment of society. It is an indictment of—well, not so much what America is doing to Europe, as what the whole of Western civilization is doing to itself. The J'accuse! is unanswerable.

Dudley Fitts. NR. Feb. 9, 1953. p. 19

Rexroth has invented a form with some help from Pound and Williams of short lines without rhyme. It is hard as prose and lithe as lyric. The combination, with an individualistic and controlled rhythm, makes it possible for the author to sustain his matter indefinitely.

The perfection of this new medium is striking. It enables Rexroth to express his most subtle philosophical generalizations, his strongest passions, the multifarious nature of his ideas with a kind of absolute accuracy. The lines are hard and clear, precise and lean, with continuous tensile strength and nothing fuzzy.

Richard Eberhart. NYT. Feb. 15, 1953. p. 25

I, for one, no longer object to this kind of plain, tight metrical practice as much as I did when discovering the great verbal musicians of our age. It has a good deal of variety of its own and is as essential a medium for his feeling as Cummings' syntactical whoopla for his, or Stevens' whimsical extravagance for his. If Rexroth sells short the more elaborate traditions, he does so consciously, and with a born affinity for other traditions no less important to the health of poetry. Rexroth's California, like Winters' and Jeffers', is a tradition in itself, a well-loved fastness from which a poet can hurl transcontinental thunderbolts at anything and everything that gets between him and the sun.

> R. W. Flint. *NR*. Feb. 18, 1957. p. 19

The poetry of self-exploration, which usually comes early, came late in Rexroth's writing   career. It is retrospective in character. . . . Elegies and epistles. Memories of his first wife, Andrée, who died young. Reliving their love in memory, trying to bridge the sense of separation with unmailable letters. . . . Trying to relate the personal experience to the social experience. . . . Trying to convince himself that in abandoning the "social" poem . . . or the "public speech" . . . he was still performing the function of the social poet. . . . And arriving at the "religious anarchism" which he would have us believe has been "the point of view . . . in all my work" from the beginning.

> Lawrence Lipton. *Poetry*. June, 1957. pp. 173–4

Kenneth Rexroth is the strongest of the West Coast anarchist poets because he is a good deal more than a West Coast anarchist poet. He is a man of wide cultivation and, when he is not too busy shocking the bourgeois reader . . . , a genuine poet. If fate had made Rexroth a Mormon or a Rhode Island Republican lawyer, he would still be able to write excellent poems. . . . Almost everything I have ever read by Rexroth has been worth reading, even when he was indulging himself, even when the piece was only half-finished, and even when he was both wrong and wrongheaded.

> M. L. Rosenthal. *Nation*. Sept. 28, 1957. pp. 199–200

The fineness of Kenneth Rexroth's *In Defense of Earth* depends on several virtues which are rare in this year but which are apparent in almost every one of the Rexroth poems: a lyric-minded-ness that has been prepared by many disciplines to summon up its music; a learning that eats the gifts of the world, knowing . . . how many cultures must be drawn on to make human fare; and that quality which has been talked about so much in speaking of Kenneth Rexroth and of those he has known in San Francisco: rage. . . . There is little enough control around anywhere this year, and less commitment. The sound of commitment comes through as the voice of anger. . . . Kenneth Rexroth is dealing with the plans of women and men in these magnificent poems, which are harsh, full of grace and certainty and grief: poems of the mountain nights.

Muriel Rukeyser. SR. Nov. 9, 1957. p. 15

See *Signature of All Things, The Dragon and the Unicorn,* and *In Defense of Earth* (poems); also *Behind the Mountain* (verse plays) and *Bird in the Bush* (essays).

RICE, ELMER (1892–)

Plays

Mr. Rice's vision of the world may infuriate you. . . . You cannot miss it; you cannot withdraw yourself from its coherence and completeness. Examine his play (*The Adding Machine*) scene by scene, symbol by symbol. The structure stands. There are no holes in its roof. It gives you the pleasure of both poetry and science, the warm beauty of life and love, the icy delight of mathematics. I am aware of the fact . . . that my profound sympathy with Mr. Rice's substance necessarily colored my reaction to his play. Not, however, to its form, not to the heartening fact that here is an American drama with no loose ends or ragged edges or silly last-act compromises, retractions, reconciliations. The work, on its own ground, in its own mood, is honest, finished, sound.

Ludwig Lewisohn. Nation. April 4, 1923. p. 399

Street Scene is, at bottom, conventional in form. Yet the swift, accurate, quickly changing manner of its acting, the finely adapted setting which shadows it and gives it an exciting unity, and the genius of the direction—Mr. Rice did this job himself—make it as new as even the very best of the downright stylized experiments. *Street Scene* proves what many of us have long suspected, that a new form in itself may not be a creation at all, that a traditional form, hammered and polished and fused in a white heat of imagination . . . will glow with as new a light as the wildest expedition into constructivism, expressionism, or any other rebellion born in the travail of dramatic experiment in Berlin or Moscow.

Robert Littell. TA. March, 1929. pp. 164–5

In everything he has written—melodrama, smart drama, expressionist drama, realist drama, he has shown himself a perfect technician. . . . With this equipment, and the gradual deepening of purpose which is evident through his writing, it is not idle to expect that Elmer Rice's major work in the theatre is yet to be done. The least that he can give is a chronicle of American scenes done in an American way, a procession of characters whose externals of manner and speech are perfectly reproduced. . . , but in his latter plays he has given evidence that he has the power to quicken these characters with the kind of life that makes "pure music" out of "program music."

Meyer Levin. *TA*. Jan., 1932. p. 62

In contrast to *Street Scene* which was universal, Elmer Rice's latest play, *We, the People,* is of a particular day and mood. It is vibrantly of the present moment, almost hysterically so at times. It is a play of angry and ironic protest against the broader aspects of social injustice in times like these and against special and particular forms of injustice and hypocrisy. Hot fury runs through it like a fever, the more so because delusions are often mixed with realities and half truths with honest statements of fact. The delusions and half-truths concern chiefly the inner motives of some of the leading characters. The honest facts relate to happenings recorded with tragic monotony in every edition of every newspaper. . . . The play provides a stirring experience, and makes an appeal, no matter how prejudiced it may seem, to the fires of self-examination which are slowly kindling beneath the agony of our day.

Richard Dana Skinner. *Com*. Feb. 8, 1933. p. 411

As art *We, the People* has now and again precisely the limitations that Mr. Rice's plays have often had. I am surprised that so many judgments of the new piece have turned on the talking, the haranguing, the raw statement of causes and thoughts. This is what Mr. Rice did in *Street Scene* and in *The Left Bank,* though the love story and the various esthetic considerations eased the tedium of a lack of creation in the dramatist. . . . This talk without creation appeared and heavily, in the young heroine's long speech in the last act of *Street Scene,* and almost constantly in *The Left Bank*. As a matter of fact, the new play has less of it, what with the push of the many scenes to be presented.

Stark Young. *NR*. Feb. 15, 1933. p. 19

With *Two on an Island* Mr. Rice, I think, resumes his place among the best of our comic writers, along with the Messrs. Behrman, Barry, and Kaufman. . . . Neither the comic insight nor the wit of Mr. Rice is like that of any of the others, and it rests, one might say, on a broader base, derives from the spirit of a larger mass of people. It is not merely that his favorite characters are landladies, taxi drivers, and the

like, persons whose knowingness is combined with an innocent un-
sophistication. It is also that the whole flavor of his writing is more
robust, more earthy, less narrowly local, and less highly specialized
in spirit if not in manner. Of the four he is the most inclusively American, and without him the quartet would represent far less completely
than it does the comic spirit of this nation.

Joseph Wood Krutch. Nation. Feb.. 3, 1940. p. 136

Elmer Rice is a heavy-set man with reddish hair who does not look
anywhere near fifty one. A serious, conscientious person, he still has
a lot of humor—the wry, understated kind—and his quietness makes it
hard to imagine him ever blowing up about anything. Nevertheless he
has always been mixed up in controversies; he is a great man for
taking a stand about anything, from the destructive influence of the
critics on the theatre to world problems of today. . . . Politically
Elmer Rice has always been firmly and vocally to the Left. Which is
consistent, because it would be odd if a man who has always been a
persistent experimentalist in art forms should turn out to be, ideo-
logically, a conservative.

Elizabeth-R. Valentine. NYT mag. Sept. 12, 1943. p. 15

Elmer Rice in Dream Girl has broken away from his usual preoccupation with the state of the nations to contemplate fondly, and at great
length, the naive charms of a sweet young thing as she wrestles with
her adolescent problems. . . . Mr. Rice plays exclusively with the
surface of this young girl's mind. She is not asleep; she is merely indulging in the kind of futile and entirely volitional day dreaming to
which we are all prone. She fancies herself in all sorts of heroic attitudes—a prisoner in the dock, a prostitute, a great actress reciting the
"quality of mercy" speech. As a result the play is a tour-de-force in
quick changes and continuous action but it lacks psychological and
emotional content.

Rosamond Gilder. TA. Feb., 1946. pp. 78–9

In the half-bakery of Broadway, the belated recognition of the science
of psychiatry usually results in a kind of convention of disorder the moment the faculty of imagination (healthy or otherwise) is summoned
by one or other members of a cast. Immediately, enormous, unidentifi-
able, tenanted visions—often in the form of ballets—are sprung out of
nowhere and swirled and swooped for no discernible reason other than
ART, one supposes, or POETRY, or some equivalent miscalculation.
In his depiction of a heroine who spends a long day largely dreaming it,
while Mr. Rice has given himself almost unlimited opportunities for

flight and figment, he has, I think, got off on the right foot. Beginning with *character,* his fantasies are naturally ordered: the dreams fit into the day so to speak; there are no figurations too alarming, interesting, or expensive for the size of the figurer; all the shadows are owned. If the case-history seems somewhat simple, nevertheless it is true, and its people are alive.

Kappo Phelan. *Com.* Feb. 15, 1946. p. 457

Novels

Here in a satire (*Voyage to Purilia*) which is both nimble-witted and pervasive, and which at times attains the implacable complexity of a nightmare, the author of *Street Scene* pays his respects to that planet known to astronomers as Purilia, where life is so utterly different from that of earth as to be almost incomprehensible. Not since Merton of the Movies announced that his wife was his best pal and his severest critic has there been anything as detached and scarifying as this excursion into the unplumbed vacuity of the celluloid. This is satire of a high order, so high that it at times suggests the Golden Ass of Apuleius.

John Carter. *NYT.* March 23, 1930. p. 2

Mr. Elmer Rice's *Voyage to Purilia* is an amusing satire on the American film. It is a short book, gracefully and gaily written. Mr. Rice, according to his diary, sets off in an aeroplane for the undiscovered country, known to no terrestial map, where cinema scenarios come into being. From the first moment when he gets among the "soft, pink mists" and the unceasing sentimental music that surround the new planet, until the moment when his Purilian bride, much to his disappointment, dissolves on the altar steps in the Nirvana of a fade-out, there is no experience known to humanity, and yet there is no situation or sentiment that is not an admired commonplace of the movies.

Hubert Griffith. *NSN.* Sept. 27, 1930. p. 764

The theatre novel is traditionally a bête noir. . . . Now, in *The Show Must Go On,* Elmer Rice has done very well with the subject. And what could be more appropriate, for he can write as one in authority and not as the scribe. This makes his story, apart from its other qualities, as complete and clinical a primer of how our American theatre runs in its every aspect as any aspirant thereto could desire. It reveals, also, the lofty concept of the theatre artist's obligation to his craft that has always distinguished Mr. Rice and made him one of the most constructive, as well as gifted, people in it. . . . He does not write a distinguished prose but in most other respects, such as characterization and dialogue and story sense, his talents as dramatist carry over into the narrative medium.

Edmund Fuller. *SR*. Oct. 15, 1949. p. 15

See *The Adding Machine, Street Scene, Counsellor-at-Law,* and *Dream Girl* (plays); also *Voyage to Purilia* and *The Show Must Go On* (novels).

RICHTER, CONRAD (1890–   )

Mr. Richter, unmoved by the stormier phases of frontier life, is attracted by small authenticities, by the unaffected kindliness of simple people who face life with bare hands, by a sort of temperature refinement which is characteristic of isolated people, by a romanticism which sees something vague and incomprehensible in the daily walk, by the pathos which hangs about those who play a lone hand.

It must be a careless reader who fails to realize that here is an admirably trained intellect with fine perception of character reproducing impressions of life; not the life of today, but of a past neglected by historians and enshrined in forgotten newspapers.

Charles J. Finger. *SR*. Aug. 8, 1936. p. 7

Though there is a slight element . . . of sententious platitudinizing . . . there is much more than that. There is research, sincerity, imagination and beauty of writing. It is escape literature of a high-class sort . . . that is, it sets the mind free and refreshes it with images and figures from an innocent, half legendary world; a world as far removed from us as if it were another planet, but real all the same, and comforting as rain in a parched land. . . . Richter makes skilful use of his evidently profound historical studies, and the picture of pioneer life he builds up is extraordinarily concentrated, detailed and vivid.

Rosamond Lehmann. *Spec*. May 17, 1940. p. 694

Mr. Richter has hoarded up every savorous and homely detail of the life of the early nineteenth century . . . and now pours them out. The result is as American as goldenrod or Indian pudding. . . . (His novels are) written with infinite care to make the atmosphere and background authentic and convincing. The furniture and utensils in the cabin, the phrases of the dialogue, the hymns sung at the prayer meeting—all seem just right. But one might admire Mr. Richter for his exactitude on these points and still not count him a good novelist. However he does succeed in making the stuff of life flow in the veins of most of the people who inhabit these careful settings of his.

Theodore M. Purdy. *SR*. April 13, 1946. p. 72

In his handling of the past Conrad Richter is an artist in prose. His short, compact novels demonstrate the fact that story-telling need not be subordinated to documentation of history, for reality of the imagination can be made more compelling than the appearance of fact. To him a story is always a record of human experience, regardless of time or setting. In short, he has been writing novels while other and more popular writers were turning out sword-and-musket romances or historical theses dressed up as fiction.

Dayton Kohler. EJ. September, 1946. p. 364

Conrad Richter has been steadily piling up a record for solid and distinguished achievement. His writing is distinguished and poetic both as to character and image. It is intensely atmospheric and backed in the case of the historical novels on sound research. Moreover he has the supreme gift of novelists in creating a world of utter reality in which the reader is able to lose himself completely after the first page or two.

Louis Bromfield. NYHT. April 23, 1950. p. 5

In 1928 Conrad Richter, thirty-eight years old and all his novels yet unwritten, moved from Pennsylvania to New Mexico. The Southwest was not wholly new to him; from early boyhood he had heard tales of New Mexico from relatives who had lived there in territorial times. And having moved two thousand miles away, he did not forget his ancestral country. As a writer he found himself inhabiting both backgrounds and looking back to a vanished past: to the late eighteenth century in the Allegheny frontier and to the late nineteenth century in New Mexico. The two lands, so unlike to the senses, he found alike in their demands upon the people who would possess them and in the opportunity they offered for bold, far-reaching actions. . . . To both his eastern and western frontier settings Conrad Richter brings a chivalrous respect. The great forest and the high plains are the frontiersman's adversaries, and at the same time they are his magnificent birthright.

Walter Havighurst. SR. May 25, 1957. p. 14

The Trilogy—The Trees, The Fields, The Town

Mr. Richter's indubitable learning is worn so lightly that one has no sense at all that this is a "historical" novel or that its people are playing character parts in a costume play. You feel them as individuals, some of whom lived by the forest; others, to subdue it; and still others to be killed by it. In a setting so alien that it is hard for city folks to realize it, he shows movingly what were those other ways in which these Americans found joy, terror, and satisfaction in living, in which they earned their livelihood, showed their love of family and home.

Mary Ross. NYHT. March 3, 1940. p. 2

Mr. Richter saw his trilogy, both structurally and humanly, in the shape of one of those trees, the fate which symbolizes the entire progress in Sayward's mind. *The Trees,* in which Sayward must turn mother and father to her brothers and sisters in their forest hut, is a kind of trunk to the whole, a direct and simple tale of a life narrow and strong and dark. In *The Fields,* with the coming of neighbors and clearings, and the development of Sayward's own life as wife and actual mother, there is a branching out of purposes and interests and a brightening of atmosphere. And now, in *The Town,* the longest and most complex story of the three, comes the leafing out of the many who flourish better in the sun of man's laws than in the primeval gloom of nature's.

Walter Van Tilburg Clark. *NYT.* April 23, 1950. p. 4

Like all good works of fiction Conrad Richter's fiction means different things to different people. Simply stated, his trilogy is the story of the realization of the great American dream. In the time between the Revolution and the Civil War a port of timber by a river grew to be Americus, a prosperous town with a waterfront, many churches, and a railroad; and in this town there was a fine brick house where died a rich old woman who remembered the green twilight of the great forest and how it was to live from the woods with neither bread nor salt. The pioneers have conquered everything—trees, Indians, loneliness, mud, distance, ignorance, poverty—for some everything is conquered except ambition, death, fear of change, and such things as ugliness and the smell of the waterfront.

Harriette Arnow. *SR.* May 16, 1953. p. 13

See *Sea of Grass, The Trees, The Fields, The Town, Always Young and Fair,* and *The Lady* (novels).

ROBERTS, ELIZABETH MADOX (1886–1941)

Again and again of course she returned (and still returns) to Kentucky; I never saw her there. But wherever she is, it evidently underlays the outbranching experience, folded shadowily into the typical scenes of an author's life—an immense territorial ghost. Its past, still animated in her imagination, accompanied the present. One who knew her but had never traveled to Louisville and beyond was always aware of it, as vivid in her talk, her shepherdess's far-sighted gaze, the archaic foldings of her hands, as on the most evocative pages; in her company one never seemed to be altogether where one was in reality, with that spiritual landscape in the air! And with herself, though always keeping in character, it also underwent impressive changes.

Glenway Wescott. Bkm. March, 1930. p. 13

Miss Roberts' work is free of sentimentality, but its realism, like that of Chaucer, is permeated with romance, with glamour. This is possible because she has discarded the poor old worn-out duality of body and mind from which the sordidness of realism springs. Her leading characters, to whom she entrusts the task of directly or obliquely conveying her idea, experience life with their whole bodies indivisible, think with their whole bodies. This extraordinary sensitiveness not only enriches common experience, but establishes also a community of living between the character and the grasses, the cows, the birds, amidst which she works.

J. D. Robins. CF. Nov., 1930. pp. 66–7

Her language, it should be said at once, is in itself a thing of perpetual delight—taut with wit as well as languorous with longing for certitude. It is the mixture of these elements in it that accounts for its pre-eminence over the language of other southern novelists today who try perhaps to do the same thing Miss Roberts is doing. They fail because they lack her complexity of mind which, after everything else is said, is the thing we come back to when we are explaining the excellence of a novelist or artist of any kind. Her language is the language of her own mind; and so is everything in her novels typical of her own character.

Mark Van Doren. EJ. Sept., 1932. p. 528

The time is ripe, I think, to evaluate the work of Elizabeth Madox Roberts in the novel. Let me say at the outset that I consider her to be a writer of genius, one who at her best has written scenes which stand with the finest in the history of fiction. I draw no qualifications to this—I say the finest and I mean the finest, whether in the Russian, French, or English novel. I think that this occasional mastery of hers has not yet received its due recognition, and I think too that her work as a path-breaker in the art of fiction has not yet been fully understood. At the same time I am equally of the opinion that her shortcomings have not been adequately discussed. She has received high praise which was not high enough; but also, along with some very invalid adverse criticism, there has been insufficient mention of certain weaknesses which have kept Miss Roberts from reaching her potential stature as a creative artist. . . . They are in part the product, it seems to me, of a too great turning inward—an ever present danger to the mystically inclined mind. The very habits of thought which give depth and power to her work are also those which obscure it. . . . Her style, as everyone who knows her work is aware, is extraordinarily perceptive, rich in the power of suggestion, and sustained by subtle and very beautiful rhythms. But it is sometimes and, I think, increasingly, indirect and tenuous.

J. Donald Adams. *VQR.* Jan., 1936. pp. 80–90

The critical neglect of Elizabeth Madox Roberts during the last few years of her life and since her death in 1941 is indeed hard to account for. . . . Though Miss Roberts did not write so much as Cather, her four best novels are on the whole quite as good as the four best of Cather; in fact, in some ways, especially in her poetic imagination and her gift for penetrating satire, Miss Roberts is decidedly superior to Cather. Indeed Miss Roberts' poetic imagination, or what E. M. Forster in reference to D. H. Lawrence has called "the rapt bardic quality," makes her best work worthy of comparison in this respect with the best of Lawrence and Faulkner.

Harry Modean Campbell. *SWR.* Autumn, 1954.

p. 337

The Time of Man

I have compared this novel to Reymont's tetralogy and, putting the relative smallness of the scale aside, Miss Roberts' book does not suffer much from the comparison. Like Reymont, Miss Roberts seems absolutely saturated in her material and capable of using it with a freedom which suggests rather an intimate experience than any laborious documentation. Moreover she seems to owe little to any of the schools of fiction which have hitherto busied themselves with the treatment of American provincial life. Her mood is original, powerful, and without ever verging upon sentimentality, tender.

Joseph Wood Krutch. *SR.* Aug. 28, 1926. p. 69

Poetry

Miss Roberts's art consists most often in juxtaposing simple physical details of a landscape or situation in such a way that they act upon and limit each other definitely and minutely, without being at any point similar or parts of each other. They are simply carefully ordered parts of a whole, and bear in every case an intimate relationship to the sound movement. . . . Occasionally she lets a rhythm that has already been used in this manner carry over its emotion as a sort of superimposed comment upon lines, the content of which is too far removed from the physical to fuse with sound.

Yvor Winters. *Poetry.* April, 1923. p. 47

Miss Roberts's most characteristic invention is a poem of the following kind. . . : a combination of an impulsive feeling, somewhat indeterminate in its object—longing, the sense of being haunted—with an objective and even minute picture of agricultural activity. The feeling is given especially in the lilting rhythm, either moderately lilting, as with anapests among iambs, or strongly lilting, breaking down ordinary double-meters into amphimacer and amphibrachs, to the point of song. . . . At her best, Miss Roberts is deep in the forty years of the American Renascence, drawing on both its inspiration of expressing feeling by pictures and feeling and thought by actuality.

Paul Goodman. *Poetry*. Oct., 1940. pp. 43–5

See *The Time of Man, My Heart and My Flesh, The Great Meadow,* and *Black Is My True Love's Hair* (novels); also *Under the Tree* and *Song in the Meadow* (poetry).

ROBERTS, KENNETH (1885–1957)

Surely in these novels the reader enjoys a remarkable visualization of place and incident. One never loses touch with the people or their story. The secret of this power is probably in the apt use of a vast store of historical details gathered through years of study. This power of keeping the object clearly before the reader is also, I believe, a direct result of Mr. Roberts' years of experience as a newspaperman. Journalism is a good training for a novelist, for it teaches him to get the necessary details for a clear view of an incident and for a coherent story. One also enjoys knowing that in Roberts' novels the specific details of history are the authentic results of sound research.

Chilson H. Leonard. *Kenneth Roberts* (Doubleday).

1936. p. 16

His earlier books, the stories of Arundel and the two sea stories, are conventional historical narratives, traditionally romantic in outline but original and realistic in detail, unreflective, rapid, and usually superficial in their feeling for history. By superficial I do not mean to derogate from Mr. Roberts' rich inventiveness nor to deny that he has a fine eye for the characteristic, the picturesque, and the historically appropriate; I mean that he has been indifferent to the energies and movements of which the events he describes were a specific expression, that he has not bothered about their relation to the age.

Bernard De Voto. *SR*. July 3, 1937. p. 5

For something like twenty years Kenneth Roberts has been reminding Americans of their heritage—how once men discovered that this was a mighty continent, a land of untold wealth for hardy people, with huge forests to be turned into homes, fertile lands to till, great rivers for fish and traffic, abundance of wild life and mountains full of metals. The hardy men came, his romances report, from several nations, to fight and scheme against one another and the original possessors, and against the wily boys from home with an eye to their own main chance. In spite of his Saturday Evening Post background of affiliations and ideas, Kenneth Roberts has written some good novels about this country; the black and white demarcations of his pamphleteering shade off into the lighter and darker grays of reality in his best fiction.

B. E. Bettinger. *NR*. July 14, 1937. p. 287

One of my numerous and heretical opinions is that Kenneth Roberts has no particular talent for writing fiction. As a novelist he gets by, I think, as in the Arundel series and in *Northwest Passage,* wholly because he is primarily a most excellent nonfiction writer. . . . He gets some fire and force into his yarns out of pure resentment against the myths handed down from one to another, by the academic historians. . . . If we decide we are going to have history and put it into books, let it be history, not legend. Roberts feels that way about it, and I'm for him.

The thing that makes him good in this respect, of course, is the thing that militates against his being a very good writer of fiction. Fiction . . . is not concerned with facts or even with minor truths: it is concerned with the universal truths.

Burton Rascoe. *Nwk*. June 20, 1938. p. 31

Mr. Roberts' . . . best talents lie in the swift narration of some tale of heroic exertions or resistances. Nobody better than he can bring a battle, a siege, a toilsome march, a wrestle with overmastering moral and material forces, vividly before us. He has a fine power of visualization, an even finer faculty for enlisting the reader in the ardors and endurances of some embattled body of men. When it comes to the presentation of gentler scenes, whether in drawing rooms, courts, or congresses, he is much less effective. Nor is he skilled in the integration of a far-reaching and highly varied piece of fiction.

Allan Nevins. *SR*. Nov. 23, 1940. p. 5

He is a hater of shams, pretensions, self-deceptions, fallacies; and he particularly hates the persistent distortion of history. In what would be for him the best possible world, every history would be written with a fine impartiality and by a neutral party. He is tireless in hunting out proof that Colonials during the Revolutionary period were (a) dauntless heroes, or (b) blovalating politicians and self-seekers; the choice depending on which misconception he is at the moment engaged in setting right. He is equally tireless in proving that all British and Tories were (a) cultivated and intelligent gentlemen abused by the Colonials, or (b) tyrannical rascals abusing the Colonials.

For Ken, who expects from the historian a remote impartiality, himself always has a thesis to demonstrate. His thesis is the unrecognized truth; and he will with the most laborious research write a book to prove that on a given subject everyone who believes what everyone else believes is wrong!

Ben Ames Williams. Introduction to *The Kenneth Roberts Reader* (Dutton). 1945. p. ix

I wish Mr. Roberts had a clearer idea of what to eliminate from his first drafts. His novels, even the best of them, have a tendency to sprawl, and in this case (*Lydia Bailey*), as in *Northwest Passage,* there are a beginning, a middle, and an end, and then without pause for breath, another beginning and middle and end. It adds up to too much, and in the protraction, in the constant shift from one background to the next, the main characters lose their orientation, they become flat rather than forceful, the victims of romance rather than of a reality.

Edward Weeks. *At.* Feb. 1947. p. 130

Kenneth Roberts is a big, hearty, vital, opinionated, hasty-tempered man. He hates politicians, hypocrisy, corruption, cowardice, and tyranny. He loves food, action, valor, independence, and the very stuff of history itself. All this is plain as a pikestaff in his books. He is uninterested in, or incapable of, the subtleties of fiction as an art. His plots are crude and clumsy, his virtuous characters only stilted puppets. But he is a superb chronicler of violence, battle, massacre, rape, flight, and pursuit. He is wonderfully effective in his portraits of picturesque, eccentric, lusty men of action. And always his enormous relish for the life of the past endows his work with a living background of interest in itself.

Orville Prescott. *YR.* Spring, 1947. p. 573

Though his novels . . . suffer from unnecessary repetitions and occasional lags, they have a definite advantage over most other period novels, and this is the unobstrusive introduction of a fundamental human problem—namely the clash of the attitude of loyalty with independent pragmatic judgment in one and the same person. . . . It is true that this conception does not appear to be strong enough to lift these novels to the plane of an irrational and feverish search for some kind of non-pragmatic values as, say, in Thomas Wolfe's novels, but it carries enough weight to keep the intelligent reader's attention and sympathy through the stories.

Heinrich Straumann. American Literature in the
Twentieth Century (Hutchinson). 1951. p. 67

This "implacable detestation of false men and evil measures," this moral impatience which he attributes to America, severely cripples Mr. Roberts' imagination. No doubt his intolerance is well grounded in reason and experience, and it will be as Richard Wilbur puts it, that, "In a time of continual dry abdication/ And of damp complicities" Mr. Roberts' narrow rectitude is the proper tonic. I doubt it, though.

Thomas E. Curley. Com. Feb. 10, 1956. p. 496

See *Arundel, Boon Island, Captain Caution, Lively Lady, Northwest Passage,* and *Oliver Wiswell* (novels).

ROBINSON, EDWIN ARLINGTON (1869–1935)

He has an ascetic hatred for the trite word, the facile phrase, the rhetorical cadence. His individual idiom—as clearly marked as John Donne's, whom he resembles in many ways—was apparent from the first. . . . The thought is packed very tight, except in the humorous diffusion and willful Wordsworthian flatness of occasional passages in the monologues. The athletic sparseness of epithet, the suppression of climaxes, the projection of the planes of the poem beyond the lines of the poem itself—these are Robinsonian characteristics that will continue to repel some readers as certainly as they fascinate the adepts.

Bliss Perry. NYT. Dec. 21, 1919. p. 765

Robinson had discovered that simply by making a plain statement of certain important things, he achieved a poetic effect unlike anything known to poetry except possibly the ballad. . . . Robinson wrote in the old meters. He often employed stock poetic phrases. But all the stanza forms he used resolved themselves to the level of the ballad statement of fact, and stock poetic phrases were an ironic reflection on the poverty of a life of which the phrase was the sole grandeur.

Samuel Roth. Bkm. Jan., 1920. pp. 507–8

Now Mr. Robinson is a dyed-in-the-wool New Englander, and that must never be forgotten. His tenacity of purpose is thoroughly New England, so is his austerity and his horror of exuberance of expression. His insight into people is pure Yankee shrewdness, as is also his violent and controlled passion. He is absolutely a native of his place, the trouble was that he was not a native of his time. He was twenty years ahead of his time, and that advance has set the seal of melancholy upon him; or, to speak in the cant of the day, it has wound him in inhibitions which he has been unable to shake off.

Amy Lowell. *Dial*. Feb., 1922. p. 133

Mr. Robinson, even in youth, was a poet of failure and regret. He was preoccupied with New England in decay. In the moonlight of an eternal autumn he sat brooding on the poor ghosts of men—brooding sadly rather than in grief. . . . And since Mr. Robinson began in autumn he has never had his rightful spring. He was old from the very first. When his time came for him to be really old, his trees were doubly bare.

Edmund Wilson. *Dial*. May, 1923. p. 516

If the psychology of failure, or of that uncertain middle ground between spiritual success and failure, is Robinson's recurrent motive, it may be interesting to study his attitudes and his methods in presenting that motive in art. It is heroic, not ignoble, struggle that engages him, or if not heroic, at least the struggle of highly strung, sensitive souls to fulfil their manifest destiny; ending either in acceptance of compromise, or in tragic spiritual revolt that induces some kind of dark eclipse. The form is usually narrative, with the poet as the narrator, under some assumption of friendship or at least neighborliness; but in the longer poems we have, as a rule, monologue and dialogue, the characters unfolding their perplexities, or recording their action upon each other, in long speeches which are not talk, as talk actually ever was or could be, but which are talk intensified into an extra-luminous self-revelation; as if an x-ray, turned into the suffering soul, made clear its hidden structural mysteries.

Harriet Monroe. *Poetry*. Jan. 1925. p. 210

Robinson's portrait of the American failure (a failure arrived at through the misapplication of New England pragmatism) is so complete, that the fact many of his books became best sellers must be a source of quiet amusement to him. There lies the irony more profound than anything Robinson has written. He remains, as always, the most unshaken, the most unmoved of America's critics, his clinical finger piercing an open wound. He has made his one discovery, has patented it; sometimes the statement produces poetry, sometimes merely words, but there it is; and it would take another reincarnation of Robinson to deny it.

Horace Gregory. *Poetry*. Dec., 1934. pp. 160–1

His artistry has much of the Yankee in it: on the one hand, its laconic, word-sparing quality and its tendency to understatement; on the other, its gift for circumlocution when this device will either conceal or veil what the Yankee has in mind or what is in his mood. . . . Moreover, it is this trait of expressing by indirection that makes Robinson seem more exclusively intellectual than he actually is. The man who does not wear his heart on his sleeve is not therefor heartless, but he is bound sometimes to produce that impression. And the man who on occasion talks by indirection or . . . so curtly that he throws away everything but the meaning—and keeps that to himself, does not always suffer from a tertian ague of tongue-tiedness and verbosity.

Percy H. Boynton. *Literature and American Life*
(Ginn). 1936. pp. 804–5

His lyric perceptions, like his human values, are rooted in the known and possible—the capacities of a man which survive even in his sorriest condition of stultification and confusion. . . . He is a realist not only in conscience but in style and diction; in *milieu* as much as in imagery; and this gives him his license to explore the problems of abstract casuistry and moral contradiction which he filed down into that style of attenuated rumination, impassioned hair-splitting, and bleak aphorism which will always remain unmistakably his own.

Morton D. Zabel. *Literary Opinion in America*
(Harper). 1937. p. 405

Edwin Arlington Robinson personified winter. Abandoning New England, he had carried to New York an aura of blight, desolation, decay, and defeat. His view of the world was wintry,—so was his life,—and his style and his personality were bleak and bare. Had there ever been a poet who loved life less or found so little joy in the turning of the seasons? In the down-east phrase, Robinson was "master chilly."

Van Wyck Brooks. *New England: Indian Summer*
(Dutton). 1940. pp. 490–1

Because his own poetry was based so firmly on his personal and sensitive appreciation of what was unchanging and available in the poetry of the past, Robinson was finally able to contemplate the future with some equanimity. Subsequent revolutions in taste have somewhat impared the reputation he finally won toward the end of his career, but these revolutions have also shown that some of Robinson's poetry did attain the stature at which he aimed and that it will not be quickly forgotten. There can be little doubt that his best work is now part of the ideal order by which he always wished to be measured.

Edwin S. Fussell. *Edwin Arlington Robinson*
(California). 1954. p. 186

Shorter Poems

Mr. Robinson's shorter poems are many and various, and the perfection they reach is remarkably many-sided. In blank verse, in talkative rhyme, in suave epigram, in running eloquence he has found his forms; in men of all conditions and characters he has found his material. But he is still consistent . . . in his presentation of the problem which existence is. A little light in a great deal of darkness, a wisp of music in a universe of irregular and ominous drums—it is in such images that he tells . . . of man's never wholly vain struggle for self-respect.

Mark Van Doren. *Edwin Arlington Robinson*
(Literary Guild). 1927. pp. 49–50

As with the passage of time their quality stands out from the bulky later work that tends to hide them, as the nation in maturing, gains in respect for the intellectual and contemplative virtues and sees behind material satisfactions the tragedy of human condition and feels the glory of art that in accepting tragedy transcends it, Robinson's figure will grow.

Emery Neff. *Edwin Arlington Robinson* (Sloane).
1948. p. 259

See *Collected Poems*.

ROETHKE, THEODORE (1908–1963)

A good poet can be recognized by his tense awareness of both chaos and order, the arbitrary and the necessary, the fact and the pattern. . . . By such a test Mr. Roethke is instantly recognizable as a good poet. . . . Many people have the experience of feeling physically soiled and humiliated by life; some quickly put it out of their mind, others gloat narcissistically on its unimportant details; but both to remember and to transform the humiliation into something beautiful, as Mr. Roethke does, is rare.

W. H. Auden. *SR*. April 5, 1941. pp. 30–1

Theodore Roethke uses flowers, wind, water, and such materials of art and nature to express his views of them and of larger issues. . . . These serve him as images often presented with the clear sharp colors of the objects and then are transformed into symbols of human struggle or contemplation. . . . Mr. Roethke does evoke the turbulent anxieties of a young man and the return of a hard-won equilibrium with many lines of considerable talent.

Eugene Davidson. *YR*. Summer, 1948. p. 747

What Roethke brings us . . . is news of the root, of the minimal, of the primordial. The sub-human is given tongue; and the tongue proclaims the agony of coming alive, the painful miracle of growth. Here is poetry immersed in the destructive element.

Stanley Kunitz. *Poetry*. Jan., 1949. p. 225

He meets, in his way, the problem which Eliot met in another by expanding his poetry to encompass theological doctrine, and thereby including a terminology which, within the Roethke rules, would be ungainly (unless used ironically—and children don't take to irony). Eliot added winds of doctrine. Roethke "regressed" as thoroughly as he could, even at considerable risk, toward a language of sheer intuition.

Kenneth Burke. *SwR*. Jan., 1950. p. 102

With many a writer who affects to plumb the depths of his own unconsciousness, one feels that after he has dived into the bathysphere, he is only too apt to emerge with nothing but the bathetic—or the banal—and that if he comes up with something rich and strange, or only grotesque, one cannot feel sure but that he has planted his deep-sea bucket in advance with a few specimens of starfish and sea-urchins, not to mention an old boot or two, just to make it look better. Mr. Roethke is more convincing; he has established, and this is a matter of technique as surely as feats of prosody, avenues of communication to his own unconsciousness. . . . Adept at breathing, so to speak through his gills, Mr. Roethke seems to me a little less sure of himself when it is time to use his lungs.

Rolfe Humphries. *Nation*. March 22, 1952. p. 284

By the controlled restriction of his theme, the intense hyperbolical sexual wit, the almost perceptual level of his language, Roethke asks of us the most delicate reading even for sympathetic appreciation, let alone an evaluation. He has launched a brilliant and to a large degree victorious assault upon deadening abstractions in poetry.

Frederick Brantley. *YR*. Spring, 1952. p. 476

Roethke's work is his own. His shorter poems are distinguished not so much by their matter . . . but by their tone. He manages to escape the pedestrian flatness of some of his fellows and the strained intellectualiam of others. He has as much to say of the interior landscape as of that without, and writes with particular acuteness of the nameless malaise of the spirit. His work gains from the fact that his childhood was intimately bound up with the life of a Michigan greenhouse, which physically and otherwise, was to afford the material for some of his best lyrics. . . . Shifting cadences and homely images taken from childhood memories of the floriculturist's world, meanings as evasive as some secretive animal and equally frightening, produce unusual and powerful effects. These poems are an account of the journey through the dark wood—here symbolized by stagnant water, among other forms of death—into the light that clothes the visible in the garments of eternity.

Babette Deutsch. Poetry in Our Time (Holt). 1952.
pp. 182–3

Roethke's is the poetry of therapy; it dances its way from madness (symbolized by the wet riot of vegetable roots and the grossness of flesh) to a reflective calm (winter and distance). It is the richness and variety of Roethke's rhythm together with the shock and clarity of his broken phrases that persuades. Roethke slams into his dance, arms in air and ranting like a sibyl. His style seems most nearly founded on Christopher Smart, Blake, the Elizabethan rant, and the backwoods brag, all scattering free, but always with a sense of breaking through a tremendous formal control. Roethke's strength is that he never talks about his subject matter but enters and performs it. The best measure of his achievement is that there are now a subject, a rhythm, and a kind of perception that are specifically Roethkean.

John Ciardi. Nation. Nov. 14, 1953. p. 410

Mr. Roethke has accepted the evolutionary story as a chart for his poetic voyage. And derived much joy from this newly-discovered closeness to the rest of earth's creatures. . . . Indeed, one of the striking things about Mr. Roethke's poetic stance is this very joyousness. . . . There is considerable experimentalism, the odd originality of the child . . . which, however, is at least partially backed by a symbolism more than childlike.

Gerard Previn Meyer. SR. Jan. 16, 1954. p. 19

A very good poet is Theodore Roethke. From the precise statements of Open House (1941) through the sensuous wilderness of Praise to *the End* (1951) he has arrived at the wild precision of his most recent verse. . . . Never, in Roethke's "free verse," is there a hint of the arbitrary; every line is glued in place, as fixed as in his regular forms. . . . He is more accomplished outside conventional forms than any poet since Wallace Stevens.

Donald Hall. *NWW* 7. 1955. pp. 236–7

It is sufficiently clear by now that Theodore Roethke is a very important poet. . . . These poems appear, at first glance, to be uncontrollable and subliminal outcries, the voices of roots, stones, leaves, logs, small birds; and they also resemble the songs in Shakespearean plays, Ophelia's songs perhaps most of all. This surface impression is genuine and ought not to be disregarded. But it is only the surface, however moving, and as such it can be misleading or superficial. The reader who supposes that Roethke is really a primitive lyric poet loses or misses a great deal. . . . Throughout his work, Roethke uses a *variety* of devices with the utmost cunning and craft to bring the unconsciousness to the surface of articulate expression.

Delmore Schwartz. *Poetry*. June, 1959. p. 203

See *Open House, The Lost Son, Praise to the End, The Waking,* and *Words for the Wind* (poetry).

RUKEYSER, MURIEL (1913–   )

Theory of Flight is one of those rare first volumes which impress by their achievement more than by their promise. It is remarkable poetry to have been written by a girl of twenty-one, and would do credit to most of her elders. . . . Here is a well-stored, vigorous mind attempting to bring its world into some kind of imaginative and human order. . . . Miss Rukeyser's poems are among the few so far written in behalf of the revolutionary cause which combine craftsmanship, restraint, and intellectual honesty.

Philip Blair Rice. *Nation*. Jan. 29, 1936. p. 134

Miss Rukeyser's first book is remarkable for its self-confidence and lack of hesitation. At twenty-one, she has already covered much of the technical ground of modern American verse, and has learned how to pick up everything she feels capable of consolidating into a poem. . . . Miss Rukeyser's verse, however, unlike that of the immediately preceding generation of modernists, does not emanate from the decorative or phenomenalistic fascination alone; it contains a moral will, a will to make itself useful as statement, and a will to warm itself against the major human situations of our day. Thus the subjective, rarely quieted in her, is redirected towards recurrent themes of class-oppression, death, the historical background, revolution.

Harold Rosenberg. *Poetry*. May, 1936. pp. 107–8

Though at first consideration she seems typical of our young class-conscious poets, she will be found to transcend them in nearly every respect. Her materials, like her contemporaries', is every-day life. . . . Her viewpoint, like theirs, has the clearness and objectivity of a photograph. But she is far more aware what an adaptable instrument the camera is, and achieves effects the poetic realist of the past never dreamed of. . . . Where her confreres tend to grasp only broad social phenomena, or only isolated examples, she captures both the general meaning and the specific detail, plays one against the other, thereby reaching a truer, more moving analysis.

Kerker Quinn. *NYHT*. Feb. 20, 1938. p. 12

There are moments in *US 1* that are pretty dull, but that's bound to be the character of all good things if they are serious enough: when a devoted and determined person sets out to do a thing he isn't thinking first of being brilliant, he wants to get there even if he has to crawl on his face. When he is able to—whenever he is able to—he gets up and runs. . . . (But) I hope Miss Rukeyser does not lose herself in her injudicious haste for a "cause," accepting, uncritically, what she does as satisfactory, her intentions being of the best. I hope she will stick it out the hardest way, a tough road, and invent! make the form that will embody her rare gifts of intelligence and passion for a social rebirth the chief object of her labors.

William Carlos Williams. *NR*. March 9, 1938.
pp. 141–2

What most distinguishes Muriel Rukeyser's third book, *A Turning Wind,* from her earlier work is an extension of method and point of view, which has greatly enriched her poetry and at the same time introduced a corresponding, though not, I believe, a necessary obscurity.

The extension of viewpoint may best be described in simplification as a shift of emphasis from the concrete to the abstract, from the immediate concern with evidence of social decay and its remedies to the more speculative concern with its causes, particularly psychological. . . . One reason, I believe, for the occasional failure to communicate is that Miss Rukeyser has not yet been wholly successful in extending her method to keep pace with the extension of viewpoint and subject matter.

Philip Horton. *NR*. Jan. 22, 1940. p. 123

What is exciting about Miss Rukeyser's work is the vitality and large-ness of her ideas and feelings, and the amazing but controlled origi-nality of her methods of expressing them. . . . Hers is an original and startling talent for the bright and expanding image, the concrete phantasy, the magical reality of a world of machines, cities, social forces, and nervous complexities. . . . Even when one cannot put his words on what all her "sources of power" are, one feels she has power. Beauty and thought are tremendously exciting even when we cannot measure their height, or compass their horizons.

Mildred Boie. *At*. Feb., 1940. Unpaged

If Muriel Rukeyser is—as I believe she is—the most inventive and challenging poet of the generation which has not yet reached thirty, it is because of her provocative language fully as much as because of her audacious ideas. . . . *Theory of Flight* announced a new symbolism as well as a new speech. The style was swift, abrupt, syncopated; it matched the speed of the strepitant post-war world, the crazy energy of murderous machines, the "intolerable contradiction" of flight. . . . For her the images of war and industry are all too natural. . . . It is the "agonies of decision" which Miss Rukeyser expresses for more than her own generation. . . . In the midst of desperate remedies and clamoring negatives, she affirms the life of people and the life of poetry—the life of the spirit giving all processes and inventions, the creative life which is the double answer to living slavery and to the wish for quick escapes, comforting death.

Louis Untermeyer. *SR*. Aug. 10, 1940. pp. 11–3

One of the most interesting phases of the transformation of the social poet in years of stress is the change in his use of language. In the case of Muriel Rukeyser, it moves from that of simple declarative exhortation, in the common phrases of the city man, to that of a gnarled, intellec-tual, almost private observation. In her earlier usage, images are apt to be simple and few; the whole approach is apt to be through the medium of urban speech. In the latter work, images become those of the psychologist, or of the surrealist, charged with increasing complica-tion of symbols; the first are public, the last, even though they may represent universal issues, are privately conceived and privately en-dowed.

John Malcolm Brinnin. *Poetry*. Jan., 1943. p. 555

The dilemma of conflict rising from an unresolved dualism in view-point has characterized Muriel Rukeyser's recent work. . . . Hers is a poetry of confusion in a confused world—a poetry which submits to that confusion—falls back upon the non-rational: the myth, the dream, the supernatural; or selects as its mouth-pieces a "drunken girl," a "madboy," a "child." By so doing, the poet seemingly justifies lack of organization, disassociated images, abrupt shifts in person and tense, and enigmatical meaning. . . . It seems to me her poems are much more effective when she forgets myth, symbol and dream . . . and turns to factual events or experiences common to the majority of men and women today.

Ruth Lechlitner. *NYHT*. Dec. 31, 1944. p. 4

Muriel Rukeyser is a forcible writer with a considerable talent for emotional rhetoric, but she has a random melodramatic hand and rather unfortunate models and standards for her work—one feels about most of her poems pretty much as one feels about the girl on last year's calendar. . . . One feels, with dismay and delight, that one is listening to the Common Siren of our century, a siren photographed in a sequin bathing suit, on rocks like boiled potatoes, for the week-end edition of PM, in order to bring sex to the deserving poor. . . . Yet all the time the poem keeps repeating, keeps remembering to repeat, that it is a *good* girl—that it is, after all, dying for the people; the reader wanders, full of queasy delight, through the labyrinthine corridors of the strange, moral, sexual wish-fantasy for which he is to be awarded, somehow, a gold star by the Perfect State.

Randall Jarrell. *Nation*. May 8, 1948. pp. 512–3

In a time of shrinking poets and shrinking critics here, at any rate, is one capable in both poetry and criticism, who expands and embraces. . . . Miss Rukeyser disowns little or nothing. With her poet's knack of seeing the symbolic meanings in events and the connections latent in them, and with various and deep reading she adduces and enriches from every quarter of contemporary life, from punctuation to the blues, from Fenellosa to Leadbelly. . . . Yet I have a disturbing sense that in these recent poems Miss Rukeyser's motile, ringing energies are becoming over-agitated. Frenetic is too harsh a word, but her images and rhythms, like Shelley's, seem humid and driven by a general passion behind and so external to all particular items of our experience.

James R. Caldwell. *SR*. March 11, 1950. p. 26

See *Selected Poems;* also *Life of Poetry* (criticism) and *One Life* and *Willard Gibbs* (biography).

SALINGER, J. D. (1919–   )

J. D. Salinger's writing is original, first rate, serious and beautiful. . . . He has the equipment for a born writer to begin with—his sensitive eye, his incredibly good ear, and something I can think of no word for but grace. There is not a trace of sentimentality about his work, although it is full of children that are bound to be adored. He pronounces no judgments, he is simply gifted with having them passionately. . . . What this reader loves about Mr. Salinger's stories is that they honor what is unique and precious in each person on earth.

Eudora Welty. *NYT*. April 5, 1953. p. 4

Salinger is an extreme individualist with a pleasing disregard for conventional narrative form and style. . . . Above all Salinger appears to be ravenously interested in human beings, whom he depicts with an understanding, without either sentimentality or condescension, something unusual in so young a writer. Even his weaker stories are peopled with memorable minor characters, people who appear on stage for a few moments only, but who are endowed with lives of their own.

William Peden. *SR*. April 11, 1953. pp. 43–4

The special quality of Mr. Salinger's stories is humaneness. He engages the reader's civilized sympathies for the puzzled and troubled individuals whose sensibilities civilization has injured. There is little perception of the tragedy of life or, as Faulkner has put it, of the human heart in conflict with itself. Mr. Salinger's is the tradition of Chekhov applied to middle-class niceties and influenced by the standards of The New Yorker. . . . What he does do, he does well, but the scope of these stories is strictly limited. They are more concerned with a slice of life, an impression of it, than with life itself. For the most part, one discovers the problem of sensibility isolated, misdirected, misunderstood, and at last interpreted in a flash of insight.

Gene Baro. *NYHT*. April 12, 1953. p. 6

J. D. Salinger's closest resemblance is to F. Scott Fitzgerald—that is, close in one sense. Salinger is at home with the details of upper middle-class life, and, like Fitzgerald, there is much grace, lightness of touch, and bitter-sweet emotion in his stories. But since Salinger is his own man, and hardly an imitation, the analogy with Fitzgerald ends at a certain point; there is a bitterness and intensity in the young writer's work which is subtly wedded to the charm, and the combination makes Fitzgerald seem romantically old-fashioned by comparison. But both writers have that particular poignance which results from a lyrical identification with subject matter set off by a critical intelligence; they are both lovers, so to speak, who are forced to acknowledge that they have been "had," and this gives their work the emotion of subtle heartbreak.

> Seymour Krim. *Com.* April 24, 1953. p. 78

Salinger's fiction convicts us, as readers, of being deeply aware of a haunting inconclusiveness in our own, and in contemporary, emotional relationships—members all of the lonely crowd. His characters exist outside the charmed circle of the well-adjusted, and their thin cries for love and understanding go unheard. They are men, women, and adolescents, not trapped by outside fate, but by their own frightened, and sometimes tragi-comic awareness of the uncrossable gulf between their need for love and the futility of trying to achieve it on any forseeable terms.

Salinger's short stories are all variants on the theme of emotional estrangement.

> David L. Stevenson. *Nation.* March 9, 1957. p. 216

In January, 1953, after a year and a half of literary fame and literary silence, Salinger published in the New Yorker a story called "Teddy," which began his latest phase. It reads *methodically;* as if the impulse had first been to write something that was not a story. It has dialogue of a kind then new to his work but now his standard: no longer seducing our belief and lighting up characters with things we had heard but not listened to, but expounding an ordered set of ideas as plainly as can be done without actually destroying the characters into whose mouths they are put. The ideas are mostly Zen.

In the stories Salinger has published since then . . . poignant, beautifully managed philosophic dialogues, really—the doctrine is developed, sometimes in the language of Christian mysticism (after Meister Eckhart) and sometimes as a rather high-flying syncretism.

> Donald Barr. *Com.* Oct. 25, 1957. p. 90

What Salinger has seen in American life is the extraordinary tension it sets up between our passion to understand and evaluate our experience for ourselves and our need to belong to a community that is unusually energetic in imposing its understanding and values on its individual members. Whatever one may think of Salinger's answer to the problem, this view of American life is important; it has a long and distinguished history. But Salinger's achievement is not that he has grasped an abstract idea of American experience, important as that idea may be in itself; it is that he has seen this idea working in the actual life of our time, in our habitual activities, in the very turns of our speech, and he has found a way to make us see it there, too.

Arthur Mizener. *Harper*. Feb., 1959. p. 90

For the college generation of the Fifties, Salinger has the kind of importance that Scott Fitzgerald and Ernest Hemingway had for the young people of the Twenties. He is not a public figure as they were; on the contrary, his zeal for privacy is phenomenal; but he is felt nevertheless as a presence, a significant and congenial presence. There are, I am convinced, millions of young Americans who feel closer to Salinger than to any other writer.

In the first place, he speaks their language. He not only speaks it, he shapes it, just as Hemingway influenced the speech of countless Americans in the Twenties. . . . In the second place, he expresses their rebellion.

Granville Hicks. *SR*. July 25, 1959. p. 13

There are many writers, like J. D. Salinger, who lack strength, but who are competent and interesting. He identifies himself too fussily with the spiritual aches and pains of his characters; in some of his recent stories, notably "Zooey" and "Seymour: An Introduction," he has overextended his line, thinned it out, in an effort to get the fullest possible significance out of his material. Salinger's work is a perfect example of the lean reserves of the American writer who is reduced to "personality," even to the "mystery of personality," instead of the drama of our social existence. . . . The delicate balances in Salinger's work, the anxious striving, inevitably result in beautiful work that is rather too obviously touching.

Alfred Kazin. *Harper*. Oct., 1959. p. 130

See *The Catcher in the Rye* (novel) and *Nine Stories*.

See Supplement at end of text for additional material.

SANDBURG, CARL (1878–   )

The free rhythms of Mr. Carl Sandburg are a fine achievement in poetry. No one who reads *Chicago Poems* with rhythm particularly in mind can fail to recognize how much beauty he attains in this regard. But the more arresting aspect of Mr. Sandburg's achievement is, for myself, the so-called imagistic aspect. . . . At first these poems may seem too innocent of self-interpretation to mean anything, too im-

pressionistic to compel the name of beauty—to give that completion
which has no shadow and knows no end beyond itself. But such exquisite realization of the scenes that gave Mr. Sandburg the mood of beauty
is in itself a creation of the beautiful.

> Francis Hackett. *Horizons* (Huebsch-Viking). 1918.
> pp. 304–5, 309

The "natural rhythms of a manly life" that Plato insisted upon . . .
just as they tumble roughly along in Mr. Sandberg's vibrant verse,
beat out from the very unpoetic look of this poet. And when he talks
—there is no jabber nor gesticulation nor studied modulation in his
talk—and when his eyes burn out their black fire, your attention is
gripped by that same honest man-to-man sincerity which he is able
to put into the grinding, crashing, angular words of his unrhymed
free-rhymed verses, and you can understand more clearly why his verse
must be unrhymed, free-rhymed, unfettered. . . . Mr. Sandburg's
poems are Mr. Sandburg. They are powerful, live, brutal, gentle, and
human—and so is he.

> Walter Yust. *Bkm.* Jan., 1921. pp. 286, 290

There must be some powerful principle of life in the man, that he can
make one feel so much. There must be some rocky strength, some
magnetic iron in him, that compels, despite coatings of muck and dust,
and draws iron to iron. For Sandburg is an almost rudimentary artist.
His successful effects are almost sparks of fire out of a chaos, sudden
tongues of flame that leap out of smoking matter and subside as suddenly again. He appears to be as nearly unconscious as an artist can
be and still remain a creator; it is well-nigh in spite of his technique that
he manages to communicate.

> Paul Rosenfeld. *Bkm.* July, 1921. p. 393

Buried deep within the He man, the hairy, meat eating Sandburg there
is another Sandburg, a sensitive, naive, hesitating Carl Sandburg, a
Sandburg that hears the voice of the wind over the roofs of houses at
night, a Sandburg that wanders often alone through grim city streets
on winter nights, a Sandburg that knows and understands the voiceless
cry in the heart of the farm girl of the plains when she comes to the
kitchen door and sees for the first time the beauty of prairie country.

The poetry of John Guts doesn't excite me much. Hairy, raw meat
eating He men are not exceptional in Chicago and the middle west.

As for the other Sandburg, the naive, hesitant, sensitive Sandburg—
among all the poets of America he is my poet.

> Sherwood Anderson. *Bkm.* Dec., 1921. p. 361

Sandburg is alien to most of the Anglo-Saxon elements in American life. Its aspects which he chooses to describe are those precisely which distinguish it from life in England. . . . He avoids the language along with everything else that is English. He never wrote an American dictionary, but he does something even more hazardous and exciting: he writes American. With earlier authors American was a dialect; it was the speech of the comedian and the soubrette; the hero, when serious, declaimed his Sunday-best Oxford. The case is opposite with Sandburg. . . . Sandburg writes American like a foreign language, like a language freshly acquired in which each word has a new and fascinating meaning.

Malcolm Cowley. Dial. Nov., 1922. pp. 565–6

Sandburg, for all his strength, is not without his weakness. . . . In giving way to a program of mysticism, Sandburg gives the unconscious an absolutely free hand; he lets it dictate its unfettered—and, one might almost add, its unlettered—fantasies. There are times, more frequent than one might wish, when he completely fails to guide the current of his thought; it directs or misdirects him so that he follows blindly what, too often, is merely a blind alley. . . . But though the meaning is not always clear, there is no mistaking the emotion. It is implicit in every line; a concentrated exaltation, rich in its sweeping affirmations, rich in suggestive details.

Louis Untermeyer. American Poetry since 1900
(Holt). 1923. pp. 86–7

Sandburg's profoundest belief about the world is that the universe is mainly cruel and capricious, that meaning is given it only by the lives of men—pitiful and noble lives which are continually being thwarted by death or disease or the facts of the social order. . . . As Sandburg, because he sets so high a value on men, is continually brought to the thought of death, so, like other mystics, he prizes silence above noise, introspection above activity. . . . He feels keenly that ideas are frail, values are fragile, language is inadequate.

Howard Mumford Jones. VQR. Jan., 1927. pp. 112,
116, 121

Of tenderness, of human feeling, of generous and robust sentiment, there is notoriously a great deal: of strong, sharp and ardent emotion, of the specific passion and intensity of poetry, there is singularly little. This verse, you feel, is the work of a man whose emotional nature, like his intellectual life, has never found the earth and air in which it could develop freely and expansively. His strength has lain in his closeness to the people, but they are a people whose impulses and affections have been nipped and stunted . . . like wild flowers on a stock farm; and of so cramped an emotional existence this too cool, too inexpensive, too phlegmatic poetry—this poetry of half-lights and understatement and ironic anti-climaxes—is the inevitable expression.

Newton Arvin. *NR*. Sept. 9, 1936. p. 120

Sandburg's poetic instrument is exactly fitted to his purposes: it simply happens that those purposes are too vaguely poetic to make the instrument become anything more than the loose, amorphous, copious, semi-prose medium that it still remains after twenty-five years of use. And one may suppose that if he had exerted more labor on the task of filing and concentrating his verse, giving one phrase or anecdote the pith now thinned out over twenty, he would have arrived at something more fixed and specific in his social beliefs. . . . The potentialities of an epic judgement lie in Sandburg's materials, but he has not realized them.

Morton D. Zabel. *Poetry*. Oct., 1936. pp. 43–4

Carl Sandburg petered out as a poet ten years ago. I imagine he wanted it that way. His poems themselves said what they had to say, piling it up, then just went out like a light. He had no answers, he didn't seek any. Without any attempt at the solace which the limitations of art (as with a Baudelaire) might bring the formlessness of his literary figures was the very formlessness of the materials with which he worked. That was his truth. That was what he wanted truthfully to make plain, that was his compulsion. That form he could accept but at a terrible cost: failure deliberately invited, a gradual inevitable slackening off to ultimate defeat.

William Carlos Williams. *Poetry*. Sept., 1951. p. 346

In all his poetry a single effort was represented—that of refounding his derived romanticism, its vision and imaginative ecstasy upon the common realities of a labor and populist experience. This latter remained for him a fixed element, one he would not place in perspective and seemingly could not alter. . . . Consequently, the only mobile or adaptable part of his work lay in its other half—the essentially rhetorical and willful exercise of fancy to embellish and stage impressively his obdurate poetic matter. Like the other midwesterners, Sandburg was a poet of subject. Where his subject was itself arresting, moving, and satisfying, his poem likewise could achieve these qualities.

Bernard Duffey. *The Chicago Renaissance in American Letters* (Michigan State). 1954. pp. 216–7

Increasingly Sandburg disregards the metaphor for direct statement. Now poetry of statement may be very great poetry, as Dryden and Pope have shown us, but it must by its nature be a poetry diamantine in its hardness and brilliance. Sandburg lacks any technique in this sense, and consequently his late ideological poetry fails. . . . Early or late, however, wherever the metaphor of itself exercises absolute control of the poem—as in "Chicago," "The Harbor," "Fog," "Cool Tombs," and "Grass"—Sandburg attains technical success. It is an extremely limited success as an imitator of Whitman and as one of the Imagists.

Nicholas Joost. *Com.* Jan. 16, 1958. p. 382

Everybody loved Carl Sandburg in our town. Nobody knows where he went. . . . Compare "I Am the People, The Mob" with *The People, Yes.* It's enough to make you weep. In the early poem you see so clearly behind the abstraction the stark individuals of the other poems in *Chicago Poems.* Behind the second *People* is only mush. . . . It is a terrible pity, but after about 1925 there is nothing of value. Since most of the prose comes after that, Sandburg the historian, novelist, autobiographer, writer of children's stories simply does not exist for literature. I suppose the last thing was the *Songbag.*

Kenneth Rexroth. *Nation.* Feb. 22, 1958. pp. 171–2

See *Complete Poems* and *The New American Songbag;* also *Always the Young Strangers* (autobiography) and *Abraham Lincoln* (biography).

SANTAYANA, GEORGE (1863–1952)

To him no ties are morally binding but those of common thoughts and purposes. Instead of allowing the accident of family, country or profession to dictate his affection and his future, he has followed his affinities and aspirations. Even the age he has chanced to live in has not kept him from communing with the ancients he admires. . . . He seems to know all that is worth knowing, to feel everything that touches the human heart. He writes with the calm of an ancient philosopher, the passion of a mystic poet, the insight into eternal and intimate things which belongs to the great dead. He writes as if he had lived a long time ago and were writing for all time to come.

Van Meter Ames. *Proust and Santayana* (Willett). 1937.
pp. 50, 80. Used by permission of Harper and Brothers

Without prejudicing in the least the question of the respective validities of the ways of thought and action idealized in the *Life of Reason* and the *Realms of Being,* one cannot ignore the fact that the period in which the second work was written witnessed the disintegration of the world whose stability seemed so assured during the years when he composed that philosophic masterpiece, the *Life of Reason.* He has experienced not so much a metaphysical conversion as a moral revulsion before the tremendous changes in the world he once knew. The situations that are difficult to master when approached as tasks and challenges he has forever settled, in his own mind, by converting them into spectacles.

Sidney Hook. Nation. Nov. 2, 1940. p. 424

He was not, as he says in a well-known sonnet, "born to be beatified by anguish," but "to stand perplexed aside from so much sorrow." Still, there are many cherished writers who experienced neither anguish nor joy but something in the middle ground that helped them to ruminate on life and on the symbols that have been evolved for the explanation of it, writers who often seem to be more knowledgeable, less dense, for the limitation of their experience. Santayana, not only by temperament but by his own plan of life, seems to have been destined for the middle way. Anyhow, he has gone that way and has brought out of it a curious wisdom, something that is a combination of the mundane with the disinterestedly spiritual. His mind has never been distorted by the strain of too intense feeling or by impetuosity, by too much work or a too imprudent sense of duty.

Mary M. Colum. SR. April 21, 1945. p. 8

Although a materialist, Santayana considers himself devout and worshipful. He loves the rites and ceremonies of the Catholic Church. He loves its dogmas, knows them to the last detail, and dwells on them with unreserved emotion. But he does not think they are true. He thinks they express in a symbolic way ideals that are needful to spirits in finding their way through a material world. . . . I do not think going through the motions of religion without genuine belief is a peculiarly Catholic phenomenon—or even a peculiar phenomenon. The peculiar thing about Santayana is his candid confession, or rather bold celebration, of it. He makes a sincerity of being insincere. He is devout with no object of devotion. He is religious without any religion.

Max Eastman. AM. Nov., 1951. p. 38

The dominating interest of Santayana, throughout his whole repertory of writings, is psychological. His consistent concern is with the events that occur in the human psyche and in the human spirit. . . . Santayana's moral system, as developed in *The Life of Reason* and in the other volumes which cluster around *The Life of Reason,* seems precisely to accomplish the post-Lockean goal of delineating the structure of human nature, with the added security of an assumed material world as the sum of the existing. Thus, it satisfies at once the demands of a modern faith and those of a humane sensibility. Among philosophical systems of the century, it is uniquely acceptable to persons whose taste may be described as literary and traditional, and whose religion is scientific naturalism. Its aesthetic is marked by unconcern for fashionable, arbitrary, or occult doctrines of poetry and fine art.

Charles T. Harrison. *SwR*. Spring, 1953. pp. 209, 212

It can hardly be said that Santayana writes like one inspired, or like one with a zeal for either understanding or reforming the world. . . . His style reminds one more of the soliloquy of a dreamer who has never taken the world or even the facts of human life and achievement with intense seriousness or been overly disturbed by the prospect and actuality of catastrophes that have threatened human happiness and existence. The acute observations of, and the definite reactions to, the most crucial problems of living (which form a large part of his contribution to philosophy) are expressed in prose that seems so effortless and such a delight in itself that often one must, as Kant said of Rousseau's writings, read his essays and books several times in order to give attention to the matter rather than to the beauty of the style.

Willard E. Arnett. *Santayana and the Sense of Beauty*
(Indiana). 1955. pp. 202–3

It was not Santayana's abstract "message" that explains his magic. It was not even the limpid and epigrammatic prose in which he stated it. It was the mixture of irony and sympathy he brought to his great theme, the unrelenting standards combined with the unillusioned acceptance of men as they are; it was the glinting wisdom, and the literary imagination which evoked the inner experience of men living in the most disparate moral climates. Most of all, it was the expression of a frankly relativistic moral outlook that was nevertheless Dantesque in its stringent declaration of preferences, its comprehensiveness, and its consistency. Here was a man with the sobriety of Aristotle writing with the poetry and excitement of Plato on the only things which give anything else meaning—human ideals.

Charles Frankel. *SR*. Jan. 7, 1956. p. 11

The Last Puritan

His attitude to the world of ideas no less than of the senses has always seemed to be an artist's rather than a philosopher's, and this, while no doubt making him an object of suspicion to his fellow thinkers, makes his philosophical writings enjoyable to the layman. It is notable, too, that he has (again unlike a philosopher) a sensitiveness to literature that has produced first class literary criticism. . . . His novel is therefore really a novel, not an arrangement of mouthpieces for philosophic speeches; the moral tensions he is interested in arise of themselves from the fable and call for little explication; and in his handling of them one is aware only of the (duly self-effacing) artist. The social fable is extended in all directions by the frequent symbolic implications, and behind the overt action one may sense an allegory of the moral life of man.

Q. D. Leavis. *Scy.* Dec., 1935. p. 322

Unashamedly old-fashioned in its method, and in its quiet thoroughness, *The Last Puritan* makes the average contemporary novel, even the best, look two-dimensional by contrast. It has the solidarity of a *Tom Jones* or *Clarissa Harlowe,* does for the New England scene, or a part of it, what those novels did for eighteenth-century England, and with the same air of easy classic competence. Nor is it quite fair to call it old-fashioned: for Santayana's employment of a kind of soliloquy-dialogue is an extremely interesting invention technically, and very skillfully done.

But the whole book is a delight, so richly packed with perceptions and wisdom and humans, not to mention poetry, that it can be read and reread for its texture alone.

Conrad Aiken. *NR.* Feb. 5, 1936. p. 372

The characters are seen only from certain aspects, and are seldom physically vivid. And the dialogue is like none heard in the novel for a generation. It is an exchange of soliloquies or finished essays; it is full of unblushing self-explanation or exposition, not for the benefit of the person ostensibly addressed, but for the reader; and nearly always it is much too intelligent and clairvoyant. . . . These long, explicit, uninterrupted speeches are a device of compression: we come to assume that what is said in one long speech by a character is the meat of what he really said over the course of a whole evening or a week; and the unnatural intelligence and articulateness of everyone is a refreshing relief from the current convention of laconic obtuseness or incoherent stream of consciousness.

Henry Hazlitt. *Nation.* Feb. 26, 1936. p. 255

Readers must approach this book with a tolerance of fancy. The epicurean wisdom of Peter Alden, the emotionalism and naïveté of Fraulein Irma, the fervid Catholicism of Caleb Wetherbee—these must be accepted as significant on their own account and not merely as supplementary to the narrative, because it is these elements which the author has either fused in his thought or systematically excluded from it. The import of this novel is primarily philosophical—of greater value to many readers than its author's abstract works, being as Mario says, a picture painted, and "all the truer for not professing to be true." Mr. Santayana has here realized imaginatively a suggestion he made in a paper over twenty years ago—that one way for a philosopher to justify his system would be for him to acknowledge its personal basis. The proponent, if such he could be called, of any system would merely set forth his cognitive and moral experience, imparting to others that kind of knowledge which any keen observer might arrive at.

Justus Buchler. NEQ. June, 1936. p. 282

Except for William James . . . Santayana's thought would never have taken just the turn it did. . . . It is true that, from Santayana's point of view, America had a merely negative and astringent value for him, and a deep-rooted American will not feel that either *The Last Puritan* or *Persons and Places* does justice to what was most creative in America. . . . American readers of these books can make their own reservations, mainly in silence, and meanwhile there is much to be learned from them. No one but Santayana could have seen what he saw in the New England of the Age of Howells: his memories of those decades have a fictional sharpness, a precision of imagery, a piercing psychological quality that one finds in few comparable American autobiographies.

Newton Arvin. Nation. Jan. 29, 1944. p. 133

Poetry

The world has scarcely any objective existence for him. Though in weaving his similitudes he uses the traditional apparatus of flowers and stars, mountains, rivers, and the sea, these things are pure ideas to him, divested of all material attributes. . . . The pageantry of life means little or nothing to him. He has no vision for external nature, but only for the summaries, essences, abstracts of phenomena, recorded in the concave of his soul. . . . Theoretically, this characteristic ought to imply a serious defect in Mr. Santayana's work; practically I find it no defect at all, but rather a source of distinction. It is a relief, for once in a way, to escape from the importunate details of the visible world into a sphere of pure thought and pure melody.

William Archer. Poets of the Younger Generation
(John Lane). 1902. pp. 373–4

The joy of his verse is not so much its delicacy as its brilliance and the temper of its strength. His manner is the manner of swordsmanship, and the blade, though daintily raised, bites in. He is an exquisite in thrust and parry and a master of the subtle feints of fence, but there is more than swordplay in his skill. There is sometimes a desperate courage in the stab of a phrase as though he drove against a shadowy antagonist always at point to strike and overwhelm. . . . But for all its intensity the poetry of George Santayana never fails of a fine restraint and an unobtrusive mastery of form. His glimpses of reality are labored into closely articulated epigrams, and his phrases of wonder or of doubt or grief are inevitable unities, perfect to the uses of his will.

Archibald MacLeish. Bkm. Oct., 1925. pp. 188–9

Among philosophical personalities the most urbane and humanistic since Socrates may well be Mr. Santayana. I imagine he is what Emerson might be if Emerson had had a philosophical instead of a theological background; in other words if his Harvard had been the Harvard of today or yesterday. As an Emerson disturbs the theologians, a Santayana disturbs the philosophers—an admirable function. Each speaks luminously, and that dismays his professional colleagues and drives them to speak primly; and each pours out an incessant gnomic wisdom, so that the colleagues look a little innocent or empty. The likeness goes further: each possesses the technical accomplishment of verse. But here the report is not so favorable. Emerson was too much the theologian to be quite released by poetry, and Mr. Santayana is imprisoned with all his graces in the net of his intellectualism. They do not command the freedom of poets.

John Crowe Ransom. The World's Body (Scribner).
1938. p. 304

One must of course be attuned to the sensitiveness of such a temperament as Santayana's to detect the emotion which the sonnets and certain of the other more personal verses reveal. One must share his aesthetic responsiveness, his sincere deference in the presence of beauty, his delight in quiet contemplation, his high seriousness. Santayana's Muse asks no plaudits of the crowd, desires no throng of admirers or followers. His poetry is personal and aloof, the discourse of a man with his soul, a soliloquy hardly more than a whisper, or perhaps a prayer.

George W. Howgate. George Santayana
(Pennsylvania). 1938. p. 85

See The Sense of Beauty and The Life of Reason (philosophy); also Poems and The Last Puritan (novel).

SAROYAN, WILLIAM (1908–   )

Mr. Saroyan is excited, eager, clever, honestly introspective, . . . narcissistic, wistful, humane, tender and the very reverse of naïve while affecting naïveté. He is an original. I see no traceable influence upon him except that of Sherwood Anderson, the untutored, homely honesty of whose early writings Mr. Saroyan has apparently absorbed. . . . There is evidence . . . that a new, refreshing, and interesting talent is in the first experimental stages of creation. . . . It is an apollonian and eager talent, entertaining us and leaving us expectant.

Burton Rascoe. NYHT. Oct. 21, 1934. p. 9

It is obvious . . . that Saroyan is not what is called "a good writer"; people who smack their lips over good writing will never come within smacking distance of him. But it's equally obvious that what he's shouting about is not just his bumptious Armenian self but something vital. The rub comes in deciding whether he's a blasphemer or a buffoon. Or, perhaps, neither. . . . A good deal of Whitman's writing was promissory, a great deal of it sheer brag. The professors have mummified him into a literary figure, but he was better than that. He could hardly write his name in their language; but he made his mark. William Saroyan is the same sort of fellow.

T. S. Matthews. NR. March 18, 1936. p. 172

Saroyan takes you to the bar, and he creates for you there a world which is the way the world would be if it conformed to the feelings instilled by drinks. In a word, he achieves the feat of making and keeping us boozy without the use of alcohol and purely by the action of art. . . . These magical feats are accomplished by the enchantment of Saroyan's temperament, which induces us to take from him a good deal that we should not take from anyone else. With Saroyan the whole thing is the temperament: he hardly ever tries to contrive a machine. The good fairy who was present at his christening thus endowed him with one of the most precious gifts that a literary artist can have, and Saroyan never ceases to explain to us how especially fortunate he is.

Edmund Wilson. NR. Nov. 18, 1940. p. 697

My Name Is Aram, in its highly original way, has linked itself to one of the most fertile lines of the American literary tradition; while at the same time adding a new element of the utmost importance for an imaginative study of America as America is. It is an Armenian book, charged with the Christianized orientalism of the Armenians, rich in the highly humorous contrasts of their ideal of living in a California environment, written with the naïve blend of spirituality and realistic cynicism that one finds in Arabic popular literature. And at the same time it is intensely American. . . . I should vote, indeed, for this story of an Armenian boyhood as the most truly American book of the year.

Henry Seidel Canby. *SR*. Dec. 28, 1940. p. 5

Someone soon will have to make an analysis of his very personal style, for though one might say of it that it is in the Hemingway tradition, there is something added, or is it taken away? For the art is most definitely one of subtraction, of shearing away the trimmings; it becomes an art of inarticulateness, where the silences say more than the words. . . . The writer, of course, has to fill in the significance of the silences, and that is where the art comes in; and he has to manage the business without your noticing what he is after. Mr. Saroyan knows how to do it.

Bonamy Dobrée. *Spec*. March 28, 1941. p. 354

He can be charming, he can be vastly amusing, he can be tender and innocent and even sometimes, as if by accident or inspiration, profound, but he can never be quite satisfying. Mr. Saroyan is a complete romantic. His fancifulness, his ecstatic love and admiration for children and even half-wits, his enthusiasm, his delight, his wonder at everything and anything, his faith in the promptings of the heart over those of the head . . . , his conviction that good always drives out sickness and evil and that love conquers all, makes him difficult to argue with. One can only disagree.

Wallace Stegner. *NYT*. Feb. 28, 1943. p. 7

No one in any serious sense believes in him any longer as a major prophet.

Saroyan might well have been one. He arrived on the American literary scene at a time when the public was tired of the destructive and cynical dicta of post-war novelists. He tried to affirm by his puckish humor, his Armenian folk-tales, his fables and his naive emotionalism that nothing mattered in the world except love and being true to yourself. He failed because a depression followed the war and another world war followed the depression. . . . We look today at Saroyan's men and women. . . . We love their primitive honesty, but . . . feel . . . that he is a gifted teller of fairy-tales, or parables, which have little relation to a world faced with continual revolution, starvation, and the threat of another war.

Harrison Smith. *SR*. June 1, 1946. pp. 7–8

At best Saroyan's fiction gives expression to a philosophy of life which is typically Californian, and also is central to the American transcendental tradition. Unlike the muckraking and socialistic writing of Upton Sinclair, Saroyan has no axe to grind, no gospel to preach. Unlike the naturalistic and sociological fiction of John Steinbeck, Saroyan treats human nature and social injustice without violence and anger. But because he rejects the utopian socialism of Sinclair and the revolutionary violence of Steinbeck, Saroyan does not adopt the pessimistic nihilism of Robinson Jeffers. Rather he reaffirms the old American faith of Emerson and Whitman, who, skeptical both of social reformers and of prophets of doom, proclaimed that the world could be reformed only by reforming the individual, and that this could not be accomplished by social compulsion and physical violence but only by personal freedom and loving tolerance.

Frederic I. Carpenter. *PS*. Winter, 1947. p. 96

Unlike his contemporaries of the late Nineteen Thirties he was given neither to political ranting nor to standardized thinking. In virtually everything he wrote—and he was astonishingly prolific—there was a curious twist of poetry and flashes of genuine humor and imagination. He was almost completely original, seeming to derive from no one at all, and the naïveté that was part of his style contained a winning charm that reflected the pleasant egoism of youth. In addition, he had mastered the integrate art of playwriting from the beginning, a technical feat at which many a fine novelist failed.

Thomas Quinn Curtiss. *NYT*. Nov. 20, 1949. p. 5

Saroyan's concept of goodness, once synonymous with love and gratitude, has become linked with man's tenacity, his will to live. And because this new optimism has a firmer basis in fact and bears out a dramatic element in life, his plays, with all their fantasy, have grown in plausibility. . . . Saroyan's outlook seems to have taken a Shavian turn (and not surprisingly, since Shaw is the one writer he admires). But with one important difference, that Saroyan's faith in the Life Force does not stem from dialectic but from his intuitive feeling of the ultimate meaning of things and events.

Nona Balakian. *NR*. Aug. 7, 1950. p. 20

I should say that Saroyan at his best turns out a peculiar literary version of schizophrenia. He writes of a world of strangers and loose ends in which there is no real human contact; it is a world in motion, but the laws of motion are suspended and none of the common patterns persists. Ordinary human feelings, such as hunger and loneliness—the two with which he is most often preoccupied—are presented in a minimum of setting, a social void, in which they are laid bare of the usual association. The attention is concentrated on the isolated action or emotion, which is, in turn, distorted, blown out of its common proportions, by being projected out of context. . . . The distortion heightens the expressive effect, and what comes through . . . represents a perception which - is frequently absent in the more crowded "realistic" view of the universe. . . . But "human kind cannot bear very much reality," and Saroyan can't stand even his own. He is in constant flight from it.

Isaac Rosenfeld. NR. Dec. 8, 1952

He has not merely, by some august fortuity, happened, chanced or blundered upon a public; he may be said to have charmed one into existence and, by his blend of oddity with persuasive strength, bound his readers to him along his way. . . . Probably since O. Henry nobody has done more than William Saroyan to endear and stabilize the short story, as it were, to guarantee it, to rescue it from its two extremes of possible disrepute—that of being purely esthetic, divorced from life, or purely commercial, divorced from virtue. Also, does not this writer tilt against the deadening uniformity of society, constituting himself the spokesman of the odd man out, the champion of the misfit, the chronicler of the bum? Herein may lie some part of his fascination for those who do not dare deviate, but might wish to. Here, one may infer is a tempting, disturbing, repeated manifestation of innocence, on the part of somebody who has never sold out—the inspired, sometimes flamboyant alien, for whom nothing is yet quite normal in the American scene, and who flutters and dips in Americanism, like a bird in a birdbath, without being in any way processed by it.

Elizabeth Bowen. NR. March 9, 1953. p. 18

See *My Name is Aram* and *The Human Comedy* (novels); also *The Daring Young Man on the Flying Trapeze* and *The Assyrian* (short stories) and *The Time of Your Life* and *The Cave Dwellers* (plays).

SARTON, MAY (1912–   )

Poetry

A good part of Miss Sarton's poems are love sonnets. . . . To achieve the high polish which these sonnets possess it has been necessary for the poet to employ a good many pre-fabricated emotions, just as the sonnet form itself lends a ready-made gloss to the verse. The result is that the whole performance inevitably calls up Millay *et al.*, in their second April moods, and Miss Sarton's sonnets seem to stem from literary rather than personal emotions. . . . The finest piece of work in every way is a lyric in ten fluid parts, "She Shall Be Called Woman." This poem seems to me to reveal that secret access that women have into the core of their sensations and feelings. And it is certainly from that heightened consciousness that their best and unique work always comes. It is to be hoped that Miss Sarton's future writing will take its departure from this point.

Sherman Conrad. *Poetry*. July, 1937. pp. 229–31

Done with something of the eighteenth-century care for the sedate, un-emotional line, her poems suggest the even lawns and precise gardens of the time of Queen Anne and the first of the Georges, before the turbulence of the romantic movement rushed in from the left to bewilder and overturn a strictly ordered world. Nevertheless, there is at the same time more emotion beneath the surface of Miss Sarton's dignified verses than was common in eighteenth-century poetry. The result of this slightly paradoxical combination is interesting. Let one try to visualize a butterfly imprisoned within a cake of ice and one will have a fairly good parallel to the poems.

Percy Hutchison. *NYT*. March 5, 1939. p. 5

May Sarton is an artist of remarkable powers. She is one of those rare poets who, in making use of simple combinations of words—and of the words of our common speech at that—has achieved a vocabulary and style as distinctly her own as any poet now writing. . . . She has drawn upon the whole stream of English literature to develop her subtle cadences and delicate, all-but-inaudible rhythms. . . . One wonders at the extreme simplicity of her statement (for such simplic-ity needs courage), and the more one wonders the more one is aware of the great gifts set forth. . . . Whatever life-images Miss Sarton chooses to turn into poetry become poetry. Her work is worth the ad-miring attention of everyone who considers himself a reader.

Martha Bacon. *SR*. April 17, 1948. p. 50

I suspect that what has always been considered the admirable simplicity of May Sarton's poetry is something more than that. . . . She demon-strates a great range of feeling and subject, an unusual strength in describing what comes before her eyes and touches her heart. Whether she speaks of zinnias or swans or the irradiating light of Provence, she testifies to a deep experience of reality which far surpasses purely speculative philosophy. . . . Her words . . . are never deadened by artifice or pose. The ease with which images in her poetry transpose notions provides the notions or the abstractions with their own firmness and poetic vigor.

Wallace Fowlie. *NR*. Dec. 14, 1953. p. 19

May Sarton's *In Time Like Air* is, to a poet at least, a book to carry in the pocket and reread with delight, the sort in which a second reading will disclose things undiscovered at first. What is the difference between this book and run-of-the-mill verse? It is partly a matter of personality, partly, perhaps, a matter of intellectual heritage, in no small degree a matter of the best kind of virtuosity. In Miss Sarton's writing there is passion, discretion, grief, joy, music and the intimation of delight. What gives her work its great distinction is its willingness to achieve its aims by simplicity when simplicity serves best and by elaboration when elaboration is proper. . . . Miss Sarton's extraordinary gift is her ability to make the actualities of physical existence and motion serve as the imaginative metaphor pointing to metaphysical reality.

Raymond Holden. *NYT*. Dec. 22, 1957. p. 4

Novels

Only a poet and, perhaps, only a young poet could have written this beautiful and distinguished first novel (*The Single Hound*). In it May Sarton has created a little world of some half dozen people and she has given them rich, bountiful life, not only pregnant with meaning for this present instant of time in which she has placed them, but deeply rooted in that humanity which is ageless. . . . Here, as in her poems, May Sarton's aim is to arrive at what she calls "transparency." She has, also, in *The Single Hound* exemplified a way of life and enunciated a literary creed.

Jane Spence Southron. *NYT*. March 20, 1938. p. 6

Hinged on irony, *Faithful Are the Wounds* swings open onto tragedy. The movement of the book is, in its classical climbing and clearing shape, toward light and truth. It has none of that intellectual wasp sting that such a subject might afford itself. It is a quiet and ever-deepening penetration into the roiled darknesses of uncommitted passion, of jelled fervors in the cold air of doubt; it touches that reserve that jails the modern conscience in its own dubious safety from which it can utter only the cry of "Why can't love help?". . . . Miss Sarton's method, even as that of her men and women who crave the light of day against self-inflicted darkness, is to turn to light what is shadowed, raise to the level of the common ground what is half-buried underground.

William Goyen. *NYT*. March 13, 1955. p. 6

In her new novel, *Faithful Are the Wounds,* May Sarton moves from the world of purely personal relationships, brought to glowing life and examined in minute detail, to one of the most violently burning public questions of our day, democratic dissent in a time of national crisis. Yet the change is much less than the statement implies. . . . Once again the kaleidoscope of feeling is turning throughout and once again the reader feels himself constantly in the presence of a master of English fiction. There is a maturity here, a command, command of the language first of all, and of the situation, the character, the change and growth, that make one terribly impatient with much that the American novel is now bringing forth.

Frank Getlein. *Com*. April 8, 1955. p. 19

The Birth of a Grandfather is not a "woman's novel," a lending library favorite; it is much too precisely observed, truly told and serious minded. But it is limited to much the same material as these contrivances, the feminine world of family and home. What is worse, the delineation of its male characters is weakened by what may well be a conscientious scruple; a refusal (since one is not male) to try to see these characters in male terms, because such an effort would involve invention almost in the sense of falsification.

For a novelist as finely observant, as capable, as Miss Sarton, such scruples are nonsense.

Elizabeth Janeway. *NYT*. Sept. 8, 1957. p. 4

The author has long considered the difficulty of achieving personal harmony through human relationships. All her books, and much of her poetry, have shown preoccupation with the growth of personality, the ability or lack of it to communicate love, or, for that matter, to feel it in the first place, the acceptance of birth and death as cyclical parts of man's continuity. These are primary concerns, usually wrapped in the thunderclouds of *Sturm und Drang*. But Miss Sarton's style is quiet, her dialogue true and sure. She describes no scene "folkloristically" yet each has abundant authentic detail. And her situations, though low-keyed, are basic, alive with their own kind of tension, drama, and suspense.

Frances Keene. *SR*. Sept. 14, 1957. p. 50

See *The Lion and the Rose* and *In Time Like Air* (poetry); also *The Single Hound, A Shower of Summer Days,* and *Faithful Are the Wounds* (novels).

SCHULBERG, BUDD (1914–   )

What Makes Sammy Run? is brilliantly effective because it is completely of this time, expressing the beliefs and hopes that begin to
stand out in this period, marked in it by the threat of complex defeat.
The dialogue is a bit freer, less reticent than even that dialogue that
shocked the dear innocent early public of Hemingway. The style is un-
sweated, but colorful. The story is constantly pointed up with incident.
. . . It is unquestionably one of the most interesting and promising
first novels to appear in several years.

Robert Van Gelder. NYT. Mar. 30, 1941. p. 6

If you have frequently looked with fascination at the unmistakable
lineaments of big business and have tried to solve the mystery of what
must have been the living transformation of the individual into the
corporation, then you will follow the quest for the answer to the question posed in the title of Mr. Schulberg's book. . . . The book in uneven; the first part is badly written and developed. . . . Toward the
end Mr. Schulberg does say what he wants to say, the writing is good,
the plot blooms, and the form is there. Hollywood, that junction of
theater and audience, is more honestly, amusingly, and instructively
covered than in any other book I know.

L. P. Lazarus. Nation. April 19, 1941. p. 477

Budd Schulberg's new book is a hard-boiled successor to his first and
tough little novel, *What Makes Sammy Run?* Just as full of heels and no-
goods, and as fast, slangy and wisecracking, *The Harder They Fall* is
in many ways a much better novel than *Sammy*. . . . Out of the
elements of the Carnera story Schulberg has created a brilliant novel
—the first of the modern prize ring, I believe, to be a worthy contender
for literary honors. . . . Schulberg owes something to Hemingway,
F. Scott Fitzgerald, and Jerome Weidman, and the readers of the
sports pages also will recognize rhythms of sports columnist Jimmy
Cannon. . . . But the final product is a Schulberg original, a switch on
the American success story wherein bad boy makes good.

John Horn. NYT. Aug. 10, 1947. p. 3

What gives *The Harder They Fall* its impressive quality is the realism
and the scientific accuracy of the deadly picture of a sordid business.
Schulberg knows the atmosphere, the history and the technique of the
ring and the psychology of its fighters, promoters, hangers-on and pub-

lic. Even the sentimentalism, the sadness and the rare examples of bravery are credible, because the author sees not only the ugliness but the fascination of the racket that is a sport. . . . Schulberg hates the sordidness, cruelty and corruption of the so-called fight game, but he can get as sentimental as the next man about the battered and punch-drunk veterans of an earlier day and just as excited about a good battle between a couple of fighters who really fight.

Richard Watts, Jr. *NR*. Aug. 11, 1947. pp. 27–8

The Harder They Fall is the story of an American heavyweight and of how he got his. . . . Not since Hemingway's "Fifty Grand" has there been a story so idiomatic, so physically cruel, so underscored with the disgust of the corrupted. The atmosphere at Stillman's gym, the Sunday luncheon at Nick's country place, Barry Winch playing gin rummy, the sparring of George Blount—these are descriptions or bits of low comedy incomparably well done. I cannot question the tough reality of the episodes—not even the corny scenes with Shirley, a boxer's widow, who would probably be even cornier in real life. But I do wonder whether there is enouch change of pace and enough high relief in the book to keep the reader coming.

Edward Weeks. *At*. Sept., 1947. p. 120

Mr. Schulberg's gamy, grimy opus is hard-fisted writing at its brass-knuckle, kidney-punching best. . . . *The Harder They Fall* is an exposé of the prize-fighting business in this country. . . . This, too, is a part of American culture, a conspicuous part; and Mr. Schulberg's combination of contemptuous hatred and reluctant fascination makes for good reading. . . . With no subtleties of characterization, but with wonderfully authentic atmosphere, he has written a scathing indictment of a so-called "sport." And in the process he has never allowed his indignation to get in the way of his story-telling.

Orville Prescott. *YR*. Autumn, 1947. p. 191

The thirty-six-year-old Mr. Schulberg is a sensitive and gentle companion. In fact, his gentleness transforms itself into an exacting concern in the modulations of an idea—such shadings and qualifications lending to Mr. Schulberg's speech a hesitant and touchingly tormented character. At the same time, within this muted atmosphere that Mr. Schulberg can't help but create, there exists an awareness in his companions that Mr. Schulberg is possessed of a remarkably powerful chest, that he is, as well, the proud possessor of a promising prize-fighter—all of which combines into a nice paradox.

Harvey Breit. *NYT*. Nov. 5, 1950. p. 28

Schulberg has moved up from the heels of *What Makes Sammy Run?* and the punks of *The Harder They Fall.* The flashy, erratic style of those novels often obscured the maturity of his implied judgements, his ability to open people up so that you can decide what makes *them* run. These gifts are more richly displayed, more fully developed in *The Disenchanted.* There are weaknesses: the book seems uneven in spots, too long, and trite and awkward when Schulberg is trying to recreate some scenes with which he appears personally unfamiliar. But there are episodes of great power and vividness, in which the thoughtful reader can discern some penetrating observations on the evils of casting stones.

Paul V. Farrell. *Com.* Nov. 10, 1950. p. 124

Because Budd Schulberg is a sound journalist who draws upon material he has lived with or authenticated, the twenty entries in *Some Faces in a Crowd* are packed with verisimilitude. Few observers know more about Hollywood . . . or about the boxing business. . . . He is suspicious of all Head Men, depicted here as uneasy end-products of a dog-eat-dog process among phonies, ingrates, bullies, eccentrics, and dreamers right out of the final scene of *The Iceman Cometh.* He believes that fame is fleeting, loyalty about as rare as the whooping crane, and moments of glory illusion.

In Schulberg land, the heels are at work, the realities are squalid, and the prognosis is dreary.

James Kelly. *SR.* May 16, 1953. p. 14

His . . . stories . . . differ from popular magazine fiction chiefly in the way they end. The characters have to take the responsibility for what they do. They have to pay moral costs and face defeats. . . . Mr. Schulberg is like the popular magazine writers, however, in his style and in the ingredients out of which his fictions are made. He obviously admires Hemingway and Lardner and Fitzgerald, but he does not feel their need to get things just right, to see the thing as what in itself it truly is. . . . Villainy is made a little too easy to be against in these stories. Villainy is, nevertheless, very clearly seen and very dramatically presented. And virtue is very clearly seen, too, especially in the war stories.

Robert Gorham Davis. *NYT.* May 17, 1953. p. 5

Schulberg . . . seems congenitally unable to see the world except through the special lenses developed by Hemingway (the sentimentalized prize fight and the brutalized deep-sea fishing stories) or Fitzgerald (the beautiful rich girl with a suicidal drive). . . . Schulberg is another of the Jewish writers like Weidman and Shaw whose work has skimmed close to the solid shores of genuine American literary achievement. These writers, in a sense which can serve only as an initial, temporary excuse, have been incapacitated from realizing their promise by a lack of a serious and active artistic tradition, something they give hints of recognizing; but, instead of seeking one, as, say, Lionel Trilling has done, in the depths of history and in the classical values, instead of dealing with the lack as part of the process of developing an authentic idiom, they have casually gone for their guidance to the popular culture heroes.

Morris Freedman. Cmty. Oct., 1953. pp. 389–92

See *What Makes Sammy Run?*, *The Harder They Fall*, *The Disenchanted*, and *Waterfront* (novels); also *Some Faces in a Crowd* (short stories).

SCHWARTZ, DELMORE (1913–   )

Concerned with fundamentals, with the problem of identity, of knowledge and belief, haunted by the noise time makes, able to write wittily and movingly, Mr. Schwartz is betrayed by a failure of concentration. His diffuseness is perhaps inevitable to a sensitive person pausing before a mirror which reflects his face against the background of this distracted twentieth-century scene. . . . He shows himself open to more perceptions than he can properly control. They crowd upon him so thickly that the effect, which should be one of richness and depth is sometimes that of confusion. But at his best, and his best is very good, he exhibits a sensibility and an intelligence rare in his generation.

Babette Deutsch. NYHT. March 5, 1939. p. 21

In the story which opens *In Dreams Begin Responsibilities,* and in the lyrics which make up the third section, the author displays not only a mastery of technic that is precisely suited to his poems' intention, but also a rare sensitivity of perception, an urgent humanity, and such an honesty of expression as is rare in a day when the manners of poetry ape the sliding faithless manners of international diplomacy. It is hard to believe that this is a first book, the work of a very young man. . . . Almost without exception the short poems achieve the equilibrium between Thing Said and Way of Saying that is the mark of the finest poetry.

Dudley Fitts. SR. April 29, 1939. p. 29

Schwartz is an authoritative poet, which is to say that he is much more than a poet of the decade. His achievement is threefold. First of all, he has orchestrated the central theme of his decade more richly, more consistently, and more intelligently than any of his contemporaries. Beyond this, Schwartz differs from most of his contemporaries in having a genuinely creative attitude of mind that enables him always to project and to resolve the tensions of his poetry in terms of real experience. He rejects the easy solutions offered by ideologies; his use of ideas is always dramatic rather than didactic; he takes the hard way—to a solution in terms of poetry.

Moreover, Schwartz develops his solution in an original verse tone that modifies the English poetic tradition in using it.

George Marion O'Donnell. *Poetry*. May, 1939. p. 107.

Much that he has done has been self-conscious rather than conscious of larger meanings than the self. He is not alone in the fault. A whole school of younger poets rely on learning rather than vision. But it is time that Mr. Schwartz find, if he is ever going to, the rhythms and images characteristic of him and of him alone, the convictions which he holds, the vision, not so narcissistic, which makes his voice worth listening to. If he does not do this he will remain one of the several bright young poets who have risen to some fame rather too easily because of their ability to handle form and to echo current ideas and patterns of belief. On a few occasions this poet has written movingly, but more often he has only composed in the more modern forms of poem, play, or short story.

Eda Lou Walton. *NYHT*. Nov. 23, 1941. p. 32

Schwartz adumbrates a theme of the first importance and value: the infinite possibilities, logically and ethically studied of human individuality. This and its uncompromising technical skill are what make the poem not only a document but positive. "You lie in the coffin of your character," one of the ghosts says . . . ; but another asks, "Who can recover actuality? And who can win his way to criticism?" If *Genesis* is a statement of this question, it creates confidence that the answer, too, will be aesthetically valid. Despite occasional garrulous aridity, it suggests as a whole a genuinely tragic view of life, which needs stating more than ever against the prevalent falsettos uttering or claiming to dispel premature indifference and despair.

Frank Jones. *Nation*. Aug. 14, 1943. p. 187

These stories (in *The World Is a Wedding*) are written, for the most part, in a monotonous, even awkward prose. For a writer with a reputation as a poet, they are surprisingly deficient in imagery, or the visual sense. But one soon notices in the explicit themes, in the abstract language, in the political references, and in the tone of polite discussion, a deliberate direction halfway between traditional fiction and the philosophical dialogue.

In a number of instances Schwartz brings it off beautifully; in any case, it's a direction along which writers, here and there, are feeling their way, and one which should have happy consequences for the form and content of fiction.

John Farrelly. *NR*. Aug. 2, 1948. p. 27

Delmore Schwartz writes fiction as a poet and not as a chronicler. For him, the history of the New York Ashkenazim from the nineties to the present is symbolic of what has happened to man everywhere. . . . I have read no fiction of late whose content seems so completely lived and comprehended—all communicated in the sparsest and barest of prose, a whole society, the generations, breathing and talking endlessly. Given this concern with most of the central anxieties of modern life, it would be easy for the author to fall into self-pity. Except for two unfortunate stories . . . , an intellectual astringency keeps Mr. Schwartz out of this kind of difficulty.

Ernest Jones. *Nation*. Sept. 11, 1948. p. 294

With a deceptive sparseness and formality of style Delmore Schwartz writes of Jewish middle class family life in New York in this century. His stories, moving from room to room inside the dry vastness of the city, show families divided against themselves, and individuals, who, though terribly interdependent, will never know each other directly in love or friendship. He describes the search for love in these people, even as they fall away from it, their feelings of guilt and self-defense even as the desire to be rid of them, and their resignation even in their frustration. . . . In a comparatively few pages some of the stories encompass generations of family tensions and frustrations without apparent strain. But the style, though quiet, has a kind of muted eloquence which testifies even more strongly to this author's talent.

John Hay. *Com*. Sept. 17, 1948. p. 551

Pleasure in reading Schwartz comes in recognition of worldly values. . . . Schwartz has long been a poet of the city. No illusions are left about it. We feel that we have been dragged through its least place in reading him, for nothing is spared in the depiction of truth. We accept, the gross, the banal, the sentimental, the sensual. . . . There is little of fury or rage, much of philosophic understanding, and a hard-worked control over what is being said. The poems erect substantial orders to mirror the actual urban world, urban life, and the foibles of both.

Richard Eberhart. *NYT*. Nov. 5, 1950. p. 2

In mercilessly identifying the sources on which he draws, and in choosing as his central theme the chasm between poetry and life and between man and man, he battles for his identity as poet. (Occasionally, when his verse gets very good, it is as if his verse had chosen him and not he it, in the very same way that Rilke became the "speaking mouth" of his visions.) In celebrating the American continent, the astonishment of the child still alive in him; in debunking America, in satirically stripping the mask of reality from its surface, and only then going on to praise its unveiled beauty and its grandeur, he struggles for his identity as an American. And in taking his origins as the point of departure for his attempt to make himself part of the world, part of the human environment and of the universe of the intellect, he battles for his identity as a Jew.

Heinz Politzer. *Cmty*. Dec., 1950. p. 568

No other young poet has realized the inadequacy of Christianity (and the Judaism from which it derives) in the modern Western world with the same appalling consciousness that he has. . . . In his own quiet American way Delmore Schwartz is the desperate counterpart of Rimbaud, whose *Une Saison en Enfer* he has translated. Both are aware that the supports of their respective cultures are tottering and new beliefs must be found to nourish the religious impulse of man. . . . Schwartz is not unaware of the literary value of his heritage. . . . Schwartz makes of Jewishness a symbol of the modern situation. The alienated man apprehends experience as the Jew lives in the modern Christian world, both through a glass darkly.

Morton Seiff. *JSS*. Oct., 1951. pp. 311–2, 316

See *The World Is a Wedding* (short stories) and *Summer Knowledge* (poems).

SCOTT, WINFIELD TOWNLEY (1910–   )

Winfield Townley Scott is a striking poet working with an original key which was provided him by the techniques of our modern school, but one who exists in an isolated sphere in the same way that Chirico does in contrast to other surrealist painters. Scott's stark contrast to the surrealist poets like Parker Tyler, Weldon Kees, etc., is that he never builds beyond a single phenomenon, whereas they struggle to find a magnet for a series of phenomena. . . . The strange portions of his work, in concept, I feel have been affected through John Wheelwright's influence and the subtle shifting of musical phrases by simulating the poetry of Dylan Thomas. Like Wheelwright's, it is a felt poetry as well as thought, uneven and inclusive and highly original. I expect that he will grow in stature.

Maurice Swan. *NYT.* Jan. 18, 1942. p. 5

By whatever critical formulas Scott's poetry is approached and discussed, it would be an obtuse, tired reviewer who could fail to sense the genuineness of this poet's mind, the liveness of the poetic experience he records and makes. . . . For the searcher of speech patterns, they are there, not as indelible and local as Frost's perhaps, and sometimes out of control, but very close and real. The danger of prose "draining the air" is successfully overcome in almost every poem. There are enough verses presenting awareness and criticism of twentieth-century environment to meet the demands of the critic who believes modern verse must mirror the times to the last neon tube and microphone.

Marshall Schacht. *Poetry.* April, 1942. p. 47

When he is not celebrating individualists of that region whose transcendentalism enables the poets to include heaven and earth within their "regionalism," Mr. Scott is reducing the general to the individual (what John Peale Bishop called "minute particulars") in the manner of all true poets.

Mr. Scott's eye is acute; his powers of observation show to good advantage in a number of poems. In the transcendental mode he finds wide meaning in narrow corners of nature; his landscapes extend infinitely.

Gerard Previn Meyer. *SR.* Oct. 9, 1948. p. 32

The Dark Sister is a figure from the Norse saga's *Long Island Book,* the source of all we know about the discovery of America by Lief Ericson in the year 1000. . . . Winfield Scott has been accurate to the mood of the story. We forget that we know so little of our past, what ancestors we come from. . . . Scott has used a long line and diction well suited to the rough speech of his sailor characters who were under their mistress' domination throughout the voyage.

William Carlos Williams. *Nation.* Feb. 22, 1958. p. 171

Scott's newest book, his seventh, is *The Dark Sister,* a saga not only because it is about Leif Ericson's half sister, Freydis, and the Viking exploration to the new world, but because in this poet's language, narration, and sweep a saga truly rises out of Vinland. The hero is not human, but infinitely greater, the land itself bigger than all the human beings who came to it or were to come for centuries. Scott's descriptive passages of weather, forests, the sea are more the climate of the poem than "passages," but they thrust under our very feet and into our blood. . . . Scott's realization in words of that clean cold land and time is his triumph in this poem.

John Holmes. SR. April 12, 1958. p. 70

Though Winfield Townley Scott has published admirable verse for over twenty years, *The Dark Sister* is his masterpiece and one of the remarkable poems of recent times. It has excitement and depth. With a control of his medium that almost never falters, he handles characterization, narrative, and landscape with equal power in the flexible cadences of his verse. . . . The work is written in loose three-part measures—largely dactyls and amphibrachs with some fine spondees that have almost a quantitative effect. The form is sufficiently fluid to meet the demands of the content, and is notably satisfactory in the seaborne and windswept passages.

Robert Hillyer. NYT. March 9, 1958. p. 10

Both the conscious skill of understatement and the fine sea-rhythm (somewhat like the best of Jeffers) are present in the new long poem *The Dark Sister*. This is a narrative poem which—I don't know how to suggest the uncomfortable suggestion—tries to be an epic. I enjoyed reading *The Dark Sister*. It is an important contribution to the solution of the problem which seems to fret the good poets of Mr. Scott's generation: the long poem. Its narrative line is always clear, its characterizations are adequately distinct from one another, its heroine is a real four-square howling bitch who would plainly devour her litter. Moreover, Mr. Scott has achieved scenes which are startlingly dramatic.

James Wright. Poetry. Oct., 1958. pp. 47–8

See *Mr. Whittier and Other Poems* and *The Dark Sister* (poetry).

SHAPIRO, KARL (1913–   )

As a member of the generation that grew up between the wars, I can't help taking a certain collective pride in the poems of Karl Shapiro. They would be good poems in any generation, but for mine they express with such unusual accuracy and poignancy a set of hitherto faintly

articulated attitudes that they arrive as a kind of culmination. The bitterness may be more concentrated in the poems of Kenneth Fearing.
The aloof nobility of Spender . . . or the desperate humility of James
Agee may not be here quite equalled. But the peculiar affirmations
and negations of this generation are focused by Shapiro for the first
time in a characteristic idiom. . . . Like Hart Crane, Shapiro sees life
with an acute urgency. But unlike Crane, in the mirror of a well-de-
veloped social conscience. And unlike the Marxists, without wishful
distortions.

Selden Rodman. NR. Dec. 21, 1942. p. 834

The manner and especially the diction of Shapiro's writing is all from
Auden. . . . In Shapiro . . . the borrowed style is an aid and not an
obstacle; the result is a growing originality.

The source of this originality is undoubtedly Shapiro's inexhaustible power of observation. He can see a great deal, he has taken a long,
cunning, and intelligent look at the important objects of modern life,
and has serious and important feelings about what he sees. Yet this
strength has, like most virtues, its danger and its weaknesses. There is
not only a sameness of tone and feeling in a good many of these poems
but also a tendency to rely too much on dramatic observation, organized merely as a succession of items, to solve all problems and provide
the insight which the subject requires.

Delmore Schwartz. Nation. Jan. 9, 1943. pp. 63–4

The notable thing about *Person, Place, and Thing* was a firmness of
mood and singleness of purpose. Its well-written satires on industrial
society were not great poetry or even on their way to being that;
they were in the best sense "minor." And Shapiro was able to be a
successful minor poet in our time because, while renouncing the larger
myth-making pretensions of modern poetry, he nevertheless maintained
the modernist defiance of middle-class civilization. The ground of self-
assurance is now giving way, it is clear, under pressure of the war and
prolonged soldiering. . . . There is in his work growing contempt for
conscious artistry and intellect, an eagerness to present himself as
passionately immersed in the folk life of the soldier.

F. W. Dupee. Nation. Sept. 16, 1944. pp. 327–8

Shapiro is a developing craftsman, applying himself conscientiously to
problems of poetic technique and illustrating the results in his verse.
Much of his work is still in the experimental stage: his technique is
sometimes inept, his poems sometimes don't come off at all. But on
the whole he is coming along very nicely, and has already produced a

few really good poems. Let us remember, incidentally, that very few people indeed produce any really good poems, though many spend a lifetime trying. . . . Shapiro is doing all right, working his passage to salvation the hard way.

David Daiches. *Poetry.* Aug., 1945. pp. 266–7, 273

Whatever else one may conclude about the merits or demerits of Mr. Karl Shapiro's remarkable tour de force, *Essay on Rime,* and perhaps all the more because it is certain to be violently liked or disliked for an immense variety of reasons, whether esthetic, psychological, sociological or philosophic, one feels assured of one thing: this little book is destined to become a kind of literary watershed. . . . His "attack" is, one dares to use the word, masterly. As for the poem itself, and the prosody, if one finds it sometimes *too* near the prose level, and certainly oftener pedestrian than equestrian, and if it far too seldom delights the ear, nevertheless it is very cunningly calculated for its purpose: and it is questionable whether, by tightening and formalizing it further, more might not have been lost than gained. Let us be properly grateful to Mr. Shapiro. He has put himself in an enviable and dangerous position, at the head of his generation.

Conrad Aiken. *NR.* Dec. 3, 1945. pp. 752–4

He isn't a liar, he isn't an ape, he isn't just sad over the state of the world and the stars, he doesn't even bother to concern himself with humanity, or economics, or sociology or any other trio.

He's almost painfully interested in writing as it has been, masterfully, in the world and as it may be (under changed and changing conditions) in the world again. He keeps on the subject. And that's rare. More power to him. I hope he finds her rarest treasures—I am not jealous.

William Carlos Williams. *KR.* Winter, 1946. p. 125

There is something in the nature of his subject matter and his kind of diction which can easily reduce his poetry—and often does—to its lowest common denominator. . . . (Yet) Shapiro has done enough already to prove that he is much more important than the mistakes he makes. He has the personal vigor and the personal capacity—as few young poets in America have—to make his way forward through his work. . . . When you have read a good amount of his verse you are sure that he is a real poet, really feeling things and really sure that he is feeling them. He has the vocation. I say this as my last word for I am confident that in the development of Karl Shapiro as a poet this strength, this integrity, this personality will have the last word.

Henry Rago. *Com.* Jan. 16, 1948. pp. 352–3

Mr. Shapiro is a difficult poet to estimate, because whilst there are elements of technical accomplishment in his poetry which obviously command admiration, there are also elements of crudeness and insensitivity which make him vulnerable to a purist approach, and his very violence makes one uncertain of his power. Nevertheless he is a poet of rare intellectual strength, he has an exceptional power of being able to think of a poem as a single idea, and he has an interesting and perhaps passionate personality which his poetry at present partly conceals. If he were as preoccupied with the single word as he is with the stanza, he would gain enormously. At present he is too inclined to throw his words away on the wings of his stanzas. He is certainly one of the very few poets writing today whose development is an exciting subject for speculation.

Stephen Spender. *Poetry*. March, 1948. pp. 316–7

He can be tenderly emotional, savagely spiritual, and bitterly intellectual without apparently worrying over who is going to think him what.

It seems to me from his works so far . . . that Mr. Shapiro has equipped himself to handle the dark matter at the roots of the tree of poetry and the metaphysical sap of the trunk and branches as well as the mystical flower and fruit. If his apparent assumption that the poet is, in large part, an antisocial madman does not keep him too far from compassionate experience of his world, I feel that he may turn out to be that rarest of all sea-serpents, a poet whose work will be more substantial, more valid, and more perfect twenty years from now than it is today.

Raymond Holden. *SR*. March 20, 1948. p. 16

He paraphrases Descartes' famous sentence thus: *"Sentio ergo sum."* The prominence of feeling in his work is one of the elements that distinguish it from that of Auden, the cogitative contemporary from whom he learned so much. His ability to absorb and transmute this influence among others is an index of his gift. So, too, is his aptitude for making the common places of American culture in war and in peacetime come alive through his plain words and vibrant rhythms. Nor does one need to reread his lines on the "University" (of Virginia) and on "Jefferson" in the light of Warren's major work in order to appreciate that Shapiro recognizes the ambiguity that attends the human effort, even at the peak of its glory.

Babette Deutsch. *YR*. Winter, 1954. p. 281

Fortunately, the Good Lord made Karl Shapiro a genuine poet even though He skimped somewhat on the logical and critical endowment.

Despite the traumatic basis of their movement into compassion, a number of his poems reach beautiful resolution. Others explode ponderous themes—the ease with which we forget history's most dreadful lessons, the incommunicability of certain essential differences of tradition and life-principles, and so on—without losing their buoyancy and independent character as works of feeling with a design independent of doctrinal interests. Indeed, when Shapiro succeeds it is through his vibrant language and rhythm, his unabashed candor, and his irresistible emotional force that *will* bring out his true meanings even when he himself is not quite sure of them.

M. L. Rosenthal. *Nation.* July 5, 1958. p. 15

See *Person, Place, and Thing, V-Letter, Essay on Rime, Trial of a Poet,* and *Poems of a Jew* (all poetry).

SHAW, IRWIN (1913–)

He strikes a fine balance between the sentimentality of the soft-boiled and the sentimentality of the hard-boiled. The warmth of feeling, the heart, the humanity that underlies his stories is genuine and moving. The pathos is not cheap and the humor is not facile. . . . Shaw's stories are contemporary to a degree and New Yorkerish to a degree. There are in them elements that in other writers would be merely a modish despair, a modish heartbreak, a modish "social consciousness." But Shaw's genuine warmth and rightness of feeling, his mature and discriminating sensibility, gives the best of them what one feels is a solid and lasting quality.

H. N. Doughty, Jr. *NYHT.* Jan. 25, 1942. p. 6

Mr. Shaw has throughout his career been a clear spokesman of his well-meaning generation. . . . As an artist he has been an exemplary citizen—devoted, energetic, too intelligent to be too pious yet too pious to be disturbing, his talents as a writer beautifully tuned to the intellectual pitch of his society. But at last, after its long period of sounding on one note—the note of political decency—this society gives signs of having to recognize the existence of a much fuller scale of human motives and values. . . . This is the new freedom that now appears, if only by hints, in Mr. Shaw's novel (*The Young Lions*). . . . Mr. Shaw has the novelist's power—if he has the courage to release it—to overturn the conventions of truth and dig up a few of the real facts about people and the societies they create.

Diana Trilling. *Nation.* Oct. 9, 1948. p. 409

Mr. Shaw's people seem wonderfully alive, even when the author descends to caricature and burlesque. Like Dickens, Mr. Shaw has created, prodigally, a crowded gallery of memorable people. Like Dickens, too, he handles scenes superbly; from the crummy atmosphere of a third-rate New York hotel to the oppressive heat of an Army newspaper office in Algiers, his stories are firmly anchored in time and space. And he communicates experience with a narrative felicity and sincerity which redeem even a frequently far-fetched sentimental or one-sided situation.

William Peden. *SR*. Nov. 18, 1950. p. 28

I am inclined to believe that nothing Mr. Shaw might write could be wholly lacking in interest of one kind or another. For one thing, he always *does* observe and he always *does* feel, and even when he is facile in observation and sentiment he is not insincere. And then he has established himself in a position which guarantees at least the historical or sociological or cultural interest of whatever he writes. He has undertaken the guidance of the moral and political emotions of a large and important class of people, those whom he once called "the gentle people." These are men and women usually of a middling position in our society. They are involved with ideas because modern life seems to make their very existence depend upon the involvement, but they are modest in what they demand by way of ideas and are quite willing to settle for attitudes. . . . In general and almost as a function of his good will Mr. Shaw has been content to tell his audience that decency is a kind of simplicity, that modern life is ghastly because it is an affront to simplicity, and that the simple virtues are all we have for our defense.

Lionel Trilling. *SR*. June 9, 1951. p. 8

He is essentially a master of episode. . . . And it is in the short story . . . that his talents have found their most congenial scope.

Many of his stories deal with Jews. Some relate their sufferings in pogroms and concentration camps, their aspirations and agonies in Palestine. The better ones, as stories, deal with their everyday life in America. . . . Shaw's material is fresh. His people come in off the streets; they are not literary derivatives. His emotional restraint often makes them seem superficial and reduces their griefs and tragedies to an indiscriminate misery. But, where his pity overcomes his self-restraint and still evades his indignation, he has produced some of the best short stories in contemporary literature.

Bergen Evans. *EJ*. Nov., 1951. pp. 490–1

The group for whom he writes often appear as characters in his fiction . . . the well-heeled beneficiaries of mass communications with their regrets and "higher" yearnings. . . . It is part of Irwin Shaw's uncanny flair for what is topical in this world (which is the world of everyone, for its writers smuggle daily into their copy these bootleg ideas) that has brought him on the long journey from *Bury the Dead* to *Lucy Crown.* In a way, he is vindicating his repeated protest that he was not ever *really* a propagandist, though he wrote against war when pacificism was the reigning passion of the young (in *Bury the Dead*), then for a war against fascism when feeling had shifted in that direction (in his sadist-sentimental parable *The Gentle People*), about Nazis and non-conformists in World War II when the age demanded The Big War Book once more (in *The Young Lions*), about McCarthyism and Communism when the newspapers were trying to persuade us we could think of nothing else (in *The Troubled Air*). When no one seems to care about political subjects for the moment, or when at least they have ceased to sell, Shaw can give up politics without a quiver of regret and return to the human subject, to sex and the family, as if he had never left home. . . . At the end of this road is *Lucy Crown,* the book an author like Shaw writes when the times no longer provide him with an ostensible public subject and he must do his best with his own *Ladies' Home Journal* kind of imagination.

Leslie A. Fiedler. Cmty. July, 1956. pp. 71–3

The Young Lions

It was for this image, I suspect, that Shaw wrote his book: to tell what the army did to a nice sensitive bookish young man named Private Noah Ackerman. Noah's ordeal at the hands of his violently anti-Semitic company in Florida has haunted the reviewers into awe-stricken prose. . . . What they all mean to say, I think, is that they have gotten something really new out of a war novel; they have had a shocking emotional discovery of the cruelty in our society from a Jewish writer who is, for all his easy Broadway skill, driven by his experience as a Jew. Shaw has put into the story of Private Noah Ackerman all that Jews have felt in these last years with such particular anguish, and to see Noah there, a shy and liberal intellectual slowly petrifying into another Jew on the cross, is to awaken with horror to a victim who is more real than the millions of victims we read about, for he is familiar and yet absolutely alone.

Alfred Kazin. Cmty. Dec., 1948. p. 497

The Young Lions is a more mature work than *The Naked and the Dead* and a more complete novel than *The Gallery;* yet it shares their common weakness. On the first level, Shaw seems to be making a passionate and deeply human affirmation of the power of decency and justice to survive and even triumph amid the misery and horror of modern war. Yet if we look closely, it becomes apparent that these values do not arise out of the experience presented in the novel but remain outside and above it. Shaw, like Mailer and Burns, has seen the need for belief, but he has been able to objectify the need only and not the belief itself.

John W. Aldridge. *SR*. Feb. 12, 1949. p. 8

See *The Young Lions* and *Lucy Crown* (novels); also *Mixed Company* and *Tip on a Dead Jockey* (short stories).

SHERWOOD, ROBERT (1896–1955)

Plays

Reunion in Vienna is, of course, far more than another dramatization of a Vienna waltz. It is so much more that I have had moods while reading it (and it should be read as well as seen) of thinking that it is the wisest and ripest comedy ever written in America. I cannot at the moment think of another that moves with such a lively grace and still keeps an intelligent head on its shoulders. . . . Sherwood has so often been compared with Shaw that the association of their names is no longer flattering to either, and yet Shaw has done so many things with a provocative badness that it is a satisfaction to see the same things done with a graceful finality. *Reunion in Vienna* is as modern as the latest theory of the neuroses, and yet it is a modernism that is now mature enough to have languors and regrets and nostalgias.

Thomas H. Dickinson. *SR*. May 14, 1932. p. 728

In theatrical variety and unexpectedness of effect there is no living English-speaking dramatist the superior of Robert Sherwood. It is rare to find one of his plays which does not appeal to more than one class of people; most of them appeal to five or six. His plays are a veritable grab-bag of comedy-tragedy-melodrama-farce with always a seasoning of serious meaning. . . . Unlike most Broadway playwrights, Mr. Sherwood has both beliefs and feelings, and unlike the propaganda brethren, he has a subtle mind and a sensitivity of impression which makes him at home in the region of the ironic. Moreover, he knows the world, the great world as well as the work-a-day one.

Grenville Vernon. *Com*. April 10, 1936. p. 664

Reunion in Vienna (is) the first play in which Sherwood showed an aptitude for developing a good theatre situation after he had created it. From this point on, you begin to see clearly in your mind's eye the people of whom he wrote, and although you do not always see them as people walking beside you in the world, they remain with you in the shape of the actors who took part in his plays. If they are not yet people of the real world, they are real people of the theatre world, and for certain plays, such as *Reunion in Vienna,* that is quite enough.

Edith J. R. Isaacs. *TA.* Jan., 1939. pp. 34–7

In *Abe Lincoln in Illinois* Robert E. Sherwood is tracing the career of Lincoln from the Thirties and New Salem, Illinois, to the day he entrained for Washington to be inaugurated President. It has been called the best play about Lincoln ever written, which it probably is; the best play by Mr. Sherwood, which is a matter open to argument; and the greatest play by any living American, which it probably is not. But it is a very moving story of one of the world's great figures.

Lewis Nichols. *NYT.* Feb. 26, 1939. p. 18

What Sherwood most wished to tell (in *Abe Lincoln in Illinois*), I think, is summed up in a sentence Speed wrote to Herndon, "He must believe he was right, and that he had truth and justice with him, or he was a weak man; but no man could be stronger if he thought he was right." To show us the weak Lincoln, to show us the gradual infiltration of a belief in the truth and justice of the cause he was called on to lead, an infiltration which met the resistence of doubts and broodings curiously suggestive of Hamlet, and finally to show the emergence of a man who was the champion of democracy as the justice of God, was Mr. Sherwood's task. With what under the circumstances is a minimum of historical invention, this task he has brilliantly performed, brilliantly because he has given us a three-dimensional character and because he has not forgotten, also, that he is writing a play which must be effective in the theatre.

Walter Prichard Eaton. *Com.* March 3, 1939. p. 526

There Shall Be No Night is more than a good play. It is one of those events in the theatre that explain its survival and justify the faith of those who see in it one of the highest forms of human expression. . . . The play burns with passion. It is, of course, special pleading. . . . It deals with events that are not only current news but actually, in themselves, violently tragic. Yet these elements are usually obstacles rather than aids to dramatic writing. Mr. Sherwood, in undertaking this subject, dared to measure his artifices against Finland's flaming actualities. It is to the credit of his skill as a craftsman and his discipline as an artist, joined to the skill and discipline of his cast, that the attempt has proved successful.

Rosamond Gilder. *TA*. June, 1940. p. 399

Sherwood's world is very pessimistic. He hears the feet of trampling legions stamping out the vestiges of Western civilization. You cannot escape the feeling that, as in *The Petrified Forest,* he still believes that the old civilization is crumbling. The battle he proposes (in *There Shall Be No Night*) is a last ditch stand, which may leave the forces of destruction in triumph. . . . Sherwood believes in the liberal idea of freedom, the democratic ideals to which he testified in his patchwork quilt of Lincolnia, *Abe Lincoln in Illinois*. When he sees these ideals menaced by the philosophy of force, all he can say is fight. Science might save us and religion perhaps, but, anyway, we have to fight.

Robert C. Healey. *CW*. Nov., 1940. pp. 179–80

Among the personalities of the literary world none is more currently conspicuous than Robert Sherwood, and few are more representative of this age both by their revolts and by their conformities. In the theatre he is not only one of the masters of his craft, but the one playwright in the lobby or in the haunts of the after-theatre set who overshadows celebrities of the acting profession without so much as a word on his part to call attention to himself. In the political world he is, barring Archibald MacLeish, the one writer who has found a place both in the government and in the scrimmage line of public controversy. . . . And he is perhaps most significant, in the casual way in which only Sherwood can be significant, as a phenomenon of the liberal mind at work in our day.

John Gassner. *At*. Jan., 1942. p. 26

My firm conviction (is) that Mr. Sherwood's plays have always lagged one pace behind his own ever-increasing seriousness. By his own confession he wrote the highly diverting *Reunion in Vienna* in order not to think of certain things which troubled him. By the time he had got to *The Petrified Forest* and *Idiot's Delight* he could no longer wholly disregard them, and in *There Shall Be No Night* he thought that he had gone completely over to responsible seriousness. Actually, however, he has never permitted himself to go beyond journalism, and I risk the assertion that his present concern with specific political issues is as much an "escape" from deeper questions too puzzling and too painful to think about as *Reunion in Vienna* was an escape from the relatively more serious things even then struggling in his mind for recognition.

Joseph Wood Krutch. *Nation*. Nov. 24, 1945. p. 562

Written during the lull between two World Wars, *Idiot's Delight* is uncanny in its detailed forecasting of the shape the second was to take. The author was also singularly successful, it now becomes evident, in mirroring the precise attitudes of the period and their vulnerability in the face of events to come: the Marxist brotherliness which, in its fanaticism, was quickly adaptable to the needs of nationalism; the other-worldliness of science, which was to find itself not so much above politics as it had supposed; the British complacency, which was to respond so quickly, almost matter-of-factly, to any challenge to the status quo; and so on. More interesting than any of these things, however, is the sense of helplessness which pervades the play, the mood of surrender to idiocy as though idiocy were the only remaining characteristic of the human race.

Walter Kerr. *Com*. June 8, 1951. p. 213

He was a lean, tall man, six-feet-seven, who surveyed the foibles and the errors of mankind with a kindly and somewhat melancholy glance. . . . Courteous to everyone, he had a sharp tongue for isolationists. He wrote with a complete absorption and astonishing rapidity, producing five plays in two years. . . . During the years of uneasy peace and war he came to his full stature, a kindly man of impeccable honesty, courageous, eloquent in the cause of democracy, and a humorist with a touch of irony. It is often said after a man's death that "we shall not see his like again." It is true of Robert Sherwood.

Harrison Smith. *SR*. Nov. 26, 1955. p. 31

No stranger could ever encounter Bob without becoming aware that he was in the presence of a formidable brain and personality. No friend of Bob's ever found him lacking in warmth, sympathy or time when there were troubles to be met. Though he was no opportunist, though he said what he thought whenever it was useful, he made few enemies. Many stood in awe of him because of his deft and pungent tongue, but apt as he was in attack or retort, Sherwood was readier still to give mercy, happier to be tolerant than to be angry.

Maxwell Anderson. *Time*. Nov. 28, 1955. p. 26

Roosevelt and Hopkins—History

He writes a book that is a pleasure to read; and not the least of his merits is that being a playwright, professionally concerned with exploring the complexities of character, he knows enough about it to know how much he does not know. He attempts no "psychograph" of Roosevelt; Hopkins was a far simpler character, but Sherwood does not always explain him; he merely sets down the record—all of the record. Nothing is extenuated; what needs extenuation seems to some of us trivial beside the accomplishment, but Sherwood sets it down anyway; it happened, and he reports all that happened, good and bad.

Elmer Davis. *SR*. Oct. 23, 1948. p. 7

This is an amazing book Mr. Sherwood has written. It is intimate, wonderfully intimate, and yet it is history, full-scaled and far-flung. Immediately it takes its place—a high honor—on the same slim shelf with Winston Churchill's *The Gathering Storm*. The rolling periods are deliberately missing. . . . A different kind of eloquence replaces Mr. Churchill's. It is the eloquence of extreme simplicity. It is as unlike Mr. Churchill's as was Mr. Roosevelt's—a fact which is not surprising since in the preparation of his speeches Mr. Roosevelt depended so often on Mr. Sherwood's aid. . . . The prose is unembellished and swift-moving. . . . It speaks the democratic idiom, movingly, effectively, sometimes humorously.

John Mason Brown. *SR*. Nov. 13, 1948. pp. 54–5

See *Reunion in Vienna, The Petrified Forest, Idiot's Delight,* and *Abe Lincoln in Illinois* (plays); also *Roosevelt and Hopkins* (history).

SINCLAIR, UPTON (1878–   )

The fierce and humorless intensity of Upton Sinclair's youthful masterpiece *The Jungle* has here (in *Oil!*) given place to a maturer kind of writing, with a surprising new tolerance in it for the weaknesses of human nature, and a new curiosity which fills it with the manifold richness of the American scene on every social plane. It restores Upton Sinclair to us as a novelist, and it constitutes one of the great achievements in the contemporary discovery of America in our fiction.

Floyd Dell. *NYHT*. June 12, 1927. p. 7

All the figures in Mr. Sinclair's world are automata except the sublime and tormented hero who is at war with them. There is only one thing in Mr. Sinclair's world that he treats with that respect which is due to reality. That is his own conception of his own mission among men. Everything else is stage properties and supers. . . . He has erected a structure of theories in front of his eyes which is so dazzling that nothing in the outer world is clearly visible to him. . . . He is a noisy and voluble saint, but none the less authentically a saint. He has consecrated himself to his own mission. He is a brave man, too, and spasmodically and spectacularly a rather dashing fighter against oppression. . . . I do not happen to admire deeply his type of saintliness, and so perhaps cannot do him full justice.

Walter Lippmann. *SR*. March 3, 1928. pp. 642–3

As art Sinclair's novel, *Boston,* is worthless; as propaganda it is superb. He has a theme and a character that ride triumphant over technical disabilities. And he has a living conscience. As he works toward a climax, the pretense of fiction gradually falls away and in the last magnificent chapters the book becomes a piece of glorified reporting. Concurrently, the heat of the author's indignation rises steadily higher until, at the end, the reader is left with the sense of having himself been cleansed and purified by fire and humbled by great tragedy.

R. N. Linscott. *SR*. Dec. 1, 1928. p. 425

The difficulty with Sinclair's characters and situations is not in recognizing them, but in *feeling* them. His characters are rational—or cerebral if you will—rather than emotive creations. One can see them—but not experience them. This is partly due to the fact that, in the main, they are types instead of individuals, types that you know. . . . Sinclair tends to portray his characters in terms of straight lines instead of in terms of all those zigzags of personality, those intricate and irrational contradictions of self, which create individuality in life as well as in fiction.

V. F. Calverton. *Nation*. Feb. 4, 1931. pp. 132–3

From *The Jungle* (1906) to date he has repeatedly thrust a sharp knife into most of the sore spots of our contemporary civilization: the packing-house filth, the newspaper racket, the oil scandal, "Massachusetts justice," etc. etc. . . . Sophisticated readers, professors and critics, hold that Mr. Sinclair's novels are not "literature"—whatever that may mean. . . . If a passionate interest in the substance of all great literature—life, if a wide acquaintance with its special manifestations of the writer's own day, if a deep conviction about the values underlying its varied phenomena and the ability to set them forth, count in the making of enduring literature, all these Mr. Sinclair has demonstrated again and again that he possesses.

Robert Herrick. *NR*. Oct. 7, 1931. p. 213

Mr. Sinclair has never pretended to be a professional literary critic. He has been a creative artist and a pamphleteer. To those readers who dislike his work he is the latter exclusively. But to the world at large he takes his place as one of the great literary men of the day. His works are almost immediately translated into French, German, Spanish, Swedish, Chinese, Japanese, and Russian, which is a testimony to his popularity, if not to his art. His books contribute to the forming of opinions about America in almost every country on the globe.

C. Hartley Grattan. *Bkm.* April, 1932. p. 61

Sinclair's moral strength has never let him escape an awareness of the degradation and humiliation that are the normal lot of the oppressed in our republic, and his honesty has never let him remain silent about them. . . . (Yet) Sinclair has scarcely attempted to interpret working-class life since *The Jungle*. His typical story is that of a rich young man who gets mixed up in the radical movement, and the drama lies in the dissolution of his ruling class dogmas.

Robert Cantwell. *NR.* Feb. 24, 1937. pp. 70–1

Because his faults are always so conspicuous and never the fashionable ones, Mr. Sinclair has been either dismissed or patronized by the majority of critics and literary historians. Yet I am willing to wager that his chances of survival are as good as those of any living American author. . . . Sinclair is a master of narrative. Like the Victorians, whose habits of underscored characterization and chatty comment he has always imitated, he has the trick of making you want to find out what happens next. . . . With his own kind of magic, Sinclair rushes you from scene to sceen, and you have to go on to the end.

Granville Hicks. *NR.* June 24, 1940. p. 863

I respect him . . . because he has retained an old-fashioned and innocent love for mankind. Do you think it possible for a man to be too good to become a great novelist? . . . Sinclair . . . is so kindly and trusting—till each new disillusionment—and so convinced that men are naturally good unless distorted by the property system, that you deplore his villains instead of hating them. They are merely products of their environment. . . . Sinclair doesn't believe in Satan; at heart he doesn't even believe in Heinrich Himmler. He is a capable writer when explaining the connections between economics and politics, but he never casts much light on the connection between politics and the human soul.

Malcolm Cowley. *NR.* Jan. 11, 1943. p. 58

(*Presidential Agent*) is an extraordinary and gigantic job . . . of collation, selection, synthesis, craftsmanship, and interpretation, and one that could only have been done by a novelist as mature and practiced and experienced in thinking as its author. Desperately and nervously exciting, moreover; as desperately and nervously exciting as the desperate times in which we live. . . . Here is the first time that any novelist has had the courage to take the present monstrous shape of evil and show it in its proper proportions and in its inevitable final weakness when it meets courage, endurance, and intelligent good-will.

Struthers Burt. *SR*. June 10, 1944. p. 8

Mr. Sinclair is a major figure—and I make the statement ungrudgingly. He is a thoroughly American personality. A fluent—a fatally fluent—writer with an unconquerable desire to preach and teach, he has a heart honorably moved by human suffering. . . . His insight into society is sometimes shrewd, and his prophecies are occasionally correct. Above all, his courage is . . . the courage of American individualism, which has nothing to do with the socialism of Mr. Sinclair's dream.

But when Mr. Sinclair explicitly or implicitly demands that one's sympathy for his courage be translated into one's admiration for him as a literary artist, one can only deny the confusing plea.

Howard Mumford Jones. *At*. Aug., 1946. p. 151

The secret of Upton Sinclair nobody yet knows—except to the degree that he still represents a flourishing of those provincial rebels, freethinkers, and eccentrics who in the 1900's, from Robert Ingersoll to Veblen, marked the climax of our earlier agrarian and mercantile society. But what is the secret of the Lanny Budd series? . . . Mr. Sinclair's familiar villains are here, to be sure, including the international bankers, the Fascists, and the military. Yet there is very little sense of evil in this entire chronicle of modern corruption and decay. Even Hitler has sense enough to listen to Lanny Budd. . . . This central view of life, which corresponds to our own earlier dreams of national destiny and to the Europeans' wildest fancy, seems to me the main element in the success of the Lanny Budd novels.

Maxwell Geismar. *SR*. Aug. 28, 1948. p. 13

See *The Jungle, Oil!, Boston,* and *The Presidential Agent* (novels).

STAFFORD, JEAN (1915–   )

From time to time there appears on the American literary scene an exceptional and original feminine talent. Several over the past few years have exhibited brilliant facets, but Jean Stafford is the first in many

years to spread before our eyes a radiant stylistic network of dazzling
virtuosity.

Elizabeth Bullock. *CS*. Sept. 24, 1944. p. 1

There is no doubt that Jean Stafford, author of *Boston Adventure,* is a
remarkable new talent. This is not to say that her first novel is a completely satisfying experience but that Miss Stafford brings to the writing
of a novel an unusual native endowment; I would find it hard to name
a book of recent years which, page for page or even sentence for sentence, was so lively and so clever. By the light of any one of the in-
candescent moments of *Boston Adventure,* it may turn out that the
book as a whole is strangely disappointing, reminding us that in the final
analysis no amount of skill as a writer substitutes for the total novelistic
power. But for its manner, for the way in which it stands up to the
literary job, Miss Stafford's novel unquestionably demands a place for
itself in the best literary tradition.

Diana Trilling. *Nation*. Sept. 30, 1944. p. 383

Miss Stafford's remarkably fine novel (*Boston Adventure*) has been
praised for its range and perception, its style, and for a distinction, as
I see it, that springs from the meeting of genuine personal culture with
deep independence of sight. It has also, because of certain echoes,
been analyzed for its Proustian qualities. But not enough has been said
of the real Proustian epic in it. . . . Here, at last, is a novel in which
sensibility is not sacrificed to representation; in which the inwardness
of man, at once the deposit of events and the shaper of them, is func-
tionally related to bold and objective visual power.

Alfred Kazin. *NR*. Oct. 23, 1944. p. 538

(*The Mountain Lion*) is an even finer novel than *Boston Adventure,*
though less brilliant. It does not have the startling wealth of anecdote
which Jean Stafford offered in her first novel; but it has a deeper richness of child-myth and child-lore—charms against the adult world,
rhymes, ritualistic "dialogues" and shared "jokes," intimations of mortality—and the statement it makes of good and evil, innocence and
experience, is tantalizing in its possibilities of extension. In this narrower plot, the author has found, paradoxically, greater freedom of
perception and utterance: her style here is cleaner and more athletic.

Henry Rago. *Com*. April 4, 1947. p. 618

Miss Stafford writes with brilliance. Scene after scene is told with unforgettable care and tenuous entanglements are treated with wise
subtlety. She creates a splendid sense of time, of the unending after-
noons of youth, and of the actual color of noon and of night.

Refinement of evil, denial of drama only make the underlying truth more terrible.

Catherine Meredith Brown. SR. March 1, 1947. p. 15

The Catherine Wheel—her third and perhaps most complex novel—is supported by few of those subsidiary virtues which gave vitality and idiosyncrasy to her earlier work; for all the elaborate rendition of locale and *decor,* it never really aims—as did *Boston Adventure*—at a systematic investigation of the social fact, nor does it attempt to frame a specialized personal crisis with the masterly precision of *The Mountain Lion*. Its scope is defined by intentions at once more limited and more ambitious than these: Miss Stafford has sought to convey, through two subtly interwoven though distinct narratives, a vision of emotional anarchy assaulting a world of "traditional sanctity and loveliness"—a vision in which the individual disaster is simultaneously symptom and result of the larger social decline. . . . Miss Stafford has written a novel to compel the imagination and nurture the mind; she has also written one in which pity and terror combine to reach us in the secret, irrational places of the heart.

Richard Hayes. Com. Jan. 25, 1952. pp. 404–5

In her superbly controlled novel (*The Catherine Wheel*) Miss Stafford has shown a modern martyrdom; her story discloses the secret torture of two persons, a child and a woman, both caught in a tragic circumstance during a tranquil summer on the coast of Maine. . . . The village in this novel is named Hawthorne, but even without that reminder it is clear that Miss Stafford is concerned with the identical plight that Nathaniel Hawthorne pondered in his stories—the tragedy of human isolation, the devious, painful, perilous struggle for harmony and understanding. *The Catherine Wheel* is a novel of great restraint and of great beauty.

Walter Havighurst. SR. Jan. 26, 1952. p. 11

In each of her novels, she has begun with what her art and imagination can really create: a densely detailed, spatially narrated image of a place, some people, and their relationships, dramatizing the whole in a diffused, remembered time, rather than any too tyrannical chronological time. But then, toward the end, she seems to feel the need for a "memorable act," for some abruptly theatrical violence, which not only intrudes improbably upon the soft-grained texture she has been building up, but for which frankly she has no taste or instinct. . . . The result is false, mutilating, and unworthy of her.

Robert Phelps. NR. March 10, 1952. p. 21

Character is most important in these stories, but character does not play out a drama of isolated sensibility. Instead, Miss Stafford's people are seen, as it were, in a full round of experience, are set with their problems and conflicts in a milieu that is vital and charged both with intimate and external meaning. To an unusual degree, there is a significant rapport and reciprocal influence between these characters and their environments, and from this ability of Miss Stafford's to relate aspects of character with the details of scene and situation comes a major strength of these stories, their compelling believability.

Gene Baro. *NYHT*. May 10, 1953. p. 3

Maladies and misfortunes of one sort or other cause Miss Stafford's characters to retreat from the world of customary urges and responses into a never-never land of dreams and unfulfilled desires, a land where sickness is king and despair his consort. Within its boundaries, Miss Stafford writes with certainty, understanding, and beauty. Like her three novels, (her) stories within their impeccable frame-work, are meaningful and complex. They remind me of children's Japanese flower-shells which when submerged in water open silently to disgorge a phantasmagoria of paper flowers, richly colored, varied and vaguely grotesque in contrast to the bland, unrevealing walls of their temporary habitations.

William Peden. *NYT*. May 10, 1953. p. 5

See *Boston Adventure, The Mountain Lion,* and *The Catherine Wheel* (novels); also *Children Are Bored on Sunday* (short stories).

STEGNER, WALLACE (1909–   )

Mr. Stegner, who has not published any long fiction before this novelette (*Remembering Laughter*), has built a narrative which comes startlingly close to perfection. In many ways it will remind everyone who reads it of *Ethan Frome*. It has the same quiet strength and simplicity in structure and style. The characterizations are not as mature or subtle as those in Mrs. Wharton's novelette, but they are well-realized, and this story has dramatic relief from the tragic mood in Alec's tall tales and the opulence of the farm life.

There is no use to mention the assurance and calm competence that Mr. Stegner brings to his first book—it has to be read to be believed.

Phil Stong. *SR*. Sept. 25, 1937. p. 5

The passing generation of writers examined man with a minifying glass, made him smaller, baser, more miserable than life-size. Inevitably, the characters became too small to be seen; and new writers are returning to their only possible tool, the magnifying lens, and establishing man once more above the ground. In this tradition Mr. Stegner has written a rich and moving study (*On a Darkling Plain*). Perhaps it is in spite of himself that he is romantic, mystical, compassionate, and warm. The interbellum generation has been taught by the war generation to distrust these qualities; but in Mr. Stegner—as in Steinbeck, Wolfe, and Saroyan—they are what we value most.

Milton G. Lehman. NR. Feb. 26, 1940. p. 284

Stegner is prepared to give an inside view of the great Northwest as it was passing from the pioneer to the settled agricultural stage. In numerous tales he has faithfully worked this mine, without really striking pay dirt until the present moment. . . . With *The Big Rock Candy Mountain* the author takes a real hold on his subject. . . . Mr. Stegner has felt the spell of mountain and prairie, of drought, flood and blizzard; he can write of moving accidents and hairbreadth escapes which give us the feel of frontier life better than phrases about the stars and seasons.

Joseph Warren Beach. NYT. Sept. 26, 1943. p. 4

The Big Rock Candy Mountain is not a conscious rediscovery of American values. Mr. Stegner is as amused at small-town cussedness as was Sinclair Lewis, but he knows that satire accomplishes nothing. In a larger sense, however, his book is an extraordinary study in American folkways. The language, the psychology, the customs of his characters are essential and characteristic, largely because, knowing them, he takes them for granted and does not dissect and analyze. His, to be sure, is a masculine world, just as, despite the tenderness with which the wife is treated, this is a masculine book.

Howard Mumford Jones. SR. Oct. 2, 1943. p. 11

Mr. Stegner is a regional writer in the usual sense that a certain geographical area engages him. Three subjects particularly intrigue him: memories of a prairie boyhood; a sudden and often belated revelation to one character of the incubi that haunt another; and what might be called the He-man pastoral, a highly American form found at its purest in the work of Sherwood Anderson and in such stories as Hemingway's "Big Two-Hearted River," and Faulkner's "The Bear."

Harry Sylvester. NYT. Jan. 1, 1950. p. 15

Mr. Stegner writes beautifully about almost any kind of rural landscape, whether it be a birch-and-maple forest in Vermont, an apricot ranch in

California, or the "endless oceanic land" of Saskatchewan. . . . At their most effective, his landscapes leap at you with a vividness that reminds you of the first time the eye doctor dropped the right lens in your test frame.

In his quiet way, Wallace Stegner is one of the most talented writers in our midst.

Richard Match. *NYHT*. Jan. 1, 1950. p. 4

Stegner is always the quiet, sure workman, slipping in almost unnoticed bits of poetry and little ironies and sage observations as the story moves along, but, though almost unnoticed, the little touches dig in, take hold, do their work on the subconscious mind of the reader. But he is at his best, when he is aroused, when he gets his waters to rolling and roiling, for then he gets up on that high plateau that most of his *The Big Rock Candy Mountain* represents.

Feike Feikema. *CS*. Jan. 9, 1950

Wallace Stegner is a thoroughly skilled writer who belongs to a tradition which takes the short story seriously, but not too seriously. Even his least successful stories are characterized by a well-disciplined, essentially conservative craftsmanship. Neither an entertainer nor an artist *per se,* he seldom fails to respect either his characters or his readers. In short, serious as his approach to short fiction may be, he does not allow his story to be submerged by message or overshadowed by technique.

William Peden. *SR*. Jan. 21, 1950. p. 17

The psychological or regional not-at-homeness of Stegner's main characters makes the stories dominantly reflective in tone. The changes are mostly inner. What begins as condemnation of others becomes self-criticism. A deepened sense of what others are and need results in a deepened and chastened sense of self. Such detachment and reflectiveness are not likely to go with passionate commitment, and the stories do not usually drive dramatically to some final outer resolution. They are wise and humane as well as observant, however, and teach what must happen in ourselves before we can love and understand others, and by what steps we can move toward effective sympathy with those who, most needing love, are most unlovable.

Robert Gorham Davis. *NYT*. Oct. 26, 1956. p. 6

His gifts are of a distinguished, though completely unspectacular kind. They include a cool steadiness of insight into the complexities of the human condition and an extraordinary flexibility in making the idiom of the moment bespeak many subtleties of judgement. . . . Stegner always turns away from the shattering climax. When his point is made he breaks off, sometimes abruptly. This is as it must be with a writer to whom nothing is more offensive than the second-hand affirmative unless it is the garish, improbably bloody tragic resolution.

James Gray. *NYHT*. Nov. 4, 1956. p. 4

See *Remembering Laughter, On a Darkling Plain,* and *The Big Rock Candy Mountain* (novels); also *Women on the Wall* and *City of the Living* (short stories).

STEIN, GERTRUDE (1874–1946)

We find . . . that Miss Stein's method is one of subtraction. She has deliberately limited her equipment. . . . Obviously, any literary artist who sets out to begin his work in a primary search for music or rhythm, and attempts to get this at the expense of (the) "inherent property of words," obviously this artist is not going to exploit the full potentialities of his medium. He is getting an art by subtraction; he is violating his *genre*. . . . Miss Stein continually utilizes this violation of the *genre*. Theoretically at least, the result has its studio value. . . . By approaching art-work from these exorbitant angles one is suddenly able to rediscover organically those eternal principles of art which are, painful as it may be to admit it, preserved in all the standard textbooks.

Kenneth Burke. *Dial*. April, 1923. pp. 409–10

In her detachment, her asceticism, and her eclecticism, Miss Stein can only remind us of another American author who lived in Europe and devoted himself more and more exclusively to the abstract. The principal difference between Henry James (whom Miss Stein reads more and more these days) and Gertrude Stein is that the former still kept within the human realm by treating moral problems. . . . Moreover, what Miss Stein has in common with James she has in common with Poe, Hawthorne, Melville, and several other important and characteristic American writers: an orientation from experience toward the abstract, an orientation that has been so continuous as to constitute a tradition, if not actually *the* American tradition. Of this tradition it is possible to see in Miss Stein's writing not only a development but the pure culmination.

William Troy. *Nation*. Sept. 6, 1933. pp. 274–5

I was delighted to see that Miss Stein never mentioned her style, never said that she had a philosophy, and that her point of view was merely the natural way she had of walking and speaking English; even in her boldest creations she acted spontaneously and enjoyed the fun of amusing herself. I was surprised first because our French wits rather liked wondering at themselves and even being shocked at themselves but certainly explained to everybody how marvelous and queer they were. On the contrary this woman whose mind was so rich and so new seemed never to have time to stop, look and listen at herself. All her actions and all her attention she kept in herself. All her personality she carried inside herself, inside this space and this time which was herself.

Bernard Fay. Preface to Gertrude Stein's *The Making of Americans* (Harcourt). 1934. pp. xii–xiii

I have never heard talk come more naturally and casually. It had none of the tautness or deadly care that is in the speech of most American intellectuals when they talk from the mind out. If sometime you will listen to workingmen talking when they are concentrating upon the physical job at hand, and one of them will go on without cease while he is sawing and measuring and nailing, not always audible, but keeping on in an easy rhythm and almost without awareness of words—then you will get some idea of her conversation.

John Hyde Preston. *At.* Aug., 1935. p. 192

She had the easiest, most engaging and infectious laugh I have ever heard. Always starting abruptly at a high pitch and cascading down and down into rolls and rolls of unctuous merriment, her hearty laugh would fill the room and then, as it gradually dwindled into chuckles and appreciative murmurs, the silence that followed seemed golden with sunlight. Her laugh was boisterous but I have never known it to offend even the most delicately attuned, for it was so straight from the heart, so human, so rich in sound.

Bravig Imbs. *Confessions of Another Young Man* (Henkle-Yewdale). 1936. pp. 118–19

It is little surprising that the ideas of William James have influenced his pupil. It is remarkable, however, to realize that Stein has, from her first work forward, created in an aesthetics which did not have its formal doctrination until as late as two decades after her first experiments with it. It is to be understood literally that the rudiments of a pragmatic aesthetic appeared in her work before contemporary philosophers, including William James, had expounded such an aesthetic. It was, then, with the voice of annunciation that she said, in 1926, "naturally no one thinks, that is no one formulates until what is to be formulated has been made."

Robert Bartlett Haas. Foreword to Gertrude Stein's *What Are Masterpieces* (Conference). 1940. p. 21

Her writing is harder than traditional prose, as a foreign tongue is harder than a native tongue; at first glance we catch a word here and there, or a phrase or two, but the over-all meaning must be figured out arduously. Yet a tension is created, a question asked and in Miss Stein at her best, dramatic context mounts to a climax and then a conclusion. It's pure creative activity, an exudation of personality, a discharge, and it can't be defined more exactly. The mysterious surge of energy which impels a boy who is idling on a corner to race madly down the street is part and parcel of the same thing. When people call it elementary, they mean elemental.

W. G. Rogers. *When This You See Remember Me*
(Rinehart). 1948. pp. 69–70

I recall having a tormented feeling when first hearing the musicians of India playing for the dancing of Shankar. The music went on and on, like the babbling of a brook, always going on, always slightly, but ever so slightly, different, but mostly always the same. One waited almost nervously for a crescendo, a period, a climax, but one waited in vain; and gradually as the expectation was thwarted, as one gave up expecting, it was a soothing music as the babbling of a brook may be soothing, and then gradually as one listened more intently it was an intensely interesting, even a revealing music. There was no blare of horns, but it was none the less interesting. Miss Stein's prose is like that.

George Haines IV. *SwR*. Summer, 1949. p. 413

"In writing a word must be for me really an existing thing." Her efforts to get at the roots of existing life, to create fresh life from them, give her words a dark liquid flowingness, like the murmur of blood. She does not strain words or invent them. Many words have retained their original meaning for her, she uses them simply. Good means good and bad means bad—next to the Jews the Americans are the most moralistic people, and Gertrude Stein is an American Jew, a combination which by no means lessens the like quality in both. Good and bad are attributes to her, strength and weakness are real things that live inside people, she looks for these things, notes them in their likenesses and differences. She loves the difficult virtues, she is tender toward good people, she has faith in them.

Katherine Anne Porter. *The Days Before* (Harcourt).
1952. p. 39

In almost all literature until Gertrude Stein, the act of composition has been used to recall, recreate, analyze, and celebrate an Object Time, the time in which the "thing seen" is happening. This is true whether this Object Time is in the historical past . . . or the historical present. . . . In Gertrude Stein, just the reverse is true. In almost everything she wrote, it is the Subject Time, the time in which she is happening as she sees and writes, which is realized. . . . When she says "The time of the composition is the time of the composition," she means exactly that. The time that goes on in her writing is *not* the time in which her "thing seen" is going on. Her complete works might very aptly be called, "A la recherche du temps présent."

Robert Phelps. *YR*. Summer, 1956. p. 601

She never relinquishes the strictest, most intimate relationship between her words and her thought. . . . The aphoristic style and the conciseness of the formulas express the energy of this writer's consciousness, which appears almost excessive. Her language is affirmed in slow tempo, with a marked degree of solemnity, as it seeks to acquire a certain weight of one-syllable words. It represents finally a summation of things felt, lived with, possessed. It is common language and yet it relates an experience of intimacy which is the least communicable of all experiences. A word used by Gertrude Stein does not designate a thing as much as it designates the way in which the thing is possessed, or the way whereby the poet has learned to live with it.

Wallace Fowlie. *SR*. Dec. 22, 1956. p. 21

If these works are highly complex and, for some, unreadable, it is not only because of the complicatedness of life, the subject, but also because they actually imitate its rhythm, its way of happening, in an attempt to draw our attention to another aspect of its true nature. Just as life is being constantly altered by each breath one draws, just as each second of life seems to alter the whole of what has gone before, so the endless process of elaboration which gives the work of these two writers (Stein and Henry James) a texture of bewildering luxuriance —that of a tropical rain-forest of ideas—seems to obey some rhythmic impulse at the heart of all happening.

In addition, the almost physical pain with which we strive to accompany the evolving thought of one of James's or Gertrude Stein's characters is perhaps a counterpart of the painful continual projection of the individual into life.

John Ashberry. *Poetry*. July, 1957. p. 252

See *Selected Writings;* also *The Autobiography of Alice B. Toklas;* and *Three Lives* and *The Making of Americans* (fiction).

STEINBECK, JOHN (1902–   )

He is primarily a masculine writer. . . . He has proved himself an original and highly individualistic force. His books provoke the masculine mind because of his fearless grappling with ideas and human passions as well as sacred taboos. The dry rot of gentility has never touched him and neither sex nor a woman's honor nor romantic love loom large as a man's serious problems in his view.

Edmund C. Richards. *NAR*. June, 1937. p. 409

Steinbeck abhors and abjures the tag "mystic" which some critics have used in describing him. He is deeply concerned with the problem of Good and Evil, not in any conventional, moral, or philosophical sense but as phenomena in life and as animating principles in life. I have heard him use no word indicating the nature of his beliefs and intimations; but I should vaguely describe them as comprising a curious, very modern Manicheanism, derived perhaps in part from the Indians of the West Coast he has known since boyhood, from acute observation of cause and effect operating among primitive or untutored men, and from a frank facing of the evidences of his own hidden resources of mind and will.

Burton Rascoe. *EJ*. March, 1938. pp. 213–4

Surely no one writes lovelier stories, yielding a purer pleasure. Here are tragedy and suffering and violence, to be sure, but with all that is sharp and harsh distilled to a golden honey, ripe and mellow. Even cruelty and murder grow somehow pastoral, idyllic, seen through this amber light, as one might watch the struggles of fish and water snakes in the depths of a mountain pool. Beyond question, Steinbeck has a magic to take the sting out of reality and yet leave it all there except the sting. Perhaps it is partly the carefulness of his art, with endless pains devising and arranging every detail until all fits perfectly and smooth and suave as polished ivory. But probably it is more the enchantment of his style, of that liquid melody which flows on and on.

T. K. Whipple. *NR*. Oct. 12, 1938. p. 274

The variability of the form itself is probably an indication that Mr. Steinbeck has never yet found the right artistic medium for what he wants to say. But there is in his fiction a whole substratum which does remain constant and which gives it a certain basic seriousness that that of the mere performer does not have. What is constant in Mr. Steinbeck is his preoccupation with biology. He is a biologist in the literal sense that he interests himself in biological research. . . . Mr. Steinbeck almost always in his fiction is dealing either with the lower animals or with human beings so rudimentary that they are almost on the animal level; and the close relationship of the people with the animals equals even the zoophilia of D. H. Lawrence and David Garnett. . . . The chief subject of Mr. Steinbeck's fiction has been thus not those aspects of humanity in which it is most thoughtful, imaginative, constructive, but rather the processes of life itself.

Edmund Wilson. *NR*. Dec. 9, 1940. pp. 785–6

Handling complex material rather too easily, he has been marked by the popularizing gift—this indigenous American blessing which has, however, in the case of so many literary figures (a William Lyons Phelps, a Woollcott, a Louis Bromfield, as well as Steinbeck himself) become a blessing not altogether unmixed. In Steinbeck's work the false starts and turns, the thwarting problems of material and of the artist in the process of penetrating it, which usually mark the effort to portray truth, these are singularly lacking. If Steinbeck has reminded us of a Thomas Wolfe rejoicing in the mournful questioning of youth which wants no answers, he has never, like Wolfe, found himself disturbed by the final enigma of existence itself. For Steinbeck, Wolfe's famous stone is a stone, a leaf a leaf, and the door is sure to be found.

Maxwell Geismar. *Writers in Crisis* (Houghton).
1942. p. 260

Much of Steinbeck's basic position is essentially religious, though not in any orthodox sense of the word. In his very love of nature he assumes an attitude characteristic of mystics. He is religious in that he contemplates man's relation to the cosmos and attempts, although perhaps fumblingly, to understand it. He is religious in that he attempts to transcend scientific explanations based upon sense experience. He is religious in that from time to time he explicitly attests the holiness of nature. . . . Nineteenth century fears that the development of naturalism meant the end of reverence, of worship, and of "august sentiments" are not warranted in the case of Steinbeck. . . . Steinbeck is, I think, the first significant novelist to begin to build a mystical religion upon a naturalistic basis.

Woodburn O. Ross. *CE*. May, 1949. pp. 436–7

Steinbeck illustrates vividly the kind of moral impasse to which the idea of relativity applied to the field of cultural investigation has brought us while at the same time widening the grounds of tolerance in a way we can only approve. Since what is good in terms of our culture may be a positive bad in another, we can safely apply the term "good" only to those motives which appear in common at the most primitive level. This is precisely what Steinbeck does. His paisanos in *Tortilla Flat,* Mack and the boys in *Cannery Row* and most of the characters in *The Wayward Bus* gain a certain vitality (which his less earthy characters do not have) as a result of their uninhibited response to organic drives; but this involves their almost complete emancipation from social responsibility and a disregard of everything which culture has added to human life.

Blake Nevius. *PS.* Summer, 1949. pp. 307–8

We have been right all along in suspecting that there are nearly two Steinbecks. There is the Steinbeck of *Grapes of Wrath,* of *In Dubious Battle,* and of a number of short stories, an angry man whose anger has put a real tension in his work; and there is also the Steinbeck who seems at times to be only a distant relative of the first one, the warm-hearted and amused author of *Tortilla Flat, Cannery Row, The Wayward Bus, The Pearl,* capable of short stretches of some really dazzling stuff but, over the length of the book, increasingly soft and often downright mushy. In other words, Steinbeck has achieved his success by working within the limitations which are perhaps self-imposed on him by his temperament. They tie him down to an exclusive preference for one type of character, which recurs with surprising consistency throughout his work, and to a maximum of two emotional attitudes, one compounded of some delight and much compassion toward the people he writes about, the other of compassion and wrath.

W. M. Frohock. *The Novel of Violence in America* (Southern Methodist). 1950. p. 147

Those who have written about Steinbeck have disagreed far more widely—and deeply—than they have about any other important writer of our time. . . . There is at least one notable characteristic of Steinbeck's writing on which otherwise conflicting critics agree: he is a man in whom the faculty of pity is strong and close to the surface. . . . It may turn out . . . that the essence of Steinbeck-man and Steinbeck-writer lies in these two quite uncomplicated truths: he earnestly wishes to make people understand one another and he is able, like Blake, to "seek love in the pity of others' woe."

Joseph Henry Jackson. Introduction to *The Short Novels of John Steinbeck* (Viking). 1953. pp. vii-viii

I think we have been wrong about Steinbeck. We have let his social indignation, his verisimilitude of language, his interest in marine biology lead us to judge him as a naturalist. Judged by the standards of logical consistency which naturalism demands, his best books are weak and his poorer books are hopeless. Steinbeck is more nearly a twentieth-century Dickens of California, a social critic with more sentiment than science or system, warm, human, inconsistent, occasionally angry but more often delighted with the joys that life on its lowest levels presents.

Hugh Holman. *NR*. June 7, 1954. p. 20

If Steinbeck's characters seldom achieve true novelistic reality, it is precisely because they are so little individualized, so little individuals and finally so little human. Their emotions always remain obscure and somewhat opaque, situated, it seems, under the diaphragm or around the solar plexus; it is hard to picture them, even in a distant time, reading a clear consciousness of themselves. . . . We may say that there is something false and suspicious, at any rate monstrous, in the very innocence of Steinbeck's heroes. . . . Because of this very amputation, Steinbeck's universe and the artistic domain in which he can succeed will be perforce very limited. . . . One cannot help wondering whether there are very great possibilities open to a "novelist of animality," however perfect his art may be and however deep the bond of sympathy between his subject and himself.

Claude-Edmonde Magny in *Steinbeck and His Critics*, edited by F. W. Tedlock and C. V. Wicker (New Mexico). 1957. pp. 225–7

See *Tortilla Flat, In Dubious Battle, Of Mice and Men, Grapes of Wrath, Cannery Row, The Wayward Bus,* and *East of Eden* (novels); also *The Long Valley* (short stories).

STEVENS, WALLACE (1879–1955)

Stevens is precise among the shyest, most elusive of movements and shadings. He sees distinctly by way of delicacy the undulations of the pigeon sinking downward, the darkening of a calm under water-lights, the variations of the deep-blue tones in dusky landscapes. Quite as regularly as the colors themselves, it is their shades of difference that are registered by him. . . . Yet this fastidious, aristocratic nature possesses a blunt power of utterance, a concentrated violence, that is almost naturalistic. . . . But sensation alone is liberated to new intensity by Stevens's forms. Emotion, on the contrary, is curiously constrained by them within a small range of experience and small volume of expression. . . . Stevens's rhythms are chiefly secondary rhythms.

Scarcely ever is his attack a direct and simple one. Generally, it is oblique, patronizing and twisted with self-intended mockery.

Paul Rosenfeld. *Men Seen* (Dial). 1925. pp. 152–5

Wallace Stevens gains elegance in large measure by his fastidiously chosen vocabulary and by the surprising aplomb and blandness of his imagery. He will say "harmonium" instead of "small organ," "lacustrine" instead of "lakeside," "sequin" instead of "spangle"; he will speak of "hibiscus," "panache," "fabliau," and "poor buffo." The whole tendency of his vocabulary is, in fact, toward the lightness and coolness and transparency of French, into which tongue he sometimes glides with cultivated ease.

Gorham Munson. *Destinations* (Sears). 1928. p. 81

Stevens is more than a dandy, a designer, and esthete. Each of these persons is a phase of a central person, each a mask in a masquerade at the heart of which philosophy and tragi-comedy view the world with serenity. If the earth is a tawdry sphere, America a tawdry land, the relation of human to human the most tawdry of all, Stevens refuses to despair. . . . Behind the veils there is always a meaning, though the poet employs supersubtlety for veiling the meaning as well. No one hates the obvious more. No one knows better than he that all these things have been felt and thought and known before. One can only improvise on material used over and over again and improvise for oneself alone.

Alfred Kreymborg. *Our Singing Strength* (Coward-McCann). 1929. pp. 501–2

(Stevens) give us, I believe, the most perfect laboratory of hedonism to be found in literature. He is not like those occasional poets of the Renaissance who appear in some measure to be influenced by a pagan philosophy, but who in reality take it up as a literary diversion at the same time that they are beneath the surface immovably Christian. Stevens is released from all the restraints of Christianity, and is encouraged by all the modern orthodoxy of Romanticism: his hedonism is so fused with Romanticism as to be merely an elegant variation of that somewhat inelegant System of Thoughtlessness. His ideas have remained essentially unchanged for more than a quarter of a century, and on the whole they have been very clearly expressed, so that there is no real occasion to be in doubt as to their nature; and he began as a great poet, so that when we examine the effect of those ideas upon his work, we are examining something of very great importance.

Yvor Winters. *The Anatomy of Nonsense* (Allan Swallow). 1943. p. 119

Wallace Stevens lives in a world from which the elemental, the super-natural, and the mythical have been drained, and in which the deeper instincts of the human race are consequently starving. Somehow, by his own mind and senses, man must find sustenance, must make terms with air and earth, must establish some relation between himself and the world about him. . . . Whether expressed in the splendor and gaudiness of *Harmonium,* or in the more restrained, more abstract verse of his latest volume, the answer is the same. It lies in the cultivation of sensibility and in the affirmation of that sensibility through works of the human imagination. . . . He is not merely the poetic dandy that he has been called. His interest in the precisions of poetic technique arises from what we might call his dedication to the mission of the poet in the modern world.

Louise L. Martz in Modern American Poetry, edited by
B. Rajan (Harcourt). 1952. pp. 94–6, 108

The liveliness of his interest, the depth of his concern, the intensity and subtlety of his connoisseurship are alike directed to what the imagination can make of our physical, factual pluriverse. "Piece the world together, boys, but not with your hands," he enjoins us. And proceeds to show us the how of it. He considers a snow man, a moun-tain, two pears on a dish, a man reading, a woman looking at a vase of flowers, particulars peculiar to a certain occasion in Hartford, in Florida. Speaking of these, delighting in their suggestiveness, com-municating his own private exhilaration, he presents the quality of a given hour, the genius of a place, the scene and its habitants, the climates and weathers of the soul. As a result, the reader enjoys the liberating experience of a traveler: he is allowed to make the exotic to some extent his own; he learns to clothe with becoming strangeness what is native and intimate. . . . It is all a matter of words. Occa-sionally it is a matter of non-words. Some of Stevens's most celebrated poems are composed in traditional metrics or in free cadences to which we have long been accustomed. They are saved from monotony by his fine ear and by the fact that his vocabulary is singularly personal. It moves between colloquial speech and what he calls the "poet's gib-berish," this last a dazzling medley of allusive, witty, half-foreign resonances and purely aural titillations.

Babette Deutsch. NYHT. Oct. 3, 1954. p. 3

In a sense . . . Wallace Stevens has spent a lifetime writing a single poem. What gives his best work its astonishing power and vitality is the way in which a fixed point of view, maturing naturally, eventually takes in more than a constantly shifting view could get at.

The point of view is romantic, "almost the color of comedy"; but "the strength at the center is serious."

Samuel French Morse. NYT. Oct. 3, 1954. p. 3

The starting point of Stevens's poems is often the aesthetic experience in isolation from all other experiences, as art is isolated from work, and as a museum-is special and isolated in any modern American community. And if one limits oneself to the surface of Stevens's poetic style, one can characterize Stevens as the poet of the Sunday: the poet of the holiday, the week-end and the vacation, who sees objects at a distance, as they appear to the tourist or in the art museum. But this is merely the poet's starting point. Stevens converts aestheticism into contemplation in the full philosophical and virtually religious sense of the word.

Delmore Schwartz. NR. Nov. 1, 1954. p. 16

Opulence—it is the quality which most of us, I expect, ascribe before all others to the poetry of Wallace Stevens: profusion, exotic abundance, and luxuriance. We carry in our minds an image of poems which teem with rich, strange, somehow forbidden delights, omnifarious and prodigious. . . . Stevens is Elizabethan in his attitude towards language, high-handed in the extreme. . . . Stevens is the delighted craftsman whose delight is, in part, the access of gratification which comes upon the exercise of mastery. His pleasure is endless because it is part of his work, past and present; it is transmissable because we too, in reading his poems, share that mastery.

Hayden Carruth. Poetry. Feb., 1955. pp. 288–92

It is clearly too soon to estimate the value of Stevens's poems with justice, and nothing short of a detailed essay would make plausible what will surely seem personal and an over-estimation, my own conviction that the more than 500 pages of Stevens's Collected Poems makes a book as important as Leaves of Grass. The very charm and beauty of Stevens's language mislead the reader often: delighted with the tick and tock, the heigh ho of Hoon and Jocundus, "jubilating," "in the presto of the morning," the reader often missed the basic substance, the joy that for the moment at least the poet has grasped "the veritable ding an sich at last": for Stevens was essentially a philosophical poet, the rarest of all kinds, seeking always "in a good light for those who know the ultimate Plato," to see and possess "the nothing that is not there, and the nothing that is."

The primary philosophical motive leads to a major limitation—the meditative mode is a solitude which excludes the dramatic and narrative poet's human character and personality. But it also leads to a great access: Stevens, studying Picasso and Matisse, made the art of poetry visual in a way it had never been before, and made him the first poet to be influenced, very often in the same poem, by Shakespeare, Cubism, the Symbolist movement, and modern philosophy since Kant.

Delmore Schwartz. *NR*. Aug. 22, 1955. pp. 21–2

Technically Stevens was not, as were many of his contemporaries, an experimentalist. He did not write staid classroom lines that can be regularly scanned, but they lie, for all that, in regular units of 2s and 3s and 4s quite according to custom. There is an intrinsic order which they follow with a satisfying fidelity which makes them indefinably musical, often strongly stressed by Stevens, his signature.

His is not strictly speaking a colloquial diction, but there are especially in his later works no inversions of phrase, "for poetic effect," no deformities of the normal syntax.

William Carlos Williams. *Poetry*. Jan., 1956.

pp. 235–6

One of the fascinating questions about the life and work of Wallace Stevens concerns the connection between his successful business career, as vice-president of the Hartford Accident and Indemnity Company, and his poems. At first glance it seems incredible that these particular poems . . . so full of references to painting and sculpture and music, to faraway places and figures of fantasy, should have been written by a man who spent his days dealing with the intricacies of insurance law. But a closer reading of his work suggests that there is no essential paradox after all. Stevens is a man completely at home in his environment; he lives in modern city society without any impulse to overturn or to escape. He is, indeed, the singer of suburban life.

Partly because some of his well-known early poems picture the tropical luxuriance of Cuba or Florida or Mexico, relatively little attention has been paid to the fact that he habitually refers to the New England landscape in writing about the nature of reality. Still less noticed is the fact that he describes the kind of natural world enjoyed by the man who lives in a town or suburb—who has a lawn on which crickets sing and rabbits sit at dusk, a hedge of lilac and dogwood, a park nearby where he can watch the swans on the lake, and a summer vacation when he can go abroad or get to the New Hampshire hills or the coast of Maine.

Elizabeth Green. *SR*. Aug. 11, 1956. p. 11

O my people, burn, burn back to grace!
. . . But a light blinked and the business fronts fell past us;
a religion of chromium and plate glass windows
raising its monstrances of golden junk

called the dead poet from his imaginings:
"Soit!" he chimed back from the pixie passion
that made his belltowers tinkle as they bonged.
"Waa-wallee-waa!", the whistle learned to say.
. . .
By bong and tinkle he dwarfed back the fronts
of the age's skew and sooty imagination.
Now he is dead; one gone of the three truest*
and poverty, drowned in money, cannot care.

John Ciardi. SR. Aug. 11, 1956. p. 13

* STEVENS, FROST, W. C. WILLIAMS.

See *The Collected Poems;* also *The Necessary Angel* (essays).

STYRON, WILLIAM (1925–   )

The brilliant lyric power of William Styron's *Lie Down in Darkness* derives from the richest resources of the Southern traditions. Although ostensibly a story of psychological and moral breakdown, it is primarily a novel of place and must be judged in terms of its successful evocation of place. Like his best older contemporaries, Faulkner and Warren, Styron possesses a poetic sensibility of the very highest order. Through it he is able to respond to and project back into language those intricate relationships between natural setting and human agony which, at least since Hardy's heath and Conrad's sea, have formed the heart of our greatest fiction.

In fact, so completely does Styron dramatize these relationships that one feels justified in saying that the Southern landscape against which the action is portrayed is the most successfully realized character in the novel.

John W. Aldridge. NYT. Sept. 8, 1951. p. 5

Despite its echoes of familiar authors, *Lie Down in Darkness* is satisfying work. It is planned with mature intelligence, it is written in a style everywhere competent and sometimes superb, and its slow and powerful stream is fed by insights into human beings beyond the capacity of better-known novelists. . . . Mr. Styron has fertility of imagination, he knows how to manage a long novel, and in the economy of his tale he proves himself a craftsman of the first water. . . . And though no system of morality can be explicitly drawn from these pages, Mr. Styron believes there is a moral law. Few recent writers have had the courage of this affirmation, and few have had the capacity to mingle beauty, wisdom and narrative art as he has done.

Howard Mumford Jones. *NYHT*. Sept. 9, 1951. p. 3

I should say at once that *Lie Down in Darkness* is a remarkable and fascinating novel—the best novel of the year by my standards—and one of the few completely human and mature novels published since the Second World War. . . . The story itself moves on several levels at once, as all good novels do; the characters, like images seen through a prism, are reflected from every side until the distortions of their personality are finally resolved in not their own view of themselves but the novelist's central and sympathetic view of them. But Mr. Styron is particularly good on the visual level of his craft; we are *at* all these ghastly parties, ceremonials, and festivals of a middle-class business society that has inherited the trappings of the planter aristocracy. . . . The writing itself, graceful and delicate, is rigorously controlled as the medium through which the story is revealed—not as a medium for its author's personality.

Maxwell Geismar. *SR*. Sept. 15, 1951. pp. 12–3

Lie Down in Darkness starts out a bleak and black book and it ends up as one; there is no catalyst here. That is why I have no affection for it. I am profoundly aware, though, that in wanting to cite its perhaps inevitable defects, I have placed my criticism in an improper focus.

For example, the book is not bleakly written. On the contrary, it is richly and even (in the best sense) poetically written. . . . If . . . there exists a fugitive sense that the author has gone to Joyce for his structure and to Faulkner for his rhetoric, it is only fugitive and consequently intelligent and probably assimilated. Not least among its virtues, the novel is deeply absorbing. It is a basically mature, substantial, and enviable achievement, powerful enough to stay with you after you have shut it out.

Harvey Breit. *At*. Oct., 1951. pp. 79–80

William Styron . . . has tasted and—to his credit—very nearly digested a number of writers of what might be called the "stream of words" tradition: notably Thomas Wolfe, James Joyce and William Faulkner.

Yet from what at first appears as chaos he has subtly evolved a pattern. As form the pattern is the elaborate and skillful use of flashback: the minute advance of a funeral procession while memory strips back the life now ended. As subject the pattern clarifies once again into the theme of the sterility of modern life: this time in Tidewater, Virginia and in a family less intellectual than country club.

Ruth Chapin. CSM. Oct. 4, 1951. p. 15

Many of the new writers have been learning their craft from William Faulkner; that is among the leading tendencies of the day; but I can't think of any other novel that applies the lessons so faithfully, or, for that matter, with so much natural authority and talent. . . . It is a general rule that novels which stay close to their literary models have no great value of their own, but *Lie Down in Darkness* is an exception; in this case the example of Faulkner seems to have had a liberating effect on Styron's imagination. One might even say that his book is best and most personal when it is most Faulknerian.

Malcolm Cowley. NR. Oct. 8 ,1951. pp. 19–20

Mr. Styron is twenty-six, a year or so younger than Mann was when he published *Buddenbrooks*. His first novel, *Lie Down in Darkness,* is a book of astonishing stature, as mature in conception as the work which now seems in the perspective of fifty years to have been so clear a harbinger of Mann's future achievement.

This is naturally not to say that Styron is, or will become, a great novelist—fifty years being about the shortest period in which such judgements can be hazarded. But *Lie Down in Darkness* suggests that his talents are equal to it, if he has luck and energy and capacity for growth to match. It ranks him at once as a member, and by no means the least considerable member, of that distinguished group of Southern writers whose names are generally headed by Faulkner and Wolfe.

Margaret Wallace. IW. Nov., 1951. p. 325

One would . . . welcome some insight into the expanding area . . . of comfort and complacency. . . . Is it possible to say *No* without ignoring the comfortable reality? One way is indicated by William Styron's fine story "Long March" which appeared in *discovery No. 1*. Styron focuses on the experience of several reserve officers recalled to duty during the Korean emergency, and so he manages to place our flannel-suited careers in some historical perspective. He provides only one or two quick glimpses of domestic contentment, but since they are set against a panorama of remorseless military idiocy, they take on a wonderfully delicate power. To these men suddenly back in combat dress our lives between wars seem but a childish revery—placid, mindless, comfortably unreal.

Leo Marx. NR. Oct. 31, 1955. p. 20

See *Lie Down in Darkness* (novel); and "The Long March" (novelette).

TATE, ALLEN (1899–   )

Poetry

Allen Tate is a poet who seldom achieves Frost's perfection of style, but he has other qualities. He is too intelligent and cosmopolitan to find in his region, the South, the absolute satisfaction that Frost discovers in his attachment to New England. Indeed, he remains unreconciled to pretty much everything: our literature, our civilization, our wars. . . . If, then, Tate lacks Frost's repose, he also lacks his complacency. If his work is a perpetual experiment, a poetry labored out of intractable material by the naked will, it is invariably *interesting*. . . . And it is Tate, not Frost, who influences the younger poets.

F. W. Dupee. Nation. April 21, 1945. p. 466

Increasingly over the past quarter of a century, the name of Allen Tate has come to stand for a singular integrity of outlook. At all times he has given the impression of a poet who knows his own mind and intends to use it in his poetry. In consequence, he has been accused of a certain coldness; but hardly a line of Tate is not informed by passionate sincerity, though it may be controlled by a fine irony or educed by emotions which many readers outside the South of his fathers find inexplicable.

Gerard Previn Meyer. SR. March 20, 1948. p. 24

Allen Tate's poems are beautiful examples of what a hard, select intelligence can press out of rather deadly insights—but insights that are self-consistent and profound. . . . In his poetry, Tate traverses a hall of metaphysical fears and memorial pieties, at one end of which is The South and at the other The Abyss. . . . Tate's finest poems . . . are fruitless lyrics, and they impose astringent judgements upon the world and time we inhabit. Our nature as Americans is a divided nature, and if we listen carefully we may learn from this Tennessean accurate symbols of the guilt that returns and returns to us.

Robert Fitzgerald. NR. April 26, 1948. pp. 31–2

There are no trivia in Tate's *Collected Poems*. Every line seems to have found its inevitable final form, even if this took years of tinkering by the master workman. . . . Hart Crane once urged Tate to be true to "your language" in "so pure a way that it will be noticeable, and you will do well enough." Today Crane's prophecy has been more than fulfilled by Tate's long aesthetic asceticism, his uncompromising devotion to language.

Peter Viereck. At. Nov., 1948. pp. 96–8

His poems, all of them, even the slightest, are terribly personal. Out of splutter and shambling comes a killing eloquence. Perhaps, this is the resonance of desperation, or rather the formal resonance of desperation. I say "formal" because no one has so given us the impression that poetry must be burly, must be courteous, must be tinkered with and re-cast until one's eyes pop out of one's head. How often something smashes through the tortured joy of composition to strike the impossible bull's-eye! The pre-Armageddon twenties and thirties with all their peculiar fears and enthusiasms throb in Tate's poetry; imitated ad in-finitum, it has never been reproduced by another hand.

Robert Lowell. SwR. Autumn, 1959. p. 559

Criticism

Tate . . . is a Catholic by intellectual conviction (though not by com-munion), he is Southern Agrarian by social background, he is a man of letters trained in the Late Romantic or Symbolist tradition—and these are three positions that cannot be reconciled anywhere short of Nir-vana. The South, for example, was not in its great days hospitable ei-ther to Romantic poetry or to any other forms of creative literature . . . it was and remains hostile to Rome. Today if Tate carried his praise of traditional religion to the logical point of joining the Church, he would be alienating himself from his own people. . . . He would be forcing himself to reject many poets whom he still admires, with a divided mind. It almost seems that his essays are being written by three persons, not in collaboration but in rivalry (and we are given occasional hints of a fourth, a disciple of Schopenhauer rich in Yogi wisdom and prepared to reject the whole world as a realm of unmiti-gated evil).

Malcolm Cowley. NR. April 29, 1936. p. 348

Mr. Tate's method (is) . . . a method of unrelenting definition and redefinition which makes for criticism that is at once stimulating and exhausting. For it is one of the tacit assumptions of this criticism that the critic must never permit himself to become emotional, even when he is dealing with emotional subjects, and the reader must respond by pretending to remove any such suspicion from his mind. He must meet the critic on his own plane of dialectic logic, however difficult that may be, and in Mr. Tate's case it is very difficult indeed.

William Troy. *Nation.* June 10, 1936. p. 747

Let us return to certainties and pieties which can enlist our allegiance; let us revive the magic power inherent in tradition; let us rebuild the foundations of our ruined faith. This is substantially Tate's credo, and it is, what he intended it to be, "reactionary." . . . Whether or not Allen Tate is entitled to speak for the South, he does not represent the advanced thought of his time. He is a sectional prophet, a provincial thinker. . . . Because his call to tradition is no more than a repudiation of the present and a nostalgic flight to the past . . . and because he has lent himself to the service of economic obscurantism, he is guilty of that treason to the intellectuals which is so alarming a symptom of contemporary thought.

Charles Glicksberg. *SwR.* Summer, 1937. pp. 294–5

Mr. Tate is an earnest and subtle critic who turns his inquiring eye on past and present literature with the pure intention of perceiving it and its problems with clarity—of noting necessary distinctions, eliminating confusion and misapprehensions, and illuminating the distinctive qualities of artistic literary expression. He is often rather like a man with a powerful pair of field-glasses reporting to his friends (who lack such aids) what he sees: his friends, not being able to see through the glasses, cannot always quite make out from his description of what he sees exactly what he is describing; but they do know that he is giving an honest and careful report of what is visible to him.

David Daiches. *SR.* Dec. 25, 1948. p. 10

I do not see how to avoid saying that Allen Tate is our finest literary intelligence, though remarks like this have about them what Mr. Tate himself calls "an edifying generality": they make their subject sound remote and inhuman. . . . All we ought to mean by this "edifying generality" is that the demonstrated variety and order of Mr. Tate's awareness are greater than those of any other literary man in America . . . . Nothing could, however, be less fair to him than to make him sound remote and awful, for no one sees more clearly than him the danger of the kind of abstraction which, existing in isolation from nature, operates like a honoric hyperbole, a device for creating false gods and imaginary ghosts.

Arthur Mizener. *NR.* April 13, 1953. p. 18

Fiction

It is a curious story which Allen Tate unfolds (in *The Fathers*), subtly and delicately, all the notes muted. It is a story which lends itself readily enough to the allegorical suggestion, and the rhythm of the prose reminds us that a poet wrote it. It is concerned with imponderables, with the meanings behind the formal speeches and codes, with clashing philosophies of life symbolized by people who would never use the term. It is a psychological horror story, but it is the psychology of Henry James rather than of William Faulkner; despite the catastrophe that overwhelms all the characters it is concerned with life rather than death, with significance rather than with futility.

Henry Steele Commager. NYHT. Sept. 25, 1938. p. 5

Mr. Tate's prose moves with a finely balanced rhythm that is a definite aid to the narrative flow of the story, and which is almost always subtle enough not to obtrude itself into the reader's consciousness. It is a style well suited to the material, handled so skillfully that it never seems at all mannered and, while it often makes for a separate kind of beauty, it remains a part of the vital texture of the novel. . . . Of the innumerable novels that have come out of the South in the past decade or two, I think Mr. Tate's very easily challenges comparison with the best and the most penetrating.

Herschel Brickell. NYT. Sept. 25, 1938. p. 2

The prose is straightforward and, sentence by sentence, of the utmost simplicity. Yet the air of the narrative is charged, and behind the words, behind the imaginary narrator, who is rather a simple fellow —we are aware of a mind sharp and intense, clear as to its own situation, yet so caught in difficulties that it seems devious; secure in its own courage and yet in the midst of combat never ignorant of the imminence of defeat. . . . Mr. Tate is not unaware of the conflict in which he is involved. Because he is a poet and because it is as clear in his mind as it is confused in his emotions, he has created out of it, first in his poetry, and now in his prose, a dramatic irony, which for intensity is scarcely to be surpassed among his contemporaries.

John Peale Bishop. NR. Nov. 9, 1938. pp. 25–6

The central tension of *The Fathers,* like that of its design, is a tension between the public and the private life, between the order of civilization, always artificial, imposed by discipline, and at the mercy of its own imperfections, and the disorder of the private life, always sincere, imposed upon by circumstances, and at the mercy of its own impulses. We see, on the one hand, the static condition a society reaches when, by slow degrees, it has disciplined all personal feeling to custom so that the individual no longer exists apart from the ritual of society and the ritual of society expresses all the feelings the individual knows. We see, on the other hand, the forces that exist—because time does not stand still—both within and without the people who constitute a society, that will destroy the discipline of its civilization and leave the individual naked and alone.

Arthur Mizener. SwR. Autumn, 1959. p. 606

See Poems 1922-1947; also On the Limits of Poetry and The Forlorn Demon (criticism) and The Fathers (novel).

TAYLOR, PETER (1917–   )

All but two of these stories (The Long Fourth) concern the mores of family life in Nashville, Tennessee, but they also, except when making a tangent with the ethos of their special social and political landscape, concern all United States family mores. The tensions, affections, longings, the "shoddiness, stupidity and even cruelty" are equally true for any family confronted with the attack of modern industrial forces on inherited standards. . . . Occasionally one has the feeling that the stories are rather attenuated, perhaps because their action is not violent but quiet—almost quotidian. . . . It is a tribute to Mr. Taylor's talent that by his rendering of atmosphere, nuances of character and barely perceptible conflicts he is able to keep such episodes from rebuffing the reader.

Hubert Creekmore. NYT. March 21, 1948. p. 6

What Mr. Taylor is really doing, with honesty and sureness and beauty, is to experiment, both technically and psychologically, with very different approaches to extremely difficult definitions. For all its deceptively unstartling appearance, his method is quite as odd and daring as that in any of Picasso's paintings of double-headed women or seemingly capricious groupings of objects.

Mr. Taylor is inquiring into those relations through which things take on their meaning, and he makes his inquiry, not in unfamiliar language, but through connections so unfamiliar that he shakes the reader into emotional insecurity.

Marjorie Brace. SR. March 27, 1948. p. 18

If Taylor even remembers, he refuses to tell a story the way it was told before. He refuses, moreover, to exploit his material to the limit, to manufacture characters, drama, suspense—in short, he won't traffic in what is known as a "strong story line." He refuses to be electric. He knows that life itself has a very weak story line. To render it truly he distils it, though again not as you might think: his work is not remarkable for its form and conciseness. He likes to take a while to get a story underway. He has a feeling for naming his characters. He has the poet's gift for finding the clichés of a nation and getting his characters to say them so that they almost sound like something else (as when one uses them oneself).

J. F. Powers. Com. June 25, 1948. p. 262

No description of the mere materials or events of A Woman of Means can indicate the particular kind of excitement it possesses. The kind of excitement is the excitement of being constantly on the verge of deep perceptions and deep interpretations. Mr. Taylor follows closely the contour and texture of event, and sometimes for a considerable space the reader feels that he is engaged with an ordinary realistic, objective narrative. However, Mr. Taylor's method is to intersperse tantalizing flashes, to break the ordinary texture of things and then quickly close the rent before the eye has caught the full significance of what lies beyond the curtain.

Robert Penn Warren. NYT. June 11, 1950. p. 8

What right has Mr. Taylor, one asks oneself, to be so good at drawing people, and at probing deep into the secrets of their relationships, without doing more with them? Why aren't these small kindly anecdotes, so delightfully told, collected more carefully into a mounting tension? They lie like pins spilled out of a box on to the floor, and one waits for the small but subtle magnet, which must surely be at work, to draw them together. But something has gone wrong. Either the magnet is not powerful enough or else it is being held too far away.

Robert Kee. NSN. Dec. 2, 1950. p. 566

Peter Taylor . . . is possibly the most interesting and accomplished new writer to have come out of the South in the last ten years. . . . Mr. Taylor's comedy is quiet, his drama subtle and generally muted. Passion, violence and the more extreme aberrations are absent from his fiction. . . . And yet he fascinates, entertains and enlightens us as only a first-rate writer could. Immersed in his wonderfully lucid pages, we come to feel that this is not realism, but reality itself.

Dan Wickenden. NYHT. May 2, 1954. p. 4

Most of (the stories) treat family problems, the emotional relationships that make for happiness or unhappiness in domestic life, or the mutual obligations of married couples, relatives, servants and friends both to the quick and the dead. Mr. Taylor is particularly skillful in showing how the beauty of family life vanishes in the absence of free interchange in sympathy and affection among people destined to live under the same roof. . . . Mr. Taylor never preaches, but he has a message and a valuable one: If the sanctity of the home is preserved, all will be well with mankind.

Frank H. Lyell. NYT. May 2, 1954. p. 5

The Widows of Thornton . . . is as free of ugliness as . . . lingering nutmeg and as unpretentious as coldwater cornbread. . . . Mr. Taylor, Tennessee-born, has created a wistful, clinging but utterly nondepraved image of the Deep South that some of us his regional contemporaries have kept trying to recall from our childhood but were beginning, after Capote and Tennessee Williams, to doubt ever existed. . . . He has suggested that his stories may explain why a Southerner of the blood never entirely leaves home. But they are more than that, a tender and perceptive treatment of clanspeople of the same name but different pigment, drawn so close together from their beginnings that their real beauty is in each other and not in themselves.

Mack Morris. SR. May 8, 1954. p. 14

Peter Taylor writes of a Southern world everywhere present and tangible, but subtly, the center of his fiction is displaced in time: the mind, solaced by the wit, the elegiac temper and tender sensibility of these histories of fine consciences, is yet compelled to view them with an astonishing spaciousness of perspective. For what Mr. Taylor has achieved is the portrait of a complex society held in the most fastidious dramatic suspension; the past impinging upon and molding the present, the present rebelling against the tyranny of the past, the noisy warring of both in the abused heart.

Richard Hayes. Com. Dec. 17, 1954. p. 317

See *A Woman of Means* (novel); also *The Long Fourth* and *The Widows of Thornton* (books of short stories).

THURBER, JAMES (1894–1961)

Mr. Thurber's pets are, as the town knows, priceless, both pictures and prose. Here are super-beasts. Animals plus. I can stare at them over and over, acquiring new edification every minute. They are springboards to the infinite, or something like that. They run the gamut, too. For starkly sinister qualities, the bedridden cat which "follows every move I make" is almost too terrific to contemplate. . . . And surely Ibsen at his worst never thought of anything half so horribly symbolic as Mr. Thurber's night prowling horse.

Will Cuppy. NYHT. Feb. 8, 1931. p. 6

He has a style combining accuracy, liveliness, and quiet—qualities which do not often go together. He has a sense of the wildly incredible things that happen to human beings who think all the time that they are acting with the greatest prudence and common sense. It is this sense that his people imagine themselves to be moving steadily and reasonably under their own motivations when they are really being as near lunatic as you can be, unconfined, that makes Mr. Thurber an exceptionally interesting writer. . . . I think this is the reason that no matter how the extravagant situations pile up, you always have the feeling that Mr. Thurber is telling the literal truth.

Gilbert Seldes. SR. Nov. 18, 1933. p. 269

Many of Mr. Thurber's characters spend their lively existence in a state of mania. Haunted by hallucinations, they bound distractedly between the monstrous and the absurd. . . . Noting these manifestations, people who have absorbed psycho-analytic patter (by conversational osmosis rather than by study) are always sure to do a certain amount of eyebrow-raising over Mr. Thurber's themes. Obviously aware of that popular preoccupation he continues to exploit it with amiable ruthlessness. A Joyce in false-face, he strews hilarious pages with characters who take their subconscious out on a bender. . . . There's beautiful method in his madness.

C. G. Poore. NYT. Nov. 24, 1935. p. 3

Mr. Thurber's score on honesty and originality is high. In prose, he speaks his mind with a complete lack of pose not often encountered. A good many humorists get into a formula—he never has. . . . His style of drawing is completely his own. Even an unsigned Thurber is as unmistakable as an unsigned kangaroo. . . . Mr. Thurber's brand of humor lays him open to . . . ingenuous assaults. Because it has a fine cuckoo quality that is part of humor itself, it is often described as crazy. Many reviewers use words like "haywire humor," "zany" and "daffy" to describe what is a definite—and conscious—distortion of reality.

Stephen and Rosemary Benét. NYHT. Dec. 29, 1940. p. 6

In a few sentences the bold labels and solid outlines of one's fellow human beings have sagged alarmingly and nothing remains except an amoeba-like form with a startled eye in which ones sees, only too plainly, one's own reflections. A sinking feeling accompanies the laughter of anyone engaged in reading Thurber; the jokes have all been salvaged from dreams. Bump!—it is oneself that has slipped on the banana skin. Whether the word for this suffering and awareness of catastrophe is humour, I don't know. Thurber does make me laugh, but I become engulfed, I am less and less sure of myself as I read on.

G. W. Stonier. *NSN*. Dec. 19, 1942. p. 414

When we view Thurber's prose as a whole, our first impression may be of rout, of frightened people, dogs and rabbits running . . . away from whatever faces them when they get up in the morning— old lettuce leaves, empty ration books, their own faces in the shaving mirror, anything familiar that haunts them. Their first impression, however, is deceptive. Man, Thurber thinks, is standing his ground, perhaps because he sees no better place to run to. . . . He tries to observe and report the fundamental disorder in the universe. Other interpreters of the modern scene attempt to suggest the truth through exaggeration, but Thurber sees that no amount of understatement can conceal the oddness of what happens.

Dan S. Norton. *NYT*. Feb. 4, 1945. pp. 1, 18

There is not much wit in Thurber's writing, although there is plenty of it in his conversation. Occasionally in a story he permits himself a relatively brilliant or sparkling metaphor. . . , but for the most part he confines himself to the almost businesslike description of incongruous situations that are often blended with pathos. . . . He writes so naturally and conversationally that it is hard to realize how much work goes into his stories. His art is in fact extremely conscious, and it is based on a wide knowledge of contemporary writing. . . . Besides learning to write with an easy flow and coherence that very few authors achieve, he also learned to omit everything inessential, including the winks, the rib-nudgings and the philosophical remarks of older American humorists. He achieves a sort of costly simplicity, like that of well tailored clothes or good conversation.

Malcolm Cowley. *NR*. March 12, 1945. p. 362

A large part of his comedy is the slow exfoliation of dilemma. It deals with people who live in a world of mist, as if they were seeing objects through a rainy windshield. Thurber's comedy not only depends on this obfuscation both of sense and value. It is part of our own obfuscation. His comedy is disturbing, therefore, because whatever else it does it identifies his people with ourselves. No one living, surely, comes so close as he does to making the personally comic shake hands with the tragic. Because this bifocal vision is our own, Thurber is able to make the stumbling of his people the stumbling of ourselves.

Francis Downing. *Com.* March 9, 1946. pp. 518–9

Thurber might be called a sprite, if sprites have sophistication. He has been repeatedly classified as a humorist. He clearly is one, though clearly also one who does not think life, even ordinary life, is a joke, nor does he find the absurdities for which he has an unfailing eye, unfailingly delicious. These essays . . . may be called roughly the prose poetry of humorous exasperation. Mr. Thurber's writing displays exasperation at once amiable and savage with all sorts of things, for instance—and repeatedly—with the pompous inefficiency of bureaucrats, both public and private. . . . We are all, Mr. Thurber seems to be saying, involved in the maddening silliness of a foolishly complicated world.

Irwin Edman. *NYHT*. Nov. 1, 1953. pp. 1, 8

Thurber's relationship to politics has never been an overt one, yet a political climate informs all his later work, either directly or by implication . . . The early fables contained a few stories . . . which were direct attacks on the indifference with which the democratic nations faced the spreading power of the Nazis. These old fables sound just as topical today, although at the moment the foxes and the wolves . . . will sound more like the Russians than the Germans, for it is any dealers in oppression who mask their ruthlessness in fine phrases that are the target of Thurber's anger.

Gerald Weales. *Com.* Jan. 18, 1957. p. 410

When he is anatomizing the English language, or engaging in the rueful self-mockery that makes neurosis respectable and almost attractive, or reminiscing with wistful charm about his family and friends in Columbus, Ohio—then Thurber is in a class by himself, and criticism by his inferiors becomes presumptuous. . . . Thurber's great talent lies in his intuitive grasp of the unconscious (always, of course, carefully controlled by his craft); and when he deals with facts, with objective reality, he is generally reducing his powers, not expanding them.

Sydney J. Harris. *SR.* Nov. 30, 1957. p. 26

See *The Thurber Album, Thurber Country, My World and Welcome To It, The Thurber Carnival, Fables for Our Time,* and *Further Fables for Our Time.*

TRILLING, LIONEL (1905–   )

Mr. Trilling has . . . , if I am not mistaken, written one of the first critical studies (*Matthew Arnold*) of any solidarity and scope by an American of his generation. And he has escaped the great vice of that generation: the addiction to obfuscatory terminology. Dealing in a thoroughgoing fashion with the esthetic, the philosophical and the socio-political aspects of his subject, he is almost entirely free from the jargons of any of these fields. I believe he has been influenced by the fashion in a little neglecting the literary aspect of Arnold as well as the biographical. . . . But if Mr. Trilling has followed the fashion, it is evidently not due to lack of competence. His observations on Arnold's style are admirably phrased as well as just.

Edmund Wilson. NR. March 22, 1939. p. 200

Mr. Trilling likes to move out and consider the implications, the relevance for culture, for civilization, for the thinking man today, of each particular literary phenomenon which he contemplates, and this expansion of the context gives him both his moments of greatest perception and his moments of disconcerting generalization. . . . It is civilization, we feel, that he really wants to talk about, and though, of course, all discourse about literature is and should be ultimately discourse about civilization, we sometimes feel that Mr. Trilling is stretching and forcing his literary material to allow himself to move over quickly to the larger issues.

David Daiches. NYHT. April 3, 1955. p. 4

As a conscious liberal Mr. Trilling is reluctant to commit himself to any single critical attitude. He cherishes a freedom to experiment, to use a combination of methods and a diversity of standards as tools at his disposal. . . . If there is one angle of insight which appeals to Mr. Trilling more than another, however, it is the Freudian. He even goes to the length—surely hyperbolic—of asserting that his pleasure in responding to a short treatise by Freud is difficult to discriminate from the pleasure afforded by a couplet from Yeats. Yet he also keeps his admiration this side of idolatry and on several occasions indicates his clear awareness of the limitations of Freudian concepts when applied to the interpretation of literary masterpieces.

George F. Whicher. NYHT. April 9, 1950. p. 5

Within his frames of knowledge and conviction his thinking is active, straightforward, and seldom clouded. Best of all, perhaps, he does not despise common sense as an instrument too common for an intellectual use. He does not employ jargon. He recognizes "the dangers which lie in our most generous wishes." . . . My respect for Mr. Trilling is so great that I can take no pleasure in hunting out his possible faults, but he exhibits, to my mind, one defect that should not be ignored—parochialism. He is parochial, I think, when he declares that "it is the plain fact that there are no conservative or reactionary ideas in general circulation."˜. . . . What he is really saying here is that he cannot believe in the genuineness of any political ideas save those to which he can himself subscribe. . . . However . . . his political bias does not corrupt his literary judgements.

Ben Ray Redman. *SR*. April 15, 1950. pp. 44–5

Mr. Trilling is outstanding, in the higher ranks of criticism, for his freedom from pedantry and his alertness to the intimate connection between the world of literature and life itself. Working with the insights of a flexible, undoctrinaire modernism, he has shown himself to be a resolute and perceptive researcher into the problems of modern life. . . . To the fatuous optimism of the doctrinaire progressive, Trilling opposes the deep truth of James's moral imagination, with its awareness of disaster, and the tough psychology of Freud, which invites a more complex estimate of human motives than liberalism has made.

Charles J. Rolo. *At*. June, 1950. pp. 82–4

Lionel Trilling is not only an accomplished interpreter of the nineteenth century; he is, in his own right, a thoughtful mind of the mid-twentieth. The distance between this position and the mentality of the early twentieth century may be gauged by the very breadth of sympathy with which Mr. Trilling, Professor of English at Columbia, treats the commitments and sanctions of mid-Victorianism.

Not that his mood is nostalgia for the past; rather it is a pathos of the present, an urgent awareness of "our modern fate" well calculated to impress contemporary readers. . . . Something can be gained by revaluation—which, in these cases, means higher evaluation —of writers whose sense of individuality struggled against the encroachments of conformity.

Harry Levin. *NYT*. Feb. 13, 1955. p. 3

Mr. Trilling dares to bring scholarship into criticism; and therefore he is one of the few critics in this country who can write limpidly, humanely, undogmatically about any and every book that interests him, and who can be interested in any and every kind. While he takes care not to confuse the effects of a book upon himself with the book itself, he is not afraid to entertain relativity; he boldly sets forth a writer's in-

tention, unperturbed by the cry of "fallacy!" So he is constantly instructive, eminently readable, always refreshing.

Perry Miller. *Nation*. March 5, 1955. p. 203

This is, in fact, real criticism, which can only be addressed to those
who are directly on a level with the critic himself; they need not have
read exactly the same books, but he has to assume that they have the
same quality of interest in the subject as he has. Professor Trilling is a
master of this procedure, for all that his tone is not conversational or
intimate, but rather Arnoldian, without sharing Arnold's tendency to
nag or preach. And, far more than Arnold, he has the true critic's
gift of describing *exactly* the thing he is talking about. . . . His criticism, at bottom, is not technical, nor aesthetic, but moral. What makes
a great book great, for him, is the spiritual and moral health it embodies.

John Wain. *Spec.* July 29, 1955. pp. 171–2

The Middle of the Journey—Novel

The Middle of the Journey is not a *tendenz* novel; yet it defines the
tendency of our lives, and can be most easily discussed in its moral
rather than its dramatic terms.

This temptation is to be resisted, for the dramatic terms are always
in the fore, and sometimes almost as brightly as in a comedy of manners. Certainly it is a book of great wit, and it is difficult to think of any
recent novels which are at all like it. From older writers one detects,
perhaps predictably, the influence of E. M. Forster, especially in
the effective combination of wit and gravity, and in the somewhat frosty
detachment of style.

Mark Schorer. *NYT*. Oct. 12, 1947. p. 40

What Mr. Trilling has written is, quite overtly, a dialectical novel.
. . . His language is analytical, his structure polemic, his sequence of
scenes and confrontations among characters virtually syllogistic. Yet it
is a remarkable testimony to his skill and sincerity and to the tenacious
probity of his thinking, that he has been able to keep his plotting
sharply dramatic; that as we read we lose our sense of lacking familiar
fictional ingredients; and that we become profoundly absorbed in his
story, not only as a brilliantly sustained argument but as the record of an
essential experience and milieu of our age. . . . It is a book that
brings the best critical intelligence now discernible in America into play
with an absolutely honest creative talent.

Morton Dauwen Zabel. *Nation*. Oct. 18, 1947.
pp. 414–5

Because the level on which perception takes place in the novel is immeasurably higher than what is seen in most popular fiction, the writing will make considerable demands upon the reader. The reviewer for *Time,* who found the style rather too "gray," simply did not notice that Mr. Trilling's material forces him to a line of greater length and more complex contour than one finds, say, in John O'Hara or James Cain. Mr. Trilling's writing is well up to the high intelligence and peculiar tact which direct it, and in some places . . . it is literally perfect. . . . Mr. Trilling's novel stands as the testament of a real human being, struggling with the complexities of human thoughts and human feelings and moving in a journey which has meaning and purpose only as long as it remains human.

Henry Rago. *Com.* Nov. 14, 1947. pp. 121–2

See *Matthew Arnold, E. M. Forster, The Liberal Imagination, The Opposing Self,* and *A Gathering of Fugitives* (criticism); also *The Middle of the Journey* (novel).

TWAIN, MARK (1835–1910)

We who remember Mark Twain when his light first rose above the horizon cannot help thinking of him as a humorist above everything else, for it was as such he rose, and as such his radiance increased. We soon came to know that he was also a philosopher and after a while that he was a story-teller, but for all that and despite our added knowledge of him, we still think first of his brightness, and often forget that his surface may be inhabited or that he has an influence upon our tides.

Frank R. Stockton. *Forum.* Aug., 1893. p. 677

In his books Mark Twain has set forth, and in himself he embodies, the traits, the humors, the virtues, of a distinct people. So regarded, he has in our literature no equal, and in life he has had but one superior, Abraham Lincoln. This is the explanation of Mark Twain's fame. There are few things as interesting, as attractive, as instructive, as the man who, without sacrificing a jot of his own individuality, stands out as the type of his country.

Henry Dwight Sedgwick. *The New American Type*
(Houghton). 1908. pp. 293–4

To accept him is almost equivalent to accepting the American flag. . . . Not by his subtlety, . . . nor his depth, nor his elevation, but by his understanding and unflinching assertion of the ordinary self of the ordinary American did Mark Twain become our "foremost man of letters." . . . When Mark Twain, robust, big-hearted, gifted with the divine power to use words, makes us all laugh together, builds true romance with prairie fire and Western clay, and shows us that we are at one on all the main points, we feel that he has been appointed by Providence to see to it that the precious ordinary self of the Republic shall suffer no harm.

Stuart P. Sherman. Nation. May 12, 1910. pp. 478–80

Mark Twain was great in many ways and especially in four—as a humorist, as a story-teller, as a stylist and as a moralist. Now and again his humor was fantastic and arbitrary, perhaps even mechanical; but at its richest it was irresistible, rooted in truth, sustained by sincerity and supported by a manly melancholy—which became more plainly visible as he broadened his outlook on life. His native gift of story-telling, the compelling power of his narrative, was cultivated by conscious art, until one could not choose but hear. . . . As a master of English prose he has not received the appreciation he deserved. . . . And his sturdy morality, inspired by a detestation of sham and of affectation as ingrained as Molière's, ought to be evident . . . to all who have meditated upon "The Man Who Corrupted Hadleyburg."

Brander Matthews. NAR. June, 1910. pp. 834–5

Mark Twain is not all of Samuel Clemens. He was much more than humorous. He was a great fictionist and a rough-hewn stylist uttering himself in his own way, which was a large, direct and forceful way. No amount of Old World contact could destroy his quaint drawl, and not all his reading nor his acquired personal knowledge of other writers could conventionalize his method. He remained the mid-Western American and literary democrat to the last. . . . Every letter of his speech was vital with the breath of his personality.

Hamlin Garland. NAR. June, 1910. p. 833

The art which premeditatively determines the scope of its venture so that one sees at every step the curvature of its rounding up—in a word the literary art—was foreign to Mark Twain's nature. . . . He always wanted room—the whole open sky—for his action. . . . Mark inherited from nobody but, if not as purposeful, he was as masterful as Rabelais, Cervantes, and Swift were. He was not learned and literary as those men, and had not their kind of conscious purpose, but there was a strain of earnestness in all his work—a Western strain. . . .

Mark Twain, like Lincoln, was a native of the West and, like him, though in so different a vein, was gigantically in earnest.

Henry M. Alden. *Bkm.* June, 1910. p. 367

So far as I know, Mr. Clemens is the first writer to use in extended writing the fashion we all use in thinking, and to set down the thing that comes into his mind without fear or favor of the thing that may be about to follow. . . . He would take whatever offered itself to his hand out of the mystical chaos, that divine ragbag, which we call the mind, and leave the reader to look after the relevancies and sequences for himself. . . . He has not attempted to trace the threads of association between the things that have followed one another. . . . An instinct for something chaotic, ironic, empiric in the order of experience seems to have been the inspiration of our humorist's art.

William Dean Howells. *My Mark Twain* (Harper).
1910. pp. 166–8

One of Mark Twain's best attributes as a commentator on style, on man, on religious beliefs and on the ways of nations is his capacity for profound admiration. He has no poor provincial grudges against the souls and gifts of other peoples. He could praise well. . . . He had besides a certain essentially masculine faculty, in which no author has equaled him in many hundreds of years. . . . He could curse well. . . . To curse in a fine, forthright style and spirit seems to require at once more intensive and more extensive moral information—more knowledge of the states of Heaven and Hell and of excellence and splendor and miserableness and meanness in mortal character than has ever been acknowledged. Mark Twain will long gratify his country as a magnificent, an immortal execrator.

Edith Wyatt. *NAR.* April, 1917. pp. 614–5

There was a reason for Mark Twain's pessimism, a reason for that chagrin, that fear of solitude, that tortured conscience, those fantastic self-accusations, that indubitable self-contempt. . . . It is as old as Milton that there are talents which are "death to hide," and I suggest that Mark Twain's "talent" was just so hidden. That bitterness of his was the effect of a certain miscarriage in his creative life, a balked personality, an arrested development of which he was himself almost unaware, but which for him destroyed the meaning of life.

Van Wyck Brooks. *The Ordeal of Mark Twain*
(Dutton). 1920. p. 14

My suspicion is that it was the secondary social and conventional forces enveloping him after his early success and marriage and playing on this sympathetic, and, at times, seemingly weak humanist, succeeded for a time in diverting him almost completely from a serious, realistic, and I might say Dostoevskian, presentation of the anachronisms, the cruelties, as well as the sufferings, of the individual and the world which, at bottom, seem most genuinely to have concerned him. For, to a study of these he would have turned, had it not been, I think, for the noisy and quite vacuous applause accorded him as Genius Jester to the American booboisie. And by that I mean almost the entire American world of his time.

Theodore Dreiser. *EJ*. Oct., 1935. p. 621

Mark had only one discipline to which he had rigorously and success-fully submitted himself—language. Mark's English is superb, his taste in diction impeccable. He boasted of it and was right. His terse, simple, effective style, his words chosen with a lively sense of values, his ac-curacy and his force, never fail except in an occasional purple passage when he strains after an artificial beauty which was not his forte. He writes . . . better English than Henry James, both by word and by rhythm, though with far less assistance from a flowing vocabulary.

Henry Seidel Canby. *Turn West, Turn East*
(Houghton). 1951. p. 191

It might be said that a humorist by temperament, for example Ben-jamin Franklin, is a man serenely adjusted to his environment, while a wit like Jonathan Swift is not. Clemens himself—"Mark the Double Twain," as Dreiser called him, all his engaging self-contradictions mak-ing him a "human philopena" like his extraordinary twins, Luigi and Angelo—partook of both natures. And so, while one side of his creative nature lived and moved upon the level of his boyhood, in almost per-fect control of his materials, the other battled with clumsy valor upon the darkling plain of his maturity. By instinct he knew what a boy was like, from having been one himself in a river town in the golden age be-fore the War; but to the question, What is Man? his self-taught phi-losophy yielded no better answers than that Man is either a knave or an illusion, "wandering forlorn among the empty eternities."

Dixon Wector. *Sam Clemens of Hannibal*
(Houghton). 1952. p. 265

All that the surrealists were later to yearn for and in their learned way simulate, Twain had stumbled on without quite knowing it. . . . In the chamber of horrors of our recent fiction, the deformed and dwarfed and dumb have come to stand as symbols of our common plight, the failure of everyone to attain a purely fictional norm. Toward this insight, Twain was fumbling almost without awareness, believing all along that he was merely trying to take the curse off of a bitterness he could not utterly repress by being what he liked to think was "funny."

Leslie A. Fiedler. *NR.* Aug. 15, 1955. p. 17

The loneliness of Twain's childhood is reflected everywhere in his work. As has often been observed, loneliness is the peculiar quality of a great deal of American writing and comes out in many forms . . . but in Twain, loneliness almost without exception takes the form of alienation from the family. . . . With the possible exception of Poe's fantasies of being buried alive, there is no other corpus of American writing that reverts so often as does Twain's work to the nightmare of being utterly cut off.

Kenneth S. Lynn. *YR.* Spring, 1958. pp. 422–3

Huckleberry Finn

Into its making went oral narrative and Washoe burlesque, practice with native characters and their speech, formulas of the journalist and lecturer, viewpoints of the westerner, and experiences of the Hannibal boy and the river pilot. In this novel humor is deepened with pathos and matured into wisdom. Here romance and realism are held in delicate balance. Men are seen and satirized with full sympathy. The heroic is balanced with the humble; the loyal and good with the selfish, craven, and false.

Edgar Marquess Branch. *The Literary Apprenticeship*
of Mark Twain (Illinois). 1950. p. 199

If Mark Twain lacked art in Arnold Bennett's sense (as Arnold Bennett pointed out), that only shows how little art in Arnold Bennett's sense matters, in comparison with art that is the answer of creative genius to the pressure of profoundly felt and complex experience. If *Huckleberry Finn* has its examples of unintelligence that may accompany the absence of sustained critical consciousness in an artist, even a great one, nevertheless the essential intelligence that prevails, and from the poetic depths informs the work, compels our recognition—the intelligence of the whole engaged psyche; the intelligence that represents the integrity of this, and brings to bear the wholeness.

F. R. Leavis. *Cmty.* Feb., 1956. pp. 128–9

See *Huckleberry Finn, Tom Sawyer,* and *Pudd'nhead Wilson* (novels); also *Life on the Mississippi* (autobiography) and "The Mysterious Stranger" (short story).

VAN DOREN, MARK   (1894–   )

Poetry

We have only a few poets who have the inclination or the courage to be simple. Mr. Van Doren is one of them—his poems have that much maligned and refreshing quality of wholesomeness. They are like a lake breeze, cool milk, fresh bread and honey; though there is nothing remarkable about any of them either in subject matter or in content, almost all of them give genuine delight. . . . And though the poems have not enough individuality to win ardent admirers or vituperative assailants, they will undoubtedly and deservedly please the many who look to poetry for delicacy of feeling and charm of expression.

Marion Strobel. *Poetry*. Feb., 1925. pp. 279–80

The poetry of Mark Van Doren, an Illinois metaphysician transplanted to Connecticut, affords additional relief to readers sated with the vertigo of bookish poets. A few vital factors have saved Van Doren from growing dull: he lives on a farm and knows nature intimately; his principal masters are such commonsense Yankees as Emerson and Frost; and he has an eye and ear of his own and a style deleted of the "high-falutin," and devoted to an Anglo-Saxon rendering of concrete images. He may sound rather dry at first, but as one grows accustomed to his precision, one is moved by his passion and the wisdom of his deductions —deductions often left to the imagination.

Alfred Kreymborg. *Our Singing Strength* (Coward).
1924. p. 599

If an equivalent of these poems could be found in another medium, it would be in the art of etching. There is no music, or at most an abstract music. The tones are delicate grays and austere blacks and whites. Only a few strokes meticulously and economically drawn, are needed to suggest the bleakness of a landscape or the angularity of a person. The suasion is of the mind and not of the senses, yet the poet is concerned less to develop an idea than to suggest an evaluation. . . . If there is such a thing as a main stream of letters, they are doubtless not at its center. Yet subtlety and justness of psychological insight, precision of language, and neatness of forms are qualities that are not too abundant at any time; they are particularly rare today.

Philip Blair Rice. *Nation*. Nov. 13, 1937. pp. 537–8

In his first five books of poetry, Mark Van Doren proved himself a careful craftsman with a sharp eye for the homely and a mind aware of the profound implications of the casual. . . . Yet for all the solid writing, the formal excellence, there are disturbing imperfections: monotonous verbal patterns, stanzas weakened by mannered feminine rhymes, themes overwritten. . . . But the chief defect results from an ear no longer sufficiently naive: lack of resonance. . . . However, it is easy to pick flaws in the work of a truly prolific artist. Although Mark Van Doren has written no single lyric to be compared with, let us say, Louise Bogan's "The Mark" . . . the level of his achievement has been remarkably high.

Theodore Roethke. SR. Nov. 17, 1937. p. 52

He is in the English tradition; his master, we can hardly doubt it, Dryden. He has the ease of Dryden, as he has the sanity; though he has always clarity, he does not have a comparable radiance. He has his own grace, but does not give that sense of inexhaustible strength which, more than anything else in Dryden, contributes to the impression of manly nobility. Mr. Van Doren is more easily resigned. He has come late to the English tradition, as he is rather belated in coming to his particular New English material. The style he has made for it is properly autumnal and dry.

John Peale Bishop. Nation. Dec. 23, 1939. p. 714

Mr. Van Doren thinks best through small objects seen as symbols and writes best in the short line and lyric vein.

His philosophy, also, is more attuned to the interval than the aeon. His cosmology would seem to be influenced by a conception of the universe that reduces Man to a passing and time-bound phenomenon among the slackening suns, thus increasing the importance, from the human point of view, of the small portion of life alotted him. A melancholy more delicate than pessimism evokes lost opportunities for joy and all the carnage of our years; a happiness less robust than optimism remembers the sensitiveness of childhood and takes comfortable refuge in the homely intimacies of earth.

Robert Hillyer. NYT. March 14, 1948. p. 6

Mr. Van Doren has somehow managed to remain undisturbed by technical revolutions, and, like Robert Frost, presents in his poetry the lively record of an individual sensibility without seeming to feel the need for any severe wrestling with language. His technical equipment is, on the whole (or at least on the surface), traditional, as far as verse forms and figures of speech go; but style and tone are often wholly original, and Mr. Van Doren is frequently able to achieve a strangely impressive significance with what seems at first sight an excessively conventional means of expression. At his best, the conventionality is superficial, and the freshness and originality of vision, which continually give new twists to traditional kinds of expression come across most convincingly.

David Daiches. *YR*. Summer, 1953. p. 629

Mr. Van Doren, hemmed in by the American world of business technology, chooses what is perhaps the most difficult strategy of all: to write poetry that employs rhyme and metre but keeps mainly within the rhetorical limits of informal prose. In this he follows Robinson and Frost, but relies less than Robinson on a strong rhythmic movement, less than Frost on colloquial effects (using no contractions, for instance, except in dialogue). He has so perfected his method that he is able to develop a highly subjective train of thought, sometimes at length, sustaining elusive figures and conceits, while keeping the alert tone and perfectly even temper of conversation.

George Dillon. *Poetry*. Aug., 1955. p. 289

Criticism

To understand the difference between these essays (in *The Private Reader*) and the run of criticism today is to discriminate not between methods but between persons, not between intentions but talents. Trying to become a science, criticism today has failed to be even a human communication. But the work in this volume is a communication, for Mr. Van Doren has the nobility that comes from discovering it in others and the wit that can define failure and pass beyond it. . . . Among good critics Mr. Van Doren has always stood out as The Great Neutral, and that neutrality is the secret and condition of his quality. For if his is an ardent mind, it is also a very tidy one; and if it is never aloof, it always lives on its own track; a mind exact and generous and often piercing in its intuitions, but very careful never to overreach, to say too much; ambitious only to stop on the necessary point made, the observation perfectly seen.

Alfred Kazin. *NYHT*. March 29, 1942. p. 2

Mr. Van Doren is a good critic in any sense of the word, for he has the ability to say interesting and illuminating things about books. He has also read deeply, so that he can fit any new book he reads into the framework of literature. And one would want to say more of all this were not one more impressed with how Mr. Van Doren can fit what he reads into the framework of life. One always gets the feeling that a man is writing . . . , as well as a critic. . . . His opinions, like his prose, are cool and dry; he is masculine in his tastes, with no foolish or neurotic sensibilities.

Louis Kronenberger. *Nation*. May 16, 1942. p. 576

One of the few pieces of definitive literary criticism written in this country during the present century (is) Mark Van Doren's *John Dryden*. . . . Mr. Van Doren has explored the bases of Dryden's power with an industry steadily illuminated by good sense. His book is packed with ordered information, none of which is superfluous to his intention. . . . On the first appearance of this assured masterpiece of criticism T. S. Eliot declared: "It is a book which every practitioner of English verse should study." The poetry of the last quarter-century has been the poorer in that his advice has not been taken.

George F. Whicher. *Nation*. March 2, 1946. p. 266

Nathaniel Hawthorne is quite as largely critical as it is narrative; indeed, in the end, it is essentially a criticism of Hawthorne's work to which a good deal of biography has been made to contribute. Criticism of the sort it is could hardly be less perfunctory, more alert, awake, and attentive than Mr. Van Doren's: nothing is taken for granted, and no piece of Hawthorne's work, not even the slightest sketch, slips past Mr. Van Doren's eye in careless companionship with some other piece to which it may bear an apparent resemblance but which in fact is of an unequal quality. . . . Criticism of this writer's beautiful—if undeniably wavering and variable—work will as time goes on, be more laborious and more intensive than Mr. Van Doren's; it seems unlikely ever to be juster.

Newton Arvin. *SR*. April 30, 1949. pp. 11–2

See *Selected Poems* and *New Poems;* also *The Private Reader, John Dryden* and *Nathaniel Hawthorne* (criticism).

VAN DRUTEN, JOHN (1901–1957)

If *Young Woodley* is neither a great nor a powerfully imagined play . . . it is at least a delightful and gentle thing, one of the happiest of late seasons in our theatre, one of the most lovable and memorable. Its sensitive observation, its simplicity and directness are admirable. Its picture is not so much that of youth rebellious, jazzy, ruthless, which we have been treated to so abundantly of late, but, what is more universal and poignant by far, of youth with all its passionate urgency, its surprised solitude, its brutality and confusion and rank, wild growth.

Stark Young. *NR*. Dec. 23, 1925. p. 134

After All, by John Van Druten, of *Young Woodley* renown, is a fine comedy in the proper sense of that much misused word. . . . There is nothing farcical or even melodramatic about *After All;* it is simply a keenly observant and delicately ironical study of the conflict between the generations in an upper middle-class English family. Whether you will like it or not depends on whether you believe there is a place for that sort of thing on the stage. . . . *After All* is really what in painting is known as *genre.* It depicts, or should depict, a small portion of a portion of life.

Otis Chatfield-Taylor. Outlook. Dec. 16, 1931. p. 502

If you can imagine a combination of the charm of Sir James Barrie, the realistic directness of George Kelly and the whimsical touch of Philip Barry, you will have a fairly good idea of what Mr. Van Druten achieves in *There's Always Juliet.* Like Philip Barry, he appreciates the importance of unspoken words, and also the significance of sheer nonsense and banter covering up much deeper emotions. He has George Kelly's particular facility for making his characters utterly natural and familiar both in speech and action. But above all he has the James Barrie trait of endowing his characters with a quite intangible and yet insistent charm.

Richard Dana Skinner. Com. Mar. 2, 1932. p. 495

When sex now triumphs in the theatre, it wears the trappings of romance, as did *There's Always Juliet,* in one sense the most daring production of the season. Think of the audacity required to present supposedly ultra-sophisticated Broadway with three acts of unmitigated love-making, object matrimony! Such effrontery is almost unbelievable. But the very novelty of what really wasn't a play at all, but only a duologue, resulted in a success more than justifying the iconoclasm. . . . *There's Always Juliet* was a pronounced hit, possibly because Everywoman saw in it something of her own romance, either as it was or as she wished it might have been. And romance has survived every change the world has seen.

Louise Maunsell Field. NAR. Aug., 1932. pp. 174–5

Mr. Van Druten is a prolific playwright who has managed to achieve a considerable success both here and in London. . . . Nice people in their nicer—and quieter—moments he understands very well. When nothing more is required than a pleasant picture of pleasant domesticity he has a style of his own, and no one can make the tea table more genuinely agreeable than he. But he is not really at home anywhere except in the drawing room, and even there he is lost if the drawing-

room atmosphere is disturbed by so much as a gentle draft from anywhere outside the walls which were built to inclose quiet affection and
polite self-control. Resigned regret on the one hand, a mild determination on the other, make the limits over which his characters can move
without losing all verisimilitude.

Joseph Wood Krutch. Nation. April 24, 1935. p. 490

Mr. John Van Druten is one of the few men now writing for the stage
who knows how to write high comedy. His touch is at once delicate
and sure; his sense of comedy, particularly on the distaff side, keen and
subtle; his dialogue witty, often distinguished. Perhaps the war will
end this type of writing; a general leveling process will certainly end it;
but if end it does, the world will be the poorer. It presupposes a certain
amount of leisure, a willingness in the audience to forget for the moment social questions and to interest itself in the interplay of human
character. High comedy may not be, in the critical jargon of the day,
important, but it is one of the marks of a civilized society.

Grenville Vernon. Com. Jan. 10, 1941. p. 303

Mr. Van Druten is a playwright who pulls no punches in exposing the
shoddier aspects of his characters, but his sympathies run deep. Within
the narrow confines of his play (*Old Acquaintance*) . . . he does a
remarkable job of steering a group of civilized people through situations
which bring out their pettiness and jealousies, without stripping them of
their essential kindliness and decency. For all the smartness of the
writing and sophistication of the plot, such as it is, Mr. Van Druten's
play conveys a peculiarly warm conviction that humanity, even on its
less rarefied levels is capable of a modest sort of nobility.

Robert Bendiner. Nation. Feb. 1, 1941. p. 137

The Voice of the Turtle (has) three actors, one entirely realistic set, no
plot to speak of, almost no action, certainly no music and dance. And
this . . . is theatre. . . . A gem of purest ray—and serene, too—set
neatly, with an expert's touch, in the circlet that is to hold it; a light,
deft play as winningly acted as it is wisely directed, making no greater
claim than what it so amply accomplished—that of being a good example of good theatre. *The Voice of the Turtle* . . . is a pleasant
study of pleasant people. Like Mr. Van Druten's earlier *There's Always Juliet,* it concerns love at first sight and has about as much or as
little plot as that former excursion into the same subject. It is chiefly engaging for its amiable conversation, (and) for the discernment with
which its characters are revealed.

Rosamond Gilder. TA. Feb., 1944. p. 73

The Voice of the Turtle, in short, is an apotheosis of the sex life and irresistible in its implications. . . . It is convincing, infinitely appealing, and beautifully indifferent to the morality held sacred by the bluenoses. Yet the latter seem to have not the slightest suspicion of the fact and not a voice has been lifted against it. That is Van Druten's triumph. For he has written it so very skillfully; he has, without the least chicanery or subterfuge, gone about his business with such deceptive immaculateness and simplicity; and he has so astutely avoided any slightest sense of smirk or vulgarity that he has managed to make the moralists themselves not only eat his play but digest it and like it.

George Jean Nathan. AM. April, 1944. p. 465

Mr. Van Druten is a dramatist who cannot write a play without some merits. In an age that has proved itself tragically uncivilized, he continues to be a highly civilized talent. He is a craftsman who enjoys the challenges of his medium. He is at his best when working as a miniaturist. His perceptions are charming. He understands the human significance of the smallest values. . . . He wears his sophistication lightly. His wit is gentle. His audacities have a way of remaining respectable. He talks of passion in crumpet tones. He remains somewhat Victorian in tone even when in word he is the champion of the unlost weekend.

John Mason Brown. SR. Dec. 15, 1945. pp. 15–6

Van Druten is a kind of Katherine Mansfield among playwrights. Genteel, polished, mannerly, he illuminates tiny corners of middle-class life, recites a small, simple story in hushed library tones, tells us very little directly, and sends us out of the theater with disquieting reverberations echoing softly in our ears.

Irwin Shaw. NR. Nov. 3, 1947. p. 36

See *Young Woodley, There's Always Juliet,* and *The Voice of the Turtle* (plays).

VIERECK, PETER (1919–   )

Poetry

With the energy, high spirits, and optimism of a young man, he has set out to conquer a space for the humane and reasonable wherever it can be found amid the encircling gloom, and he is often remarkable capable of doing it. . . . His pleasure in words occasionally leads him to dubious puns—neurosis-new roses—and neo-Swinburnian rhymes that overpower the poem. But for the most part, both in phrasing and form, the sense of craftsmanship is evident throughout the book.

Eugene Davidson. *YR*. Summer, 1949. p. 726

He is a linguist, widely read, a man of zest and wit with a beautiful control of language. . . . I enjoyed Viereck's lively historical sense, his love of fun, and the skill with which he restates the traditional and great poetic themes. Unlike most young poets, he is more impressive collected than when read in single poems. He seldom over-extends himself in the grand effect.

Edward Weeks. *At.* Aug., 1949. p. 83

Viereck has something of an insight into the tensions of poetry, into the struggles of the formative spirit, and into the spiritual area of romanticism; but he has mounted too shrilly and too athletically the stilts of "romanticism-classicism," and has taken this opposition, not so much as something from which one could learn, but as an article of faith and a source of poetry.

J. H. Johnston. *Com.* Aug. 5, 1949. p. 418

The poems are lively . . . and a few of them sustain a neat, coarse clarity and a satiric turn of fancy that is not disagreeable. . . . The appearance of these qualities, and the appeal they seem to have, are evidences of a shift long under way from visionary concentration in poetry . . . to a drier and airier attitude, a more epigrammatic vein. In Viereck's case . . . the shift is so indiscriminate that on the whole it looks more like a relapse. . . . Viereck has as yet written very little to which one could wish to return often or with serious interest.

Robert Fitzgerald. *NR*. Aug. 8, 1949. p. 17

Whatever Viereck touches takes on a freshness and excitement. He writes about the Dawn Horse and the function of the poet with an equal mixture of gravity and mockery. He puts the scrawled phrase "Kilroy was here" into rhyme with adventurous daring and epic spirit. He is amusing and arousing in the same breath. He is an experimenter who rarely yields to the speciously spectacular, a writer who respects tradition without being submerged in it, a genuine wit who is, at the same time, a poet of emotional power.

Louis Untermeyer. *Modern American Poetry*
(Harcourt). 1950. pp. 686–7

Viereck may well be described as the principal standard-bearer of the tradition of humanistic democracy in this country. . . . Combining high wit and high seriousness, Viereck has escaped the lugubriousness ever present in the work of many of his elders. His poetry, weaving together classical myths and wartime legends such as that of Kilroy, brings to the mind the aspect of Alexander Pope that appears in "The Rape of the Lock." Like (Robert) Lowell, his enemy is Satan— not the Biblical Satan, but the modern masked Satan who denies his own existence.

Anthony Harrigan. *SAQ*. Oct., 1950. p. 486

In opposition to one poetic fashion of the Forties—the fashion of anxious psychologizing, interrupted by metafidgets—Viereck set himself off. Ostensibly as a "classicist," but in reality as something rarer in our time and more difficult to maintain on a high level—an ambitious and intelligent romantic, one of the few new poets impatient to put the gains of the two previous generations to the service of big themes, in a style remarkable and exciting for its ability to work into one context the dramatic and the didactic, the humorous and the lyrical, the topical and the fantastic.

Maurice English. *Poetry*. May, 1954. pp. 89–90

It was partly Viereck's ingenuity in the use of conventional form that aroused so much interest. . . . His attack on the more arid and drooping kind of "modernism" has been frontal, and his admirers have cheered his championship of a new and rather reactionary poetic future wherein poetry, with Eliot and Pound finally vanquished in open combat, could once more "communicate" to a large and eager audience. . . . He still displays a strong belief in his own powers, both poetic and polemic, and he is still full of vigor and zest, but much of his originality seems to be stiffening into eccentricity. . . . Tricks come more and more into evidence.

Louise Bogan. *Selected Criticism* (Noonday). 1955.
p. 395

From the beginning he had been hard to classify. There was much that was rollicking, wild, and sometimes raucous in his initial book of verse. But half-concealed by technical fireworks and plain vitality was a quieter, more tranquil Viereck, the lyricist gravely recording the eternal flow of life and experience.

It is the lyricist who is now coming into his own. . . . The latent lyricism of the poet has become incarnate in language which evokes from the reader an equal response of mind, heart, and the wistful senses.

Chad Walsh. *NYT*. Oct. 28, 1956. p. 37

Prose

His aim is a foursquare blow at the standardized thinking of both the Right and the Left in contemporary America. . . . He is glib, sassy, and provocative. . . . You will have to enjoy the dexterity with which he bursts so many half-truths and slides his sword behind the arras of so many hidden fallacies.

Thurston Davis. *Am.* March 14, 1953. pp. 652–3

Mr. Viereck is full of energy, full of zest in hate and love, in fact a man who evokes . . . the word "Renaissance," not the nice humanism of an Erasmus, but a Rabelaisian piling-up of pearls and rubbish. . . . Mr. Viereck himself is clearly a more astounding paradox than any he has written. This defender of the middle way, this classicist, this lover of French *mesure* writes most unbridled and unbuttoned books, books sewed together with all sorts of odds and ends, books that froth and foam with anger at the stupidity of the race—or at least of those of the race he knows best, his fellow intellectuals.

Crane Brinton. *JHI.* June, 1953. p. 461

In each essay Mr. Viereck arrives at the conclusion that neither of the two large opposing points of view under examination is sufficient, and he proposes a mean between them that will combine the best of both. Despite the impression of mechanical formula that such a procedure is bound to give, when Mr. Viereck speaks about specific works of poetry his taste is always good and his judgement disinterested. . . . Everywhere, in fact, his notions are sober and considered. Yet the language in which he states his moderation is neither moderate nor restrained, and sometimes not even intelligible.

Steven Marcus. *Cmty.* Aug., 1954. p. 175

See *Terror and Decorum, Strike Through the Mask, The First Morning,* and *The Persimmon Tree* (poetry); also *Dream and Responsibility* and *The Unadjusted Man* (prose).

WARREN, ROBERT PENN (1905–   )

Trite as it is nowadays to stigmatize an author as a dual personality, I cannot help pointing to a duality in Warren that may well constitute his major problem: it is his combination of critical and creative power. I am far from suggesting that the critical and the creative are of their nature antipathetic and I am fully ready to grant that what makes

Warren remarkable among American writers is his double endowment. The problem lies precisely in his being so two-sidedly gifted; he evidently finds it difficult to combine his two sorts of awareness. There is Warren, the critic, the cosmopolitan, the scholar, the philosopher; and there is Warren, the raconteur, the Kentuckian, the humorist, the ballad maker. . . . Warren is a faulty writer, but he is worth a dozen petty perfectionists. Though commonly associated with "formalists" and "classicists" in_criticism, he is close to the type of romantic genius: robust, fluent, versatile, at his worst clever and clumsy, at his best brilliant and profound.

Eric Bentley. KR. Summer, 1948. p. 424

Mr. Warren draws the themes for his books from historical incidents in the South. . . . His novels are crammed with blood and thunder in the tradition of historical fiction, but his stories take on the depth and universality of a parable, because the characters seek to learn the causes of their plight, the reasons for the rules of society, and the philosophical ideas which seem tenable in a morally, politically, and economically confused world.

Harry R. Warfel. American Novelists of Today
(American). 1951. p. 442

The wide range of his subjects, the treatment of problems that touch upon the fundamentals of human existence, the vitality of his characters, the skill with which he creates suspense and atmosphere, and the richness of his language, are characteristics that one does not often find together in a modern writer. . . . Like Hemingway and Steinbeck, he believes in the principle of solidarity as an essential value, but different from them, he stresses its inevitable clash with other elements of human behavior, above all with those of ambition, love of power, physical desire. He stands for the fundamental honesty that is so vital an issue for the generation between the two wars, but he realizes that the process of arriving at some truth may have devastating effects on the seeker.

Heinrich Straumann. American Literature in the
Twentieth Century (Hutchinson). 1951. pp. 114–5

I find all of the novels of Robert Penn Warren to be variations on a single theme, symbolized in the polarities of violence and order. He could not have chosen two concepts more arresting to the modern reader or more deeply imbedded in the history of his country and his region. . . . Robert Penn Warren has uncovered the historical sources of American violence and made them available for literary purposes, all four novels taking off from violent episodes in history that are used to illuminate modern meanings. But in writing tragedy, though the downward plunge into action takes up the most space and provides the greatest interest, violence alone is not enough. The tragic note cannot be struck without a positive world view. . . . For Warren murder, rape, and arson are simply the most effective dramatic means of developing one half of his theme: that *violence is life without principle.* Nor, to illustrate the other half, does he use orderliness for its own sake (there are no police chiefs or private detectives among his heroes); to him *order is living by principles,* even when the particular effort to do so falls far short of perfection.

Charles R. Anderson in Southern Renascence, edited
by Louis D. Rubin, Jr. and Robert D. Jacobs (Johns
Hopkins). 1953. pp. 207–9

Both the rhetoric and the "smart-aleck" commentary of *All the King's Men* have been roundly condemned by critics, usually without reference to their functional significance. . . . The cynical smart-aleck pose is Jack's defense against an alien world, the "fancy writer" the smothered and hence exaggerated ideal of himself. The two continually warring elements are further overlaid by the retrospective reflections of the mature philosophic Jack of the book's end. . . . Warren's ear is uncommonly acute, but the most valuable faculty he possesses is human insight, a shrewd and at the same time sympathetic ability to penetrate imaginatively into the inner life of his characters. In the most caustic vignette offered through Jack Burden's squinted eyes, the pity of human wastage is never lost. Warren's sense of "irreducible evil" and of human frailty permits an extremely wide range to a natural sympathy that is completely devoid of sentimentalism—ironic in the Richards sense that it is immune to irony.

John M. Bradbury. Accent. Spring, 1953. pp. 87–9

Beneath the dulled-rust-red, short-clipped hair his face was astonishingly compact: slits of eyes almost lashless, taut skin over hard cheekbones, spare modeled nose, straight line of mouth—the "entire consort" a sculpture in granite. The hard-knit, barrel-chested torso added more if that were possible, to the impression. But when Mr. Warren talked, the shock was the discovery in each subsequent moment of how much warmth and wit and wisdom, of how much humanity, there issued from that stony image.

Harvey Breit. The Writer Observed (World). 1956.
p. 131

/ What he has managed to create (in *All the King's Men*) is a work of literature that is a fully realized "concrete universal," a work which presents particulars everywhere concretely imaged yet having together a kind of universal relevance or reference—a work of the order of *Crime and Punishment* or Pope's satires or the *Oedipus Tyrannus*. . . . Such creation always depends upon a unified, integral imaginative grasp which apprehends reality in many dimensions or on many levels simultaneously. A concrete-universal cannot be schemed into existence; it issues from a sensibility aware of the implication of the universal in the concrete and a narrative skill or felicity which is able to exhibit, not merely assert or weakly suggest, their fusion. It is Warren's particular distinction to have created such a work in these times of fragmented sensibility.

Neal Woodruff, Jr. *All the King's Men: A Symposium*
(Carnegie Institute of Technology). 1957. p. 62

The need to accept the consequences of eternity's terrible intrusion on time has always been Warren's major theme, just as the place he has always seen it with the fullest particularity is the South, at some point where the contemporary life of football games and state cops, political manipulation and television exploitation tangles with the older life of the red-necks and the hunters, the Baptist ministers and the ballad singers. With this novel (*The Cave*) he has come back to the life of *Night Rider* and *All the King's Men,* where there is never world enough and time to love in but God's plenty of both to die in.

Arthur Mizener. *NYT.* Aug. 23, 1959. p. 1

Poetry

The poetry of Robert Penn Warren can best be studied as the esthetic expression of a mind in which tradition and the forces destroying tradition work in strong opposition to each other—ritual and indifference to ritual; self-knowledge and indifference to or inability to achieve self-knowledge; an inherited "theological" understanding of man and the newer psychological or social understanding, illustrated perhaps in the religious concept of evil and the liberal belief in man's ultimate power to control "evil" forces. There are two major pulls at work in shaping his idiom, the older belief in a morally integrated human being and the naturalist belief in a being formed by ill-understanding forces. The former pull expresses itself in a body of poems, and in some of his prose, as a provincial, homogeneous and consistent view that in another age might have achieved the epic proportions we associate with poetry as vision, the latter pull expresses itself in fictional characters of a low order and in a poetic idiom of a considerably less imaginative vitality.

William Van O'Connor in A Southern Vanguard,
edited by Allen Tate (Prentice-Hall). 1947. p. 92

Warren, as he is in the pristine sense a religious and moral writer, has worked directly towards the centre of the "modern problem," the fundamental ˉnature of our guilt. The probing of that cancerous tissue is done solely in terms of imagery and dramatic situation. Even Warren's attitude to the craft of poetry reflects one facet—the deathly divorce between metaphor and statement—of the disintegration theme; for his poetry is dedicated to the wedding of concept and image. Shying from abstract analysis of the conflicts within the world, he has approached his material in the structural terms of tragedy. . . . Warren's form is the tragedy and the vision which informs and bloods the drama (for his method is invariably dramatic rather than discursive) is a stark but sympathetic one of the "divided man." . . . Many of the poems, one might say, are explorations of the problem of knowledge. They receive much of their force from the ironic contrast between the purity of experience and man's commentary upon it. Man is consistently relating himself to Nature, but man's peculiar position is that, if only from his ability to suffer regret and attempt definition, he is over and above Nature.

Frederick Brantley in Modern American Poetry,
edited by B. Rajan (Dobson). 1950. pp. 66, 75

(Warren's poems) use an aristocratic and slightly archaic diction comparable to Ransom's, and they may have learned from him some of their suave irony. But, more essentially, they show how much a poet can still profit from Marvell. They are as different as possible from Cummings. Despite Cummings's distaste for abstractions, his lyrics hardly more than name the wonders of love and beauty, and thus, except for their eccentric syntax, are little thicker in texture than the songs of tin-pan alley. Warren, on the contrary, has devoted his whole attention to crowding his lines with the greatest specific gravity thˆy will bear, so that they will not merely assert the uniqueness of an experience but will convey the actual burden of that experience, both as it has been felt and as it has been thought about.

F. O. Matthiessen. The Responsibilities of the Critic
(Oxford). 1952. pp. 121–2

I think highly of Mr. Warren's poetry. There is a subtlety about it that is not readily apparent. I said earlier . . . that his rhythms resembled those of Mr. Ransom with the graciousness squeezed out of them. That is not literally true. The oftener one reads the poems—not all of them to be sure—the more aware he becomes of a new music. There is graciousness in the rhythms, but it is less obvious. The reader who has not freed himself from a subservience to the music of the iambic foot will find some of his rhythms strange. He, however, who joys in the fact that English and American poetry is returning to the rhythms natural to English, before the leaden-eared nineteenth century critics uttered inanities about the dominance of the iambic line, particularly the iambic pentameter, will delight in the subtle music of Mr. Warren's verse.

> James G. Southworth. *More Modern American Poets*
> (Blackford). 1954. pp. 118–9

See *Night Rider, At Heaven's Gate, All the King's Men, World Enough and Time, Band of Angels,* and *The Cave* (novels); also *Selected Poems, Brother to Dragons,* and *Promises* (poetry).

> See Supplement at end of text for additional material.

WELTY, EUDORA (1909–   )

She proceeds with the utmost simplicity and observes with the most delicate terseness. She does not try mystically to transform or anonymously to interpret. The parallel forced upon us, particularly by those of Miss Welty's stories which are based on an oblique humor, is her likeness to Gogol. . . . Like Gogol, Miss Welty opens the doors and describes the setting, almost inch by inch. . . . Miss Welty's method can get everything in; nothing need be scamped, because of romantic exigencies, or passed over, because of rules of taste. Temperamentally and by training she has become mistress of her material by her choice of one exactly suitable kind of treatment, and—a final test of a writer's power—as we read her, we are made to believe that she has hit upon the only possible kind.

> Louise Bogan. *Nation*. Dec. 6, 1941. p. 572

Now I happen to think that to make a ballet of words is a perversion of their best function and I dislike—because it breeds exhibitionism and insincerity—the attitude toward narrative which allows an author to sacrifice the meaning of language to its rhythms and patterns. . . . Miss Welty constantly calls attention to herself and away from her object. . . . This is the sin of pride—this self-conscious contriving— endemic to a whole generation of writers since Katherine Mansfield and most especially to the women of that generation. . . . I have spoken

of the ballet quality of Miss Welty's stories: in this connection I am reminded of the painter Dali and—via Dali—of the relationship between
the chic modern department store and much of modern fiction.

Diana Trilling. *Nation*. Oct. 2, 1943. pp. 386–7

It is her profound search of human consciousness and her illumination
of the underlying causes of the compulsions and fears of modern man
that would seem to comprise the principal value of Miss Welty's work.
She, like other best writers of this century, implies that the confusion
of our age tends to force individuals back upon conscience, as they
have not been since the seventeenth century; for in the intervening
centuries, values were more closely defined, behavior was more outwardly controlled. Miss Welty's prose fiction, like much of the poetry
and fiction of this era that seeks to explore the possibilities of the imagination, is comparable to the rich prose of Sir Thomas Browne; and
reminiscent of the poetry of the seventeenth century.

Eunice Glenn in *A Southern Vanguard,* edited by
Allen Tate (Prentice-Hall). 1947. pp. 89–90

From her earliest stories, Miss Welty's writing has had a high degree of
individuality. Her memory for colloquial speech is unbelievably accurate, and her antic imagination, coupled with her profound compassion
and understanding, gives us people much realer than real, stranger, yet
more believable than the living.

Herschel Brickell. *SR*. Aug. 27, 1949. p. 9

Amongst the younger generation, there are very few novelists indeed
whose work is plainly based on the conception of the absolute autonomy of imagination. In fact, Eudora Welty, a Southern writer, appears
to be the only one with an undisputed talent for this kind of writing, and
she is also the most promising one, because, unlike James Branch Cabell's and Gertrude Stein's, her fantasies appear entirely normal and
her style practically without mannerism. The reason for this achievement lies undoubtedly in the fact that Eudora Welty possesses the
faculty of moving imperceptibly from the world of fantasy into everyday life and back.

Heinrich Straumann. *American Literature in the
Twentieth Century* (Hutchinson). 1951. p. 125

Let us admit a deep personal preference for this particular kind of
story, where external act and the internal voiceless life of the human
imagination almost meet and mingle on the mysterious threshold between dream and waking, one reality refusing to admit or confirm the

existence of the other, yet both conspiring toward the same end. This is not easy to accomplish, but it is always worth trying, and Miss Welty is so successful at it, it would seem her most familiar territory. There is no blurring at the edges, but evidence of an active and disciplined imagination working firmly in a strong line of continuity, the waking faculty of daylight reason recollecting and recording the crazy logic of the dream.

> Katherine Anne Porter. *The Days Before*
> (Harcourt). 1952. pp. 107–8

There is one young woman who is accepted as "different" and "authentic" even by the best celebrants of the black mass in Taos and Carmel and Greenwich Village and Norfolk: the Eudora Welty who, with her two recent volumes of short stories, *A Curtain of Green* and *The Wide Net,* has become possibly the most distinguished of the new storytellers. Oh yes, she has heard of Symbolism, but her writing is as clear —and free of obscenity—as the Gettysburg Address.

> Sinclair Lewis. *A Sinclair Lewis Reader*
> (Random). 1953. p. 212

The best of Eudora Welty's fiction bears little direct resemblance to that of any other writer. In it the reader feels the form and pressure of a coherently organized view of the world in which the author lives, and perhaps she has inherited that view from Faulkner; but the deep, inward response of her characters to the conditions of existence is her unaided achievement. If we began by wondering how her gift would thrive in Faulkner's gigantic shadow, we end by deciding that it has grown and flourished all the more for being rooted in prepared ground.

> Robert Daniel in *Southern Renascence,* edited by
> Louis D. Rubin, Jr. and Robert D. Jacobs (Johns
> Hopkins). 1953. p. 315

Miss Welty revels in working in terms of conscious ambiguity; she leaves the last word unsaid, the ultimate action unconsummated. Writing with swift, sure, and often devastating understanding of her characters, and indulging a humor which is at times like the despairing cry of a child being swallowed up by quicksand, she has created out of artifice and artistry a world unmistakably her own and authentically real.

> William Peden. *SR*. Jan. 16, 1954. p. 14

Miss Welty's writing is "feminine" in both the best and the worst senses: it is sympathetic, generous and intuitive; it is also fragile, verbose and hypersensitive. The author, it could be said, rarely gets to the heart of her material, but is very good around the smaller veins.

Jean Holzhauer. *Com.* April 29, 1955. p. 109

Miss Eudora Welty . . . deals in overtones and moments of implication; she . . . compels our acceptance by the spell of words and symbols. The significance of her characters and scenes lies as much in the past behind them and in the future before them as in the moment snatched from the moving reel and set before us in a vivid "still." . . . The unsaid and the implied are essentially human, and human sophisticated at that, for although the characters of her creation are usually simple folk the reader is never for a moment unconscious of Miss Welty's sophisticated eye. Here is a wonderfully clear vision, humorous, tender, and always shaping the raw experience before her to our satisfaction. Nevertheless, as I read each successive book of Miss Welty's, I am less and less satisfied. She is so entirely successful on her own home ground, but she hardly ever wins an away match.

Angus Wilson. *NSN.* Nov. 19, 1955. p. 680

See *A Curtain of Green, The Wide Net, The Golden Apples,* and *The Bride of Innisfallen* (short stories); also *The Robber Bridegroom, Delta Wedding,* and *The Ponder Heart* (novels).

WESCOTT, GLENWAY (1901–   )

(*The Apple of the Eye*) is a book almost exclusively of emotional propulsion. Indeed, it even becomes a drenching in emotions, those softer, readier emotion which we designate usually as "feminine," an experience purely of "delight and tears" (to borrow one of his chapter heads) and is thus a kind of revival in letters, an atavism, albeit a revival which is done with such force, such conviction, that one is caught unawares and before he knows it is deeply involved in these partings (by death and locomotion), this girl like a wilted flower left to perish, these stutterings of love, the sleep-walking in the moonlight, the call, or lure, of the city over hills and plains. . . . In method, Mr. Wescott's chief contribution is the bringing of a greater and more sensitive vitality to a type of book in which the typical novelist would feel very much at home.

Kenneth Burke. *Dial.* Dec., 1924. pp. 513–4

About *The Grandmothers* I feel it difficult to remain calm. Its appearance at this time is comparable to the occasions when *The Spoon River*

Anthology and *Winesburg, Ohio* were first given to the public. Indeed, it bears some superficial likeness to both of those books. . . . *The Grandmothers* is a novel not only with its roots in the American soil, but it is a novel of those roots and of that soil. It is a novel that gives a new significance to American life. It should inculcate a finer patriotism and a deeper sense of pride of country than all the Fourth of July orations ever delivered.

Burton Rascoe. *Bkm.* Sept., 1927. pp. 86–7

(*The Grandmothers* is) altogether a magnificent record of failure, a stately elegy on lives too fine for success, but in no real sense a novel. A scheme which gives to each life a chapter and to each chapter the import of the whole permits neither movement nor design. But as autobiography, the book provides a not unworthy complement to *The Education of Henry Adams.* The prose, though less spontaneous than in his first novel, is Mr. Wescott's principal accomplishment. He lavishes on the sad and wasted figures in his collection a sort of valedictory elegance, which more than anything else should compensate them for the many losses, the many humiliations.

William Troy. *NR.* Sept. 14, 1927. p. 105

Glenway Wescott opens a family album and out of its portraits he makes a book (*The Grandmothers*). From its stained pages ghosts emerge, each with a story. History repeats itself to him—the history of a group of people all bound by ties of blood or marriage, settlers in Wisconsin. The scene has the strong quality of those early days, there is that somber sense of the land, of the growth of the soil and of those who took root there.

Each ghost becomes in turn the shadow of an earlier wraith who left a heritage of energies and impulses. Each life yields its hidden drama; the past gives up its secret. Out of the cross threads of passion is woven the material of this novel. Out of it the author cuts the pattern of the race.

Halle Schaffner. *Survey.* Nov. 1, 1927. p. 161

His is a vision that may be at times extravagant and is certainly open to the charge of cloudy mysticism—but it is a vision, moving and troubling, of a wide, brooding land that (we are at last realizing it) calls not for a Dreiser but for a Dostoevsky. . . . More important than any individual story is the sense they all give of a beautiful and trained style, a style at times over-poetic and at times over-mannered, but which bears within itself many of the qualities of greatness. It is not too much (and certainly not much) to say that Mr. Wescott's prose is among the most beautiful being written in America today.

Clifton Fadiman. *Bkm.* Oct., 1928. pp. 220–1

The Wisconsin of Glenway Wescott is more than a geographical region with natural boundaries of hills and rivers, a landscape of highways and farms. He sees it also as a symbol of narrowness because the old pioneer spirit has dwindled to the restlessness of discontent. . . . Wescott seems to write while remembering, his mind filled with images of places and people seen but half-forgotten, stories heard long ago and recalled in tranquil recollection. . . . He saw the late twilight of the pioneering epoch and he has watched with moving, troubled gaze the effects of those factors that are transforming rural Wisconsin into an urban landscape. . . . He is always the observer, watching, remembering, attempting to explain the implications of a national birthright.

Dayton Kohler. *Bkm.* April, 1931. p. 143

The intimate routines of the family, love's power to survive its own abuses, to arrest the flux and establish continuity, filled the younger Wescott with frank wonder and curiosity. And he used to astonish the sophisticated twenties by exhibiting all this, the stuff of average human experience, as something very rare, almost a mystery. He was the poet of the family album; a repentant Ishmael, to whom his artist's exclusion from the tribe had become a burden. . . . But Wescott the emergent artist has become Wescott the mature spectator, coolly ironic where he used to be impassioned and devout. Clearly he has set out to transcend the nostalgic lyricism of his early work and to bring to bear upon his favorite themes a more complex experience and a more objective method. . . . One hopes . . . that he will not permit his newly acquired irony to dissipate the intensity and peculiar visionary idealism which have always been his strength.

F. W. Dupee. *NR.* Dec. 9, 1940. pp. 807–8

The Pilgrim Hawk, with which Glenway Wescott returns to fiction after a twelve-year absence, is less a story of love than a fable. . . . The dramatic substance of his scenes and characters does not manage to sustain the elaborate commentary he has imposed on it. The annotation becomes too elaborate, strained, ingenious, and self-conscious. A tendency toward a worrying preciosity of inference and analysis is never genuinely subdued to the natural volition of events and personalities, and the result becomes too patently contrived and at times almost desperately *voulu.* This is not to minimize the beauty of many of its pages, the great superiority of its style and feeling to the general ruck of fiction, and its always subtly considered, often brilliant observations.

Milton Dauwen Zabel. *Nation*. Dec. 21, 1940. p. 636

In *Apartment in Athens* Glenway Wescott writes fiction transcendentally, aware that, whatever their ultimate reality, events are known only in individual consciousness, and that social and political developments can be fully understood, fully responded to, fully shared, only as they are related to archtypes, partly unconscious, within the individual. What Wescott is doing imaginatively is so important that we don't mind the failures in surface realism or in information about Greece. But on a higher level the lack of convincing Greekness is still a defect.

Robert Gorham Davis. *NR*. April 16, 1945. p. 526

We don't expect a writer of Mr. Wescott's caliber to use his talents in the service of propaganda, and I especially didn't expect him to propagate hatred. To the writer of real creative power there is usually something deeply antipathetic in the act of subordinating free creativity to indoctrination, and where there is as much critical awareness of style as in all of Mr. Wescott's work, I would have expected—though, I now see, mistakenly—to find enough critical awareness of self to save an author from guilty gestures. We are told that Mr. Wescott calls *Apartment in Athens* his war work. It is the kind of war work we commonly look for, not at the head or heart of intellectual and artistic life, but at its fringes, where conscience seems to exist only to be uneasy.

Diana Trilling. *Nation*. March 17, 1945. p. 312

See *The Apple of the Eye, The Grandmothers,* and *The Pilgrim Hawk* (novels); also *Good-bye, Wisconsin* (short stories).

WEST, NATHANAEL   (1906–1940)

It is easy enough to indicate the materials which Mr. Nathanael West has used in his grotesquely beautiful novel, *Miss Lonelyhearts*. But it is a far more difficult matter to convey some notion of the intensely original incandescence of spirit which fuses these simple elements. Chapter after brilliantly written chapter moving like a rocket in mid-flight, neither falls nor fails. The book itself ends with the sudden, swift delumination of a light going out.

Florence Haxton Britten. *NYHT*. Apr. 30, 1933. p. 6

Mr. West pierces beneath the surfaces of his material. The tragic lives of his characters impress us even more powerfully because they are made to seem stupid and comic. We may laugh with the author at these people, but we recognize the essential seriousness which has given his writing its impetus. . . . Mr. Dreiser would have made a tragedy out of this material; Mr. West, in making a satiric comedy of it, has perhaps given a more adequate rendering of men whose warped lives do not offer any theme considerable enough for tragedy.

T. C. Wilson. *SR*. May 13, 1933. p. 589

His new novel, *The Day of the Locust,* deals with the nondescript characters on the fringe of Hollywood studios. . . . And these people have been painted as precisely and polished up as brightly as the figures in Persian miniatures. Their speech has been distilled with a sense of the flavorsome and the characteristic which makes John O'Hara pedestrian. Mr. West has footed a precarious way and has not slipped at any point into relying on the Hollywood values in describing the Hollywood people. . . . The doings of these people are bizarre, but they are also sordid and senseless. Mr. West has caught the emptiness of Hollywood; and he is, as far as I know, the first writer to make this emptiness horrible.

Edmund Wilson. *NR*. July 26, 1939

Here is a book (*The Day of the Locusts*) that attempts to do a great deal more than just pillory the foibles and flimflammery of the movie industry. While its setting is Hollywood and the miasma of the studio naturally permeates the lives of the people concerned, Mr. West has sketched an acidulous melange of Southern Californian grotesques, including . . . some samples of the queer folk you don't read so much about: the Middle Westerners who have saved up a few thousand dollars and moved to California to end their days basking in its vaunted sun. These people, mostly middle-aged, often semi-invalid, invariably bored with their self-chosen life of idleness, inhabit an appalling spiritual wasteland . . . There is abundant material here for scathing satire or careful social study, and the principal objection to *The Day of the Locusts* is apt to be that it merely scratches the surface.

Louis B. Saloman. *Nation*. July 15, 1939. pp. 78–9

West's contemporaries were realists; he was a kind of superrealist. He often used enormous incongruities to make his points, which gave him a kinship with French writers of the school of Rimbaud and with the later surréalistes; but instead of documenting his perceptions with magnifying-glass clarity, he preferred to distill them into images and situations painfully barren of minutiae. He was an extreme pessimist, which may have been the reason why he never reached a wide audience while he was alive.

Richard B. Gehman. At. Sept. 19, 1950. p. 69

West's Hollywood is made up of degeneracy and brothels, of failure and sexual desire, of cock-fighting and third-rate boarding houses. But more than anything it is made up of significant boredom, of an etiolated ennui: the whole canvas on which the motiveless actions take place acquires a Breughal-like stillness, as if all the monstrous things going on were part of a very ordinary pattern. And, indeed, the pattern of all West's books is ordinary; it is only the extraordinary stylized grotesques on the edge, the narrative logic that touches the rim of fantasy, that charge it with the nervous garishness, the disproportionate perspective that, like the beautiful hunchbacks in *Balso Snell,* mock normality with their own freakishness.

Alan Ross. Introduction to The Complete Works of
Nathanael West (Farrar). 1957. pp. xxi–ii

West's symbols and grotesques are perhaps more disturbing even than Kafka's, because they more strongly resemble the real. His satire never loses its sting because it is always more real than satirical. He delves more deeply than Melville into the ingrained confidence game of American civilization, the ever-widening split between aspiration and actuality that keeps our public statements, from school days on, from corresponding with the way things are. . . . West treats serious subjects flippantly; but that is better than treating trivial subjects, such as the "romance of business," seriously. He is like a perky little wind that blows, now this way, now that, until all the fog of illusion is dispelled from the land.

William Bittner. Nation. May 4, 1957. pp. 394–6

The recognition grows that West wrote about something more than pseudo-surrealist characters inside the Trojan horse, a demented writer giving advice to the unloved, a bumpkin determined to act out all the Horatio Alger stories, a group of Hollywood grotesques. He had to write about something. He could not simply and starkly proclaim: here in America is a great emptiness, a vacuum sucking us all in and forcing us to die of spiritual bends. He did not tell, he showed. . . . He sensed what Paul Tillich calls "the shaking of the foundations." Like an expressionistic artist, he saw the breaking up of life's surface, and in his prose he drew the fragments.

Richard L. Schoenwald. Com. May 10, 1957.
pp. 162–3

Nathanael West's saving grace was that, as a man and as a writer, he practiced the fine art of detachment. Although he was as concerned as his colleagues with the ills of Depression America (once he was arrested for joining a picket line in front of a New York department store), he rarely permitted the period's numerous teapot tempests to intrude on his serious writing. As a writer, his preoccupation was with the moral bankruptcy that underlay the surface ills. Specifically, he wrote of the dreams by which man attempts to live and of the violence which perverts these dreams.

Roger H. Smith. SR. May 11, 1957. p. 13

He had the gift of a grotesquely accurate imagination, so much admired in the Nineteen Twenties, but the chief reason why his work is remembered is simply that he could write. He wrote as carefully as if he were chiselling each word in stone, with space around it. He wrote as if he were composing cablegrams to a distant country, with the words so expensive that he couldn't waste them, and yet with the need for making his message complete and clear. In rereading his works one is always surprised to find how short they are. The proof of their value is that they occupy more space in one's memory than they do on the printed page.

Malcolm Cowley. NYT. May 12, 1957. p. 5

See *The Complete Works of Nathanael West.*

WHARTON, EDITH   (1862–1937)

I take to her (Mrs. Wharton) very kindly as regards her diabolical little clevernesses, the quality of intention and intelligence in her style, and her sharp eye for an interesting *kind* of subject. . . . She *must* be tethered in native pastures, even if it reduces her to a back-yard in New York.

Henry James. Letters, edited by Percy Lubbock
(Scribner). 1920. v. 1, p. 396

One of Mrs. Wharton's greatest distinctions is that she is not sentimental; when she succeeds in awakening an emotion in the reader, it is a legitimate one; and she accomplishes it by her art, not through parade of her own feelings. . . . She is detached from her plot. She can stand over and away from her structure and let the story tell itself, absorbing all our attention with a few light touches, and giving finality to all of them. The tenseness of her style and the manner in which she combines eagerness with discipline, poise, and perfection of phrase with lack of mannerism, are the tangible bases of her talent. She plots her stories, sees in her mind's eye the persons who participate in them, how they look, dress, and act, what their background is. She seeks to tell the truth about them, impartially and unemotionally.

Joseph Collins. *Taking the Literary Pulse* (Doran).
1924. pp. 54–5

Despite her artistry . . . Mrs. Wharton has failed as the eighteenth century failed, by her insistence upon definitions of life in terms of the artificial, in terms of civilization rather than in the fundamentals of Nature. Of the great, quivering, suffering, laboring human mass, she knows little. . . . Nature unadorned she views with all the horror of an Addison or a Pope.

Fred Lewis Pattee. *The New American Literature*
(Century). 1930. p. 253

Mrs. Wharton . . . has been far too much the professional novelist to sustain the qualities which first and very justly brought her fame. These were . . . an unflagging distinction of manner and a very high and very penetrating wit. Nor was this all. Her people were very much alive and several of her earlier books at least have that virtue so immensely rare in our letters: architectonic beauty, beauty of inner structure. Yet her work is fading and crumbling and will probably be almost forgotten until a time so detached from the present arises that people can go back to a little of it as to something quaint and sweet and lavendered, wondering that at so late an age a woman as intelligent as Edith Wharton could have taken seriously the conventions of a small and unimportant social group, could have in ultimate judgement identified herself with these futile and fugitive notions and confronted the moral world with the standards of a silly and cruel game.

Ludwig Lewisohn. *Expression in America* (Harper).
1932. p. 466

Nothing was ever more unmistakable in Edith than the quality of the foundations of her culture. She was never delayed in trifling with the easy, the showy, the quickly and cheaply rewarding; she went straight for the best, and no time lost; and she set up her standards once for all, to serve her lifetime. She seemed to be excused the long labor of trying the wrong turnings, following the wrong leads, discarding misfits, such as most of us have to worry through with patience; and this was fortunate, for she had no patience at all or any time for second thoughts and anxious renewals, only an eagerness, never exhausted, for further exploration and acquisition . . . She was all that was right and regular in her smooth clan-plumage, but the young hawk looked out of her eyes. . . . She actually grasped what she was about, this one, as she settled down to her work and stuck to it; and on fire as she was with her ambition, her head was cool, she knew her place, and her pride in it was as sound as her modesty. The sagest and sternest of the craftsmen must admit that she meets them on their ground.

> Percy Lubbock. *Portrait of Edith Wharton* (Appleton-Century). 1947. pp. 13, 244

In the stories of Mrs. Wharton, men are condemned for their paucity of understanding. The lament which sounds from Mrs. Wharton's fiction is not that women must inhabit a man's world, but that, because of man's unperceptiveness, each sex is consigned to a different world. . . . Men are the visitors who never arrive. Women wait for them their life long, women who demand neither the vote nor economic equality, women who seldom clamor for a single standard of sex morals. What the women of Edith Wharton's novels crave is an understanding presence, and that man is never able to accord. . . . For the man of Edith Wharton's conceiving, woman is always walled away, by his own blindness; so that she, unbeheld, finally ceases to behold.

> Josephine Lurie Jessup. *The Faith of Our Feminists* (R. R. Smith). 1950. p. 80

Especially in her earlier work, Edith Wharton is chiefly concerned with the overpowering effect of social and tribal conventions on the individual. She adheres to the assumption that the reality of these conventions is stronger than Man, who, though he may not always perish in this conflict, will be fatally injured in his happiness. If, in addition to this conception, the role played by blind chance is taken into account, the criteria of a determinist attitude are obvious. It may, however, be necessary to point out that for those readers to whom the cruelty of social conventions is not a reality, a good deal of Edith Wharton's art will be lost.

> Heinrich Straumann. *American Literature in the Twentieth Century* (Hutchinson). 1951. pp. 54–5

There was something odd in the resentment with which she seemed to exaggerate the vulgarity of the vulgar and the illiteracy of those whom she disliked. It was as if, in some way, she felt that she was menaced by them, as if she was in some fashion on the defensive, and certain it was that, as a writer, she was not at ease with American life when she left the small magic circle of her old New York. As a rule she could not yield herself to her native world as it actually was, she felt obliged to see it in terms of England, so that she constantly suffered lapses in which her people and scenes no longer corresponded with the reality they assumed to present.

> Van Wyck Brooks. *The Confident Years* (Dutton).
> 1952. p. 278

It is interesting to see how Henry James's insistence on "form" in the novel was simplified by his friend and follower, Mrs. Wharton, into mere adherence to plot. The plot must proceed, through all its ramifications, even though characters be wrenched out of shape to serve it. Minor figures, put in purely to prop up the plan, soon are shuffled away, and are featureless from the beginning. The long arm of coincidence snaps up the roving actors and places them down neatly in surroundings cleverly arranged to suit their situation. . . . Mrs. Wharton's work formed a bridge from the nineteenth-century novel to the magazine fiction of the present where, in a superficially arranged scene, manners, clothes, food, and interior decoration are described carefully and at length; how she contained in herself, as it were, the whole transitional period of American fiction, beginning in the bibelot and imported-European-culture era of the late nineties, and ending in the woman's-magazine dream of suburban smartness.

> Louise Bogan. *Selected Criticism* (Noonday).
> 1955. p. 84

See *The House of Mirth, Ethan Frome,* and *The Age of Innocence* (novels).

WHEELOCK, JOHN HALL (1886–   )

He acknowledges the message of Whitman, even as every musician must feel the impress of Wagner, every sculptor the force of Rodin. . . . It is just because Mr. Wheelock is so much in touch with today that he seems so often to be speaking with the accents of Whitman. But, though he too insists on the glory of the commonplace . . . , he strikes out for a freedom of style and utterance entirely his own. . . . At its best Mr. Wheelock's poetry is clear, revealing and full of that high realism which is the color of life. He has something of the vision which uplifts sensuality, and enough of the realist's passion to save mysticism from itself, and humanize it.

> Louis Untermeyer. *NYT.* Dec. 29, 1912. p. 800

At its best the poetry of John Hall Wheelock has been notable for a gravity in feeling and reflection which has given it, at times, a sober romantic beauty quite its own in character. . . . Abstaining from experiment is his privilege, probably his advantage. . . . The grandiose, the ingenious, the clever and exciting elements of the art are not for him. With a firm lonely sobriety he now addresses a life sombrely shaded. . . . In his ripe unbaffled sincerity there is still a true, if uneventful, meditative beauty.

Morton Dauwen Zabel. Poetry. Feb., 1927. pp. 280–2

Mr. Wheelock knows how to be alone and how to make friends with humanity and the distant suns in the vast silence that is himself. . . . This poet can trace the line in the marks a mouse's feet make in the dust or in the rays of a star in outer space, and can see them as foliations of the same scroll. He can handle the mystic magnitudes, yet he can be private in his tenderness as well. Without the ancient theological designs, he can find deity.

Robert P. Tristram Coffin. NYHT. Dec. 13, 1936. p. 18

His eclecticism is enormously wide; but if ghosts as dissimilar as Wordsworth, Matthew Arnold, Tennyson, Blake, and even Sydney Lanier, sometimes rise from his pages, they are conjured before us by the magic of a genuine intuition; and their intrusion cannot dissipate the conviction we have of witnessing the impact upon a man of sensibility and surcharged feeling of a world physically real . . . His most marked virtues are due to his amazing instinct for representing moods with appropriate cadences; and to capacities which have prolonged through years those excitements in physical living, that élan from tragedies, which, in most of us, escape after youth.

Evelyn Scott. Poetry. May, 1937. pp. 102–3

John Hall Wheelock shows himself a devoted and sincere disciple of the art, but more notable for the sense of exaltation with which he writes than for his actual performance of the page. . . . Mr. Wheelock's whole poetical stock seems to consist of rapturous but undifferentiated, unparticularized feeling; and as the emotion is undefined, so the expression is indistinct, putting up with all manner of phrases from the common sentimental store. . . . At times the genuineness of his emotion proves communicable, and then the reader comes on a passage in which a sense of exalted participation in the sum of things is truly given. This is Mr. Wheelock's poetry at its best; at its all too frequent worst it is a poetry of pink mist.

Theodore Morrison. At. June, 1937. Unpaged

He sings; his concept of poetry is ecstatic, vatic; even in his latest work the grand public manner of his youthful poems compels though less overtly, the gesture of composition.

Because the manner is grand, and because the purity of the emotion finds, at moments of greatest intensity, modes of declamation that are just and persuasive, we find from the very beginning poems and parts of poems that have the definitive rightness. These are the passages that establish Mr. Wheelock—not in the vatic tradition, where I suspect he would like to be, but in the soberer tradition of poets who enforce a more human response. The less oratory, the more conviction.

Dudley Fitts. *NYT*. Sept. 9, 1956. p. 10

It is, of course, not simply his preference for accepted forms that makes Mr. Wheelock a traditionalist. He writes about the human condition not as it has been affected by such thinkers as Marx, Freud, and Einstein, by the dazzle that the hydrogen bomb and the IBM diversely provide, but in terms that would have been understood by men living in Jerusalem in the first century of our era or in Athens five centuries earlier. Recent ideological and technological revolutions have not been big enough, however, to silence the old questions about the half-known self and the great unknown Other. . . . Poems that speak feelingly of these matters, with candor and with the force bred of economy, have a durable value. Mr. Wheelock's most carefully wrought lyrics belong.

Babette Deutsch. *Poetry*. Feb., 1957. pp. 320–1

John Hall Wheelock's career as poet is a curious one. It is not exceptional for a lyric poet to be prolific in his youth—as Wheelock was—and then run thin and dry in his forties—as Wheelock did. . . . But what is really curious, and all but unique, is the revival of his talent in the past ten years; better still, the improvement of it. . . . The effort is to bring the language into a simpler, more natural tone; and to make, one can say, better sense. It is this effort—to abandon rhetoric, to walk without the embroidered coat—which makes the . . . new poems . . . so much more meaningful reading, so much more *real*. One can say "against" some of the recent poems that the pulse is low and the language meandering, but on the whole their fresher vocabulary guarantees an immediacy and poignancy never achieved in the earlier work.

Winfield Townley Scott. *SR*. March 2, 1957. p. 20

See *Poems, Old and New.*

WHEELWRIGHT, JOHN BROOKS (1897–1940)

Despite their mathematical whiskers, Wheelwright's unconventional sonnets are patently integral, the forms of an experience. Long, in instances singing, in other instances staccato breaths or periods sustained by an individual, racy, infrequently exalted idiom harmoniously compose them; and these harmonies—in some cases somewhat cryptically but in others clearly and fully—convey a fresh grasp of life, particularly of the ways, fortunes, and tragedies of friendship.

> Paul Rosenfeld. *Nation*. Oct. 15, 1938. p. 386

He is called hag-ridden, exhibitionist, skillful, dignified like a Greek, a leader of a revolutionary school; it is further stated that he has no ear and that his language is bald. Some make of him a mystic; others are satisfied that he comes from New England—and that almost as an accusation. . . . He seems a poet, for he infuses and infuriates. He is skillful, for he is called a heretic. In brief, he claims attention for his Christian attitudes as well as for his Marxist politics; and both, fused into his poetry, easily run riot with the critical fanciers of the laissez-faire in verse. . . . It is to the accomplished Deed that Wheelwright gives his strange allegiance and his stranger art.

> Harry Roskolenko. *Poetry*. August, 1940. pp. 278–81

Technically, Wheelwright . . . was a most versatile poet. He was equally adept at handling a metaphysical conceit and a dramatic monologue. In some of his shorter poems he even appears as the terrible man —there is no adequate, single word to describe him—who deliberately mixed his metaphors. . . . In all capacities, however, he was a precise writer, one who avoided unnecessarily expansive language and who achieved his effects by sharp contrasts, clever juxtapositions.

> E. Reed Whittemore. *NYHT*. Aug. 17, 1941. p. 13

John Wheelwright was not able or not willing to practice the necessary insincerities of communication; this absolute honesty sanctioned the bewildering, misleading, and seemingly captious items that fill his poems, underneath which the reader will often look in vain for the directive logic, poetic or otherwise, that should organize and sustain them. . . . The short satirical and epigrammatical poems are particularly good of their kind. There the poet, being forced to revolve his poem around a single point, hasn't the pretext for divagation and must concentrate what he says into one small, but very sharp, bite. The gnomic flavor of Wheelwright's poetry makes the bite all the sharper—once it is felt.

Clement Greenberg. Nation. Aug. 30, 1941. p. 186

On the technical side, John Wheelwright is a genuinely advanced poet; he has thoroughly explored the tradition, and the recent extensions of the tradition, and his final products are by and large richly original, formally ambitious, and modern in a mature and respectable sense. His themes and perceptions spring typically from the operation of a well-sharpened intellect upon the objective world, with the result that the poems never try to lift themselves by their own platitudes, nor do they ever open their hearts to the amateur of emotions of the good-old-fashioned kind. . . . Wheelwright is an intellectual poet, and by this I mean not merely that he is an intelligent poet, but that the themes of his poetry are quite often the propositions of philosophical argumentation.

E. S. Forgotson. Poetry. Oct., 1941. pp. 45–6

Wheelwright had sense, satire, sensibility and the salt of literature that made him one of the best of the recognizable minor poets. Had he lived, he would have perfected his New England acerbity, his tart sort of common sense that we badly need, but, as he writes in another context:

Then I departed as I came, tearing roses
and trampling the gooseberries and the strawberries.

Peter Monro Jack. NYT. Dec. 14, 1941. p. 5

Very nearly all of Wheelwright's verse lacked the presence and the unforced control of a "melodic ear," and unlike Marianne Moore, he had yet to find a "light rhyme" or its equivalent with which to define his particular art of writing verse. Some of his effects were "experimental" and inventive, others seem to have been studiously premeditated, still others had an air of seeming accidental, and the great majority were dominated by a prose rhythm that had yet to achieve its maturity. But at the center of the verse where a number of Wheelwright's epigrams remained half-formed and half-concealed, a personality that had created its own speech emerged: the speech was often critical and it welcomed controversy, and it was persistent in its effort to write poetry with ideas and not with words.

Horace Gregory and Marya Zaturenska. A History of
American Poetry (Harcourt). 1947. pp. 348–9

It is part of Wheelwright's integrity, of course, that he gave no palm to halfway measures. He hounded Truth. Therefore the didactic note in all his poetry, his effort to objectify and dramatize. The image is never for its own sake: sense must be made of it—a thing said. His obituary poems on Hart Crane, Crosby, and Miss Lowell say definitive things; like all his best poems, they survive with a remarkable solidarity. Where his thought attained the vigor of eloquence, neither matter nor manner damaged by the other, he wrote poems which repeatedly reward attention and which should give him a yet unsuspected importance in the history of American poetry.

Winfield Townley Scott. NMQ. Summer, 1954. p. 195

See *Rock and Shell, Mirrors of Venus, Political Self-Portrait,* and *Selected Poems* (all poems).

WILBUR, RICHARD (1921–   )

Wit of the kind he is aiming at—the Swiftian or Eliotesque kind—demands more intellectual incisiveness and emotional "blackness" than Mr. Wilbur is at present able to muster. His true domain is the borderland between natural and moral perception, his special gift for the genteel, non-metaphysical conceit which illuminates the hidden correspondences between natural and moral phenomena. Characteristically, two of Mr. Wilbur's favorite devices stem from Marianne Moore: the lingering over minute particulars and the sudden introduction of anecdotal units into straight narrative or meditative sequences . . . where the "anecdote," so far from merely winding up the poem, both climaxes and clinches it.

F. C. Golffing. Poetry. Jan., 1948. pp. 221–2

His poems are full of affirmation, delight in the shapes and colors of the visible world; water and light are favorite symbols. Mr. Wilbur's turn of mind is philosophic as well as sensual; his epithet is neither the fashionably verbal nor the obsolescent conventional; he has considerable variety of manner and a meet sense of proportion in the way he fits manner to theme. The danger he may face . . . is that of finding things a little too easy, of having forms come facile, however quick, to suit the demands of the not quite deep, really, levels of emotion.

Rolfe Humphries. Nation. Dec. 9, 1950. p. 536

Some of these poems are pieces of pure gaiety, some present uncrossed felicity. Most of them are about gratifying objects. All of them are charged with responsiveness to the lusters, the tones, of the physical world, and show the poet alert to less apparent matters. The scenes are alive with light, be it the light coined by "the minting shade of the trees" that shines on clinking glasses and laughing eyes, or one of a wintrier brightness. They shiver and sway happily with the sound of winds and waters. Yet they are apt to close upon a somber chord, to admit an intrusive shadow.

Babette Deutsch. *NYT*. Feb. 11, 1951. p. 12

Mr. Wilbur always keeps firm control over the shape of his poems, and it is a shape determined jointly by the ear and by the mind, so that the poems resolve themselves to a conclusion both musically and intellectually. He is at his best with the longer line and the slower cadence, in subjects which take their origin in scenes observed or remembered. Occasionally observation gives way too readily to exclamation. . . . But this is not a common fault, and for the most part he moves from description to comment so subtly yet naturally that the texture of the poem remains even and a descriptive poem has become a meditative or even a philosophic one before the reader is aware.

David Daiches. *NYHT*. Feb. 18, 1951. p. 4

The precise quality of the poems is a delicate suspension. He performs an extraordinary feat of balance. His poems are strong and yet are sensitively wrought so that in general the reader gets a fine, real sense of the world.

There is a sense of mastery but of struggle, of order claimed from chaotic forces never allowed to assume disproportion, yet valued as formative. . . . One returns to the idea of balance, of orderliness, of excellence, of elegance, of a good centrality, nothing excessive, nothing divisive, which is to say that Wilbur has achieved a natural and full harmony in his poetry.

Richard Eberhart. *NYT*. June 24, 1956. p. 5

Now with *Things of This World,* his enormous gifts grown into their mature assurance, Wilbur certainly emerges as our serenest, urbanest, and most melodic poet. To say Wilbur has matured is not to imply that he will not accomplish finer things yet, and I would suggest for instance that in his search for a serene diction he might place less reliance on such adjectives as "clear," "pure," "calm," and "graceful." It is exactly the qualities described by these adjectives that best describe the best Wilbur poems, but it is very much to the point, I believe, that in those best poems the clarity, purity, calm, and grace emerge thing-wise and self-living, not by adjectival assertion.

John Ciardi. *SR*. Aug. 18, 1956. p. 18

Imagination as a word has tended to associate with the bodiless. "Imaginary" and "fictional" are synonyms. In Wilbur's previous work, the attempt is to divest objects of being or relevance and create a world of the imagination independent of objects. Here we find imagination in another function, applied to things not to uncover an inner reality superior to the outer, but to present their gaudiness and to celebrate sensuous enjoyment of them. If we "imagine excellence" it is in order to "try to *make* it." . . . There has been a steady intellectual growth, and a movement away from the destitution of formalism into the beginnings of something else; from a self-delighted loveliness (and the poems, let it be insisted, really *are* lovely) not to any "affirmation" as Life editors would have it, but toward the discovery of some "things of this world."

Donald Hall. *Poetry*. Sept., 1956. p. 403

Mr. Wilbur used to be a kind of backward-looking, forward-aspiring fellow. If it were a spring day, he perversely wanted it to be an autumn one. . . . But all is changed now. In his newest work he stands squarely in the midst of the things of this world and likes all of what he sees, smells, hears, touches, and tastes. . . . If *Things of This World* is marked by Wilbur's new-found sense of reality, it still exhibits what have come to be the trademarks of his work—formal elegance, unusual although never grotesque imagery, control, quiet gaiety, and an agile imagination. Now that Wallace Stevens is dead, Williams seems headed toward being the dandy of American verse.

Leah Bodine Drake. *At*. June, 1957. p. 78

See *The Beautiful Changes, Ceremony*, and *Things of This World* (poetry)

WILDER, THORNTON (1897–   )

Before we read him, we are likely to think that he is one of those contemporary writers who seem still to date from the nineties—that he is simply another "stylist," another devotee of "beauty"—that we shall, in fact, find him merely a pretty or a precious writer; but Wilder, when we come to read him, turns out to be something quite different. He certainly possesses that quality of "delightfulness" of which Saintsbury has said that Balzac didn't have it, but that Gérard de Nerval did. But he has a hardness, a sharpness, a precision, quite unlike our Cabells, our Dunsanys, our Van Vechtens and our George Moores. He has an edge which is peculiar to himself and which is never incompatible with a consummate felicity.

Edmund Wilson. *NR*. Aug. 8, 1928. p. 304

The Bridge of San Luis Rey can be sacrificed without loss. . . . Its fatalism seems specious, trivial, and even dishonest, as though consistency in the Maker's ways were trumped up to serve the ends of plot. *The Cabala* is much better, though questionable in that general air of selectness which it has in common with the society novels of writers like Marcel Prévost . . . and Paul Bourget. . . . And the work is vitiated at the close by that superficial coquetting with the mystic which mars *The Bridge* as a whole.

Kenneth Burke. *Bkm*. Aug., 1929. p. 562

That so exquisite a writer and so intense an inventor should devote his arts entirely to moral, as distinct from political, purposes is an admirable but, in the present state of things, a rare characteristic. . . . Through a combination of qualities almost unheard of in England but not uncommon in France, all Mr. Wilder's virtues, even the tidy flamboyance of his prose and the pagan revels of his intellect, arise from this smack of the evangelist in him.

E. G. Twitchett. *LM*. May, 1930. p. 32

Wilder has concocted a synthesis of all the chambermaid literature, Sunday school tracts and boulevard piety there ever were. He has added a dash of the prep-school teacher's erudition, then embalmed all this in the speciously glamorous style of the late Anatole France. He talks much of art, of himself as Artist, of style. He is a very conscientious craftsman. But his is the most irritating and pretentious style pattern I have read in years. It has the slick, smug finality of the lesser Latins; that shallow clarity and tight little good taste that remind one of nothing so much as the conversation and practice of a veteran cocotte.

Michael Gold. *NR*. Oct. 22, 1930. p. 267

He was a dramatist before he became a novelist, and his prose has always shown the discipline of the theater. His novels were never completely satisfactory in form: they were panel novels—long, vivid character sketches linking dramatic scenes. The quality of his imagination and his interest in character portrayal were both dramatic in spirit.

Dayton Kohler. *EJ*. Jan., 1939. p. 4

Thornton Wilder possesses several distinctive virtues as a creative literary artist, but unfortunately none of them has much to do with his actual skill as a writer. He has an adventurous mind, which makes him try new and interesting fields without resting comfortable on already won laurels. He is of an independent nature, which leads him to write as he pleases without being intimidated by critics or public. He is ambitious, which makes him do difficult and arresting things, even if not always seeming too well equipped for them. He has versatility, which results in his knowing his way about in both the novel and the drama. And he knows the advantage of leisure, which enables him to take his time about polishing his work, even to the extent of allowing fourteen years to elapse between novels.

Richard Watts, Jr. NR. March 1, 1948. p. 22

Mr. Wilder has been unfairly ignored by serious literary critics. . . . He is a humorist who knows the underlying seriousness of comic events, a satirist who loves the human race. True, his style has sometimes been pretentious, and his stories slow-paced; but he deserves our respect as an artist. The bold attempt of his whole career has been nothing less than the re-establishment of human values in a world which, he believes, desperately needs them. Consistently he has attempted to write literature which, having a value of its own, would still not be an end in itself. He deserves our admiration for accepting as his task the difficult artistic problem of suiting fable to idea and sound to sense, producing thus an integrated whole.

Joseph J. Firebaugh. PS. Autumn, 1950. p. 438

Though Wilder, when we look closely, has a mark of his own, his work strikes one as that of an "arranger" rather than a creator. His arrangements are artful, attractive, scrupulously calculated, and unmistakably gifted. They are delightfully decorative patterns created from the raw material dug up by other men. To put it another way, he arranges "flowers" beautifully, but he does not grow them. In this sense, he resembles certain modern Frenchmen rather than one of our own playwrights.

What is American in Wilder's plays are their benign humor, their old-fashioned optimism, their use of the charmingly homely detail, the sophisticated employment of the commonplace, their avuncular celebration of the humdrum, their common sense, popular moralism, and the simplicity—one might almost say simple-mindedness—behind a shrewdly captivating manipulation of a large selection of classic elements.

Harold Clurman. Nation. Sept. 3, 1955. p. 210

Mr. Wilder's play is, in a sense, a refutation of its thesis. *Our Town* is purely and simply an act of awareness, a demonstration of the fact that in a work of art, at least, experience *can* be arrested, imprisoned, and preserved. The perspective of death, which Mr. Wilder has chosen, gives an extra poignancy and intensity to the small-town life whose essence he is trying so urgently to communicate. . . . The perspective is, to be sure, hazardous; it invites bathos and sententiousness. Yet, Mr. Wilder has used it honorably. He forbids the spectator to dote on that town of the past. He is concerned only with saying: this is how it was, though then we did not know it.

Mary McCarthy. Sights and Spectacles (Farrar).
1956. p. 28

I think that if the play (*Our Town*) tested its own theme more remorselessly, the world it creates of a timeless family and a rhythm of existence beyond the disturbance of social wracks would not remain unshaken. . . . I think, further, that the close contact which the play established with its audience was the result of its coincidence with the deep longing of the audience for such stability, a stability which in daylight out on the streets does not truly exist. . . . To me, therefore, the play falls short of a form that will press into reality to the limits of reality, if only because it could not plumb the psychological interior lives of its characters and still keep its present form.

Arthur Miller. At. April, 1956. p. 39

He is our great unsocial and antihistorical novelist, the artist of the anachronism. . . . Wilder does not think of history as an irreversible process of a river in flood; he thinks of it as a series of recurrent patterns, almost like checkerboards set side by side. . . . Wilder has written a dozen books, each strikingly different from all the others in place and time, in mood, and even more in method, yet all the books embody or suggest the same feeling of universal experience and eternal return. *Everything that happened might happen anywhere, and will happen again.* That principle explains why he is able to adopt different perspectives in different books, as if he were looking sometimes through one end of a telescope and sometimes through the other.

Malcolm Cowley. SR. Oct. 6, 1956. pp. 50–1

Although Wilder has been hysterically popular in Germany since the end of the war, when the State Department sent *Our Town* on tour as a "representative example" of "modern American theatre" . . . , his star has risen even higher since he received the Peace Prize at the Frankfurt Book Fair in 1957. . . . The vitalistic cosmic optimism of *The Skin of Our Teeth* provides the contemporary German with the psychological reassurance he demands. Shocked and terrified by the situation in which he finds himself as the primary European target of bombs dispatched from opposite directions, the middle-class German reader flees to the lap of Wilder.

Paul Fussell, Jr., Nation. May 3, 1958. pp. 394–5

See *The Cabala, The Bridge of San Luis Rey, Heaven's My Destination,* and *The Ides of March* (novels); also *Our Town* and *The Skin of Our Teeth* (plays).

WILLIAMS, TENNESSEE (1914–   )

No play can be truly flawless and certainly *The Glass Menagerie* is not so. Mr. Williams has replaced action in his script with the constant flow of human attitudes, relations and ideas across the stage; there are bound to be a few slow moments in the parade. There is one particular instance of too-obvious symbolism. . . . For every flaw, however, there are twenty brilliancies, even in the matter of symbolism.

Otis L. Guernsey, Jr. NYHT ts. Apr. 8, 1945. p. 1

A Streetcar Named Desire emerges as the most creative American play of the past dozen years. . . . What *A Streetcar Named Desire* has is the abundance of a good novel. . . . Life has density in this drama of a woman's tragic effort to clothe her nakedness. . . . The author's viewpoint combines a sharp sense of reality, a naturalistic fearlessness in the face of what is gross in individual life and society, and a just compassion. The handling of the dramatic elements is remarkably astute, since the author keeps wave after wave of revelation hurtling through the play. . . . But what stands out as most contributory to the making of a memorable play is the over-all effect of humanity seen in the round.

John Gassner. Forum. Feb., 1948. pp. 86–7

There are a number of superficial resemblances between the two plays (*The Glass Menagerie* and *A Streetcar Named Desire*) that have established Tennessee Williams as one of the finest of modern dramatists: both deal with the grotesque, an anachronistic refinement of a moribund Southern society; both make incidental mention of Moon Lake Casino and other names from the landscape of his memory. . . . Williams says that Southern women are the only remaining members of our populace who can speak lyrical dialogue without sounding highflown.

Paul Moor. Harpers. July, 1948. p. 71

Although Tennessee Williams writes a gentle style, he has a piercing eye. . . . The insight into character is almost unbearably lucid. Although it derives from compassion, it is cruel in its insistence on the truth. . . . He is a writer of superb grace and allusiveness, always catching the shape and sound of ideas rather than their literal meaning. As its title suggests, *Summer and Smoke* deals in truths that are unsubstantial. But as Mr. Williams sees it, these are the truths that are most profound and most painful, for they separate people who logically should be together and give life its savage whims and its wanton destructiveness.

Brooks Atkinson. NYT tp. Oct. 7, 1948. p. 33

Williams is, of course, one of two or three good playwrights writing today. . . . But why does he arrange his dramas like inquisitions, with torture preceding the confession and death following? Why is his world recognizable only fitfully, and why does he flagellate his heroines so? Does Mr. Williams mean that the original sin they have committed is that they are women? . . . One understands and is moved by his tragedies and his luckless people, and is sympathetic to his sense of the disaster that lies at the heart of our world; one understands and even partially accepts—but why does it seem all wrong?

Alfred Hayes. NYHT. Oct. 22, 1950. p. 14

Tennessee Williams, to come right out with it, seems to me not only the finest playwright now working in the American theatre but in one very strict sense the *only* playwright now working in the American theatre. Alone among his contemporaries he works as an artist and a poet: he makes plays out of images, catching a turn of life while it is still fluid, still immediate, and before it has been sterilized by reflection. Arthur Miller, for instance, builds a better play, but he builds it out of bricks; Williams is all flesh and blood. He writes with his eyes and his ears where other men are content to pick their brains—poetry with them is an overlay of thought, not a direct experience—and his plays emerge in the theatre, full-bodied, undissected, so kinetic you can touch them.

Walter Kerr. Com. Feb. 23, 1951. p. 492

With a pen that smokes and burns, Mr. Williams has created some horribly memorable chapters in the history of what one of his characters calls the "mad pilgrimage of the flesh." . . . He began as a poet, and perhaps it is as the poet of the blasted, the doomed, and the defeated that he will be remembered. . . . At his best . . . Tennessee Williams is in a class by himself. Even at his worst he creates magical, terrifying, and unforgettable effects; his only limitations appear to be self-imposed.

William Peden. SR. Jan. 8, 1955. p. 11

Living vitally in illusion is the substance of nearly all the important people in nearly all of Williams's work. . . . Williams explores in fiction and the theatre the *true* world behind the apparent one. . . . He pushed aside the great iron door and discovered there, behind the pulsating machine of modern technology, the throbbing human heart. It is this care for the individual man and woman and child and cornered cat which warms the lines of his plays and stories, which makes each example of his writing useful and moving. . . . The more he illuminates that inner and contrived world, however, the more he actually reveals of the brutal daylight outside.

Paul Engle. NR. Jan. 24, 1955. p. 27

He has said that he only feels and does not think; but the reader's or spectator's impression is too often that he only thinks he feels, that he is an acute case of what D. H. Lawrence called "sex in the head." And not only sex. Sincerity and Truth, of which he often *speaks* and *thinks,* tend to remain in the head too—abstractions with initial capitals. His problem is not lack of talent. It is, perhaps, an ambiguity of aim: he seems to want to kick the world in the pants and yet be the world's sweetheart, to combine the glories of martyrdom with the comforts of success. If I say that his problem is to take the initial capitals off Sincerity and Truth, I do not infer that this is easy, only that it is essential, if ever Mr. Williams's great talent is to find a full and pure expression.

Eric Bentley. NR. Apr. 11, 1955. p. 29

The crises of Williams are never common. They are the creation of a very strange and very special imagination, potent enough to impose itself on an audience and hold it in a common trance. He is a theater magician, invoking the lightning of emotion, releasing the doves of instinct, holding in fanlike suspension a brilliant pack of cards peopled with symbols and specters. . . . And I doubt whether the emotional exhaustion that is the residual effect of seeing a play by Tennessee Williams . . . is either illuminator or catharsis. It is a shock treatment administered by an artist of great talent and painful sensibility who illumines fragments but never the whole. He illuminates, if you will, that present sickness which *is* fragmentation.

Marya Mannes. Reporter. May 19, 1955. p. 41

Mr. Williams's plays involve, in a most vexing and intimate way, the problem once defined by Stark Young as that of "scraping back to the design." The early works, with their slight yet audible music, elude the charge, but in the later plays—ambitious statements about personality and suffering and society—one has somehow the insupportable sense that life is being obscurely practiced upon, the substance of feeling coerced into new and bizarre patterns. Not alone Mr. Williams's emphases nourish this unease, but the gathering awareness of his startling omissions, too. Yet subtly, this consciousness of nullity is modified by the curious presence of an impulse, the burden of some serious concern and intention making itself felt through layers of modish sensiblity and gratuitous shock.

Richard Hayes. *Com.* June 3, 1955. p. 230

It occurs to me that we might well now regard Tennessee Williams as perhaps our great expert today in *Realpsychologie*. For, in such theatricals as *The Rose Tattoo* and *Baby Doll,* what he has undertaken is to strip the human animal of all moral refinements and to present the "true" animal, the "fine, wild" animal at whom we laugh, however, because for all the wildness the animal functions like a kind of clock, automatically, that is, giving heed to the promptings of natural impulse. But the major point to be made, it seems to me, is that the ribaldry, unsalacious as it really is, is utilized for the sake of what it is often Williams's major purpose to do; namely, to laugh at the very notion that human life might have a dimension of tragic significance.

Nathan A. Scott, Jr. *CC.* Jan. 23, 1957. p. 112

See *The Glass Menagerie, A Streetcar Named Desire, Summer and Smoke, The Rose Tattoo,* and *Orpheus Descending* (plays); also *The Roman Spring of Mrs. Stone* (novel); *One Arm and Other Stories;* and *In the Winter of Cities* (poetry).

See Supplement at end of text for additional material.

WILLIAMS, WILLIAM CARLOS (1883–1963)

He can give himself, William Carlos Williams, such as he is, without either simple or inverted pride; give himself in his crassness, in his dissonant mixed blood, in absurd melancholy, wild swiftness of temper, man-shyness; Americano, Jerseyite, Rutherfordian; give himself with a frankness, a fearlessness, a scientific impersonality, that is bracing as a shock of needle-spray. . . . And, in moments, of felt power, in moments of conscious toughness and sharp will, he breaks "through to the fifty words necessary," and briskly, laconically, like a man with little time for matters not absolutely essential to the welfare of the universe, brings into clarity the relation existing between himself and the things seen by him.

Paul Rosenfeld. *Port of New York* (Harcourt). 1924.
pp. 109–11

Surely Williams's savagery is a unique essence in modern American letters. He has perceived his ground, he has made a beginning, he is riding the forces of his locality. Determinedly, he seeks to be a Daniel Boone of letters, a Sam Houston in method, and an Aaron Burr in personal psychology. What threatens him—be it puritanic pressures or the hard exigencies of combining literature with medicine—he barks at it: the dog with a bone in its throat is symbolic of his attitude toward all that might interrupt or diminish his poetic pursuit.

Gorham Munson. *Destinations* (Sears). 1928. p. 134

For the most part, so completely in fact that one must search out the rare exceptions, Williams's verse has been unrhymed; in temper it has been at the furthest remove from "professional" verse; it has been protestant, yet formal, and the virtues of even his slightest pieces have been those of presenting definite objects and scenes before the eye of the reader. . . . Williams's search for "an honest man," as well as an instruction to others "to stand out of my sunlight," are the kinds of truth that Williams sought in verse. The search may at times seem wantonly naive, and at times it has resulted in incomplete and "experimental" poems, but we may be certain that Williams has never falsified his language; and he has made an ethical distinction between the uses of artifice and art. Craftsmanship, not artifice, has been his concern, and perhaps no writer of the twentieth century has yielded so little to the temptations that mere artifice places within his path.

Horace Gregory and Marya Zaturenska. *History of American Poetry* (Harcourt). 1947. pp. 208–12

Although his lines rarely descend to slang, they are full of the conversational speech of the country; they express the brusque nervous tension, the vigor and rhetoric of American life. Even when they are purposely unadorned and non-melodic they intensify some common object with pointed detail and confident, if clipped, emotion.

Louis Untermeyer. *Modern American Poetry*
(Harcourt). 1950. p. 275

Life is more than art for Dr. Williams, as the object is prior to the word. He is no goldsmith making timeless birds. Part of the exhilaration in reading his poetry comes of its formal and logical incompleteness (this is at the same time its greatest drawback). Many of his poems seem notes to a text—to the dense and fluid text of reality; they seem gestures and exclamations in appreciation of something beyond the poem, insistences that we use our senses, that we be alive to things.

Richard Wilbur. *SwR*. Winter, 1950. p. 139

Examined from the perspective of an ideal academic poet like say, Bridges, Dr. Williams appears to be groping about under a very low ceiling indeed. . . . Truthfully pleading his inability to handle traditional coin traditionally, Williams improvises, issues a fluid currency of his own. . . . Incoherence, then, is the principal "cost," to use a favorite word with Williams, incoherence raised to a level where it corresponds to Eliot's diffidence or Pound's tactlessness, a quirk which can sometimes reveal the poetry, sometimes conceal it, sometimes ruin it altogether, but which is also absorbed into the success of passage after passage, poem after poem.

R. W. Flint in *Kenyon Critics,* edited by John Crowe
Ransom (World). 1951. pp. 335–40

Williams has found his end in his beginnings. He has devoted himself to the American scene as it met the eye of a doctor practicing in the provinces. . . . He gives the inner quality of things not by transferring to them his feeling about them, nor by a kind of damp sentiment from which even so inward a poet as Rilke was not wholly free. He gets at the essence, as apprehended not *behind* but actually *by means of* the phenomenon: the reality grasped by devoted concentration on its manifest being.

Babette Deutsch. *Poetry in Our Time* (Holt). 1952.
pp. 109–10

It is necessary to love this man because he teaches life the richness of its own combinations. The world is his mistress, made beautiful by his love. The fact of her is his passion. No poet since Donne has banged so avidly at Things, at the hammer and take of the world upon the senses. Everything, even his own aesthetic, has been shattered in the name of Things.

John Ciardi. *Nation*. April 24, 1954. p. 368

He is one of the most tensile, dynamic, and kinaesthetically engaging of poets; his quick transparent lines have a nervous and contracted strength. Often they move as jerkily and intently as a bird, though they can sleep as calmly as a bird, too; they do not have the flowing and easy strength, the rhythmic powers in reserve, the envelopment and embodiment of some of the verse of old poets. But sometimes they have a marvelous delicacy and gentleness, a tact of pure showing; how well he calls into existence our precarious, confused, partial looking out at the world—our being-here-looking, just looking! And if he is often pure presentation, he is often pure exclamation, and delights in yanking something into life with a galvanic imperative or interjection. . . . He loves to tell the disgraceful or absurd or obscene or piercing or exhilarating or animally delightful truth. He is neither wise nor intellectual, but is full of homely shrewdness and common sense, of sharply intelligent comments dancing cheek-to-cheek with prejudice and random eccentricities; he is somebody who, sometimes, does see what things are like, and he is able to say what he sees more often than most poets.

> Randall Jarrell. *Poetry and the Age* (Knopf). 1955.
> pp. 236–7

After more than thirty books and at his present age Williams exercises his whole personality to unlock a remarkable lyrical lore of love. His love is inclusive of many things, attitudes, and feelings. It has the qualities of sincerity, knowledge, and acute perception. It is mature man speaking direct truth. Yet I do not mean that there is not a great deal of strategy in the way he makes his verses.

> Richard Eberhart. *SR*. Feb. 18, 1956. p. 49

Paterson

A man spends Sundays in the park at Paterson, New Jersey. He thinks and looks about him; his mind contemplates, describes, comments, associates, stops, stutters, and shifts like a firefly, bound only by its own milieu. The man is Williams, anyone living in Paterson, the American, the masculine principle. . . . The park is Everywoman, any woman, the feminine principle, America. . . . "Paterson" . . . is about marriage. . . . Everything in the poem is masculine or feminine, everything strains toward marriage, but the marriages never come off, except in the imagination and there, attenuated, fragmentary, and uncertain.

> Robert Lowell. *Nation*. June 19, 1948. pp. 692–3

It may be simply the effect of time, but at this writing "Paterson I" seems to me better than "Paterson II" and both of them better than "Paterson III," though the difference is small. What cannot be enough insisted on is that in this poetry, which operates by what Crane called "metaphorical logic," the whole is always greater than the sum of the parts. "Paterson" is planned, though more loosely than *Ulysses,* "Four Quartets," or the "Cantos." Successive books have worked fresh material into the mythic, rhythmic, and metaphorical pattern established in the first, so that the effect, though cumulative, is not oppressively so. We don't feel the clouds of a portentous Greatness gathering over us.

> R. W. Flint in *Kenyon Critics,* edited by John Crowe
> Ransom (World). 1951. p. 335

If "Paterson" is rarely as good as Pound's work at his best, it is far more alive than the drearier sections of the "Cantos." Both poets are concerned with communication, and with the forces obstructing and debasing it. The great difference is that for Williams the time is not antiquity or the renaissance, but now (he sees its old roots): the scene is no foreign country, but is the provincial factory town on the Passaic in all the sordidness of its abused beauty and energy.

> Babette Deutsch. *Poetry in Our Time* (Holt). 1952.
> pp. 104–8

The organization of "Paterson" is musical to an almost unprecedented degree: Dr. Williams introduces a theme that stands for an idea, repeats it over and over in varied forms, develops it side by side with two or three more themes that are being developed, recurs to it time and time again throughout the poem, and echoes it for ironic or grotesque effects in thoroughly incongruous contexts. . . . Everything in the poem is interwoven with everything else, just as the strands of the Falls interlace: how wonderful and unlikely that this extraordinary mixture of the most delicate lyricism of perception and feeling with the hardest and homeliest actuality should ever have come into being!

> Randall Jarrell. *Poetry and the Age* (Knopf). 1955.
> pp. 203–9

See "Paterson" (Books I-IV), *Collected Earlier Poems, Collected Later Poems,* and *The Desert Music;* also *Selected Essays, Autobiography, The Build-Up* (novel), and *Make Light of It* (short stories).

See Supplement at end of text for additional material.

WILSON, EDMUND (1895–   )

The distinction of Edmund Wilson's critical writing, at a period of low pressure in this field, resides in his skepticism, his candor, and his boldness. Where most other professional critics, in America, are content to remain journalists, timid or compromised through intangible connections with the literature-business, Wilson is a widely read, laborious, and willing adventurer into the forest of modern art. Here, amid these shadows, the others may remain ignorant or bewildered, conceiving or relating nothing to any recognizable suite of ideas—or simply grow humoristic, like Mencken; Wilson attacks his chosen material with intelligence and with high energy, scrutinizing the product, demanding of it insistently, almost clamorously, what is its meaning and what is its intention.

> Matthew Josephson. *SR.* March 7, 1931. p. 642

The ability to tell what a book is about remains Mr. Wilson's greatest distinction, his almost unrivaled skill, among living students of literature. His explorations have steadily widened; he has risked the formulations but surmounted the limitations of historical, sociological, and psychiatric method; he has brought the rich sympathies and recognitions of his earlier investigations to a steadily sounder and more penetrating use. . . . He writes criticism of one kind and one of the best kinds, but it continually requires supplementing and extension by specifically aesthetic analysis and normative evaluation. But there are only two or three other contemporaries who have been as scrupulous in making the matter of modern literature available, in defining historical and categorical relationships, and in arriving at the sense of the elements and complexities of creative genius which must be realized before the full scope and richness of books can be determined by whatever keener instruments or methods of dissection.

Morton Dauwen Zabel. Nation. Oct. 11, 1941. p. 350

Honesty is perhaps the most admirable of all Edmund Wilson's gifts. He is as sympathetic and just as he can be: where his sympathy fails him, as it does when he approaches Paul Elmer More in a tone of continued flippant severity, and where his justice fails him, as it does in his estimate of the narrow scholarship of Housman, it is because, like every man he is held within the bonds of his temperament, and within those of the social pressures about him. The reader is sure that the critic has done his utmost to release himself from such bonds, that he has never wantonly tightened them, as almost all of his contemporaries have done. He has never asked himself what the party-line would be— Marxist, or Freudian, or bohemian—and he has never allowed a scruple for abstract logic (if one said such and such about Henry James in 1938, must one say this and that about Edith Wharton in 1941?) to come between him and his material.

E. K. Brown. UTQ. Oct., 1941. pp. 110–1

Edmund Wilson has a genuine feeling for the chthonic, the underground aspects of a literature. He has learned to hold his Freudianism like a gentleman. Dislike of people, despair of life, the cultivation of private values, and other trappings of romantic individualism are fashionable today; and Edmund Wilson has successfully kept two jumps ahead of the fashion. A technique which mingles the methods of fiction with those of criticism, and a willingness to subordinate inconvenient facts in the interest of an interpretation have helped him in this project. The prose style of Edmund Wilson is sensitive though sesquipedalian, his reporting is accurate and perceptive, he has read more than most journalists, and he is not afraid to use his reading.

Robert Adams. *SwR*. Spring, 1948. p. 286

Sometimes Wilson is guilty of gratuitous waspishness and sometimes he is glaringly condescending. Occasionally he employs a tank attack against a molehill (the syntax of *Mission to Moscow*), and once or twice, notably in Maugham's case, he carries depreciation to very questionable lengths (granted Maugham's lifelong love affair with the cliché, some of ·his work is surely not *completely* second-rate). But by and large, Wilson tellingly points up the failings and limitations in the work of well-known writers—O'Hara, Saroyan, and Steinbeck, for instance— without losing sight of their qualities. His loathing of commercialism and championship of the nonpopular; his respect for writers who toil for the *mot juste;* the slightly romantic feeling he projects of the glamour and dignity in the calling of letters—all this I find admirable and it outweighs Wilson's crotchets.

Charles J. Rolo. *At.* Nov., 1950. p. 98

How Wilson gets time to do anything but sit and read, one marvels. What keeps him from being merely an omnivorous reader is the intensity of his passion for literature. And. he can find it in the most unlikely places, because in his view literature has little or no relation to the so-called "subject matter." . . . The great works of our time, he asserts, may and must express the despair and anguish of ·these years, but instead of discouraging they fortify. . . . His passion for literature is definitely not aestheticism: his chase has an end in view. . . . If Wilson makes anything that may be called mistakes—he says that all critics have failings—it is out of excess of devotion to the ideals which he feels came into their own with the rationalists of the twenties.

Perry Miller. *Nation*. Jan. 27, 1951. pp. 87–8

If it is a crime for a critic of literature to be also a good writer then by all means let us shoot him, or at least ban his books; but if it should happen to be a virtue then, if only in a whisper, perhaps we should honor it. It seems likely that Mr. Wilson had to sweat over his early writing just in order to beat out his competitors, win magazine-space for himself, and earn a living. This is simply not true of the formal or college-professor critics: not dependent on writing for a living, concerned with criticism as an extension of knowledge rather than as an art, they were never called upon to compress or season their thought for *practical* reasons, as was Wilson. The result is that while several of these critics are more original than Wilson, the results of their thinking are rarely consolidated with his tested generalship and authority.

Seymour Krim. *HdR*. Spring, 1951. p. 152

Wilson was always bringing fascinating and profitable writers to our attention, and he never made us feel that he was displaying his own subtlety and wit and invention at their expense. In these later days a good many critics seem to be yielding to the vice of ostentation; criticism has exfoliated until the work of art is sometimes smothered beneath it, like a tree covered with fox grapes and Virginia creeper. Wilson kept trying to strip off the critical misconceptions and reveal the tree in its proper form. He kept inviting his readers to join him in a search for intellectual heroes, since—as he told us time after time—the existence of such men gives meaning and value to our lives.

Malcolm Cowley. NR. Nov. 10, 1952. pp. 17–8

I suppose literary history will class Wilson as a social critic, and recently there has been a tendency, mostly on the part of the younger formalist critics, to brush him aside as an extra-literary critic, who has not done enough to illuminate immediate literary texts and problems. . . . I think the criticism of him on this score has been very unfair and represents a sectarian judgement. For, if Wilson, like Parrington and other social critics, has taken literature as a part of history, unlike most of them he has not dissolved literature into history. . . . Actually his method has been to find the basic mood and intention of a literary work, and then to connect it with the pattern of the author's life, and literary tradition and social history. . . . On purely literary grounds, it is amazing to see how many of Wilson's judgements have stood up, which is, I am sure, the final test of a critic's accomplishment.

William Phillips. AM. Nov., 1952. pp. 106–7

I cannot think of any other critic who would be capable of writing intelligently about Faulkner, Sartre, Tolstoy, and Shakespeare, about such eccentricities as manuals of conjuring and the biography of Houdini, about both burlesque shows and Emily Post, about both best sellers and obscure difficult authors, and—here is a peculiar and rather touching speciality of Wilson's—about interesting near-failures like John Jay Chapman. . . . He writes about so many things because he has a multitude of active and growing ideas, and because he chooses the new intellectual experiences that will feed them. . . . He believes in the mind, and the taste, and the fancy. He dislikes the tyrants who try to throttle them or starve them or exploit them, and he enjoys every activity which sends blood through them, lets them expand, gives them hope and laughter, precision and purpose.

Gilbert Highet. People, Places, and Books (Oxford).
1953. pp. 33–5

The high place of Edmund Wilson in modern American literary criticism has been slow of recognition because he has always seemed to play the role of counselor, interpreter and friend to his fellow writers and readers rather than that of lawgiver or of chronicler. . . . Yet he has been from the twenties down to the present, a leading voice among those critics who cling to the conception of art as an expression of its own creator and of the culture which produces him. An historical critic rather than a literary historian, he has done more than anyone else in his time to make the master works of his contemporaries intelligible to their own readers and to assign to them the values which posterity in many cases must accept.

Robert E. Spiller. *Nation*. Feb. 22, 1958. p. 159

His extraordinary gift for turning every assignment into a superb literary article is a symbol of his inability to lose himself, as so many writers did, in a purely human situation. The reins are always tight, and the horses always go the same way. On the other hand, Wilson's detachment certainly never made him incurious. The secret of his durability as a writer is his patient, arduous effort to assimilate, to clarify for himself and others, subjects from which he feels excluded by temperament. . . . Amid the laziest minds in the world he is the most Puritanical of intellectual students, the most exacting in the correctness of his language and his learning.

Alfred Kazin. *Reporter*. March 20, 1958. p. 44

See *Axel's Castle, To the Finland Station, The Triple Thinkers, Classics and Commercials, The Wound and the Bow,* and *The Shores of Light* (criticism)

WINTERS, YVOR (1900–   )

Poetry

His poetry is gaunt, gray and harsh. It is also cold, with that burning cold that belongs to ice. . . . There is an integrity about it which derives from the poet's metaphysical passion—a passion colored by his sharp apprehension of physical things, and having its issue in a profound disenchantment with the world. He conveys it by means of a few spare, precise images. In some thirty words he will give you the essence of a moment. But these moments are an effectual screen for eternity. Time, Space, and the mind that spins them are Mr. Winters's ultimate concern.

Babette Deutsch. *Bkm*. June, 1928. p. 441

Mr. Winters remains one of the best of the imagist school, but limited by that school. He is afraid to trust himself in any extension of language beyond absolute clarity and precision, and he therefore loses much in power. He remains one of the most interesting and contemporary of our poets, despite the fact that his critical mind does his poetic mind some injury. He states more clearly than any other poet the modern dilemma: the gradual loss of feeling through too much of "print."

Eda Lou Walton. *Nation*. Dec. 17, 1930. p. 680

Mr. Winters's work is precise, scrupulous and taut; no syllable is wasted: the intellectual element does not exclude emotion, though it controls it. The metrics are formal, the rhymes strict; seldom does a word seem rhyme-fetched, rather than intended. The poet's ear is good. If his poems seem cold—or, anyway, cool—it is worth remembering that it can be with poems as with women: some like them so, at least sometimes.

Rolfe Humphries. *NYT*. April 23, 1944. p. 24

In his own generation he has the eminence of isolation; among American poets who appeared soon after the first world war he is, Crane being dead, the master. If he has been neglected—when he has not been ignored—the reasons are not hard to find. He has conducted a poetic revolution all his own that owes little or nothing to the earlier revolution of Pound and Eliot, or that goes back to certain great, likewise neglected Tudor poets for metrical and stylistic models. . . . He is a Renaissance humanist of the pre-Spenserian school of metaphysical rhetoricians, the school of Greville and Raleigh: a poet whose moral imagination takes, without didacticism, the didactic mode, striving for precision in language and, in verse, for formal elegance.

Allen Tate. *Nation*. March 2, 1953. pp. 17–8

His best poetry is "occasional." It takes off from something observed or remembered, or from a contemporary occasion, and by a combination of perception and meditation wrings some human meaning out of it. This meaning is often oblique, often delicate, quite different from the great commonplaces of the Victorian or eighteenth-century poets. Nor does it reach out through deliberate symbolic echoes and ironic parallels to include all of civilization, as the early Eliot so often did. Winters works by limitation; the meaning which each of his poems achieves is precise and restricted; and perhaps his most remarkable technical accomplishment is his control, his ability to stop (not only in terms of length but also in terms of depth) when he has said enough.

David Daiches. *YR*. Summer, 1953. p. 629

Criticism

Mr. Winters started with a basis of ideas which he has never found reason to abandon, either creatively or critically. His is a centrifugal progress. He has had the courage to work outward from hard absolutes of meaning and intuition toward the surfaces of sense, and thus toward the periphery of a complete and comprehending sensibility. To express this sensibility perfectly is to achieve style. Mr. Winters's difficulties have been chiefly of two kinds: in communication because the initial meaning or intuition has not always found a genuine sensible embodiment; and in persuasion, because, even when it has, the requisite passion and conviction of style have too often been lacking.

Morton Dauwen Zabel. *Poetry*. Jan., 1931. p. 226

Yvor Winters, writing like a combination of a medieval scholastic and a New England divine, is a critic of a type that one has become accustomed to regard as practically extinct. . . . Evidently Mr. Winters began with a temperamental distaste for the general atmosphere of distress, the hectic experimentation with forms and with style, that has characterized so much contemporary verse. But to this situation he responded with that mechanism of the mind which consists in reacting to any phenomenon by celebrating its opposite. . . . Mr. Winters is narrow, dogmatic, parochial; and these are all the defects of his method. But it would be unjust not to mention the virtues of these defects: the sharpening of focus on important problems, the formulation of useful distinctions, and the construction of definitions that at least provide a springboard for discussion.

William Troy. *Nation*. Feb. 20, 1937. p. 216

When Mr. Winters is actually talking about the work of the American experimental poets, how it failed and even how it could have been improved, when he talks about meter and convention or any technical matter, he makes only normal mistakes and produces a great many pertinent and stimulating facts. . . . Mr. Winters's system of absolutes, his coinage of intellectual counters, is not much better than other systems or much worse; but it is more bare-faced, candid and uncompromising than most; hence more irritating and I should say easier, in a good cause, to ignore. When he translates his absolutes back into the genuine but ultimately provisional elements of his feeling for poetry, he will always be at the level of his best.

Richard P. Blackmur. *NR*. July 14, 1937. p. 285

To watch him taking a critical misjudgement apart gives the same kind of pleasure that we get from seeing a first-rate woodman split a log—

the great secrets being merely to start the opening wedge in the right place and then to hit it hard enough. Mr. Winters has no lack of sharp, smooth wedges to start where they will do the most good, and his style can be on occasion a two-handed sledge to sink them home. . . . Those who perceive how much Mr. Winters has as a critic cannot well help wishing that he had everything. What he does not at present seem to have in normal measure is the rounded man's appreciation of writing that is consummate in a small way. His canons are serious to severity and he is little tolerant of the playful, the trifling, the frankly artificial, the droll, the merely mellifluous.

Wilson Follett. *NYT*. Dec. 4, 1938. p. 36

To his earlier perversities . . . Winters adds an intemperate denigration of the poetry and criticism of T. S. Eliot. . . . This seems to me not only mistaken but ungenerous, since I cannot help but feel that Winters shares both Eliot's literary and religious traditionalism and his method of employing arresting *obiter dicta* which contain valuable insights even when the essays in which they blossom are elaborately wrong-headed.

What I find of value in Winters's criticism is precisely what I have found (but in a larger measure) in Eliot's: a love of good writing and an occasional articulation of that passion, despite theories and posturing.

George Mayberry. *NR*. July 12, 1943. pp. 51–2

Winters is what Kierkegaard said *he* was—a corrective; and Winters's case for the rational, extensive, prosaic virtues that the age disliked, his case against the modernist, intensive, essentially romantic vices that it swallowed whole, have in his late criticism become a case against any complicated dramatic virtues. Winters's tone has long ago become that of the leader of a small religious cult, that of the one sane man in a universe of lunatics; his habitual driven-to-distraction rages against the reprobates who have evidenced their lunacy by disagreeing with him go side by side with a startled, giant admiration for the elect who in a rational moment have become his followers.

Randall Jarrell. *NYT*. Aug. 24, 1947. p. 14

See *Collected Poems;* also *In Defense of Reason* (criticism).

WOLFE, THOMAS (1900–1938)

Some of Mr. Wolfe's material is not subordinated to the intention of the book. What is his intention? On what is the mass of material fo-

cussed? What is to give it form? His novels are obviously autobiographical. This means that the binding factor should be, at least in
part, the personality of the narrator, or since Mr. Wolfe adopts a disguise, of the hero, Eugene Gant. . . . The hero is really that nameless fury that drives Eugene. The book is an effort to name that fury
and perhaps by naming it to tame it. But the fury goes unnamed and
untamed. Since the book is formless otherwise, only a proper emotional
reference to such a centre could give it form. Instead, at the centre
there is this chaos that steams and bubbles in rhetoric and apocalyptic
apostrophe, sometimes grand and sometimes febrile and empty; the
centre is a maelstrom, perhaps artificially generated at times; and the
other tangible items are the flotsam and jetsam and dead wood
spewed up, iridescent and soggy as the case may be.

Robert Penn Warren. *AR*. May, 1935. pp. 199–202

Mr. Wolfe has power, passion, a singular fearlessness, the ability to
create individual scenes of brilliant truth, a genius for lyrical prose un-
equalled in contemporary letters, insight into certain types of characters
and problems. But Mr. Wolfe the artist has advanced scarcely a step
since *Look Homeward, Angel*. He is full of self pity. If he is a genius,
he is still an adolescent genius. His universe is utterly or mainly subjective, and the result is a transcript of experience curiously true in
some particulars, curiously false in others.

Howard Mumford Jones. *SR*. Nov. 30, 1935. p. 13

His imagination has provided him with a great theme and his accurate
memory flashes infinite exact detail of the life which he intends to make
his book. But he cannot control the theme or reduce his substance to a
medium. He will write neither poetry nor prose, but both. He will
not be content with the literal autobiographic description of men and
events which his journalistic sense supplies so readily but must intersperse with passages of sheer fantasy or poetical uplift. He will stick
neither to fiction nor to fact. Hence the reader never enters into that
created world of the real novelist which has its own laws, its own
atmosphere, its own people, but goes from here to there in Mr. Wolfe's
own life, seeing real people as he saw them, and often recognizing
them . . . not as created characters but as literal transcripts from the
life. So that the effect is always of being in two worlds at one time, fiction and fact, until curiosity takes the place of that ready acceptance
of a homogenous life in the imagination which a fine novel invariably
permits.

Henry Seidel Canby. *Seven Years' Harvest*
(Rinehart). 1936. p. 168

Something of the homefolk's first resistance to the book about the home town may lie behind the criticism of Wolfe's books as undisciplined and formless. I suspect in some such criticism a wish, like Asheville's, to have a native story a little nicer, a trifle neater, more ordered and patterned in delicacy and decorum. And now at his death I expect that the suggestion will be strenuously stirred that had he lived Tom Wolfe's big, sprawling, powerful, pouring prose would have been served in neater packages of sweeter stuff. It is possible to say anything about the dead. In Wolfe's case, they may even make him a classicist who might have been. But our loss will remain the unbounded vitality, the uncaptured power which made his books and his world and all his Gants and Pentlands alive. Form and discipline undoubtedly in important respects he lacked; it is lacking also in the confusion which is as much a part of American life as Tom Wolfe was.

Jonathan Daniels. *SR*. Sept. 24, 1938. p. 8

Wolfe wrote *great* American novels, he wrote great *American* novels, and, loosely speaking, he wrote great American *novels*. But he fails to measure up in the fourth respect: he did not write *the* great American novel. . . . Wolfe was not of the artistic temperament to write such a work. The author of The Great American Novel must be dramatic and omnipresent; Thomas Wolfe was lyrical and uni-present. For him there was only one world and he was at the center of it. . . . But his . . . gravest limitation was his genius. . . . The genius of Thomas Wolfe was too much. He was driven by a restlessness which kept him from achieving that cool perfection which often comes easy to lesser men.

Thomas Lyle Collins. *SwR*. Fall, 1942. p. 504

The career of Thomas Wolfe is the spectacle of a novelist who began with the sole concern to transfer to others his fascination with his own family as material for fiction, who turned thereafter in the same simplicity of intention to his own relationships with persons outside his family, but who poured into these relationships all the disorders of the contemporary world until he was forced at the end to attempt their solution in a letter to his editor on social views, in which his work as a writer culminated and, it may be said, his life concluded.

Edwin Berry Burgum. *VQR*. Summer, 1946. p. 421

Even among the most famous representatives of the more serious contemporary literature that I know, Thomas Wolfe, it seems to me, is the only one endowed with the prophetic Ethos and the poetic Pathos of the true genius. He is the only one consciously transmuting his own discovery of life and of the world into a message of religious intensity.

He had consented to be "God's lonely man." He knew from the start that "genius can bring death." There must have been in him from his early youth this feeling of being consecrated, fated, and inevitable.

Even beyond his own artistic testimony, it is a most poignant human experience to witness this Pilgrim's Progress from the exalted rhapsodic lyricism, the youthful turmoil and ecstasy of his first book to the manly composure, the profound ethical awareness of his "Credo" in the last chapter of *You Can't Go Home Again*.

Franz Schoenberger. *NYT*. Aug. 4, 1946. p. 1

Wolfe's poetry is not calmly and quietly intense; his main theme is the theme of being lost in America, and it is treated by a poet who is still lost. His perspective of America itself is out of joint: distances and spaces are magnified, a trip from New York to North Carolina becomes a journey "down the continent"; much of his America is an abstraction. He has some of the naturalistic pantheism, the feeling that man and soil are intensely bound together in essence which marks so much Western literature since Zola and which makes him sound occasionally like Jean Giono, just as he shows at times some of the enthusiasm for being American, if not the faith democratic, of Walt Whitman. Now and again he reveals a feeling for, though not much knowledge of, the history of our people—the feeling that this land is something apart because the dust of his ancestors is mixed with its dust. But mostly his complaint is that these things do not mean more to him than they do, that he really has no place and "no door where he can enter," and that meanwhile he is being swept along by the stream of life. The answer to his eternal question is not the answer of Whitman and Crane and Paul Engle. The one thing that he can be sure of, the one door that must open for him, is death.

W. M. Frohock. *SWR*. Autumn, 1948. p. 357

Disillusionment, the hindsight of the self-deluded and the half-blind, was not one of Thomas Wolfe's qualities. No one ever accused him of being blind in any degree. His fault, if fault it was, was that he saw too much. Till the day he died he retained that luminous gift which all bright children seem to possess up to a certain age: the ability to look at life and see it as it really is, with all its many and ever-changing faces, its mystery and wonder, its exhilaration and stark terror, its endless contrasts of beauty and ugliness, its haunting interplay of good and evil, its flashing colors and subtly shifting shadows.

Edward C. Aswell. *SR*. Nov. 27, 1948. p. 34

In the style of Wolfe is his essence. It is for this that we read him—not for his narrative, not for philosophy, not for the desire to study more intently the nature of human thought and behavior. The narrative is dictated by the circumstances of his own life, and he runs wild as an unsheared hedge. The philosophy is half-baked—a sequence of ideas held today because of yesterday's impressions, and just as likely to be altered tomorrow. . . . We read Wolfe primarily for his rhetorical poetry, which he delivers from his great height with the authority of a prophet who has seen the clouds open to reveal a calligraphy of fire upon the white spaces of the air.

Pamela Hansford-Johnson. *Hungry Gulliver*
(Scribner). 1948. p. 20

It is largely through his effort to find permanence in flux that the novels of Thomas Wolfe may be considered "modern" in their treatment of time. In Wolfe's novels time becomes a rushing all-erosive river, which, nevertheless, may be arrested or turned back by the memory. Like Proust, Wolfe seeks to recapture the past through memory, including unconscious memory, and to show the sensations and moods that recollections of the past evoke in the present. Or again, like Joyce in *Finnegan's Wake,* he opposes a linear conception of time with a cyclical one, wherein the eternal is repeated through apparent change.

W. P. Albrecht. *NMQ.* Autumn, 1949. p. 320

The four novels of Wolfe's tetralogy echo the voice of time. Like the great railroad sheds, they harbor its sound. For Wolfe was secure only when he was in motion and never so sure of himself as when he was on a moving train. His books came from the huge railroad stations of his mind where "the voice of time remained aloof and imperturbed, a drowsy and eternal murmur," and where the train whistle "evoked for him a million images: old songs, old faces, and forgotten memories." Involved with Proustian metaphysics Wolfe was not, but as the taster of life and time his experience was much the same as Proust's. And for both of them the sudden and vivid resurrection of the lost moment, through a present sensory impression, was the central time-experience.

Margaret Church. *PMLA.* Sept., 1949. p. 638

His aim was to set down America as far as it can belong to the experience of one man. Wolfe came early on what was for him the one available truth about this continent—that it was contained in himself. . . . He could—and it is the source of what is most authentic in his talents—displace the present so completely by the past that its sights and sounds all but destroyed surrounding circumstances. He then lost the sense of time. For Wolfe, sitting at a table on a terrace in Paris, contained within himself not only the America he had known; he also held, within his body, both his parents. They were there, not only in his memory, but more portentously in the make-up of his mind. They loomed so enormous to him that their shadows fell across the Atlantic, their shade was on the cafe table under which he stretched his long American legs.

John Peale Bishop in Kenyon Critics, edited by John
Crowe Ransom (World). 1951. pp. 3–4

See *Look Homeward Angel, Of Time and the River, The Web and the Rock,* and *You Can't Go Home Again* (novels).

WRIGHT, RICHARD   (1909–1961)

Story Magazine offered $500 for the best book-length manuscript submitted by anyone connected with the Federal Writers' Project. The prize was awarded to Richard Wright, a young, serious, quiet-spoken Negro born in Natchez and haphazardly educated in Chicago. His book (*Uncle Tom's Children*) published last week, consists of four long stories. . . . I found them both heartening as evidence of a vigorous new talent, and terrifying as the expression of a racial hatred that has never ceased to grow and gets no chance to die.

Malcolm Cowley. NR. April 6, 1938. p. 280

Violence has long been an important element in fiction about Negroes, just as it is in their life. But where Julia Peterkin in her pastorals and Roark Bradford in his levee farces show violence to be the reaction of primitives unadjusted to modern civilization, Richard Wright shows it as the way in which civilization keeps the Negro in his place. And he knows what he is writing about. . . . The essential quality of certain phases of Negro life in the South is handled here vigorously, authentically, and with flashes of genuine poetry.

Sterling A. Brown. Nation. April 16, 1938. p. 448

Mr. Wright has laid bare, with a ruthlessness that spares neither race, the lower depths of the human and social relationships of blacks and whites; and his ruthlessness so clearly springs not from a vindictive desire to shock but from a passionate—and compassionate—concern with a problem obviously lying at the core of his own personal reality that while the reader may recoil he cannot escape from the conviction that this problem is part of his reality as well.

Margaret Marshall. Nation. March 16, 1940. p. 367

Wright does not see the whole of life steadily and thoroughly: he sees only a segment of life, and even this limited part he views in its most violent and horrible aspects. To this restricted perspective may be traced the battering redundancy, the morbid melodrama, the over-wrought excitement and the inflated calamities that sometimes appear in his work. In his limited field, nevertheless, he is generally a realistic analyst and thoughtful interpreter of social ills and, above all other American novelists, is the sensitive painter and perspicacious spokes-man of the inarticulate black millions of this century.

Hugh M. Gloster. Negro Voices in American Fiction
(North Carolina). 1948. p. 234

All through *The Outsider,* Mr. Wright keeps telling us that the least important thing about his hero is that he is a Negro. . . . He is trying to portray modern man in his existential loneliness . . . but in fact, in-stead of "universalizing" the Negro, he simply denies the Negro's ex-perience and reality. . . . Mr. Wright, it turns out, is unable to say anything at all about being a Negro except that to be a Negro is to be incoherent, and to do violence and murder. . . . Emptying his hero's life of all content except that existentialist content which evades reality through the pretense of trying to grapple with it on its "deepest" level—he has left us with only the familiar old black chasm.

Steven Marcus. Cmty. Nov., 1953. pp. 457–8

(Gertrude Stein) had never heard of Wright until her return to Paris after its liberation from the Nazis. Her book *Wars I Have Seen* was pub-lished soon after that, and among the reviews she saw was a laudatory one by Wright in *PM.* Asking a G.I. friend who this admirer of hers was, she was given a copy of *Black Boy* from the army library.

"I was very excited and wrote for the rest of his stuff," she told me. "I found Wright was the best American writer today. Only one or two creative writers like him come along in a generation. Every time he says something it is a distinct revelation."

Ben Burns. Reporter. March 8, 1956. p. 23

Many literary men have fought crusades; Wright is a crusader who fights with words. It makes a difference and it accounts for the spe-cial quality of his fiction. *The Long Dream* is not a badly-made book, as you will discover if you try to pull it to pieces. It is very strong, but its workmanship is careful only where care is needed for Wright's purposes. Elsewhere the book is boldly hammered together—not as a work of art but as the scaffolding for an idea. . . . He writes now with much more control than he once showed; his ear is wonderfully acute and his judgement of emotional degree and balance is subtle, varied, and exciting.

Robert Hatch. *Nation*. Oct. 25, 1958. p. 297

Native Son

Its swift rise to murder, its ruthless staging of a scene where race preju-dice and palpable injustice capture the reader's sympathy, and the re-fusal of its author to make his chief character anything but a criminal, dangerous to society, all reveal a creative mind of unusual power, dis-cipline, and grasp of large ideas. The question, which first concerns vice and viciousness and crime, slowly becomes ethical, political, and psychological without once separating itself from an intensely human content.

Henry Seidel Canby. *SR*. March 23, 1940. p. 8

Native Son, the most perdurable and influential novel yet written by an American Negro, is at the same time one of the masterpieces of modern proletarian fiction. Taking as its leading character a traditional "bad-nigger" stereotype usually accepted as a representative Negro by mis-informed whites and frequently viewed with nausea by supercilious blacks, the book seeks to show that the individual's delinquency is pro-duced by a distorting environment rather than by innate criminality. Having this purpose, *Native Son* may rightly be regarded as the most significant probing of the plight of the lower-class Northern urban Negro in contemporary American literature.

Hugh M. Gloster. *Negro Voices in American Fiction*
(North Carolina). 1948. p. 233

Elements of heredity, of social environment both black and white, of blind chance and misdirected attempts on the part of the whites to break down the colour bar, are brought together to drive the coloured hero of *Native Son* to the murder of a white girl and of his own sweet-heart until he is caught, brought to trial, and sentenced to death. The dramatic development and straightforward characterization, as well as the absence of any false sentiment or propagandistic tone, make the novel more effective than most writing in this field. The book gives one of the rare examples of what can be achieved by the technique of pure reporting applied with a consistent attitude and an adequate subject matter.

Heinrich Straumann. *American Literature in the Twentieth Century* (Hutchinson). 1951. p. 50

See *Uncle Tom's Children* (short stories); also *Native Son, The Outsider,* and *The Long Dream* (novels) and *Black Boy* (autobiography).

SUPPLEMENT

BALDWIN, JAMES

Baldwin is a man possessed by the necessity of coming to grips with himself and his country. He is also concerned with forcing our nation—with which he has had a turbulent love affair—to come to grips with itself. Because he is a gifted black man in an environment controlled by whites, his view of life is especially illuminating. He is, as he has said in a recent radio discussion, "the maid" in the American house. He is the outsider within, the agonized repository of the family's most intimate secrets.

Julian Mayfield. NR. Aug. 7, 1961. p. 25

I'm sure that Baldwin doesn't like to hear his essays praised at the expense (seemingly) of his fiction. And I'm equally sure that if Baldwin were not so talented a novelist he would not be so remarkable an essayist. But the great thing about his essays is that the form allows him to work out from all the conflicts raging in *him,* so that finally the "I," the "James Baldwin" who is so sassy and despairing and bright, manages, without losing his authority as the central speaker, to show us all the different people hidden in him, all the voices for whom the "I" alone can speak. . . . To be James Baldwin is to touch on so many hidden places in Europe, America, the Negro, the white man—to be forced to understand so much.

Alfred Kazin. Contemporaries (Little). 1962. pp. 255–6

While any evalution of Baldwin as writer must consider both his essays and his novels, it is, hopefully, for the latter that he will be remembered. Since the essays, for the most part, deal with contemporary problems, they will become historical; that is, again hopefully, they will cease to apply to current situations. Yet it is partly on the basis of the essays that one has faith in his value as a novelist, for some of the resources on which he must draw are revealed most sharply in the essays. What seems to be the case is that Baldwin has yet to find the artistic form that will reveal the mystery, that will uncover the truth he knows is there. If he does, if his intention and accomplishment become one, if his intellectual grasp is matched by his imaginative, he will be a writer whose measure it will be difficult to take.

James Finn. Com. Oct. 26, 1962. p. 116

James Baldwin has written, in *Another Country,* the big novel everyone has thought for years he had in him. It is a work of great integrity and great occasional power; but I am afraid I can do no more than the damned compact liberal majority has done, and pronounce it an impressive failure. Spiritually, it's a pure and noble novel; though it's largely populated by perverts, bums, queers, and tramps, with only an occasional contemptible square interspersed, I wasn't much distressed by their comings, couplings, and goings. They are looking for love in some fairly unlikely ways and places, but the commodity is a rare one, and we can't afford to overlook possibilities. No, the book's faults are mainly technical. One of them has to do with the difficult question of dialect. Most of Mr. Baldwin's characters are of the hipster persuasion, or at least on the near fringe of hipsterism, and the patois he makes them talk has most of the faults of artifice and few of the merits of originality. In effect, their argot is dull and uninventive. We are supposed to feel about many of these characters that they're proud, sensitive, suffering souls; it is thoroughly depressing to find, when they open their lips flecked with anguish, that, man, they talk like trite. They're always mouthing about "making it" and if they could break the shackles of their degenerate dialect, it's indeed conceivable that they might make a phrase or an image or something.

Robert M. Adams. PR. Spring, 1963. pp. 131–2

When Baldwin records, with finest notation, his exacerbated sense of what it is like to be a Negro; when he renders, with furious conviction, the indignities and humiliations which attend his every step, the stiffening and perpetual pressure which closes in upon a Negro simply because he is one; when he conveys his sense of the social climate by which the Negro comes despairingly to know, from earliest childhood, the atmosphere in which desperation is bred, that he is a pariah, a little more than animal, but less than human—then, I have no doubt, there can scarcely be a Negro who does not listen to him with full assent. But when we listen to any of Baldwin's voices—his passionately exhortatory warning or his pleading—it is not the voice, nor is it the tone of reason we are hearing, for Baldwin is not a "reasonable" man; it is a lamentation and a curse and a prayer.

Saul Maloff. Nation. March 2, 1963. p. 181

See also *Another Country* (novel); and *Nobody Knows My Name* and *The Fire Next Time* (essays).

BELLOW, SAUL

In all his work thus far Bellow has been moving toward a hedged affirmation. . . . In qualified terms he has revived the cult of personality and, paradoxically, given us the clue to the social history of the post-war years. Preoccupied with what it feels like, what it takes, what it means to be a human being, Bellow has made man the vital center of his work. No guiding philosophical conception shapes his image of man; he is concerned with man alive. Augie says in one of his introspective passages, that he seeks simplicity, and one is reminded of Thoreau's simplify! simplify! . . . So it is with Bellow, who wants no confining philosophy or myth, who has no patience with passing social phenomena, who finds the essentials of human experience in human beings seeking themselves and seeking love. And fleeing annihilation.

Chester E. Eisinger. *Accent.* Summer, 1958. pp. 202–3

It appears that although Bellow's insistence on being free is not a complete view of human destiny, neither is it simply a piece of naïvety or moral irresponsibility, as has sometimes been suggested. He believes that if we ever define our character and our fate it will be because we have caught up with our own legend, realized our own imagination. Bellow's fertile sense of the ever-possible conversion of reality and imagination, fact and legend, into each other is the source of the richness and significance of his writing. He differs in this respect from the traditional practice of American prose romance, which forces the real and imaginary far apart and finds that there is no circuit of life between them. Bellow differs, too, from the pure realist, who describes human growth as a simple progress away from legend and toward fact.

Richard Chase. *Cmty.* April, 1959. p. 327

For Bellow, as for Malamud and some of the other fine novelists of the time, personality is back in the middle of the novel, not where their great predecessors—Proust, Joyce, and to somewhat lesser extent, Mann—put it, as part of the thematic scheme which apportions the size and intensity of every element. *Henderson* is a kind of bridge between *Augie, Seize the Day,* and these thematic novels; the difficulty is that the bridge must bear the weight of constant invention, invention which can draw hardly at all on the home detail in which the other novels luxuriate. . . . Bellow readers, used to commodity markets, Mexican resorts, Evanston haberdasheries, and the Machiavellians and con-men who in vintage Bellow load the pages, must go into another gear. They will be helped by the fact that *Henderson* is a stylistic masterpiece.

Richard G. Stern. *KR.* Autumn, 1959. p. 660

Bellow's artistic progress reveals itself in the stages his heroes mark. . . . The movement . . . is towards a resolution of the conflict between self and world; the movement is from acid defeat to acceptance, and from acceptance to celebration. All these heroes are in some way or other outsiders to the world they inhabit; all are on intimate terms with pain; and all affirm the sense of human life. The affirmation has· an ironic knowledge of its limits. For if Joseph (of *Dangling Man*) is the eternal victim, he is victim to his own lack of resolution; and if Henderson is the eternal savior, he is at the same time a bungling and grotesque redeemer. Thus does the progress of Bellow's hero maintain a sense both of hope and humility. And thus does it disclose to us a *form* of human courage.

Ihab H. Hassan. *Critique*. Summer, 1960. pp. 35–6

The matter has become more and more apparent, but since the beginning all Bellow's heroes have started in a gesture of escape from burdens, an extreme romantic gesture. It is a gesture which in its extremity brings Bellow into touch with one of the defining impulses of American character, into touch with at least all the classic Redskins of American letters, from Leatherstocking to Whitman to Mark Twain to Hemingway, all those who light off for the woods, the open road, the Territory, and into touch perhaps with the Palefaces, too. (The extreme need to escape burdens, to be free of all the clutter, is certainly as well a distinction of Hawthorne and Henry James.) Bellow's hero is tempted frequently to epiphanies of love for mankind in general, though never for things, and his motion is brought to various thematic significances, but he is in the first instance activated by the need to rid himself of the weight of the chaos.

Marcus Klein. *KR*. Spring, 1962. p. 211

See also *Herzog* (novel).

FAULKNER, WILLIAM

Faulkner had what (giving up the attempt to define it more closely) we call genius. It is what Herman Melville had when he wrote *Moby Dick* and rarely manifested thereafter. We know that genius seldom lasts, but we are always saddened when it goes.

On the other hand, if something has been lost (in *The Mansion*), something has been gained. In his note Faulkner says that "the author has learned, he believes, more about the human heart and its dilemma than he knew thirty-four years ago." Indeed he has. He has learned, for one thing, to respect deeply the human capacity for sheer endurance. He has also acquired compassion. . . . The Snopeses, it turns out, are not personifications of greed or anything of the sort; they are poor sons of bitches like the rest of us.

Granville Hicks. *SR*. Nov. 14, 1959. p. 21

Faulkner is right in assuming that the hope in man's will to endure and prevail has been the subject of his fiction all along; but this will is variously represented, and the degree and quality of context in which we see it vary considerably from the beginning of his career to the present. He moves from what is almost a total lack of awareness to a vague and fleeting insight into human beings—to the point where the meaning of existence is not only seen but overtly defined. Throughout this progress, however, there are many uncertainties which upset the calculation, and his characters are frequently seen missing their chances and blundering badly despite their sense of dedication. This is one among many reasons for the value of Faulkner's work; it appears an endless variety of new experiments in the means to express not only man's worth but the elaborate stratagems he is guilty of using to conceal it.

Frederick J. Hoffman. *William Faulkner* (Twayne).
1961. pp. 117–8

Evil for Faulkner involves the violation of the natural and the denial of the human. . . . Yet Faulkner is no disciple of Jean-Jacques Rousseau. He has no illusions that man is naturally good or that he can trust to his instincts and emotions. Man is capable of evil, and this means that goodness has to be achieved by struggle and discipline and effort. Like T. S. Eliot, Faulkner has small faith in social arrangements so perfectly organized that nobody has to take the trouble to be good. Finally Faulkner's noblest characters are willing to face the fact that most men can learn the deepest truths about themselves and about reality only through suffering. Hurt and pain and loss are not mere accidents to which the human being is subject; nor are they mere punishment incurred by human error; they can be the means to deeper knowledge and to the more abundant life.

Cleanth Brooks. *MR*. Summer, 1962. p. 712

The European reader finds something uniquely American in Faulkner, and obviously no European could have written his books; the few European commentators that I have read seem to me to glorify William Faulkner in a provincial American (or Southern) vacuum. I believe that as his personality fades from view he will be recognized as one of the great craftsmen of the art of fiction which Ford Madox Ford called the Impressionistic Novel. From Stendhal through Flaubert and Joyce there is a direct line to Faulkner, and it is not a mere question of influence. Faulkner's great subject, as it was Flaubert's and Proust's, is passive suffering, the victim being destroyed either by society or by dark forces within himself. Faulkner is one of the great exemplars of the international school of fiction which for more than a century has reversed the Aristotelian doctrine that tragedy is an action, not a quality.

Allen Tate. *SwR*. Winter, 1963. p. 162

FROST, ROBERT

I think of Robert Frost as a terrifying poet. Call him, if it makes things any easier, a tragic poet, but it might be useful every now and then to come out from under the shelter of that literary word. The universe that he conceives is a terrifying universe. . . . But the *people,* it will be objected, the *people* who inhabit this possibly terrifying universe! About them there is nothing that can terrify; surely the people in Mr. Frost's poems can only reassure us by their integrity and solidity. . . . They affirm *this* of themselves: that they are what they are, that this is their truth, and that if the truth be bare, as truth often is, it is far better than a lie. For me the process by which they arrive at that truth is always terrifying. The manifest America of Mr. Frost's poems may be pastoral; the actual America is tragic.

Lionel Trilling. PR. Summer, 1959. pp. 451–2

The conditions which circumscribe Frost's poems are those of a world not yet dominated by urban, industrialized, bureaucratized culture—the very world which, seeing its inevitable coming, Emerson and his kind strove to confront and save for man before it would be too late. Frost glances at this world, only to turn to a one he knows better. In that world the proper life style—which in turn generates the literary style—is that of Frost's characteristic protagonists: individuals who again and again are made to face up to the fact of their individualism as such; who can believe that a community is no more than the sum of the individuals who make it up; who are situated so as to have only a dim sense, even that resisted mightily, of the transformations which the individual might have to undergo if he is to live fully in the modern world and still retain his identity as an individual. But, of course, Frost's protagonists refuse to live fully in the modern world and will have little or nothing to do with such transformations. Frost's work is in the end a series of expressions of that refusal and assessments of its cost.

Roy Harvey Pearce. KR. Spring, 1961. pp. 261–2

Let the School System make a whited saint of Mr. Frost if it must; and as, alas, it will. The man himself remains an *hombre*. If he is half radiance he is also half brimstone, and praise be. His best poems will endure precisely because they are terrible—and holy. All primal fire is terrible—and holy. Mr. Frost could climb to heaven and hear the angels call him brother—*frater,* they would probably say—but he could as well climb Vesuvius and equally hear every rumble under his feet call out to him.

The darkness in his poems is as profound as the light in them is long. They are terrible because they are from life at a depth into which we cannot look unshaken.

John Ciardi. SR. March 24, 1962. pp. 15–6

A question arises from Frost's *Collected Poems* . . . : what are the possibilities for a poetry based upon nothing more than a shared sense of human fact? Is this enough? Will it serve instead of those other "certainties" which are, for many readers, insecure?

Frost would seem to answer "Yes." Yeats relied on nervous improvisations or religious patterns hired for the occasion of the poem. . . . Frost committed himself to the common ground he *knew* existed between himself and his putative reader. He knew that if he were to tell a pathetic story in a few common words whose weightings were part of our blood, we would respond feelingly. And that was something. Frost has spent a lifetime seeing how much he could say on those terms. He is the poet most devoted to bare human gesture.

Denis Donoghue. YR. Winter, 1963. p. 216

See also *In the Clearing*.

GOLD, HERBERT

Mr. Gold has an extraordinary talent for style, but also a weakness for it; he is in danger of becoming a *stylist*. As Shakespeare, according to Dr. Johnson, would sometimes trade all sense for the achievement of a pun, Gold will trade it for a frill, or sometimes even a trill. His style is by nature a vehicle of warm and intelligent humor, and when it is properly limited, leashed, and pommeled into obedience, it does its work well and charmingly. Gold can be very, very funny; or expressive; or even brilliant in little perfect flashes of incidental observation or conversation. . . . But often there is a regrettable muddying of perception by style—an over-styling that blinds or distracts or blurs the eye that is supposed to see something more clearly with the style's help.

Richard Foster. HdR. Spring, 1961. pp. 146–7

Gold has emerged as a kind of literary hipster, far too cunning to be taken in by any hipster nonsense, but who in his unsentimental coolness, pitiless sense of the contemporary, and inside dopsterism has links with the type.

Even more important, Gold, like very few of our major writers, has tried to stretch language to meet the new requirements of our time. He has used an idiom that is highly permutable, strained perhaps, too shifty; but it reaches out to encompass new states of mind that writers in an easier time did not have to cope with. At its best, it is taut, keyed-up, nervously inventive; at its worst, it is merely artsy-smirky, a pushy, obtrusive prose. And it defines Gold's stance: the novelist as wise guy. . . . Herbert Gold leaves us where we were before. There is a terrible emptiness everywhere. If the older generation of writers dealt with the loss of values, Gold's characters seem never to have had them.

David Boroff. *SR*. April 20, 1963. pp. 45–6

Mr. Gold is "that most happy fellow" in America, the master of "the going thing." His stories and novels are zeroed in on a new generation who suffer early sorrow, make an early marriage, father children at an early age, and then—surrounded by the symbols of middle-class domesticity—find their hearts festering with unrealized adolescent desires. Divorced in their early thirties, cut adrift in a hustling world that "understands" but never helps, these martyrs to the American fixation on "love" wobble desperately between fantasies of suicide and a second, better union.

The one man who speaks consistently to their condition—who describes it minutely in all its embarrassingly familiar detail and yet never betrays its poignant optimism—is Herbert Gold.

Albert Goldman. *NR*. June 8, 1963. p. 23

See also *Therefore Be Bold* and *Salt* (novels), *Love and Like* (short stories), and *Age of Happy Problems* (essays).

HELLER, JOSEPH (1923–   )

Heller's satire cuts a wide swath. He takes after a variety of bureaucrats, makes fun of security checks, ridicules psychiatrists and army doctors in general. Sometimes he shoots way over the mark, but often his aim is good. There are several extremely funny passages, the humor usually rising out of the kind of mad logic that seems to Heller the essence of modern warfare. . . . But . . . Heller has introduced so many characters, tried to deliver so many knockout blows, and written in such a variety of styles that the reader becomes a little dizzy.

Granville Hicks. *SR*. Oct. 14, 1961. p. 32

Below its hilarity, so wild that it hurts, *Catch-22* is the strongest repudiation of our civilization, in fiction, to come out of World War II. That the horror and the hypocrisy, the greed and the complacency, the endless cunning and the endless stupidity which now go to constitute what we term Christianity are dealt with here in absolutes, does not lessen the truth of its repudiation. . . . To compare *Catch-22* favorably with *The Good Soldier Schweik* would be an injustice, because this novel is not merely the best American novel to come out of World War II, it is the best American novel that has come out of anywhere in years.

Nelson Algren. *Nation*. Nov. 4, 1961. p. 358

Considering his indifference to surface reality, it is absurd to judge Heller by standards of psychological reality (or, for that matter, by conventional artistic standards at all, since his book is as formless as any picaresque epic). He is concerned entirely with that thin boundary of the surreal, the borderline between hilarity and horror, which, much like the apparent formlessness of the unconscious, has its own special integrity and coherence. Thus, Heller will never use comedy for its own sake; each joke has a wider significance in the intricate pattern, so that laughter becomes a prologue for some grotesque revelation. This gives the reader an effect of surrealistic dislocation, intensified by a weird, rather flat, impersonal style, full of complicated reversals, swift transitions, abrupt shifts in chronological time, and manipulated identities . . . , as if all mankind was determined by a mad and merciless mechanism.

Robert Brustein. *NR*. Nov. 13, 1961. p. 13

Catch-22's comedy, fantastically inventive, controlled, patterned and structured even when it seems all wild improvisation and top-that-one-if-you-can surrealism, is one long, bludgeoning attack on the hero, or what little was left of him in the tradition of twentieth-century fiction before Heller's demented fliers came along.

Heller does not try to dissolve the Achilles dilemma (to live a long, undistinguished, tame life or a hot, glorious, heroic and therefore short one) in a way that so much of the literature of anti-heroism does. He does not say, "Nonsense. It's a false and artificial choice. Everyone knows there are others." On the contrary, Heller's nuthouse comedy and grotesque tragedy are dedicated to the Falstaffian proposition that it's better to be a live coward than a dead hero.

Melvin Seiden. *Nation*. Nov. 18, 1961. pp. 408–9

Joseph Heller's *Catch-22* is an extraordinary book. Its basic assumption is that in war all men are equally mad; bombs fall on insane friend and crazy enemy alike. . . . Ostensibly a black farce about an American bomber squadron stationed on an island in the Mediterranean towards the end of the Second World War; it is, in fact, a surrealist *Iliad,* with a lunatic High Command instead of gods, and a coward for hero. . . . Epic in form, the book is episodic in structure. Each chapter carries a single character a step nearer madness or death or both, and a step, too, into legend. The action takes place well above the level of reality. On leave or in action the characters behave with a fine disregard for the laws of probability. Yet . . . within its own terms the book is wholly consistent, creating legend out of the wildest farce and the most painful realism, constructing its own system of probability.

Julian Mitchell. Spec. June 15, 1962. p. 301

In *A Modest Proposal,* however horrifying Swift's suggestions may be, however explicit his instructions for braising or roasting a fat infant, author and reader are fully aware that the suggestions are unreal, that Swift writes as he does precisely because he knows that his readers will agree with him that such things are beyond comprehension, and will therefore agree with him that other real attitudes and acts are equally intolerable and must be reformed. No such sense sustains us in *Catch-22.* The scenes Heller describes are real; they are close enough to our experience to convince us that the fundamental horror is true, and neither author nor reader can console himself with the rationalization that this is an imaginary horror and that it is meant only to inspire reform in some other area.

John H. Muste. Critique. Fall, 1962. p. 22

See *Catch-22.*

HEMINGWAY, ERNEST

I am tempted to guess that future literary historians may go back to *The Old Man and the Sea* as their convenient marker for the end of one kind of serious fiction in American writing, the novel of formal structure, with a solidly presented central character and with a definite conclusion; a fiction which asserted easily understood and elemental human values. In its Darwinian stoicism, *The Old Man and the Sea* is an epitome of all Hemingway's previous work. In the tight organization of its events, it is the epitome of a whole generation of novel writing. It is also the kind of novel with which the most serious young writers of today have parted company.

David L. Stevenson. Nation. Nov. 1, 1958. p. 308

As somebody who has never been concerned with "rating" Hemingway's works but has simply been grateful for whatever joy his writing has offered, I might as well throw in a word about those critics who took an injured, censorious tone when discussing the life that Hemingway led in later years and what they considered a decline in his work. They sometimes sounded as if they thought that Hemingway made a point of letting them, specifically, down, in order to disport himself as a public figure, whereas, as I saw it, he was heroically and uncompromisingly occupied day after day with writing as hard as *he could* and as well as *he could* until the day he died. And when he was unable to write or was between books, he still did what *he could,* which was to live life to the full and then, with that limitless generosity of his, make his private experience public, so that everybody else could also have a wonderful time.

Lillian Ross. Portrait of Hemingway (Simon). 1961. p. 16

He made the man who could follow him no farther than his own well-lit door, feel, standing in it, the dark precipitous edge where life drops in one moment to utter nothingness. As though a man must earn his death before he could win his life.

No American writer since Walt Whitman has assumed such risks in forging a style, and the success of these risks was not accidental. For they were risks assumed in living, and thereby derived a tension that no merely literary risk could have achieved.

They were not amateur's chances, such as that proposed by one of the beatnik saints in assuming that writing resembled driving with headlights out and a noseful of pot. The chances Hemingway took were professional, being measured, and were then governed by an iron control. They were the kind of chances by which, should they fail, the taker fails alone; yet should they succeed, succeed for everyone.

Nelson Algren. Nation. Nov. 18, 1961. p. 387

And I looked up into Hemingway's smile—the teeth yellowish and widely spaced, but bared in all the ceremonious innocence of a boy's grin. He was suddenly, beautifully, twelve years old. A tough, cocky, gentle boy still, but also a fragile, too-often-repaired old man, about (how could one help knowing it?) to die. It puzzled me a little to discover him, who had never been able to invent a tragic protagonist, so much a tragic figure himself—with meanings for all of us, meanings utterly different from those of his myth, meanings I would have to figure out later. . . . Yet he seemed, too, as we had always suspected, one who had been *only* a boy and an old man, never what the rest of us for too wearily long must endure being—all that lies between.

Leslie Fiedler. PR. Summer, 1962. p. 404

LOWELL, ROBERT

The voice of Robert Lowell's poetry has always had the authority of the extreme. No conflict is glossed over or rationalized by a system of ideas. His religion was always entirely eschatological: the world he describes, ancient or modern, is never influenced by religion but only threatened by it. It is as if he could bear to contemplate this world because he could momentarily expect its total destruction or total delivery.

Thus, the one thing this poet never worried about in his writing was how to go on living. This has given him great strength, which he still has. The new poems have abandoned the myths of eschatology and the masks of heroes, but the violence and the guilt, the unalleviated seizure of experience, these remain. This is why, perhaps alone of living poets, he can bear for us the role of the great poet, the man who on a very large scale sees more, feels more, and speaks more bravely about it than we ourselves can do.

John Thompson. KR. Summer, 1959. p. 487

The persistent refusal of happiness, the constant indulgence of a guilty conscience, would make a dreary spectacle if it were not for a certain knowing humor and a certain poise of style in the offender. But Lowell is not only the hunger artist practicing an art of famine because he doesn't like food; he knows he is something like that and makes a conscious role of it. The prose memoirs are the most triumphant example of his essential composure. The surface of them is all anecdote and caricature, malign and dazzling; but the interior is solid social analysis of a family, a society, a period; and when completed the work will probably excel any poet's autobiography since Yeats's. The portraits and memories in verse are excellent in their command of a cadenced as opposed to metrical medium and they are exceedingly lively. But given their intense response to what they describe, they suffer a little from being inconclusive as to the meaning of it all. . . . They represent, perhaps, major poetry pulling in its horns and putting on big spectacles and studying how to survive.

F. W. Dupee. PR. Summer, 1959. p. 475

Lowell is still the wonderful poet of "The Quaker Graveyard in Nantucket," the poet of power and passion whose striving aesthetic of anguish belies the "frizzled, stale, and small" condition he attributes to himself. He may be wrong in believing that what has happened to New England's elite is necessarily an embodiment of the state of American culture, the whole maggot character of which he feels he carries about in his own person. But he is not wrong in looking at the culture through the window of psychological breakdown. Too many other American poets, no matter what their social class and family history, have reached the same point in recent years. Lowell is foremost among them in the energy of his uncompromising honesty.

M. L. Rosenthal. *Nation*. Sept. 19, 1959. p. 154

Robert Lowell is a . . . Lowell, and comes out of the heart of Lowell country—Beacon Hill. His memoir (*Life Studies*), though acerb and wise and tender, has above all that extraordinary subtlety of upper-class commentary on itself (something you don't find in so good a book as *The Late George Apley*) that is possible to Americans who don't really know anyone beyond themselves but who have the gift of experiencing and expressing their own situation to the depths. It is this that made Henry Adams, with all pretentiousness, such a marvelous autobiographer; Robert Lowell has only, poker-faced, to write "In 1924 people still lived in cities" for us to know exactly where we are. . . . He specializes in place, in eloquent vertigo, in stylizing the communion with self that is the essence of dramatic monologue, and I can't think of any poet of his generation who has polished the dramatic sense, rare enough, to such acuteness.

Alfred Kazin. *Contemporaries* (Little). 1962.
pp. 226, 228

See also *For the Union Dead* (poetry).

MAILER, NORMAN

Norman Mailer is one of the few postwar American writers in whom it is possible to detect the presence of qualities that powerfully suggest a major novelist in the making. Anyone trying to describe these qualities would be likely to dwell on Mailer's extraordinary technical skill, or on the boldness and energy of his mind, or on his readiness to try something new whenever he puts pen to paper. What seems even more remarkable, however, is that his work has responded to the largest problems of this period with a directness and an assurance that we rarely find in the novels of his contemporaries. Mailer is very much an American, but he appears to be endowed with the capacity for seeing himself as a battleground of history —a capacity that is usually associated with the French and that American writers are thought never to have. He is a man given to ideologies, a holder of extreme positions, and in this too he differs from the general run of his literary contemporaries, so many of whom have fled ideologies to pursue an ideal of sensible moderation both in style and philosophy.

Norman Podhoretz. *PR*. Summer, 1959. p. 371

Norman Mailer, trying in *The Deer Park* to compose a novel about the malaise of our years, avoided the cumbersomeness of the traditional social novel but could find no other structure that would give coherence to his perceptions. Mailer tried to embody his keen if unstable vision in a narrative about people whose extreme dislocation of experience and feeling would, by the very fact of their extreme dislocation, come to seem significant. But in its effort to portray our drifting and boredom full-face, in its fierce loyalty to the terms of its own conception, *The Deer Park* tended to become a claustrophobic work, driving attention inward, toward its own tonal peculiarities, rather than outward, as an extended parable.

Irving Howe. *PR*. Summer, 1959. p. 431

On one of his sides he rejoices in that "appetite for life" which he admires in James Jones. Sheer experience, experience for its own sake, leads him on. And just as this makes him a comparative rarity among younger writers today, so it constitutes his living relation to the older American writers—his living one, that is, as distinguished from the relation by way of familial piety and emulation. But on another side he has an equal hunger for ideas, a hunger that is not so well satisfied by what he can produce in the way of intellectual nourishment. The various forms of enlightenment which the older writers brought to bear on their experience seem to have crystallized for Mailer, into a vague, self-conscious sort of wisdom. This has sought to express itself in appropriate ideas, Marxist or Nietzschean (hip has Nietzschean roots, as Norman Podhoretz implies) or Freudian. Of these the Freudian is Mailer's most pervasive source of ideas and images. . . . But the Freudian ideas, like those of other derivation, often operate not to reinforce and clarify his experience but to embarrass and devitalize it.

F. W. Dupee. *Cmty*. Feb., 1960. p. 131

If Mailer is an existentialist he is an odd one, for he clearly cannot tolerate existence. He is enraged at his own freedom because it is finite. He will settle for nothing short of an omnipotence which would enable him to actualize every possibility. Failing that, he yearns to become fate itself in the hope that it might extinguish his miserable finitude. A mystic of the bottom, he seeks to be consumed by the "spirit of the flesh," not only "nearer to" but *identical* with "that God which every hipster believes is located in the senses of the body." Rape, murder, and suicide are not merely antisocial acts; they are *defiant* acts which seek to annihilate existence. Although the murderer ordinarily seeks to destroy only a single person, the *quality* of his passion is infinite. It is not so much his action as the *infinity* of the murderer's passion which intrigues Mailer. As he half-knows, he is obsessed not simply with violence, but with *death*.

George Alfred Schrader. *YR*. Winter, 1962. pp. 275–6

MALAMUD, BERNARD

Mr. Malamud's people may seem to approach us guilelessly, and the language in which we are told about them may seem to have no pretension; but we soon find out that in the world of simple people with simple problems that he has created, nothing is simple. . . . Mr. Malamud can force us to recognize him as a true writer, in the way that we do recognize the true writer: by his ability to make us feel as we read that usually, and by choice, we move in a moral twilight of habit, flippancy, and sentimentality, half-blind and half-insensible to the sights of the world. . . . We acknowledge his power . . . when we acknowledge that humble and simple though his characters are, they have an awareness of a kind that is much rarer and subtler and more difficult to communicate than anything that usually goes under the heading of "intelligence."

Dan Jacobson. *Cmty.* Oct., 1958. pp. 360–1

Although Malamud captures the elusive tones and shadows of the traditional Yiddish tale, he is not at all a teller of tales in the traditional manner. He is an extremely self-conscious short story writer, keenly sensitive to the formal demands of the short story, and unwilling to let a character vignette or Aleichem-like evocation of atmosphere embody his vision. His manner is frequently that of the teller of tales, but his technique of structure is poetic and symbolic. He seems, as it were, to construct his stories backwards—beginning with his final climactic image and then manipulating his characters into the appropriate dramatic poses which will contribute to the total significance of that image.

Earl H. Rovit. *Critique.* Winter-Spring, 1960. pp. 5–6

It would be merely sentimental and pious to suggest that those qualities of his work (following *The Natural*) which have been so steadily remarked upon—the pity and the tenderness, the compassion and love, as in *The Assistant* and many of the stories in *The Magic Barrel*—are Jewish properties and that the writer who expresses and conveys them is, therefore, a Jewish writer. They do not in themselves make for art; without art they may, indeed, only suffocate; and Malamud, whose instinct is for that center of passion where feeling is most exacerbated, is almost always in absolute control of his difficult art, though he takes the greatest risks in creating his rarefied atmosphere.

"Levitation," in fact, is one of his favorite words. In that thin air between natural earth and outer space everything is permitted, all rules are suspended, but only so long as the artist can keep his characters there by his own centrifugal force. If we say that Malamud's world is like no other, it is because the world he creates occupies the air exactly between the real and the absurd, where only saints and lunatics are, and where the right gesture—of movement, of language, of syntax, of metaphor— can save one's life, or some other.

Saul Maloff. NR. Nov. 18, 1961. p. 407

In general, the special achievement of Malamud's technique has been the movement back and forth between the grimly plain and the fantastic, the joining of the natural to the supernatural, the endowing of the abstracted version of the commonplace with the entanglements of a dream. His most impressive prose has been a similar mixture of a hard common speech, twisted by Yiddishisms or by his own syntax so that it vibrates, and lit here and there by a sudden lyrical image. The solidity of his best work has come from an obsessive mood and vision which from moment to moment seems to take the place of the realist's eye for physical detail. . . . By-passing contemporary reality, then, and the techniques of realism, Malamud has relied instead mainly upon his memories of ghetto life and his idiosyncratic imagination to create situations of sufficient density —and intensity—for his moral concerns. His excursions beyond the ghetto life have been noticeably less sure and distinguished.

Theodore Solotaroff. Cmty. March, 1962. p. 201

See also *A New Life* (novel).

MILLER, HENRY

It is difficult to say how far such an instinctive writer as Miller has realized his own importance. Probably he arrived at it through a process of trial and error: looking for a fixed point in a world of shadows he found only himself, and in the depths of himself nothing but a longing, nihilistic and pre-natal, a violent attraction toward the darkness of the womb. There is, however, no doubt that his transition from the objectivity of the third person to the subjectivity of the first, from a narrative to an auto-biographic style, from reticence on certain subjects to the most brutal frankness, was deliberate and conscious. With him the American novel, which with many of the imitators of Hemingway, Faulkner and Saroyan had become merely a literary machine, reached a turning point. Like the spring-time rush of a turbid and riotous mountain stream breaking up the winter's ice (or if you prefer it like the filthy gush from a drain bursting up through the cracks in the surface of a road), we see in Miller the moment when that precarious balance between American society and its opponents, which had never been completely achieved, broke down altogether.

Alberto Moravia. SwR. Summer, 1960. pp. 474–5

Henry Miller can use the language. He writes strong, biting, memorable, vivid prose. . . . Style, style, style: brushwork, the drive of the hand into the clay, the thrust of the lines of structure against each other, the movement of the musical phrase between keys and modes, the balance and rivalry of colors, the rise and fall and timing of an actor's voice—style is a chief aim of all artists in all media. This Henry Miller has achieved: he is a wonderful stylist.

Spontaneous, his style appears. He writes prose which often seems to run absolutely naturally, like the flow of eager conversation or a rapidly written letter or the current of nonlogical ideas in one's own mind. If in the future he is remembered for anything more than his interest in obscenity, he will be recalled as an agile, often graceful, sometimes powerful manipulator of word and phrase and sentence and paragraph, and sometimes (although less often) of those larger units which are called chapters.

Gilbert Highet. Horizon. Nov., 1961. pp. 104–5

The form he uses is sometimes called "the autobiographical novel," but this is a misnomer; the word "autobiographical" obtains merely because the narrator (that is the created <i>I</i>) sounds so very real. It is now generally recognized that all that is dramatically engaging—whether tragic or comic —must appear to stem from a bedrock of reality. In narrative, this means a straight-faced delivery. This straight face can extend as it does with Miller, beyond the work itself, so that, when questioned about it he can say: "Oh yes, that's all real, that really happened, that's <i>me</i> I'm writing about, etc." which is, of course, nonsense, but, in any case, does not alter the new form which he has brought into being. This form—the narrative using a wholly created, but entirely convincing <i>I</i>—is one of the great forms of the future, even as it is today, in the work, for example, of William Burroughs and John Rechy.

Terry Southern. Nation. Nov. 18, 1961. pp. 400–1

Miller is always good when he can praise anything. In however addle-pated a way, he loves life. Though his recipe for happiness is one that for any thoughtful person just wouldn't work, nevertheless happiness is what he wants.

What is more, Miller has developed a style that is very well fitted for this continual act of celebration. He writes a hurrying, turbulent prose that gives the impression of complete spontaneity, but only the most naïve reader will imagine that such prose can be produced without a great deal of hard work. The rhythms never get out of hand, the pauses are varied with considerable skill, and the words are chosen with great effectiveness. If this is anti-art, it is at least not anti-craft.

John Wain. *NR*. Dec. 1, 1962. p. 22

He is childlike, sensitive, very proud, high-spirited, totally uncritical, alternately gay to the point of euphoria and despairing to the point of sui-cide. He curses a civilization that he does not understand, reviles a coun-try he is unable to leave, and dismisses as worthless all the major authors he has never taken the trouble to read. He refuses to make any effort to commercialize himself, to "earn a living," but harasses his acquaintances to support him ("You call yourselves my friends") in petulant open letters —and they do. I do not pretend wholly to understand such a man—even Durrell, who should of all people be able, all too obviously fails. But his letters . . . , cleared of the cant and rhetoric of his books, offer as clear a picture as we are ever likely to get. They prove, at least, if proof were needed, that the Dirty Old Man who still represents the greater part of his public image is really only a fractional, though integral, fragment of the whole—a whole that is huge, unchanging, probably unique, and the closest thing our century is likely to produce to a genuine Noble Savage.

David Littlejohn. *Reporter*. April 11, 1963. p. 45

See also *Lawrence Durrell and Henry Miller: A Private Correspondence.*

MORRIS, WRIGHT

It is said of [Morris] that he is the darling of the Litry and *Ceremony in Lone Tree* does show signs, like Morris's earlier books, that he has read other writers beside himself, including Faulkner and perhaps even Nabakov. . . . The defense of Morris need not rest, however (as it has done in the past), entirely on his wit, or on his power to create out of emptiness a living scene, or even on his eye for such boondocks of the age as the castrating Female. His strongest claim is that alone among Amer-ican writers he has an intuitive sense of the present quality of [the] life of the middle . . . a sense of waves of *kitsch,* buried Calvinism, bogus hatred (of the city), bogus love (for the tough old mountain men, The Pioneers), fear of the bomb and disbelief in the bomb that now torment and titillate the millions who still sit in kitchen chairs instead of kitchen bar stools.

Benjamin DeMott. *PR*. Fall, 1960. p. 758

Like Morris himself, his characters have to rediscover the past, seeking both "the durable dreams of American life" and the significance of their own youthful experiences, if they are to grow and achieve self-knowledge. The degree of self-awareness they attain depends not only upon their own capacities but also upon Morris's "escape from nostalgia." As he examines, re-examines, and probes the past, Morris also seeks the means to reveal it. He discovers a number of symbols that recur throughout his novels; he experiments with several techniques, discarding some, developing others, until he finally finds a form that both contains and expands his theme. Thus the growth of the artist parallels the growth of the man. It is in this insistent and progressive examination of the role of the past in American experience, plus the development of a creative method for rendering this theme, that the importance of Wright Morris can be found.

Arthur E. Waterman. *Critique*. Winter, 1961–2. p. 24

Morris has been called a "nay-sayer" by Leslie Fiedler, the highest honor Fiedler can bestow on one of his contemporaries. Though the epithet is applicable, it may be indicative not of the strength of Morris's vision, but of its final limitation. He lacks the over-riding compassion which enables Bellow, for example, to redeem his lost sufferers in the midst of impossible circumstances, in spite of everything. Morris's world, in which the past and the future merge in malevolent conspiracy, denies the human being his presumption of dignity.

Although Morris's universe is nihilistic, his theme impotence, his characters fools and madmen, he renders experience with great richness of detail and evocation, bringing it to life to expose its essential deadness. If his view of reality is limited, it is no more limited than Hemingway's; it is only less simple, less readily appealing. Though in recent years Morris has received a fair amount of critical approbation, he is still undervalued. He may see life through a narrower window than the greatest writers, but he sees its incompleteness distinctly, and he sees it whole.

Jonathan Baumbach. *Critique*. Winter, 1961–2. p. 71

He says big things, big enough to win the respect of the most serious reader, but they are not particularly hard sayings. . . . There is in his novels a constant, explicit dialectic between two worlds—between what is really real and what, in our ordinary experience, merely seems so. Almost obsessed, from the beginning, with the poignance of a human life caught in a changing, shifting world, he has in most of his novels gone back to the past, caught the lives of his characters in flux, and tried to fix them by a transforming vision of whatever is timeless beneath or above the changing surface. . . . The particular values shift from work to work, and we can be sure that they will continue to shift. . . . But the varied quest can, for Morris, be summarized without too much distortion under three heads: 1. Men escape the phony and find reality whenever they do anything heroic, courageous, full of audacity. . . . 2. But it is not enough to be merely brave; the unimaginative hero is soon caught in his own clichés. . . . What can save him is inventiveness, imagination. . . . 3. Finally—to come to a value that in some modern novelists has been unique and supreme—one can touch reality by achieving love.

Wayne C. Booth. *AS*. Autumn, 1962. pp. 610–2

Also see *Ceremony in Lone Tree, What a Way to Go,* and *Cause for Wonder* (novels).

PORTER, KATHERINE ANNE

Katherine Anne Porter is conventionally praised for her humanity and warmth and for the stoic virtues which her people show in the face of life's hardships. It is true that she sets up the stoic as the best of behavior. It is also true that the dignity and compassion of her characters are strikingly apparent. But Miss Porter's world is a black and tragic one, filled with disaster, heartbreak, and soul-wrecking disillusionment. The most noble of her characters . . . must submit in the nature of things to sorrows which are not ennobling but destructively abrasive of joy, love, and hope; all of them end with a bleak realization of the Everlasting Nay. They are confronted by the thing "most cruel of all," which in its enormity transcends all other sorrows—the obliteration of hope. The tiny particle of light must always be snuffed out in the depths of the whirlpool.

James William Johnson. *VQR*. Autumn, 1960. p. 611

[*Ship of Fools*] is a vast portrait gallery, with portraits of all sizes hung here and there on the wall, high and low; and some of the portrayed ones seem to dance down out of their frames, some tumble out, some fight their way out, with fearful vitality. I can think of only one possible reason for anyone's not liking this book: just at the start the characters are almost too strong, one shrinks from them a little. No, you may say, I do not wish to spend another page with this smug glutton, or this hypochondriac drunkard, or this lachrymose widow; no, not another word out of that girl in the green dress! But presently, having read a certain number of pages, you feel a grudging sympathy with one and all, or a rueful empathy, or at least solidarity, as a human being.

Glenway Wescott. *At*. April, 1962. p. 48

Her contemptuous and morbid attitude toward human sexuality plays a large part in deflecting her sensibility to its incessant quarrel with human nature and in leading it by inevitable stages to a vision of life that is less vice and folly than a hideously choking slow death. For Miss Porter's versions of political action, artistic creation, religious belief, teaching, and so forth are no less skewed and embittered than her versions of copulation. Further, this clammy connection between sex and evil appears to rule out any feeling toward her characters other than a nagging exasperated irony, and to remove the possibility of any struggle toward deeper insight. As a result, the consciousness that is operating in the book, for all its range of view, is standing, so to speak, on a dime, and has little contact with the sources of imaginative vitality and moral power that renew a long work of fiction.

Theodore Solotaroff. *Cmty.* Oct., 1962. p. 286

Life—which to Miss Porter means personal relationships—is a hazardous affair, however cautiously we try to live it. We walk a tightrope, never more than a step away from possible disaster, so strong and so intimately connected with our need for other people are the primitive impulses of violence and egoism and so thin is the net of civilized behavior that is between us and the pit. Indeed, if in trying to civilize ourselves we have been trying to make order out of chaos, Miss Porter seems to be saying that we have succeeded only in becoming more systematically and efficiently, though less directly violent; the more definite and clear-cut the code by which we live and expect others to live, the more clearly even our ordinary actions reflect the violence that is only imperfectly submerged and that may erupt savagely and nakedly at any time.

Marjorie Ryan. *Critique.* Fall, 1962. p. 94

See also *Ship of Fools* (novel).

POWERS, J. F. (1917–   )

Even though the expert technique of these stories is as unemotional and photographic as the later Hemingway, consisting mainly of placing the model in a good clear light and shooting, the collection as a whole leaves one with the impression that the author has a disciplined distaste for materialism and bullying, and that he believes that these two traits account for most of the frustrations and woes of contemporary man, whether in the church or out of it.

Eunice S. Holsaert. *NYT.* May 4, 1947. p. 20

He avoids the stereo-typed two-dimensional layout, the affected obliquity which keeps everything on the same level, and the colorless neutrality which makes such an obvious pretense of "objectivity." He is unabashedly inside his story, focusing on objects, catching nuances for us, and heightening the volume when he wishes. . . . His perceptions are interesting not only for their acuteness but for the mass of dense particulars which they penetrate.

Henry Rago. Com. Aug. 22, 1947. pp. 457–8

Of all modern writers known to me who have dealt with Catholic religious life J. F. Powers . . . is far and away the best. He has his own peculiar technique for handling the subject. Unlike the sentimentalists and satirists, he rarely glances at religion itself, as though it were a light too strong for his eyes. He is interested mainly in the pettiness and vulgarity of a mechanical civilization. . . . After the darkness of so much American fiction this book (*The Presence of Grace*) produces a peculiar shock of delight. Having lived with Mr. Powers's first book, *Prince of Darkness,* for some years, I can testify that it is not a delight that disappears as the shock diminishes. Powers is among the greatest of living storytellers.

Frank O'Connor. SR. March 24, 1956. p. 22

Competitiveness is central in Powers's work, whether he is using the secular world or the tight world of the Church. . . . The competitive agitation leads to a distinctive developmental pattern in Powers's stories. Most typical is a centripetal movement that begins on the outskirts of things, with the inconspicuous, literal, mundane detail, and slowly whirls in toward a still point of revelation that in a sense negates all hierarchies. The protagonist is at least temporarily freed of the compulsion to maintain self, sees himself and others as victims of a condition endemic to humanity, glimpses and responds to a motivation that operates as an antidote—that is, there is a release from the pressure of self-interest, with the concomitant experiencing of compassion and even of love.

George Scouffas. Critique. Fall, 1958. p. 42

What made these stories so remarkable was maturity. American fiction is always striking an attitude or being "psychological" or just reporting the violence of some unusual experience. Mr. Powers's work was about a *world;* it constantly yielded literary vanity to the truth and depth of this world. He was subtle, funny, precise, and always unexpected. The book seemed to come out of a longer background than most young American writers of fiction ever own. . . . I admire Mr. Powers very much—story after story is worked out to the finest possible point; this is work that manages by fusing intelligence and compassion, to come out as humor.

There is real love in his heart, but he knows that the *heart* does not write short stories, and that the beauty of grace can appear only against the background of the horrid daily element, which is gravity.

Alfred Kazin. *Contemporaries* (Little). 1962. pp. 223–5

In this novel (*Morte D'Urban*), as in many of his best-known short stories, Powers writes about the Catholic Church with an air of great authority. He writes as an insider, though certainly not *for* insiders. The Order of St. Clement may be his invention, but it is as real as Yoknapatawpha County. Having created a little world of his own, with its particular beliefs and customs, he can write a comedy of manners. There are no dramatic incidents and no large issues, but we do have a quiet, steady revelation of character, a revelation superb in its subtlety and depth. . . . His faith permits him to look with tolerance on the foibles of good men and to recognize the virtues of bad ones.

Granville Hicks. *SR*. Sept. 15, 1962. p. 21

It seems pretty generally agreed that Satire Is Dead. I'm delighted to inform you that you must revise your opinion, because J. F. Powers has written a book (*Morte D'Urban*) which is satire in the pure sense—not a symbolic action in the manner of Joyce or Kafka, not a psychological comedy in the manner of Kingsley Amis or Peter de Vries, though all these can be turned to critical ends—but a pure satire which will nevertheless please the most sophisticated literary tastes. Powers has done something quite remarkable: he has revived the satire of the Great Age —from Erasmus to Swift, let's say, reverting to tradition—within a modern context of style and attitude. In fact, the stylishness almost—but not quite—obscures the point that his book is a classical satire against mankind based on the exploitation of types.

Hayden Carruth. *NR*. Sept. 24, 1962. p. 24

From the start, nearly twenty years ago now, when his writing began to excite the admiration of the readers of *Accent,* it was evident that the stories of J. F. Powers had a very special quality, a rare richness of theme and perception; and, for all their liberal zeal and satirical intent, often an even rarer gentleness of tone. . . . Powers's theme remains truly haunting; it is one that might be framed as a question: how can the spirit express itself in nature without compromise, without debasement, since one is so distant from the other, and each one is obedient to different laws? Again: can a mind manipulate its work in the world without becoming completely worldly itself? . . . Powers has found the formula for his fiction in all this. He regularly sees the priest in a worldly role. The necessity of this role makes Powers's satire kind. The contradictions implied make his irony deep.

William H. Gass. *Nation*. Sept. 29, 1962. pp. 182–3

The characters in *Morte D'Urban* have the tangibility that real people have for us in those rare moments when the fog of abstraction and self-absorption lifts, and they come illuminated out of the fog with Powers's rare combination of irony, sympathy and humor. . . . Yet the novel is not simply a gallery of memorable portraits; characters are revealed in action and interaction. Few writers today have as acute a sense of the drama of interpersonal relations as Powers has. . . . *Morte D'Urban* is not simply an anecdotal display of a central character by a writer whose ear for American speech is as good as O'Hara's; in it character and theme are dramatized in a significant complex. . . . It is Powers's version of that most Christian of ironies: the Fortunate Fall.

John P. Sisk. *Critique*. Winter, 1962–3. pp. 101–2

Powers's is a world of the living all too living, and only in such a world can the ethical consideration bear much weight. For the purposes of fiction, he effects a divorce between faith and morals. The question is not whether faith, in the measure his characters have it, makes them greatly better or greatly worse than those outside the fold. The question is whether those inside the fold can sustain the moral life at the level of average good will, self-respect, and taste. If this approach is necessary to Powers as a moral realist, it is also congenial to him as a story teller; and his love of narration in all shapes, sizes and degrees of seriousness is obvious. Stories within stories, ranging from rectory-table anecdotes through biblical parables to scraps of radio serials caught from the airwaves, thicken the fictional atmosphere. Each sentence tends to be an event; yet every event, like every firm but fluent sentence, is an open door into the next half-expected, half-shocking encounter. Thus does J. F. Powers coax stories out of the shabby rectories of his not altogether mythical Minnesota.

F. W. Dupee. *PR*. Spring, 1963. p. 114

The Prince of Darkness and *The Presence of Grace*, necessary preliminaries to *Morte D'Urban*, have few faults and present less of the big world than Powers's novel. *Morte D'Urban* is not woven tightly; it overuses narrative bridges; it hurries its concluding section; it sometimes exhibits an overindulgence in clever ambiguities; its experiments with the play form within a novel achieve the partial success that calls attention to technical dexterity rather than to the heart of the matter. Yet these faults seem slight flaws as I think back over the experiences of reading the novel.

Err though he may, Powers *has* gone on from the smaller provinces where a cat whimsically evaluates or outwits a priest, even beyond the short importance of a good Franciscan's death with his "will amenable to the divine," beautiful though it may be. Here is J. F. Powers's large world, fully peopled with the Clementines he invented and those they contend against and try to tend and live with. Here, fully imagined, is the tragic and comic world where Father Urban lives within, above, and beneath his own and the Order's scheme of values, forgetting and remembering and learning about the God who gives him rein and pulls him to heel.

Harvey Curtis Webster. *KR*. Winter, 1963. p. 167

See *The Prince of Darkness* and *The Presence of Grace* (short stories) and *Morte D'Urban* (novel).

ROTH, PHILIP (1933–   )

It's not far from Newark to Short Hills—or from the Bronx to Westchester—but the gap is sometimes unbridgeable, no matter how steep a toll one is prepared to pay. It is about the middle-class Jewish residents of both these worlds that Philip Roth writes in his first book, *Goodbye, Columbus.* . . . Philip Roth surveys the role of the Jew in modern American society with keen perception. Underlying his stories is the Jews' century-old tragic sense of life, leavened with warmth and humor, and with compassion. There are no excesses of sentimentality or bitterness: his characters cannot be typed as either Molly Goldbergs or Sammy Glicks.

If there is any doubt in my mind, it concerns the validity of these stories for the non-Jewish, or even the non-Eastern, reader. For so much depends on a familiarity with the peculiarly parochial surroundings and the subtle speech inflections.

Arnold Dolin. *SR*. May 16, 1959. p. 31

In some ways Jews may be thin-skinned and sensitive but in others they have a capacity to mock themselves mercilessly. That is why there are so many superb comedians among them. That is also why their best writers have written of them with an awareness of the thin line between the ludicrous and the pathetic, the comic and the tragic. Among those who have recently exploited this vein is Bernard Malamud. Now Philip Roth joins this company with a short novel and five short stories . . . marked by a comic, almost a caricaturist's, view of character, and effects that are at once funny and dreadful. At his most serious he has an original and most disturbing capacity for converting farce into nightmare.

Milton Rugoff. *NYHT*. May 17, 1959. p. 3

What many writers spend a lifetime searching for—a unique voice, a secure rhythm, a distinctive subject—seem to have come to Philip Roth totally and immediately. At 26 he is a writer of narrow range but intense effects. He composes stories about the life of middle-class American Jews with a ferocity it would be idle to complain about, so thoroughly do they pour out of his own sense of things.

Mr. Roth's stories do not yield pleasure as much as produce a squirm of recognition: surely one feels, not all of American Jewish life is like this, but all too much is becoming so. Anyone who might object to these stories insofar as they are "reports" about a style of life cannot do it on the ground that Mr. Roth is hard-spirited—for given his material what else can he be?—or that he is unskilled—for, like so many other young writers these days, he has quickly absorbed the lessons of modern crafts-manship, perhaps a bit too quickly. If one is to object to these stories on non-literary grounds, out of a concern for the feelings or reputation of middle-class American Jews, it can be done only by charging that, in effect, Mr. Roth is a liar. And that, I am convinced, he is not.

Irving Howe. *NR*. June 15, 1959. p. 17

Goodbye, Columbus is a first book but it is not the book of a beginner. Unlike those of us who came howling into the world, blind and bare, Mr. Roth appears with nails, hair, and teeth, speaking coherently. At twenty-six he is skillful, witty, and energetic and performs like a virtuoso. His one fault, and I don't expect all the brethren to agree that it is a fault, is that he is so very sophisticated. Sometimes he twinkles too much. The *New York Times* has praised him for being "wry." One such word to the wise ought to be sufficient. Mr. Roth has a superior sense of humor (see his story "Epstein"), and I think he can count on it more safely than on his "wryness."

Saul Bellow. *Cmty*. July, 1959. p. 77

The best of the *New Yorker* story writers, like John Cheever, always make me feel that, keen as they are, there is a whole side to their observa-tions of American society that is entirely fantastic, imaginative, almost visionary, and so belongs to themselves alone. Roth, though emphatically not tailored to the *New Yorker,* involuntarily fits it because of a certain excess of intellectual theme over the material. There are too many sym-bols of present-day society, too many quotable bright sayings; the stories tend too easily to make a point. . . . I admire the edge and fierceness of Mr. Roth's mind, but his book (*Goodbye, Columbus*) leaves me worried about his future. For he has put so much of himself into being clear, decisive, straight, his stories are consciously so brave, that I worry whether he hasn't worked himself too neatly into a corner. He shows himself too anxious in each story not only to dramatize a conflict but also to make the issue of the conflict absolutely clear.

Alfred Kazin. *Contemporaries* (Little). 1962. pp. 261–2

That Roth is a careful observer and has a good ear is known to every reader of *Goodbye, Columbus,* but these gifts can be abused, and in the novel (*Letting Go*) Roth has abused them. Line by line the writing is fine, but that does not save long stretches from being unpardonably dull and quite superfluous. . . . What the book seems to demonstrate is not that contemporary civilization is a disaster but that many people manage to mess up their lives—which isn't news. . . . Let me make it clear that Roth is still a figure to be reckoned with. This is the kind of bad book that only a good writer could have written. But, after *Goodbye, Columbus,* with its vitality and sureness of touch, *Letting Go* is a disappointment.

Granville Hicks. *SR*. June 16, 1962. p. 16

Letting Go is not just a book that displays the virtues of *Goodbye, Columbus* at far greater length. It is also a deliberate and almost too fully achieved realization of the sense of life that Mr. Roth shares to a large extent with his whole generation and in very obvious ways with such writers as Saul Bellow, Harvey Swados, and William Styron (and with Jack Kerouac, too, who provides an unintentional parody of it). This sense of life is oddly self-conscious and limited, despite the talent and insight of these writers, as if they had spent more of their lives with the *Paris Review* crowd or in Iowa City or some similar "creative writing" center than was good for them as writers. It is almost exclusively personal. There is a great deal about the public life in these writers, but they always see that life as an unjustifiable, inexplicable—if immovable—obstacle to the realization of the private self, which is inexhaustibly queried, analyzed and suffered over by everyone in their books, as it might be in some incredibly brilliant soap opera or undergraduate short story.

Arthur Mizener. *NYT*. June 17, 1962. p. 1

If there is any fault with this novel (*Letting Go*), it is that Mr. Roth is too lavish with his gifts. His talent for swift and concise characterization is such that he tends to bring minor characters unnecessarily into the foreground of the action. The result is that the book becomes too diffuse. In a few remarkable pages near the beginning he has given us Paul and Libby to the life; we know the kind of history they will have, and we hardly need the remorseless accumulation of detail with which Mr. Roth follows their fortunes. Complex as their personalities are, their life together is too threadbare and starveling to carry the weight of a saga.

William Barrett. *At*. July, 1962. p. 111

Perhaps it would have been as well for Philip Roth if he hadn't been cited again and again as a leading member of the new school of American-Jewish novelists. Without so portentous a label hung round his neck, he might never have been lured into writing such tawdry, incoherent stuff. . . . Writers like Bellow and Malamud derive their blend of warmth and irony both from the intensity of the past, and from their ambiguous relationship with that past. From Jewish experience they abstract a metaphor for 20th century man: rueful, displaced, tragi-comic. Mr. Roth has borrowed a few externals from this tradition, but his high-gloss prose suggests another line of descent. He really belongs with a very different group of American-Jewish writers, the slick professionals like Irwin Shaw, Jerome Weidman, or even Herman Wouk.

John Gross. *NSN*. Nov. 30, 1962. p. 784

What grieves Roth most is the awareness that normalcy has, like a Procrustes' bed, truncated the range of life, excluding on the one hand the embrace of aspiration, the exhilaration of wonder, and on the other the acceptance of suffering. From this sadness grows Roth's ferocity, directly mainly against those who deny life, against the cowards who fear it, against all who would reduce it to safe insignificance, against all who flee from self and suffering—to seek repose is a travesty of all the realities of life and the potential of man. Roth is committed to his unheroic heroes who yearn and aspire, who want to climb out of the morass "up the long marble stairs that led to Tahiti."

Joseph C. Landis. *MR*. Winter, 1962. p. 261

See *Goodbye, Columbus* (stories) and *Letting Go* (novel).

SALINGER, J. D.

He has always been open, of course, to the charge of being soft-centered. To youth and laziness he promises a release into the utopia where every difficulty and agony is understood to be a result of the barbaric insensitivity of Others; at the heart of his myth lies the conviction that no one of merit ought to *work,* that all truly decent folk spring full-brained from the womb and therefore need only to master a few great texts of anti-knowledge—weapons with which to belabor knaves and scholars. Putting it another way: the world of most Salinger stories connects (in its assumptions) not with the general world but with those odd communities that grow up around conservatories and museum schools—societies in which youngsters who haven't read a word of Shakespeare or Spinoza argue violently about Wilhelm Reich or Edmund Begler, M.D., pleasingly pleased with themselves.

Benjamin De Mott. *HdR*. Winter, 1961–2. pp. 626–7

Salinger offers no difficult visions; he's guaranteed not to disturb. He permits his reader to eat his cake and have it too—secure in the knowledge that he deserves better cake, but there is none to be had. Salinger is not concerned with genuine (or at least, possible) alternatives to the values and life-styles he deplores. His technique for handling the individual vs. society situation is simply to divide the world between the sensitive few and the vulgar many. You, my reader, he assures us, belong to an elite —not because you want to live differently, but because you are sensitive. You have religious experiences, you have special affinities with little girls, you can't stand phonies, you *understand*. You are so sensitive it's a wonder you go on. In fact, Salinger implies, *you are a hero and your heroism is not based on heroic action but on mere existence*.

Jeremy Larner. *PR*. Fall, 1962. p. 597

Before the present volume (*Franny and Zooey*), Salinger had always presented madness as a special temptation of males; perhaps because, in the myth he was elaborating, it is a female image of innocence that, at the last moment, lures his almost-lost protagonists back from the brink of insanity: a little girl typically, pre-pubescent and therefore immune to the world's evil, which, in his work, fully nubile women tend to embody. The series which begins with "Esme" goes on through "A Perfect Day for Banana-fish," where the girl-savior appears too late to save Seymour, oldest of the Glass family; and reaches an appropriate climax in *Catcher in the Rye,* where the savior is the little sister and the myth achieves its final form. It is the Orestes-Iphigenia story, we see there, that Salinger all along has been trying to rewrite, the account of a Fury-haunted brother redeemed by his priestess-sister; though Salinger demotes that sister in age, thus downgrading the tone of the legend from tragic to merely pathetic.

Leslie Fiedler. *PR*. Winter, 1962. p. 130

How did Salinger get hung up on the idea that the Glass menage had to produce a Messiah? It's not really his line of work at all. His concern from the first was with the incoherently, callowly genuine; and with this theme he made excellent fun. But to be a prophet in the wilderness, Saint Salinger Cornishhensis, he simply isn't equipped; he's got nostalgia, he's got confusion, but he has neither faith nor the structured intellect which properly produces it. Having promised a revelation for so long, he's more or less bound to oblige; and the sort of mouse his mountains are liable to yield may be guessed from the wretched rodent that squeaks forth at the end of *Seymour, an Introduction*.

Robert M. Adams. *PR*. Spring, 1963. p. 129

See also *Franny and Zooey* and *Raise High the Roof Beams, Carpenters* (each two stories).

UPDIKE, JOHN (1932–   )

Leaving the contrapuntal music of the poets, the invitation is to hear a young man in a lonely pasture play the ocarina. He plays it exceedingly well; and should you wish to hear it again tomorrow you may suddenly find that his notes have overtones which at first escaped you, that his seemingly disparate little airs are somehow interrelated, and that now and then his music is coming at you from all directions, the way the sound of a winter wren in Canada will flood the valley. You should have your wits about you too, for the player is obviously an unusual individual who deserves but does not ask for an unusual audience. . . . [John Updike] has developed a maturity of technique; and in almost every instance he approaches an idea with the wariness of a sportsman after woodcock. Furthermore, he is a graceful border-crosser (light verse to poem) as Auden has been; as Betjeman and McGinley frequently are.

David McCord. *SR*. Aug. 9, 1958. p. 32

John Updike is a poet; his prose is lean and lapidary—in some cases almost engineered, like a fine, jeweled watch. Its unfragile delicacy is exactly what is needed to convey his insights whole, as in a picture or a poem. The abused word "artistry" may be here correctly applied. . . . It is a world seen neither with the brain nor the heart—or the guts—but with the understanding eye of the caring nonparticipant. It is characterized by a perceptive delicacy in which emotion is implied—as sound is implicit in a taut but unplucked string. The prime operative factor is, perhaps, a kind of genteel—almost stylish—super-awareness, with elegantly conveyed insights taking the place of events.

A. C. Spectorsky. *SR*. Aug. 22, 1959. pp. 15, 31

We are in a necessary period of non-solution in the novel, of anti-literature, which is essentially a resistance to tying neat knots, offering explanations, coming up with big solid counterweights to the miseries of life, providing alternative existences such as have come more and more to be demanded of fiction, that is to say, heroes to whom the reader can latch on and be carried right out of his mean, stifling *nonliterary* days and years. Updike, like the new French *alittérateurs,* doesn't want the novel to perpetuate itself as a compensation, a branch of philosophy or a rival of science, a *way out.* . . . *Rabbit, Run* gives off little of the air of implementing a plan which mars some of the work of Alain Robbe-Grillet or Nathalie Sarraute, for example. But it is all theorem or at least nothing else is there, no tying together of loose threads, no conclusions you can put on a shelf, no road-maps, no reinforcement of attitudes or beliefs. Only a distinguished balancing-act over a void, a major image of precarious life being true to itself.

Richard Gilman. Com. Oct. 28, 1960. p. 128

Updike frequently gives the impression that he has six or seven senses, all of them operating at full strength, and his writing is an attempt to register as precisely and originally as possible all the intelligence these senses send him. Struggling for a kind of hyperexpression, he mints an unceasing flow of almost invariably surprising images, which he then molds into uncluttered phrases, sentences, paragraphs, and pages that move with a sense of rhythm, timing, timbre, and volume that is impeccable. An irresistible tension is set up—a verbal rather than a narrative tension—and the reader immediately becomes a part of it, a trick dog who willingly sees, hears, smells, and feels exactly what Updike commands him to.

Whitney Balliett. NY. Nov. 5, 1960. p. 222

Despite the cleverness of his verse and the possibly overcivilized restraint of his fiction, Updike avoids a simple facile sophistication through his acute awareness of the "dislocations of modern life" and his religious sensitivity. A professed Congregationalist deeply familiar with theological and speculative problems, this Janus-faced writer combines a startling literacy, stylistic virtuosity, wit, and a profound melancholy in a way that is almost Joycean in quality.

Evelyn Geller. WLB. Sept., 1961. p. 67

Updike is not merely talented; he is bold, resourceful, and intensely serious.

His seriousness is not immediately apparent because he so often chooses to work with materials that seem slight and commonplace. . . . He is a most redoubtable explorer of the mysteries of the commonplace. . . . One of Updike's characters asks, "What is the past, after all, but a vast sheet of darkness in which a few moments, pricked apparently at random, shine?"

Updike's aim is to preserve certain of these moments, not out of nostalgia but because they give meaning to life. His Jamesian eagerness to let no experience be wasted is heightened by his sense of impermanence.

Granville Hicks. *SR*. March 17, 1962. p. 21

There is in John Updike's writing the kind of visceral understanding that can whiten a world to being in the flicker of a phrase or in a sudden crackle of speech. . . . He understands—better than foundries of sociological discourse can ever understand—the arcane folk rituals of adolescence. . . . And because John Updike writes of a more representative American experience, he tells us something other than what that fellow chronicler of the young, J. D. Salinger, tells us. For if Salinger reflects what the young would like to be, Updike tells us what they are.

Richard W. Murphy. *Horizon*. March, 1962. p. 84

Like the stories, the novels come close to being mere delicate restatements of the great current theme of isolation: millions of throbbing souls seeking fulfillment, identity, and, alas, happiness through love. Updike avoids reiterating the commonplace neurosis mainly because he is talented and intelligent. Also he is quiet and restrained. He has a commonsense perception of the ridiculous in things, and he is true to his personal vision. Ultimately the common thread running through all his works is the location of the human disease in the ego. But if we are all trapped in ourselves, unenlightened idealists in a real world, we are inevitably so. Except for old Hook in *The Poorhouse Fair* and a few matter-of-fact but terribly limited women, the people in the Updike world not only cannot communicate with each other, but they feel no need to.

J. A. Ward. *Critique*. Spring-Summer, 1962. p. 29

Updike shares with Agee a prickly, almost painful sensitivity to objects and relationships and a gift for precise and vivid prose. . . . With prose as sharp as music and jagged as rocks, Mr. Updike writes about the first furtive sexual explorations and drugstore obscenities of the adolescent. The ground is familiar enough, but the familiar is constantly undergoing transformation by his extraordinary perception. Events like a high-school basketball game or the manipulation of a pin-ball machine by a delinquent "with an absolute purity of ambitionlessness" become, somehow, occasions of significance and even of beauty.

Updike brings to fiction unusual powers of vision and style and accommodates these powers to a wide range of effects. Sometimes he writes in a vein of intense fantasy reminiscent of Dylan Thomas's unfinished *Adventures in the Skin Trade*, at others with the comic hypertension that is found in Kingsley Amis's novels at their best.

Peter Buitenhuis. *NYT*. April 7, 1963. p. 4

Now . . . it should begin to be clear how Updike is commenting not only beautifully but also meaningfully on our times. The baroque grandeur of Faulkner's world and the chivalric simplicity of Hemingway's seem far removed from the mainstream of American life as the second half of the twentieth century churns along; so indeed, do the rarified ruminations of J. D. Salinger's fragile Glasses. Updike, by contrast, is writing about something rather more pertinent—how most of us really live in this depressing sort of a world.

Does it follow, as *Time* and Updike's other detractors suggest, that small people necessarily have small problems?

The people Updike has written about . . . are enmeshed in the desperate facts of their condition. Their problems are just that—the desperation of their condition from which there is no ready escape. By weight of numbers alone, these problems take on a towering dimension, and one measure of Updike's achievement, it seems to me, is the quantity of joy and dignity he is able to detect in these drab existences without denying that very drabness.

Richard Kluger. *NYHT*. April 7, 1963. p. 8

See *The Carpentered Hen* (poems), *Pigeon Feathers* and *Same Door* (short stories) and *The Poorhouse Fair, Rabbit, Run* and *The Centaur* (novels).

WARREN, ROBERT PENN

In reading Warren's fiction and poetry I often have the sense that this theme of "the true life," of the necessary contradiction between man's nature and man's values, offers an image of stoical struggle that is necessary to Warren. He refuses the sanctions of orthodox Christianity, which proclaim spiritual values as absolute truths, and the naturalistic interpretation of values as pragmatically necessary to man. For Warren values are something that man *insists* on heroically and arbitrarily in the face of everything. There is no *system* of values that he believes in; there is only the last-ditch faith in values themselves as they emerge through the activity of literature. At the heart of literature is the essential faculty of poetic imagination, which works through symbols that are recollections of our ancient connections with a spiritual world.

Alfred Kazin. *PR*. Spring, 1959. p. 315

Warren's right to be regarded as an intellectual is indisputable; he is a formidable and influential critic; he has won general recognition as a poet;

he has taught at some of our best institutions. Moreover, from the point of view of either structure or style, his novels could serve as texts in writing courses. . . . Even the most skeptical of his critics, I suppose, would agree that Warren's fundamental intentions as a novelist are completely serious. He simply tries, as nineteenth-century novelists commonly tried and twentieth-century novelists commonly don't try, to entertain the reader who is looking merely for entertainment and at the same time to reward one who is willing to make some effort of intellect and imagination. . . . He tells a story and the story is fascinating in its own right, but it is not for the story's sake that he tells it. All his skill as a story-teller—his mastery of narrative form, his wonderfully racy style—serves his real purpose. He is concerned with the deepest realities of the human spirit.

Granville Hicks. *SR*. Aug. 22, 1959. p. 13

The theme that has principally exercised his imagination is that of the "incompleteness" of man, the struggle to reconcile the idea and the need of unity with the facts of multiplicity in human experience. He has, on the one hand, an immense fascination with the varieties of human possibility, with man becoming. But, opposed to this—Warren's formulation of the problem is, I think, basically a moral one—there is the old Hawthornian, post-Puritan hatred of hypocrisy, the profound feeling that man, a man, should be what he seems. And it is from this opposition that the peculiar tension of his fiction derives—the conflict between the psychological and merely sensual, human richness of the story, with its endless complications of mere plot, that threatens continually to get out of hand, and the continually and rather desperately reimposed philosophical order, the precarious balancing of antinomies.

John Edward Hardy. *VQR*. Autumn, 1960. pp. 587–8

Warren's typically personal view rejects the state worship and general dehumanization which he associates with giantism in industry and pyramided cities. Yet his special agrarianism cannot abide either that naïve optimism, kin to the frontier dream of perpetually renewed innocence, which sprang from Jeffersonian neglect of man's dark ancestry.

These broad themes emerge with all the conviction that fullness of style at once intense and delicate can provide. They have been grounded by Warren in everyday particulars of a South which lends itself to metaphor and metaphysical expansion. . . . The excruciating self-consciousness and willful complexity of the South, its ferment of tensions, its acceptance of complicity (even its rejection of the Negro often seems motivated less by denial of guilt than by fear of retribution)—these provide Warren with handy symbols for the fate of the modern self, subsectioned by Freud and indexed in depth by Jung. The malices of society are used to dramatize the inward twist of shadows in any man, anywhere.

Leonard Casper. Robert Penn Warren: The Dark
and Bloody Ground (U. of Washington). 1960. pp. 6–8

See also *You, Emperor, and Others* (poetry).

WILLIAMS, TENNESSEE

In his continued self-analysis Williams makes use of standard dream symbols—largely sexual. Added to these are personal symbols. The playwright is at his best when he is creating symbols out of situations rather than superimposing them or hauling in irrelevant or traditional ones. One of Tennessee Williams's outstanding talents is his ability to see his life and his world metaphorically. The most exciting Williams symbols are those fashioned from his own experience.

The author's enthusiasm for metaphor and symbolism comes partially from modern psychology and partially from an enduring regard for the French symbolist poets. . . . The use of symbolist atmosphere and musical accompaniment provides stimulating contrasts to the realism of his characterization and dialogue. Because his sense of theatre restricts him to a basic realism, he seldom allows the atmosphere of his plays to thin out into a symbolist fog. It has been hard for Williams to use other influences effectively, but in his use of symbolism his talent and his literary tastes are happily united.

Nancy M. Tischler. Tennessee Williams:
Rebellious Puritan (Citadel). 1961. pp. 294–5

The universe is the great antagonist in Tennessee Williams. It is as malignant as it is implacable. It has, through time, destroyed a way of life and a tradition that once meant civilization and has evolved a society that is grasping, repressive and destructive. Anything that was honorable is gone and the codes of the past have become anachronistic and ridiculous in the present. The standard bearers of this tradition are hopelessly inadequate in a world which calls for Jim O'Connor's "zzzzzzzzzp!" and yet if there is to be any meaning in life it will have to come, Williams is saying, from the codes and traditions which his ragged cavaliers and tattered ladies are waving in the face of impending darkness.

This is the credo of the romantic, the cry of Don Quixote charging the windmills and Lord Byron making his final stand for Greek independence. But if Williams devoutly believes in the romantic revolt against the Philistines, he has no illusions about the triumph of this insurrection. While sympathizing with his romantics he is at the same time able to see and understand the futility of their quest. Williams is the romantic and the realist, and his best work is marked by this important juxtaposition of beliefs.

> Benjamin Nelson. *Tennessee Williams: The Man and His Work* (Ivan Obolensky). 1961. pp. 288–9

It is from [the] conflict between the need to condemn and the desire to pardon that the weakness of Williams's work stems, for it is ironically the strength of his moral temper that forces him to censure what he wishes to exalt. Williams is passionately committed to the great Romantic dictum inherent in his neo-Lawrentian point of view, that the natural equals the good, that the great natural instincts that well up out of the subconscious depths of men—and particularly the sexual instinct, whatever form it may take—are to be trusted absolutely. But Williams is too strong a moralist, far too permeated with a sense of sin, to be able to accept such an idea with equanimity. However pathetic he may make the martyred homosexual, however seemingly innocent the wandering love-giver, the moral strength that led Williams to punish the guilty Blanche impels him to condemn Brick and Chance. But because he is condemning what he most desires to pardon, he must sometimes in order to condemn at all, do so with ferocious violence.

> Arthur Ganz. *AS*. Spring, 1962. p. 294

Though Williams has not, so far as I know, delivered himself of a single pronouncement on the question of integration, though his signature is never to be found on a petition or a full-page ad in the New York *Times,* he seems to have located the trouble spots more precisely than Arthur Miller, for instance, who deals so conscientiously with social questions. Williams is American in his passion for absolutes, in his longing for purity, in his absence of ideas, in the extreme discomfort with which he inhabits his own body and soul, in his apocalyptic vision of sex, which like all apocalyptic visions sacrifices mere accuracy for the sake of intensity. Intensity is the crucial quality of Williams's art, and he is perhaps most an American artist in his reliance upon and mastery of surface techniques for achieving this effect.

> Marion Magid. *Cmty*. Jan., 1963. p. 35

WILLIAMS, WILLIAM CARLOS

I have emphasized Williams's simplicity and nakedness and have no doubt been misleading. His idiom comes from many sources, from speech and reading, both of various kinds; the blend which in his own invention is generous and even exotic. Few poets can come near to his wide clarity and dashing rightness with words, his dignity and almost Alexandrian modulations of voice. His short lines often speed up and simplify hugely drawn out and ornate sentence structures. I once typed out his direct but densely observed poem, "The Semblables," in a single prose paragraph. Not a word or its placing had been changed, but the poem had changed into a piece of smothering, magnificent rhetoric, much more like Faulkner than the original Williams.

Robert Lowell. HdR. Winter, 1961–2. p. 534

In Williams we have a poet who refuses to belittle the American genius for mechanical inventiveness; who developed the concept of a poem machine to achieve artistic expression in the American idiom; but who sees at the same time the moral and spiritual toll it has exacted from our culture because we have made a machine-world geared to such high speed and efficiency that we are losing our ability to see and touch the simple, the natural. It is for this reason Williams would make St. Francis of Assisi our patron saint. He asks us to realize our humanity in the scientific age. He sees the objective poem, in which the poet like the linguistic scientist has put his speech to the test of human need, as a means toward that goal. "But before I extol too much and advocate the experimental method," he warns, "let me emphasize that, like God's creation, the objective is not experimentation but *man*. In our case, poems!"

Mary Ellen Solt. MR. Winter, 1962. p. 317

It is Dr. Williams's distinction that he is willing to incur time and again the enormous risk of dispensing with the protections poetry has traditionally devised for itself. Eschewal of safety, in fact, has come to seem to him a matter of honour. He will have no special vocabulary, around which common speech has learned to tiptoe; he will not suffer attention to be lulled by a metric of recurrences; there are not even privileged subjects to which the poem addresses itself, or approved planes of consciousness on which it functions. The Williams poem at the first word takes its life in its hands and launches itself from a precipice, submitting itself to accelerations it does not seek to control, and trusting its own capacity for intimate torsions to guide it into the water unharmed. It is not surprising that so many of his poems get shattered; the miracle is that he succeeds with half his attempts, that indeed he ever succeeds. For the gravitational field to which he entrusts his poems is the enveloping tug of impassioned daily speech, which precipitates into a void whatever it gets hold of.

Hugh Kenner. MR. Winter, 1962. p. 328

William Carlos Williams may well turn out to be one of the most significant writers of our time. . . . It would be easy to say, as some have already said, that Williams, like Walt Whitman, loves life—sees all that his eyes will let him see and shrinks from none of it, lovingly presenting the whole in inconspicuous language. But this would be to talk sentimentally about a writer who is almost never guilty of sentimentality. . . . Williams simply has no sense of a capacity for contamination. He treats the flesh with respect because he seems to believe that flesh, even at its worst, has a capacity for dignity; and under the term *flesh* he would include not only people but dogs, chickens, rocks, pine trees, and wet ferns.

Yet if this were all Williams had, he would be neither a good writer nor a good physician. He would merely be avoiding the other kind of sentimentality that those writers are guilty of who speak glibly of the autonomy of the word. In fact, one gets the impression from reading these stories that one liberates the other: the word becomes respectable for serving as the matrix by which the object is made knowable, and the marriage of the two means a generation of love for both.

J. A. Bryant, Jr. SwR. Winter, 1963. p. 121

William Carlos Williams, poet and physician. Trained to crises of sickness and parturition that often came at odd hours. An ebullient man, sorely vexed in his last years, and now at rest. But he had this exceptional good luck: that his appeal as a person survives in his work. To read his books is to find him warmly there, everywhere you turn.

In some respects, the physician and the poet might be viewed as opposites, as they certainly were at least in the sense that time spent on his patients was necessarily time denied to the writing of poetry. But that's a superficial view. . . . The point is this: For Williams any natural or poetic concern with the body as a sexual object was reinforced and notably modified by a professional concern with the body as a suffering or diseased object. . . . The same relation to the human animal in terms of bodily disabilities led him to a kind of democracy quite unlike Whitman's, despite the obvious influence of Whitman upon him.

Kenneth Burke. NYR. Spring, 1963. p. 45

INDEX TO CRITICS

See page 618 for Index to Supplement.

ABBOTT, Herbert Vaughan
Hearn, 222

ADAMIC, Louis
Jeffers, 258

ADAMS, Franklin P.
Lardner, 278; Parker, 373

ADAMS, J. Donald
Hersey, 232; Howells, 240; Roberts, E., 400

ADAMS, Leonie
Bogan, 68

ADAMS, Phoebe
Kerouac, 267

ADAMS, Robert
Wilson, 540

AIKEN, Conrad
Bodenheim, 65; Dickinson, 134; Eberhart, 151; Fletcher, 190; Gregory, 215; Lowell, A., 297; MacLeish, 309; Santayana, 423; Shapiro, 443

ALBRECHT, W. P.
Wolfe, 549

ALDEN, Henry M.
Howells, 238; Twain, 491

ALDINGTON, Richard
Pound, 380

ALDRIDGE, John W.
Bellow, 46; Burns, 88; Cowley, 111; Farrell, 166; Morris, 355; Shaw, 448; Styron, 473

ALEXANDER, Sidney
Kantor, 266

ALGREN, Nelson
Dreiser, 149; Farrell, 166

ALLEN, Charles
Porter, 380

AMES, Van Meter
Santayana, 420

AMSTER, Leonard
Bowles, 71

ANDERSON, Charles R.
Warren, 505

ANDERSON, Maxwell
Sherwood, 451

ANDERSON, Quentin
James, 254

ANDERSON, Sherwood
Lewis, 283; Sandburg, 417

ANGOFF, Charles
Hersey, 233; Mencken, 333

ARCHER, William
Santayana, 424

ARNETT, Willard E.
Santayana, 422

ARNOW, Harriette
Richter, 398

ARROWSMITH, William
Bishop, J., 60; Hersey, 234

ARVIN, Newton
Benét, 47; Howells, 239; Mencken, 330; Sandburg, 419; Santayana, 424; Van Doren, 497

ASHBERRY, John
Stein, 464

ASWELL, Edward C.
Wolfe, 548

ATKINS, Elizabeth
Millay, 336

ATKINS, John
Hemingway, 229

ATKINSON, Brooks
Williams, T., 532

AUDEN, W. H.
Brooks, C., 76; Roethke, 407

BACON, Leonard
Howard, 236

BACON, Martha
Sarton, 430

BAILEY, Robeson
Benét, 50

BAKER, Carlos
Capote, 98; Hemingway, 231

BALAKIAN, Nona
Saroyan, 428

BALDWIN, Charles C.
Anderson, S., 18

BARO, Gene
Jones, 261; Salinger, 414; Stafford, 458

BARR, Donald
Goyen, 213; Jackson, 246; Salinger, 415

BARRETT, William
Miller, H., 345

BARRIE, J. M.
James, 251

BARRY, Iris
Capote, 97; March, 319; Pound, 382

BARZUN, Jacques
James, 252

BATES, Ernest Sutherland
Barnes, 35

BAYM, Max I.
Adams, 1

BEACH, Joseph Warren
Caldwell, 94; Stegner, 459

BECKER, Carl
Adams, 4

BELLOW, Saul
Behrman, 42

BENDER, R. J.
Fisher, V., 182

BENDINER, Robert
Van Druten, 499

BENEDICT, Ruth
Hersey, 232

BENÉT, Rosemary
Marquand, 323; Thurber, 483

BENÉT, Stephen Vincent
Marquand, 323; Thurber, 483

BENÉT, William, Rose
Hayes, 219; Kantor, 264; Kreymborg, 273; Lewis, 284; Masters, 328; Moody, 347; Patchen, 375

BENSON, Arthur Christopher
James, 250

BENTLEY, Eric
O'Neill, 370; Warren, 504; Williams, T., 533

BENTLEY, Phyllis
Buck, 81

BERRYMAN, John
Brooks, C., 77 Fitzgerald, F., 186

BETTINGER, B. E.
Roberts, K., 402

BIANCHI, Martha Dickinson
Dickinson, 133

BISBEE, Thayer Donovan
Marquand, 324

BISHOP, John Peale
Cummings, 132; Fearing, 175; Fisher, V., 181; Fitzgerald, F., 183; Hemingway, 227; Patchen, 375; Tate, 479; Van Doren, 495; Wolfe, 550

BITTNER, William
West, 516

BLACKMAN, Ruth Chapin
Malamud, 317

BLACKMUR, R. P.
Adams, 3; Aiken, 11; Brooks, C., 77; Crane, H., 117; Cummings, 128; Dickinson, 135; Doolittle, 138; Eliot, 159; Fletcher, 191; James, 253; Moody, 348; Pound, 383; Winters, 544

BLAKE, Howard
Crane, H., 119

BLANKENSHIP, Russell
Lindsay, 290; Lowell, A., 298

BLAU, Herbert
Ginsberg, 205

BODE, Carl
  Cummings, 129
BODENHEIM, Maxwell
  Pound, 381
BOGAN, Louise
  Lowell, R., 302; Porter, 378;
  Viereck, 502; Welty, 508; Whar-
  ton, 520
BOIE, Mildred
  Rukeyser, 412
BONTEMPS, Arna
  Cullen, 126; Hughes, 243
BOWEN, Elizabeth
  Sarton, 429
BOWER-SHORE, Clifford
  Saroyan, 54
BOYD, Ernest
  Lewis, 283
BOYNTON, Percy
  Bierce, 52; Cabell, 91; Cather,
  102; Hearn, 223; Masters, 327;
  Robinson, 406
BRACE, Marjorie
  Taylor, 480
BRADBURY, John M.
  Warren, 505
BRADY, Charles A.
  Capote, 95
BRADY, Mildred Edie
  Miller, H., 342
BRANCH, Edgar Marquess
  Twain, 493
BRANTLEY, Frederick
  Roethke, 408; Warren, 507
BREIT, Harvey
  Agee, 6; Bellow, 43; Capote, 96;
  Hemingway, 229; Jackson, 247;
  Patchen, 375; Schulberg, 434; Sty-
  ron, 474; Warren, 505
BRICKELL, Herschel
  Fisher, V., 180; Tate, 479; Welty,
  509

BRIDGES, Horace James
  Lewisohn. 288
BRINNIN, John Malcolm
  Eberhart, 151; Fitzgerald, R., 189;
  Rukeyser, 412
BRINTON, Crane
  Viereck, 503
BRITTEN, Florence Haxton
  West, 514
BROMFIELD, Louis
  Richter, 397
BRONSON, John
  Fisher, V., 180
BROOKS, Cleanth
  Bishop, J., 59
BROOKS, John
  Auchincloss, 23; Kerouac, 266
BROOKS, Robert C.
  London, 293
BROOKS, Van Wyck
  Bierce, 52; Dreiser, 148; Heming-
  way, 228; Howells, 240; James,
  251; Lowell, A., 300; Mencken,
  332; Millay, 336; Robinson, 406;
  Twain, 491; Wharton, 519
BROSSARD, Chandler
  McCarthy, 304
BROWN, Calvin S.
  Aiken, 9
BROWN, Catherine Meredith
  Stafford, 457
BROWN, E. K.
  Cather, 102; Wilson, 539
BROWN, John Mason
  Barry, 39; Hellman, 226; How-
  ard, 235; Kingsley, 269; Odets,
  366; O'Neill, 370; Sherwood, 452;
  Van Druten, 500
BROWN, Sterling A.
  Wright, 550
BRYANT, Arthur
  Lindsay, 292

BRYHER, Winifred
Doolittle, 137; Moore, Mne., 349

BUCHLER, Justus
Santayana, 424

BULLOCK, Elizabeth
Stafford, 456

BULLOCK, Florence Haxton
Kerouac, 266

BURGUM, Edwin Berry
Wolfe, 547

BURKE, Kenneth
Caldwell, 92; Cowley, 108; Gregory, 214; Roethke, 408; Stein, 461; Wescott, 511; Wilder, 528

BURNS, Ben
Wright, 551

BURNS, David
Cummings, 130, 131

BURT, Struthers
Boyle, 74; Sinclair, 455

CABELL, James Branch
Glasgow, 208; Mencken, 333

CALDWELL, James R.
Rukeyser, 413

CALMER, Ned
Jones, 261

CALVERTON, V. F.
Sinclair, 453

CAMPBELL, Harry Modean
Roberts, E., 400

CANBY, Henry Seidel
Benét, 49; Boyle, 73; Buck, 83; Cather, 101; Glasgow, 207; James, 253; Lindsay, 291; Lowell, A., 299; Parker, 372; Saroyan, 427; Twain, 492; Wolfe, 546; Wright, 552

CANTWELL, Robert
Boyle, 74; Lewis, 284; Sinclair, 454

CARMER, Carl
Barry, 38

CARPENTER, Federick I.
Saroyan, 428

CARPENTER, Richard C.
Boyle, 75

CARROLL, Latrobe
Cather, 99

CARRUTH, Hayden
Blackmur, 62; Eberhart, 153; MacLeish, 311; Stevens, 471

CARTER, Everett
Garland, 201; Howells, 241

CARTER, John
Rice, 395

CASSIDY, T. E.
Baldwin, 32

CATHER, Willa
Crane, S., 122

CESTRE, C.
Babbitt, 31

CHAMBERLAIN, John
Cowley, 109; Hughes, 242

CHAPIN, Ruth
Goyen, 211; Styron, 475

CHASE, Cleveland B.
Anderson, S., 19, 21

CHATFIELD-TAYLOR, Otis
Van Druten, 498

CHIAROMONTE, Nicola
Miller, H., 342

CHILDS, Herbert Ellsworth
Masters, 328

CHURCH, Margaret
Wolfe, 549

CIARDI, John
Aiken, 10; Auden, 28; Bogan, 68; Burke, 86; Cullen, 126; Kunitz, 275; MacLeish, 311; Millay, 336; Pound, 385; Roethke, 409; Stevens, 473; Wilbur, 526; Williams, W., 536

CLANCEY, William P.
McCullers, 307

CLARK, Barrett H.
Howells, 237

CLARK, H. H.
Fisher, D., 178

CLARK, Walter Van Tilburg
Guthrie, 218; Richter, 398

CLEGHORN, Sarah N.
Fisher, D., 179

CLURMAN, Harold
Behrman, 42; Hellman, 225; Inge,
245; Kingsley, 270; Miller, A.,
338; Odets, 366; O'Neill, 371;
Wilder, 529

CODMAN, Florence
Bowles, 71

COFFIN, Robert P. Tristram
Wheelock, 521

COHEN, Morris
Lewisohn, 289

COLBRON, Grace Isabel
London, 293

COLLINS, H. P.
Doolittle, 137

COLLINS, Joseph
Lowell, A., 297; Wharton, 518

COLLINS, Thomas Lyle
Wolfe, 547

COLUM, Mary
Boyle, 74; Brooks, V., 78; Jarrell,
254; March, 319; Millay, 337;
Santayana, 421

COMMAGER, Henry Steele
Glasgow, 208; Kantor, 265; Tate,
479

CONNOLLY, Cyril
Capote, 95

CONRAD, Joseph
Crane, S., 121

CONRAD, Sherman
Sarton, 430

COOKE, Alistair
March, 320; Mencken, 333

COOKE, Delmar Gross
Howells. 239

COOPER. Frederic Taber
Bierce, 50

COOPERMAN, Stanley
Hughes, 243

CORBIN, John
O'Neill, 368

COUCH, W. T.
Caldwell, 93

COUGHLAN, Robert
Faulkner, 173

COUSINS, Norman
Hersey, 233

COWLEY, Malcolm
Aiken, 8; Algren, 13; Auden, 25;
Bodenheim, 64; B o g a n, 67;
Brooks, V., 81; Buck, 83; Burke,
86; Caldwell, 94; Cozzens, 113;
Crane, H., 119; Dos Passos, 142;
Fast, 168; Faukner, 172; Fitz-
gerald, F., 187; Frost, 197; Hayes,
220; Hearn, 223; McCarthy, 303;
Norris, 360; Sandburg, 418; Sin-
clair. 454; Styron, 475; Tate, 477;
Thurber, 484; West, 517; Wilder,
530; Wilson, 541; Wright, 550

COX, Sidney
Frost, 199

COXE, Louis O.
Cozzens, 112; Jarrell, 257

CRANE, R. S.
Brooks, C.. 78

CREEKMORE, Hubert
Taylor, 480

CUMMINGS, E. E.
Eliot, 159

CUPPY, Will
Thurber, 483

CURLEY, Thomas E.
Roberts, K., 404

CURTISS, Thomas Quinn
Saroyan, 428

DAICHES, David
Cather, 103; Ciardi, 105; Eberhart, 151; Eliot, 162; Hughes, 243; James, 252; Lowell, R., 301; Shapiro, 443; Tate, 478; Trilling, 486; Van Doren, 496; Wilbur, 526; Winters, 543

DAMON, S. Foster
Lowell, A., ˉ298

DANGERFIELD, George
McCullers, 306

DANIEL, Robert
Welty, 510

DANIELS, Jonathan
Wolfe, 547

DAVIDSON, Donald
Fletcher, 192

DAVIDSON, Eugene
Fearing, 176; Patchen, 377; Roethke, 408; Viereck, 501

DAVIS, Arthur P.
Cullen, 127

DAVIS, Elmer
Sherwood, 452

DAVIS, Elrick B.
Guthrie, 218

DAVIS, Robert Gorham
Bellow, 45; Bowles, 71; Guthrie, 217; Nin, 357; Schulberg, 435; Stegner, 460; Wescott, 514

DAVIS, Thurston
Viereck, 503

DE CASSERES, Benjamin
Markham, 322

DELL, Floyd
Anderson, S., 18; Barnes, 35; Dreiser, 147; Millay, 355; Sinclair, 452

DEMPSEY, David
Jones, 261

DENNEY, Reuel
Eberhart, 153

DENNIS, Patrick
Inge, 245

DE TOLEDANO, Ralph
Bowles, 72

DEUTSCH, Babette
Bogan, 67; Cummings, 129, 131; Doolittle, 138; Eliot, 157; Fowlie, 193; Jarrell, 255; Lowell, R., 301; Moody, 348; Pound, 384; Roethke, 409; Schwartz, 436; Shapiro, 444; Stevens, 470; Wheelock, 522; Wilbur, 526; Williams, W., 536, 538; Winters, 542

DE VOTO, Bernard
Cozzens, 112; Frost, 196; Lewis, 284; Roberts, K., 401

DEWING, Arthur
Hemingway, 230

DICKINSON, Thomas H.
Sherwood, 448

DILLON, George
Cullen, 125; Van Doren, 496

DOBRÉE, Bonamy
Eliot, 162; Saroyan, 427

DOGGETT, Frank A.
Doolittle, 137

DOOLEY, William Germain
Morris, 354

DOUGHTY, H. N., Jr.
Shaw, 445

DOWNER, Alan S.
O'Neill, 370

DOWNING, Francis
McCullers, 307; Thurber, 485

DRAKE, Leah Bodine
Wilbur, 527

DREISER, Theodore
Twain, 492

DREW, Elizabeth
Crane, H., 118; Moore, Mne., 350; Ransom, 386

DUBOIS, Arthur E.
Burke, 84

DUDLEY, Dorothy
Dreiser, 147

DUFFEY, Bernard
Sandburg, 419

DUFFUS, R. L.
Edmonds, 155

DUNCAN, Robert
Doolittle, 139

DUPEE, F. W.
Agee, 6; Shapiro, 442; Tate, 476;
Wescott, 513

DURGIN, Cyrus
Capote, 96

EAMES, Ninetta
London, 293

EASTMAN, Max
Benét, 48; Cummings, 128; Santayana, 421

EATON, Walter Prichard
Behrman, 40; Kingsley, 269;
O'Neill, 369; Sherwood, 449

EBERHART, Richard
Bishop, E., 56; Doolittle, 139;
Rexroth, 390; Schwartz, 439; Wil-
bur, 526; Williams, W., 537

ECKMAN, Frederick
Ginsberg, 204

EDEL, Leon
Adams, 3; Blackmur, 63; Brooks,
V., 80; James, 253

EDMAN, Irwin
Lewisohn, 288; Parker, 374; Thurber, 485

EISENGER, Chester E.
Bellow, 44

ELDER, Donald
Lardner, 279

ELIOT, T. S.
Babbitt, 31; James, 249; Pound,
383

ELLIOTT, G. R.
Babbitt, 31; Frost, 195

ELLMANN, Richard
Cozzens, 114

ELTON, William
Lowell, R., 300

ENGLE, Paul
Benét, 50; Lowell, R., 300; Williams, T., 533

ENGLISH, Maurice
Viereck, 502

ESTY, William
Barnes, 34

EVANS, Bergen
Shaw, 446

EVANS, Oliver
McCullers, 307

FADIMAN, Clifton
Bierce, 54; Cather, 99; Hemingway, 226; Lardner, 277; Marquand, 325; Wescott, 513

FAGIN, N. Bryllion
O'Neill, 371

FARRAR, John
March, 320

FARRELL, James T.
Algren, 13; Hemingway, 228;
Lardner, 278; Levin, 280

FARRELL, Paul V.
Schulberg, 435

FARRELLY, John
Burns, 88; Schwartz, 438

FAY, Bernard
Stein, 462

FEIKEMA, Feike
Stegner, 460

FELD, Rose
Barnes, 36; Fast, 168; Levin, 282;
McCullers, 306

FERGUSON, Otis
Edmonds, 155; Odets, 365

FERGUSSON, Francis
Cozzens, 112

FIEDLER, Leslie A.
Algren, 13, 14; Capote, 98; Shaw, 447; Twain, 493

FIELD, Louise Maunsell
Van Druten, 498

FINGER, Charles J.
Richter, 396

FIREBAUGH, Joseph J.
Wilder, 529

FISCHER, John
Cozzens, 113

FISHER, Dorothy Canfield
Guthrie, 217

FISKE, A. Longfellow
Lindsay, 292

FITTS, Dudley
Aiken, 11; Barnes, 37; Blackmur, 61; Cullen, 126; Fearing, 176; Garrigue, 202; Jeffers, . 261; Moore, Mrl., 353; Rexroth, 390; Schwartz, 436; Wheelock, 522

FITZGERALD, E. J.
Aiken, 9

FITZGERALD, F. Scott
Lardner, 278; Mencken, 329

FITZGERALD, Robert
Frost, 198; Patchen, 374; Pound, 383; Tate, 476; Viereck, 501

FLANAGAN, John T.
Masters, 329

FLANNER. Hildegarde
Jeffers, 259

FLETCHER, John Gould
Aiken, 8; Auden, 24; Bodenheim, 64; Gregory, 216; Kreymborg, 272; Lindsay, 299

FLEXNER, Eleanor
Anderson, M., 16; Barry, 38; Howard, 236

FLINT, R. W.
Dreiser, 148; Rexroth, 391; Williams, W., 536, 537

FLOWER, B. O.
Markham, 321

FOLLETT, Wilson,
Bierce, 52; Winters, 545

FONER, Philip S.
London, 295

FORD, Ford Madox
Bogan, 67; Crane, S., 122, 124

FORGOTSON, E. S.
Patchen, 376; Wheelwright, 524

FOSTER, Edward
Anderson, M., 16

FOWLIE, Wallace
Bishop, E., 57; Gregory, 216; Sarton, 431; Stein, 464

FRANK, Joseph
Barnes, 37; Bishop, J., 59

FRANK, Waldo
Kreymborg, 271

FRANKEL, Charles
Santayana, 422

FRANKENBERG, Lloyd
Bishop, E., 55; Moore, Mne., 350

FRASER, G. S.
Eberhart, 152

FREEDMAN, Morris
Moody, 346

FREMANTLE, Anne
Miller, H., 343

FROHOCK, W. M.
Caldwell, 95; Farrell, 165; Faulkner, 172; Hemingway, 228; Steinbeck, 467; Wolfe, 548

FULKERSON, Baucum
Fletcher, 191

FULLER, Edmund
Clark, 108; Jeffers, 257; Rice, 396

FULOP-MILLER, Rene
Nin, 358

FUSSELL, Edwin S.
Robinson, 407

FUSSELL, Paul, Jr.
Wilder, 531

GABRIEL, Gilbert W.
Miller, A., 338

GALANTIERE, Lewis
MacLeish, 308

GALE, Zona
Garland, 200

GARLAND, Hamlin
Howells, 238; Norris, 359; Twain, 490

GARNETT, Edward
Crane, S., 121, 122, 123

GARRIGUE. Jean
Goyen, 212

GARRISON, W. E.
Markham, 322

GASSNER, John
Barry, 40; Behrman, 42; Hellman, 226; Howard, 237; Miller, A., 339; Odets, 365; Sherwood, 450; Williams, T., 531

GAY, Robert M.
Edmonds. 156

GEHMAN, Richard B.
West, 516

GEISMAR, Maxwell
Algren, 12; Bellow, 43; Brooks, V., 81; Burns, 88; Cather, 101, 103; Cozzens, 115; Dos Passos, 143; Dreiser, 148; Faulkner, 174; Fitzgerald F., 185; Glasgow, 209; Hemingway, 230; Hersey, 232, 234; Jones, 262; Lardner, 278; Lewis, 287; London, 296; March, 320; Mencken, 332; Nin, 358; Norris, 361; Sinclair, 455; Steinbeck, 466; Styron, 474

GETLEIN, Frank
Farrell, 167; Sarton, 432

GIESE, William F.
Babbitt, 30

GILBERT, Rudolph
Jeffers, 259, 260

GILDER, Rosamond
Rice, 394; Sherwood, 450; Van Druten, 499

GILMAN, Lawrence
Masters, 326

GLEASON, Ralph
Kerouac, 267

GLENN, Eunice
Welty, 509

GLICKSBERG, Charles I.
Ellison, 164; Jones, 262; Lindsay, 289; Miller, H., 343; Tate, 478

GOLD, Herbert
Kerouac, 267; Malamud, 316

GOLD, Michael
Dos Passos, 140; Wilder, 528

GOLDMAN, Eric F.
Mencken, 334

GOLFFING, F. C.
Burke, 85; Wilbur, 525

GOODMAN, Paul
Roberts, E., 401

GORDON, Caroline
O'Connor, 362

GORMAN, Herbert
Bodenheim, 65; Hearn, 223; Pound, 381

GOSSE, Edmund
James, 250

GOULD, George M.
Hearn, 222

GOYEN, William
Malamud, 316; O'Connor, 361; Sarton, 432

GRATTAN, C. Hartley
Bierce, 53; Farrell, 166; Lewis, 286; Norris, 359; Sinclair, 454

GRAVES, Robert
Ransom, 386

GRAY, James
Stegner, 461

GREEN, Elizabeth
Stevens, 472

GREENBERG, Clement
Eliot, 163; Wheelwright, 524

GREENE, James
O'Connor, 363

GREENSLET, Ferris
Hearn, 221

GREGORY, Horace
Aiken, 10; Anderson, S., 22; Bishop, J., 58; Bodenheim, 66; Cummings, 128, 130; Doolittle, 139; Fitzgerald, R., 189; Fletcher, 191; Robinson, 406; Wheelwright, 524; Williams, W., 535

GRIFFIN, Hubert
Rice, 395

GRUDIN, Louis
Bodenheim, 63

GUERARD, Albert
Burke, 85

GUERNSEY, Otis L., Jr.
Williams, T., 531

GURKO, Leo
Caldwell, 94; Marquand, 324

HAARDT, Sara
Glasgow, 206

HAAS, Robert Bartlett
Stein, 462

HACKETT, Francis
Lindsay, 290; Sandburg, 417

HAINES, George, IV
Stein, 463

HALL, Donald
Jarrell, 255; Lowell, R., 302; Rukeyser, 410; Wilder, 527

HALLINE, Allan H.
Anderson, M., 17

HALSBAND, Robert
Jackson, 247; McCarthy, 303

HANSEN, Harry
Anderson, S., 21

HANSFORD-JOHNSON, Pamela
Wolfe, 549

HARDY, John Edward
Brooks, V., 78

HARRIGAN, Anthony
Viereck, 502

HARRINGTON, Alan
Gold, 209

HARRINGTON, Michael
Cummings, 129

HARRIS, Sydney J.
Thurber, 485

HARRISON, Charles T.
Santayana, 422

HART, Elizabeth
March, 318

HARTER, Evelyn
Boyle, 73

HARTLEY, Anthony
Babbitt, 28

HARTLEY, Lodwick
Porter, 379

HARTLEY, Marsden
Dickinson, 133

HARVEY, Alexander
Howells, 238

HATCH, Robert
Hersey, 233; Inge, 244; Wright, 552

HATCHER, Harlan
Cather, 99, 102; Eberhart, 150; Faulkner, 170; Marquand, 323

HAVIGHURST, Walter
Bishop, E., 55; Richter, 397; Shaw, 457

HAY, John
Schwartz, 438

HAY, Sara Henderson
Auchincloss, 22; Garrigue, 203; Miller, A., 337

HAYAKAWA, S. I.
Cummings, 131

HAYES, Alfred
Williams, T., 532

HAYES, Richard
Bowles, 70; Capote, 98; Inge, 244; Kreymborg, 270; Miller, A., 340; Stafford, 457; Taylor, 482; Williams, T., 534

HAZEL, Robert
Caldwell, 95

HAZLITT, Henry
Dos Passos, 140; Santayana, 423

HEALEY, Robert C.
Sherwood, 450

HENRY, David D.
Moody, 348

HERMAN, Barbara
Crane, H., 118

HERRICK, Robert
Moore, Mrl., 453

HEWES, Henry
Inge, 244; Miller, A., 341

HEYWARD, Du Bose
Hughes, 241

HEYWOOD, Robert
Fowlie, 194

HICKS, Granville
Auden, 24; Baldwin, 33; Bellow, 46; Cabell, 90; Cozzens, 112, 115; Cummings, 130; Dos Passos, 142; Dreiser, 149; Garland, 201; Gold, 210; Jones, 264; Lindsay, 293;

Malamud, 317; Marquand, 324; Salinger, 416; Sinclair, 454

HIGGINSON, Thomas Wentworth
Dickinson, 133

HIGHET, Gilbert
Wilson, 541

HILLYER, Robert
Scott, 441; Van Druten, 495

HILTON, James
Hayes, 221; Jackson, 246

HOAGLAND, Clayton
Aiken, 12

HOFFMAN, Charles G.
Norris, 361

HOFFMANN, Frederick J.
Crane, H., 120

HOGGART, Richard
Auden, 27

HOLDEN, Raymond
Jarrell, 255; Sarton, 431; Shapiro, 444

HOLMAN, Hugh
Steinbeck, 468

HOLMES, John
Eberhart, 152; Scott, 441

HOLT, Edgar
Lewis, 283

HOLZHAUER, Jean
Welty, 511

HONIG, Edwin
Moore, Mrl., 353

HOOK, Sidney
Santayana, 421

HORN, John
Schulberg, 433

HORTON, Philip
Barnes, 36; Crane, H., 117; Rukeyser, 412

HOWARD, Joseph Kinsey
Guthrie, 217

HOWE, Irving
Adams, 3; Anderson, S., 20, 22; Ellison, 164; Faulkner, 174; Howells, 241; Mencken, 333

HOWELLS, William Dean
Crane, S., 121; Garland, 199; Norris, 359; Twain, 491

HOWGATE, George W.
Santayana, 425

HUGHES, Charlotte
Hellman, 225

HUGHES, Langston
Baldwin, 33

HUGHES, Riley
O'Connor, 363

HUGHES, Serge
Fowlie, 194

HUME, Robert A.
Adams, 2

HUMPHRIES, Rolfe
Fearing, 175; Fitzgerald, R., 188; Frost, 197; Millay, 336; Rexroth, 389; Roethke, 408; Wilbur, 525; Winters, 543

HUNEKER, James Gibbons
James, 249·

HUTCHENS, John K.
Fast, 169; March, 321

HUTCHISON, Percy
Sarton, 430

HYAMS, Barry
Odets, 367

HYMAN, Stanley Edgar
Blackmur, 62; Brooks, V., 80; Cozzens, 111; March, 319

HYNES, Sam
Pound, 385

IMBS, Bravig
Stein, 462

INGALLS, Jeremy
Fowlie, 193

IRISH, Marian D.
Adams, 1

ISAACS, Edith J. R.
Behrman, 41; Hellman, 225; Odets, 365; Sherwood, 449

ISAACS, J.
Eliot, 161

ISHERWOOD, Christopher
Porter, 379

JACK, Peter Monro
Bishop, 56; Bodenheim, 66; Kantor, 264; Wheelwright, 524

JACKSON, Joseph Henry
Steinbeck, 467

JACOBSON, Dan
Ginsberg, 205; Kerouac, 267

JAMES, Henry
Wharton, 517

JANEWAY, Elizabeth
Cozzens, 115; Sarton, 432

JARRELL, Randall
Aiken, 11; Auden, 27; Blackmur, 61; Ciardi, 105; Frost, 198; Gregory, 215; Lowell, R., 302; Marquand, 324; Moore, Mne., 350; Ransom, 388; Rukeyser, 413; Williams, W., 537, 538; Winters, 545

JESSUP, Josephine Lurie
Glasgow, 208; Wharton, 519

JOHNSON, Gerald W.
Lewis, 285

JOHNSON, J. H.
Viereck, 501

JOHNSON, Wendell
Fisher, V., 182

JONES, Ernest
Schwartz, 438

JONES, Frank
Benét, 49; Schwartz, 437

JONES, Howard Mumford
Adams, 3; Cather, 100; Glasgow, 207; Porter, 379; Sandburg, 418;

Sinclair, 455; Stegner, 459; Styron, 474; Wolfe, 546

JONES, Llewellyn
Lindsay, 291

JOOST, Nicholas
Sandburg, 420

JOSEPHSON, Matthew
Wilson, 538

KALLICH, Martin
Dos Passos, 142

KANG, Younghill
Buck, 82

KARP, David
Baldwin, 34

KAUFMAN, Lenard
Hayes, 221

KAZIN, Alfred
Agee, 6; Anderson, S., 20; Barnes, 36; Cabell, 91; Cather, 100; Crane, S., 122, 124; Dos Passos, 144; Dreiser, 147; Farrell, 165; Fast, 168; Faulkner, 171; James, 251; Levin, 281; Lindsay, 289; Mailer, 315; Malamud, 316; Ransom, 388; Salinger, 416; Shaw, 447; Stafford, 456; Van Doren, 496; Wilson, 542

KEE, Robert
Capote, 97; Taylor, 481

KEENE, Frances
Sarton, 432

KEES, Weldon
Fearing, 174

KELLY, James
Algren, 15; Burns, 87; Gold, 209; Schulberg, 435

KENNARD, Nina H.
Hearn, 223

KENNER, Hugh
Pound, 385

KERR, Walter
Barry, 39; Odets, 366; Sherwood, 451; Williams, T., 532

KILBY, Clyde S.
Kerouac, 268

KIRCHWEY, Freda
Fisher, D., 177; Miller, A., 340

KIZER, Helen Buller
Lowell, A., 296

KLEIN, Alexander
Capote, 96

KNIGHT, Grant C.
London, 296

KNOPF, Paul
Fast, 170

KOHLER, Dayton
Edmonds, 155; McCullers, 307; MacLeish, 310; Richter, 397; Wescott, 513; Wilder, 528

KREYMBORG, Alfred
Crane, H., 116; Cummings, 127, 130; Hayes, 219; Jeffers, 258; MacLeish, 310; Stevens, 469; Van Doren, 494

KRIM, Seymour
Salinger, 415; Wilson, 540

KRONENBERGER, Louis
Adams, 5; Eliot, 162; Mencken, 332; Parker, 373; Ransom, 388; Van Doren, 497

KRUTCH, Joseph Wood
Anderson, M., 17; Barry, 38; Behrman, 41; Caldwell, 93; Hellman, 224; Howard, 236, 237; Kingsley, 269; Lewis, 285; Lewisohn, 288; McCarthy, 305; Odets, 364; O'Neill, 371; Rice, 394; Roberts, E., 400; Sherwood, 451; Van Druten, 499

KUNITZ, Stanley
Aiken, 8; Fearing, 176; Gregory, 214; Ransom, 389; Roethke, 408

LA FARGE, Oliver
Capote, 98

LAING, Dilys
Ciardi, 106

LAKE, Kirsopp
    Adams, 1
LANGDALE, E. G.
    Jackson, 247
LANGE, Victor
    McCarthy, 305
LASK, Thomas
    Fast, 169; London, 295
LAS VERGNAS, Raymond
    Goyen, 212
LAWRENCE, D. H.
    Lowell, A., 298
LAZARUS, L. P.
    Schulberg, 433
LEAVIS, F. R.
    Twain, 493
LEAVIS, Q. D.
    Santayana, 423
LECHLITNER, Ruth
    Agee, 5; Rukeyser, 413
LEE, Alwyn
    Miller, H., 344
LEE, C. P.
    Lindsay, 292
LEHMAN, Milton G.
    Stegner, 459
LEHMANN, Rosamond
    Richter, 396
LEONARD, Chilson, H.
    Roberts, K., 401
LERNER, Max
    Levin, 282
LESLIE, Shane
    Adams, 5
LEVENSON, J. C.
    Adams, 4
LEVIN, Harry
    Trilling, 487
LEVIN, Meyer
    Malamud, 316; Rice, 393

LEVIN, Peter R.
    Levin, 282
LEWIS, Charlton M.
    Moody, 346
LEWIS, Sinclair
    Dos Passos, 140; Welty, 510
LEWIS, Wyndham
    Faulkner, 170
LEWISOHN, Ludwig
    Anderson, S., 19; Cabell, 90;
    Dreiser, 146; O'Neill, 367; Rice,
    392; Wharton, 518
LINSCOTT, R. N.
    Sinclair, 453
LIPPMANN, Walter
    Mencken, 330; Sinclair, 453
LIPTON, Lawrence
    Rexroth, 391
LISTER, Richard
    Marquand, 325
LITTELL, Robert
    Cummings, 131; Edmonds, 156;
    Hemingway, 230; Kantor, 265;
    Rice, 392
LITTLE, Carl Victor
    Morris, 354
LOCKE, Alain
    Hughes, 242
LOGGINS, Vernon
    Cabell, 91; Caldwell, 93; Crane,
    S., 121, 123
LONDON, Joan
    London, 294
LOVE, Paul
    Fast, 168
LOVETT, Robert Morse
    Aiken, 11; Moody, 347
LOWELL, Amy
    Fletcher, 190; Robinson, 405

LOWELL, Robert
Jarrell, 255; 256; Ransom, 387;
Tate, 477; Williams, W., 537

LOWES, John Livingston
Lowell, A., 299

LUBBOCK, Percy
James, 250; Wharton, 519

LUCCOCK, Halford E.
Dos Passos, 141

LUHRS, Marie
Parker, 372

LYELL, Frank H.
Taylor, 482

LYND, Robert
Lindsay, 290

LYNN, Kenneth S.
Twain, 493

LYONS, Hilary H.
Clark, 106

LYTLE, Andrew
Faulkner, 173

McCARTHY, Mary
Wilder, 530

McGOVERN, Hugh
Patchen, 377

MacLEISH, Archibald
Benét, 49; Lowell, A., 297;
Santayana, 425

McLOUGHLIN, Richard
Capote, 97

McNAUGHTON, Ruth Flanders
Dickinson, 135

McWILLIAMS, Carey
Bierce, 53

MAGNY, Claude-Edmonde
Steinbeck, 468

MAINE, Harold
Miller, H., 343

MALOFF, Saul
Farrell, 167

MALONEY, John J.
Bowles, 69

MANDEL, Siegfried
Hayes, 220

MANFRED, Frederick F.
Lewis, 286

MANN, Dorothea Lawrence
Fisher, D., 178; Glasgow, 206

MANNES, Marya
Williams, T., 533

MANSFIELD, Margery Swett
Kreymborg, 272

MARCHAND, Ernest
Norris, 360

MARCUS, Steven
Baldwin, 33; Ellison, 164;
Viereck, 503; Wright, 551

MARINI, Myra
Boyle, 73

MARKHAM, Edwin S.
Howells, 238

MARSH, Fred T.
Bishop, J., 58; Farrell, 167;
Fisher, V., 180; Guthrie, 218;
McCullers, 306; March, 319

MARSHALL, Margaret
Dos Passos, 144; Guthrie, 217;
Porter, 379; Wolfe, 550

MARTIN, Edward S.
Howells, 238

MARTZ, Louise L.
Stevens, 470

MARX, Leo
Styron, 476

MASTERS, Edgar Lee
Lindsay, 292

MATCH, Richard
Bellow, 44; Stegner, 460

MATTHEWS, Brander
Twain, 490

MATTHEWS, T. S.
Saroyan, 426

MATTHIESSEN, F. O.
Bishop, J., 58; Eliot, 158;
James, 252; Warren, 507

MAXWELL, William
Clark, 106

MAYBERRY, George
Winters, 545

MAYNE, Ethel Coburn
James, 249

MENCKEN, H. L.
Bierce, 51; Dreiser, 146;
Garland, 200; Lardner, 277

MERCIER, Louis J. A.
Babbitt, 29

MERCIER, Vivian
Kunitz, 275

MERRICK, Gordon
Malamud, 318

MEYER, Gerard Previn
Bishop, J., 60; Burke, 86; Ciardi,
104; Eberhart, 153; Roethke, 409;
Scott, 440; Tate, 476

MICHAUD, Régis
Cabell, 90

MILLARD, Bailey
Markham, 321

MILLETT, Fred B.
Aiken, 9; Fletcher, 192

MILLER, Arthur
Wilder, 530

MILLER, Henry
Fowlie, 193

MILLER, Perry
Trilling 488; Wilson, 540

MILLSPAUGH, C. A.
Fitzgerald, R., 188

MINER, Ward L.
Faulkner, 172

MIZENER, Arthur
Auden, 24; Cowley, 110; Dos
Passos, 145; Eberhart, 152; Fitz-
gerald, F., 185, 186; Jarrell, 256;
MacLeish, 310; Marquand, 325;
Salinger, 416; Tate, 478, 480;
Warren, 506

MONRO, Harold
Doolittle, 136

MONROE, Harriet
Benét, 48; Bodenheim 65; Cummings, 127; Dickinson, 133;
Fletcher, 190; Frost, 195; Kreymborg, 270; MacLeish, 309; Masters, 326; Millay, 334; Moore,
Mne., 349; Pound, 381; Robinson,
405

MOODY, Minnie Hite
Lewisohn, 288

MOOR, Paul
Williams, T., 531

MOORE, Harry T.
Fisher, V., 181; Levin, 281

MOORE, Marianne
Bishop, E., 55; Bogan, 68; Dickinson, 135; Pound, 382

MORE, Paul Elmer
Babbitt, 30; Eliot, 160; Hearn, 221

MORGAN, Lucy Ingram
Fisher, V., 181

MORRIS, Alice S.
Jackson, 247

MORRIS, Lloyd
Capote, 96; Cowley, 110; Dreiser,
145; Farrell, 165; Faulkner, 171;
Fisher, D., 177; Fitzgerald, F.,
185; Howells, 240; Lewis, 285

MORRIS, Mack
Thurber, 482

MORRIS, Wright
Ellison, 163

MORRISON, Theodore
Wheelock, 521

MORSE, Samuel French
Stevens, 471

MORTON, Frederic
Farrell, 167

MUIR, Edwin
Miller, H., 341

MUMFORD, Lewis
Brooks, V., 79

MUNSON, Gorham
Babbitt, 28; Brooks, V., 79;
Crane, H., 116; Frost, 196;
Moore, Mne., 349; Stevens, 469;
Williams, W., 535

MURRAY, William
Morris, 355

MUSGROVE, S.
Eliot, 160

NASH, Ogden
Parker, 373

NATHAN, George Jean
Anderson, M., 15; O'Neill, 370;
Viereck, 500

NATHAN, Leonard
Fearing, 177

NATIONS, Leroy J.
Bierce, 51

NEALE, Walter
Bierce, 53

NEFF, Emery
Robinson, 407

NEMEROV, Howard
Bishop, E., 56; Cozzens, 114;
Garrigue, 203; Ransom, 387

NEVINS, Allan
Edmonds, 155; Fast, 169; Guthrie,
216; Roberts, K., 402

NEVIUS, Blake
Steinbeck, 467

NICHOLS, Charles H.
Barnes, 34

NICHOLS, Lewis
Sherwood, 449

NICKERSON, Hoffman
Babbitt, 30

NOEL, Joseph
London, 294

NORTON, Dan S.
Auden, 26; Thurber, 484

NUHN, Ferner
Garland, 201

NYREN, Dorothy
Kerouac, 268

O'BRIEN, Justin
Fowlie, 194

O'CONNOR, William Van
Crane, H., 120; Warren, 507

O'CONOR, Norreys Jephson
Fowlie, 192

O'DONNELL, George Marion
Schwartz, 437

ORWELL, George
Miller, H., 344

O'SHEEL, Shaemas
Markham, 322

PARK, Charles E.
Lewisohn, 287

PARTRIDGE, A. C.
Eliot, 157

PATRIDGE, Eric
Bierce, 52

PATERSON, Isabel
Cozzens, 111

PATTEE, Fred Lewis
Wharton, 518

PATTERSON, Jack
Nin, 356

PAUL, Elliot
Hemingway, 227

PAYNE, William Morton
Moody, 346

PEDEN, William
Bowles, 72; Goyen, 212; Jackson,
248; Malamud, 317; Salinger, 414;

Shaw, 446; Stafford, 458; Styron, 460; Welty, 510; Williams, T., 533

PEFFER, Nathaniel
Buck, 82

PERLES, Alfred
Miller, H., 344

PERRY, Bliss
Robinson, 404

PETERKIN, Julia
Hughes, 242

PETERSON, Houston
Aiken, 8

PETERSON, Virgilia
Buck, 82

PEYRE, Henri
Fowlie, 194; Jarrell, 257

PFAFF, William
Mailer, 314

PHELAN, Kappo
Miller, A., 338; Rice, 395

PHELPS, Robert
Stafford, 457; Stein, 464

PHELPS, William Lyon
Fisher, D., 178; Masters, 327

PHILLIPS, William
Wilson, 541

PICKREL, Paul
Agee, 7; Clark, 107; Jones, 262; Lardner, 280; Marquand, 325

PLOMER, William
Parker, 374

PODHORETZ, Norman
Bellow, 47; Ginsberg, 204; McCarthy, 304; Malamud, 315

POLITZER, Heinz
Schwartz, 439

POORE, C. G.
Thurber, 483

PORTER, Katherine Anne
Boyle, 73; Cather, 101; Goyen,

211; Pound, 384; Stein, 463; Welty, 510

POUND, Ezra
Frost, 195; James, 248

POWELL, Lawrence Clark
Jeffers, 258, 260

POWERS, J. F.
Fitzgerald, F., 184; Taylor, 481

POWYS, John Cowper
Masters, 327

POWYS, Llewelyn
Dreiser, 146; Millay, 334

PRAGER, Charles M.
Howard, 235

PRATT, Julius W.
Masters, 327

PRESCOTT, Orville
Hayes, 220; Roberts, K., 403; Schulberg, 434

PRESTON, John Hyde
Millay, 335; Stein, 462

PRITCHETT, V. S.
Bowles, 70

PRUETTE, Lorine
McCarthy, 303; McCullers, 308

PURDY, Theodore M.
Richter, 396

QUINN, Arthur Hobson
Fisher, D., 179; Glasgow, 207; Howells, 239

QUINN, Kerker
Fitzgerald, R., 188; Rukeyser, 411

RAGO, Henry
Brooks, V., 80; Garrigue, 202; Shapiro, 443; Stafford, 456; Trilling, 489

RAHV, Philip
Algren, 13; Boyle, 74; Levin, 281; Miller, H., 342

RAINE, Kathleen
Barnes, 37; Dickinson, 136

RAINER, Dachine
Baldwin, 33; Mailer, 314

RALEIGH, John Henry
Baldwin, 32

RANSOM, John Crowe
Brooks, C., 77; Burke, 85; Eliot, 161; Santayana, 425

RASCOE, Burton
Babbitt, 29; Barnes, 35; Lardner, 277; Mencken, 331; Roberts, K., 402; Saroyan, 426; Steinbeck, 465; Wescott, 512

RAW, Ruth
Garland, 200

RAY, David
Jones, 263

REDDING, J. Saunders
Baldwin, 32

REDMAN, Ben Ray
Hemingway, 230; McCullers, 308; Trilling, 487

REXROTH, Kenneth
Bogan, 68; Ciardi, 106; Ginsberg, 205; Miller, H., 344; Sandburg, 420

REYNOLDS, Quentin
Hersey, 232

RHODES, Harrison
Hearn, 222

RICE, Jenning
Edmonds, 156

RICE, Philip Blair
Benét, 48; Cullen, 126; Fitzgerald, R., 187; Masters, 328; Millay, 335; Porter, 379; Rukeyser, 410; Van Doren, 494

RICHARDS, Edmund C.
Steinbeck, 465

RICHART, Bette
Moore, Mne., 351

ROBBINS, F. L.
Lewisohn, 288

ROBINS, J. D.
Roberts, E., 399

RODMAN, Selden
Bishop, E., 56; Eberhart, 153; Fearing, 175; Garrigue, 203; Hayes, 219; Jeffers, 259; Rexroth, 389; Shapiro, 442

ROELOFS, Gerrit H.
Adams, 2

ROETHKE, Theodore
Van Doren, 495

ROGERS, W. G.
Stein, 463

ROLO, Charles J.
Agee, 7; Auchincloss, 23; Bowles, 70; Capote, 99; Dos Passos, 143; Ellison, 164; Goyen, 211; Jones, 263; McCarthy, 305; Nin, 358; Trilling, 487; Wilson, 540

ROSE, G. B.
Moody, 346

ROSENBERG, Harold
Anderson, M., 16; Bierce, 55; Rukeyser, 411

ROSENBERGER, Coleman
Bishop, E., 56; Ciardi, 104

ROSENFELD, Isaac
McCarthy, 304; Nin, 357; O'Connor, 362; Patchen, 376; Saroyan, 429

ROSENFELD, Paul
Anderson, S., 18; Cummings, 132; Fitzgerald, F., 183; Nin, 357; Porter, 378; Sandburg, 417; Stevens, 469; Wheelwright, 523; Williams, W., 535

ROSENTHAL, M. L.
Eberhart, 154; Fearing, 176; Ginsberg, 204; Jarrell, 254; Kunitz, 275; Miller, H., 345; Rexroth, 391; Shapiro, 445

ROSKOLENKO, Harry
Garrigue, 203; Kreymborg, 272; Masters, 329; Wheelwright, 523

ROSS, Alan
  West, 516

ROSS, J. D.
  Burns, 87

ROSS, Mary
  Lowell, A., 297

ROSS, Nancy Wilson
  Kerouac, 268

ROSS, Woodburn O.
  Steinbeck, 466

ROTH, Samuel
  Robinson, 404

ROTHMAN, Nathan L.
  Boyle, 75; Fisher, V., 183

ROURKE, Constance
  Lindsay, 291

ROVERE, Richard H.
  Miller, A., 341

RUBIN, Louis D., Jr.
  O'Connor, 363

RUGOFF, Milton
  Algren, 14; Blackmur, 62; Cowley,
  110; Dos Passos, 141; Hersey,
  233; Malamud, 317

RUHL, Arthur
  March, 318

RUKEYSER, Muriel
  Rexroth, 392

SALOMAN, Louis B.
  West, 515

SALOMON, I. L.
  Ciardi, 105

SANDEEN, Ernest
  Ciardi, 105

SAPIR, Edward
  Dickinson, 134

SAROYAN, William
  Mencken, 331

SARTRE, Jean-Paul
  Dos Passos, 143

SAXON, Lyle
  Faulkner, 173

SCHACHT, Marshall
  Scott, 440

SCHAFFNER, Halle
  Wescott, 512

SCHEVILL, James
  Anderson, S., 21

SCHNEIDER, Daniel E.
  Miller, A., 340

SCHOENBERGER, Franz
  Wolfe, 548

SCHOENWALD, Richard L.
  West, 516

SCHORER, Mark
  Aiken, 12; Clark, 108; Fitzgerald,
  F., 184; Kunitz, 274; Lewis, 286;
  Nin, 356; Trilling, 488

SCHULBERG, Budd
  Algren, 12; Fitzgerald, 184

SCHWARTZ, Delmore
  Aiken, 10; Bellow, 46; Blackmur,
  62; Dos Passos, 144; Eliot, 161;
  Jarrell, 256; Lardner, 280; Pound,
  382; Roethke, 410; Shapiro, 442;
  Stevens, 471, 472

SCHWARTZ, Edward
  Bellow, 43

SCOTT, Eleanor M.
  Morris, 354

SCOTT, Evelyn
  Wheelock, 521

SCOTT, Nathan A., Jr.
  Williams, T., 534

SCOTT, Winfield Townley
  Aiken, 9; Fitzgerald, R., 188;
  Gregory, 216; Moore, Mne., 351;
  Morris, 356; Rexroth, 390; Wheel-
  ock, 522; Wheelwright, 525

SCOTT-JAMES, R. A.
  Auden, 26

SCUTTON, Mary
Auchincloss, 23

SEDGWICK, Henry Dwight
Twain, 489

SEIDEN, Melvin
Gold, 210

SEIFF, Morton
Schwartz, 439

SEIFFERT, Marjorie Allen
Kreymborg, 271

SELDES, Gilbert
Lardner, 279; Thurber, 483

SERGEANT, Elizabeth Shepley
Lowell, A., 298

SHACKFORD, Martha Hale
Moody, 347

SHAFER, Robert
Dreiser, 150

SHAPIRO, Charles
Levin, 282

SHAPIRO, Karl
Jarrell, 255

SHAW, Irwin
Van Druten, 500

SHEA, Albert A.
Miller, A., 339

SHERMAN, Stuart
Dreiser, 149; Glasgow, 206; Lardner, 277; Twain, 490

SHERRY, Laura
Kreymborg, 271

SHIRER, William
Hersey, 232

SIEVERS, W. David
Barry, 40; Hellman, 226; Inge, 245

SIMONS, John H.
O'Connor, 362

SINCLAIR, May
Doolittle, 136 Moody, 346

SINCLAIR, Upton
Mencken, 331

SKINNER, Richard Dana
Howard, 235; O'Neill, 369; Rice, 393; Van Druten, 498

SLATER, Montague
O'Neill, 371

SMITH, A. J. M.
Kunitz, 274

SMITH, Bernard
Brooks, V., 79

SMITH, Harrison
Burns, 88; Lewis, 285; Miller, H., 343; Saroyan, 427; Sherwood, 451

SMITH, Peter Duvall
Eberhart, 152

SMITH, Roger H.
West, 517

SNELL, George
Bierce, 54; Dreiser, 150; Faulkner, 171; Fisher, V., 182

SNOW, Edgar
Buck, 83

SOUTHRON, Jane Spence
Sarton, 431

SOUTHWORTH, James G.
Auden, 25; Warren, 508

SPENCER, Theodore
Cummings, 129; Ransom, 388

SPENDER, Stephen
Auden, 27; Eliot, 157; Lowell, R., 302; Shapiro, 444

SPILLER, Robert E.
Howells, 240; Wilson, 542

STALLINGS, Sylvia
Goyen, 212; O'Connor, 362

STAUFFER, Donald A.
Burke, 85

STEEGMULLER, Francis
Jarrell, 257

STEGNER, Wallace
Saroyan, 427

STEIN, Gertrude
Anderson, S., 19

STEPANCHEV, Stephen
Garrigue, 202

STEPHAN, Ruth
Fearing, 175

STERLING, George
Bierce, 51

STEVENS, Wallace
Ransom, 387

STEVENSON, David L.
Agee, 7; Salinger, 415

STEVENSON, Elizabeth
Adams, 2

STOCKTON, Frank R.
Twain, 489

STONE, Jerome
Goyen, 213

STONG, Phil
Stegner, 458

STONIER, G. W.
Thurber, 484

STRACHEY, Julia
McCarthy, 303

STRAUMANN, Heinrich
Roberts, K., 404; Warren, 504; Welty, 509; Wharton, 519; Wright, 552

STRAUSS, Harold
Levin, 281

STROBEL, Marion
Van Doren, 494

SUGRUE, Thomas
Fisher, V., 182

SULLIVAN, A. M.
Lewisohn, 289; Markham, 323

SULLIVAN, John F.
Blackmur, 63

SULLIVAN, Richard
Burns, 87; Kantor, 265

SULZBERGER, Cyrus L., II
Moore, Mrl., 352

SWADOS, Harvey
Clark, 107; Gold, 209; Jones, 263; Morris, 354

SWAN, Maurice
Scott, 440

SWEENEY, John L.
Gregory, 215

SYKES, Gerald
Boyle, 72

SYLVESTER, Harry
Kreymborg, 272; London, 295; Malamud, 315; Stegner, 459

SYRKIN, Marie
Levin, 282

TAGGARD, Genevieve
Dickinson, 134; Parker, 372

TALLANT, Robert
March, 320

TATE, Allen
Benét, 47; Bishop, J., 57; Cowley, 109; Crane, H., 117, 119; Kantor, 264; Kreymborg, 271; Millay, 335; Porter, 378; Pound, 382; Winters, 543

TAYLOR, Frajam
Patchen, 377

TEMPLE, Jean
Hearn, 223

THOMPSON, Dorothy
Lewis, 286

TINDALL, William York
Auden, 26

TITTLE, Walter
Lardner, 276

TOWNE, Charles Hanson
Markham, 322

TRILLING, Diana
  Bellow, 44; Capote, 97; Fast, 169;
  Shaw, 445; Stafford, 456; Welty,
  509; Wescott, 514

TRILLING, Lionel
  Cather, 100, 103; Fitzgerald, F.,
  185; O'Neill, 369; Shaw, 446

TROY, William
  Stein, 461; Tate, 478; Wescott,
  512; Winters, 544

TUTTLE, Allen E.
  Hearn, 224

TWAIN, Mark
  Howells, 238

TWITCHETT, E. G.
  Wilder, 528

UNTERMEYER, Jean Starr
  Patchen, 376

UNTERMEYER, Louis
  Auden, 26; Bodenheim, 64;
  Brooks, C., 76; Cummings, 128;
  Dickinson, 134; Gregory, 214;
  Jeffers, 259, 260; Lindsay, 291;
  Lowell, A., 299; Lowell, R., 301;
  Moore, Mrl., 352; Patchen, 377;
  Rukeyser, 412; Sandburg, 418;
  Viereck, 501; Wheelock, 520;
  Williams, W., 535

VALENTINE, Elizabeth R.
  Rice, 394

VAN DE WATER, Frederic F.
  Fisher, D., 179

VAN DOREN, Carl
  Cabell, 89; Caldwell, 92; Garland,
  200; Lewis, 284; Lindsay, 290

VAN DOREN, Mark
  Barnes, 36; Bogan, 66; Cullen,
  124; Parker, 373; Roberts, E.,
  399; Robinson, 407

VAN GELDER, Robert
  Schulberg, 433

VAN GHENT, Dorothy
  Gold, 210

VAUGHAN, Virginia
  Burns, 88

VAZAKIS, Byron
  Fitzgerald, R., 189

VERNON, Glenville
  Barry, 39; Odets, 364; Sherwood,
  448; Van Druten, 499

VIERECK, Peter
  Frost, 198; Hayes, 219; Tate, 477

VIVAS, Eliseo
  Burke, 84; James, 252

VOGT, William
  Edmonds, 154

VON ABELE, Rudolph
  Cummings, 129

VON HOFMANSTHAL, Hugo
  O'Neill, 368

WADE, Mason
  Dos Passos, 141

WAGENKNECHT, Edward
  London, 295; Norris, 359

WAGONER, David
  Kunitz, 275

WAIN, John
  Trilling, 488

WALCUTT, Charles Child
  Algren, 14

WALKER, Franklin
  Norris, 360

WALL, Vincent
  Anderson, M., 16

WALLACE, Margaret
  Styron, 475

WALSH, Chad
  Morris, 356; Viereck, 502

WALTON, Eda Lou
  Agee, 5; Bishop, J., 57; Buck, 82;
  Ciardi, 104; Cullen, 125; Fitz-
  gerald, R., 187; Gregory, 213;
  Kunitz, 273; MacLeish, 309;
  Markham, 322; Masters, 328;

Moore, Mrl., 352; Schwartz, 437;
Winters, 543

WANNING, Andrew
Fitzgerald, F., 184

WARD, John W.
Cozzens, 114

WARFEL, Harry R.
Boyle, 75; Warren, 504

WARREN, Austin
Babbitt, 30

WARREN, C. Henry
Frost, 196

WARREN, Robert Penn
Auden, 25; Bellow, 44, 45; Bishop,
J., 58; Fletcher, 191; Moore, Mrl.,
351; Patchen, 375; Ransom, 386;
Taylor, 481; Wolfe, 546

WARSHAW, Robert S.
Odets, 365

WATTS, Richard, Jr.
Schulberg, 434; Wilder, 529

WAUGH, Evelyn
Hemingway, 228

WEALES, Gerald
Thurber, 485

WEBSTER, Harvey Curtis
Bellow, 45; Cullen, 127; Ellison,
163; Morris, 355

WECTOR, Dixon
Twain, 492

WEDEK, Harry E.
Hearn, 224

WEEKS, Edward
Kantor, 265; Roberts, K., 403;
Schulberg, 434; Viereck, 501

WELLS, Henry W.
Brooks, C., 76; Crane, H., 120;
Moore, Mrl., 353; Ransom, 387

WELTY, Eudora
Salinger, 414

WESCOTT, Glenway
Roberts, E., 399

WEST, Herbert Faulkner
Miller, H., 342

WEST, Jessamyn
Cozzens, 113

WEST, Ray B., Jr.
Clark, 107; Porter, 380

WEST, Rebecca
Fisher, D., 177

WHARTON, Edith
James, 251

WHEELWRIGHT, John
Blackmur, 60; Frost, 196

WHICHER, George F.
Brooks, C., 77; Gregory, 215;
Trilling, 486; Van Doren, 497

WHIPPLE, T. K.
London, 294; Steinbeck, 465

WHITALL, James
Doolittle, 138

WHITE, Antonia
Burns, 89

WHITEHEAD, Robert
Odets, 367

WHITTEMORE, Reed
Bogan, 69; MacLeish, 311; Wheelwright, 523

WICKENDEN, Dan
Jackson, 248; Taylor, 481

WILBUR, Richard
Williams, W., 536

WILDER, Amos N.
Crane, H., 117

WILKINSON, Marguerite
Fletcher, 190

WILLIAMS, Ben Ames
Roberts, K., 403

WILLIAMS, Blanche
Cabell, 89

WILLIAMS, Oscar
Blackmur, 61; Hayes, 218

WILLIAMS, Tennessee
Bowles, 69, 70

WILLIAMS, William Carlos
Burke, 84; Doolittle, 138; Pound,
384; Rexroth, 390; Rukeyser, 411;
Sandburg, 419; Scott, 440; Shapiro, 443; Stevens, 472

WILSON, Angus
Welty, 511

WILSON, Edmund
Anderson, M., 15; Crane, H., 116;
Eliot, 159; Hemingway, 227;
Lardner, 276; Mencken, 330; Mil-
lay, 337; Robinson, 405; Saroyan,
426; Steinbeck, 466; Trilling, 486;
West, 515; Wilder, 527

WILSON, James Southall
Glasgow, 207

WILSON, T. C.
Fitzgerald, R., 187; West, 515

WINSTER, Archer
Edmonds, 154

WINTERS, Yvor
Babbitt, 29; Crane, 118; Eliot,
158; Frost, 197; Jeffers, 258;
Kunitz, 273; Moore, Mne., 349;
Moore, Mrl., 351; Roberts, E.,
400; Stevens, 469

WOOD, Clement
Cullen, 125

WOODBRIDGE, Homer E.
Anderson, M., 17

WOODRUFF, Neal, Jr.
Warren, 506

WOOLLCOTT, Alexander
Parker, 374

WOOLF, Virginia
Lardner, 279

WRIGHT, James
Kunitz, 276; Scott, 441

WRIGHT, Richard
Hughes, 243; McCullers, 306

WYATT, Edith
Twain, 491

WYATT, Euphemia Van Rensselaer
Inge, 244; Miller, A., 339

WYCKOFF, Elizabeth
Fisher, D., 178

YAFFE, James
Auchincloss, 23

YEZIERSKA, Anzia
Lewisohn, 287

YOUNG, Philip
Hemingway, 229, 231

YOUNG, Stark
Barry, 38; Behrman, 41; Hellman,
225; Kingsley, 269; Miller, A.,
338; Odets, 364; O'Neill, 368;
Rice, 393; Van Druten, 497

YOUNG, Vernon
Clark, 107

YUST, Walter
Fitzgerald, F., 186; Sandburg, 417

ZABEL, Morton Dauwen
Benét, 48; Bishop, J., 59; Cowley,
109; Eliot, 160; Gregory, 214;
Kunitz, 274; MacLeish, 310;
Moore, Mne., 349; Robinson, 406;
Sandburg, 419; Trilling, 488; Wes-
cott, 514; Wheelock, 521; Wilson,
539; Winters, 544

ZATURENSKA, Marya
Cummings, 128, 130; Wheelwright, 524; Williams, W., 535

ZOLOTOW, Maurice
Inge, 245

Index to Supplement

ADAMS, Robert M.
  Baldwin, 556; Salinger, 584
ALGREN, Nelson
  Heller, 563; Hemingway, 565
BALLIETT, Whitney
  Updike, 585
BARRETT, William
  Roth, 581
BAUMBACH, Jonathan
  Morris, 573
BELLOW, Saul
  Roth, 580
BOOTH, Wayne C.
  Morris, 574
BOROFF, David
  Gold, 562
BROOKS, Cleanth
  Faulkner, 559
BRUSTEIN, Robert
  Heller, 563
BRYANT, J. A., Jr.
  Williams, W., 592
BUITENHUIS, Peter
  Updike, 586
BURKE, Kenneth
  Williams, W., 592
CARRUTH, Hayden
  Powers, 577
CASPER, Leonard
  Warren, 589
CHASE, Richard
  Bellow, 557
CIARDI, John
  Frost, 561
DEMOTT, Benjamin
  Morris, 572; Salinger, 583
DOLIN, Arnold
  Roth, 579

DONOGHUE, Denis
  Frost, 561
DUPEE, F. W.
  Lowell, 566; Mailer, 568; Powers, 578
EISINGER, Chester E.
  Bellow, 557
FIEDLER, Leslie
  Hemingway, 565; Salinger, 583
FINN, James
  Baldwin, 555
FOSTER, Richard
  Gold, 561
GANZ, Arthur
  Williams, T., 590
GASS, William A.
  Powers, 578
GELLER, Evelyn
  Updike, 585
GILMAN, Richard
  Updike, 585
GROSS, John
  Roth, 582
GOLDMAN, Albert
  Gold, 562
HARDY, John Edward
  Warren, 588
HASSAN, Ihab H.
  Bellow, 558
HICKS, Granville
  Faulkner, 558; Heller, 562; Powers, 577; Roth, 581; Updike, 586; Warren, 588
HIGHET, Gilbert
  Miller, H., 571
HOFFMAN, Frederick J.
  Faulkner, 559
HOWE, Irving
  Mailer, 568; Roth, 580

JACOBSON, Dan
  Malamud, 569
JOHNSON, James William
  Porter, 574
KAZIN, Alfred
  Baldwin, 555; Lowell, 567; Powers, 577; Roth, 581; Warren, 587
KENNER, Hugh
  Williams, W., 592
KLEIN, Marcus
  Bellow, 558
KLUGER, Richard
  Updike, 587
LANDIS, Joseph C.
  Roth, 582
LARNER, Jeremy
  Salinger, 583
LITTLEJOHN, John David
  Miller, H., 572
LOWELL, Robert
  Williams, W., 591
McCORD, David
  Updike, 584
MAGID, Marion
  Williams, T., 590
MALOFF, Saul
  Baldwin, 556; Malamud, 570
MAYFIELD, Julian
  Baldwin, 555
MITCHELL, Julian
  Heller, 564
MIZENER, Arthur
  Roth, 581
MORAVIA, Alberto
  Miller, H., 571
MURPHY, Richard W.
  Updike, 586
MUSTE, John H.
  Heller, 564

NELSON, Benjamin
  Williams, T., 590
O'CONNOR, Frank
  Powers, 576
PEARCE, Roy Harvey
  Frost, 560
PODHORETZ, Norman
  Mailer, 567
RAGO, Henry
  Powers, 576
ROSENTHAL, M. L.
  Lowell, 567
ROSS, Lillian
  Hemingway, 565
ROVIT, Earl H.
  Malamud, 569
RUGOFF, Milton
  Roth, 579
RYAN, Marjorie
  Porter, 575
SCHRADER, George Alfred
  Mailer, 568
SCOUFFAS, George
  Powers, 576
SEIDEN, Melvin
  Heller, 563
SISK, John P.
  Powers, 578
SOLOTAROFF, Theodore
  Malamud, 570; Porter, 575
SOLT, Mary Ellen
  Williams, W., 591
SOUTHERN, Terry
  Miller, H., 571
SPECTORSKY, A. C.
  Updike, 584
STERN, Richard G.
  Bellow, 557

STEVENSON, David L.
  Hemingway, 564
TATE, Allen
  Faulkner, 559
THOMPSON, John
  Lowell, 566
TISCHLER, Nancy M.
  Williams, T., 589
TRILLING, Lionel
  Frost, 560

WAIN, John
  Miller, H., 572
WARD, J. A.
  Updike, 586
WATERMAN, Arthur E.
  Morris, 573
WEBSTER, Harvey Curtis
  Powers, 579
WESCOTT, Glenway
  Porter, 574

continued from front flap

Dickinson who began their careers in the 19th century but are inadequately covered or neglected in the famous eight-volume set of literary criticism compiled by Charles Wells Moulton and completed in 1904. Since publication of that English-oriented work, American writing has developed into a literary force receiving international recognition, and long deserving a volume for itself.

As a critical key to modern American literature and as a guide to first readings in each author covered, this new, up-to-date *Library of Literary Criticism* will be an indispensable addition to every home or library bookshelf.

ABOUT THE EDITOR:

Dorothy Nyren, well known in the library field, is now Coordinator of Adult Services for the Brooklyn (N.Y.) Public Library. Formerly head librarian in Concord, Massachusetts, and in Northbrook, Illinois, she is a regular reviewer of contemporary American writers for *Library Journal, Books Abroad,* and other publications. Holder of a master's degree in American literature from Boston University and an M.S. in library science from Simmons College, she is also co-editor (as Dorothy Nyren Curley) of *Modern Romance Literatures,* another title in this series.